# CRIMINAL LAW

**JOHN L. WORRALL**

*University of Texas at Dallas*

**JENNIFER L. MOORE**

*DeSales University*

**PEARSON**

Boston   Columbus   Indianapolis   New York   San Francisco   Upper Saddle River
Amsterdam   Cape Town   Dubai   London   Madrid   Milan   Munich   Paris   Montreal   Toronto
Delhi   Mexico City   São Paolo   Sydney   Hong Kong   Seoul   Singapore   Taipei   Tokyo

*Editorial Director:* Vernon R. Anthony
*Senior Acquisitions Editor:* Eric Krassow
*Development Editor:* Elisa Rogers, 4development
*Editorial Assistant:* Lynda Cramer
*Director of Marketing:* David Gesell
*Senior Marketing Manager:* Cyndi Eller
*Senior Marketing Coordinator:* Alicia Wozniak
*Marketing Assistant:* Les Roberts
*Senior Managing Editor:* JoEllen Gohr
*Senior Project Manager:* Steve Robb
*Senior Operations Supervisor:* Pat Tonneman
*Creative Director:* Andrea Nix

*Senior Art Director:* Diane Y. Ernsberger
*Text and Cover Designer:* PMG
*Cover Image:* PMG
*Media Project Manager:* Karen Bretz
*Full-Service Project Management:* Sherrill Redd, Aptara®, Inc.
*Composition:* Aptara®, Inc.
*Printer/Binder:* Edwards Brothers Malloy
*Cover Printer:* Lehigh/Phoenix Color Hagerstown
*Text Font:* Sabon LT Std

Credits and acknowledgments for content borrowed from other sources and reproduced, with permission, in this textbook appear on the appropriate page within the text.

**Library of Congress Cataloging-in-Publication Data**
Worrall, John L.
    Criminal law/John L. Worrall, Jennifer L. Moore.
       p. cm.
    ISBN-13: 978-0-13-138317-3
    ISBN-10: 0-13-138317-5
    1.  Criminal law—United States.      I.  Moore, Jennifer L.      II.  Title.
    KF9219.W67 2013
    345.73—dc23

                                             2011041411

10 9 8 7 6 5 4 3 2

**PEARSON**

ISBN 10:      0-13-138317-5
ISBN 13:    978-0-13-138317-3

**For my wife, Sabrina, and my kids, Dylan and Jordyn.**
*J.W.*

**For my husband, Brian, my family, and the students who served as my inspiration.**
*J.M.*

> **Easy to teach, easy to learn.** Each module in this text is a stand-alone unit that represents a course objective and includes information on a topic, the theory or research behind the topic, and the practical application of that information. This flexible, consistent format allows instructors to easily move from module to module and teach in the order of their choice. The modular format also enables students to learn the material in smaller segments that are easier to absorb than an entire chapter at once. This allows for better retention of critical concepts and linkage of theory and research.

# PREFACE

Welcome to the first edition of *Criminal Law*. We have both taught criminal law for several years, leading us to become quite familiar with the many books available in a relatively crowded market. The more we have become familiar with these texts, the more we saw an increasing need to write our own book, one that adopts a fresh and contemporary take on criminal law. We also determined that there is a need for a new format for teaching the subject matter. The format we have adopted is modular in nature.

## DISTINGUISHING FEATURES

### Modular Organization

Our book's modular format sets it apart from others on the market. Like chapters in a traditional text, modular chapters begin with a set of chapter objectives. Learning objectives, however, are then broken up and organized into modules. Each module is a stand-alone section. There are two to seven modules per chapter in our book. Each module follows a consistent organization and contains the following elements:

1. "Core Concepts" sections that include standard criminal law content, covering all major topics

2. "Court Decision" sections that feature excerpts from real cases followed by critical thinking questions

3. "Your Decision" exercises affording the reader an opportunity how to decide a particular case

4. A concise bulleted summary

Each chapter concludes with a list of learning objectives, review questions, and key terms, organized by module. Chapter synthesis questions are also included at the very end of each chapter. This summary format gives readers the ability to quickly link specific terms, questions, and objectives to the modules associated with them.

Presenting material in modular format makes it easier for students to absorb the information (in smaller chunks as opposed to an entire chapter at once), and gives instructors the flexibility of assigning the modules they feel are most pertinent. It also ensures that each main topic in the text is supported by an application ("Your Decision") and, where relevant, a case example ("Court Decision").

### Interesting and Controversial Cases

We make liberal use of interesting, fresh, and controversial cases. A large number of our cases were decided in the last two to three years, making the material as current as possible. In regard to key Supreme Court cases, examples integrated in the book include the Virginia Military Institute case, *United States* v. *Virginia*, which addresses the constitutionality of prohibiting women from attending military academies. In addition, Chapter 2 highlights the Supreme Court's ruling on lethal injection in *Baze* v. *Rees*. Many other contemporary and controversial cases appear throughout the book. The cases are specifically targeted to engage young students with unique and relatable factual scenarios and encourage lively class discussions.

## Exercises

Each module contains scenarios that emulate the approach taken in Singer and LaFond's *Criminal Law: Examples and Explanations* (Wolters Kluwer) and Worrall's *Criminal Procedure: From First Contact to Appeal* (Pearson). Students are presented with a hypothetical scenario that puts them in the position of judge, prosecutor, defense counsel or jury. We call this feature "Your Decision." Two such exercises appear at the end of each module. *Answers are available to instructors in the instructor's resource materials.* This promotes classroom discussion.

## SUPPLEMENTS

*Criminal Law* is supported by a complete package of instructor and student resources.

- *MyCrimeKit* Web site (**www.MyCrimeKit.com**). This online supplement offers book-specific learning objectives, chapter summaries, flashcards, and practice tests, as well as video clips and media activities to aid student learning and comprehension. Note: An access code is needed for this supplement. Students can purchase an access code at **www.MyPearsonStore.com** or from the MyCrimeKit site at **www.MyCrimeKit.com**.

- *eBooks. Criminal Law* is available in two eBook formats, *CourseSmart* and Adobe Reader. *CourseSmart* is an exciting new choice for students looking to save money. As an alternative to purchasing the printed textbook, students can purchase an electronic version of the same content. With a *CourseSmart* eTextbook, students can search the text, make notes online, print out reading assignments that incorporate lecture notes, and bookmark important passages for later review. For more information, or to purchase access to the *CourseSmart* eTextbook, visit **www.coursesmart.com**

- *TestBank* and *MyTest*. These supplement represent a new standard in testing material. Whether you use the basic *TestBank* in the Instructor's Manual or generate questions electronically through *MyTest*, every question is linked to the text's learning objective, page number, and level of difficulty. This allows for quick reference in the text and an easy way to check the difficulty level and variety of your questions. *MyTest* can be accessed at **www.PearsonMyTest.com**.

- *Interactive Lecture PowerPoint presentation.* This supplement will enhance lectures like never before. Award-winning presentation designers worked with our authors to develop *PowerPoints* that truly engage the student. Much like the text, the *PowerPoints* are full of instructionally sound graphics, tables, charts, and photos that do what presentation software was meant to do: support and enhance your lecture. Data and difficult concepts are presented in a truly interactive way, helping students connect the dots and stay focused on the lecture. The *Interactive Lecture PowerPoints* also include in-depth lecture notes and teaching tips so you have all your lecture material in one place.

- *Instructor's Manual with Case Briefs and Test Bank.* This instructor's manual contains case briefs, proposed responses to the You Decide questions in the text, and a test bank with answer key. The authors have prepared a pack of case briefs that correspond to the excerpted cases that appear in each chapter. These case briefs essentially serve as a one-page summary of the key elements of the various cases, similar to the approach used by students during law school. We feel this is an important addition because it aids the instructor in preparing for class. One difficulty often encountered by instructors in courses that use the "text-case" approach is remembering all of the details of each case for class. These briefs provide summaries of the key material and greatly decrease the preparation time needed. In addition, they make switching to the new text an easier transition.

To access supplementary materials online, instructors need to request an instructor access code. Go to **www.pearsonhighered.com**, click the Instructor Resource Center link, and then click Request IRC access for an instructor access code. Within 48 hours of registering you will receive a confirming e-mail including an instructor access code. Once you have received your code, go to the site and log on for full instructions on downloading the materials you wish to use.

# ABOUT THE AUTHORS

**John L. Worrall** is Professor of Criminology and Program Head at the University of Texas at Dallas. A Seattle native, he received both his M.A. (criminal justice) and Ph.D. (political science) from Washington State University, where he graduated in 1999. From 1999 to 2006, he was a member of the criminal justice faculty at California State University, San Bernardino. He joined University of Texas at Dallas in the fall of 2006. Dr. Worrall has published articles and book chapters on a variety of topics, ranging from legal issues in policing to crime measurement. He is also the author or coauthor of numerous textbooks, including *Introduction to Criminal Justice* (with Larry J. Siegel, 13th ed., Cengage, © 2012) and *Criminal Procedure: From First Contact to Appeal* (4th ed., Prentice Hall, © 2013); coeditor of *The Changing Role of the American Prosecutor* (SUNY, © 2009); and editor of the journal *Police Quarterly*.

**Jennifer L. Moore** is Assistant Professor of Criminal Justice at DeSales University in Center Valley, Pennsylvania. She obtained her B.A. in government from Dartmouth College in Hanover, New Hampshire, and her J.D. with honors from Emory University School of Law in Atlanta, Georgia. Prior to entering academics, Professor Moore practiced at a large law firm in Atlanta, Georgia. Her legal practice included corporate litigation, antitrust litigation, and white-collar criminal defense. Professor Moore has also published articles on a wide range of legal topics, with a specific focus on criminal law issues.

# ACKNOWLEDGMENTS

Many people contributed to this project. We would like to thank everyone at Pearson and its vendors, including Eric Krassow, Elisa Rogers, Steve Robb, Sherrill Redd, and Evelyn Perricone.

We would also like to thank the reviewers. They were John Anderson, California State University, Fullerton; Maria Daniel, Community College of Philadelphia; Judith Fitzgerald, Bowie State University; David Graff, Kent State University; Michael Kwan, Salt Lake Community College; Michael Raymond, New Hampshire Technical Institute; Elvira White, Livingstone College; and Stanley Yeldell, Rowan University of New Jersey.

Finally, we would like to thank our families for their continued love and support.

# BRIEF CONTENTS

# CONTENTS

# 1

# THE BASICS OF CRIMINAL LAW

*Learning Objectives*

## MODULE 1.1 PRELIMINARY INFORMATION
- Define crime and criminal law.
- Explain the difference between substantive criminal law and criminal procedure.
- Identify the goals of the criminal law.
- Describe the various classifications of crime.

## MODULE 1.2 SOURCES OF CRIMINAL LAW
- Identify the sources of the criminal law.

## MODULE 1.3 REACHING A VERDICT
- Describe the adversarial system.
- Identify courtroom participants.

## MODULE 1.4 COURT ORGANIZATION
- Describe the structure of the U.S. legal system, including jurisdiction.

## MODULE 1.5 LEARNING CRIMINAL LAW WITH REAL AND HYPOTHETICAL CASES
- Outline the stages of a criminal case.
- Explain the practical meaning of a verdict.

MODULE

# 1.1    PRELIMINARY INFORMATION

*Learning Objectives*

- **Define crime and criminal law.**
- **Explain the difference between substantive criminal law and criminal procedure.**
- **Identify the goals of the criminal law.**
- **Describe the various classifications of crime.**

## CORE CONCEPTS

**criminal law** Specifies what kinds of behavior are illegal, what punishments are available for dealing with offenders, and what defenses can be invoked by individuals who break it.

**Criminal law** is the bedrock of the American criminal justice system. It specifies what kinds of behavior are illegal, what punishments are available for dealing with offenders, and what defenses can be invoked by individuals who find themselves on the wrong side of the law. Without the criminal law, there would be no crimes, no criminals, and perhaps no means of controlling undesirable behavior. Certainly violence would still exist, property would still be stolen, and order would still be threatened, but these activities, harmful as they are, would not be considered illegal. Our system of criminal laws ensures that something can be done in response to behaviors that are widely deemed unacceptable.

The study of criminal law forces us to confront some deep and profound questions. Most of us can agree that murdering another human being is wrong. Most of us can agree, too, that harming children, destroying others' property, and breaking into occupied dwellings are not behaviors society is willing to accept. The list of taboos goes on. Yet there are many other activities that are not widely regarded as inappropriate. For example, some people feel—and the criminal law reflects this feeling—that recreational marijuana use should be illegal. Others, though, feel that they should be able to use the drug to their heart's content so long as it does not harm others. This poses a question: At what point is the line between legal and illegal behavior drawn? There is no easy answer.

There are many other deep questions that arise in the study of criminal law. And they, too, have no easy answers. For example, why is it justifiable for society to punish people for their wrongdoing? More specifically, at what point is it acceptable for government to take away the life or liberty of a person who does harm to others? Conversely, when is it acceptable for a person to take another's life? Should one individual be held liable for the actions of another? When is it acceptable to commit an otherwise harmful act? Can certain individuals be excused for their transgressions? These are the questions this book sets out to answer. But to answer such questions, we must first lay a foundation for the study of criminal law.

# Comparing Crimes to Civil Wrongs

**crime** Anything the criminal law defines as illegal.

This book—and the study of criminal law—focuses squarely on the concept of **crime**. Unfortunately, there is no easy way to define crime, other than to say it is anything that lawmakers define as criminal. There is no clear "consensus" in society as to what should be deemed criminal. There is no single underlying moral dimension to what is criminal, either. There is no single value system that prevails. Many crimes are defined as such because the overwhelming majority of people feel they should be. Crimes, then, are little more than behaviors that lawmakers, who in the United States are our elected representatives, consider illegal.

The concept of crime is perhaps more easily understood by looking to state penal codes and their stated *purpose* for the criminal law. For example, in Pennsylvania, the stated purposes of the criminal law, according to Section 104 of that state's Crimes Code, are:

1. To forbid and prevent conduct that unjustifiably inflicts or threatens substantial harm to individual or public interest.
2. To safeguard conduct that is without fault from condemnation as criminal.
3. To safeguard offenders against excessive, disproportionate, or arbitrary punishment.
4. To give fair warning of the nature of the conduct declared to constitute an offense, and of the sentences that may be imposed on conviction of an offense.
5. To differentiate on reasonable grounds between serious and minor offenses, and to differentiate among offenders with a view to a just individualization in their treatment.

Crimes need to be distinguished from torts. Even though many crimes are committed against other individuals, the criminal law treats them as offenses against society as a whole. This is why most criminal law cases contain the name of the person charged and the governing authority that is tasked with charging the alleged criminal. Cases such as *People* v. *Smith*, *Commonwealth* v. *Jones*, or *State* v. *Wallace* reflect this arrangement. In contrast, a **tort** is a private wrong or injury. In a tort situation, a court will provide a remedy in the form of an "action," or a lawsuit between the two parties, the victim and the so-called **tort-feasor**. Tort actions are brought by victims to compensate them for their injuries. This compensation is usually financial. In contrast, criminal cases are brought for the purpose of punishing wrongdoers.

**tort** A private wrong or injury.
**tort-feasor** One who commits a **tort**.

# Comparing Criminal Law to Criminal Procedure

**criminal procedure** A vast system of laws and guidelines that detail how suspected and accused criminals are to be processed and handled by the criminal justice system.

The substantive criminal law is separate and distinct from the law of criminal procedure. **Criminal procedure** is a vast system of laws and guidelines that detail how suspected and accused criminals are to be processed and handled by the criminal justice system. Constitutional guidelines pertaining to search and seizure, confessions and interrogations, due process, and the like are all important in criminal procedure. Also, as its name suggests, criminal procedure emphasizes *procedure* over substance. A course on criminal procedure will arm you with an understanding of how criminal justice officials are supposed to process criminal suspects, criminal

**defendant** The individual charged with committing a crime.

defendants (the individual charged with a crime is called the **defendant**), and even the convicted. In contrast, criminal law is about the *substance* of the law, what it prohibits and what types of individuals can be punished for violating it.

Criminal-law class is not where you learn about vehicle searches, witness identification, *Miranda* warnings, and sobriety checkpoints. Instead, criminal law focuses on equally critical topics, including the basic elements of crime, the defenses available to criminal conduct, the rules governing criminal activity that stops short of completion, and liability for people who conspire together in furtherance of their illegal actions. Criminal law is also where you build an understanding of the differences between the many types of illegal activity named in criminal statutes at the federal, state, and local level. For example, what is the difference between robbery and burglary? When is a person guilty of first-degree murder instead of second-degree murder? What sets terrorism apart from homicide?

# Goals of the Criminal Law

Some people regard the criminal law as an instrument of oppression. Others are quick to claim that the poor criminal offender stands no chance against the deep pockets of the state. There is a measure of truth to such impressions, as they are closely tied to criminal law's goal of punishing wrongdoers. Yet our system of criminal laws is built on other goals as well. These include community protection and offender protection.

## Offender Punishment

**punishment** The infliction of unpleasant consequences on an offender.

Punishment is widely considered a key goal of the criminal law. Some even consider it the *only* goal.[1] What is **punishment**? There is no readily agreed-upon definition, but one that suffices is this: the infliction of unpleasant consequences on an offender on the grounds that he or she *deserves* it. This definition treats punishment as an end to itself. Sometimes, however, punishment is considered a means to another end, such as deterrence, rehabilitation, or even harm reduction. For example, we might choose to punish an offender not just to prevent that person from committing additional crimes, but also because we want to send a message to the community that such crimes are not tolerated.

Punishment is most often associated with a retributive theory of punishment, the view that offenders must be made to suffer, whether by confinement, death, or some other method for their indiscretions. A famous Pennsylvania Supreme Court case, *Commonwealth* v. *Ritter*[2] further described **retribution** in this way:

**retribution** A theory of punishment that believes offenders must be made to suffer, whether by confinement, death, or some other method for their indiscretions.

> This may be regarded as the doctrine of legal revenge, or punishment merely for the sake of punishment. It is to pay back the wrong-doer for his wrong-doing, to make him suffer by way of retaliation even if no benefit result thereby to himself or to others. This theory of punishment looks to the past and not to the future, and rests solely upon the foundation of vindictive justice. It is this idea of punishment that generally prevails, even though those who entertain it may not be fully aware of their so doing. Historically, it may be said that the origin of all legal punishments had its

---

[1]M. Moore, *Placing Blame: A General Theory of the Criminal Law* (New York: Oxford University Press, 1997).
[2]*Commonwealth* v. *Ritter*, 13 Pa.D. & C. 285 (1930).

**Figure 1.1**
How Criminal Law Promotes Community Protection

root in the natural impulse of revenge. At first this instinct was gratified by retaliatory measures on the part of the individual who suffered by the crime committed, or, in the case of murder, by his relatives. Later, the state took away the right of retaliation from individuals, and its own assumption of the function of revenge really constituted the beginning of criminal law.

The Old Testament also captures the essence of retributive theory in Leviticus 24:17, 19–20 (King James Version):

> And he that killeth any man shall surely be put to death. . . . And if a man cause a blemish in his neighbor; as he hath done, so shall it be done to him; Breach for breach, eye for eye, tooth for tooth.

## Community Protection

**utilitarian** In terms of criminal law, the notion that the criminal law should maximize the net happiness of society.

Another goal of the criminal law is community protection. This stems from a **utilitarian** perspective. As Jeremy Bentham once argued, the purpose of all criminal laws is to maximize the net happiness of society.[3] Utilitarianism thus requires that we look beyond the offender and beyond the somewhat limited goal of punishment for punishment's sake. It is concerned with society's interest in protecting itself and providing for the general welfare, or simply community protection. By what means, then, is community protection a goal of the criminal law? Through incapacitation, deterrence, rehabilitation, restoration, and denunciation (see Figure 1.1).

**incapacitation** The act of removing an individual from society so that person can no longer offend.

**Incapacitation,** or the act of removing an individual from society so he or she can no longer offend, serves an important community protection function. Clearly depriving a person of contact with most, if not all, law-abiding individuals hampers the individuals' ability to offend, yet incapacitation is distinct from the "payback," or "eye-for-an-eye" character of retribution. The court case *Commonwealth* v. *Ritter* elaborated on incapacitation in this way:

> To permit a man of dangerous criminal tendencies to be in a position where he can give indulgence to such propensies would be a folly which no community should suffer itself to commit, any more than it should allow a wild animal to range at will in the city streets. If, therefore, there is danger that a defendant may again commit crime, society should restrain his liberty until such danger be past, and, in cases similar to the present, if reasonably necessary for that purpose, to terminate his life.[4]

**specific deterrence** The idea that when an offender is locked up, that person cannot commit crimes out in society.

When an offender is locked up, that person cannot commit crimes out in society. This is the concept of **specific deterrence**. Specific deterrence also serves, it is hoped, to discourage the offender from committing additional crimes once he or she is released from confinement (if this ever occurs). It is presumed that the offender's incarceration will cause that person to "think twice" before offending again. This

---

[3]J. Bentham, *An Introduction to the Principles of Morals and Legislation*, J. Bowring, ed. (1843).
[4]M. D. Wolfe, ed., *Holmes-Laski Letters* (Cambridge, MA: Harvard University Press, 1953), p. 806.

way specific deterrence is a utilitarian goal. It maximizes, we hope, the net happiness of society either because a dangerous individual is removed from the community or sees the error of his or her ways on release.

**General deterrence** also protects society, more so than specific deterrence. General deterrence is concerned not with the offender, but with other would-be offenders. The assumption is that when would-be offenders see a criminal held accountable, they opt to abide by the law for fear of suffering the same fate. Whether general deterrence actually occurs is up for debate. Many offenders are not aware of or do not pay attention to the consequences other criminals face. General deterrence *assumes* that the criminal law helps protect the community through its ability to *prevent* criminal activity.

**general deterrence** The assumption that when would-be offenders see a criminal held accountable, they opt to abide by the law for fear of suffering the same fate.

While society may benefit from general deterrence, the offender may not. For example, should offenders be locked up for the sole purpose of sending a message to others? Supreme Court Justice Oliver Wendell Holmes raised this concern:

> If I were having a philosophical talk with a man I was going to have hanged (or electrocuted), I should say, "I don't doubt that your act was inevitable for you but to make it more avoidable by others we propose to sacrifice you to the common good. You may regard yourself as a soldier dying for your country if you like. But the law must keep its promises."[5]

**rehabilitation** A planned intervention intended to bring about change in an offender.

The criminal law also protects society via **rehabilitation**. Rehabilitation is typically defined in terms of a "planned intervention that is intended to change offenders for the better."[6] For example, requiring a drug abuser to complete a treatment program may benefit society in the long run because the individual may desist from drug use. Yet incarceration can also serve a rehabilitative function, or so some people think. The logic goes like this: If a criminal is locked up, that person will have plenty of time to reflect and understand the harm that he or she has caused. Rehabilitation can also be considered punishment, as it is not uncommon for a judge to order a convicted criminal to get psychiatric care, participate in vocational training, or attend anger management meetings, even though the offender may have no desire to do so.

**restoration** The practice of having offenders "face up" to the harm they have caused.

**restorative justice** "A process whereby all the parties with a stake in a particular offence come together to resolve collectively how to deal with the aftermath of the offence and its implications for the future."

**Restoration** is concerned with getting offenders to "face up" to the harm they have caused. Most often, restoration is associated with the practice of **restorative justice**, which has been defined as "a process whereby all the parties with a stake in a particular offence come together to resolve collectively how to deal with the aftermath of the offence and its implications for the future."[7] Often, the offender will be brought before the victim in some controlled setting and be made aware of the harm that the offender has caused. Then, typically, an agreement is reached such that the offender can (1) repair the harm inflicted and then (2) successfully reenter the community. Clearly there are community protection benefits associated with successfully implemented restorative justice initiatives.

---

[5]Ibid.
[6]J. L. Worrall, *Crime Control in America: What Works?* (Boston, MA: Allyn & Bacon, 2008), p. 228.
[7]J. Braithwaite, "Restorative Justice: Assessing Optimistic and Pessimistic Accounts," in M. Tonry, ed., *Crime and Justice: A Review of Research* (Chicago, IL: University of Chicago Press, 1999), p. 5.

**denunciation** When society expresses its abhorrence of the crime committed.

Finally, the criminal law helps ensure community protection via **denunciation**. Denunciation occurs when society expresses its "abhorrence of the crime committed."[8] In democratic societies, criminal laws presumably express the majority's view as to what is and is not acceptable. Elected representatives enact statutes in response to society's preference, which means the resulting criminal laws serve to express society's condemnation of unacceptable forms of conduct. This denunciation further serves a community protection function in the sense that would-be offenders come to understand (we hope) what activities the majority frowns on. Of course it doesn't always work this way, but the same can be said of restoration, rehabilitation, general deterrence, and even specific deterrence.

## Offender Protection

It is tempting to get caught up in the "unpleasant" effects on the offender of the criminal law. Whether offenders are locked up, made to pay for their actions, treated, or shunned by the community, they find themselves on the "losing" side. But it is important to note that the criminal law also serves the important goal of *protecting* offenders, too. One way this occurs is via the prevention of vigilantism. Having a formal system of criminal laws helps ensure that the *state* seeks justice rather than private individuals. In earlier times, people took matters into their own hands and avenged wrongdoing as they saw fit. Nowadays, such actions are prohibited. Victims still retaliate some of the time and take the law into their own hands, but such actions are uncommon and discouraged in modern society. The criminal law thus protects offenders from the threat of victims coming after them.

The criminal law also protects offenders by ensuring proportionate and nonarbitrary punishment. Statutes spell out the gradations of various crimes (e.g., first-degree murder, second-degree murder), a topic we will consider in some depth throughout this book. These statutes also spell out the range of acceptable punishments, ensuring at least *some* protection against wildly differing sentences between offenders. There are still examples of unequal treatment that persist, especially pertaining to racial and ethnic disparities in criminal justice,[9] but the criminal law at least *helps* ensure a measure of equal treatment.

Offenders also benefit from elaborate procedural protections, including the right to counsel, the right to a speedy trial, the right to an impartial jury trial, the right to a public trial, the right to confrontation, and the right to compulsory process. These protections, however, stem more from the rules of criminal procedure—and particularly the U.S. Constitution—than they do from the criminal law. In any case, offenders these days rarely find themselves subjected to the arbitrary whims of the state. The opposite is true. The criminal law continues to grow and involve, both in response to new harms and out of concern for protecting those who find themselves charged with law violations.

---

[8]D. Lanham, B. Bartal, R. Evans, and D. Wood, *Criminal Laws in Australia* (Sydney, Australia: The Federation Press, 2006), p. 14.

[9]See, e.g., S. Walker, C. Spohn, and M. DeLone, *The Color of Justice: Race, Ethnicity, and Crime in America*, 4th ed. (Belmont, CA: Wadsworth, 2007); R. J. Sampson and J. L. Lauritsen, "Racial and Ethnic Disparities in Crime and Criminal Justice in the United States," in M. Tonry, ed., *Crime and Justice: A Review of Research* (Chicago, IL: University of Chicago Press, 1997), pp. 311–374.

# The Classification of Crimes

We raised two important issues earlier in this chapter. One was that crimes are defined as such by legislative bodies. Another was that while there is no consensus over what should be illegal, there is a certain measure of agreement when it comes to more harmful types of behavior, such as murder. With this backdrop, we can begin to make sense of criminal law by classifying crimes. Criminal statutes tend to classify crimes in terms of felonies and misdemeanors, the former being more serious than the latter. This classification scheme, however, is somewhat arbitrary and may not reflect the true harms that one crime causes compared to another. For that reason, it is helpful to think of the "evil" that underlies a certain type of activity. Some behaviors are simply more evil than others.

## Felonies and Misdemeanors

**felony** A crime punishable by death or confinement in prison for *more than* 12 months.

**misdemeanor** A crime punishable by a fine or a period of incarceration *less than* 12 months.

The classification of crimes into felonies and misdemeanors is age old, popular, and found in nearly every penal code. In general, a **felony** is a crime punishable by death or confinement in prison for *more than* 12 months. Obviously, death is reserved for the most serious felonies, such as first-degree murder. Lesser felonies, such as theft of goods valued at a certain amount, result in imprisonment rather than capital punishment. A **misdemeanor**, by contrast, is a crime punishable by a fine or a period of incarceration *less than* 12 months.

Importantly, a crime is defined as a felony or a misdemeanor based on possible, not actual, punishment. For example, in one case, a woman was sentenced to one year in prison for driving under the influence, but the judge "probated" her sentence, meaning he suspended it, and instead required her to serve 120 days in home confinement. She later argued she was a misdemeanant, not a felon, but an appeals court said that "a person whose . . . felony sentence is reduced . . . does not become a misdemeanant by virtue of the reduction but remains a felon."[10]

Why should we care about the distinction between felonies and misdemeanors, other than by the punishments that can be imposed? A key reason is that trial procedures differ for felonies and misdemeanors. For example, jury trials are not required in misdemeanor cases where the punishment does not exceed six months' confinement.[11] Also, felony trials tend to be more drawn out and elaborate because of the stakes involved, which could include capital punishment for the offender in serious cases. Another reason it is important to classify crimes in this way is because certain offenses require it. For example, some statutes define burglary in terms of unlawful entry with intent to commit a felony inside. If a misdemeanor is committed inside, then the crime is not burglary. We look at burglary in more detail in Chapter 10.

## *Malum in Se* versus *Malum Prohibitum*

**malum in se** An act that is wrong or evil in itself.

**malum prohibitum** An act that is wrong or evil because it is defined as such.

*Malum in se* (or the plural form, *mala in se*) is a Latin phrase meaning "wrong or evil in itself." In contrast, **malum prohibitum** (or *mala prohibita*) means "wrong or evil because it is defined as such." This distinction goes back to the criminal law's moral underpinnings we discussed earlier. Certain crimes are simply wrong in themselves.

---

[10]*Commonwealth* v. *Rhodes*, 920 S.W. 2d 531 (1996), p. 533.
[11]*Baldwin* v. *New York*, 399 U.S. 66 (1970).

For example, it is all but impossible to convince someone that an unjustified and inexcusable murder is acceptable. Other examples of *mala in se* offenses include robbery, larceny (theft), and rape.

The line between what is wrong in itself and what is wrong because legislators defined it that way is difficult to draw. Is drug possession wrong in itself? What about speeding? Speeding arguably poses risks to other drivers, so is speeding inherently wrong? If not, could it be once a driver exceeds a certain speed, say 100 miles per hour? There are no easy answers. The distinction between *malum in se* and *malum prohibitum* is largely academic these days because for the majority of offenses, it is difficult to objectively place them in one category over another.

## YOUR DECISION

1. On New Year's Eve, George Schultz was out celebrating with his friends in New York City and drank at least seven mixed cocktails. After the ball dropped in Times Square, George began to drive home while still under the influence of alcohol. Accidentally, he crashed into Janette Lucas, a cocktail waitress who was walking to the subway after work. Janette was killed in the accident. Her family thinks George Schultz should be held to account for his actions. Would they pursue a civil or a criminal case? Why?

2. Armed with a Swiss Army knife, Jeffrey Biggins robbed the local convenience store and made off with $700 in cash. The police were able to apprehend Biggins and charged him with the crime of armed robbery, which has a potential prison sentence of up to five years. Biggins pled guilty to the crime. Since this was Biggins' first criminal offense, the judge sentenced him to six months in prison and 100 hours of community service. Is the crime of armed robbery a felony or a misdemeanor? Why?

## Summary

- Crime is anything that lawmakers define as criminal.
- Torts are wrongs between individuals; crimes are offenses by an individual against society as a whole (even though there are real victims).
- The criminal law is separate and distinct from criminal procedure.
- Criminal law specifies what kinds of behavior are illegal, what punishments are available for dealing with offenders, and what defenses can be invoked by individuals who find themselves on the wrong side of the law.
- Criminal procedure is a vast system of laws and guidelines that detail who suspected and accused criminals are to be processed and handled by the criminal justice system.
- The first goal of the criminal law is punishment. Punishment is most often associated with retribution, the view that offenders must be made to suffer, whether by confinement, death, or some other method for their indiscretions.
- The second goal of the criminal law is community protection.
- The criminal law promotes community protection because of the utilitarian perspective, which holds that the purpose of all criminal laws is to maximize the net happiness of society.

- The community is protected from criminals via incapacitation, deterrence, rehabilitation, restoration, and denunciation.

- The third goal of the criminal law is offender protection. Offenders are protected against vigilantism and arbitrary punishment.

- A felony is a crime punishable by death or confinement in prison for *more than* 12 months. A misdemeanor, by contrast, is a crime punishable by a fine or a period of incarceration *less than* 12 months.

- *Malum in se* (or the plural form, *mala in se*) is a Latin phrase meaning "wrong or evil in itself." In contrast, *malum prohibitum* (or mala prohibita) means "wrong or evil because it is defined as such."

**MODULE**

# 1.2     SOURCES OF CRIMINAL LAW

*Learning Objective*

- **Identify the sources of the criminal law.**

**CORE CONCEPTS**   We have already offered a definition of "criminal law" and mentioned statutes and penal codes in passing, but we have *not* just yet discussed where the criminal law comes from, other than to say there are some moral underpinnings and that, today, crimes are mostly defined as such by legislatures. What are the origins of the criminal law? There many of them, some ancient, others more modern. Here we look at five sources of the criminal law: early legal codes, the common law, modern statutes, the Model Penal Code, and constitutional sources. Each is best viewed as a piece of the criminal-law puzzle (see Figure 1.2).

**Figure 1.2**
Sources of the Criminal Law

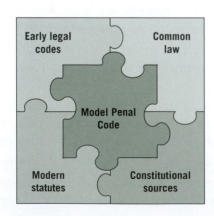

**Code of Hammurabi**
The earliest known example of a formal written legal code. It expressed a strong "eye-for-an-eye" philosophy on punishment.

## Early Legal Codes

Perhaps the earliest known example of a formal written legal code was the **Code of Hammurabi**. Also known as Hammurabi's Code and assembled by the sixth Babylonian king, Hammurabi, in 1760 B.C., the code expressed a strong eye-for-an-eye philosophy. To illustrate, here is the seventh of the code's "code of laws":

If anyone buy from the son or the slave of another man, without witnesses or a contract, silver or gold, a male or female slave, an ox or a sheep, an ass or anything, or if he take it in charge, he is considered a thief and shall be put to death.[12]

Roman law provides another example of formally codified legal principles. The so-called **Twelve Tables** (450 B.C.) was the first secular (i.e., not regarded as religious) written legal code.[13] The code was named as such because the laws were literally written onto 12 ivory tablets. The tablets were then posted so all Romans could read them. The Twelve Tables, like Hammurabi's Code, contained a strong element of retributive justice. One of the laws, "*Si membrum rupsit, ni cum eo pacit, talio esto*" translates as follows: "If one has maimed another and does not buy his peace, let there be retaliation in kind."[14]

Despite their shortcomings and harsh character, these early legal codes are important because they signaled the emergence of formalized "law." And while it is difficult to define the term with precision, **law** generally refers to formal rules, principles, and guidelines enforced by **political authority**. This political authority is what began to take dispute resolution out of the hands of citizens and put it under control of governments. Legal codes have changed and evolved considerably over the years, but the use of political or governmental authority to enforce such codes has remained pretty constant.

**Twelve Tables** The first secular written legal code.

**law** The formal rules, principles, and guidelines enforced by political authority.

**political authority** Another term for *governmental authority*.

## Common Law

**common law** Also known as *case law* or *judge-made law*, the law developed in early England by judges who wrote down their decisions and circulated them to other judges. The law "in common."

**special law** In contrast to **common law**, the laws of specific villages and localities that were in effect in medieval England and that were often enforced by canonical (i.e., religious) courts.

After the Norman conquest of England (A.D. 1066), King William and his Norman dukes and barons moved quickly to consolidate their hold over newly won territories. One method was to take control of the preexisting legal/court system. Once they did this, the judges in their courts not only issued decisions but also wrote them down. These decisions were subsequently circulated to other judges. The result was a measure of uniformity from one court to the next. This was literally the law "in common" throughout England, and it came to be known as the **common law**.

The common law can be better understood when it is contrasted with **special law**, which refers to the laws of specific villages and localities that were in effect in medieval England and that were often enforced by canonical (i.e., religious) courts. Under the reign of Henry II (1154–1189), national law was introduced, but not through legislative authority as is customary today. Rather, Henry II implemented a system whereby judges from his own central court went out into the countryside to preside over disputes. They resolved these disputes based on what they perceived as custom. The judges effectively created law, as there was no democratic law-forming process in place at the time.

---

[12]Ancient History Sourcebook, *Code of Hammurabi*, c. 1780 B.C., from http://www.fordham.edu/halsall/ancient/hamcode.html (accessed January 1, 2010).
[13]O. J. Thatcher, ed., *The Library of Original Sources* (Milwaukee, WI: University Research Extension Co., 1901), Vol. III: *The Roman World*, pp. 9–11.
[14]Ibid.

**precedent** In general, some prior action that guides current action. In the context of courts, letting judges' decisions be guided by earlier decisions.

**stare decisis** A Latin term meaning "to stand by things decided," or to adhere to precedent.

As more and more judges began to record their decisions, the principles of *stare decisis* and precedent were developed. **Precedent** refers, generally, to some prior action that guides current action. In the common law context, this meant that judges' decisions were guided by earlier decisions. Precedent thus ensured continuity and predictability. If decisions changed radically from one judge to the next or from place to place, or both, the "common" law would be anything but common. It was also easier for judges to fall back on earlier decisions; otherwise they would have to continually reinvent the wheel. **Stare decisis**, which is Latin for "to stand by things decided," is thus the formal practice of adhering to precedent.

While the common law is usually viewed as a legal concept, it also had social implications: The medieval judge was entrusted with the collective wisdom, values, and morals established by the community and was trusted to apply them to solve disputes between citizens. Even when appointed by the king, the medieval judge represented the community and applied the community's (not the king's) law, thereby maintaining its age-old customs and values.

## Modern Statutes

Modern statutes differ from early legal codes because they exist at different levels of government and come in several different forms. The United States Code contains federal laws, and violations of its provisions can lead to federal prosecution. States have their respective codes. Other units of government, such as counties and cities, often have their own ordinances. These legal codes exist in several varieties. States such as California list criminal offenses in more than one code. There, most crimes are spelled out in the Penal Code, but the Health and Safety Code criminalizes drug-law violations. The state has 29 separate legal codes![15]

Having multiple criminal codes at various levels of government makes it nearly impossible to develop a full understanding of the criminal law. This book cannot thoroughly cover the criminal code of each state, as it would be excessively lengthy. Of course, an attorney who wishes to practice criminal law in a particular state will need to become well versed in the laws of his or her state, but for a general introduction to criminal procedure, we cannot afford to delve too deeply into the laws of any given state. Fortunately, there is considerable overlap in the criminal laws of various jurisdictions.

**American Law Institute** A private organization of lawyers, judges, and legal scholars that wrote and adopted the **Model Penal Code**.

## The Model Penal Code

In our federal system of government, each state is free—within certain constitutional limitations—to develop its own common and statutory law. This led to considerable variation from state to state. In 1962, however, the **American Law Institute**, a private

[15]See, e.g., http://www.leginfo.ca.gov/calaw.html (accessed January 1, 2010).

**Model Penal Code** A model set of criminal laws adopted by the American Law Institute for states to emulate as they see fit.

organization of lawyers, judges, and legal scholars, adopted a **Model Penal Code**. The Code was intended to serve as just that, a "model" for states to follow. Since 1962, several states have adopted the Model Penal Code, either in whole or in part. This is beneficial in at least two respects. First, it promotes consistency across the states. Second, it makes the study of the criminal law more manageable. As such, we will introduce, throughout this book, criminal law concepts through the lens of the Model Penal Code. But bear in mind that the federal system has not adopted it, nor has California, the nation's most populous state.

## Constitutional Sources

Constitutions are perhaps the most significant source of law. Unlike penal codes, constitutions generally do not prohibit actions on the part of private citizens. Rather, constitutions generally place limits on government authority. They define, in broad terms, government structure and organization; they also spell out various rights that people enjoy, how government officials will be selected, and what roles various government branches will take on.

The U.S. Constitution is so important to the criminal law that we devote all of Chapter 2 to it. In particular, we will look at the Constitution's prohibition against so-called *ex post facto* laws. We will look in detail at the concept of equal protection and consider issues of vagueness and overbreadth in the criminal law.

**Bill of Rights** The first ten amendments to the U.S. Constitution.

The **Bill of Rights** (see Figure 1.3), consisting of the first ten amendments, also announces important limitations on government authority with respect to the investigation and prosecution of crime. The Fourth Amendment, for example, spells out warrant requirements, and the Fifth Amendment protects people, in part, from being forced to incriminate themselves. The Eighth Amendment prohibits cruel and unusual punishment.

While the federal Constitution receives the most attention from its status as the supreme law of the United States, it is important to note that each state has its own constitution. These often mirror the federal Constitution, but they often go into much more detail. Some states use an initiative process, where every November voters can decide the fate of proposed constitutional amendments. Other states have used their constitutions to more clearly spell out what they consider prohibited actions, whereas a close read of the federal Constitution suggests the founding fathers intended something different. In any case, constitutions work together with legal codes, administrative regulations, and the common law to provide an interesting basis for criminal justice as we know it.

State constitutions can be more restrictive than the U.S. Constitution, but no state can relax protections spelled out in the U.S. Constitution. For example, the U.S. Constitution's Fourth Amendment spells out search warrant requirements, but the Fourth Amendment is vague in terms of whether a warrant is required in all circumstances. In theory, a state could require warrants for *all* searches, but as a practical matter, most states have followed the U.S. Constitution's lead (and the Supreme Court's interpretation of it).

**Figure 1.3**
Bill of Rights

### Amendment I

Congress shall make no law respecting an establishment of religion, or prohibiting the free exercise thereof; or abridging the freedom of speech, or of the press; or the right of the people peaceably to assemble, and to petition the government for a redress of grievances.

### Amendment II

A well regulated militia, being necessary to the security of a free state, the right of the people to keep and bear arms, shall not be infringed.

### Amendment III

No soldier shall, in time of peace be quartered in any house, without the consent of the owner, nor in time of war, but in a manner to be prescribed by law.

### Amendment IV

The right of the people to be secure in their persons, houses, papers, and effects, against unreasonable searches and seizures, shall not be violated, and no warrants shall issue, but upon probable cause, supported by oath or affirmation, and particularly describing the place to be searched, and the persons or things to be seized.

### Amendment V

No person shall be held to answer for a capital, or otherwise infamous crime, unless on a presentment or indictment of a grand jury, except in cases arising in the land or naval forces, or in the militia, when in actual service in time of war or public danger; nor shall any person be subject for the same offense to be twice put in jeopardy of life or limb; nor shall be compelled in any criminal case to be a witness against himself, nor be deprived of life, liberty, or property, without due process of law; nor shall private property be taken for public use, without just compensation.

### Amendment VI

In all criminal prosecutions, the accused shall enjoy the right to a speedy and public trial, by an impartial jury of the state and district wherein the crime shall have been committed, which district shall have been previously ascertained by law, and to be informed of the nature and cause of the accusation; to be confronted with the witnesses against him; to have compulsory process for obtaining witnesses in his favor, and to have the assistance of counsel for his defense.

### Amendment VII

In suits at common law, where the value in controversy shall exceed twenty dollars, the right of trial by jury shall be preserved, and no fact tried by a jury, shall be otherwise reexamined in any court of the United States, than according to the rules of the common law.

### Amendment VIII

Excessive bail shall not be required, nor excessive fines imposed, nor cruel and unusual punishments inflicted.

### Amendment IX

The enumeration in the Constitution, of certain rights, shall not be construed to deny or disparage others retained by the people.

### Amendment X

The powers not delegated to the United States by the Constitution, nor prohibited by it to the states, are reserved to the states respectively, or to the people.

**YOUR DECISION**

1. Carrie Raymond is a first-year associate at a large criminal-defense law firm in Philadelphia. The firm recently received a new client—a famous football player charged with extortion. The partner on the case has asked you to research Pennsylvania extortion law. Where should you look? What sources should you use?

2. Martin Drake is being charged with first-degree murder in Florida and wants to raise the defense of insanity. Drake and his lawyer believe that he has the best chance of winning under the Model Penal Code's "substantial capacity" test for insanity. Drake's lawyer asks the Florida court to apply the Model Penal Code's test. Does the trial court in Florida need to use the Model Penal Code test? Why or why not?

## Summary

- Five sources of criminal law are early legal codes, the common law, modern statutes, the Model Penal Code, and constitutional sources.

- One of the earliest known examples of a formal written legal code was the Code of Hammurabi.

- The so-called Twelve Tables was the first secular written legal code.

- Common law is "the law in common," meaning that as one judge wrote down a decision and circulated it to other judges, consistency developed as these judges began to apply the same principles.

- The common law was not unique to any particular place; it was the law "in common" throughout England.

- Special law refers to the laws of specific villages and localities.

- The United States Code contains federal laws, and violations of its provisions can lead to federal prosecution.

- States have their own legal codes that define what is and is not criminal.

- Other units of government, such as counties and cities, often have their own ordinances that define legal and illegal behaviors.

- The Model Penal Code, developed by the American Law Institute, is a *sample* legal code that many states have adopted.

- States adopt their own penal codes, adopt the Model Penal Code, or adopt a combination of each.

- Constitutions are perhaps the most significant source of law.

- Unlike penal codes, constitutions generally do not prohibit actions on the part of private citizens. Rather, constitutions generally place limits on government authority.

- The U.S. Constitution, including the Bill of Rights, is very influential in American criminal law.

# 1.3

# REACHING A VERDICT

*Learning Objectives*
- **Describe the adversarial system.**
- **Identify courtroom participants.**

## CORE CONCEPTS

This book, like many other criminal-law books, makes extensive use of cases involving actual people charged with and convicted of crimes. The problem is that most published court decisions hail from the appellate courts—after someone has been convicted. This is a critically important point to keep in mind. Nearly every published criminal-law case, including those already referenced in this chapter, involve some person who was already convicted of a crime and who decided to appeal that conviction for one reason or another.

As you know by now, the appellate stage of the criminal process comes *after* adjudication, that is, after the defendant has been tried and convicted in court. It is thus easy to lose sight of some of the important procedures and considerations that lead up to the publishing of a court case. In this section we look at several of them: the adversary system, the burden of proof in criminal trials, presumptions, the roles of the prosecutor and the defense attorney, and the roles of the judge and jury.

## Adversary System

**adversarial justice system** A system of justice that pits two parties against each other in pursuit of the truth.

Ours is an **adversarial justice system**. It is adversarial because it pits two parties against each other in pursuit of the truth. Our adversarial system is not what it is, however, because attorneys love to hate each other. Rather, adversarialism owes to the many protections our Constitution and laws afford people.

When criminal defendants assert their rights, this sometimes amounts to one side saying the other is wrong, which ultimately leads to an impasse that must be resolved by a judge. If the defendant's attorney seeks suppression of key evidence that may have been obtained improperly, the prosecutor will probably disagree; after all, such evidence could form the basis of his or her case. The judge must rule to settle the matter. This is the essence of adversarialism—two competing sets of interests (the defendant's and the government's) working against each other.

Why else is ours an adversarial system? Another more fundamental explanation lies in the founding fathers' concerns with oppressive governments. Adversarialism promotes argument, debate, and openness. With no defense attorneys and only prosecutors having any say in a defendant's case, there would be untold numbers of rights violations, rushes to judgment, and so on.

Hollywood loves to make it look like prosecutors and defense attorneys cannot stand each other, and they are constantly springing surprise witnesses on one another, arguing with each other to the point of fighting, and so on. While it is true that some prosecutors and defense attorneys are not the best of friends, most know each other and work together on a routine basis. Some prosecutors were once defense attorneys and vice versa. These days, collaboration is popular, too, as prosecutors and defense attorneys are coming to realize that the traditional hard-line adversarial approach to meting out justice is not always helpful for the accused.

## Inquisitorial Justice

**inquisitorial system** The opposite of an adversarial system. The accused does not enjoy the same protections and decision-making authority is placed in the hands of one or very few individuals.

Adversarial justice can be better understood when compared to its opposite, namely inquisitorial justice, which is characteristic of an **inquisitorial system**. There are several features of inquisitorial systems that differ from adversarial systems. First, inquisitorial systems do not provide the same protections to the accused (e.g., right to counsel); second, inquisitorial systems place decision making in the hands of one or a very few individuals. Third, juries are often the exception in inquisitorial systems. Finally, the attorneys in inquisitorial systems are much more passive than in adversarial systems, and judges take on a more prominent role in the pursuit of truth.

Inquisitorial justice is often likened to justice from the past, such as in medieval England, and particularly at the hands of the early Christian church. For the most part, this perception is accurate, but some borderline inquisitorial systems are very much alive and well in this day and age, even in modern industrialized nations. For example, in France, the *juge d'instruction* (i.e., investigating magistrate) engages in fact-finding and performs investigations in cases of serious and complex crimes. American judges, in contrast, focus on legal matters, and in trials by jury, they never engage in fact-finding.

Until as recently as 1996, China had a full-blown inquisitorial system. Since the Chinese adopted significant reforms to their legal system, that has changed. As one researcher observed:

> [U]nder China's inquisitorial system, judges were required to engage in evidence-gathering and criminal investigations. Judges in the post-reform period, however, should be more likely to serve as impartial adjudicators who hear evidence and arguments from both sides and render a decision based solely on this information.[16]

**burden of proof** The requirement that a particular party convince the jury with regard to a particular issue. In the criminal law context, the burden of proof falls on the prosecutor to establish the defendant's guilt.

## Burden of Proof

**burden of persuasion** In a criminal case, the requirement that the prosecution persuade the jury that the defendant committed the crime.

The **burden of proof** in a criminal prosecution first falls on the government. This means that it is the government's responsibility to prove that a person committed a crime. The prosecution must *persuade* the jury that the defendant should be held accountable. This is known as the **burden of persuasion**. Related to the burden of

---

[16]H. Lu, "Confessions and Criminal Case Disposition in China," *Law and Society Review*, Vol. 37 (2003), p. 555.

**burden of production**
One party's (the prosecutor's in a criminal case) obligation to present sufficient evidence to have the issue decided by a fact-finder. The burden of production is a question of law.

**directed verdict** A judge's order that one side or the other wins without the need to move on to fact-finding (in which the defense would introduce evidence, call witnesses, and so on).

**proof beyond a reasonable doubt**
The standard of proof necessary in a criminal case, roughly akin to 95% certainty.

**preponderance of evidence** The standard of proof in a civil case, equivalent to "more certain than not."

**presumption** A fact assumed to be true under the law.

**presumption of innocence** A bedrock presumption in the American criminal justice system, the notion that the accused is not guilty until proven as such in a criminal trial.

proof is the **burden of production**. The burden of production is one party's (the prosecutor's in a criminal case) obligation to present sufficient evidence to have the issue decided by a fact-finder. The burden of production is a question of law. If the prosecutor does not meet the burden of production, the case may result in a **directed verdict**, which is a judge's order that one side or the other wins without the need to move on to fact-finding (in which the defense would introduce evidence, call witnesses, and so on).

In a criminal case, the prosecutor must present **proof beyond a reasonable doubt** that the defendant committed the crime, which is roughly the same as 95% certainty. In contrast, the burden of proof in a civil case falls on the plaintiff, the party bringing suit. Also, the standard of proof in a civil trial is lower. It is generally the **preponderance of evidence,** roughly akin to "more certain than not."

If proof beyond a reasonable doubt amounts to 95% certainty, then reasonable doubt is that other 5%. It is in the defense's interest to exploit that 5%, to get members of the jury thinking that there is a *chance* the defendant did not commit the crime. If the defendant chooses to assert a defense, then the burden of proof for doing so falls on the defendant. For example, if the defendant in a murder trial claims he was insane at the time of the crime, then it will be his burden to prove as much. The prosecution's only obligation is to prove each element of the crime charged.

## Presumptions

A **presumption** is a fact assumed to be true under the law. In the world of criminal law, there are many types of presumptions. Conclusive presumptions require that all parties agree with something assumed to be true. An example of this would be that a child born to a married couple who live together is the couple's child. It is likely that both parties to a case would agree to this presumption. In contrast to this kind of a conclusive presumption, a *rebuttable* presumption is one that could reasonably be disagreed with. Here is an example of a rebuttable presumption: "Because a letter was mailed, it was received by its intended recipient." This is rebuttable because the letter could actually be lost because of a mistake made by the post office.

Every person charged with a crime is assumed, in advance, to be innocent, which is known as the **presumption of innocence**. The presumption of innocence is both a presumption of law (because it is required from the outset) and a rebuttable presumption (because the prosecutor will present evidence to show the defendant, or the person charged with the crime, is not guilty). The presumption of innocence is a bedrock legal principle. One classic court decision put it this way:

> The presumption of innocence is not a mere belief at the beginning of the trial that the accused is probably innocent. It is not a will-o'-the-wisp, which appears and disappears as the trial progresses. It is a legal presumption which the jurors must consider along with the evidence and the inferences arising from the evidence, when they come finally to pass upon the case. In this sense, the presumption of innocence does accompany the accused through every stage of the trial.[17]

Presumptions are essential to the smooth operation of criminal justice. They serve, basically, as substitutes for evidence. Without them, every minute issue that

---

[17]*Dodson v. United States,* 23 F.2d 401 (1928).

**Figure 1.4**
Common Presumptions

- *Presumption of sanity.* All defendants are presumed sane; the burden falls on the defense to prove otherwise.
- *Presumption of death.* It is presumed that a person who has disappeared and is continually absent from his or her customary location (usually after seven years) is dead.
- *Presumption against suicide.* It is assumed that when a person dies, the cause is not suicide.
- *Presumption of a guilty mind following possession of the fruits of crime.* The jury can usually infer guilt if a person is caught "red-handed" with the fruits of crime.
- *Presumption of knowledge of the law.* Ignorance is not a defense to criminal liability.
- *Presumption of the regularity of official acts.* It is assumed, for example, that a proper chain of custody exists, unless the defense can show otherwise.
- *Presumption that young children cannot commit crimes.* Some states presume that children under a certain threshold age (e.g., age seven) cannot form criminal intent and thus cannot commit crime.
- *Presumption that people intend the results of their voluntary actions.* If a person voluntarily shoots another, the jury can presume the shooter intended to do so.

could possibly be disputed would come up during trials. For example, it is presumed that a child born to a married couple who live together is the couple's child. Without presumptions such as these, the process would be slowed down considerably because every minor event, no matter how likely, would have to be proven in court. (Figure 1.4 shows popular presumptions that arise in criminal justice.)

## The Prosecutor and the Defense Attorney

**opening statements**
The statements made by both the prosecutor and defense attorney at the outset of a criminal trial wherein each side lays out for the jury, in overview form, what they will prove throughout the trial.

Trials begin with **opening statements**. In their opening statements, both the prosecutor and the defense attorney lay out for the jury, in overview form, what they will prove throughout the trial. Opening statements are a crucial part of the trial. They give the attorneys a chance to bond with the jury. Studies indeed reveal that jurors frequently decide in favor of the party they are most impressed with during the opening statements phase of the trial[18]; they also give attorneys an early shot at summarizing the whole argument that lies ahead. This may resonate better with the jury than a long, arduous process of rolling out exhibit after exhibit and witness after witness. See Figure 1.5 for a summer of the full trial process.

### The Prosecutor

**direct evidence** Evidence that proves a fact without the need for the juror to infer anything from it.

Once opening statements have concluded, the government (via the prosecutor) has the opportunity to present its case. As prosecutors make their case, they present evidence. Evidence can be thought of in several different ways. **Direct evidence** is "evidence that

---

[18]J. J. Eannace, "Art—Not a Science: A Prosecutor's Perspective on Opening Statements," *The Prosecutor*, Vol. 31 (1997), pp. 32–37.

**Figure 1.5**

Summary of Steps in a Criminal Trial

*Source:* Reprinted from Larry J. Siegel, Frank Schmalleger, and John L. Worrall *Courts and Criminal Justice in America* (Upper Saddle River, NJ: Pearson, 2011)

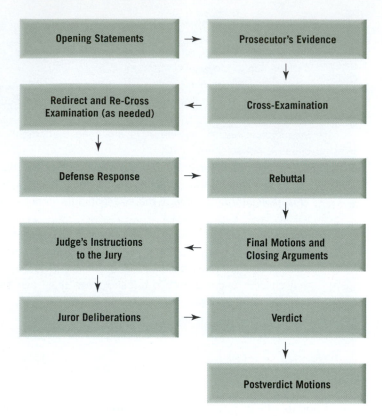

proves a fact without the need for the juror to infer anything from it"[19]; an example of direct evidence is testimony by a witness that the accused committed the crime. By contrast, **circumstantial evidence** is "evidence that *indirectly* proves a fact."[20] An example of circumstantial evidence is evidence of the defendant's ability to commit the crime or that person's possible motive*s*; for instance, the prospect of receiving a life insurance settlement could serve as someone's motive to kill.

It is also useful to think in terms of real, testimonial, and demonstrative evidence. **Real evidence** refers to "any tangible item that can be perceived with the five senses."[21] Real evidence can consist of everything from clothing and footprints to weapons and drugs as well as documents, contracts, letters, and the like, and it can include scientific evidence, such as blood samples, fingerprints, and lab test results. **Testimonial evidence** refers to what someone says, usually someone who is under oath and giving testimony in a trial. Finally, **demonstrative evidence** is evidence that seeks to demonstrate a certain point, such as drawings, diagrams, illustrations, and computer simulations that are used to help jurors understand how a crime was likely committed.

Not just any of these forms of evidence will do. In the case of real evidence, what is introduced must be relevant, and evidence is relevant when it sheds light on a matter that is in dispute. Real evidence also has to be competent, meaning it was not

**circumstantial evidence** Evidence that indirectly proves a fact.

**real evidence** "Any tangible item that can be perceived with the five senses."

**testimonial evidence** Most often, testimonial evidence consists of verbal statements given by someone who is under oath.

**demonstrative evidence** Evidence that seeks to demonstrate a certain point (e.g., drawings, illustrations).

---

[19]J. L. Worrall and C. Hemmens, *Criminal Evidence: An Introduction* (Los Angeles: Roxbury, 2005), p. 71.
[20]Ibid.
[21]Ibid.

**material evidence**
Evidence that "is relevant and goes to substantial matters in dispute, or has legitimate influence or bearing on the decision of the case."

secured illegally or in violation of the Constitution. Finally, real evidence must be material. **Material evidence** is "that which is relevant and goes to substantial matters in dispute, or has legitimate influence or bearing on the decision of the case."[22] Distinguish between relevant and material evidence in this way: The former relates to the issue in question; the latter is concerned with how significant the evidence is.

## The Defense Attorney

Once the prosecution rests its case, the defense gets its turn. The main concern is with establishing reasonable doubt to ensure the prosecution fails to meet its burden. One strategy that the defense may resort to is challenging the prosecution's scientific evidence; another may be to present on one of many affirmative defenses. **Affirmative defenses** are those that go beyond simply denying that a crime took place or that the defendant committed it; examples include everything from alibi defenses and self-defense to duress and entrapment. We look at these defenses in some depth later on (Chapters 4 and 5).

**affirmative defense**
A criminal law defense that goes beyond simply denying that a crime took place or that the defendant committed it.

Interestingly, a defendant in a criminal trial cannot be compelled to testify under *any* circumstances because defendants enjoy absolute Fifth Amendment protection from self-incrimination during criminal proceedings. However, once a defendant takes the stand, he or she can be compelled to answer questions related to the facts of the case at hand.[23]

# The Judge and the Jury

The judge presides over the proceedings, from before trial all the way through to the reading of the verdict. Judges are required to remain neutral and detached throughout the proceedings. Before reading the verdict, the judge will give instructions to the jury (in a jury trial). This section examines the role of judges and juries in the criminal process.

## The Role of the Judge

**trier of law** One who is tasked with resolving any legal matter that comes before a court, most often a judge. Opposite of a trier of fact.

Judges are often described as **triers of law** (or *finders of law*), meaning that they are generally tasked with resolving any *legal* matter that comes before the court. For example, if one of the attorneys in a civil case goes too far in questioning a particular witness, such as by leading the person in a particular direction, the judge will make a ruling on the propriety of such action if the opposing party objects; in other words, the judge will determine whether the questioning can proceed. In a criminal case, the defendant's attorney may seek exclusion of evidence that was allegedly obtained improperly, and the judge, being familiar with the Fourth Amendment and relevant state and local rules governing the admissibility of evidence, will decide on the matter. His or her decision will amount to applying the law, either as spelled out in statutes or as interpreted by other courts' decisions.

---

[22]Ibid., p. 407.
[23]See, e.g., *Brown* v. *United States*, 356 U.S. 148 (1958); *Rogers* v. *United States*, 340 U.S. 367 (1951).

**trier of fact** Someone who listens to the evidence and renders a decision, a judge in a bench trial or a jury member in a jury trial. Opposite of trier of law.

The opposite of a trier of law is a **trier of fact** (or *finder of fact*), someone who listens to the evidence and renders a decision. Assuming there is a jury trial, jurors are the triers of fact; in a criminal case, they listen to the facts presented by the prosecution and the defense and then render a decision based on which side made the more convincing case. (Remember that the "facts" presented by the prosecution and the "facts" presented by the defense can differ because what happened before the trial is often disputed.) Since jurors were not present for the crime, they are forced to interpret the facts as presented to them by the prosecution and defense. Jurors' decisions ultimately affect whether the defendant will be held accountable for the crime. At no point does a jury decide on what the law says or how it is to be interpreted. At the most, members of a jury may be presented with different options for verdicts, but these options are presented to them by a judge.

In some cases, judges serve as triers of law *and* fact. This occurs in a bench trial, a trial in which the judge basically replaces the jury. Sometimes defendants waive their constitutional right to a jury trial. In other situations, especially those involving low-level offenses like misdemeanors, jury trials are rare, if not barred altogether, which requires that the judges do more than just decide on the legal minutia in the cases. Judges even act as triers of fact to some extent in jury trials, especially in the sentencing phase. They weigh aggravating and mitigating factors and settle on a sanction that is fair relative to the crime in question, something which requires at least some degree of attention to what happened during the case or at least to what the defendant's background was leading up to the case.

**The Judge's Instructions to the Jury.**     Once final motions and closing arguments have been made, the judge will give instructions to the jurors before they head off to deliberate. First, the judge gives the jurors something of a crash course in basic legal principles, discussing burdens and standards of proof. Second, the judge discusses the specific offenses in question, and the particular elements of each. Third, if an affirmative defense was raised, the judge will advise the jury of the standards or tests that need to be used to determine whether such a defense is meritorious. Finally, the judge will inform jurors of the verdicts that can be selected and may also discuss the prospect of a guilty verdict for a lesser included offense. In the homicide context, for example, jurors may find the defendant guilty of second- instead of first-degree murder. Second-degree murder is less serious than first degree, but its elements are the same as first-degree murder (deliberate killing); first-degree murder just adds premeditation.

All of this is usually preceded by a charging conference. In a criminal case, this is where the prosecutor, defense attorney, and judge meet out of earshot of the jury to decide on what the instructions to the jurors will be. Jury instructions are important insofar as they can serve as the basis for an appeal, that is, if what the judge tells the jury is wrong, then the defendant may have a basis for challenging a conviction. Unfortunately, even if the judge's instructions to jurors are flawless, getting jurors to understand them is a different matter entirely—researchers have found that many jurors, even well-educated ones, have difficulty comprehending the instructions that they are given.

## The Jury

The Sixth Amendment states, in part, that the "accused shall enjoy the right to a speedy and public trial, by an impartial jury of the state." While this seems straightforward on its face, it is a qualified right. In *Duncan* v. *Louisiana*, the Supreme Court prohibited jury trials for petty offenses, and in *Baldwin* v. *New York*, the Court announced its reason for this: The "disadvantages, onerous though they may be," of denying a jury trial for petty crimes are "outweighed by the benefits that result from speedy and inexpensive nonjury adjudication."[24]

The right to a jury trial can also be waived. If the case is particularly inflammatory or is one with which the community is intimately familiar, then obtaining a fair jury may be difficult, so in such a situation, the defendant may opt for a bench trial. Interestingly, the waiver of the right to a jury trial can be vetoed by the trial judge, that is, the judge can require a jury trial even if the defendant desires otherwise; often, such a veto comes at the request of the prosecutor. Indeed, the Supreme Court has upheld at least one federal statute permitting vetoes of this nature.[25]

Assuming the right to a jury trial applies and that the right is not waived, jury selection takes place. The process behind selecting an impartial jury is rather complicated. Before ***voir dire*** (the process of examining potential jurors for bias) commences, a list of potential or prospective jurors must be compiled, and the creation of this list is critical; without an impartial list, the final jury will not reflect a fair cross section of the community. Once a list is put together, then a panel of jurors is selected. This is where individuals are selected, usually randomly, for jury duty. Think of jury selection, then, as a three-stage process: A list of potential jurors must be compiled, potential jurors are selected from that list, and only then is the jury itself chosen from the potential jurors selected.

There are three main steps in the *voir dire* process. *Voir dire* usually begins with the judge asking questions concerning potential jurors' familiarity with the case, attitudes toward one or other party to the case, demographic information, and so on. This is often done to guide the attorneys in their *voir dire* questioning. Next, during *voir dire*, both the defense and the prosecution have an unlimited number of so-called **challenges for cause**, which are used to exclude potential jurors from service on the jury because of bias or a similar reason. For example, if a member of the jury panel is related to the defendant, a challenge for cause will almost certainly succeed, or if the potential juror served on a past jury in a case dealing with a similar crime, a challenge for cause could probably succeed. Next, each attorney is afforded a certain number of **peremptory challenges**. These call for removal of potential jurors without any type of argument. Think of the peremptory challenge as a fall-back measure. If, say, the defense fails with a challenge for cause to exclude a potential juror whom it believes will be biased against the defendant, a peremptory challenge can be used—in fact, peremptory challenges can be used to exclude potential jurors for any reason whatsoever.

**voir dire** The process of examining potential jurors for bias.

**challenge for cause** The opportunity for a prosecutor or defense attorney to excuse a prospective juror for cause (e.g., racial prejudice). Challenges for cause are unlimited.

**peremptory challenge** The opportunity for a prosecutor or defense attorney to excuse a prospective juror for any reason. Peremptory challenges are limited, and race cannot be used as a basis for exercising peremptory challenges.

---

[24]*Baldwin* v. *New York*, 399 U.S. 66 (1970), p. 73.
[25]*Singer* v. *United States*, 380 U.S. 24 (1965).

A defense attorney addresses the jury.
© Rich Legg/iStockphoto.com

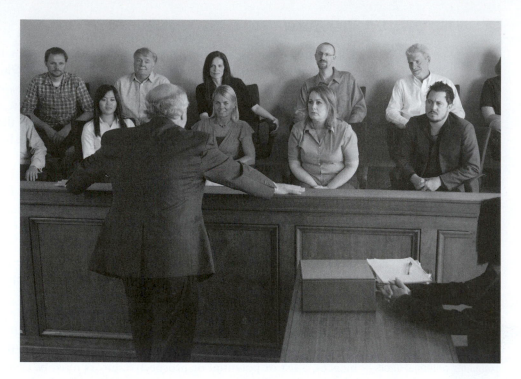

### Jury Decision Making.

Once the jury leaves the courtroom to deliberate, this becomes the "black box" phase of the criminal process. Jury deliberations, as we mentioned earlier, are secretive. If jurors need anything (such as to view an exhibit a second time), they will ask the bailiff; otherwise, jurors are more or less shut off from the rest of the courtroom actors. The reason for this should be obvious: Preserving the jury's neutrality and objectivity is of paramount concern. As we saw earlier, however, it is somewhat naive to think of jurors as entirely objective and concerned solely with the facts as presented.

If the jury cannot reach a verdict and becomes hopelessly deadlocked, this is known as a **hung jury**. If this occurs, the result is generally a **mistrial**, and a new trial will then be held. Mistrials can occur for various reasons, not just deadlocked juries, as this explanation illustrates: "[A mistrial is] a trial which has been terminated and declared invalid by the court because of some circumstance which creates a substantial and uncorrectable prejudice to the conduct of a fair trial, or which makes it impossible to continue the trial in accordance with prescribed procedures."[26]

Juries rarely become deadlocked in their deliberations, meaning that rates of hung juries are exceptionally low.[27] Even so, in the event that a jury cannot reach an agreement, one result may be an **Allen charge** (named after the Supreme Court's decision in *Allen* v. *United States*,[28] which is a set of instructions given to jurors after they become deadlocked that instructs them to reexamine their opinions in an effort to reach a verdict.

**hung jury** A deadlocked jury, one that cannot reach a verdict.

**mistrial** An end to the trial, such as a when the jury becomes hopelessly deadlocked. A new trial is usually held.

**Allen charge** Instructions given to jurors after they become deadlocked that instructs them to reexamine their opinions in an effort to reach a verdict.

[26]Search Group., Inc., under Law Enforcement Assistance Administration, *Dictionary of Criminal Justice Data Terminology* (Washington, DC: U.S. Department of Justice, 1976), p. 132.
[27]P. L. Hannaford, V. P. Hans, and G. T. Munsterman, "How Much Justice Hangs in the Balance? A New Look at Hung Jury Rates," *Judicature*, Vol. 83 (1999), pp. 59–67.
[28]*Allen* v. *United States,* 164 U.S. 492 (1896).

**Jury Nullification.** Sometimes juries act strangely and run amok, returning decisions that are altogether opposite of what would be expected by tradition, process, or law. They sometimes return a guilty verdict in cases where the defendant is clearly not guilty and/or return a not-guilty verdict in cases where the defendant is guilty. This practice of either ignoring or misapplying the law in a certain situation is known as **jury nullification**. Jury nullification sounds counter to the way the jury system should operate, but there can be an upside to it. Back in 1997, an Aurora, Illinois, bar owner, Jessie Ingram, booby-trapped his bar after it was burglarized three times. He put warning signs outside the windows that had been broken during previous burglaries announcing that anyone entering the premises without permission would be subject to electric shock. One burglar ignored the signs and broke a window; on climbing through it, he was shocked to death by a piece of electrified steel that Ingram had adhered to the windowsill. The grand jury refused to indict Ingram on homicide charges (interestingly, though, he was later held civilly liable for the burglar's death). This was a grand jury case, not a trial jury case, but the same logic applies—sometimes justice can be served (or so the grand jurors felt) by going somewhat counter to what the law requires.

There is precedent for jurors ignoring the law and deciding what they feel is best. During Prohibition, for example, jurors routinely refused to convict people charged with liquor-law violations.[29] But jury nullification can also live up to its negative connotations. Historically, southern juries often refused to convict white defendants who were charged with offenses against black victims despite the presence of evidence that would warrant conviction.[30] Some have argued that jury nullification can also be used for political purposes and has little to do with the facts of the case at hand or even with juror characteristics. For example, the acquittal of O. J. Simpson may have been little more than an effort on jurors' part to show that the Los Angeles Police Department (LAPD) was racist.[31]

Is jury nullification really a problem? One study showed, for example, that as penalties become more severe, jurors become less likely to convict, possibly suggesting nullification.[32] In another study, researchers used mock jurors to decide the fate of a hypothetical physician who was accused of knowingly transfusing a patient with blood he knew hadn't been screened for human immunodeficiency virus (HIV); the researchers found that the jurors were less likely to convict if the penalty was severe (e.g., prison instead of a fine).[33] These studies do not provide clear evidence of jury nullification, but they at least illustrate there can be apprehension on jurors' part to apply the law to the letter, meaning jurors sometimes do what *they* think will best serve the ends of justice.

**jury nullification** Jurors' practice of either ignoring or misapplying the law in a certain situation.

---

[29]A. Scheflin and J. Van Dyke, "Jury Nullification: The Contours of Controversy," *Law and Contemporary Problems*, Vol. 43 (1980), pp. 51–115.

[30]See, e.g., W. W. Hodes, "Lord Brougham, the Dream Team, and Jury Nullification of the Third Kind," *University of Colorado Law Review*, Vol. 67 (1996), pp. 1075–1108.

[31]J. Rosen, "The Bloods and the Crits: O.J. Simpson, Critical Race Theory, the Law, and the Triumph of Color in America," *New Republic*, December 9, 1996, pp. 27–42.

[32]N. L. Kerr, "Severity of Penalty and Mock Jurors' Verdicts," *Journal of Personality and Social Psychology*, Vol. 36 (1978), pp. 1431–1442.

[33]K. E. Niedermeier, I. A. Horowitz, and N. L. Kerr, "Informing Jurors of Their Nullification Power: A Route to a Just Verdict or Judicial Chaos?" *Law and Human Behavior*, Vol. 23 (1999), pp. 331–351.

**jury vilification** The opposite of jury nullification.

The flipside of jury nullification has been called **jury vilification**[34]: "Juries may return verdicts that reflect prejudiced or bigoted community standards and convict when the evidence does not warrant a conviction."[35] Jury vilification is exceptionally rare; more often, if a person is unjustifiably convicted, the decision is more likely from jurors' failure to understand important dimensions of the case.

## YOUR DECISION

1. Jodie Matthews is the lead prosecutor on a murder trial that is currently in the process of jury selection. Juror 2, Lane Smith, claims that he was a college roommate of the defense attorney. Juror 6, Jack Sproule, is wearing a T-shirt that reads "Down with the Police." And Juror 12, Mary Murphy, is falling asleep during the questioning process. Jodie is trying to decide which of these jurors, if any, to eliminate. What types of challenges, if any, could Jodie use to eliminate these potential jurors?
2. Amy Jones was physically and mentally abused by her husband, Mark, for the last ten years of their marriage. Amy routinely ended up in the hospital as a result of Mark's terrible beatings. One evening while Mark slept, Amy finally decided she'd had enough. She shot Mark in the chest, killing him instantly. At her murder trial, Amy presented gruesome evidence regarding the abuse she suffered during her marriage. She failed, however, to prove that she was in any danger at the moment she killed Mark. You are on the jury and feel that Mark "got what he deserved" and would like to find Amy not guilty. If you find Amy not guilty, are you engaging in jury nullification? Why or why not?

## Summary

- An adversarial system pits two parties (prosecution and defense) against one another in the pursuit of the truth.
- The American system of justice is adversarial.
- An inquisitorial system is the opposite of an adversarial system.
- The burden of proof in a criminal trial is proof beyond a reasonable doubt.
- A presumption is a fact assumed to be true under the law.
- The most widely known presumption in American criminal law is the presumption of innocence.
- The prosecutor presents the government's case.
- The defense attorney represents the defendant and seeks to establish reasonable doubt in the minds of the jurors (or judge in a bench trial).
- Judges (called triers of law) are tasked with resolving *legal* matters that come before the court and making sure the law is followed.

[34]I. A. Horowitz, N. L. Kerr, and K. E. Niedermeier, "Jury Nullification: Legal and Psychological Perspectives," *Brooklyn Law Review*, Vol. 66 (2001), pp. 1207–1249.
[35]Ibid., p. 1210.

- The practice of either ignoring or misapplying the law in a certain situation is known as jury nullification.
- Jury vilification occurs when jurors convict if the evidence does not warrant a conviction.

# COURT ORGANIZATION

### Learning Objective

- **Describe the structure of the U.S. legal system, including jurisdiction.**

**CORE CONCEPTS**

The criminal law lies dormant until someone is charged with a crime. Once someone is charged with violating the law, as we have seen, a trial takes place. Trials take place at different levels, however. Federal criminal trials involve suspected violations of federal law. State criminal trials apply to violations of state laws. To further gain a grasp of this arrangement, it is important to consider both the structure and hierarchy of the court system in the United States.

## Dual Court System

**dual court system** The American court system, one that separates federal and state courts.

**dual federalism** A system in which the only powers of the federal government are those explicitly listed, with the rest being left to the states.

**cooperative federalism** A system of federalism in which the lines between federal and state power are blurred.

Ours is a **dual court system** that separates federal and state courts. The dual court system is advantageous and desirable because it parallels federalism, a system of government where power is constitutionally divided between a central governing body (i.e., the federal government) and various constituent units (i.e., the states). Federalism requires that laws are made by the central governing authority and by the constituent units. In the United States, the federal government makes law, but federalism also gives the states power to make their own laws.

A quick glance at the U.S. Constitution reveals a system of **dual federalism,** where the only powers of the federal government are those explicitly listed, with the rest being left to the states. In reality, however, ours is more of a system of **cooperative federalism,** meaning some of the lines between federal and state power are blurred. Article I, Section 8, of the U.S. Constitution gives the federal government the power to regulate interstate commerce, but this authority has been interpreted broadly such that the federal government can control much of what happens at the state level.

While a dual court system is desirable from a federalism standpoint, it also promotes complication and confusion. It would be neat and tidy if the federal criminal law was separate and distinct from state criminal law, but in reality both overlap. For example, certain criminal acts, such as those involving firearms, are violations of *both* federal and state criminal law. This leads to confusion over where it would be best to try offenders or whether they should be tried twice in the two different systems.

# Court Levels

**courts of limited jurisdiction** Courts that have jurisdiction over relatively minor offenses and infractions. A traffic court fits in this category.

**courts of general jurisdiction** Courts that try several types of cases, so-called trial courts.

**superior courts** The name commonly used for courts of general jurisdiction. Often found at the county level.

**intermediate appellate courts** Courts to which verdicts from courts of general jurisdiction can be appealed.

**state supreme court** The highest court in a state.

**district court** Federal trial court. There are 94 in the United States, the District of Columbia, and the U.S. territories.

**U.S. Court of Appeals** The federal appellate court. There are 13 in the United States: 12 regional courts, and 1 federal circuit.

**U.S. Supreme Court** The highest court in the federal system.

The dual court system is only part of the story. At each level, there is a distinct court hierarchy. States often have limited jurisdiction courts (such as traffic courts), trial courts, appellate courts, and supreme courts. At the federal level, there are trial courts, appellate courts, and the U.S. Supreme Court. Each trial court adjudicates different offenses. Appellate courts consider different matters depending on where they lie in the court hierarchy. Appeals from state courts can sometimes be heard in the federal courts. Higher-level courts can control the actions and decisions of lower courts, but not the other way around. Despite the apparent complexity, each court has its place.

There is no way to succinctly describe all the variations in state court structures, but, generally, they resemble one another. Typically, the lowest-level courts in a given state are **courts of limited jurisdiction**, which have jurisdiction over relatively minor offenses and infractions. A traffic court fits in this category. Next are the trial courts, also called **courts of general jurisdiction**, which try several types of cases. Courts of general jurisdiction are often county-level courts and are frequently called **superior courts**. At the next highest level are the **intermediate appellate courts**; verdicts from courts of general jurisdiction are appealed to these courts. Finally, each state has its own **state supreme court**, the highest court in the state. Figure 1.6 shows California's relatively simple court structure. Importantly, state courts try cases involving state laws (and, depending on the level of the court, some county, city, and other local ordinances).

The *federal* court structure can be described succinctly because, for our purpose, it consists of three specific types of courts. Federal courts try cases involving federal law. The lowest courts at the federal level are the so-called **district courts**. There are 94 federal district courts in the United States (as of this writing), including 89 district courts in the 50 states and 1 each in Puerto Rico, the Virgin Islands, the District of Columbia, Guam, and the Northern Mariana Islands. At the next level are the **U.S. Courts of Appeals**. There are 13 of these so-called circuit courts of appeals: 12 regional courts and 1 for the federal circuit. Each is charged with hearing appeals from several of the district courts that fall within its circuit. Figure 1.7 illustrates how the U.S. Courts of Appeal are divided geographically in the United States. Finally, the **U.S. Supreme Court** is the highest court in the federal system.

To reiterate a point raised earlier, most of the cases we will look at in this book hail from either the appellate courts or the Supreme Court. Again, this is because trial courts rarely publish their decisions. This point cannot be overemphasized because there are untold numbers of cases that never make their way into criminal law texts or classrooms simply because they are not published.

**Figure 1.6**

The Court System of California

*Source:* Reprinted from Larry J. Siegel, Frank Schmalleger, and John L. Worrall, *Courts and Criminal Justice in America* (Upper Saddle River, NJ: Pearson, 2011).

## The Relationships Among Courts

Higher courts have considerable influence over lower courts because of the hierarchical structure pointed out in the previous section. At the state level, for example, appellate and supreme courts issue decisions that lower courts are required—on their face—to abide by. Yet lower courts do not always "follow the rules" to the letter. Also, many of them have developed various means to cope with influential decisions from the higher courts.

Nearly all high-court decisions are subject to interpretation simply by the way they are written. For example, in the famous school desegregation case of *Brown* v. *Board of Education*,[36] Chief Justice Warren's implementation order (also called an *implemen-*

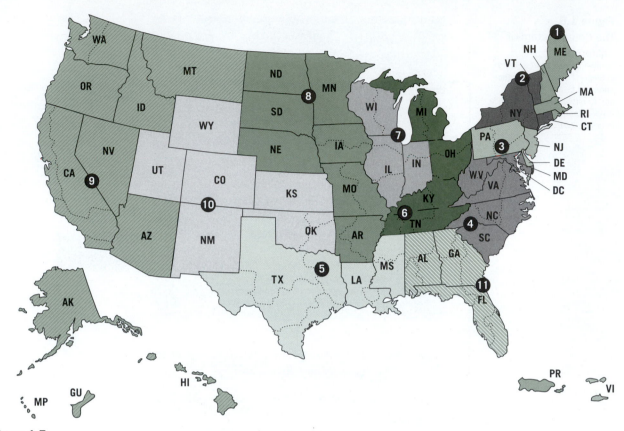

**Figure 1.7**
Geographic Boundaries of the U.S. Courts of Appeal
*Source:* Administrative Office of the U.S. Courts, http://www.uscourts.gov/Court_Locator.aspx (accessed April 25, 2011)

*tation decree,* issued following the Court's opinion in the case, spelling out details on how the decision was to be implemented by the lower courts) said the following:

> [T]he cases are remanded to the District Courts to take such proceedings and enter such orders and decrees consistent with this opinion as are necessary and proper to admit the parties to these cases to public schools on a racially nondiscriminatory basis with all deliberate speed.[37]

What is meant by "all deliberate speed"? There was no easy answer to this question, which meant the lower courts had considerable license to interpret it. The implementation order also referenced a "prompt and reasonable start toward full compliance with the ruling."[38] What did Chief Justice Warren mean by this? Again, there was no easy answer, and the result was room for interpretation by the lower courts.

Consider a criminal justice example. In the landmark *Katz v. United States*[39] decision, the Supreme Court defined a search as consisting of government action that infringes on a "reasonable expectation of privacy." What is a reasonable expectation of privacy? Yet again, there is no easy answer.

---

[36]*Brown v. Board of Education,* 347 U.S. 483 (1954).
[37]*Brown v. Board of Education,* 349 U.S. 294 (1955), p. 301.
[38]Ibid., p. 300.
[39]*Katz v. United States,* 389 U.S. 347 (1967).

Lower courts employ a range of methods for dealing with higher-court decisions simply because of how many of the former there are. Researchers are mixed on the issue of how compliant lower-court judges are with higher-court decisions.[40] A number of studies have found that lower-court judges' decisions closely mirror those of the higher courts and that they follow the same ideological trends.[41] But other researchers have found that lower-court judges frequently resist higher-court decisions with which they disagree.[42] For those judges who resist higher-court decisions, they tend to employ two strategies:

- *Ignore the higher court's decision altogether.* This type of defiance is rare. A judge may act in this way by disposing of a case on procedural grounds before the point where the controversial higher-court decision may need to be applied. For example, the judge could decide the plaintiff in a civil case does not have standing to sue.

- *Implement a higher court's decision sparingly.* Most cases are factually distinct from one another. Little twists and turns in the facts can make one case seem sufficiently different that a judge will not apply a controversial higher-court decision and thus "distinguish" the case before him or her, effectively issuing a new decision.

## YOUR DECISION

1. James Garfalo was arrested for selling 10 grams of cocaine to an undercover police officer. At his jury trial in the state trial court, James was convicted and sentenced to two years in prison. James believes his constitutional rights were violated during the trial and wishes to appeal. What court will hear James's appeal? Assume instead that James's trial happened in a federal district court. What federal court would here his appeal?

2. Assume the U.S. Supreme Court issues an opinion declaring that the Sixth Amendment to the U.S. Constitution requires all criminal defendants to have a trial with 24 jurors instead of the traditional 12. The lower courts are not happy with this decision because their jury boxes only accommodate 12 people comfortably, not 24. Do the lower courts have to follow the U.S. Supreme Court decision? Why or why not?

[40]D. R. Songer, J. A. Segal, and C. M. Cameron, "The Hierarchy of Justice: Testing a Principal-Agent Model of Supreme Court-Circuit Court Interactions," *American Journal of Political Science*, Vol. 38 (1994), pp. 673–696.

[41]For just a few examples, see L. Baum, "Response of Federal District Judges to Court of Appeals Policies: An Exploration," *Western Political Quarterly*, Vol. 3 (1980), pp. 217–224; S. C. Benesh, *The U.S. Court of Appeals and the Law of Confessions: Perspectives on the Hierarchy of Justice* (New York: LFB Scholarly, 2002); J. Gruhl, "The Supreme Court's Impact on the Law of Libel: Compliance by Lower Federal Courts," *Western Political Quarterly*, 33 (1980), pp. 502–519; D. Songer and R. S. Sheehan, "Supreme Court Impact on Compliance and Outcomes: *Miranda* and *New York Times* in the United States Courts of Appeals," *Western Political Quarterly*, Vol. 43 (1990), pp. 297–319.

[42]See, e.g., J. W. Peltason, *Fifty-Eight Lonely Men: Southern Federal Judges and School Desegregation* (New York: Harcourt Brace, 1961); N. T. Romans, "The Role of State Supreme Courts in Judicial Policy Making," *Western Political Quarterly*, Vol. 27 (1974), pp. 38–59.

## Summary

- America's is a dual court system that separates federal and state courts.
- America is characterized by cooperative federalism, meaning some of the lines between federal and state power are blurred.
- The dual court system, while ideal from a federalism standpoint, promotes complication and confusion (e.g., in the precise relationship between the courts).
- There is a distinct court hierarchy at both the state and federal levels.
- States often have limited jurisdiction courts (such as traffic courts), trial courts, appellate courts, and supreme courts.
- At the federal level, there are trial courts, appellate courts, and the U.S. Supreme Court.
- Higher courts have considerable influence over lower courts because of the hierarchical structure of court systems.
- Lower courts do not always "follow the rules" to the letter; many have developed creative means to cope with influential decisions from the higher courts.

MODULE

# 1.5    LEARNING CRIMINAL LAW WITH REAL AND HYPOTHETICAL CASES

### Learning Objectives

- **Outline the stages of a criminal case.**
- **Explain the practical meaning of a verdict.**

**CORE CONCEPTS**    It is not sufficient to introduce criminal-law concepts without linking them to real-world cases that affect actual people. Throughout this book, we bring our discussions and definitions to light with a careful look at criminal-law cases decided in high-level courts throughout the United States. This approach suffers from a key limitation, however. It is one we have pointed out twice already in this chapter. Namely, all published cases involve people who have been convicted of a crime. This leaves unanswered the question of whether the individual ever should have been convicted—or even charged—in the first place.

## Understanding Case Citations and How to Locate a Case

Being able to find court cases requires that readers be familiar with legal citations as well as the publications in which cases can be found. Legal citations are somewhat cryptic, but can be deciphered with relative ease. The following is the citation format used throughout this text:

*Miranda* v. *Arizona*, 384 U.S. 436 (1966)

*Miranda* and *Arizona* refer to the parties to the case. Importantly, the party listed first is the one initiating the action. In this case, *Miranda* appealed his conviction, which is why he is listed first. The legal citation format that follows the parties is interpreted as follows: The first part, *384*, is the volume; the second part, *U.S.*, is the publication in which the case can be found; the third part, *436*, is the page on which the case starts; and the fourth, *1966*, is the year that the decision was published.

After you become familiar with case citations, it is necessary to learn where the cases can actually be found. First, most university libraries have one or several of the so-called reporters. They can be found in bound form on the library shelves. These days, most university libraries have access to subscription databases, such as Lexis Nexis or Westlaw, which contain cases from nearly all courts across the country. Electronic databases like these are quickly replacing the older bound form.

For those who do not enjoy reading actual court decisions, other sources of legal information may be useful. For example, legal dictionaries and encyclopedias offer clarification of important legal concepts. Legal digests identify and consolidate legal issues, provide commentary on and interpret cases, and otherwise "digest" complex material. Finally, law reviews are useful places to find discussions of various aspects of the law as well as opinions on and interpretations of court cases.

## Making Sense of Court Cases

One of the more frustrating aspects of criminal law, especially for those who have little familiarity with the law or legal jargon, is the sometimes laborious task of tracing the progress of a criminal case. If final decisions were reached in a single court, then criminal law would be vastly simplified. In reality, however, a single case can bounce back and forth between trial and appellate courts, sometimes for years. Indeed, many U.S. Supreme Court decisions concern matters that occurred a decade or more ago. Thus, it is of particular importance for students of criminal law to learn how to trace a criminal case.

There are several essential steps to tracing the progress of a criminal case. First, it is necessary to have a basic understanding of the nation's court structure. This requires knowing where the criminal trial in question took place. If it took place in a federal circuit court, then tracing the progress of the case will be fairly easy. As you read earlier, there are only three possible courts—district court, circuit appellate court, and the Supreme Court—that may have handed down decisions on the matter. If the case originated in state court, however, it can be decidedly more difficult to trace the case over time. Familiarity with the state court structure is needed, as well as an understanding of how cases can jump back and forth between the state and federal courts, which will be discussed later in this section.

Second, to adequately follow the progress of a criminal case, it is also necessary to understand the legal jargon, beginning with the parties to the case. The *parties* to the case are the people involved. At the trial level, the parties of interest are the defendant (as defined earlier, the person charged with the crime in question), and the **prosecutor**, or the official representing the government. At the appellate level, these parties are no longer called *defendant* and *prosecutor* but rather **appellant** and **appellee**. The *appellant* is the party that appeals; both the prosecutor and defendant can appeal, but the defendant appeals more often than the prosecutor. The *appellee*

**prosecutor** The official who charges the defendant and is tasked with representing the government in court.

**appellant** The party of appeals.

**appellee** The party appealed against.

**reverse** In the appeals context, what happens when an appellate court nullifies or sets aside a lower court's verdict.

**vacate** In the appeals context, basically the same as a reversal.

**remand** In the appeals context, what happens when an appellate court sends a case back to the lower court for further action consistent with its decision.

**affirm** In the appeals context, the act of an appellate court agreeing with a lower court's decision.

(sometimes called the *respondent*) is the party appealed against. Most cases favor the defense on appeal, as the prosecution is permitted to appeal only in very limited circumstances because of certain constitutional constraints, such as double jeopardy (discussed in the next chapter).

Next, to follow a criminal case, it is essential to have an understanding of how cases are decided and what possible decisions can be reached. At the trial level, two decisions can result: guilty and not guilty. At the appellate level, however, the picture becomes more complex. Assume, for example, that a defendant is found guilty in a federal district court and appeals to one of the circuit courts of appeals. Assuming that the court agrees to hear the case, it can hand down one of several decisions. It could **reverse** the lower court's decision, which is akin to nullifying or setting it aside. Sometimes the appellate court **vacates** the lower court's decision, which is basically the same as reversing it. A reversal does *not* always have the effect of setting the defendant free, however. The appellate court could also **remand** the case back to the lower court. When a case is remanded, it is sent back to the lower court for further action consistent with the appellate court's decision. Cases can also be reversed and remanded together. The appellate court can also **affirm** the lower court's decision, in which case it agrees with the lower court.

If there was only one appellate court, tracing the progress of a case would be fairly simple. Unfortunately, multiple appellate courts exist, which means the decisions from court to court can change. This is a very important point. Assume, for example, that a defendant is found guilty in a state trial court. The defendant could appeal to the state's intermediate appellate court, which could reverse the defendant's conviction. The case could then go to the state's supreme court, which could reverse the appellate court's decision and basically uphold the defendant's conviction. Finally, the case could go to the U.S. Supreme Court, which could again reverse the defendant's conviction. Believe it or not, this is a fairly simple progression. Nothing prevents a single case from going from the trial court to the appellate court, back to the trial court, up to the appellate court again, then up to the state supreme court, back to the intermediate appellate court, and so on.

It is essential to understand what has happened with a criminal case before making any claims as to its importance or influence. In other words, doing incomplete legal research can be a recipe for disaster. If, for instance, a researcher finds a state supreme court decision that supports a point he or she wants to make but that decision was later reversed, say, by the U.S. Supreme Court, whatever argument that researcher makes in reliance on that state supreme court case will be inaccurate. Thus, in tracing the progress of a criminal case, it is necessary to understand whether the issue in question has been resolved or may currently be on the docket of an appellate court, which could render an altogether different decision.

## Understanding the Parts of a Court Opinion

In tracing a criminal case, especially when interpreting one decided at the appellate level, it is important to understand the components of a published decision. An appellate court often consists of a panel of judges who may not always agree with one another, even though the court reaches a single decision. For example, a 5–4 decision by the U.S. Supreme Court is one in which the Court reached a single decision because

**opinion** The rationale for an appellate court's decision subscribed to by the majority of judges or justices, usually authored by one judge or justice.

**concurring opinion** An opinion that agrees with the majority decision but for different reasons.

**dissent** A minority opinion that is at odds with the majority opinion

of a majority, but four of the justices disagreed. The **opinion** is the voice of the five justices (or the voice of the majority of the judges in a lower appellate court decision), although one or more of the five may opt to write a **concurring opinion**, which supports the majority's decision but with different legal logic. The four remaining justices will probably write a **dissent**, in which they argue why they disagree with the majority's decision. If they wanted to, each of the four minority justices could write his or her own individual dissent. Either way, it is important to distinguish between a given court's opinion and possible concurring and dissenting opinions.

In addition to the opinion and dissent (if there is a dissent), cases also include a prior history, the disposition, the judges who decided the case, the attorneys who represented the government and the defendant, the facts of the case, the decision, and the procedural history. Sometimes these elements are clearly spelled out. Other times some of them are "buried" within the case. For example, the facts of the case, the recounting of what happened, are often included near the beginning of the opinion. Likewise, decisions do not always stand out in their own section. They are often included in the language near the end of the opinion. And unfortunately, no case is the same in the next, and multiple formats are followed. It thus takes a certain amount of practice to read cases.

## Editing Cases for Readability

Most published cases contain a wealth of information, some of which is not useful or necessarily pertinent to the introductory study of criminal law. This is especially true of cases in Lexis Nexis, Westlaw, and other electronic databases. For example, Lexis Nexis cases include "headnotes," case summaries, and other bits of information not found in the original published case. This can make it difficult for the nonlawyer to determine where the Lexis Nexis contribution ends and the actual case begins.

Even the original published case may include information that is not particularly helpful or necessary for introductory criminal-law classes. This sometimes includes references to other cases, some footnotes, page numbers found in the original print version, and so on. Much of this material can be safely edited out to enhance the case's readability. Where necessary in this book, we have taken out some of this material and include ellipses (e.g., . . . .) to denote that we have done so.

In an effort to further improve readability, we have edited all cases such that (1) only the essentials are presented and (2) they follow a fairly consistent format. Many cases are far too long to reprint in a textbook like this. As such, we have edited many cases for length. In these situations, a triple asterisk (e.g., * * *) will denote where we have done so. Also, we follow a format that includes the following elements: (1) parties of the case; (2) citation; (3) court where the case was decided; (4) prior history; (5) disposition; (6) judges; (7) opinion, including who wrote it; and (8) dissent or concurrence, if any. The disposition is the decision, but the decisions also appear, as we indicated earlier, toward the end of the opinion.

The accompanying Court Decision box includes a sample case. Note how it contains each of the elements just listed. This was a case involving a defendant who was found guilty of selling illegal drugs. He appealed, claiming entrapment (an issue we will look at in more depth later). Note that the disposition was "judgment affirmed." This means his conviction was upheld, that the Supreme Court of Illinois felt he was not entrapped.

**COURT DECISION**

*People v. Toler* 185 N.E. 2d 874 (Ill. 1962) Supreme Court of Illinois

**Background:** Defendant (Toler) appealed the decision of the Criminal Court of Cook County (Illinois) convicting him of the unlawful sale of narcotic drugs and sentencing him to prison.

**Disposition:** Judgment affirmed.

**Counsel:** Julius Lucius Echeles, of Chicago, for the defendant.

William G. Clark, Attorney General, of Springfield, and Daniel P. Ward, State's Attorney, of Chicago, (Fred G. Leach and E. Michael O'Brien, Assistant Attorneys General, and John T. Gallagher and Dean H. Bilton, Assistant State's Attorneys, of counsel,) for the state.

**Judges:** Mr. Justice Daily delivered the opinion of the court. Mr. Justice Schaefer, dissenting. Mr. Justice Klingbiel concurs in this dissent.

**Opinion By:** Daily

Defendant, Willie Toler, was indicted in the criminal court of Cook County on charges of having unlawfully sold narcotic drugs to Richard Tracy on June 8 and 11, 1959. Tracy, a Chicago police officer, had been introduced to defendant by Edward Unsell, a former fellow employee of defendant at a water-pumping station, and who was then working as a special employee of the State's Attorney's office. Defendant pleaded not guilty and waived a jury trial, but was subsequently found guilty after a bench trial and sentenced to the penitentiary for a term of not less than ten nor more than twelve years. Upon this writ of error the single contention made is that, under the evidence, defendant should have been discharged because he was entrapped into committing the crimes.

Past decisions of this court establish that entrapment constitutes a valid defense if officers of the law inspire, incite, persuade or lure a defendant to commit a crime which he otherwise had no intention of perpetrating . . . . At the same time, however, it is equally well settled that officers may afford opportunities or facilities for the commission of crime, or may use artifice to catch those engaged in criminal ventures, and that the defense of entrapment is not available to one who has the intent and design to commit a criminal offense, and who does commit the essential acts constituting it, merely because an officer, for the purpose of securing evidence, affords such person the opportunity to commit the criminal act, or purposely aids and encourages him in its perpetration . . . .

The testimony of the defendant paints a picture of an innocent man who, after being approached by Unsell some twenty times in an effort to get narcotics, finally succumbed to an appeal to his sympathy by Tracy. The latter told him that he worked for a dentist who had a son who was a narcotics addict, that he wanted some "good stuff," that he might need as much as three or four thousand dollars worth and that he wanted a sample. Defendant stated that he purchased narcotics, without profit to himself, to aid a narcotics addict who was sick . . . . The proof introduced by the People reflects two sales of narcotics by defendant when the funds were shown to be available, and an intent and willingness on the part of the defendant to commit the crime, shown by his ready complaisance and quick access to substantial quantities of illegal narcotics. We are of the opinion that the officer and special employee did no more than afford defendant the opportunity to commit a criminal act of his own design, and that their actions did not constitute entrapment . . . . The record also shows a circumstance hardly compatible with naivete and innocence, an elaborate system of delivery devised by defendant whereby the narcotics were never actually seen in his possession.

The judgment of the criminal court of Cook County is affirmed.

**Dissent By:** Schaefer

The evidence on the issue of entrapment in this case is not conflicting, and I think that it establishes that the defendant was entrapped. The police officer, Richard Tracy, testified as follows concerning the meeting at which Unsell introduced him to the defendant:

"A. During the course of the conversation I told Mr. Toler I was working for a dentist and this dentist had a son that was a narcotic addict and because of the new prescription law it was impossible for this dentist to obtain narcotics legally for his son and the son was in need of narcotics, and we were looking for some good stuff, some good heroin, if we could get it off the street at least this occasion because he was in pretty bad shape; we didn't think he would live very long.

Q. Indicate how much you wanted?

A. I told—we talked about getting a very large amount, possibly three or $ 4000 worth of narcotics, and at that time I indicated to Toler I would like to buy a sample for approximately $ 100, and I asked him how much stuff he could get me for $ 100."

The defendant testified that he and Unsell were close friends, and that Unsell had approached him many times, telling him that he wanted narcotics for a friend who was sick and had only a year to live.

On cross-examination, the informer, Unsell, who was called as a rebuttal witness, testified as follows:

"Q. Isn't it a fact you told the defendant, Willie Toler here, you had a customer who needed some narcotics badly because he was ill and had about a year to live?

A. Not customer, No.

Q. Did you tell him anyone?

A. Yes.

Q. Whom?"

At this point the prosecution objected on the ground that the cross-examination was going beyond the scope of the direct, and the court sustained the objection saying "This is a rebuttal witness."

There is no showing in the record that apart from the two occasions involved in this case the defendant had ever had any transactions with narcotics or that he had any criminal record whatsoever. Under these circumstances I am of the opinion that the defense of entrapment was established and that the judgment should be reversed.

Mr. Justice Klingbiel concurs in this dissent.

## Briefing Cases

As mentioned, we have taken the liberty of editing down lengthy criminal law cases for readability. While this will be helpful for building an understanding of each case, it is also important for you to brief the cases. A case brief is a short (usually one page or less) summary of the key components of a case. It is written in response to a few questions, such as:

1. What is the procedural history?
2. What are the facts?
3. What is the central issue at hand in the case?
4. What is the holding, decision, or disposition?
5. What is the reasoning the court offered in its opinion?
6. What is the essence of the dissent, if there is one?

Answers to these questions are invaluable, as they help you gain a complete grasp of a case. It is not enough to simply know what happened and what was decided. Case briefs help you identify the core issue at hand in each case. It is sometimes easy to lose sight of that issue, as cases can be long-winded, written in complex legalese, and presuppose that the reader already knows why the case is important. At the core of every case, however, is one or a few key issues. Case briefs also help you understand, in a "short and sweet" fashion, *why* the decision was reached. Opinions tend to lay out the court's reasoning over several pages. A brief encourages you to "cut to the chase" and identify, in a sentence or two, what the court was thinking. The same holds for the dissent.

Box 1–1 includes a brief of the *People* v. *Toler* case introduced earlier. Note that it is short. It is worth noting, too, that *People* v. *Toler* is itself a short case. Other cases, as you will see throughout this book, are much longer.

---

*People v. Toler*, 185 N.E.2d 874 (Ill. 1962)

**Procedural History**
This case is on appeal from the Criminal Court, Cook County to the Supreme Court of Illinois. The defendant was found guilty at the trial court.

**Facts**
Defendant Toler sold narcotics to an undercover police office, Richard Tracy. Toler had been introduced to the police officer by Edward Unsell, a friend of Toler and a special employee of the State's Attorney's office.

**Issue**

Was the defendant entrapped by Tracy and Unsell?

**Holding**

Conviction affirmed. Entrapment does not exist when a mere "opportunity to commit a criminal act of his own design" is presented to the defendant.

**Reasoning**

The court found an "intent and willingness" on the part of Toler to commit the crime when funds were shown to be available. In addition, the court stated that Toler's elaborate system of delivery indicated he was not simply a naïve and innocent victim.

**Dissent**

Justice Schaefer felt the defense of entrapment had been sufficiently established by the defendant. No evidence of Toler's propensity for criminal acts was presented. In addition, Toler was led to believe the drugs were for an ill patient with little time to live.

## The Practical Meaning of Verdicts

There are some important points that need to be borne in mind with respect to verdicts. First, the two main verdicts that can be reached in a trial, guilty and not guilty, do not speak to *factual* guilt or innocence. Just because a defendant is found not guilty does not mean he or she is innocent. It just means that the prosecution could not meet its burden of proving beyond a reasonable doubt that the defendant committed the crime. Likewise, a verdict of guilty means, simply, that the government met its burden. It does not mean the defendant is factually guilty (i.e., committed the crime), but this may certainly be the case.

Second, the "verdicts" reached at the appellate stage have equally unusual meanings. If an appellate court sides with an appellant, it is not stating the individual is innocent. Indeed, appellate courts do not focus on the "facts" of the case and decide whether a defendant is guilty or not guilty. Instead, they focus on legal issues and whether proper procedures were followed at the trial level. It is not uncommon for an appellate court to side with the appellant, who then spends the rest of his or her sentence in prison. Other times, the appellant court may require a new trial, which could result in a guilty verdict just as easily as it could result in a not-guilty verdict.

## The Value of Hypothetical Scenarios

Published cases afford readers with the benefit of 20–20 hindsight. You can read the facts of the case, identify the issue at hand, and see the appellate court's logic for either affirming or rejecting a lower court's decision. These cases leave little to the imagination because someone was already convicted, for better or worse. This does not mean, however, that we should ignore real cases. After all, published cases become law, and they affect how subsequent cases are decided.

It is also helpful to think in terms of hypothetical scenarios. A hypothetical scenario is one that doesn't let you look back through time to see how the process played out. They put you in the position of judge or juror at "square one" and force you to decide on the best course of action for dealing with a given defendant. We have presented a number of hypothetical scenarios throughout this chapter. We will present more in later chapters, especially as we delve into the substance of the criminal law. For now, here are two others that address the issues raised in this module.

## YOUR DECISION

1. Bill Graham was convicted of first-degree murder in state court and sentenced to death. He appealed, arguing that the trial judge improperly admitted evidence that led to his conviction. The appellate court agreed with Graham and reversed his conviction. Will Graham be set free? Why or why not?

2. In an 8–1 decision, a state supreme court decides that defense attorneys should not be allowed to present *any* evidence concerning a suspected rape victim's sexual history or character. Justice Herbert Loud is the lone voice of the opposition. What can he do in order to voice his displeasure with the majority's decision?

## Summary

- A U.S. Supreme Court citation looks like this: *Miranda* v. *Arizona* (384 U.S. 436 [1966]).

- The party listed first is the one initiating the action. In this case, *Miranda* appealed his conviction, which is why he is listed first. The legal citation format that follows the parties is interpreted as follows: The first part, *384*, is the volume; the second part, *U.S.*, is the publication in which the case can be found; the third part, *436*, is the page on which the case starts; and the fourth, *1966*, is the year that the decision was published.

- To trace the progress of a criminal case, it is first necessary to understand the nation's court structure.

- To trace the progress of a criminal case, it is also necessary to understand the legal jargon used in a court decision.

- At the trial level, the parties of interest are the defendant, or the person charged with the crime in question, and the prosecutor, or the official representing the government.

- At the appellate level, these parties are no longer called *defendant* and *prosecutor* but rather *appellant* and *appellee*.

- Appellate courts can issue several decisions. They *reverse* the lower court's decision, which is akin to nullifying or setting it aside. Sometimes appellate courts vacate the lower court's decision, which is basically the same as reversing it. They can also *remand* the case back to the lower court. Finally, appellate courts can *affirm* the lower court's decision, in which case they agree with the lower court.

- To summarize the parts of a published decision, we will use a U.S. Supreme Court case as an example.

- The opinion is the voice of the majority.

- A concurring opinion supports the majority's decision, but with different logic.

- A dissent (not written in a unanimous decision) is an argument that disagrees with the majority's decision.

- In addition to the opinion and dissent (if there is a dissent), cases also include a prior history, the disposition, the judges who decided the case, the attorneys who represented the government and the defendant, the facts of the case, the decision, and the procedural history.

- A case brief is a short summary of the key components of a case.

- Case briefs contain several sections, each of which answers the following questions: (1) What is the procedural history? (2) What are the facts? (3) What is the central issue at hand in the case? (4) What is the holding, decision, or disposition? (5) What is the reasoning the court offered in its opinion? (6) What is the essence of the dissent, if there is one?

- The two main verdicts that can be reached in a trial, guilty and not guilty, do not speak to *factual* guilt or innocence.

- If an appellate court sides with an appellant, it is not stating the individual is innocent.

- It is not uncommon for an appellate court to side with the appellant, who then spends the rest of his or her sentence in prison.

# Chapter Review

## PRELIMINARY INFORMATION

### Learning Objectives

· Define *crime* and *criminal law*.

· Explain the difference between *substantive criminal law* and *criminal procedure*.

· Identify the goals of the criminal law.

· Describe the various classifications of crime.

### Review Questions

1. How does a crime compare to a civil wrong?
2. In what ways is the criminal law different from the law of criminal procedure?
3. Explain the goals of the criminal law.
4. Which goal of the criminal law do you prefer, and why?
5. How are crimes classified?

### Key Terms

| | |
|---|---|
| criminal law | specific deterrence |
| crime | general deterrence |
| tort | rehabilitation |
| tort-feasor | restoration |
| criminal procedure | restorative justice |
| defendant | denunciation |
| punishment | felony |
| retribution | misdemeanor |
| utilitarian | *malum in se* |
| incapacitation | *malum prohibitum* |

## SOURCES OF CRIMINAL LAW

### Learning Objective

· Identify the sources of the criminal law.

### Review Questions

1. Identify five sources of the criminal law.
2. What effect did early legal codes have on the modern criminal law?
3. What is the common law, and why is it important?
4. At what levels of government are modern statutes found?
5. What are the constitutional sources of the criminal law?
6. Which source of the criminal law is the most influential? Why?

### Key Terms

| | |
|---|---|
| Code of Hammurabi | precedent |
| Twelve Tables | *stare decisis* |
| law | American Law Institute |
| political authority | Model Penal Code |
| common law | Bill of Rights |
| special law | |

MODULE **1.3**

## REACHING A VERDICT

### Learning Objectives

- Describe the adversarial system.
- Identify courtroom participants.

### Review Questions

1. Distinguish between *adversarial* and *inquisitorial* justice.
2. What is the burden of proof in a criminal trial? How does it compare to the burden of proof in a civil trial?
3. What are *presumptions*, and why are they important?
4. Distinguish between the roles of the prosecutor and defense attorney.
5. What is the role of the judge?
6. How does jury selection play out?
7. What is the difference between *jury nullification* and *vilification*?

### Key Terms

| | |
|---|---|
| adversarial justice system | testimonial evidence |
| inquisitorial system | demonstrative evidence |
| burden of proof | material evidence |
| burden of persuasion | affirmative defense |
| burden of production | trier of law |
| directed verdict | trier of fact |
| proof beyond a reasonable doubt | challenge for cause |
| preponderance of evidence | peremptory challenge |
| presumption | hung jury |
| presumption of innocence | mistrial |
| opening statements | Allen charge |
| direct evidence | jury nullification |
| circumstantial evidence | jury vilification |
| real evidence | |

MODULE **1.4**

## COURT ORGANIZATION

### Learning Objective

- Describe the structure of the U.S. legal system, including jurisdiction.

### Review Questions

1. What does it mean to say America's is a *dual court system*?
2. Distinguish between *dual* and *cooperative* federalism.
3. Explain the concept of *court hierarchy*.
4. Summarize the typical state court structure (i.e., what are the courts at each level and what do they do?). Do the same for the courts at the federal level.
5. Explain the relationship (real and ideal) between higher and lower courts.

### Key Terms

dual court system
dual federalism
cooperative federalism
courts of limited jurisdiction
courts of general jurisdiction
superior courts

intermediate appellate
    courts
state supreme court
district court
U.S. Court of Appeals
U.S. Supreme Court

MODULE **1.5**    **LEARNING CRIMINAL LAW WITH REAL AND HYPOTHETICAL CASES**

### Learning Objectives

- Outline the stages of a criminal case.
- Explain the practical meaning of a verdict.

### Review Questions

1. Explain the parts of a citation of a U.S. Supreme Court decision.
2. Describe the steps in tracing the progress of a criminal case.
3. Identify the parties to a case at both the trial and federal level.
4. Explain the various decisions that can be reached at the appellate level.
5. Define the parts of a published criminal case.
6. What are the parts of a case brief?
7. What is the value of the hypothetical scenarios presented throughout the book?

### Key Terms

prosecutor
appellant
appellee
reverse
vacate

remand
affirm
opinion
concurring opinion
dissent

# Chapter Synthesis Questions

1. Is it possible to define as criminal all potential harms? Why or why not?

2. The American system of criminal law is built upon several sources. What, in your opinion, are the advantages and disadvantages of this?

3. Is the adversarial system a help or a hindrance? Why do you feel this way?

4. There is a formal relationship between the courts, but reality deviates from this relationship. Should it? Why or why not?

5. In seeking to gain a grasp of a case, what are the strengths and weaknesses of relying on the full decision, an excerpted case, or a case brief?

# 2

# LIMITATIONS ON THE CRIMINAL LAW

# GOVERNMENT'S LAW-MAKING AUTHORITY AND GENERAL LIMITATIONS ON THE CRIMINAL LAW

*Learning Objectives*

- **Explain how the separation of powers and federalism limit the government's law-making authority.**
- **Describe the principle of legality.**
- **Describe the principle of lenity.**

**CORE CONCEPTS**

In Chapter 1, we pointed out that one of the goals of the criminal law is offender protection. This occurs, as you will recall, through the state's involvement in prosecuting offenders, proportionate punishment schemes, and procedural protections. Certain procedural protections, such as the right to counsel and the right to an impartial jury trial, hail from the U.S. Constitution. They are *direct* protections, as they lay out the procedures by which an individual who is arrested and prosecuted will (or at least should) be treated by the criminal justice system. There are also *indirect* means of protecting offenders. For example, the U.S. Constitution prohibits laws that are vague and overreaching. This promotes offender protection indirectly because the focus becomes a specific law rather than the treatment of one individual. Certain common law principles, namely legality and lenity, also place limits on the criminal law. These indirect methods are the focus of the present chapter. They are *indirect* protections in the sense that they are more concerned with the criminal law itself than they are with the treatment of individuals. We begin by examining general limitations on the criminal law, then we conclude with a look at various constitutional limitations. First, however, we offer a brief refresher on government's law-making authority.

## Government's Law-Making Authority

How far can the government go in terms of criminalizing behavior? For example, can a state legalize medical marijuana while the federal government makes it illegal? Alternatively, at what point should the courts get involved in deciding on whether certain statutes go "too far?" To answer these questions, we need, first, to be mindful of the separation of powers and of federalism, two key elements of the American system of government.

### Separation of Powers

As you know, the U.S. Constitution divides governmental authority into three branches: executive, legislative, and judicial. In general, the legislative branch makes the laws, the executive branch enforces the laws, and the judicial branch interprets the laws. Members of the executive branch include high-level officials like the president and his cabinet all the way down to municipal police officers and local prosecutors. The legislative branch consists mainly of Congress (the House of Representatives and the Senate) and has law-making authority. The judiciary is the court system. Some of the judiciary's key functions, especially relevant in this book, are deciding on the meaning of laws, how these laws are applied, and when and whether they become unconstitutional. In an ideal world, these three powers are separate and distinct. In reality, however, the lines between each are blurry.

There is a natural hesitancy on the judiciary's part to intrude on the legislative branch's law-making authority. This is so for at least two reasons. First, the people elect legislators, so presumably the laws reflect the interests of all people. It would run counter to this core feature of democracy for the courts to constantly meddle in legislative affairs. Second, if the courts routinely decided on matters of legislation, the result would be arbitrariness and confusion. Court A's decision could be at odds with Court B's. The courts thus *presume* that all laws are constitutional. If someone wishes to challenge the constitutionality of a statute, the burden falls on that party to bring the issue to the courts. Consequently, courts only get involved in matters of legislation when someone challenges the constitutionality of a statute.

Separation of powers is often discussed in terms of the federal government, but it is important to note that the same applies at the state and local levels. Every unit of government has its own distinct set of responsibilities, obligations, and limitations. This is important because most government employees, including those who work in criminal justice, work at either the state or local level; the number of federal positions is comparatively small.

## Federalism

**federalism** A system of government where power is constitutionally divided between a central governing body and various constituent units.

**confederation** A system of government that lacks a strong central authority

**dual federalism** An interpretation of the U.S. Constitution that suggests a system wherein the only powers vested in the federal government are those explicitly listed in the document, with the remaining powers being left to the states.

**Federalism** is a system of government where power is constitutionally divided between a central governing body (the federal government, for example) and various constituent units (the states). In a federalist system, laws are made by the central governing authority and by the constituent units. This is obviously the case in the United States. The federal government makes law, but federalism also gives the states power to make their own laws. For example, both the federal government and each state have their own legal codes regulating the conduct of citizens. This is in contrast to a unified system of government, where all power is vested in a central authority. It is also distinct from a **confederation**, where there is no strong central government.

Ours is a system of **dual federalism**, where the only powers vested with the federal government are those explicitly named in the Constitution—the rest is left to the states. This is what we might call the "textbook" definition of federalism. In reality, however, ours is more of a system of cooperative federalism, meaning some of the lines between federal and state power are blurred, or at least that they have fluctuated over time. For example, Article I, Section 8, of the U.S. Constitution gives the federal government the power to regulate interstate commerce, but this authority has been interpreted broadly such that the federal government can control much of what happens at the state level. To this day, we see plenty of federal influence over even local criminal justice activities.

Regarding what activities the federal government can criminalize compared to the state, one must become familiar with Article I, Section 8, of the U.S. Constitution (see Figure 2.1). It specifies the law-making authority of the federal government. And a quick read of Section 8 makes it clear that the federal government's law-making authority is limited. This is why criminal codes vary so much from state to state. With few exceptions, the federal government is not in the business of criminalizing the types of behaviors most state criminal codes consider illegal. Instead, its focus is more on matters of interstate commerce, relationships with other countries, taxes, currency, and the nation's defense.

The Congress shall have power to lay and collect taxes, duties, imposts and excises, to pay the debts and provide for the common defense and general welfare of the United States; but all duties, imposts and excises shall be uniform throughout the United States;

To borrow money on the credit of the United States;

To regulate commerce with foreign nations, and among the several states, and with the Indian tribes;

To establish a uniform rule of naturalization, and uniform laws on the subject of bankruptcies throughout the United States;

To coin money, regulate the value thereof, and of foreign coin, and fix the standard of weights and measures;

To provide for the punishment of counterfeiting the securities and current coin of the United States;

To establish post offices and post roads;

To promote the progress of science and useful arts, by securing for limited times to authors and inventors the exclusive right to their respective writings and discoveries;

To constitute tribunals inferior to the Supreme Court;

To define and punish piracies and felonies committed on the high seas, and offenses against the law of nations;

To declare war, grant letters of marque and reprisal, and make rules concerning captures on land and water;

To raise and support armies, but no appropriation of money to that use shall be for a longer term than two years;

To provide and maintain a navy;

To make rules for the government and regulation of the land and naval forces;

To provide for calling forth the militia to execute the laws of the union, suppress insurrections and repel invasions;

To provide for organizing, arming, and disciplining, the militia, and for governing such part of them as may be employed in the service of the United States, reserving to the states respectively, the appointment of the officers, and the authority of training the militia according to the discipline prescribed by Congress;

To exercise exclusive legislation in all cases whatsoever, over such District (not exceeding ten miles square) as may, by cession of particular states, and the acceptance of Congress, become the seat of the government of the United States, and to exercise like authority over all places purchased by the consent of the legislature of the state in which the same shall be, for the erection of forts, magazines, arsenals, dockyards, and other needful buildings;—And

To make all laws which shall be necessary and proper for carrying into execution the foregoing powers, and all other powers vested by this Constitution in the government of the United States, or in any department or officer thereof.

**Figure 2.1**
U.S. Constitution, Article I, Section 8

There are times, however, when a federal law criminalizes behavior while a state legalizes the same behavior. Whenever federal and states laws are at odds like this, the federal law supersedes. Returning to the subject of medical marijuana, this is why federal agents (at least under President Bush) routinely raided medical marijuana establishments in states like California; the latter were sanctioned under state law, but violated federal law.

# General Limitations on the Criminal Law

The early colonists brought to America the common law of England. Before there were state criminal codes, there were common law crimes. Recall from Chapter 1 that common law crimes were not the same as crimes defined by penal codes. Common law crimes were those actions that, by convention (as opposed to statute), were treated as criminal.

There is one distinct advantage to having common law crime. Namely, common law crimes offer a means of punishing inappropriate conduct that legislatures could not have anticipated or made criminal. In other words, common law crimes offer *flexibility* for handling new and unanticipated situations. Consider the English case of *Shaw* v. *Director of Prosecutions*.[1] The defendant published a "Ladies Directory" of prostitutes that contained their names, pictures, addresses, and phone numbers. At the time, prostitution was not a crime, yet the House of Lords upheld the defendant's conviction for "conspiracy to corrupt public morals." In defense of this position, Viscount Simonds argued:

> residual power to enforce the supreme and fundamental purpose of the law, to conserve not only the safety and order but also the moral welfare of the State. . . . [I]t is their duty to guard against attacks which may be the more insidious because they are novel and unprepared for. . . . Such occasions will be rare, for Parliament has not been slow to legislate when attention has been sufficiently aroused. But gaps remain and will always remain since no one can foresee every way in which the wickedness of man may disrupt the order of society.[2]

There are disadvantages to the common law, as well. First, if there is no clear precedent, or guiding past decision, the individual may not know that the conduct in question was criminal. In some cases, people only know an act is illegal *after the fact*, after the courts have defined it as such. Related to this, the common law does little to keep governmental authority in check. It gives the government wide latitude to decide what is and is not criminal—all the while without a specific code of laws. The absence of a clear set of rules thus creates uncertainty.

Today, states and the federal government maintain specific criminal codes that help overcome the weaknesses of the common law. Two distinct principles form the foundation of these codes: legality and lenity.

---

[1]*Shaw* v. *Director of Prosecutions*, House of Lords, (1962) A.C. 220.
[2]Ibid.

## Legality

The **principle of legality** is often expressed through the Latin maxim, "*Nullemcrimen, nullapoena, sinelege*." This translates into, "There is no crime without law, no punishment without law." It means that a defendant cannot be convicted of a crime unless there is specific legislation making it illegal and defining the potential punishment.

The advantage of the legality principle is that a criminal code provides prior notice to the people of what behavior is illegal. Yet its downside is a lack of flexibility, something the presence of common law crimes ensures. The criminal law has a hard time keeping pace with new actions that, although harmful, are not yet considered criminal. People are continually inventing new ways to inflict harm on others (either physically or monetarily) while legislators struggle to stay one step ahead.

Consider terrorism. With all the public pressure on the government to do something about it, prosecutors often find themselves in an awkward predicament because they are the ones who must ultimately file charges against known and suspect terrorists. The problem is that most of the available laws they would use to prosecute require completion of a criminal act. So, what is a prosecutor to do in the case of terrorism? Wait around until a serious attack occurs? Certainly not. Prosecutors have two options. One is to wait until lawmakers criminalize actions that are committed in furtherance of a criminal attack. This has happened, and continues to happen, but it certainly wasn't a major priority prior to the September 11, 2001, terrorist attacks. Another is for prosecutors to get creative in their efforts to prosecute would-be terrorists, such as by using statutes that haven't traditionally been used to target would-be terrorists.[3]

## Lenity

Related to legality is the **principle of lenity**. Lenity requires that the courts construe a statute as favorably as possible to the defendant. If there is any ambiguity in a statute, that ambiguity should benefit the defendant, not the government. In the next section, we consider several means by which lenity is applied. When statutes are overly vague, for example, that vagueness should be resolved in favor of the defendant.

See the accompanying Court Decision for more on the rule of lenity. In it we examine the case of *People* v. *Summers*, where the Supreme Court of Colorado attempts to explain an ambiguous statute.

**COURT DECISION**

*People* v. *Summers*
208 P.3d 251 (Col. 2009)

**Background:** Eugene Summers filed a motion to dismiss charges of sexual assault on a child, sexual assault on a child by one in a position of trust, and criminal attempt to commit sexual assault on a child. The District Court, City and County of Denver, denied the motion. Defendant appealed and the Supreme Court of Colorado remanded.

---

[3]R. Chesney, "Anticipatory Prosecution in the War on Terror," in John L. Worrall and M. Elaine Nugent-Borakove, eds., *The Changing Role of the American Prosecutor* (Albany: SUNY Press, 2008).

### ***I. Facts and Procedural History

The defendant, Eugene Summers, was charged with thirty-two counts of sexual assault on a child, sexual assault on a child by one in a position of trust, sexual assault on a child-pattern of abuse, and criminal attempt to commit sexual assault on a child. The acts were allegedly committed during two separate time periods—one period from August 1, 1992, to August 31, 1993, and one period from August 1, 1995, to June 30, 1996. The felony complaint charging Summers with these crimes was filed April 6, 2007. Summers moved to dismiss the charges against him, contending that they were all barred by the statute of limitations. The statute of limitations in effect at the time of the alleged crimes was ten years. However, the General Assembly amended the statute of limitations in 2002, tolling the ten-year statute of limitations for sexual assault on a child until the child victim reaches the age of eighteen. The trial court denied Summers' motion to dismiss, holding that the newly amended statute of limitations applied to Summers' case and that it had not yet run.

### II. Analysis

We are asked in this case to determine which statute of limitations applies to the sexual assault on a child charges brought against Summers. Because the plain language of the statute is ambiguous and we are unable to determine any clear intent expressed by the legislature, we hold that the rule of lenity applies and the ten-year statute of limitations in effect at the time of the alleged acts bars the charges against Summers.

### ***Legislative Intent

Because we are unable to apply the plain language of the statute, we turn to an analysis of the legislature's intent in enacting the statute. When an ambiguity appears on the face of a statute, "we may rely on other factors such as legislative history, the consequences of a given construction and the goal of the statutory scheme to determine a statute's meaning." *Frazier,* 90 P.3d at 811. In doing so, we are mindful that "[a] statute should not be construed in a manner which defeats the obvious legislative intent." *Tacorante* v. *People,* 624 P.2d 1324, 1330 (Colo.1981).

### 1. Legislative History

The confusion in this case arises out of a poorly drafted statute—the substantive provisions of the statute indicate that the statute is to apply retroactively, but the effective date clause explicitly states that the statute applies to crimes committed on or after the statute's effective date. In order to understand the conflicting provisions of the law, it is important to consider how the statute was amended.

Prior to the 2002 legislative session, the statute of limitations for sexual assault on a child in Colorado was ten years from the date of the last occurrence of the crime. The statute of limitations at the time read:

> No person shall be prosecuted, tried, or punished for an unlawful sexual offense other than the misdemeanor offenses specified in sections 18-3-402 and 18-3-404, unless the indictment, information, complaint, or action for the same is

found or instituted within ten years after commission of the offense. . . . The ten-year statute of limitations shall apply to all offenses specified in subsection (1) of this section [including the offenses with which the defendant is charged in this case] which are alleged to have occurred on or after July 1, 1979.

§ 18-3-411(2), C.R.S. (2001).

The General Assembly amended the law in 2002 to toll the ten-year statute of limitations for sexual assault on a child until the child victim reaches the age of eighteen. The substantive amendments indicated that the new statute of limitations was intended to reach back and apply to crimes committed on or after July 1, 1992. The amended statute of limitations provided:

> No person shall be prosecuted, tried, or punished for an unlawful sexual offense charged as a felony unless the indictment, information, complaint, or action for the same is found or instituted within ten years after the victim reaches the age of eighteen years. The ten-year statute of limitations shall apply to all felony offenses specified in subsection (1) of this section [including the offenses with which the defendant is charged in this case] *which are alleged to have occurred on or after July 1, 1992.*

§ 18-3-411(2)(b), C.R.S. (2002) (emphasis added).\*\*\*

In addition, section 4 of the bill provided for a retroactive effective date: "Section 4. Effective date-applicability. This act shall take effect July 1, 2002, and *shall apply to offenses committed on or after July 1, 1992." Id.* (emphasis added). This effective date was consistent with section 2 of the bill, which indicated that the new eighteen-plus-ten statute of limitations should apply to crimes committed on or after July 1, 1992.

\*\*\*Our review of the legislative history behind H.B. 02-1396 fails to clarify the legislative intent behind the bill. It is clear that the bill as initially introduced was intended to apply the new eighteen-plus-ten statute of limitations to crimes committed in the past for which the statute of limitations had not yet run. However, the original version of the bill was not enacted. The legislature, for one reason or another, changed the effective date clause to indicate that the new statute of limitations should only apply to crimes committed on or after its effective date. We must not disregard this language when determining the legislature's intent, as the words used in a statute are the best indicator of legislative intent.

### \*\*\*Rule of Lenity

Because we are unable to apply the plain language of the statute and we are unable to discern the legislature's intent behind the statutory language, we reluctantly turn to the rule of lenity—a rule of last resort invoked only "if after utilizing the various aids of statutory construction, the General Assembly's intent remains obscured." *People v. Thoro Prods. Co.,* 70 P.3d 1188, 1198 (Colo.2003). Under the rule, "ambiguity in the meaning of a criminal statute must be interpreted in favor of the defendant." *Id.* Due to our conclusion that the amended statute of limitation's coverage is ambiguous, the rule of lenity requires that we apply the flat ten-year statute of limitations in effect when the acts allegedly took place. We do not resort to the rule of lenity lightly, but we are mindful that a court should "not attribut[e] to [the legislature], in the enactment of criminal statutes, an intention to punish more severely than the language of its laws clearly imports in the light of pertinent legislative history." *Prince v. United States,* 352 U.S. 322, 329 (1957). Where, as here, both the statutory language and the legislative history leave us with no way to definitively determine the statute's intended coverage, it is not our place to choose between two competing and viable alternatives in order to usurp the General Assembly's role in making the law. Rather, we have no choice but to apply the rule of lenity in favor of the defendant. As a result, the charges against Summers are time barred and must be dismissed.

### ***IV. Conclusion

We conclude based on the rule of lenity that the eighteen-plus-ten statute of limitations applies to crimes committed on or after the statute's effective date, as stated in the effective date clause. As a result, the charges against Summers are time barred by the flat ten-year statute of limitations in effect at the time of the alleged acts. We therefore make the rule to show cause absolute and remand for proceedings consist with this opinion.

## Case Analysis

1. Specifically, what changes were made to the Colorado statute at issue in the case?
2. What is the defendant's legal argument behind his motion to dismiss?
3. Explain how the rule of lenity impacted the court's decision.

It bears mentioning that there is a downside to the rule of lenity. Many statutes are not completely clear in their wording, meaning there is plenty of room for interpretation in the language of the criminal law. As such, taken to the extreme, the rule of lenity can be used to interpret a statute in a manner that is at odds with legislative intent. For this reason, many states have abolished the rule of lenity.[4] Indeed, the Model Penal Code does not even recognize lenity, opting instead that any ambiguity in the criminal law be resolved in favor of furthering the legislative priorities behind the law, not the defendant.[5]

## YOUR DECISION

1. Dr. Feelgood, a self-proclaimed new age doctor in San Francisco, convinced his female patients that he could cure their illnesses if they had sexual intercourse with him. Unaware that he was a fraud, the women willingly complied. The rape statute in California at the time of the incidents required that the defendant act "with force or threat of force" against the victims. Can Dr. Feelgood be charged with the rape of his patients?

---

[4]J. C. Jeffries, Jr., "Legality, vagueness, and the construction of penal statutes," *Virginia Law Review*, Vol. 71 (1985), p. 189.
[5]Model Penal Code Section 1.02(3).

2. The drug trade from Central and South America is causing a dramatic increase in criminal activity in New Mexico. The New Mexico legislature wants to take action. They pass a statute with this language: "Any person found transporting illegal substances, including but not limited to, heroin, cocaine and marijuana, into New Mexico will be punished to the full extent of the law." Is this criminal statute enforceable? Why or why not?

## Summary

- Legislatures enact the law.
- Courts are naturally hesitant to intrude on the legislature's law-making authority.
- Federalism is a system of government where power is constitutionally divided between a central governing body (the federal government, for example) and various constituent units (the states).
- Ours is a system of dual federalism, where the only powers vested with the federal government are those explicitly named in the Constitution—the rest being left to the states.
- With few exceptions, the federal government is not in the business of criminalizing the types of behaviors most state criminal codes consider illegal. Instead, its focus is more on matters of interstate commerce, relationships with other countries, taxes, currency, and the nation's defense.
- The legality principle holds that there is no crime without a law prohibiting it. Legality runs counter to the common law practice of criminalizing behavior by convention rather than statute.
- The problem with legality is that the criminal law struggles to keep pace with new and emerging types of harmful behavior.
- Lenity requires that the courts construe a statute as favorably as possible to the defendant.
- Taken to the extreme, the rule of lenity can be used to interpret a statute in a manner that is at odds with legislative intent. For this reason, many states have abolished the rule of lenity.

MODULE

# 2.2

# CONSTITUTIONAL LIMITATIONS ON THE CRIMINAL LAW, PART 1

### Learning Objectives

- **Describe the Fourteenth Amendment's equal protection clause.**
- **Summarize the prohibition of *ex post facto* laws and bills of attainder.**
- **Summarize the void for vagueness principle.**
- **Explain the void for overbreadth doctrine.**

## CORE CONCEPTS

To reiterate an earlier point, the courts only get involved in reviewing statutes when there is a clear possibility that a statute violates the U.S. Constitution. There are also fairly clear dividing lines, because of federalism, between the law-making authority of the federal government and the law-making authority of the states. With this backdrop in place, we can now delve into the constitutional limitations on the criminal law. There are six of them that we will take up in this chapter: equal protection of the laws, the *ex post facto* law prohibition, the void for vagueness doctrine, the void for overbreadth doctrine, the cruel and unusual punishment provision of the Eighth Amendment, and the double jeopardy clause of the Fifth Amendment. Each places a specific limit on the criminal law. We consider the first four in this module and the last two in the next module.

## Equal Protection

**equal protection clause**
A clause in the Fourteenth Amendment of the U.S. Constitution requiring that the government justify any differential treatment on the basis of race, gender, age, sexual orientation, or other characteristic with a state interest.

The U.S. Constitution's Fourteenth Amendment requires that "no state shall deny to any person within its jurisdiction the equal protection of the laws." This is known as the **equal protection clause** and affects various aspects of criminal justice and criminal procedure, not just the criminal law. For example, convicted criminals have used the equal protection clause to challenge jury composition. In *Strauder* v. *Virginia*,[6] the Supreme Court declared unconstitutional a statute that explicitly barred African Americans from jury service. In the criminal-law context, however, equal protection challenges relate mainly to who is targeted by the statute. Essentially, a criminal statute cannot "discriminate" or treat a person differently based on a specific characteristic without a legitimate reason.

Before the end of the Civil War, many southern states retained separate systems of laws for whites and blacks. During the colonial period, black slaves who killed whites in Georgia, for whatever reason, were automatically executed.[7] At about the same time, Georgia's penal code provided that rape of a white woman by a black man was punishable by death, yet the rape of blacks was punishable "by fine and imprisonment, at the discretion of the court."[8] Likewise, a black person who assaulted a white person could be put to death, but it was considered a "minor" offense for a white person to commit the same offense against a black person. These forms of unequal treatment are absent from contemporary penal codes. Today, race-based classifications in the criminal law are not allowed.

While states no longer maintain separate penal codes for blacks and whites, there are other areas where equal protection challenges continue to creep up. For example, in *Michael M.* v. *Superior Court*,[9] the Supreme Court was tasked with deciding whether California's statutory rape law, which defined unlawful sexual intercourse as "an act of sexual intercourse accomplished with a female not the wife

[6]*Strauder* v. *Virginia*, 100 U.S. 303 (1879).
[7]*McCleskey* v. *Kemp*, 481 U.S. 279 (1987) (Brennan, J., dissenting).
[8]Ibid.
[9]*Michael M.* v. *Superior Court*, 450 U.S. 464 (1981).

Even after the Civil War and prior to the civil rights era, some states retained separate facilities for whites and blacks. This picture depicts separate drinking fountains in North Carolina, circa 1950.

Elliott Erwitt/Magnum Photos

of the perpetrator, where the female is under the age of 18 years," discriminated against males. In other words, the petitioner, Michael M., claimed that the statute unfairly discriminated against men because only men were criminally liable under the statute. On its face, this argument seems to have some merit, but the Supreme Court concluded that a more inclusive statute would complicate enforcement. It said this:

> There is no merit in petitioner's contention that the statute is impermissibly underinclusive, and must, in order to pass judicial scrutiny, be broadened so as to hold the female as criminally liable as the male. . . . [A] gender-neutral statute would frustrate the State's interest in effective enforcement, since a female would be less likely to report violations of the statute if she herself would be subject to prosecution. The Equal Protection Clause does not require a legislature to enact a statute so broad that it may well be incapable of enforcement.[10]

The Court went on to note that gender-based classifications are not "inherently suspect." It further noted that so long as they bear a "fair and substantial relationship" to legitimate state goals, such classification schemes do not violate the Fourteenth Amendment's equal protection clause. The legitimate state interest in this case was a desire to prevent illegitimate teenage pregnancies.

The *Michael M.* case raises an important point concerning equal protection, namely that the government is not required to treat *everyone* exactly the same. Though we have yet to discuss them in more detail, consider the differences between various levels of homicide. State homicide statutes treat first-degree murderers differently from those who commit negligent homicide, yet the result of each offense

---

[10]Ibid., p. 465.

is the same (i.e., the death of another). Why? One is fundamentally more serious than the next. First-degree murder requires planning and intent, while negligent homicide occurs only when a person acts negligently. It would not be fair to treat each offender as exactly the same.

Another example of a modern equal protection challenge is found in *Vacco* v. *Quill*.[11] In that case, three New York physicians challenged two seemingly contradictory sets of state statutes. One expressly prohibited physician-assisted suicide, meaning a doctor was not permitted to assist a patient in ending his or her life. The other statutes permitted a competent person to refuse lifesaving medical treatment. The distinction between the two is subtle but important. On the one hand, physicians were prohibited from actively *helping* patients end their lives. On the other hand, they were permitted to sit idly by and let the patients refuse treatment, which often resulted in death. The physicians argued that a patient's refusal to accept lifesaving treatment is basically the same as physician-assisted suicide, meaning that New York's assisted-suicide ban violated equal protection. The Supreme Court disagreed, noting a distinction between both actions:

> [W]hen a patient refuses life-sustaining medical treatment, he dies from an underlying fatal disease or pathology; but if a patient ingests lethal medication prescribed by a physician, he is killed by that medication. . . . Furthermore, a physician who withdraws, or honors a patient's refusal to begin, life-sustaining medical treatment purposefully intends, or may so intend, only to respect his patient's wishes. . . . The same is true when a doctor provides aggressive palliative care; in some cases, painkilling drugs may hasten a patient's death, but the physician's purpose and intent is, or may be, only to ease his patient's pain. A doctor who assists a suicide, however, "must, necessarily and indubitably, intend primarily that the patient be made dead." Similarly, a patient who commits suicide with a doctor's aid necessarily has the specific intent to end his or her own life, while a patient who refuses or discontinues treatment might not.[12]

The Supreme Court basically said that New York had a rational basis for treating both actions differently. Thus, there was no equal protection violation.

## Standards of Scrutiny in Equal Protection Cases

To decide whether a statute violates equal protection, the courts now apply one of three tests depending on the classification in question. If a law classifies people based on race or national origin, it is unconstitutional unless the law is "narrowly tailored" to serve a "compelling" government interest. What's more, there must be no "less restrictive" alternative available. This is known as **strict scrutiny**.[13] If a law categorizes based on sex, it is unconstitutional unless it is "substantially related" to an "important" government interest. This is known as **intermediate scrutiny**.[14] Finally, a law that classifies people on any other basis is subjected to a **rational basis** test.[15]

---

[11]*Vacco* v. *Quill*, 521 U.S. 793 (1997).
[12]Ibid., pp. 801–802.
[13]*Loving* v. *Virginia*, 388 U.S. 1 (1967), p. 11
[14]*Craig* v. *Boren*, 429 U.S. 190 (1976), p. 197.
[15]*Turner* v. *Safley*, 482 U.S. 78 (1987).

**strict scrutiny** A test used under the **equal protection clause** of the Fourteenth Amendment for classifications based on race. The law must be "narrowly tailored" to serve a "compelling" government interest. What's more, there must be no "less restrictive" alternative available.

**intermediate scrutiny** A test used under the **equal protection clause** of the Fourteenth Amendment for classifications based on gender. The law must be "substantially related" to an "important" government interest.

**rational basis** A test used under the **equal protection clause** of the Fourteenth Amendment for classifications. The law must be "reasonably related" to a "legitimate" government interest.

This means that law is constitutional so long as it is "reasonably related" to a "legitimate" government interest. See the accompanying Court Decision for more on equal protection. In it, we take a look at the 1996 Virginia Military Institute case, *United States* v. *Virginia*.

## COURT DECISION

*United States* v. *Virginia*
518 U.S. 515 (1996)

**Background:** The United States of America sued the Commonwealth of Virginia for refusing to allow women into the Virginia Military Institute. The Western District of Virginia ruled in favor of Virginia. The Fourth Circuit Court of Appeals vacated and remanded. On remand, the Western District approved a remedial plan and the Fourth Circuit affirmed. The Supreme Court granted *certiorari*.

Justice GINSBURG delivered the opinion of the Court.

Virginia's public institutions of higher learning include an incomparable military college, Virginia Military Institute (VMI). The United States maintains that the Constitution's equal protection guarantee precludes Virginia from reserving exclusively to men the unique educational opportunities VMI affords. We agree.

I

Founded in 1839, VMI is today the sole single-sex school among Virginia's 15 public institutions of higher learning. VMI's distinctive mission is to produce "citizen-soldiers," men prepared for leadership in civilian life and in military service.

***In 1990, prompted by a complaint filed with the Attorney General by a female high-school student seeking admission to VMI, the United States sued the Commonwealth of Virginia and VMI, alleging that VMI's exclusively male admission policy violated the Equal Protection Clause of the Fourteenth Amendment. Trial of the action consumed six days and involved an array of expert witnesses on each side.

In the two years preceding the lawsuit, the District Court noted, VMI had received inquiries from 347 women, but had responded to none of them. "[S]ome women, at least," the court said, "would want to attend the school if they had the opportunity. The court further recognized that, with recruitment, VMI could "achieve at least 10% female enrollment"—"a sufficient 'critical mass' to provide the female cadets with a positive educational experience." And it was also established that "some women are capable of all of the individual activities required of VMI cadets." In addition, experts agreed that if VMI admitted women, "the VMI ROTC experience would become a better training program from the perspective of the armed forces, because it would provide training in dealing with a mixed-gender army."

***Today's skeptical scrutiny of official action denying rights or opportunities based on sex responds to volumes of history. As a plurality of this Court acknowledged a generation ago, "our Nation has had a long and unfortunate history of sex discrimination." *Frontiero* v. *Richardson*, 411 U.S. 677, 684 (1973). Through a century plus three decades and more of that history, women did not count among voters composing "We the People"; not until 1920 did women gain a constitutional right to the franchise. And for a half century thereafter, it remained the prevailing doctrine that government, both federal and state, could withhold from women opportunities accorded men so long as any "basis in reason" could be conceived for the discrimination.

\*\*\*In 1971, for the first time in our Nation's history, this Court ruled in favor of a woman who complained that her State had denied her the equal protection of its laws. Since *Reed*, the Court has repeatedly recognized that neither federal nor state government acts compatibly with the equal protection principle when a law or official policy denies to women, simply because they are women, full citizenship stature—equal opportunity to aspire, achieve, participate in and contribute to society based on their individual talents and capacities.

Without equating gender classifications, for all purposes, to classifications based on race or national origin, the Court, in post-*Reed* decisions, has carefully inspected official action that closes a door or denies opportunity to women (or to men). To summarize the Court's current directions for cases of official classification based on gender: Focusing on the differential treatment or denial of opportunity for which relief is sought, the reviewing court must determine whether the proffered justification is "exceedingly persuasive." The burden of justification is demanding and it rests entirely on the State. The State must show "at least that the [challenged] classification serves 'important governmental objectives and that the discriminatory means employed' are 'substantially related to the achievement of those objectives'"). The justification must be genuine, not hypothesized or invented post hoc in response to litigation. And it must not rely on overbroad generalizations about the different talents, capacities, or preferences of males and females.

The heightened review standard our precedent establishes does not make sex a proscribed classification. Supposed "inherent differences" are no longer accepted as a ground for race or national origin classifications. Physical differences between men and women, however, are enduring: "[T]he two sexes are not fungible; a community made up exclusively of one [sex] is different from a community composed of both." *Ballard* v. *United States*, 329 U.S. 187, 193, (1946).

"Inherent differences" between men and women, we have come to appreciate, remain cause for celebration, but not for denigration of the members of either sex or for artificial constraints on an individual's opportunity. Sex classifications may be used to compensate women "for particular economic disabilities [they have] suffered," to "promot[e] equal employment opportunity," to advance full development of the talent and capacities of our Nation's people. But such classifications may not be used, as they once were, to create or perpetuate the legal, social, and economic inferiority of women.

\*\*\*For the reasons stated, the initial judgment of the Court of Appeals is affirmed, the final judgment of the Court of Appeals is reversed, and the case is remanded for further proceedings consistent with this opinion.

It is so ordered.

Justice SCALIA, dissenting.

Today the Court shuts down an institution that has served the people of the Commonwealth of Virginia with pride and distinction for over a century and a half. To achieve that desired result, it rejects (contrary to our established practice) the factual findings of two courts below, sweeps aside the precedents of this Court, and ignores the history of our people. As to facts: It explicitly rejects the finding that there exist "gender-based developmental differences" supporting Virginia's restriction of the "adversative" method to only a men's institution, and the finding that the all-male composition of the Virginia Military Institute (VMI) is essential to that institution's character. As to precedent: It drastically revises our established standards for reviewing sex-based classifications. And as to history: It counts for nothing the long tradition, enduring down to the present, of men's military colleges supported by both States and the Federal Government.

Much of the Court's opinion is devoted to deprecating the closed-mindedness of our forebears with regard to women's education, and even with regard to the treatment of women in areas that have nothing to do with education. Closed-minded they were—as every age is, including our own, with regard to matters it cannot guess, because it simply does not consider them debatable. The virtue of a democratic system with a First Amendment is that it readily enables the people, over time, to be persuaded that what they took for granted is not so, and to change their laws accordingly. That system is destroyed if the smug assurances of each age are removed from the democratic process and written into the Constitution. So to counterbalance the Court's criticism of our ancestors, let me say a word in their praise: They left us free to change. The same cannot be said of this most illiberal Court, which has embarked on a course of inscribing one after another of the current preferences of the society (and in some cases only the counter-majoritarian preferences of the society's law-trained elite) into our Basic Law. Today it enshrines the notion that no substantial educational value is to be served by an all-men's military academy—so that the decision by the people of Virginia to maintain such an institution denies equal protection to women who cannot attend that institution but can attend others. Since it is entirely clear that the Constitution of the United States—the old one—takes no sides in this educational debate, I dissent.

***In an odd sort of way, it is precisely VMI's attachment to such old-fashioned concepts as manly "honor" that has made it, and the system it represents, the target of those who today succeed in abolishing public single-sex education. The record contains a booklet that all first-year VMI students (the so-called "rats") were required to keep in their possession at all times. Near the end there appears the following period piece, entitled "The Code of a Gentleman":

> "Without a strict observance of the fundamental Code of Honor, no man, no matter how 'polished,' can be considered a gentleman. The honor of a gentleman demands the inviolability of his word, and the incorruptibility of his principles. He is the descendant of the knight, the crusader; he is the defender of the defenseless and the champion of justice . . . or he is not a Gentleman.
>
> > "A Gentleman . . .
> > "Does not discuss his family affairs in public or with acquaintances.
> > "Does not speak more than casually about his girl friend.

"Does not go to a lady's house if he is affected by alcohol. He is temperate in the use of alcohol.

"Does not lose his temper; nor exhibit anger, fear, hate, embarrassment, ardor or hilarity in public.

"Does not hail a lady from a club window.

"A gentleman never discusses the merits or demerits of a lady.

"Does not mention names exactly as he avoids the mention of what things cost.

"Does not borrow money from a friend, except in dire need. Money borrowed is a debt of honor, and must be repaid as promptly as possible. Debts incurred by a deceased parent, brother, sister or grown child are assumed by honorable men as a debt of honor.

"Does not display his wealth, money or possessions.

"Does not put his manners on and off, whether in the club or in a ballroom. He treats people with courtesy, no matter what their social position may be.

"Does not slap strangers on the back nor so much as lay a finger on a lady.

"Does not 'lick the boots of those above' nor 'kick the face of those below him on the social ladder.'

"Does not take advantage of another's helplessness or ignorance and assumes that no gentleman will take advantage of him.

"A Gentleman respects the reserves of others, but demands that others respect those which are his.

"A Gentleman can become what he wills to be. . . ."

I do not know whether the men of VMI lived by this code; perhaps not. But it is powerfully impressive that a public institution of higher education still in existence sought to have them do so. I do not think any of us, women included, will be better off for its destruction.

## Case Analysis

1. What level of scrutiny is the court using to evaluate the potential Equal Protection Clause violation?

2. How does gender discrimination differ from racial discrimination?

3. What is the main point of Justice Scalia's dissent?

## The *Ex Post Facto* Law Prohibition

**ex post facto law**
A law enacted in order to retroactively punish behavior. *Ex post facto* is Latin for "after the fact."

Just as the Fifth and Fourteenth Amendments require equal protection, the Constitution bans so-called **ex post facto** laws in Article 1, Section 9. *Ex post facto* is Latin for "after the fact," or "from after the action." Basically, an *ex post facto* law is one enacted in order to retroactively punish behavior. The ban on *ex post facto* laws makes perfect sense, as it would be unfair to punish someone for an action that wasn't illegal when it was committed. So important is the ban on *ex post facto* laws that it is found not only in the U.S. Constitution (Article I, Section 9), but also in the language of most state constitutions.

While the main type of *ex post facto* law is one that retroactively criminalizes behavior, there are three means by which a law can run afoul of the Constitution:

1. The law criminalizes an act that was legal when it was committed.

2. The law increases the punishment for an act after it was committed.

3. It takes away a defense that was available when the crime was committed.[16]

It is relatively uncommon for statutes to retroactively criminalize behavior. Legislatures carefully guard against this problem, which means that most *ex post facto* cases deal with different, sometimes more tedious issues. For example, if a new statute changes the element of a crime after it is committed, does the new statute violate Article I, Section 9? Assume a state decides to define a juvenile as someone under the age of 16, not the usual 18. Assume further that a 17-year-old committed robbery before the change. To suddenly try him or her as an adult could constitute an *ex post facto* violation.

Consider the 1970 California case, *Keeler* v. *Superior Court*.[17] In that case, Robert Keeler learned that his ex-wife was pregnant with another man's child, became very angry, and said, "I'm going to stomp it out of you." He pushed her up against a car, kneed her in the abdomen, and struck her in the face. She fainted, but by the time she regained consciousness, Keeler had departed. She managed to drive herself to a nearby hospital where a Caesarean section was performed. Doctors determined that the fetus's head was severely fractured and it was delivered stillborn. Keeler was charged with murder in violation of a California Penal Code provision that defined the offense as "the unlawful killing of a human being, with malice aforethought." The question taken up by the court was whether the fetus could be considered a human being. Keeler claimed that if a fetus is not a human being, it would be akin to an *ex post facto* violation to convict him after the fact of an act that was not considered murder when he committed it. At worst, in his view, he committed assault (or possibly an abortion), but not murder.

What did the court decide? Interestingly, it sided with Mr. Keeler. The court began with a lengthy examination of the legislative history behind the statute. It found that the law's authors felt a child in its mother's womb was not a human being. The court also noted that the state is supposed to construe statutes as favorably as possible to the defendant (recall the principle of lenity). The defendant, the court said, "is entitled to the benefit of every reasonable doubt as to the true interpretation of words or the construction of language used in a statute."[18] Against this backdrop, the court declined to interpret the statute to mean Keeler committed murder. In other words, Keeler had no "fair warning" that what he did was murder. Certainly he knew it was wrong, but the court felt he could not have known it was murder. The court said,

> This requirement of fair warning is reflected in the constitutional prohibition against the enactment of ex post facto laws. . . . When a new penal statute is applied retrospectively to make punishable an act which was not criminal at the time it was performed, the defendant has been given no advance notice consistent with due

---

[16] *Beazell* v. *Ohio*, 269 U.S. 167 (1925).
[17] *Keeler* v. *Superior Court*, 2 Cal. 3d 619 (1970).
[18] Ibid., p. 631.

process. And precisely the same effect occurs when such an act is made punishable under a preexisting statute but by means of an unforeseeable judicial enlargement thereof.[19]

*Lynce* v. *Mathis*[20] raises the issue of whether an *ex post facto* violation occurs when the punishment scheme for an offense is altered after its commission. In 1986, Kenneth Lynce received a 22-year prison sentence following a conviction for attempted murder. He was released in 1992, however, because he accumulated early release credits totaling 5,668 days, including 1,860 "provisional credits" that were awarded because of the state's prison overcrowding problem. Shortly after his release, he was rearrested pursuant to an opinion issued by the attorney general that interpreted a 1992 statute as cancelling provisional credits for people convicted of murder and attempted murder. In effect, he was required to spend more time in prison making up the 1,860 provisional credit days. Lynce challenged this, arguing that it violated the Constitution's *ex post facto* law provision. In a unanimous decision, U.S. Supreme Court sided with Lynce, holding that the 1992 statute in question violated the Constitution's *ex post facto* clause. The logic was straightforward; the new law retroactively increased Lynce's punishment by an additional 1,860 days.

A related issue arose in the case of *Garner* v. *Jones*.[21] In that case, Robert Jones, who was serving a life sentence in prison for murder, escaped and committed another murder. He was convicted and sentenced to another life term. At the time Jones committed the second murder, the state's board of pardons and parole permitted parole reviews every three years following an initial consideration after seven years. After Jones started serving his second term, the board amended its rules, which it was authorized to do by law, such that a parole review would take place every eight years for inmates serving life sentences and who were denied parole in the past. Jones was affected by this policy change and claimed that it constituted an *ex post facto* violation. The Court of Appeals for the 11th Circuit agreed with him, but the Supreme Court did not, holding that the increased interval for parole review "created only the most speculative . . . possibility of . . . increasing the measure of punishment."[22] In his concurring opinion, Justice Scalia made this argument:

> Just as the Ex Post Facto Clause gives respondent [Jones] no cause to complain that the Board in place at the time of his offense has been replaced by a new, tough-on-crime Board that is much more parsimonious with parole, it gives him no cause to complain that it has been replaced by a new, big-on-efficiency Board that cuts back on reconsiderations without cause. And the change in policy is irrelevant, in my view, whether or not the pre-existing policy happens to have been embodied in a policy statement or regulation. To make the constitutional prohibition turn upon that feature would be to ignore reality and to discourage measures that promote fairness and consistency. Such a policy statement or regulation, in the context of a system conferring complete discretion as to substance and as to the timing of hearings, upon the Parole Board, simply creates no reasonable expectation of entitlement, except

---

[19]Ibid., p. 634.
[20]*Lynce* v. *Mathis*, 519 U.S. 433 (1997).
[21]*Garner* v. *Jones*, 529 U.S. 244 (2000).
[22]Ibid., p. 251.

perhaps among prisoners whose parole hearings are held (or are scheduled to be held) while the regulation is in effect. This is not an expectation of the sort that can give rise to ex post facto concerns.[23]

We wrap up our examination of the *ex post facto* prohibition with a look at *Smith* v. *Doe*, a 2003 Supreme Court case.[24] It involved a challenge to an Alaska law that required sex offenders to register with law enforcement authorities, share certain personal information with them, and inform them as to any changes as they come up. Two convicted sex offenders challenged the statute, claiming it retroactively punished them for actions committed before the registration requirement was put in place. The Court held that Alaska's sex offender registration statute was regulatory and nonpunitive. It stated, in part, that "the Act does not subject respondents to an affirmative disability or restraint. It imposes no physical restraint, and so does not resemble imprisonment."[25]

Article 1, Section 9, of the Constitution also bans bills of attainder. A **bill of attainder** is a law that criminalizes conduct without the benefit of a trial. In other words, it is unconstitutional for Congress to perform the judicial function, to hold "trial by legislature."

**bill of attainder** A law that criminalizes conduct without the benefit of a trial.

# Void for Vagueness

The U.S. Supreme Court has repeatedly struck down laws that are so vague that a normal person could not reasonably understand them or determine when they can be applied.[26] The Court has also struck down laws that give excessive discretion to law enforcement officials to decide who is arrested or prosecuted—and to judges to decide what conduct is prohibited. In contrast to the *ex post facto* prohibition, there is no specific constitutional provision that bans overly vague laws. Instead, the **void for vagueness** doctrine is based on the Fifth and Fourteenth Amendment due process clauses. Void for vagueness cases have historically fallen into two categories—those dealing with obscenity laws and those dealing with loitering and vagrancy statutes.

**void for vagueness** A constitutional doctrine based on the Fifth and Fourteenth Amendments to the U.S. Constitution requiring that laws be written with sufficient clarity and specificity.

## Obscenity Cases

In an early case, *Winters* v. *New York*,[27] the Supreme Court was confronted with the question of whether a New York statute relating to the print and distribution of obscene articles was overly vague. A person was guilty of a misdemeanor if that person printed, published, or sold "printed paper devoted to the publication, and principally made up of criminal news, police reports, or accounts of criminal deeds, or pictures, or stories of deeds of bloodshed, lust or crime" in "such a way as to incite

---

[23]Ibid., p. 259.
[24]*Smith* v. *Doe*, 538 U.S. 84 (2003).
[25]Ibid., p. 84.
[26]*Connally* v. *General Construction Company*, 269 U.S. 385 (1926).
[27]*Winters* v. *New York*, 333 U.S. 507 (1948).

crime." A book dealer who was convicted under the statute claimed it was overly vague and succeeded. In its decision, the Court focused heavily on the "incite crime" clause. It said, in part:

> The clause proposes to punish the printing and circulation of publications that courts or juries may think influence generally persons to commit crimes of violence against the person. No conspiracy to commit a crime is required. . . . It is not an effective notice of new crime. The clause has no technical or common law meaning. Nor can light as to the meaning be gained from the section as a whole or the Article of the Penal Law under which it appears.[28]

*State* v. *Metzger*[29] is another interesting case. In it, the Nebraska Supreme Court was tasked with deciding whether a Lincoln city ordinance was void for vagueness. The law in question provided that "[i]t shall be unlawful for any person within the City of Lincoln . . . to commit any indecent, immodest or filthy act in the presence of any person, or in such a situation that persons passing might ordinarily see the same."[30] Metzger was observed standing near his apartment window naked and was convicted. He argued that nudity is not necessarily obscene and is a form of free expression guaranteed by the First Amendment. He also argued that the ordinance was overly vague. The court, focusing on the vagueness issue, noted that there is little agreement as to what constitutes an "indecent, immodest, or filthy act":

> There may be those few who believe persons of opposite sex holding hands in public are immodest, and certainly more who might believe that kissing in public is immodest. Such acts cannot constitute a crime. Certainly one could find many who would conclude that today's swimming attire found on many beaches or beside many pools is immodest. Yet, the fact that it is immodest does not thereby make it illegal, absent some requirement related to the health, safety, or welfare of the community. The dividing line between what is lawful and what is unlawful in terms of "indecent," "immodest," or "filthy" is simply too broad to satisfy the constitutional requirements of due process. Both lawful and unlawful acts can be embraced within such broad definitions. That cannot be permitted.[31]

The Nebraska Supreme Court thus invalidated the statute, declaring that it was too vague.

## Loitering and Vagrancy

Several cases have also dealt with the meaning of loitering and vagrancy statutes. For example, in *Kolender* v. *Lawson*,[32] the law at issue said that any person who "loiters or wanders upon the streets or from place to place without apparent reason or business and who refuses to identify himself and to account for his presence when requested by any peace officer so to do" is guilty of a misdemeanor. Edward Lawson was detained and arrested on approximately 15 separate occasions. He was

[28]Ibid., p. 519.
[29]*State* v. *Metzger*, 319 N.W. 2d 459 (Neb. 1982).
[30]Ibid., p. 595.
[31]Ibid., pp. 598–599.
[32]*Kolender* v. *Lawson*, 461 U.S. 352 (1983).

prosecuted only twice, however, and convicted just once. After his one conviction, he challenged the constitutionality of the statute, arguing that it was overbroad. The Supreme Court agreed, holding that "as presently drafted and as construed by the state courts, [the statute] contains no standard for determining what a suspect has to do in order to satisfy the requirement to provide a 'credible and reliable' identification. As such, the statute vests virtually complete discretion in the hands of the police to determine whether the suspect has satisfied the statute and must be permitted to go on his way in the absence of probable cause to arrest. An individual, whom police may think is suspicious but do not have probable cause to believe has committed a crime, is entitled to continue to walk the public streets 'only at the whim of any police officer' who happens to stop that individual under [the statute]."[33]

*Papachristou* v. *City of Jacksonville*[34] dealt with a similar statute, this time in Florida. The law in question, a Jacksonville ordinance, defined vagrants as any of the following:

> Rogues and vagabonds, or dissolute persons who go about begging, common gamblers, persons who use juggling or unlawful games or plays, common drunkards, common night walkers, thieves, pilferers or pickpockets, traders in stolen property, lewd, wanton and lascivious persons, keepers of gambling places, common railers and brawlers, persons wandering or strolling around from place to place without any lawful purpose or object, habitual loafers, disorderly persons, persons neglecting all lawful business and habitually spending their time by frequenting houses of ill fame, gaming houses, or places where alcoholic beverages are sold or served, persons able to work but habitually living upon the earnings of their wives or minor children.[35]

Eight defendants were convicted in Florida municipal court pursuant to the statute. Their convictions were affirmed by the Florida Circuit Court, but their appeal to the Florida appellate court was denied. They petitioned the U.S. Supreme Court for *certiorari*. The Supreme Court agreed to hear their consolidated case and reversed their convictions, holding in part that the statute "fails to give a person of ordinary intelligence fair notice that his contemplated conduct is forbidden by the statute . . . and because it encourages arbitrary and erratic arrests and convictions."[36]

The cases we just reviewed may give the impression that it is easy for defendants to challenge statutes on vagueness grounds. Nothing could be further from the truth. Courts presume that laws are constitutional. The burden of proving otherwise thus falls on the defendant. And meeting that burden is not easy, as the Ohio Supreme Court remarked:

> [The defendant] . . . must show that upon examining the statute, an individual of ordinary intelligence would not understand what he is required to do under the law. Thus, to escape responsibility . . . [the defendant] must prove that he could not reasonably understand that . . . [the law in question] prohibited the acts in which he engaged. . . . The party alleging that a statute is unconstitutional must prove this assertion beyond a reasonable doubt.[37]

---

[33]Ibid., p. 358.
[34]*Papachristou* v. *City of Jacksonville*, 405 U.S. 156 (1983).
[35]Ibid., p. 158.
[36]Ibid., p. 162.
[37]*State* v. *Anderson*, 566 N.E. 2d 1224 (Ohio 1991).

# The Void for Overbreadth Doctrine

The equal protection requirement, the ban on *ex post facto* laws, and the ban on overly vague statutes apply to all criminal laws at all times. There is another more specific limitation on the criminal law—namely, the void for overbreadth doctrine. In general, a law will be void for overbreadth if it prohibits action that would be protected in the Constitution. Overbreadth cases often involve the First Amendment.

The First Amendment addresses freedom of religion, assembly, and speech. It is the latter that is of interest to us here. The free speech clause says, "Congress shall make no law . . . abridging the freedom of speech, or of the press. . . ." Over the years, the Supreme Court has interpreted this language rather loosely to include not just things people say, but also the written word[38] and actions that communicate words and ideas. The First Amendment's free speech clause has also been made binding on the states, underscoring its importance.[39]

In general, Congress cannot ban free speech, but the Supreme Court has sanctioned such bans in a few important areas. These include certain forms of obscenity, profanity, libelous speech, and so-called fighting words.[40] These forms of free speech and expression are not sanctioned because they are not, according to the Supreme Court, an "essential element of any exposition of ideas, and are of such slight value as a step to truth that any benefit that may be derived from them is clearly outweighed by the social interest in order and morality."[41]

The Court has been confronted with a number of free speech cases over the years, mostly in the areas of seditious speech and libel, fighting words and threats to the peace, and so-called group libel, or hate speech. Before continuing, let us define some of these terms. **Libel** is defamation by the written or printed word. **Defamation**, simply, is an attack on the good reputation of another. **Seditious speech** is that which advocates rebellion against the government. (See Figure 2.2 for a list of speech that is not protected by the First Amendment.)

**libel** Defamation by the written or printed word.

**defamation** Written or spoken words that damage the reputation of the object of the speech.

**seditious speech** Speech that advocates rebellion against the government.

**Figure 2.2**
Speech that is NOT protected under the First Amendment.

- Obscenity
- Defamation
  - Libel: Written word
  - Slander: Spoken Word
- Fighting Words
- Child Pornography
- Solicitations to Commit Crimes
- True Threats
- Blackmail
- Perjury
- Incitement to Lawless Action

---

[38] *Texas* v. *Johnson*, 491 U.S. 397 (1989).
[39] *Gitlow* v. *New York*, 268 U.S. 652 (1925).
[40] *Chaplinsky* v. *New Hampshire*, 315 U.S. 568 (1942), p. 573.
[41] *Gitlow* v. *New York*, p. 572.

## Seditious Speech and Libel

Our system of government welcomes citizen protests, but seditious utterances are basically prohibited. For example, the Sedition Act of 1798 made criminal any writings that defamed, brought into disrepute, or bolstered the hatred of the people toward the government.

This is a delicate area, one in which a number of cases have been decided over the years. In one interesting case, *Brandenburg* v. *Ohio*,[42] the Court decided on the constitutionality of Ohio's Criminal Syndicalism statute. A Ku Klux Klan leader was convicted under the statute for "advocate[ing] . . . the duty, necessity, or propriety of crime, sabotage, violence, or unlawful methods of terrorism as a means of accomplishing industrial or political reform" and for "voluntarily assembl[ing] with any society, group or assemblage of persons formed to teach or advocate the doctrines of criminal syndicalism." The statute was declared unconstitutional for these reasons:

> Since the statute, by its words and as applied, purports to punish mere advocacy and to forbid, on pain of criminal punishment, assembly with others merely to advocate the described type of action, it falls within the condemnation of the First [Amendment]. . . . Freedoms of speech and press do not permit a State to forbid advocacy of the use of force or of law violation except where such advocacy is directed to inciting or producing imminent lawless action and is likely to incite or produce such action.[43]

The Court felt that because the statute did not distinguish between (1) teaching the need for violence and (2) actually calling for it, the statute infringed on the First Amendment's free speech clause.

## Fighting Words and Threats to the Peace

In *Chaplinsky* v. *New Hampshire*, the Supreme Court sanctioned a conviction under a statute that prohibited "any offense, derisive, or annoying word" addressed to anyone in a public place. The Court felt that statute was "narrowly drawn and limited to define and punish specific conduct lying within the domain of state power, the use in a public place of words likely to cause a breach of the peace."[44] The case is most famous for Justice Murphy's observation:

> [I]t is well understood that the right of free speech is not absolute at all times and under all circumstances. There are certain well-defined and narrowly limited classes of speech, the prevention and punishment of which have never been thought to raise any Constitutional problem. These include the lewd and obscene, the profane, the libelous, and the insulting or "fighting" words—those which by their very utterance inflict injury or tend to incite an immediate breach of the peace. It has been well observed that such utterances are no essential part of any exposition of ideas, and are of such slight social value as a step to truth that any benefit that may be derived from them is clearly outweighed by the social interest in order and morality.

---

[42] *Brandenburg* v. *Ohio*, 395 U.S. 444 (1969).
[43] Ibid., p. 444.
[44] Ibid., p. 573.

Protesters burn United States flag during an anti-racism demonstration in New York City Hall Park

© Richard Levine/Alamy

Importantly, the government cannot prohibit fighting words simply because they are offensive. Rather, they must have a tendency to cause acts of violence by the people against whom they are directed. Consider the case of *Gooding* v. *Wilson*,[45] a case involving a Georgia statute providing that "any person who shall, without provocation, use to or of another, and in his presence . . . opprobrious words or abusive language, tending to cause a breach of the peace . . . shall be guilty of a misdemeanor." The Court invalidated the statute, claiming that it was overly vague. It said, in part, that "the term 'breach of peace' is generic, and includes all violations of the public peace or order, or decorum; in other words, it signifies the offense of disturbing the public peace or tranquility enjoyed by the citizens of a community. . . . This definition makes it a 'breach of peace' merely to speak words offensive to some who hear them, and so sweeps too broadly."[46] In essence, the Court held that the statute was **void for overbreadth**. This is now the standard that the courts use to decide whether a statute seeking to restrict free speech runs afoul of the First Amendment.[47]

**void for overbreadth** A constitutional principal requiring that laws do not infringe on constitutionally protected behavior.

See the accompanying Court Decision for more on the role of the First Amendment in criminal law. It features the case of *Texas* v. *Johnson*, in which the Supreme Court addressed the constitutionality of a Texas criminal statute that outlawed burning the American flag.

---

[45]*Gooding* v. *Wilson*, 405 U.S. 518 (1972).
[46]Ibid., p. 527.
[47]For other cases dealing with supposed fighting words, see *Hess* v. *Indiana*, 414 U.S. 105 (1973); *Lewis* v. *City of New Orleans*, 415 U.S. 130 (1974); *Lucas* v. *Arkansas*, 416 U.S. 919 (1974); *Kelly* v. *Ohio*, 416 U.S. 923 (1974); *Karlan* v. *City of Cincinnati*, 416 U.S. 924 (1974); *Rosen* v. *California*, 416 U.S. 924 (1974); and *Eaton* v. *City of Tulsa*, 416 U.S. 697 (1974).

# COURT DECISION

## Texas v. Johnson
### 491 U.S. 397 (1989)

**Background:** Johnson was convicted in the County Criminal Court No. 8, Dallas County for desecration of a venerated object and he appealed. The Dallas Court of Appeals affirmed the conviction. The Texas Court of Criminal Appeals reversed and remanded and he Supreme Court granted *certiorari*.

Justice BRENNAN delivered the opinion of the Court.

After publicly burning an American flag as a means of political protest, Gregory Lee Johnson was convicted of desecrating a flag in violation of Texas law. This case presents the question whether his conviction is consistent with the First Amendment. We hold that it is not.

### I

While the Republican National Convention was taking place in Dallas in 1984, respondent Johnson participated in a political demonstration dubbed the "Republican War Chest Tour." As explained in literature distributed by the demonstrators and in speeches made by them, the purpose of this event was to protest the policies of the Reagan administration and of certain Dallas-based corporations. The demonstrators marched through the Dallas streets, chanting political slogans and stopping at several corporate locations to stage "die-ins" intended to dramatize the consequences of nuclear war. On several occasions they spray-painted the walls of buildings and overturned potted plants, but Johnson himself took no part in such activities. He did, however, accept an American flag handed to him by a fellow protestor who had taken it from a flagpole outside one of the targeted buildings.

The demonstration ended in front of Dallas City Hall, where Johnson unfurled the American flag, doused it with kerosene, and set it on fire. While the flag burned, the protestors chanted: "America, the red, white, and blue, we spit on you." After the demonstrators dispersed, a witness to the flag burning collected the flag's remains and buried them in his backyard. No one was physically injured or threatened with injury, though several witnesses testified that they had been seriously offended by the flag burning.

Of the approximately 100 demonstrators, Johnson alone was charged with a crime. The only criminal offense with which he was charged was the desecration of a venerated object in violation of Tex. Penal Code Ann. § 42.09(a)(3) (1959). After a trial, he was convicted, sentenced to one year in prison, and fined $2,000. The Court of Appeals for the Fifth District of Texas at Dallas affirmed Johnson's conviction, but the Texas Court of Criminal Appeals reversed, holding that the State could not, consistent with the First Amendment, punish Johnson for burning the flag in these circumstances.

\*\*\*Johnson was convicted of flag desecration for burning the flag rather than for uttering insulting words. This fact somewhat complicates our consideration of his conviction under the First Amendment. We must first determine whether Johnson's burning of the flag constituted expressive conduct, permitting him to invoke the First Amendment in challenging his conviction. If his conduct was expressive, we next decide whether the State's regulation is related to the suppression of free expression. If the State's regulation is not related to expression, then the less stringent standard we announced in *United States* v. *O'Brien* for regulations of noncommunicative conduct controls.

\*\*\*The First Amendment literally forbids the abridgment only of "speech," but we have long recognized that its protection does not end at the spoken or written word. While we have rejected "the view that an apparently limitless variety of conduct can be labeled 'speech' whenever the person engaging in the conduct intends thereby to express an idea," *United States* v. *O'Brien, 391 U.S.* at 376, we have acknowledged that conduct may be "sufficiently imbued with elements of communication to fall within the scope of the First and Fourteenth Amendments."

\*\*\*Johnson burned an American flag as part—indeed, as the culmination—of a political demonstration that coincided with the convening of the Republican Party and its renomination of Ronald Reagan for President. The expressive, overtly political nature of this conduct was both intentional and overwhelmingly apparent. At his trial, Johnson explained his reasons for burning the flag as follows: "The American Flag was burned as Ronald Reagan was being renominated as President. And a more powerful statement of symbolic speech, whether you agree with it or not, couldn't have been made at that time. It's quite a just position [juxtaposition]. We had new patriotism and no patriotism." In these circumstances, Johnson's burning of the flag was conduct "sufficiently imbued with elements of communication," *Spence,* 418 U.S., at 409, to implicate the First Amendment.

\*\*\*If there is a bedrock principle underlying the First Amendment, it is that the government may not prohibit the expression of an idea simply because society finds the idea itself offensive or disagreeable.

\*\*\*Johnson was convicted for engaging in expressive conduct. The State's interest in preventing breaches of the peace does not support his conviction because Johnson's conduct did not threaten to disturb the peace. Nor does the State's interest in preserving the flag as a symbol of nationhood and national unity justify his criminal conviction for engaging in political expression. The judgment of the Texas Court of Criminal Appeals is therefore

*Affirmed.*

Justice STEVENS, dissenting.

As the Court analyzes this case, it presents the question whether the State of Texas, or indeed the Federal Government, has the power to prohibit the public desecration of the American flag. The question is unique. In my judgment rules that apply to a host of other symbols, such as state flags, armbands, or various privately promoted emblems of political or commercial identity, are not necessarily controlling. Even if flag burning could be considered just another species of symbolic speech under the logical application of the rules that the Court has developed in its interpretation of the First Amendment in other contexts, this case has an intangible dimension that makes those rules inapplicable.

\*\*\*The value of the flag as a symbol cannot be measured. Even so, I have no doubt that the interest in preserving that value for the future is both significant and legitimate. Conceivably that value will be enhanced by the Court's conclusion that our national commitment to free expression is so strong that even the United States as ultimate guarantor of that freedom is without power to prohibit the desecration of its unique symbol. But I am unpersuaded. The creation of a federal right to post bulletin boards and graffiti on the Washington Monument might enlarge the market for free expression, but at a cost I would not pay. Similarly, in my considered judgment, sanctioning the public desecration of the flag will tarnish its value—both for those who cherish the ideas for which it waves and for those who desire to don the robes of martyrdom by burning it.

## Case Analysis

1. What crime was Johnson charged with?
2. Explain how "conduct" can be considered speech under the First Amendment.
3. What happened to the Texas Criminal Statute after the Supreme Court issued its decision?
4. What was Justice Steven's primary argument in his dissent?

## Group Libel

The courts have also sanctioned laws that ban speech that defames a certain group or class of people—or is "libelous" toward a specific group. In *Beauharnais v. Illinois*,[48] a man was convicted under a libel law for distributing a leaflet that called for keeping African Americans out of white neighborhoods. The Supreme Court held that the law complied with the First Amendment.

Subsequent decisions, however, have complicated matters. For example, in *R.A.V. v. City of St. Paul*,[49] a juvenile was alleged to have burned a cross on a black family's front lawn. He was charged with violating the city's Bias-Motivated Crime Ordinance, which made it a misdemeanor for anyone to place "on public or private property a symbol, object, appellation, characterization or graffiti, including, but not limited to, a burning cross or Nazi swastika, which one knows or has reasonable grounds to know arouses anger, alarm or resentment in others on the basis of race, color, creed, religion or gender. . . ."[50] The Court ruled that the statute was unconstitutional and decided it was overly broad because "the First Amendment does not permit [the city] to impose special prohibitions on those speakers who express views on disfavored subjects."[51]

The Court's logic in *R.A.V.* is tedious, but a few points bear mention. First, the law was limited only to race, color, creed, religion, and gender. If someone wanted to use fighting words in connection with some other ideas not covered by the law

---

[48]*Beauharnais v. Illinois*, 343 U.S. 250 (1952).
[49]*R.A.V. v. City of St. Paul*, 505 U.S. 377 (1992).
[50]Ibid., p. 380.
[51]Ibid., p. 391.

(e.g., homosexuality, criminal beliefs), that person would be allowed to. This, the Court said, is content discrimination and is prohibited. Second, the Court felt that law imposed viewpoint discrimination. Justice Scalia, author of the Court's opinion, said on this point that fighting words that "do not themselves invoke race, color, creed, religion, or gender—aspersions upon a person's mother, for example—would seemingly be usable *ad libitum* in the placards of those arguing *in favor* of racial, color, etc., tolerance and equality, but could not be used by those speakers' opponents. Finally, the Court implied that the ordinance could have been written differently and satisfied the First Amendment: "An ordinance not limited to the favored topics, for example, would have . . . "[52] helped protect the rights of groups that have, throughout history, been discriminated against.

**YOUR DECISION**

1. Concerned with its growing gang problem, the city of New York passes a law making it a crime to be a member of "a criminal street gang." Jose Perez is a 19-year-old citizen of Mexican descent. He is seen in a high-crime area wearing the color yellow, which is typically the color worn by members of the Latin Kings gang. He is arrested and charged with violating the new statute. Perez argues that the statute fails to adequately define what "a criminal street gang" is and lead to discriminatory enforcement by police. Is the New York City statute constitutional?

2. As the Olympic torch passed through Juneau, Alaska, Joseph Frederick and a number of his classmates held up a sign that read "BONG HiTS 4 JESUS." On a break from school, the high school principal confiscated the sign and suspended Frederick from school. Frederick claimed that he had the constitutional right to display the banner. Does the First Amendment protect Frederick and his classmates?

## Summary

- Constitutional limitations on the criminal law include equal protection of the laws, the *ex post facto* law prohibition, the void for vagueness doctrine, the void for overbreadth doctrine, the cruel and unusual punishment provision of the Eighth Amendment, and the double jeopardy clause of the Fifth Amendment.

- The Fourteenth Amendment states, in part, that "no state shall deny to any person within its jurisdiction the equal protection of the laws."

- The equal protection clause has been interpreted to ban separate criminal codes for separate classes of people (e.g., blacks and whites).

- As long as there is a "rational basis" for treating one group differently from the next (e.g., men and women), unequal treatment will be allowed.

- An *ex post facto* law is one enacted in order to retroactively punish behavior.

- *Ex post facto* laws are banned by the U.S. Constitution, Article I, Section 9.

---

[52]Ibid., p. 395.

- An *ex post facto* violation occurs when (1) the law criminalizes an act that was legal when it was committed, (2) the law increases the punishment for an act after it was committed, or (3) it takes away a defense that was available when the crime was committed.

- The U.S. Supreme Court has repeatedly struck down laws that are so vague that a normal person could not reasonably understand them or determine when they can be applied.

- The void for vagueness doctrine is based on the Fifth and Fourteenth Amendment due process clauses.

- Obscenity, loitering, and vagrancy statutes have been challenged on multiple occasions as overly vague.

- Statutes that are overly broad in their language and that infringe on free speech and expression violate the First Amendment.

- In general, seditious speech, certain fighting words, and "group libel," or hate speech, can be criminalized without running counter to the First Amendment.

## MODULE 2.3

# CONSTITUTIONAL LIMITATIONS ON THE CRIMINAL LAW, PART 2

### Learning Objectives

- **Describe the protections against cruel and unusual punishment.**
- **Explain the guarantee against double jeopardy.**

**CORE CONCEPTS**

## Cruel and Unusual Punishment

The Eighth Amendment to the U.S. Constitution prohibits "cruel and unusual punishment." Both the federal government *and* the states are bound by this constitutional limitation.[53] In general, the Eighth Amendment prohibits barbaric punishments and disproportionate sentencing (i.e., getting sentenced for an inordinately long time for a minor offense).

In 1910, the Supreme Court expressed a preference that "punishment for crime . . . be graduated and proportioned to [the] offense."[54] This means, basically, that a punishment that seems excessive in light of the underlying offense could be deemed unconstitutional. We say *could* because many a punishment has been sanctioned that would seem to the untrained observer a gross violation of the Eighth Amendment. Two broad classes of Eighth Amendment cruel and unusual punishments have come before the Supreme Court over the years: death penalty cases and cases challenging the length of a sentence.

---

[53]*Robinson v. California*, 370 U.S. 660 (1962).
[54]*Weems v. United States*, 217 U.S. 349 (1910), p. 367.

# Death Penalty Cases

When someone is convicted of intentional murder, the death penalty (aka *capital punishment*) is a legitimate punishment—at least, according to the courts, in the states that use capital punishment as a means of dealing with certain murderers. While the Supreme Court has never held that the death penalty constitutes cruel and unusual punishment, in a 1972 case, *Furman* v. *Georgia,*[55] the Court decided that the death penalty, as it was being carried out at the time, was unconstitutional. Each of the Court's nine justices authored separate opinions in this 5–4 decision. Three of them raised discrimination concerns: Justice Douglas argued that death penalty procedures were "pregnant with discrimination"[56]; Justice Stewart pointed out that the death penalty was "so wantonly and so freakishly imposed"[57]; and Justice White found "no meaningful basis for distinguishing the few cases in which [the death penalty] is imposed from the many cases in which it is not."[58]

The *Furman* decision was far-reaching. It brought executions to a halt and "emptied death rows across the country."[59] It also invalidated death penalty statutes in 39 states. Most of the states responded by enacting new laws aimed at curbing the discretion of judges and jurors in death penalty cases to ensure fairness and even-handedness in the process.[60] The new laws were of two varieties—some provided for the death penalty in cases of first-degree murder, and others provided for the death penalty in several offenses based on the presence of aggravating or mitigating circumstances,[61] which are now called **guided-discretion laws**.

**guided-discretion laws**
Laws that provide for the death penalty based on weighing aggravating and mitigating circumstances.

In the wake of *Furman,* the Court decided a few more death penalty cases. In *Woodson* v. *North Carolina*[62] and *Roberts* v. *Louisiana,*[63] the Court held that North Carolina's and Louisiana's mandatory death penalty statutes were unconstitutional—both states' laws gave jurors no opportunity to consider aggravating and mitigating circumstances. In contrast, the Court looked favorably on the guided-discretion laws in the states of Florida, Georgia, and Texas.[64] For example, in *Gregg* v. *Georgia,* the Court held that Georgia's statute limited the jury's discretion and thus minimized the chances that the death penalty would be arbitrarily imposed[65]:

> No longer can a jury wantonly and freakishly impose the death sentence; it is always circumscribed by the legislative guidelines. In addition, the review function of the Supreme Court of Georgia affords additional assurance that the concerns that prompted our decision in *Furman* are not present to any significant degree in the Georgia procedure applied here.[66]

---

[55]*Furman* v. *Georgia,* 408 U.S. 238 (1972).
[56]Ibid., p. 257.
[57]Ibid., p. 310.
[58]Ibid., p. 313.
[59]S. R. Gross and R. Mauro, *Death and Discrimination: Racial Disparities in Capital Sentencing* (Boston: Northeastern University Press, 1989), p. 215.
[60]S. Walker, C. Spohn, and M. DeLone, *The Color of Justice: Race, Ethnicity, and Crime in America,* 4th ed. (Belmont, CA: Wadsworth, 2007), p. 293.
[61]Ibid.
[62]*Woodson* v. *North Carolina,* 428 U.S. 280 (1976).
[63]*Roberts* v. *Louisiana,* 428 U.S. 280 (1976).
[64]*Proffitt* v. *Florida,* 428 U.S. 242 (1976); *Gregg* v. *Georgia,* 428 U.S. 153 (1976); *Jurek* v. *Texas,* 428 U.S. 262 (1976).
[65]*Gregg* v. *Georgia,* 428 U.S. 153 (1976).
[66]Ibid., pp. 206–207.

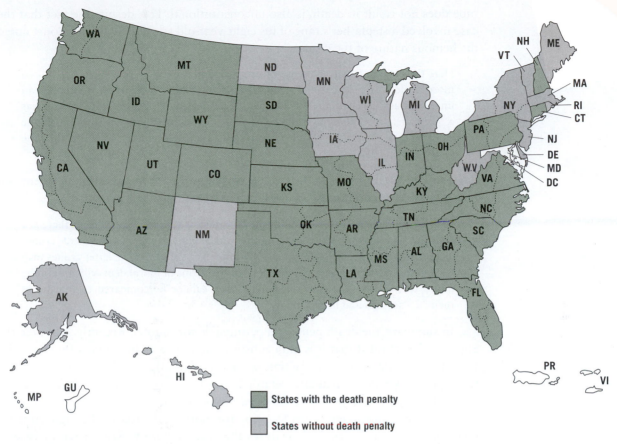

**Figure 2.3**
Death penalty use in the United States

The practical result of the *Gregg* decision was that the death penalty was reinstated. (See Figure 2.3 for a map of the United States showing use of the death penalty by state.)

Other cases have dealt with the question of whether death is an appropriate sanction for offenses other than murder. *Coker* v. *Georgia*,[67] for example, involved a man who committed two rapes, was convicted and imprisoned, escaped, and raped again. He was sentenced to death for his post-escape rape. The Supreme Court held that the sentence was grossly disproportional. Rape, the Court opined, "does not compare with murder, which . . . involve[s] the unjustified taking of human life. . . . The murderer kills; the rapist, if no more than that, does not."[68]

The *Coker* decision was limited to cases involving the rape of adult women. After the decision was handed down, several states enacted laws sanctioning the death penalty for child rapists, those convicted of raping children under the age of 12. Were such laws constitutional? The answer came only recently in the 2008 case of *Kennedy* v. *Louisiana*.[69] The Court held that even the rape of a child, where the

---

[67]*Coker* v. *Georgia*, 433 U.S. 584 (1977).
[68]Ibid., p. 598.
[69]*Kennedy* v. *Louisiana*, 128 S.Ct. 2641 (2008).

rape does not result in death, is also unconstitutional. This despite the fact that the case involved a stepfather's rape of his eight-year-old stepdaughter. The Court noted the heinous nature of the crime:

> Here the victim's fright, the sense of betrayal, and the nature of her injuries caused more prolonged physical and mental suffering than, say, a sudden killing by an unseen assassin. The attack was not just on her but on her childhood. . . . Rape has a permanent psychological, emotional, and sometimes physical impact on the child. . . . We cannot dismiss the years of long anguish that must be endured by the victim of child rape.[70]

Even so, the Court said that "[i]t does not follow . . . that capital punishment is a proportionate penalty for the crime." Why? Here is the Court's logic:

> [W]e conclude that, in determining whether the death penalty is excessive, there is a distinction between intentional . . . murder on the one hand and nonhomicide crimes against individual persons, including child rape, on the other. The latter crimes may be devastating in their harm, as here, but . . . 'in terms of moral depravity and of the injury to the person and to the public,' they cannot be compared to murder in their . . . 'severity and irrevocability.'"[71]

In summary, the death penalty is permissible for murder. Recently, however, the Supreme Court ruled that it is only constitutional in cases involving offenders who were 18 years old or older at the time of their capital offenses.[72] Also, it is unconstitutional to execute a mentally retarded murderer.[73] Capital punishment is *not* allowed in rape cases, no matter the circumstances.

See the accompanying Court Decision for more on the role of the Eight Amendment in death penalty cases. It features the case of *Baze* v. *Rees*, a recent case in which the Supreme Court reviewed the constitutionality of lethal injection as a form of execution.

---

**COURT DECISION**

*Baze* v. *Rees*
553 U.S. 35 (2008)

**Background:** Death row inmates challenged the constitutionality of the three-drug method of lethal injection. The Franklin Circuit Court in Kentucky denied the defendants relief and the Supreme Court of Kentucky affirmed. The Supreme Court granted *certiorari*.

Chief Justice ROBERTS announced the judgment of the Court and delivered an opinion, in which Justice KENNEDY and Justice ALITO join.

Like 35 other States and the Federal Government, Kentucky has chosen to impose capital punishment for certain crimes. As is true with respect to each of these States and the Federal Government, Kentucky has altered its method of execution over

---

[70]Ibid., p. 2660.
[71]Ibid., p. 2660.
[72]*Roper* v. *Simmons*, 543 U.S. 551 (2005).
[73]*Atkins* v. *Virginia*, 122 S.Ct. 2242 (2002).

time to more humane means of carrying out the sentence. That progress has led to the use of lethal injection by every jurisdiction that imposes the death penalty.

Petitioners in this case—each convicted of double homicide—acknowledge that the lethal injection procedure, if applied as intended, will result in a humane death. They nevertheless contend that the lethal injection protocol is unconstitutional under the Eighth Amendment's ban on "cruel and unusual punishments," because of the risk that the protocol's terms might not be properly followed, resulting in significant pain. They propose an alternative protocol, one that they concede has not been adopted by any State and has never been tried.

The trial court held extensive hearings and entered detailed Findings of Fact and Conclusions of Law. It recognized that "[t]here are no methods of legal execution that are satisfactory to those who oppose the death penalty on moral, religious, or societal grounds," but concluded that Kentucky's procedure "complies with the constitutional requirements against cruel and unusual punishment." App. 769. The State Supreme Court affirmed. We too agree that petitioners have not carried their burden of showing that the risk of pain from maladministration of a concededly humane lethal injection protocol, and the failure to adopt untried and untested alternatives, constitute cruel and unusual punishment. The judgment below is affirmed.

### ***A

This Court has never invalidated a State's chosen procedure for carrying out a sentence of death as the infliction of cruel and unusual punishment. In *Wilkerson v. Utah*, we upheld a sentence to death by firing squad imposed by a territorial court, rejecting the argument that such a sentence constituted cruel and unusual punishment. We noted there the difficulty of "defin[ing] with exactness the extent of the constitutional provision which provides that cruel and unusual punishments shall not be inflicted." Rather than undertake such an effort, the *Wilkerson* Court simply noted that "it is safe to affirm that punishments of torture, . . . and all others in the same line of unnecessary cruelty, are forbidden" by the Eighth Amendment. By way of example, the Court cited cases from England in which "terror, pain, or disgrace were sometimes superadded" to the sentence, such as where the condemned was "embowelled alive, beheaded, and quartered," or instances of "public dissection in murder, and burning alive." In contrast, we observed that the firing squad was routinely used as a method of execution for military officers. What each of the forbidden punishments had in common was the deliberate infliction of pain for the sake of pain—"superadd[ing]" pain to the death sentence through torture and the like.

### ***B

Petitioners do not claim that lethal injection or the proper administration of the particular protocol adopted by Kentucky by themselves constitute the cruel or wanton infliction of pain. Quite the contrary, they concede that "if performed properly," an execution carried out under Kentucky's procedures would be "humane and constitutional." That is because, as counsel for petitioners admitted at oral argument, proper administration of the first drug, sodium thiopental, eliminates any meaningful risk that a prisoner would experience pain from the subsequent injections of pancuronium and potassium chloride.

Instead, petitioners claim that there is a significant risk that the procedures will *not* be properly followed—in particular, that the sodium thiopental will not be properly administered to achieve its intended effect—resulting in severe pain when the other chemicals are administered. Our cases recognize that subjecting individuals to a risk of future harm—not simply actually inflicting pain—can qualify as cruel and unusual punishment. To establish that such exposure violates the Eighth Amendment, however, the conditions presenting the risk must be "*sure or very likely* to cause serious illness and needless suffering," and give rise to "sufficiently *imminent* dangers." *Helling* v. *McKinney,* 509 U.S. 25, 33, 34-35 (1993). We have explained that to prevail on such a claim there must be a "substantial risk of serious harm," an "objectively intolerable risk of harm" that prevents prison officials from pleading that they were "subjectively blameless for purposes of the Eighth Amendment." *Farmer* v. *Brennan,* 511 U.S. 825, 842, 846, and n. 9, (1994).

Simply because an execution method may result in pain, either by accident or as an inescapable consequence of death, does not establish the sort of "objectively intolerable risk of harm" that qualifies as cruel and unusual. In *Louisiana ex rel. Francis* v. *Resweber*, a plurality of the Court upheld a second attempt at executing a prisoner by electrocution after a mechanical malfunction had interfered with the first attempt. The principal opinion noted that "[a]ccidents happen for which no man is to blame," and concluded that such "an accident, with no suggestion of malevolence," did not give rise to an Eighth Amendment violation.

***The judgment below concluding that Kentucky's procedure is consistent with the Eighth Amendment is, accordingly, affirmed.

Justice GINSBURG, with whom Justice SOUTER joins, dissenting.

It is undisputed that the second and third drugs used in Kentucky's three-drug lethal injection protocol, pancuronium bromide and potassium chloride, would cause a conscious inmate to suffer excruciating pain. Pancuronium bromide paralyzes the lung muscles and results in slow asphyxiation. Potassium chloride causes burning and intense pain as it circulates throughout the body. Use of pancuronium bromide and potassium chloride on a conscious inmate, the plurality recognizes, would be "constitutionally unacceptable."

The constitutionality of Kentucky's protocol therefore turns on whether inmates are adequately anesthetized by the first drug in the protocol, sodium thiopental. Kentucky's system is constitutional, the plurality states, because "petitioners have not shown that the risk of an inadequate dose of the first drug is substantial." *Ante,* at 1533. I would not dispose of the case so swiftly given the character of the risk at stake. Kentucky's protocol lacks basic safeguards used by other States to confirm that an inmate is unconscious before injection of the second and third drugs. I would vacate and remand with instructions to consider whether Kentucky's omission of those safeguards poses an untoward, readily avoidable risk of inflicting severe and unnecessary pain.

## Case Analysis

1. What amendment to the U.S. Constitution is at issue in this case?
2. Explain how the process of lethal injection works.
3. Are all forms of capital punishment "cruel and unusual" by definition?
4. What was the dissent's primary argument?

## Sentence Length and the Eighth Amendment

While there is a bright line distinction between what types of offenses can result in death and what types cannot, it is substantially less clear what length of incarceration may violate the Eighth Amendment. In *Rummel* v. *Estelle*,[74] a man was sentenced to life in prison under Texas's habitual offender law. He was convicted of obtaining a check for $120.75 by false pretenses, then cashing it, but he had previously been convicted of theft on two occasions. The Supreme Court sanctioned his life sentence, stating that "the interest of the State of Texas here is not simply that of making criminal the unlawful acquisition of another person's property; it is in addition the interest . . . in dealing in a harsher manner with those who by repeated criminal acts have shown that they are simply incapable of conforming to the norms of society established by its criminal law."[75]

Contrast *Rummel* with *Solem* v. *Helm*,[76] a case involving the life sentence (without parole) of a man who was convicted of passing a "no account" check for $100.00. It was his seventh conviction. Even so, the Supreme Court decided that the sentence was cruel and unusual. It also noted that the "without parole" part of the sentence was determinative. The Court noted that Texas had a more liberal parole policy, which is why the *Rummel* sentence was deemed constitutional (he could have been paroled).

But further contrast *Solem* with the Supreme Court's 1991 decision in *Harmelin* v. *Michigan*.[77] That case involved a first-time offender who was convicted of possessing 672 grams of cocaine and sentenced to life in prison without the possibility of parole. The Supreme Court held that the sentence was constitutional. In essence, the Court felt the underlying offense was more serious than that in the *Solem* case. A similar decision was reached in *Ewing* v. *California*,[78] a case involving an application of California's punitive three-strikes laws. Ewing, a twice previously convicted felon, was sentence to 25 years to life in prison for stealing three golf clubs, each worth $399, which made his offense "grand theft," a felony under California law. The Court found no Eighth Amendment violation:

> Throughout the States, legislatures enacting three-strikes laws [have] made a deliberate policy choice that individuals who have repeatedly engaged in serious or violent criminal behavior, and whose conduct has not been deterred by more conventional approaches to punishment, must be isolated from society in order to protect the public safety. Though three-strikes laws may be relatively new, our tradition of deferring to state legislatures in making and implementing such important policy decisions is longstanding.[79]

---

[74]*Rummel* v. *Estelle*, 445 U.S. 263 (1980).
[75]Ibid., p. 276.
[76]*Solem* v. *Helm*, 463 U.S. 277 (1983).
[77]*Harmelin* v. *Michigan*, 501 U.S. 957 (1991).
[78]*Ewing* v. *California*, 538 U.S. 11 (2003).
[79]Ibid., p. 24.

These decisions make it more than a little difficult to determine when a long prison term violates the Eighth Amendment. In deciding what length of term is appropriate, courts must consider various factors, including (1) the gravity of the offense compared to the sentence, (2) the penalties imposed on other offenders in the same state for the same offense, (3) the penalties imposed in other states for the same offense, and (4) the defendant's recidivism. Courts are not required to consider all these criteria, however. To this day, there is some uncertainty as to which (if any) combination is important.

# Double Jeopardy

**double jeopardy** A principle found in the Fifth Amendment to the U.S. Constitution that prevents an individual from being tried twice for the same crime.

The constitutionally guaranteed protection against **double jeopardy** is designed to ensure that a person who has been convicted or acquitted of a crime is not tried or punished for the same offense twice. Double jeopardy occurs when, for the same offense, a person is (1) reprosecuted after acquittal; (2) reprosecuted after conviction; or (3) subjected to separate punishments for the same offense. Double jeopardy does not apply, however, to prosecutions brought by separate sovereigns. The federal government, each state government, and each Native American tribe is considered a separate sovereign.

Early English common law contains the foundations of the modern-day protection against double jeopardy. The rule of *autrefois acquit* prohibited the retrial of a defendant who was found not guilty. The rule of *autrefois convict*, on the other hand, prohibited the retrial of a defendant who *was* found guilty. These rules were adopted by the American colonies.

Today, every state provides double jeopardy protection because of the Supreme Court's decision in *Benton* v. *Maryland*,[80] in which the Court declared that the Fifth Amendment's protection against double jeopardy is a fundamental right:

> The fundamental nature of the guarantee against double jeopardy can hardly be doubted. Its origins can be traced to Greek and Roman times, and it became established in the common law of England long before this Nation's independence. . . . As with many other elements of the common law, it was carried into the jurisprudence of this Country through the medium of Blackstone, who codified the doctrine in his Commentaries. "The plea of *autrefoits acquit*, or a former acquittal," he wrote, "is grounded on this universal maxim of the common law of England, that no man is to be brought into jeopardy of his life more than once for the same offence." . . . Today, every State incorporates some form of the prohibition in its constitution or common law.[81]

## When Double Jeopardy Protection Applies

The Fifth Amendment suggests that double jeopardy occurs when a person's "life or limb" is threatened. This language has been taken to mean that double jeopardy applies in all criminal proceedings. Determining whether a proceeding is criminal, however, is not always easy. Courts will often look to the legislature's intent in writing

---

[80]*Benton* v. *Maryland*, 395 U.S. 784 (1969).
[81]Ibid., pp. 795–796.

the statute that is the basis for prosecution. For example, in *Kansas* v. *Hendricks*,[82] the Supreme Court found that a statute providing for a "sexual predator" proceeding, in addition to a criminal proceeding, did not place the defendant in double jeopardy because it provided for *civil* confinement. The Court stated:

> Because we have determined that the Kansas Act is civil in nature, initiation of its commitment proceedings does not constitute a second prosecution. . . . Moreover, as commitment under the Act is not tantamount to "punishment," Hendricks' involuntary detention does not violate the Double Jeopardy Clause, even though that confinement may follow a prison term.[83]

The courts will also examine the punitiveness of the sanctions involved in determining whether a proceeding is criminal. In *Helvering* v. *Mitchell*,[84] the Supreme Court upheld the constitutionality of a tax proceeding that was used to recover back taxes from a person *after* the person was acquitted on criminal charges. The Court declared that the proceeding was designed as a remedial sanction to reimburse the government. Because it was not considered punitive, double jeopardy did not apply.

## The *Blockburger* Rule

A rather complicated issue in double jeopardy jurisprudence concerns the definition of same offense. In *Blockburger* v. *United States*,[85] the Supreme Court developed a test that states that "[w]here the same act or transaction constitutes a violation of two distinct statutory provisions, the test to be applied to determine whether there are two offenses or only one, is whether each requires proof of an additional fact which the other does not."[86] This test came to be known as the **Blockburger rule**.

**Blockburger rule** An offense is considered the "same offense" for purposes of double jeopardy if two separate statutes that define the offense both contain the same elements.

According to the *Blockburger* rule, an offense is considered the same offense if two separate statutes that define the offense both contain elements A, B, and C. Moreover, if one crime contains elements A, B, and C, and the other has elements A and B, both are considered the same offense because neither statute requires proof of a fact that the other does not. For example, assume that the offense of first-degree murder contains elements A (premeditated), B (deliberate), and C (killing), and that the offense of second-degree murder contains elements B (deliberate) and C (killing). Both offenses are considered the same for double jeopardy purposes because second-degree murder does not require proof of another element that first-degree murder does not. If a person is convicted of first-degree murder, then, according to this example, that person cannot be charged with second-degree murder.

*Separate offenses* can be identified when, for example, one crime contains elements A, B, and C, and the other contains elements A, B, and D. Both crimes require proof of an additional element that the other does not. For example, assume the offense of joyriding contains elements A (unlawful taking), B (of an automobile), and C (the intent to *temporarily* deprive the owner of possession). Assume also that the offense of car theft contains elements A (unlawful taking), B (of an automobile), and

---

[82]*Kansas* v. *Hendricks*, 521 U.S. 346 (1997).
[83]Ibid., pp. 369–370.
[84]*Helvering* v. *Mitchell*, 303 U.S. 391 (1938).
[85]*Blockburger* v. *United States*, 284 U.S. 299 (1932).
[86]Ibid., p. 304.

D (the intent to *permanently* deprive the owner of possession). These are considered separate offenses because each offense requires proof of an element that the other does not. Thus, a person who is found guilty of joyriding can also be charged with the crime of car theft.[87]

## When Double Jeopardy Protection Does Not Apply

There are four main exceptions to the *Blockburger* rule, which means that there are four situations in which double jeopardy protection does not apply.

### Conduct Committed After the First Prosecution.
Double jeopardy does not apply if the second prosecution is based on conduct committed after the first prosecution. This was the decision reached in *Diaz v. United States*.[88] There, the defendant was convicted of assault and battery. When the victim later died, the defendant was charged with homicide. The Court stated, "The death of the injured person was the principal element of the homicide, but was no part of the assault and battery. At the time of the trial for the latter the death had not ensued, and not until it did ensue was the homicide committed. Then, and not before, was it possible to put the accused in jeopardy for that offense."[89]

### Defendant Responsible for the Second Prosecution.
If the defendant is responsible for the second prosecution, double jeopardy does not apply. In *Jeffers v. United States*,[90] the defendant was convicted in two separate trials for essentially the same offense. In the first, he was convicted of conspiring with others to distribute cocaine. In the second, he was convicted of violating drug laws. The state sought joinder on the charges (i.e., sought to combine them together such that the defendant was tried for both in the same trial), but the defendant successfully moved to have the charges tried separately. The Supreme Court sanctioned this approach because the defendant was opposed to trying both offenses in the same trial.

### Court Hearing the First Offense Lacks Jurisdiction.
Double jeopardy does not apply when the court hearing the first offense lacks jurisdiction to try the second offense. This exception came from the Supreme Court's decision in *Fugate v. New Mexico*.[91] There, the Court held that a defendant's conviction on drunk-driving charges in municipal court did not bar prosecution in a higher court for vehicular homicide tied to the same incident. The Court noted that the municipal court did not have jurisdiction to try a homicide case, so double jeopardy protections did not apply.

### Defense Plea Bargains over the Prosecution's Objection.
If the defense plea bargains over the prosecution's objection, double jeopardy protections do not apply. In *Ohio v. Johnson*,[92] the defendant succeeded in convincing the judge to dismiss

---

[87]See, e.g., *Brown v. Ohio*, 432 U.S. 161 (1977).
[88]*Diaz v. United States*, 223 U.S. 442 (1912).
[89]Ibid., p. 449.
[90]*Jeffers v. United States*, 432 U.S. 137 (1977).
[91]*Fugate v. New Mexico*, 471 U.S. 1112 (1985).

certain charges against him, over the prosecution's objection. The defendant was later tried on the dismissed charges, and the Court held that double jeopardy protections did not apply. Had the prosecution acquiesced to the dismissal, the result would have been different. Indeed, it is unlikely the defendant would have been prosecuted on the dismissed charges if the prosecution had agreed with the judge's decision.

There are still other exceptions in which reprosecution for the same offense is permissible. First, if a defendant successfully appeals a criminal conviction or otherwise succeeds in overturning a conviction, he or she may be reprosecuted. In *United States* v. *Tateo*,[93] the Court held:

> It would be a high price indeed for society to pay were every accused granted immunity from punishment because of any defect sufficient to constitute reversible error in the proceedings leading to conviction. From the standpoint of a defendant, it is at least doubtful that appellate courts would be as zealous as they now are in protecting against the effects of improprieties at the trial or pretrial stage if they knew that reversal of a conviction would put the accused irrevocably beyond the reach of further prosecution. In reality, therefore, the practice of retrial serves defendants' rights as well as society's interest. The underlying purpose of permitting retrial is as much furthered by application of the rule to this case as it has been in cases previously decided.[94]

Second, if a case is dismissed by the judge but the defendant is not acquitted, he or she may be reprosecuted. In *United States* v. *Scott*,[95] the Court held, in part, that "where a *defendant* successfully seeks to avoid his trial prior to its conclusion by a motion for a [dismissal], the Double Jeopardy Clause is not offended by a second prosecution. Such a motion by the defendant is deemed to be a deliberate election on his part to forgo his valued right to have his guilt or innocence determined by the first trier of fact."[96]

Finally, reprosecution is permissible if a *mistrial* occurs over the defendant's objections and is a "manifest necessity." That is, reprosecution is permissible following a mistrial "when the defendant's interest in proceeding to verdict is outweighed by the competing and equally legitimate demand for public justice."[97] Also, the defendant may be reprosecuted if the judge declares a mistrial with the defendant's consent or by the defendant's motion, provided that the prosecution does not agree to the defendant's consent or motion in bad faith (e.g., by intending to pursue a subsequent retrial for the purpose of subjecting the defendant to the harassment of multiple trials).[98]

## Double Jeopardy and Sentencing

Double jeopardy protection also extends to sentencing increases. First, the Supreme Court has considered whether double jeopardy is violated with the use of *consecutive punishments* (i.e., back-to-back punishments)—say, when the

---

[92]*Ohio* v. *Johnson*, 467 U.S. 493 (1984).
[93]*United States* v. *Tateo*, 377 U.S. 463 (1964).
[94]Ibid., p. 466.
[95]*United States* v. *Scott*, 437 U.S. 82 (1978).
[96]Ibid., p. 92.
[97]*Illinois* v. *Somerville*, 410 U.S. 458 (1973).
[98]See, e.g., *Lee* v. *United States*, 432 U.S. 23 (1977); *Oregon* v. *Kennedy*, 456 U.S. 667 (1982).

defendant is sentenced to a total of 10 years for convictions on two counts that each carry a 5-year sentence. The Court has held that this determination depends on legislative intent.[99] That is, provided the consecutive punishment is not for two of the same offenses, if the criminal law permits such punishment, double jeopardy does not occur.

Questions about double jeopardy have also been raised when a defendant is resentenced following some important development in the case. Increasing the sentence for the same charge (i.e., as opposed to increasing the sentence for separate charges, as in the case of cumulative punishments) after it has been imposed is permissible (1) when a conviction is reversed by an appeal[100]; (2) after the prosecution has appealed a sentence, provided there is legal authorization to do so (a rare occurrence)[101]; and (3) after discovery of a legal defect in the first sentence.[102]

In a recent—and controversial—case, *Sattazahn* v. *Pennsylvania*,[103] an individual was charged with capital murder, but the jury could not unanimously conclude that the death penalty was warranted. As required by a Pennsylvania statute, the judge then sentenced the offender to life in prison. The defendant was then retried and sentenced to death. He argued that the Fifth Amendment's double jeopardy clause was violated, but the Supreme Court disagreed. The Court argued that the deadlocked jury did not amount to a "death penalty acquittal," so it saw no constitutional problems with retrying the offender.

**YOUR DECISION**

1. Assume that a state law gives the trial judge authority to sentence to death a defendant convicted of a capital crime but also requires the judge to consider the jury's recommendation as to whether the death penalty should be imposed. Assume further that a man has been sentenced to death by the judge in his trial, even though the jury that convicted him recommended life in prison. The man appeals, claiming that the statute is unconstitutional because it does not specify the weight the judge must give to the jury's sentencing recommendation and thus permits the arbitrary imposition of the death penalty. He further claims that the judge should be forced to give "great weight" to the jury's recommendation. How should the appellate court rule?

2. The police found marijuana and growing equipment when they searched a man's house. He was prosecuted criminally, but the federal government also sought civil forfeiture of his house, pursuant to a federal law. The man challenged this action, claiming that the proposed forfeiture of his house would amount to double jeopardy, a violation of the Fifth Amendment. Does civil asset forfeiture in addition to criminal prosecution place a person in double jeopardy?

---

[99]See, e.g., *Albernaz* v. *United States*, 450 U.S. 333 (1981).
[100]*North Carolina* v. *Pierce*, 395 U.S. 711 (1969).
[101]*United States* v. *DiFrancesco*, 449 U.S. 117 (1980).
[102]See, e.g., *In re Bradley*, 318 U.S. 50 (1943).
[103]*Sattazahn* v. *Pennsylvania*, 537 U.S. 101 (2003).

## Summary

- The Eighth Amendment prohibits cruel and unusual punishment.

- The death penalty is permissible for murder, but not for murderers who were 18 years old or younger at the time of their crimes, and not for the mentally retarded. Likewise, the death penalty is not allowed in rape cases.

- In deciding whether a term of imprisonment violates the Eighth Amendment, courts must consider various factors, including (1) the gravity of the offense compared to the sentence, (2) the penalties imposed on other offenders in the same state for the same offense, (3) the penalties imposed in other states for the same offense, and (4) the defendant's recidivism.

- Double jeopardy occurs when, for the same offense, a person is (1) reprosecuted after acquittal; (2) reprosecuted after conviction; or (3) subjected to separate punishments for the same offense.

- Double jeopardy protection applies in all criminal proceedings.

- In *Blockburger* v. *United States*, the Supreme Court developed a test that states that "[w]here the same act or transaction constitutes a violation of two distinct statutory provisions, the test to be applied to determine whether there are two offenses or only one, is whether each requires proof of an additional fact which the other does not."

- Double jeopardy does not apply when (1) the second prosecution is based on conduct committed after the first prosecution, (2) if the defendant is responsible for the second prosecution, (3) when the court hearing the first offense lacks jurisdiction to try the second offense, (4) if the defense plea bargains over the prosecution's objection, and in still other situations.

- Double jeopardy protection also extends to sentencing increases.

# Chapter Review

MODULE **2.1**

## GOVERNMENT'S LAW-MAKING AUTHORITY AND GENERAL LIMITATIONS ON THE CRIMINAL LAW

### Learning Objectives

- Explain how the separation of powers and federalism limit the government's law-making authority.
- Describe the principle of legality.
- Describe the principle of lenity.

### Review Questions

1. How do the separation of powers and federalism place limitations on government's law-making authority? Be specific.
2. Explain the principle of legality.
3. How does legality run counter to common law?
4. What is lenity? How does it place limitations on the criminal law?

### Key Terms

federalism
confederation
dual federalism
principle of legality
principle of lenity

MODULE **2.2**

## CONSTITUTIONAL LIMITATIONS ON THE CRIMINAL LAW, PART 1

### Learning Objectives

- Describe the Fourteenth Amendment's equal protection clause.
- Summarize the prohibition of *ex post facto* laws and bills of attainder.
- Summarize the void for vagueness principle.
- Explain the void for overbreadth doctrine.

### Review Questions

1. What are the six constitutional limitations on the criminal law?
2. Explain how the Fourteenth Amendment's equal protection clause places limits on the criminal law.
3. What is an *ex post facto* law? Provide a specific example.
4. Offer an example of a law that could be considered "void for vagueness."
5. Offer an example of a law that could be considered "void for overbreadth."

*Key Terms*

equal protection clause

strict scrutiny

intermediate scrutiny

rational basis

*ex post facto*

bill of attainder

void for vagueness

libel

defamation

seditious speech

void for overbreadth

MODULE **2.3**    **CONSTITUTIONAL LIMITATIONS ON THE CRIMINAL LAW, PART 2**

*Learning Objectives*

· Describe the protections against cruel and unusual punishment.

· Explain the guarantee against double jeopardy.

*Review Questions*

1. What types of punishment are considered cruel and unusual?

2. Summarize the *Blockburger* rule as it pertains to double jeopardy.

3. Explain the circumstances in which double jeopardy does not apply.

*Key Terms*

guided-discretion laws

double jeopardy

*Blockburger* rule

# Chapter Synthesis Questions

1. Is government's law-making authority sufficiently limited in the United States? Why or why not?

2. Is the "quantity" of criminal law in the United States insufficient, sufficient, or overreaching? Why?

3. Are the constitutional limitations on the criminal law too many or too few? Explain your answer.

4. Does the death penalty constitute cruel and unusual punishment in your view? Why or why not?

5. At what length in years (if any) should a prison sentence be considered cruel and unusual?

6. There are certain circumstances in which double jeopardy does not apply. Is this ideal? Why or why not?

# 3

# THE ELEMENTS OF CRIMINAL LIABILITY

*Learning Objectives*

# 3.1

# INTRODUCTION TO OFFENSE TYPES

### *Learning Objective*

- **Explain the difference between conduct and result crimes.**

## CORE CONCEPTS

**general part of the criminal law** Broad principles that apply to more than one crime.

There are many types of crimes, each with their own definitions. Underlying each of them, however, are a series of basic elements. These basic elements form the foundation of the criminal law. We call these elements the **general part of the criminal law**. They are "general" because they are not unique to any one crime. For example, underlying every crime is a prohibited act or omission.

Much of the material presented in Chapter 2, including the doctrines of legality and lenity, also fits within the general part of the criminal law. Why? Each principle we introduced applies to *all* crimes. The constitutional limitations we discussed apply to all offenses as well. In the next two chapters, we will look at defenses to criminal liability. They also fall into the general part of the criminal law, as the most popular criminal defenses are not limited to any specific criminal act. We will look later on in this book at accomplice liability, attempt, conspiracy, and solicitation. These also fall into the general part of the criminal law because they have "general applicability,"[1] meaning they apply in many different situations. For example, one can attempt to commit burglary, robbery, rape, murder, and so on. There is no requirement that attempt be linked to a specific type of crime.

**special part of the criminal law** The part of law that defines specific crimes.

Contrast this with the **special part of the criminal law**, that part of the law that defines specific crimes. The special part of the criminal law names the exact elements of a crime that must be proven in court. Assume, for example, that a person is charged with knowingly killing a bald eagle. The special part of the criminal law requires a prosecutor to prove beyond a reasonable doubt that the defendant indeed killed a bald eagle—and knowingly.

This chapter is intended to connect the dots between the principles introduced in the last chapter and the content in the remaining chapters. Its purpose is to introduce the basics of criminal liability, the foundational elements of virtually every crime. Two of them, namely *actus reus* and *mens rea*, most likely sound familiar to you, as you probably read about them in an introductory criminal justice or criminology text. Other elements may be less familiar. This chapter will cover all of them.

---

[1]M. D. Dubber, *Criminal Law: Model Penal Code* (New York: Foundation Press, 2002), p. 142.

# Offense Types

Depending on what type of crime the defendant is charged with, all or only a few of the basic elements of criminal liability (*actus reus, mens rea*, concurrence, causation, and resulting harm—defined thoroughly later in this chapter) may need to be in place. There are two main crime types: conduct crimes and result crimes. It is critical to gain a grasp of the differences between each because each requires proof of a different set of elements.

## Conduct Crimes

**conduct crimes** Crimes that are complete when the criminal act and criminal intent concur. There is no requirement for resulting harm.

**Conduct crimes** are offenses for which engaging in a prohibited act constitutes the full offense. There is no requirement that any resulting harm occur, only that someone engaged in an action that was prohibited by law. An example is reckless driving. The law generally prohibits reckless driving out of concern that dangerous driver could cause harm to others, but there is no requirement that harm occur for one to be convicted of reckless driving. A more extreme example is the crime of burglary. By way of preview, burglary is basically the unlawful entry into a dwelling with intent to commit a felony inside. The crime is complete once the unlawful entry occurs. There is no requirement that a felony (such as grand theft) is actually committed.

## Result Crimes

**result crimes** Crimes that require actual harm.

**resulting harm** An essential element of a result crime. For example, the resulting harm in homicide is the killing of a human being. Without the killing, it is not homicide.

**Result crimes** are offenses that are not complete without actual harm. The classic example is murder. A person cannot be convicted of murder without the killing of another. A person's death is the actual harm. Another example is arson, which usually entails the intentional destruction of another's property by burning. Without damage by fire, the crime of arson does not occur. Result crimes thus require that elements besides just criminal conduct are in place. This is known as **resulting harm**.

**YOUR DECISION**

1. The following is a state criminal statute: "Section 1.023(a): It shall be unlawful to trespass on the property of another without consent if the property suffers physical damage. Violators of this provision face up to six months of imprisonment and may be required to pay restitution to the property owner." Does this statute describe a result crime or a conduct crime? Why?
2. The following is another state criminal statute: "Section 4.073(a)(1): In order to be guilty of any crime within the state, the defendant must commit a criminal act. This act must be committed voluntarily and without duress. An involuntary act will generally not create criminal liability." Is this statute an example of the general or special part of criminal law? Explain.

## Summary

- The general part of the criminal law is "general" because it is not unique to any one crime. For example, underlying every crime is a prohibited act or omission.

- The special part of the criminal law is that part of the law which defines specific crimes.

- Conduct crimes are offenses for which engaging in a prohibited act constitutes the full offense.

- Result crimes are offenses that are not complete without actual harm. The classic example is murder.

# THE CORE ELEMENTS OF CRIMINAL LIABILITY, PART 1: *ACTUS REUS*

### *Learning Objective*

- **Explain *actus reus* and what constitutes a criminal act.**

**CORE CONCEPTS**

There are three basic elements to criminal liability: *actus reus*, *mens rea*, and concurrence (see Figure 3.1). This module looks at *actus reus*. Module 3.3 looks at *mens rea* and concurrence. Module 3.4 then considers two other elements of criminal liability that apply in certain contexts: causation and the possibility of a circumstantial element.

## Actus Reus

**actus reus** Latin term meaning "evil act" or criminal act. One of the core requirements of a crime.

***Actus reus***, Latin for an "evil act," is the most important element of criminal liability. There cannot be a crime without some action (or inaction, as we will also see) on the part of the defendant. For example, it is not a crime to fantasize about inflicting harm on someone else. Indeed, it is not even criminal for a person to *intend* to inflict harm on another. Intention must be coupled with an action. A simple example of *actus reus* is a defendant pulling the trigger of a gun and shooting a victim. The pulling of the trigger is a criminal act, or *actus reus*. This, in a nutshell, is the essence of the *actus reus*. But there is much more to it than meets the eye.

**Figure 3.1**
Basic Elements of
Criminal Liability

## Voluntary Act

In general, a person cannot be guilty of a crime unless he or she commits a voluntary act. The issue of voluntariness is most often raised in the context of criminal defenses. If there is a chance the action in question is not voluntary, the defense bears the burden of proving as much. We will look in Chapter 5 at some so-called excuse defenses that raise the issue of voluntariness.

Modern penal codes do not necessarily name this element of criminal liability, but instead treat it as an implicit requirement. For our sake, however, it is important to explore this requirement further. As we do so, it is important to distinguish the "act" from its accompanying "voluntariness."

A criminal act is a physical movement. Such movement may be visible to the eye, such as when an assailant stabs a victim, but it could also be imperceptible. For example, someone could utter a word with minimal mouth movement and this could satisfy the *actus reus* requirement. The crime of solicitation, for example (see Chapter 7), can be completed with little more than words.

An act is considered *voluntary* when it is in some way willed by the actor. The act could be voluntary even if it is a result of habit or is inadvertent. As long as the actor had the option of acting differently, then the act will be considered voluntary. Whether the action is a force of habit or a wholly deliberate act is important when it comes to gradations of offenses, but the *actus reus* requirement is satisfied in either case. Say Larry lights a cigarette, promptly falls asleep, drops the cigarette, catches the house on fire, and manages to wake up and escape before the fire consumes the house and kills his wife. As an alternative, say Larry went into his wife's room while she was asleep, poured gasoline around the bed, lit a cigarette, and set the room ablaze, killing his wife. Clearly his actions in both scenarios were voluntary (he had the option of not lighting the cigarette in the first situation, for example), but it would be unreasonable to treat both acts in the same manner.

In most cases, it is safely assumed that the underlying act was voluntary, but ascertaining voluntariness can be difficult some of the time. Consider multiple personality disorder. In *State* v. *Grimsley*,[2] a woman drove a vehicle under the influence while she was disassociated from her primary personality. She claimed that her alternate personality was responsible for the crime, but the court disagreed, stating,

> There was only one person driving the car and only one person accused of drunken driving. It is immaterial whether she was in one state of consciousness or another, so long as in the personality then controlling her behavior, she was conscious and her actions were a product of her own volition.[3]

See the accompanying Court Decision for more on voluntariness in regards to *actus reus*. In it, we take a look at a classic case, *People* v. *Decina*, decided in 1956 by New York's highest court.

---

**COURT DECISION**

*People of the State of New York* v. *Decina*
138 N.E.2d 799 (N.Y. App. 1956)

**Background:** Defendant Decina was charged with criminal negligence in operating an automobile with knowledge that he was subject to epileptic seizures. The Supreme Court of Erie Country entered a judgment of conviction and defendant appealed. The Supreme Court (New York's intermediate court of appeals) granted a new trial based on the admission of certain evidence against the defendant. Both the defendant

---

[2]*State* v. *Grimsley*, 444 N.E. 2d 1071 (Ohio Ct. App. 1982).
[3]Ibid., p. 267.

and the prosecution appealed. The Court of Appeals (the highest appellate court in New York) found the indictment to be sufficient.

FROESSEL, Judge.

At about 3:30 p. m. on March 14, 1955, a bright, sunny day, defendant was driving, alone in his car, in a northerly direction on Delaware Avenue in the city of Buffalo. The portion of Delaware Avenue here involved is 60 feet wide. At a point south of an overhead viaduct of the Erie Railroad, defendant's car swerved to the left, across the center line in the street, so that it was completely in the south lane, traveling 35 to 40 miles per hour.

It then veered sharply to the right, crossing Delaware Avenue and mounting the easterly curb at a point beneath the viaduct and continued thereafter at a speed estimated to have been about 50 or 60 miles per hour or more. During this latter swerve, a pedestrian testified that he saw defendant's hand above his head; another witness said he saw defendant's left arm bent over the wheel, and his right hand extended towards the right door.

A group of six schoolgirls were walking north on the easterly sidewalk of Delaware Avenue, two in front and four slightly in the rear, when defendant's car struck them from behind. One of the girls escaped injury by jumping against the wall of the viaduct. The bodies of the children struck were propelled northward onto the street and the lawn in front of a coal company, located to the north of the Erie viaduct on Delaware Avenue. Three of the children, 6 to 12 years old, were found dead on arrival by the medical examiner, and a fourth child, 7 years old, died in a hospital two days later as a result of injuries sustained in the accident.

After striking the children, defendant's car continued on the easterly sidewalk, and then swerved back onto Delaware Avenue once more. It continued in a northerly direction, passing under a second viaduct before it again veered to the right and remounted the easterly curb, striking and breaking a metal lamppost. With its horn blowing steadily apparently because defendant was 'stopped over' the steering wheel the car proceeded on the sidewalk until if finally crashed through a 7 1/4-inch brick wall of a grocery store, injuring at least one customer and causing considerable property damage.

When the car came to a halt in the store, with its horn still blowing, several fires had been ignited. Defendant was stooped over in the car and was 'bobbing a little'. To one witness he appeared dazed, to another unconscious, lying back with his hands off the wheel. Various people present shouted to defendant to turn off the ignition of his car, and 'within a matter of seconds the horn stopped blowing and the car did shut off'.

Defendant was pulled out of the car by a number of bystanders and laid down on the sidewalk. To a policeman who came on the scene shortly he appeared 'injured, dazed'; another witness said that 'he looked as though he was knocked out, and his arm seemed to be bleeding'. An injured customer in the store, after receiving first aid, pressed defendant for an explanation of the accident and he told her: 'I blacked out from the bridge'.

When the police arrived, defendant attempted to rise, staggered and appeared dazed and unsteady. When informed that he was under arrest, and would have to accompany the police to the station house, he resisted and, when he tried to get away, was handcuffed. The foregoing evidence was adduced by the People, and is virtually undisputed defendant did not take the stand nor did he produce any witnesses.

\*\*\*On the basis of this medical history, Dr. Wechter made a diagnosis of Jacksonian epilepsy, and was of the opinion that defendant had a seizure at the time of the accident.

\*\*\*We turn first to the subject of defendant's cross appeal, namely, that his demurrer should have been sustained, since the indictment here does not charge a crime. The indictment states essentially that defendant, knowing 'that he was subject to epileptic attacks or other disorder rendering him likely to lose consciousness for a considerable period of time', was culpably negligent 'in that he consciously undertook to and did operate his Buick sedan on a public highway' (emphasis supplied) and 'while so doing' suffered such an attack which caused said automobile 'to travel at a fast and reckless rate of speed, jumping the curb and driving over the sidewalk' causing the death of 4 persons. In our opinion, this clearly states a violation of section 1053-a of the Penal Law. The statute does not require that a defendant must deliberately intend to kill a human being, for that would be murder. Nor does the statute require that he knowingly and consciously follow the precise path that leads to death and destruction. It is sufficient, we have said, when his conduct manifests a 'disregard of the consequences which may ensue from the act, and indifference to the rights of others. No clearer definition, applicable to the hundreds of varying circumstances that may arise, can be given. Under a given state of facts, whether negligence is culpable is a question of judgment.'

Assuming the truth of the indictment, as we must on a demurrer, this defendant knew he was subject to epileptic attacks and seizures that might strike at any time. He also knew that a moving motor vehicle uncontrolled on public highway is a highly dangerous instrumentality capable of unrestrained destruction. With this knowledge, and without anyone accompanying him, he deliberately took a chance by making a conscious choice of a course of action, in disregard of the consequences which he knew might follow from his conscious act, and which in this case did ensue. How can we say as a matter of law that this did not amount to culpable negligence within the meaning of section 1053-a?

To hold otherwise would be to say that a man may freely indulge himself in liquor in the same hope that it will not affect his driving, and if it later develops that ensuing intoxication causes dangerous and reckless driving resulting in death, his unconsciousness or involuntariness at that time would relieve him from prosecution under the statute. His awareness of a condition which he knows may produce such consequences as here, and his disregard of the consequences, renders him liable for culpable negligence, as the courts below have properly held. To have a sudden sleeping spell, an unexpected heart or other disabling attack, without any prior knowledge or warning thereof, is an altogether different situation, and there is simply no basis for comparing such cases with the flagrant disregard manifested here.

\*\*\*Accordingly, the order of the Appellate Division should be affirmed.

## Case Analysis

1. Did Decina commit a "voluntary act" that resulted in the car accident?

2. How can Decina be held criminally liable if he was suffering an epileptic seizure at the time of the accident?

3. Is it relevant that Decina knew he was subject to seizures? If so, why?

4. Is Decina's case different from a driver who suffers a heart attack or a stroke while driving? If so, why?

---

A related issue arises in the context of addiction. In *Robinson* v. *California*,[4] the U.S. Supreme Court was confronted with the question of whether a California statute that made it illegal for a person to "be addicted to the use of narcotics" was unconstitutional. The Court held that it was, arguing that the law

> is not one which punishes a person for the use of narcotics, for their purchase, sale or possession, or for antisocial or disorderly behavior resulting from their administration. It is not a law which even purports to provide or require medical treatment. Rather, we deal with a statute which makes the "status" of narcotic addiction a criminal offense, for which the offender may be prosecuted "at any time before he reforms" . . . . It is unlikely that any State at this moment in history would attempt to make it a criminal offense for a person to be mentally ill, or a leper, or to be afflicted with a venereal disease. A State might determine that the general health and welfare require that the victims of these and other human afflictions be dealt with by compulsory treatment, involving quarantine, confinement, or sequestration. But, in the light of contemporary human knowledge, a law which made a criminal offense of such a disease would doubtless be universally thought to be an infliction of cruel and unusual punishment.[5]

A similar Supreme Court case dealt with Leroy Powell, a man who was charged with violating a Texas statute that prohibited "get[ting] drunk or be[ing] found in a state of intoxication."[6] Interestingly, the Court affirmed Powell's conviction, claiming that he "was convicted, not for being a chronic alcoholic, but for being in public while drunk on a particular occasion."[7]

The differences between *Robinson* and *Powell* are subtle but important. In *Powell*, the Court was concerned with *where* the conduct took place. Powell was held liable not just because he was drunk, but because he was *found* drunk in public. In *Robinson*, however, the crime in question was limited strictly to a person's status. Status alone is insufficient to satisfy *actus reus*. In other words, any law that punishes a person merely on the chance that he or she may act is unconstitutional.

## Omission

**omission** The failure to act. In certain circumstances, an omission can satisfy the *actus reus* element of crime.

An **omission** is a failure to act. Certain omissions can satisfy the *actus reus* element of criminal liability, as well. The general rule is that, with a few exceptions, no person

---

[4]*Robinson* v. *California*, 370 U.S. 660 (1962).
[5]Ibid., p. 666.
[6]*Powell* v. *Texas*, 392 U.S. 514 (1968).
[7]Ibid., p. 532.

has a duty to act in a manner that prevents injury or loss of life to another. So, in *People* v. *Beardsley*,[8] when a man failed to come to the aid of his mistress who took a lethal dose of poison and died, he was not liable for her death. Some experts disagree with this rule, however. Graham Hughes argued, "In a civilized society, a man who finds himself with a helplessly ill person who has no other source of aid should be under a duty to summon help, whether the person is his wife, his mistress, a prostitute or a Chief Justice."[9] Others, however, feel it would be unrealistic to expect that everyone who is in a position to help should do so. In the famous Kitty Genovese case, some 38 people heard her get attacked and killed, yet none intervened—during the whole 30 minutes she cried out for help. This is surprising to say the least, but should all 38 people have been required to help? Probably not.

When can an omission satisfy the *actus reus* requirement? There are seven specific situations.

1. *Relationship.* When there is a status relationship between two parties, an omission can lead to criminal liability. For example, a woman who knew her children's father was abusing them and failed to act was guilty of child abuse by her omission.[10] Likewise, a parent who failed to seek treatment for a child, which then led to the child's death, was convicted of a homicide offense.[11]

2. *Statute.* Many states have laws that require certain officials to report actions such as child abuse. Failure to report can lead to criminal liability by omission. Some states have gone so far as to enact so-called **Bad Samaritan laws**, which make it criminal for someone to fail to come to the aid of another who is in peril.[12] See the text of Vermont's Bad Samaritan law in Figure 3.2. Bad Samaritan laws are distinctive from Good Samaritan laws, the latter of which are intended to protect people who come to the aid of those in need. For example, if Scott observes David collapse and stop breathing, attempts to perform CPR, and ends up doing more harm than good, killing David, then a Good Samaritan law would protect Scott from perhaps being sued by David's surviving family members.

3. *Contract.* If a contract sets up a special relationship between two parties and that contract is breached, criminal liability is possible. For example, if someone who is contractually obligated to care for a physically disabled person but fails to do so, a crime may occur as a result of the inaction.[13]

4. *Voluntary Assumption of Care.* If a person voluntarily assumes care of another person (without a contract), that person may be held liable for failure to act. For example, in *People* v. *Oliver*,[14] a woman took an intoxicated man into her home and allowed him to use the bathroom, knowing his intent was to inject heroin (she even gave him a spoon to help prepare his injection). He emerged from the bathroom, collapsed, and was later dragged outside, where he died. The woman was found guilty of manslaughter.

**Bad Samaritan laws**
Laws that make it a crime for someone to fail to come to the aid of another who is danger.

---

[8]*People* v. *Beardsley*, 113 N.W. 1128 (Mich. 1907).
[9]G. Hughes, "Criminal Omissions," *Yale Law Journal*, Vol. 67 (1958): 590–637, p. 624.
[10]*State* v. *Williquette*, 385 N.W. 2d 145 (Wis. 1986).
[11]*State* v. *Williams*, 484 P.2d 1167 (Wash. Ct. App. 1971).
[12]See, e.g., Vt. Stat. Ann. Tit. 12, Section 519(a) (2007).
[13]*Davis* v. *Commonwealth*, 335 S.E. 2d 375 (Va. 1985).
[14]*People* v. *Oliver*, 210 Cal. App. 3d 138 (Ct. App. 1989).

**Figure 3.2**

Vermont's Bad Samaritan Law (12 V.S.A. § 519)

# § 519. Emergency Medical Care

(a) A person who knows that another is exposed to grave physical harm shall, to the extent that the same can be rendered without danger or peril to himself or without interference with important duties owed to others, give reasonable assistance to the exposed person unless that assistance or care is being provided by others.

(b) A person who provides reasonable assistance in compliance with subsection (a) of this section shall not be liable in civil damages unless his acts constitute gross negligence or unless he will receive or expects to receive remuneration. Nothing contained in this subsection shall alter existing law with respect to tort liability of a practitioner of the healing arts for acts committed in the ordinary course of his practice.

(c) A person who willfully violates subsection (a) of this section shall be fined not more than $100.00.

5. *Creation of Peril.* If George pushes Gary, who cannot swim, into a lake, Gary struggles and cries out for help, and George fails to assist, George can be guilty of a crime. Something similar happened in *Jones* v. *State*.[15] A man raped a woman who escaped and, distraught, jumped into a creek and drowned. The man was convicted of murder.

6. *Duty to Control Conduct of Another.* Assume Larry, a business owner, knows that his delivery driver, Rick, is a reckless driver. Rick slams his delivery truck into a small car and kills the driver. Larry, through his omission (i.e., his failure to do anything about Rick's driving), may be held criminally liable.

7. *Landowner Duty.* The owner of, say, a nightclub is required to perform certain functions, such as ensure an adequate number of emergency exits. Failure to do so could lead to criminal liability in the event a fire occurs and one or more patrons die or are injured.

See the accompanying Court Decision for more on omission as a form of *actus reus*. In it, we take a look at *Commonwealth of Pennsylvania* v. *Julia Cardwell*, a case in which a mother was charged with endangering the welfare of her child.

## COURT DECISION

*Commonwealth of Pennsylvania* v. *Julia Cardwell*
515 A.2d 311 (Pa. Super. 1986)

**Background:** Julia Cardwell was convicted in the Court of Common Pleas, Philadelphia County, of endangering the welfare of her child for failing to prevent her husband from sexually abusing her daughter. The Superior Court of Pennsylvania affirmed.

This is an appeal from a denial by the court of common pleas of a writ of certiorari to the municipal court, which had convicted appellant Julia Cardwell of violating 18 Pa.C.S.A. § 4304, endangering the welfare of a child.

---

[15]*Jones* v. *State*, 43 N.E. 2d 1017 (Ind. 1942).

We are called upon to decide whether the evidence supports proof beyond a reasonable doubt of the intent element of this offense when the appellant, the child's mother, took only inconsistent and ineffectual steps to protect her child from another's severe abuse.

During the relevant time period, appellant Julia Cardwell (Julia) lived in a house in Philadelphia in a family unit with her daughter Alicia and her husband Clyde Cardwell (Clyde), Alicia's stepfather. For at least four years, beginning approximately in 1979, Clyde engaged in a pattern of sexual abuse of his stepdaughter Alicia. When Alicia was "about eleven" years old, Clyde began to buy her sexually stimulating clothing. He then began to photograph the child while clothed and in sexually explicit positions. Later, these photographic sessions included taking of photographs of Alicia either totally nude or wearing only stockings and garter belts. It was Clyde's habit to write sexually suggestive notes to Alicia on an almost daily basis.

Alicia testified that Clyde had vaginal intercourse with her on four occasions and on one occasion had attempted anal intercourse. Alicia became pregnant by Clyde twice in 1983 and had abortions both times, the second abortion occurring on October 18, 1983. There was also testimony that Clyde had sex with the child with the use of a vibrator. The last instance of intercourse occurred in 1984.

Alicia testified that she did not tell anyone about any of the sexual abuse until she told her mother after the second abortion. On cross-examination, Alicia admitted that at first she "played a sort of guessing game with [her mother]" and that it was not until some time in November, 1983, that Julia clearly understood that Clyde had been abusing Alicia.

Julia wrote two lengthy letters to Clyde in January and February of 1984, indicating her full knowledge of this abhorrent situation and warning him vaguely that she would not tolerate it. We note that Alicia testified that she and Julia were afraid of Clyde, that Clyde beat up Julia on one occasion, that he threw and broke things in the house, that he had punched a number of holes in the walls of the house, and that he carried a .357 magnum pistol, which he kept on the mantelpiece. In February of 1984 Julia moved some of her and Alicia's clothes to her mother's (Alicia's grandmother's) house. However, both Julia and Alicia remained at home with Clyde. In March 1984 Julia applied for a transfer of Alicia from her school to a school closer to Julia's mother's house. In April 1984, however, Julia's mother's house was demolished by fire, causing the death of Julia's father. The record reveals Julia took no further steps to relieve the situation until Alicia ran away from home on September 14, 1984.

On October 2, 1984, a criminal complaint was sworn against Julia Cardwell, listing Alicia as complainant and charging Julia with violating 18 Pa.C.S.A. § 4304, stating that she: "as parent supervising [Alicia]. . . knowingly endangered the welfare of said child by violating a duty of care, protection, and/or support, to wit: defendant was aware that Clyde Cardwell was having sex with complainant and taking polaroid pictures of complainant in various sexually explicit positions without reporting this to authorities. . . ."

Julia was tried and convicted in a bench trial in Municipal Court of Philadelphia. She was sentenced to one-year probation and appealed.

\*\*\*Appellant's challenge to the sufficiency of the evidence is that the evidence adduced at trial was insufficient to prove beyond a reasonable doubt the intent element of the offense of endangering the welfare of a child. This challenge is in two parts. The first part concerns the intent required by the statute defining the offense and is a matter of statutory interpretation.

18 Pa.C.S.A. § 4304, Endangering the Welfare of Children, provides:

> A parent, guardian, or other person supervising the welfare of a child under 18 years of age commits a misdemeanor of the second degree if he knowingly endangers the welfare of the child by violating a duty of care, protection or support.

Appellant alleges that this statute requires a "knowing act" of endangering the welfare of a child, and appellant implies that an omission to act cannot satisfy the statute. We do not agree. The crime of endangering the welfare of a child is a specific intent offense. The intent element required by § 4303 is a knowing violation of a duty of care. We must, therefore, interpret when an accused knowingly violates his or her duty of care.

\*\*\*This court previously discussed the issue of a parent's duty of care in the context of a challenge to the sufficiency of evidence on a conviction for involuntary manslaughter. In *Commonwealth v. Howard,* 265 Pa.Super. 535 (1979), we upheld the conviction of a mother who failed to protect her child from the physical abuse of the mother's boyfriend, who lived with them. We said in *Howard:*

> an omission to act may create criminal culpability under our Crimes Code even though the law defining the offense, as here, requires an "act," where "a duty to perform the omitted act is otherwise imposed by law." 18 Pa.C.S.A. § 301(b)(2). Here, appellant and the victim stood in the relation of parent and child. A parent had the legal duty to protect her child, and the discharge of this duty requires affirmative performance.

*Id.* at 538. In a footnote, the court added: "When a parent sees her helpless child being beaten and abused over a period of time, she is not permitted to sit back and wait until the child is in obvious need of medical attention before acting—the duty is to prevent the harm." *Id.* at 538 n. 3.

Although the charge in *Howard* was involuntary manslaughter, which requires "reckless or grossly negligent" behavior, rather than the instant charge, which requires "knowing" violation of a duty of care, we find the case instructive. Where there is a duty of care and where there is sufficient evidence that the parent knows that action is required to fulfill his or her parental duty, then a failure to act may be a knowing failure in the parent's duty of care.

\*\*\*Appellant's brief suggests that we must negate intent because Julia did "something." Therefore, the question is raised whether acts which are so feeble as to be ineffectual can negate intent. We find they cannot, and reject that argument. The affirmative performance required by § 4304 cannot be met simply by showing any step at all toward preventing harm, however incomplete or ineffectual. An act which will negate intent is not necessarily one which will provide a successful outcome. However, the person charged with the duty of care is required to take steps that are reasonably calculated to achieve success. Otherwise, the meaning of "duty of care" is eviscerated.

We conclude that a parent's duty to protect his or her child requires affirmative performance to prevent harm and that failure to act may mean that the parent "knowingly endangers the welfare of the child." 18 Pa.C.S.A. § 4304.

We hold that evidence is sufficient to prove the intent element of the offense of endangering the welfare of a child, 18 Pa.C.S.A. § 4304, when the accused is aware of his or her duty to protect the child; is aware that the child is in circumstances that threaten the child's physical or psychological welfare; and has either failed to act or has taken actions so lame or meager that such actions cannot reasonably be expected to be effective to protect the child's physical or psychological welfare.

***Order affirmed.

WIEAND, J., Concurring.
Although I join the majority's decision to affirm, it may not be amiss to suggest that the holding of the majority's decision must be confined to a great extent to its own facts. The facts in this case are disturbing. They suggest that Julia Cardwell knew that her minor daughter had twice been impregnated by her stepfather, Julia's husband, and that the child had been sexually abused by her stepfather repeatedly over a period of at least four years. Nevertheless, Julia failed to take any significant steps to protect her child from continued abuse. Although Julia's real choices in view of her not unreasonable fear of her husband were limited and difficult—she could report her husband to the authorities, she could take her daughter and leave the marital home, or she could send her daughter away—she unquestionably endangered her daughter's welfare by doing nothing to prevent the child's continued abuse at the hands of the child's stepfather.

It does not follow from the holding in this case that a parent will be made a criminal merely because he or she has been unsuccessful in preventing the abuse of a child by the parent's spouse. The criminal law should not be allowed to reach out in response to public outcry against child abuse and criminalize a parent who in good faith has attempted but has failed to confront successfully the terrible dilemma of being required to live in a family relationship with both an abused child and the abuser.

## Case Analysis

1. What crime was Julia Cardwell charged with?
2. Did the defendant ever physically abuse her daughter? If not, how can she be charged with a crime?
3. What is the main argument in Judge Wieand's concurrence?

## Model Penal Code

The Model Penal Code limits criminal liability to conduct that "includes a voluntary act or the omission to perform an act of which he is physically capable."[16] Note that this definition contains the all-important term *includes*. This means that so long as there is at least one voluntary act in a chain of acts, *actus reus* is in place. For example, a person who shotguns six beers, immediately gets in a car, and after a short distance, runs a red light and kills a pedestrian, commits at least one voluntary act (getting in the car and driving). The killing may well be involuntary if the driver does not intend to hit the pedestrian.

The Model Penal Code goes on to define an *act* as a "bodily movement whether voluntary or involuntary."[17] Actions considered involuntary under the Model Penal Code include reflexes; convulsions; conduct committed during sleep, hypnosis, or while the actor is unconscious; and "a bodily movement that otherwise is not the product of the effort or determination of the actor, either conscious or unconscious."[18] And as we indicated earlier, involuntary actions (in the absence of any voluntary ones) cannot support a criminal conviction.

In closing, we should point out that the Model Penal Code—like many penal codes—also treats "possession" as an act. This is important because possession is a passive condition, not the same as, say, taking a step. In general, it is necessary that possession be "knowing," meaning that the person charged with possession is aware that what he or she possesses is contraband. Examples of such items include illegal drugs, burglary tools, fireworks at certain times of the year and in certain places, some obscene materials, and illegal weapons.

**YOUR DECISION**

1. Jack is sitting in a crowded movie theater. Halfway through the movie, he jumps up and shouts, "Fire! We all have to get out of here! There's a fire!" In the pandemonium that ensues, several people are injured. It turns out there was no fire, however, and that Jack suffered from what is known as an "uncinate fit," a brief seizure in a part of the brain that can cause abnormal smell sensations. Is Jack guilty of a crime?
2. Joseph is a college junior rushing across campus to take his physics final exam. On his way to the classroom, Joseph passes another student passed out in the library parking lot. The student is unconscious and surrounded by a pool of blood. Joseph fears he will miss his final exam and fail the course if he stops to help, so he walks right by without intervening. The student later dies as a result of his injuries and doctors believe he would have survived if Joseph called for help. Can Joseph be charged with a crime? Why or why not?

## Summary

- *Actus reus* is Latin for "evil act." There cannot be a crime without a criminal act.

---

[16]Model Penal Code Section 2.01(1).
[17]Ibid., Section 1.13(2).
[18]Ibid., Section 2.01(2)(d).

- In general, a person cannot be guilty of a crime unless that person commits a voluntary act.

- An omission is a failure to act. Certain omissions can satisfy the *actus reus* element of criminal liability.

- An omission can satisfy *actus reus* when a special relationship is established

- An omission can also lead to criminal liability in the case of statutory relationships, in contract situations, following a voluntary assumption of care, if an omission leads to the creation of peril, when there is a duty to control the conduct of another, and when a landowner duty exists.

## MODULE 3.3 THE CORE ELEMENTS OF CRIMINAL LIABILITY, PART 2: *MENS REA* AND CONCURRENCE

### Learning Objectives

- **Explain *mens rea* and the different types of intent.**
- **Distinguish between *mens rea* and motive.**
- **Identify strict liability offenses.**
- **Summarize concurrence.**

## CORE CONCEPTS

**mens rea** Latin term meaning "guilty mind." The mental state or criminal intent of the defendant.

## *Mens Rea*

**Mens rea**, Latin for "guilty mind," is the second critical component of criminal liability. With few exceptions, a person cannot be held criminally liability unless there was some degree of intention on that person's part to commit the crime. Even the defendant's simple "knowledge" that what he or she did was morally wrong can suffice—some of the time—to meet this requirement. *Mens rea*, like *actus reus*, is exceedingly complex, as there are many levels of intent. Indeed, one expert noted that "there is no term fraught with greater ambiguity than that venerable Latin phrase that haunts the Anglo-American criminal law: *mens rea*."[19]

At one point in history, *mens rea* was irrelevant. Under early English law, a person could be held criminally responsible regardless of his or her intent. Throughout the thirteenth century and onward to present, however, *mens rea* has become a deeply entrenched component of criminal liability. The Supreme Court once remarked that "[t]he contention that an injury can amount to a crime only when inflicted by [*mens rea*] is no provincial or transient notion. It is . . . universal and persistent in mature systems of law. . . ."[20] In other words, *mens rea* is a bedrock principle of criminal law.

---

[19]G. P. Fletcher, *Rethinking Criminal Law* (New York: Oxford, 2000), p. 398.
[20]*Morissette* v. *United States*, 342 U.S. 246 (1952), p. 250.

## Traditional and Statutory *Mens Rea*

It is useful to begin with a distinction between traditional *mens rea* and *statutory mens rea*.[21] Traditional *mens rea* is concerned with culpability, or an offender's level of blameworthiness for a crime.[22] Under this view, the offender is considered morally bankrupt, perhaps even a sinner. Terms like "wicked," "evil," and "vicious" were used throughout history to describe the *mens rea* of the crime. In contrast, statutory *mens rea* is the level of intent required by a specific statute, possibly independent of any notion of morality. Today, the traditional meaning of *mens rea* has been somewhat diluted and mostly replaced with legalistic rather than moral underpinnings. Unfortunately, statutes vary widely in the terms they include to capture the *mens rea* element of criminal liability. The Model Penal Code's drafters found 76 distinct terms for *mens rea* in federal statutes alone.[23]

The distinction between traditional and statutory *mens rea* is important, as it can bear on whether someone will be held criminally liable. What if, in order to get a conviction for drug possession, the prosecutor must show that the defendant "intentionally" carried an illegal substance on his or her person? And what if the defendant did not know the substance was illegal, only that he was carrying it? Under a statutory *mens rea* requirement, the defendant's knowledge about the substance being illegal would be irrelevant. Under a *traditional mens rea* requirement, it would be important to look at the defendant's awareness that he was doing something wrong. If he had no idea he was breaking the law, then can we say he was morally blameworthy? Was he "wicked" or "evil," even though he didn't know he was doing something wrong?

## Common *Mens Rea* Terminology

Although *mens rea* defies a simple explanation, there are several terms that have appeared throughout the years in criminal codes, each of which captures its essence to some extent. The following subsections look at six of them.

**Intent.** Intent is perhaps the most straightforward conception of *mens rea*. A person who *intends* to commit a crime should be the one liable for it. When the consequences of a person's actions are desired, this is known as **direct intent**. But there are complications. What if the person intended to engage in criminal conduct but did not intend to cause harm? Say Fred pulled a gun on John, shot him, and John died. We can easily say Fred intended to pull the trigger, but did he intend for John to die? The answer is not completely clear. Maybe Fred thought the gun was empty. Maybe he knew the gun was loaded, but didn't think he would hit Fred. Maybe he just wanted to wound Fred. Maybe he meant to shoot someone else. And so on. To the extent Fred made a mistake, the law will treat his actions differently (see the Mistake section toward the end of this chapter). The other twists in this scenario present complications. For example, if Fred meant to shoot someone else, then we have a

**direct intent** Intent in which the consequences of a person's actions are desired.

---

[21] R. G. Singer and J. Q. LaFond, *Criminal Law: Examples and Explanations*, 4th ed. (New York: Wolters Kluwer, 2007), p. 53.
[22] J. Dressler, *Understanding Criminal Law*, 5th ed. (Newark, NJ: Lexis-Nexis, 2009), p. 118.
[23] Model Penal Code Section 2.02, commentary, p. 230, n. 3 (1980).

**transferred intent** The defendant's intent to harm one person is transferred to the actual victim of the crime.

**oblique intent** Intent in which the consequences of a person's actions are not desired, but should have reasonably been foreseen.

**general intent** The intent to commit the *actus reus* or criminal act of the crime only.

**specific intent** The intent to commit an act to achieve a specific criminal result.

case of **transferred intent**. More than likely, however, the "intent follows the bullet,"[24] meaning that the requisite *mens rea* was in place for Fred's conviction.

If Fred only wanted to wound John, then we have an example of **oblique intent**. This means that while Fred did not *intend* for John to die, he had to know the outcome was almost certain to occur. Consider *Regina* v. *Cunningham*.[25] In that case, Cunningham broke into a house and stole the gas meter out of the basement, causing gas to escape. A person inhaled the gas and nearly died. Cunningham pled guilty to a burglary charge and was convicted at trial of attempted murder. An appellate court reversed his murder conviction because Cunningham lacked the required *mens rea*. Cunningham did not know the gas escaped and thus did not *intend* to kill anyone. As a general rule, intent exists if someone (1) desires to commit harm and (2) knows that the harm is almost certain to occur because of his actions.[26]

Since we are on the subject of intent, it is important to point out the difference between **general intent** crimes and **specific intent** crimes. General intent crimes are those offenses that contain no specific *mens rea* component. Breaking and entering is a general intent offense. However, breaking and entering *with intent to steal* is a specific intent offense. If the statute contains language along the lines "with intent to . . . ," the offense is of the specific intent variety. But just because such a phrase is absent doesn't always yield a general intent offense. And to make matters more complicated, the same conduct can often be prosecuted under both a specific and general intent statute. Aggravated assault (defined more fully in Chapter 9) is a general intent offense, but assault with intent to kill is a specific offense. If the criminal code defines each separately, then the prosecutor decides which statute to invoke.

### Knowledge.

To *knowingly* commit a crime is not the same as *intentionally* committing one. In some cases, rather than *intending* to commit the harm, the defendant may only be required to *know* that the result is virtually certain. Some statutes even go so far as to add "knowing" or "knowingly" to the statute. For example, it is a federal offense to knowingly import any controlled substance into the United States.[27] The addition of "knowingly" thus satisfies the *mens rea* requirement.

What if someone doesn't *know* a crime is being committed, but he or she acts with "deliberate ignorance" or "willful blindness?"[28] In such situations, it is safe to say the defendant acts with knowledge. If the defendant is aware of a high probability that criminal activity is taking place and/or fails to make further inquiries as to whether criminal activity is taking place, then the defendant can be held liable. For example, if Lola agreed to drive Nancy's car from Mexico to the United States and was suspicious that drugs were hidden within it *and* failed to confirm whether her suspicions were correct, then she would most likely satisfy the *mens rea* component of the underlying offense and be found guilty.[29]

---

[24]Singer and LaFond, *Criminal Law: Examples and Explanations*, p. 57.
[25]*Regina* v. *Cunningham*, 41 Crim. App. 155 (Ct. Crim. App. 1957).
[26]*Thornton* v. *State*, 919 A.2d 678 (Md. 2007), p. 691.
[27]21 U.S.C. Section 952(a) (2008).
[28]See, e.g., *United States* v. *Lara-Velasquez*, 919 F.2d 946 (5th Cir. 1990); *United States* v. *Jewell*, 532 F.2d 697 (9th Cir. 1976); *State* v. *LaFreniere*, 481 N.W.2d 412 (Neb. 1992).
[29]See, e.g., *United States* v. *Jewell*, 532 F.2d 697 (9th Cir. 1976).

**Willfulness.**    One who commits a crime *willfully* may also commit it intentionally and knowingly. In other words, *willful* is a word without a clear meaning. *Willful* may even be synonymous with knowledge in some context. Courts have defined it as anything from "an act done with a bad purpose"[30] or with "an evil motive"[31] to "intentional violation of a known legal duty"[32] or "a purpose to disobey the law."[33]

It is possible, however, that to act willfully is simply to act by one's own will, or voluntarily, but this interpretation is too narrow. Why? If someone acts voluntarily, it does not mean that person intends for some measure of harm to occur. For reasons like this, it is rare that *willful* or *willfully* appear in criminal statutes.

**negligence** A type of *mens rea* or criminal intent in which the defendant unconsciously creates a risk of harm and does not act like a reasonable person under the circumstances.

**Negligence.**    **Negligence** is a common term in criminal law. Basically, it means that person has not foreseen any possibility that a harm would result. Negligence is concerned with taking careless risks. This means negligence is a far cry from intent. Why? Instead of acting in a morally blameworthy state of mind, the actor instead *fails* to live up to some societal expectation.

For a person to be held criminally liable for negligent behavior, it may be necessary to show that the negligence was " wanton,"[34] very serious, or not how a "reasonable person" would have acted. Another court defined negligence as that behavior

> which is denominated as gross, and which constitutes such a departure from what would be the conduct of an ordinarily careful and prudent man . . . . as to furnish evidence of that indifference to consequences which in some offenses takes the place of criminal intent.[35]

Otherwise criminal negligence looks a lot like tort negligence, a different creature altogether. Under tort law, a person who breaches a duty of care to another acts negligently. But just because someone breaches a duty of care (e.g., a lifeguard fails to notice a person drowning) does not mean that person should be criminally convicted for it. Thus, *criminal* negligence is usually something more than ordinary tort negligence.[36]

More often than not, criminal negligence comes up in the homicide context, when someone dies because of another's careless—though not necessarily intentional—behavior. In Chapter 8, for example, we will distinguish murder from different forms of manslaughter, the latter of which are sometimes considered negligence. But negligence is not a culpability standard limited only to homicide.

**Recklessness** A type of *mens rea* or criminal intent in which the defendant consciously creates a risk and chooses to act in disregard of that risk.

**Recklessness.**    **Recklessness** takes negligence to the next level. It has been defined as "a conscious decision to ignore risk, of which the defendant is aware."[37] Put differently, an offender acts recklessly if he or she knows a harmful result is likely, yet proceeds anyway. Consider a dangerous driving example: If George drives

---

[30]*Townsend* v. *United States*, 95 F.2d 352 (D.C. Cir. 1938), p. 358.
[31]*United States* v. *Murdock*, 290 U.S. 389 (1933), p. 395.
[32]*Cheek* v. *United States*, 498 U.S. 192 (1991), p. 200.
[33]*Ratzlaf* v. *United States*, 510 U.S. 135 (1994), p. 141.
[34]*State* v. *Weiner*, 194 A.2d 467 (1964).
[35]*Fitzgerald* v. *State*, 20 So. 966 (1896).
[36]For an exception, see *United States* v. *Garrett*, 984 F.2d 1402 (5th Cir. 1993).
[37]Singer and LaFond, *Criminal Law: Examples and Explanations*, p. 60.

his Corvette through a residential neighborhood at 90 miles per hour, he is certainly acting dangerously, maybe even negligently. He is only acting *recklessly*, however, if he acknowledges the risks he is posing to others *and* shrugs them off.

*Williams* v. *State* helps us gain a better sense of recklessness.[38] In that case, a woman left her two children with her boyfriend at his residence. Because the utilities were not working, a candle was lit in the children's room as they were put to sleep. At 1:00 A.M., the boyfriend woke to loud screams and saw that the room in which the children were to be sleeping was on fire. The children perished before they could be saved. The woman was convicted of injury to a child, but the Texas Court of Criminal Appeals reversed her conviction, concluding eloquently that

> there is legally insufficient evidence that appellant consciously disregarded a substantial or unjustifiable risk that her children would suffer serious bodily injury in a house fire if she took them from a house with utilities to one without utilities. Viewed objectively, this act [of] . . . leaving the girls in a room with a lit candle . . . does not involve a "substantial and unjustifiable" risk of serious bodily injury or death. There is nothing inherently dangerous about staying or sleeping in a structure that does not have utilities. Staying in a structure without utilities does not increase the likelihood of dying in a fire. . . . If taking children to spend the night in a structure without utilities is conduct that involves an extreme risk of danger for which one may be subject to criminal prosecution for injury to a child should harm befall that child, the backwoods campers of the world are in serious jeopardy. Any adult who lights a campfire that emits a spark that lands on a child's pajamas and severely burns the child can be prosecuted as a felon. Scoutmasters beware.[39]

**malice** The intent to commit a wrongful act without a legitimate cause or excuse.

**Malice.**     **Malice** is the intent to commit a wrongful act without a legitimate cause or excuse. In *Cockrell* v. *State*, a classic Texas case, malice was defined as "a condition of the mind which shows a heart regardless of social duty and fatally bent on mischief, the existence of which is inferred from the acts committed or words spoken."[40] The defendant, who had been drinking heavily, swerved off the road as he was driving and hit and killed two children who were walking on the shoulder. He was convicted of murder. In upholding his conviction, the Texas Court of Criminal Appeals noted that

> it seems to us that a person who had been proven to have taken five bottles of beer in about one hour just before the tragedy, who was admittedly not sober when he began drinking this beer, who drove out of town past city streets at sixty miles per hour, who swerved completely across a ninety foot highway to his left and crushed out the life of two innocent little boys, and then drove on away; who came back to find out what his acts had resulted in; who then spoke not a word but returned home by a circuitous route, releasing the wheel to another on the way, "turned the car over to his stepmother and went to bed,"—evidences a depraved nature, and such acts evidence wantonness and such a disregard for the rights of others, such a recklessness of action that the jury had the right there from to impute to his acts malice, and to punish him accordingly.[41]

---

[38]*Williams* v. *State*, 235 S.W.3d 742 (Tex. Crim. App. 2007).
[39]Ibid., pp. 757–758.
[40]*Cockrell* v. *State*, 135 Tex. Crim. 218 (1938), p. 224.
[41]Ibid., p. 226.

## The Role of Motive

**motive** The inducement or reason a defendant chooses to commit a crime.

**Motive** is sometimes likened to *mens rea*. Both are distinct, however. Think of motive as preceding *mens rea*. As such, it has been defined as "an idea, belief or emotion that impels or incites one to act in accordance with his state of mind or emotion."[42] Motive has also been defined as the "circumstance tending to establish the requisite *mens rea* for a criminal act and is the inducement which impels or leads the mind to indulge in a criminal act."[43] Notice how both these definitions put motive before *mens rea*. Importantly, motive is never a required element of any crime.

Motive is important in criminal law for three reasons. First, specific intent offenses (discussed in the earlier Intent section) often require proof of a specific motive. For example, in *Harrison v. Commonwealth*, a man was convicted of "willfully and *maliciously*" striking and wounding another man with a deadly weapon.[44] Motive is also important in the context of criminal defenses. Assume a defendant argues that she killed the victim out of self-defense. Self-defense is a motive that could bear heavily on whether she is convicted. She intended to kill the victim (the *mens rea*), but her motive was understandable. Finally, motive is important at the sentencing phase of the criminal process. Depending on sentencing practices in a particular jurisdiction, the judge may add or take time off a sentence based on motive. Hate crimes, for example, attach stiffer penalties for crimes committed with a particular motive.[45]

## Proving *Mens Rea*

It is one thing for a person to have the *mens rea* to support a criminal conviction. It is quite another for a prosecutor to prove it in court. The problem is that it is practically impossible to prove what a person was thinking at the time of the crime. All the prosecutor can do is present enough evidence for the jury to *infer* that the defendant acted with the required *mens rea*. This, along with *actus reus* and other elements, must be proven beyond a reasonable doubt. If jurors cannot infer *mens rea* from the defendant's actions, if they have a reasonable doubt that the defendant intended for the crime to occur, then they must acquit (or find the defendant guilty of a lesser offense if they are permitted to do so).

An example should help clarify. Assume Jack is a former military sniper and winner of numerous shooting contests. Assume further that he shot his wife and is now the defendant in a murder trial. Finally, assume he claims he did not know the gun was loaded. What is a juror to infer from this? At the least, Jack is an expert in handling guns, so his claim that the gun was unloaded may not hold much water. How would an expert shooter not know his gun was loaded? On the other hand, his argument may be convincing if there is plenty of other evidence to support his credibility. Either way, note that there is nothing the prosecutor—or anyone else—can do to give people a clear window into Jack's mental state at the time of the crime.

---

[42]*People v. Gibson*, 128 Cal. Rptr. 302 (1976), p. 308.
[43]*State v. Segotta*, 100 N.M. 18 (1983), pp. 25–26.
[44]*Harrison v. Commonwealth*, 279 Ky. 510 (1939), p. 510.
[45]See, e.g., *Wisconsin v. Mitchell*, 508 U.S. 479 (1993).

## Model Penal Code Definitions

While there is a bewildering array of *mens rea* requirements in state statutes, the Model Penal Code keeps it simple. It names four mental states, from most to least culpable: purpose, knowledge, recklessness, and negligence (also see Figure 3.3).

1. *Purpose.* A person acts purposely when "it is his conscious object to engage in conduct" or cause a particular result.[46] Purpose, according to the Model Penal Code, is the most blameworthy state of mind.

2. *Knowledge.* A person acts knowingly if he is (a) "aware" his conduct is criminal or (b) "aware that it is practically certain that his conduct will cause" a harmful result.[47] A person who acts knowingly is less culpable than one who acts with purpose.

3. *Recklessness.* The Model Penal Code defines recklessness as follows: "A person acts recklessly with respect to a material element of an offense when he consciously disregards a substantial and unjustifiable risk that the material element exists or will result from his conduct. The risk much be of such a nature and degree."[48] Here a "material element" is one of the core parts of an underlying crime. Consider murder, the intentional killing of another human being. There are two material elements: (a) intentional killing and (b) of another human being.

4. *Negligence.* The Model Penal Code defines *negligence*, the least culpable state, in this way: "A person acts negligently with respect to a material element of an offense when he should be aware of a substantial and unjustifiable risk that the material element exists or will result from his conduct. The risk must be of such a nature and degree that the actor's failure to perceive it, considering the nature and purpose of his conduct and the circumstances known to him, involves a gross deviation from the standard of care that a reasonable person would observe in the actor's situation."[49] Note that recklessness requires that the offender "consciously disregard" a risk. This requirement is not in place for negligence. Negligence only requires that the offender be "aware" of the substantial and unjustifiable risk.

## Strict Liability

**strict liability** Crimes that do not require *mens rea* or criminal intent.

In some cases, a person can be held criminally liable in the complete absence of *mens rea*. Such is the case with **strict liability** offenses. An example of a strict liability offense is selling alcoholic beverages to a minor. If someone is charged with this offense, the state need only prove the crime occurred. Intent is irrelevant. Statutory rape (or rape of an underage person) is also a strict liability offense in many jurisdictions. Thus, when Mary Kay Letourneau, a 34-year-old Seattle school teacher, had intercourse with one of her 12-year-old students, she was guilty of statutory rape even though she claimed that the boy was a willing participant.

---

[46]Model Penal Code 1:2, 229 (1985).
[47]Ibid.
[48]Ibid.
[49]Ibid.

**Figure 3.3**
Model Penal Code
Levels of *Mens Rea* and
Examples

Driving while intoxicated
is a strict liability
offense. It does not
matter whether the
person caught intended
to drive while intoxicated.
Moodboard/fotolia.com

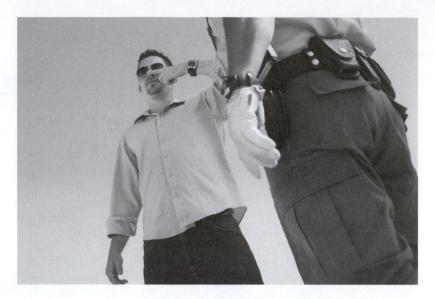

Supporters cite several arguments in favor of strict liability. One is that there is
a concern with promoting public safety and protecting people who cannot protect
themselves. During the early days of the Industrial Revolution, strict liability laws
were enacted in order to protect workers and the general public from unsafe conditions in the workplace and the community. Modern-day strict liability statutes are
rooted in this tradition. Another pro-strict liability argument is that the penalties
associated with strict liability laws are relatively mild. And this leads to another
point—namely, that since the penalties are mild, the criminal stigma that attaches in
minimal. Finally, supporters of strict liability laws feel they are beneficial in some
instances because they make it difficult for crafty criminals to escape punishment by
fooling juries with stories of their lack of intent.

Critics, however, claim that strict liability eliminates one of the fundamental
principles of criminal liability, namely *mens rea*. And in the case of regulatory strict
liability offenses (e.g., if a restaurant owner fails to conform to health standards),
there is evidence that laws are not adequately enforced and, indeed, that those who
the laws are intended to target routinely receive opportunities to correct their ways
in advance of enforcement.[50]

See the accompanying Court Decision for more on strict liability. In it, we take a
look at the case of *State* v. *Harrison* regarding the crime of driving while intoxicated.

## COURT DECISION

*State of New Mexico* v. *Thomas Harrison*
846 P.2d 1082 (N.M. App. 1993)

**Background:** Defendant Harrison was convicted for driving while intoxicated in the
District Court of Bernalillo County. The Court of Appeals affirmed the conviction.

[50]G. Richardson, "Strict Liability for Regulatory Crime: The Empirical Record," *Criminal Law Review*
(1987), p. 295.

## OPINION

### BLACK, Judge

Defendant appeals his conviction for driving while intoxicated (DWI). The issues on appeal are whether Defendant's conviction for DWI was supported by substantial evidence and what type of criminal intent must be proved in order to convict a person for DWI. Specifically, this appeal presents the Court with the issue of whether a person who is discovered unconscious or asleep at the wheel of an automobile, whose engine is on and tires are blocked, can be convicted of DWI. We hold that under those circumstances, there is sufficient evidence to support a conviction for DWI. We further hold that the criminal offense of DWI, NMSA 1978, Section 66-8-102(A), (C), is a strict liability crime. Therefore, we affirm Defendant's conviction.

### FACTS

Defendant and a friend, Jude Mari (Mari), were at a mutual friend's home. Upon preparing to leave the residence, Mari noticed that Defendant was intoxicated and offered to drive for him. They got into Defendant's car. Mari drove and Defendant was a passenger. Mari drove the vehicle for a short distance when the car stalled and would not restart. Mari testified that he steered the vehicle as close as he could to the curb and parked it. Mari further testified that he then took the keys out of the ignition, placed them under the seat, and placed bricks under the front and back tires of the vehicle. Mari instructed Defendant not to leave the vehicle and then left in search of help.

Officer Longobardi was dispatched to the area in response to a call that an individual was slumped over the steering wheel of a vehicle. Longobardi testified that upon arriving at the scene, he saw Defendant's vehicle in the southbound lane of traffic, positioned at least ten feet away from the curb. Longobardi confirmed that bricks were underneath the tires of the vehicle on the driver's side.

Longobardi testified that, upon approaching the vehicle, he saw Defendant passed out behind the steering wheel of the car. He further testified that the key was in the ignition, the ignition was turned on, the transmission was in drive, and Defendant had his foot on the brake. The officer aroused Defendant, who spoke to Longobardi in a slurred manner. Longobardi smelled alcohol on Defendant's breath and noticed that Defendant had red, bloodshot eyes. On cross-examination, the officer admitted that he did not inquire of Defendant whether he had driven the vehicle to that location, or why the car was sitting there.

\*\*\*Defendant was transported to the Bernalillo County Detention Center where he submitted to breath tests which produced readings of .17 and .15.

In the metropolitan court proceedings, Defendant was found guilty of DWI.

### \*\*\*SECTION 66-8-102 DOES NOT REQUIRE INTENT.

Defendant next argues that there was insufficient evidence to support his conviction because the State failed to prove that he intended to drive the car. Although the parties appear to use specific intent and general intent interchangeably, general intent is all that is at issue in this case. DWI does not require an intent to do a further act or achieve a further consequence, such as is ordinarily required in specific intent crimes.

Defendant argues that since he was not conscious of his wrongdoing, he cannot have the intent he says is required to sustain a DWI conviction. We disagree.

New Mexico's DWI statute states in part that "[i]t is unlawful for any person who is under the influence of intoxicating liquor to drive any vehicle within this state," and further, "[i]t is unlawful for any person who has one-tenth of one percent or more by weight of alcohol in his blood to drive any vehicle within this state." Section 66-8-102(A), (C). Our primary focus is to give effect to the intention of the legislature. In doing so, we examine the language used in the relevant statute. Section 66-8-102 makes absolutely no reference whatsoever to a required intent on the part of an accused. Rather, the statute clearly provides that the only thing necessary to convict a person of DWI is proof that the defendant was driving a vehicle either under the influence of intoxicating liquor or while he had a certain percentage of alcohol in his blood.

A strict liability crime is one which imposes a criminal sanction for an unlawful act without requiring a showing of criminal intent. The legislature may forbid the doing of an act and make its commission criminal without regard to the intent of the wrongdoer. The rationale for making an act criminal without regard to the perpetrator's intent is that the public interest is so compelling, or the potential harm so great, that the public interest must override the individual's interests. The standard for determining whether a statute is a strict liability statute involves ascertaining whether there is a clear legislative intent that the act does not require any degree of mens rea.

Obviously, the public's interest in deterring individuals from driving while intoxicated is compelling. This is due to the dangers of the practice, not only to those who operate motor vehicles while under the influence, but also to those innocent individuals who are injured or killed as a result of DWI accidents. The fact that innocent individuals are oftentimes injured or killed, and their families and loved ones made to suffer, makes the potential harm from DWI much greater than if only the irresponsible person who drove while intoxicated was put in danger. We have recognized that the policy behind the DWI statute is to prevent individuals from driving or exercising actual physical control over a vehicle when they, either mentally or physically, or both, are unable to exercise the clear judgment and steady hand necessary to handle a vehicle with safety both to themselves and the public. We believe that the legislature recognized this significant public interest and potential harm when it drafted Section 66-8-102 and made no mention of the need to prove a required intent in order to secure a conviction.

Moreover, we believe adopting Defendant's position and interpreting Section 66-8-102 as a crime requiring intent, rather than a strict liability crime, would defeat the legislature's purpose and achieve absurd results. Reduced to its essence, Defendant's argument is that he could not be convicted of DWI because he was too intoxicated to form the conscious intent to drive drunk. To allow persons charged with DWI the opportunity to present such a defense would be absurd and undoubtedly contrary to the statute's purpose.

***CONCLUSION

We believe there was substantial evidence to support the district court's finding that Defendant was in control of a motor vehicle, and therefore, driving. In reviewing the language of the DWI statute, we also believe that the legislature drafted Section

66-8-102 in order to make the act of driving while intoxicated a crime, in and of itself, regardless of the intent of the accused. Based on the above, we hold that the offense of DWI is a strict liability crime. Defendant's conviction is affirmed.

## Case Analysis

1. What level of *mens rea*, if any, is required to convict the defendant of DWI?
2. The court makes reference to "legislative intent" while interpreting the criminal statute. What is the court referring to?
3. Why would a state want to make DWI a strict liability crime?

## Concurrence

**concurrence** The *actus rea* and *mens rea* existing simultaneously.

**temporal concurrence** The *mens rea* must accompany the *actus reus* in time.

**motivational concurrence** The *mens rea* must be linked to the *actus reus* it is intended to accompany.

Though it often goes without saying, there is also a requirement that the *actus reus* and the *mens rea* occur together. This is known as **concurrence**. There are two types of concurrence: **temporal concurrence** and **motivational concurrence**. Temporal concurrence means that the *mens rea* must accompany the *actus reus* in time. Assume, for example, that Bob intends on Tuesday to kill Fred. Assume further that Tuesday turns into Wednesday and Bob changes his mind. If Bob accidentally kills Fred in a hunting accident on Wednesday, he cannot be convicted of first-degree murder because he did not *intend* to kill Fred at that time. He may be guilty of another homicide offense (see Chapter 8), but not first-degree murder. What if Bob intends to kill Fred while they are hunting, Bob shoots Fred, but Fred manages to escape, get to hospital for treatment, only to die a few hours later from massive blood loss? Is there a concurrence problem? No, because the criminal act and the *mens rea* occurred together. Only the resulting harm (Fred's death) occurred at a later point.

Motivational concurrence requires that the *mens rea* be linked to the *actus reus* it is intended to accompany. In other words, if a person intends to commit Crime A but then ends up committing Crime B, motivational concurrence is absent. Return to the hunting example, but assume that Bob and Fred went hunting with their friend, Hank. Further assume that Bob still intended to kill Fred that day, but accidentally shot and killed Hank. Bob could not be guilty of murder because he did not intend to kill Hank. This is all rather tedious, but in the end there is a simple point: For someone to be guilty of a particular crime, there can be no "mismatch" between the *mens rea* and the *actus reus*.

**YOUR DECISION**

1. Jody Sweetana is from Honolulu, Hawaii, and recently moved to New Hampshire to attend college. Jody has never seen snow or driven in winter weather. While driving home from class one snowy afternoon, Jody mistakenly believes it is safer the drive above the speed limit on the snow-covered roads. Eventually, Jody causes a major car accident and kills the driver of another vehicle. Jody has acted recklessly or negligently. Which is it?
2. Jane finds out that her husband, John, was having an affair. Devastated by the news, she plans to kill him as soon as he falls asleep. He does not fall asleep, however,

and watches television into the wee hours while Jane falls asleep. In the morning, the two make amends, but as Jane is backing her car out of the driveway to leave for work, she runs over John, mortally wounding him. Can Jane be convicted of murder? Why or why not?

## Summary

- *Mens rea*, Latin for "guilty mind," is the second critical component of criminal liability.

- Traditional *mens rea* is concerned with culpability, or an offender's level of blameworthiness for a crime.

- Statutory *mens rea* is the level of intent required by a specific statute, possibly independent of any notion of morality.

- Common *mens rea* terms include intent (even transferred and oblique intent), knowledge, willfulness, negligence, recklessness, and malice.

- General intent crimes are those offenses that contain no specific *mens rea* component.

- Specific intent crimes are those that *do* contain a specific *mens rea* component.

- Motive precedes *mens rea*.

- Motive has been defined as "an idea, belief or emotion that impels or incites one to act in accordance with his state of mind or emotion."

- Strict liability is criminal liability in the absence of *mens rea*.

- Strict liability offenses include selling alcohol to a minor and statutory rape, among many others.

- Concurrence is the requirement that the *actus reus* and the *mens rea* occur together.

- Temporal concurrence means that the *mens rea* must accompany the *actus reus* in time.

- Motivational concurrence requires that the *mens rea* be linked to the *actus reus* it is intended to accompany.

---

**MODULE**

## 3.4     OTHER ELEMENTS OF CRIMINAL LIABILITY

*Learning Objectives*

- **Explain causation.**
- **Identify a situation in which a circumstantial element is an element of criminal liability.**

## CORE CONCEPTS

**causation** The requirement that the defendant is responsible for the harm in result crimes.

To recap, the prosecutor must prove beyond a reasonable doubt that the defendant committed a criminal act with the required mental state. Concurrence between the *actus reus* and the *mens rea* is also necessary. Some crimes, however, add two more elements: causation and a circumstantial element. These additional offense elements are the topic of this module.

# Causation

**Causation**, the requirement that the defendant is responsible for the harm, applies only to result crimes. In other words, the causation requirement does not exist in the case of conduct crimes because conduct crimes do not require a harmful result. What's more, causation inquiries usually only come up in homicide prosecutions, as more often than not it is clear who caused the harm in other result crimes (e.g., rape).

Requiring a causation element in certain crimes serves a protective function. Imagine a situation in which any person who was near a homicide could be prosecuted for it. This would certainly be unfair, especially if one person was responsible for the act. The causation requirement thus helps ensure that the actual offender is prosecuted and convicted, not some innocent passerby.

It is also important to note that causation can occur not just from an overt action, but also an omission. In some cases, failure to act can result in criminal liability because such failure can result in harm. Finally, there are two main types of causation: factual causation and legal causation. The next two subsections look at each in more detail.

## Factual Causation

**factual causation** The requirement that the defendant's conduct was the cause in fact of the harm.

**Factual causation** (or "cause in fact") requires that there can be no criminal liability for a resulting harm "unless it can be shown that the defendant's conduct was the cause-in-fact of the prohibited result."[51] In order to determine factual causation, courts typically apply a "but-for," or "*sine qua non*" (Latin for "without which not") test. It requires answering a simple question: But for the defendant's actions, would the resulting harm have occurred? If the answer is no, then the defendant will be held liable. Consider this example: Sarah pulls a gun on Anne, shoots Anne in the chest, and Anne dies. We ask, "But for Sarah shooting the gun, would Anne have died?" The answer is most likely "no," which means Sarah was the factual cause of Anne's death.

In reality, the factual causation inquiry can get tedious. What if, instead, Sarah and Anne have a heated argument while at Sarah's house, Anne storms out of the house, and distracted, is hit by a car and killed. Is Sarah factually responsible for Anne's death? It is not easy to arrive at an answer because this situation confuses factual causation and *mens rea*. On the one hand, Sarah did not intend for Anne to die in this situation, yet she may not have died but for being distracted

---

[51]*Velazquez v. State*, 561 So.2d 347 (Fla. Dist. Ct. App. 1990), p. 350.

from the argument that she and Sarah had. So while we could say Sarah was the factual cause of Anne's death, *mens rea* was absent, which means Sarah could not be convicted of homicide. All pieces of the puzzle for a homicide conviction were in place except *mens rea*. In other words, this was a situation of causation without *mens rea*. As you can imagine, it is possible, too, to have *mens rea* without causation.

Another complication pertaining to factual causation arises if there are multiple actual causes of someone's death. Assume again that Sarah shot Anne, but that Anne survived for a time only to die from a botched medical procedure (say, for example, the emergency room anesthesiologist administered a lethal dose of drugs prior to Anne's surgery). Further assume, silly as it may sound, that a major earthquake struck at the precise moment the drugs were administered and that everyone in the emergency room, including Anne, was crushed to death. Who or what is the factual cause of Anne's death? We again ask the question, "But for Sarah's actions, would Anne have died when she did?" The answer is arguably yes, because of the emergency room mistake and the earthquake. In reality, in the event Anne was prosecuted for murder, the answer to the question could come down to medical testimony. The state would most likely call an expert who would argue that Anne's wounds were serious enough that she would have died regardless of whether surgery occurred. Sarah's defense attorney would probably call an expert to testify that Anne's wounds were not that serious and that the earthquake and/or anesthesiologist were responsible.

A similar issue came up in the case of *Oxendine* v. *State*.[52] Jeffrey Oxendine, Jr., a six-year-old, was killed after being the victim of two vicious attacks. In the first, his dad's girlfriend, Leotha Tyree, pushed Jeffrey Jr. into a bathtub, causing tears in his intestines, or "peritonitis," a potentially lethal condition. The next day, Jeffrey Jr.'s father, Jeffrey Oxendine, Sr., severely beat his son. Jeffrey Jr. died later that day. Both Jeffrey Sr. and Tyree were prosecuted for Jeffrey's death. Oxendine, Sr., was convicted of manslaughter, but he succeeded in having his conviction overturned because it was not clear exactly who was factually responsible for the boy's death. Why? At trial, two state medical experts offered conflicting testimony. One testified that he could not determine who was responsible for Jeffrey Jr.'s death. The other testified that Tyree was responsible, but he didn't know for sure whether Jeffrey Sr.'s actions accelerated Jeffrey Jr.'s death.

Another complication arises with respect to the notion of concurrent causation. Return to the Sarah and Anne example. Assume Sarah and another friend, Sue, both shot Anne. Sarah shot Anne in the head and Sue shot Anne in the heart. Assume further that Anne died as a result of the wounds and that each wound was mortal. Who is the factual cause of Anne's death? In like situations, rare as they may be, the "but for" test has problems. We ask, first, "But for Sarah's conduct, would Anne have died?" The answer is yes—because of the fatal wound inflicted by Sue. Next we ask, "But for Sue's conduct, would Anne have died?" The answer is also yes, so in theory, neither Sarah nor Sue was the factual cause of Anne's death. Should Sarah and Sue escape prosecution and conviction? Of course not. To get around this problem, the courts may modify the "but for" test such that a different question is asked, namely,

---

[52]*Oxendine v. State*, 528 A.2d 870 (Del. 1987).

"But for either defendant's actions, would Anne's death have occurred 'when and as it did?'"[53] This question essentially redefines the harm in question, Anne's death. Instead of "Anne's death," the concern is with "Anne's death by two mortal wounds." With the resulting harm defined in this way, Anne could not have died as she did without the fatal shots from Sarah and Sue.[54]

Consider yet another, simpler, example. *People* v. *Arzon*[55] dealt with a man who, in an effort to keep warm, started a fire on the fifth floor of an abandoned building. Firefighters were called to the scene. Meanwhile, another person started a fire on the second floor, which trapped the firefighters after they arrived. One of the firefighters died from smoke inhalation. The man who started the fifth floor fire was indicted and moved to dismiss the indictment on the grounds that he was not the factual cause of the firefighter's death. The court disagreed, reasoning that

> the defendant's conduct need not be the sole and exclusive factor . . . . [A]n individual is criminally liable if his conduct was a sufficiently direct cause of the death, and the ultimate harm is something which should have been foreseen as being reasonably related to his acts. It is irrelevant that, in this instance, the fire which had erupted on the second floor intervened, thus contributing to the conditions that culminated in the death of [the fireman]. . . . Certainly, it was foreseeable that firemen would respond to the situation, thus exposing them, along with the persons already present in the vicinity, to a life-threatening danger. The fire set by the defendant was an indispensable link in the chain of events that resulted in the death. It continued to burn out of control, greatly adding to the problem of evacuating the building by blocking off one of the access routes. At the very least, the defendant's act . . . placed the deceased in a position where he was particularly vulnerable to the separate and independent force, in this instance, the fire on the second floor.[56]

## Legal Causation

**legal causation** Also known as *proximate cause,* often the primary act that sets a chain of events in motion. Focuses on whether it is fair to hold the defendant accountable for the resulting harm.

Factual causation, to recap, is concerned with identifying who or what (e.g., an earthquake) caused a harm. There could be many factual causes, as we saw in the preceding section. **Legal causation**, or "proximate" causation, is concerned with *who should be held criminally responsible*. We basically ask a simple question: Would it be *fair* to hold the defendant responsible for the crime? If the answer is "yes," then the defendant is the legal cause. In other words, the proximate cause of a harm is the person who should be accountable for it.

A proximate cause is always the actual cause, but an actual cause is not necessarily the proximate cause. For example, a defendant could set in motion a chain of events that results in a victim's death 10 years later. Would it be fair to hold the defendant responsible when many other events likely occurred during that period? Questions like this, as we will see momentarily, routinely arise when the proximate cause is not clear.

[53]*State* v. *Montoya*, 61 P.3d 793 (N.M. 2002), p. 797.
[54]For additional examples, see *State* v. *Munoz*, 126 N.M. 371 (1998); Dressler, *Understanding Criminal Law*, pp. 187–188.
[55]*People* v. *Arzon*, 92 Misc. 2d 739 (1978).
[56]Ibid., pp. 742–743.

**direct cause** The defendant's actions are the direct causal agent that brings about the harm.

**intervening cause** Another event besides the actions of the defendant that resulted in the harm after the defendant acted.

**dependent intervening cause** A cause that is either intended or reasonably foreseen by the defendant.

**independent intervening cause** A cause that could not be intended or reasonably foreseen by the defendant.

**apparent safety doctrine** A legal principle that states the defendant is not the legal cause of a resulting harm if the victim reaches a place of "apparent safety," at which point an intervening cause of harm comes into play.

To make the distinction between factual and legal cause more clear, we also need to define what it means to be a **direct cause** and an **intervening cause**. In most cases, the defendant is the direct cause of the resulting harm. Direct causation occurs when the defendant—and only the defendant—is the causal agent that brings about a harm. An intervening cause, by contrast, is something else besides the actions of the defendant that resulted in the harm *after* the defendant acted. If there is an intervening cause that is responsible for a resulting harm, the defendant may not be the legal cause of said injury. This is because the court determines that something else is a superseding cause that had a bigger stake in the resulting injury than the defendant. Indeed, there are many considerations that come into play when deciding on matters of proximate causation. What follows are a few of them.

**Foreseeability.**    A **dependent intervening cause** (sometimes called a "responsive intervening cause") is one that is either intended or reasonably foreseen by the defendant. For example, if a carjacker draws a gun on his victim and demands the keys but the victim hits the gas pedal and flees, only to be broadsided by a city bus and killed, the carjacker-now-defendant is arguably the one who should be held responsible for the victim's death. Why? The intervening cause—namely, the victim's flight from the scene—was *dependent* on the actions of the defendant. It is safe to assume that the victim would have been more cautious pulling out into traffic but for the attempted carjacking he or she endured.

In contrast, an **independent intervening cause** (sometimes called a "superseding cause") is, as you might guess, one that could not be intended or reasonably foreseen by the defendant. Say, for example, that Joe is stabbed by Larry. Larry inflicts only one minor injury before Joe flees. Joe then goes to the hospital for treatment. While Joe is waiting for treatment, a disgruntled former employee pulls a gun and begins shooting everyone in sight. Joe is killed. Would it be reasonable to conclude that Larry was the proximate cause of Joe's death? Probably not. He could not have reasonably foreseen that a crazed gunman would enter the hospital waiting room and begin shooting.

**The Defendant's *Mens Rea*.**    The defendant's *mens rea* also deserves consideration in determining proximate causation. In *Regina* v. *Michael*,[57] a classic case, a woman wanted her child dead. She furnished poison to a nurse and told the nurse it was medicine. The nurse felt the child did not need the medicine and placed it on a mantel where, later, it was retrieved by another child and given to the intended victim, who died from it. There were two intervening causes: (1) the nurse's negligent act of placing the medicine on the mantel and (2) the other child's act of giving the poison to the victim. The mother was deemed the proximate cause of her child's death because she *intended* to kill her child.

**Apparent Safety.**    The **apparent safety doctrine** holds that a defendant is not the legal cause of a resulting harm if the victim reaches a place of "apparent safety," at which point an intervening cause of harm comes into play. In *State* v. *Preslar*,[58] a

[57]*Regina* v. *Michael*, 169 End. Rep. 48 (1840).
[58]*State* v. *Preslar*, 48 N.C. 421 (1856).

man had an argument with his wife, beat her, and later drove her away from the home and left her close to her father's house. Instead of entering her father's house, the woman decided to sleep outside in the cold. She froze to death during the night. The husband was not held criminally liable. The court said,

> If, to avoid the rage of a brutal husband, a wife is compelled to expose herself, by wading through a swamp, or jumping into a river, the husband is responsible for the consequences; but, if she exposes herself thus, without necessity, and of her own accord, we know of no principle of law, by which he is held responsible, to the extent of forfeiting his life.[59]

### Substantiality of the Intervening Cause.

If an intervening cause is substantially more significant than the actual cause, the defendant may escape criminal liability. For example, if Bill shoots Alex with a .22 caliber pistol and he dies, but at the same time Colt shoots Alex with a .50 caliber sniper rifle, a much more lethal and higher velocity weapon, would it be fair treat Bill as the proximate cause of Alex's death? Most likely not. The law will treat the *substantial* intervening case as the proximate cause, so Colt will be convicted of homicide, but Bill most likely won't be (perhaps he will be convicted of attempted murder or an analogous offense—an alternative we will consider in later chapters).

### Voluntary Victim Intervention.

Related to the apparent safety doctrine is the rule that an offender cannot be held liable if his or her victim a victim acts in a free, voluntary, and informed manner that leads to the resulting harm. You may recall the Jack Kevorkian assisted suicide case.[60] He made available a "suicide machine" that his patients could then use to kill themselves. The Michigan Supreme Court concluded that Dr. Kevorkian could not be liable for killing his patients because all he did was furnish the means for them to end their lives. (Dr. Kevorkian was eventually convicted of other crimes.) Contrast this with the case of a woman who was held against her will and sexually assaulted over a period of days. While being confined, she ingested a poisonous substance in an effort to commit suicide. She subsequently died from several causes, including ingestion of the poison. The defendant was deemed the proximate cause of the woman's death.[61] The court basically concluded that the woman was not of sound mind when she attempted to kill herself.

### Omissions.

An omission, or failure to act, can also serve as the basis for criminal liability, although this is rare. For example, in *Bowman* v. *State*,[62] the defendant, who was driving drunk, was involved in a traffic accident that killed the vehicle's passenger, who was not wearing a seatbelt. While the passenger "omitted" to wear her seatbelt, the driver was held criminally responsible.

---

[59]Ibid., p. 428.
[60]*People* v. *Kevorkian*, 447 Mich. 436 (1994).
[61]*Stephenson* v. *State*, 205 Ind. 141 (1932).
[62]*Bowman* v. *State*, 564 N.E. 2d 309 (Ind. Ct. App. 1990), affirmed in part, vacated in part, 577 N.E.2d 569 (Ind. 1991).

Dr. JackKevorkian, nicknamed Dr. Death, developed a "suicide machine" that his terminally ill patients could use to end their own lives if they so chose.

©Steven R. Nickerson KRT/Newscom

## Circumstantial Element

**circumstantial element**
Also known as *attendant circumstances*, the requirement for a specific circumstance to be present.

Some crimes contain a **circumstantial element**, or attendant circumstances. For example, in the crime of driving under the influence, the circumstance unique to that offense is "under the influence." Similarly, some jurisdictions maintain so-called felony murder rules. A person may be subjected to a murder prosecution if a person is killed (without specific intent on the offender's part) during the commission of a felony, such as robbery. In such a situation, the circumstantial element is the murder.

## YOUR DECISION

1. John and Mark robbed a bank, wearing ski masks and armed with automatic weapons. While the robbery was taking place, the 60-year-old bank manager fainted and died of a heart attack. John and Mark were unaware that the bank manager had a history of heart disease. John and Mark never physically touched the bank manager. Are John and Mark the factual and legal cause of the bank manager's death? If not, why?

2. Carrie recently learned that her husband, Brennan, is having an affair with his yoga instructor. Enraged, Carrie decides that she wants to kill Brennan and throw his body into the river. She even stays up late at night, writing in her journal and planning out his death. The next morning, Carrie has a change of heart. She decides she

would rather divorce Brennan and try to get a large alimony check every month instead of committing murder. As she is pulling out of the garage on her way to work, however, she accidentally runs Brennan over as he is retrieving the morning paper. Brennan dies as a result of his injuries. Carrie is charged with first-degree murder, which requires a specific intent to kill. Is she guilty of first-degree murder? Why or why not?

## Summary

- Causation, the requirement that the defendant is responsible for the harm, applies only to result crimes.

- Factual causation (or "cause in fact") requires that there can be no criminal liability for a resulting harm "unless it can be shown that the defendant's conduct was the cause in fact of the prohibited result."

- Legal causation, or "proximate" causation, is concerned with *who should be held criminally responsible.*

- Direct causation occurs when the defendant—and only the defendant—is the causal agent that brings about a harm. An intervening cause, by contrast, is something else besides the actions of the defendant that resulted in the harm *after* the defendant acted.

- The resulting harm is the outcome of a result crime.

- Resulting harm is not a requirement for conduct crimes.

- Many crimes contain a circumstantial element, or attendant circumstances. For example, in the crime of driving under the influence, the circumstance unique to that offense is "under the influence."

**MODULE**

# 3.5

# IGNORANCE AND MISTAKE

### *Learning Objective*
- **Distinguish between ignorance of the law and mistake.**

**CORE CONCEPTS**   Everyone makes mistakes. Suppose you engage in some action, thinking it is legal, only to find out later that it was not. Or, what if you just don't know whether a certain action is criminal and engage in it nevertheless? Should you be held criminally liable in both circumstances? Such is the essence of ignorance and mistake. In this section, we look at whether ignorance of the law is a defense. Then we consider the concept of "mistake" and distinguish it from ignorance. In doing so, we look at two types of mistake: mistake of law and mistake of fact. Finally, we consider situations in which ignorance and/or mistake can excuse a person from criminal liability.

# Ignorance of the Law

Few rules of criminal law are as well known as *ignorantia lexis non exusat*, or "ignorance of the law is no excuse." Simply, people should know the law, and it is their responsibility to refrain from acting in certain situations without checking whether a law will be violated. In other words, everyone has a "duty to inquire" about the legality of their actions. Oliver Wendell Holmes once put it this way:

> The true explanation of the rule is the same as that which accounts for the law's indifference to a man's particular temperament, faculties, and so forth. Public policy sacrifices the individual to the general good. . . . It is no doubt true that there are many cases in which the criminal could not have known that he was breaking the law, but to admit the excuse at all would be to encourage ignorance . . . and justice to the individual is rightly outweighed by the larger interests on the other side of the scales.[63]

And it does not matter if a person's ignorance of the law is something short of intentional. If ignorance is reckless or even negligent, the criminal law does not care. Criminal liability will still attach.

Not everyone agrees with the general rule. For one thing, penal codes are *massive*. Not even seasoned lawyers can list—off the top of their heads and with certainty—what actions are legal and illegal. Also, many jurisdictions have antiquated and bizarre laws on the books, some of which seem to criminalize apparently legal behavior. For example, it is a misdemeanor in Washington State to go into public with a common cold, a communicable ailment.[64] Surely someone who has a cold and must ride public transit to work is not as culpable as a murderer or rapist. Another problem is that the law is vague. Jerome Hall once remarked, in fact, that laws are so vague that we can "disagree indefinitely regarding the[ir] meaning."[65] Indeed, if the law was unambiguous, there would be no need for a book like this! But to defer to every person's subjective interpretation of the law would clearly cause problems.

Is it thus possible to reach a compromise? On the one hand, there are laws that everyone should know. On the other hand, it may be unreasonable to expect people to know about—much less be able to find and read up on—obscure laws that criminalize seemingly normal behaviors. The problem is no one could agree where the line should be drawn. It is just easier to maintain a rule that all people need to know the law. And besides, if the law is obscure, odd, disagreeable, or antiquated, it may not be enforced anyway. Just because a law criminalizes behavior does not mean prosecutors will use it!

# Examples of Ignorance

It is important to distinguish between (1) a defendant who does not know there is a law applying to his or her activity and (2) a defendant who knows there is a relevant law, but is not sure whether it applies in the exact circumstances in question. The first

---

[63]O. W. Holmes, *The Common Law* (Boston: Little, Brown, and Company, 1881).
[64]RCW 70.54.050. Also see http://www.dumblaws.com for more unusual laws from state to state.
[65]J. Hall, *The General Principles of Criminal Law*, 2nd ed. (Indianapolis: Bobbs-Merrill, 1960), p. 382.

defendant is demonstrating ignorance of the law. The second defendant is making a mistake. This section looks strictly at ignorance of the law.

Many "ignorance" cases involve aliens who are not familiar with a particular culture or its laws. For example, in *United States* v. *Moncini*,[66] the defendant, a citizen and resident of Italy, mailed child pornography to an undercover officer in the United States. Later on, when he entered the United States on unrelated business, he was arrested and convicted for a federal law violation. In challenging his conviction, he claimed that since the same conduct was not illegal in Italy, he should have been excused for his ignorance. The Ninth Circuit Court of Appeals disagreed, holding:

> Even assuming Moncini was ignorant of the law as he claims, he must bear the risk of the potential illegality of his conduct. . . . The child pornography laws are directly related to a commonly understood moral censure. The very nature of child pornography, which is commonly regulated throughout the world, should cause a reasonable person to investigate the laws of the United States before sending such material into this country. . . . This is not a case where due process prohibits convicting a defendant who has unwittingly broken the law through conduct which an ordinary person would not assume to be at least potentially criminal.[67]

In a more recent case, however, the Supreme Court moved away from this interpretation to some extent. In *Ratzlaf* v. *United States*,[68] a man owed a Reno casino over $100,000. He attempted to pay the debt in cash, but the casino reminded him that it would have to report the transaction to federal authorities (because the transaction was in an amount over $10,000). The casino then offered to drive the man around to various banks where he could obtain separate cashier's checks, each for less than $10,000, so as to avoid reporting requirements. He was charged with violating federal law and, despite claiming he was not aware that the conduct was criminal, convicted after the trial judge instructed the jury that ignorance was irrelevant. The Supreme Court disagreed, arguing that even though the defendant knew he was structuring a currency transaction to avoid reporting requirements, he didn't know this was illegal. The Court went on to note that "[b]ecause currency structuring is not inevitably nefarious, this Court is unpersuaded by the United States' argument that structuring is so obviously 'evil' or inherently 'bad' that the 'willfulness' requirement is satisfied irrespective of the defendant's knowledge of the illegality of structuring.[69]

This decision was echoed in *Lambert* v. *California*,[70] a case involving an ex-felon who was unaware of a requirement—per a local ordinance—that she register her presence in the city. The Supreme Court held that a due process violation occurred when the woman was prohibited from introducing evidence to the effect she was unaware of the ordinance. The moral of the story, then, between this and the last case is that, *some of the time*, ignorance can act as a defense. Successful ignorance defenses are *very* rare.

---

[66]*United States* v. *Moncini*, 882 F.2d 401 (9th Cir. 1989).
[67]Ibid., pp. 405–406.
[68]*Ratzlaf* v. *United States*, 510 U.S. 135 (1994).
[69]Ibid., p. 135.
[70]*Lambert* v. *California*, 355 U.S. 255 (1957).

# Mistake

In general, a mistake occurs when (1) a person knows what he or she is doing is wrong, but is not completely clear as to why, or (2) a person thinks what he or she is doing is legal, but is not correct in this knowledge. For example, assume Laura took her car to a mechanic who, in her view, charged an excessive amount for the repair.[71] She refused to pay, so the mechanic refused to give her the keys and kept the car. Laura returned after hours and, with a different set of keys, took her car. She was prosecuted for larceny. Laura made a mistake because, arguably, she knew that what she did was probably prohibited, but she may not have known that there was a state lien law that permitted the mechanic to keep her car until the bill was paid.

Or consider the case of Hank who went to the grocery store, selected 10 items from the shelves, and then visited a cashier who began scanning the items. Assume that Hank was talking on his cell phone and failed to notice that the cashier missed an item. Assume further that on leaving the store, a security guard noticed that Hank was leaving with an item that he had not paid for. Hank was prosecuted for theft. It seems he made an honest mistake. We can safely assume he knew stealing was not acceptable, but he just failed to notice that the cashier missed something.

Both of these hypothetical scenarios illustrate two different types of mistake. Laura made what is known as a **mistake of law**. She knew larceny was a crime, but she was not aware of the state lien law. Hank, on the other hand, made a **mistake of fact**. He mistakenly left the store with an item he did not pay for. Unlike Laura, however, he will most likely be acquitted. Why? Because he did not form the requisite *mens rea* to support a criminal conviction. Had the crime he was prosecuted with contained no *mens rea* component, then his mistake may not have mattered and he could have been convicted.

See the accompanying Court Decision for more on mistake of fact. In it, we take a look at the case of *Tennessee* v. *Ballinger*, in which the defendant attempts to use the mistake of fact defense in regards to a statutory rape charge.

**mistake of law** The defendant claims to misunderstand or misinterpret the law as it applies to the specific circumstances.

**mistake of fact** A misunderstanding or misinterpretation by the defendant about a relevant fact. Potentially used as a defense or to negate the *mens rea* requirement of a crime.

---

**COURT DECISION**

*State of Tennessee* v. *Charles Arnold Ballinger*
93 S.W.3d 881 (Tenn. App. 2001)

**Background:** Defendant as convicted of statutory rape and contributing to the delinquency of a minor in the Criminal Court, Bradley County. Defendant appealed claiming he was entitled to a jury instruction on the "mistake of fact" defense regarding the alleged victim's age. The Tennessee Court of Criminal Appeals reversed and remanded for a new trial.

**Opinion**

JERRY L. SMITH, Judge.
On October 14, 1998, a Bradley County Grand Jury indicted Charles Ballinger, the defendant and appellant, for statutory rape and contributing to the delinquency of a minor. Following a jury trial, the defendant was convicted on both counts. The court sentenced the defendant to serve two years for statutory rape concurrently with

---

[71]*State* v. *Cude*, 383 P.2d 399 (Utah 1963).

eleven months and twenty-nine days for contributing to the delinquency of a minor. On appeal, the defendant claims . . . that the trial court should have instructed the jury to consider mistake of fact as a defense. Because we find that statutory rape requires proof of at least a "recklessness" mens rea and that the trial court should have instructed the jury to consider mistake of fact as a defense to statutory rape, we reverse the judgment of the trial court and remand this case for a new trial.

### Factual Background

The defendant, a thirty-seven-year-old male, was a neighbor of R.S., a fifteen-year-old female. The defendant's young son was also friends with R.S.'s younger brother. On April 17, 1998, R.S. and her younger brother planned to spend the night at the defendant's home so that R.S. could babysit her brother and the defendant's son. After the defendant picked up R.S. and her brother at their home, he bought beer at a convenience store. When he arrived home, the defendant gave R.S. some beer. She became drunk and fell asleep on the couch. Later, the defendant woke R.S. and told her that he would sleep on the couch, while she could sleep in his bed. After she went to bed, R.S. awoke to discover the defendant lying next to her. He was nude, and he began rubbing R.S.'s back and stomach. He put his hands up her shirt, but she protested. The defendant put his hands in R.S.'s underwear and digitally penetrated her. Then, despite R.S.'s objections, the defendant pulled off her clothes and had sex with her. Afterward, the defendant went to sleep. R.S. stayed awake until the defendant went to work the next morning, and then she fell asleep.

Later that day, R.S. told her mother, Karen Tinsley, what had happened. Ms. Tinsley took R.S. to the hospital where a rape kit was administered. The kit, examined by a Tennessee Bureau of Investigation Forensic Serologist, revealed no semen or sperm. Afterward, police questioned the defendant, and he denied R.S.'s allegations. However, Ms. Tinsley spoke with the defendant later, and he admitted having sex with her. With Ms. Tinsley's permission, police recorded a subsequent telephone conversation that the defendant had with Ms. Tinsley. In that conversation, the defendant admitted letting R.S. drink beer. The defendant told Ms. Tinsley that R.S. wanted to have sex, that R.S. said she was eighteen, and that they had sex because "[R.S.] wanted me to." Then, the defendant changed his story and denied having sex with her.

Despite R.S.'s testimony that the defendant's actions toward her were non-consensual, the grand jury chose to indict the defendant only for statutory rape and contributing to the delinquency of a minor. Following a trial, the jury found the defendant guilty on both counts.

### ***Jury Instructions

The defendant complains that the trial court should have instructed the jury to consider the "mistake of fact" defense. Tenn.Code Ann. § 39-11-502. The state contends that mistake of fact is no defense to statutory rape, because the statutory rape statute requires no culpable mental state.

The Tennessee Code defines mistake of fact as follows: "ignorance or mistake of fact is a defense to prosecution if such ignorance or mistake negates the culpable mental state of the charged offense." Tenn.Code Ann. § 39-11-502(a). Thus, in order to determine whether mistake of fact is a defense to statutory rape, we must first determine what mental state, if any, is required for proof of statutory rape.

Statutory rape is defined as "sexual penetration of a victim by the defendant or of the defendant by the victim when the victim is at least thirteen (13) but less than eighteen (18) years of age and the defendant is at least four (4) years older than the victim." Tenn.Code Ann. § 39-13-506(a). Neither the statute nor the sentencing commission comments following the statute specify a culpable mental state. A literal reading of this statute could lead to absurd results. Because there is no requirement in the statute that the proscribed sexual penetration be unlawful, and because consent of the victim is no defense, a gynecological or proctological examination of a child between thirteen and seventeen years of age is literally prohibited by the statute.

The Legislature has provided guidance for such situations. Tenn.Code Ann. § 39-11-301 provides, in relevant part

> (b) A culpable mental state is required within this title unless the definition of an offense plainly dispenses with a mental element.
> (c) If the definition of an offense within this title does not plainly dispense with a mental element, intent, knowledge, or recklessness suffices to establish the culpable mental state.

Tenn.Code Ann. § 39-11-301(b), (c). In other words, when a mental state is neither specified nor "plainly dispensed with," the state must prove, at a minimum, that the defendant acted recklessly. In this case, because the statute defining statutory rape neither specifies nor plainly dispenses with a culpable mental state, we conclude that the state must prove that the defendant, at a minimum, recklessly engaged in sexual penetration of a victim between the ages of thirteen and eighteen and that the defendant was at least four years older than the victim.

"Reckless" as a mental element is defined at Tennessee Code Annotated Section 39-11-302(c) as follows:

> "Reckless" refers to a person who acts recklessly with respect to circumstances surrounding the conduct or the result of the conduct *when the person is aware of but consciously disregards a substantial and unjustifiable risk that the circumstances exist* of the result will occur. The risk must be of such a nature and degree that its disregard constitutes a gross deviation from the standard of care that an ordinary person would exercise under all the circumstances as viewed from the accused person's standpoint.

Therefore, in the context of a statutory rape prosecution a defendant may be said to act "recklessly" when he is aware of but consciously disregards a substantial and unjustifiable risk that the person who he is about to sexually penetrate is between the ages of 13 years and 17 years.

We turn now to determine whether the jury should have been instructed to consider mistake of fact as a defense in this case. It is well-settled that the trial court has the duty of giving a correct and complete charge of the law applicable to the facts of the case, and that the defendant has the right to have every issue of fact raised by the evidence and material to the defense submitted to the jury upon proper instructions by the trial court. Mistake of fact is not an affirmative defense; it is merely a defense. Thus, if the evidence fairly raises mistake of fact, the trial court must instruct the jury to consider the defense and that any reasonable doubt on the existence of the defense requires acquittal. The statute defining mistake of fact provides that mistake of fact shall apply "[e]xcept in prosecutions for violations of §§ 39-13-504(a)(4) and 39-13-522 [aggravated sexual battery of a child and rape of a child, respectively]." Tenn. Code Ann. § 39-11-502(a). Thus, while the Legislature has specifically excluded the defense in certain situations, it has not excluded the defense in statutory rape cases.

In this case, although the defendant testified that he did not have sex with R.S., he also testified that he thought she was eighteen years old. Based upon the evidence, the jury could have found that the defendant had sex with R.S. but, under all the circumstances was reasonably mistaken about her age, thus negating the possibility of a conclusion that the defendant acted recklessly. Thus, based on the evidence adduced at trial, we find that the trial court should have instructed the jury to consider mistake of fact as a defense to statutory rape.

Accordingly, we REVERSE the judgment of the trial court and remand this case for a new trial.

### Case Analysis

1. Explain the defense Charles Ballinger was alleging. Is there any factual evidence to support his defense?
2. Why did the court reverse his conviction?
3. Generally statutory rape is considered a strict liability crime. Explain how the court evaluates the *mens rea* requirement for the crime in Tennessee.

# When Ignorance or Mistake Can Serve as a Defense

There are three main situations in which ignorance or mistake can serve as a defense to criminal liability. First, in some circumstances, a person may be able to rely on an interpretation of the law that turns out later to be erroneous. This could include one's own reliance, reliance on an attorney's advice, or reliance on some other official's interpretation. *People* v. *Marrero*[72] offers an example of the self-reliance. In that case, a federal corrections officer was caught carrying a handgun without a permit. He cited a "peace officer" exemption in the state law he was charged with violating, which included any official or guard of "any state prison or of *any penal correctional institution.*" Though he was a federal corrections officer, he felt the state law with which he was charged should apply to him. The trial court sided with him in this regard, but the appellate court did not. As for relying on the advice of counsel, at least one court has decided that reliance on an attorney's mistaken interpretation of the law does not serve as an excuse for criminal liability.[73] While this decision was controversial, it helps

[72] *People* v. *Marrero*, 507 N.E.2d 1068 (N.Y. 1987).
[73] *State* v. *Huff*, 36 A. 1000 (Me. 1897).

avoid the problem of shady criminals seeking lawyerly advice from equally shady attorneys to support their own interpretations of the law.[74] If a person relies on an interpretation of the law made by an official or body charged with such tasks, that person will be excused from liability. The only way to succeed in this regard, however, is if the statute relied on is later ruled invalid[75] or the authorities in question are either the highest court in the jurisdiction[76] or a public officer charged with interpreting and enforcing the law, typically an Attorney General of the state.[77]

The second main situation in which a person may escape criminal liability because of ignorance or mistake concerns whether there was fair notice that the actions in question were criminal. Almost all the time, as we pointed out earlier, people are expected to know the law. In some situations, though, the law in question may be so obscure and unfamiliar that it would be unfair to hold someone liable for violating it. We return to the *Lambert* v. *California* case mentioned earlier in this section.[78] Recall that a convicted felon failed to register her whereabouts with local authorities. One point we did not raise earlier was that law required felons to register within five days of arriving in the city. The Supreme Court reversed the woman's conviction for violating the ordinance by pointing out the conduct in question was purely passive (i.e., failing to register). What the woman did, the Court felt, was not quite the same as an overt criminal act.

Finally, ignorance or mistake can—in *very* limited circumstances, mind you— excuse criminal liability if either manages to negate *mens rea*. Consider *Cheek* v. *United States*,[79] a case involving a "tax protestor" who did not file federal income tax returns for six years, even though he received income as a pilot during that time. He was charged with six counts of "willfully" failing to file a federal income tax return. Cheek testified at trial that he attended numerous "anti-tax" seminars where an attorney explained that capital gains, not wages, were considered income. In essence, he was relying on the advice of someone who, though mistaken, led Cheek to believe he was doing the right thing. Therefore, he argued that he did not "willfully" violate income tax laws. The trial judge instructed the jury that even a good faith misunderstanding like this could not serve as a defense to criminal liability, but the U.S. Supreme Court disapproved of this instruction and reversed Cheek's conviction. In essence the Court decided that Cheek's mistake *negated* the *mens rea* of the underlying offense. The Court made this argument:

> Willfulness, as construed by our prior decisions in criminal tax cases, requires the Government to prove that the law imposed a duty on the defendant, that the defendant knew of this duty, and that he voluntarily and intentionally violated that duty. . . . In this case, if Cheek asserted that he truly believed that the Internal Revenue Code did not purport to treat wages as income, and the jury believed him, the Government would not have carried its burden to prove willfulness, however unreasonable a court might deem such a belief.[80]

---

[74]See., e.g., M. Gur-Arye, "Reliance on a Lawyer's Mistaken Advice: Should it be an Excuse from Criminal Liability?" *American Journal of Criminal Law*, Vol. 29 (2002), p. 455.
[75]See, e.g., *Brent* v. *State*, 43 Ala. 297 (1869).
[76]See, e.g., State v. *O'Neil*, 126 N.W. 454 (Iowa 1910).
[77]See, e.g., *Commonwealth* v. *Twitchwell*, 617 N.E. 2d 609 (Mass. 1993).
[78]*Lambert* v. *California*, 355 U.S. 225 (1957).
[79]*Cheek* v. *United States*, 498 U.S. 192 (1991).
[80]Ibid., pp. 201–202.

It cannot be overstated how rare it is for mistake or ignorance to successfully negate *mens rea*. If it were easier for this to occur, then every criminal defendant would claim ignorance and escape conviction. What makes the Cheek case unique is the government's failure to prove that he *willfully* committed the crime—and the trial court judge's instruction to the jury that it could not even consider this aspect of the offense.

**YOUR DECISION**

1. Susan is returning from a spring break trip to Cancun, Mexico. While in Mexico, she decided to purchase cigars for her father. The cigars she ends up purchasing were actually manufactured in Miami, Florida. Believing that she has purchased authentic "Cuban cigars" that are illegal in the United States, Susan hides the cigars in her luggage and attempts to smuggle them through customs. The customs official searches her luggage and finds the cigars. Has Susan committed a crime? Why or why not?

2. Angie has just returned from a fantastic vacation to Costa Rica and she is waiting for her luggage to arrive at the baggage claim. Angie's suitcase is black with a pink ribbon tied to the handle. While she is talking on her cell phone, excitedly discussing her trip with her mother, Angie picks up a black suitcase with a pink ribbon and begins to exit the terminal. Unbeknownst to Angie, she picked up the wrong suitcase. A police officer stops Angie at the exit after a drug sniffing dog showed interest in her suitcase. The suitcase is filled with illegal drugs and Angie is arrested. Does Angie have a defense to the drug charges? If so, what defense might be applicable to her case and why?

## Summary

- Ignorance occurs when the defendant does not know there is a law applying to his or her activity.

- Mistake occurs when the defendant knows there a relevant law that applies to his or her conduct, but is not sure whether it applies in the circumstances at hand.

- In some circumstances, a person may be able to rely on an interpretation of the law that turns out later to be erroneous.

- If there was a lack of fair notice that the actions in question were criminal, a person may be able to successfully claim ignorance or mistake.

- Ignorance or mistake can—in *very* limited circumstances—excuse criminal liability if either manages to negate *mens rea*.

# Chapter Review

MODULE **3.1**

## INTRODUCTION TO OFFENSE TYPES

### Learning Objective

· Explain the difference between conduct and result crimes.

### Review Questions

1. What is the general part of the criminal law? Provide an example.
2. What is the special part of the criminal law? Provide an example.
3. Offer an example of a conduct crime *and* a result crime. Explain your answer.

### Key Terms

general part of the criminal law
special part of the criminal law
conduct crimes
result crimes
resulting harm

MODULE **3.2**

## THE CORE ELEMENTS OF CRIMINAL LIABILITY, PART 1: *ACTUS REUS*

### Learning Objective

· Explain *actus reus* and what constitutes a criminal act.

### Review Questions

1. When can an omission qualify as the *actus reus* of a crime?
2. What types of voluntary acts satisfy *actus reus*?

### Key Terms

*actus reus*
omission
Bad Samaritan laws

MODULE **3.3**

## THE CORE ELEMENTS OF CRIMINAL LIABILITY, PART 2: *MENS REA* AND CONCURRENCE

### Learning Objectives

· Explain *mens rea* and the different types of intent.
· Distinguish between *mens rea* and motive.
· Identify strict liability offenses.

### Review Questions

1. Distinguish traditional from statutory *mens rea*.
2. Provide an example of both a general and specific intent crime. Explain your answer.

3. What is the role of motive in the *mens rea* context?

4. Explain strict liability and offer an example of two strict liability crimes.

### Key Terms

| | |
|---|---|
| *mens rea* | recklessness |
| direct intent | malice |
| transferred intent | motive |
| oblique intent | strict liability |
| general intent | concurrence |
| specific intent | temporal concurrence |
| negligence | motivational concurrence |

## MODULE **3.4**   OTHER ELEMENTS OF CRIMINAL LIABILITY

### Learning Objectives

· Summarize concurrence.

· Explain causation.

· Identify a situation in which a circumstantial element is an element of criminal liability.

### Review Questions

1. Compare and contrast temporal and motivational concurrence.

2. Compare and contrast factual and legal causation.

3. What is the importance of "resulting harm" in criminal law? *When* is it important?

4. What is the circumstantial element of criminal liability? When is it relevant?

### Key Terms

| | |
|---|---|
| causation | dependent intervening cause |
| factual causation | independent intervening cause |
| legal causation | apparent safety doctrine |
| direct cause | circumstantial element |
| intervening cause | |

## MODULE **3.5**   IGNORANCE AND MISTAKE

### Learning Objective

· Distinguish between ignorance of the law and mistake.

### Review Questions

1. Provide one example each for ignorance and mistake.

2. Can ignorance serve as a criminal law defense? If so, when?

3. Can mistake serve as a criminal law defense? If so, when?

### Key Terms

mistake of law
mistake of fact

# Chapter Synthesis Questions

1. Summarize the main elements of criminal liability, distinguishing between conduct and result crimes.

2. Which is more harmful to society, a conduct crime or a result crime? Why?

3. An omission can satisfy the criminal law's *actus reus* requirement in seven specific situations. Should there be more situations or fewer in which an omission can satisfy *actus reus*? Explain your answer.

4. What is the ideal *mens rea* terminology? If there is no one best "term," why do you feel this way?

5. It is sometimes said "ignorance is no defense." Is this a fair statement? Why or why not?

6. In what situations can ignorance and/or mistake serve as defenses to criminal liability?

# 4

# JUSTIFICATION DEFENSES

*Learning Objectives*

**MODULE 4.1 JUSTIFICATION DEFENSES IN CONTEXT**
- Distinguish among failure of proof, justification, and excuse defenses.
- Explain the differences between nonexculpatory defenses and offense modifications.
- Explain the difference between a perfect defense and an imperfect defense.
- Identify three reasons for justification defenses.

**MODULE 4.2 SELF-DEFENSE AND DEFENSE OF OTHERS**
- Summarize the defense of self-defense.
- Identify recent developments that have complicated the law of self-defense.

**MODULE 4.3 DEFENSE OF PROPERTY AND HABITATION**
- Distinguish between defense of habitation and defense of property.
- Compare and contrast "make my day" laws and the castle doctrine.

**MODULE 4.4 LAW ENFORCEMENT**
- Explain the law enforcement defense.

**MODULE 4.5 NECESSITY AND CONSENT**
- Describe the necessity defense.
- Explain the defense of consent.

# JUSTIFICATION DEFENSES IN CONTEXT

*Learning Objectives*

- **Distinguish among failure of proof, justification, and excuse defenses.**
- **Explain the differences between nonexculpatory defenses and offense modifications.**
- **Explain the difference between a perfect defense and an imperfect defense.**
- **Identify three reasons for justification defenses.**

## CORE CONCEPTS

In a criminal trial, the prosecution bears the burden of proving beyond a reasonable doubt that the defendant committed the crime. This does not mean, however, that the defendant sits idly by and hopes the prosecution fails to meet its burden. Though they are not required to, most defendants usually present evidence at trial. For example, the defense attorney may cross-examine prosecution witnesses, attempting to call into question their credibility. The defendant may also assert any number of defenses, arguing why he or she should not be held liable for the crime. Such defenses are the focus of this, the second section of the book.

Defenses are broken into two general categories: justification and excuse defenses. The bulk of this chapter focuses on the former. Chapter 5 turns attention to excuse defenses. There are some defenses, however, that do not fit neatly into either of these categories. We will introduce them briefly at the beginning of this chapter and elsewhere as needed.

We begin this chapter with some general background on criminal defenses, looking not just at the various types of defenses, but also at the differences between so-called perfect and imperfect defenses and the *reasons* for defenses. After a foundation is put in place, we shift attention to the wide variety of justification defenses.

## Overview of Defenses

Defenses almost always focus on the core elements of criminal liability—*actus reus*, *mens rea*, concurrence, causation, and resulting harm (the latter two applying, again, in only the result crime context). This is particularly true of justification and excuse defenses. Each attempts to make a case that the defendant should not be held liable. But these two defense types need to be put in context against a backdrop of other defense types—namely failure of proof defenses, various "special" defenses, also called "offense modifications," and nonexculpatory defenses.[1]

## Failure of Proof

**failure of proof defense**
A defendant's acquittal is the result of the prosecution failing to prove one or more of the elements of a crime or leaving reasonable doubt in the mind of the jury.

If the prosecution fails to meet its burden of proving the various elements of an underlying offense beyond a reasonable doubt, then the result is essentially a **failure of proof defense**. That is, the prosecution's "failure to prove" one or more offense elements may result in the defendant's acquittal. Put differently, failure to prove one or more offense elements will leave "reasonable doubt" in the minds of the jury, thus meaning that the defendant could escape criminal liability, regardless of whether he or she is guilty.

A failure of proof defense *may* lead to the defendant's acquittal, but it may not. For example, assume that Fred shoots John, killing John. Fred is prosecuted for murder, but the prosecution fails to prove that Fred intended for John to die. This does not necessarily mean John will go free. John may well be convicted of a lesser homicide offense than murder (we look at the many varieties in Chapter 8).

**affirmative defense** A defense formally raised by the defendant that requires the production of evidence.

A failure of proof defense is not the same as the other leading defenses we will look at in this and the next chapter. Why? Because it is not an **affirmative defense**, or a defense formally raised at trial. The defense may not have to do *anything* and still benefit from a failure of proof. If the prosecution's evidence is weak, then the defense could just ride the trial out and wait for an acquittal. If the prosecution's evidence is modestly strong but dependent largely on witness testimony, then the defense may, at the cross-examination stage, challenge the prosecution's ability to prove the offense elements beyond a reasonable doubt.

## Justification

**justification defenses**
A group of defenses in which the defendant claims that his actions were right or justified based on the circumstances.

With **justification defenses**, the defendant accepts responsibility for the act he or she is charged with, but argues that the act was permissible under the circumstances. More formally, conduct that is criminal but "which under the circumstances is socially acceptable and which deserves neither criminal liability nor even censure"[2] qualifies for a justification defense. It is often said that justification defenses focus on the *act* rather than the actor.

Self-defense is an example of a justification defense. There are two broad categories of justification defenses: those justified by necessity and those justified by consent. An example of justification by necessity is self-defense; consent is a common defense in rape cases when the defendant argues that the victim consented. There is common thread running throughout all justification defenses:

> All of the different kinds of justification defenses share the same basic internal structure and have the same integral components. In all situations allowing a justification

---

[1]P. H. Robinson, "Criminal Law Defenses: A Systematic Analysis," *Columbia Law Review*, Vol. 82 (1982), p. 1999.
[2]P. D. W. Heberling, "Note: Justification: The Impact of the Model Penal Code on Statutory Reform," *Columbia Law Review*, Vol. 75 (1975), pp. 916.

defense, there is some adequate triggering condition that prompts the actor to violate the letter of the law. In order for the actor's responsive conduct to be justified, it must be both necessary and proportional, considering all of the circumstances.[3]

## Excuse

**excuse defenses** A group of defenses in which the defendant admits what he did was wrong but claims he should be excused from criminal liability based on the circumstances.

With **excuse defenses**, the defendant admits that what he or she did was wrong but claims that he or she should not be held responsible for the crime. Excuse defenses focus on the *actor*, not the act. The common thread running throughout excuse defenses is an argument on the defendant's part that he or she was not "normal" at the time of the crime. Note that defenses such as these provide methods of avoiding, rather than dodging, criminal liability; dodging could include fleeing the country to avoid prosecution. Also, excuse defenses, like justification defenses, are affirmative defenses that are raised at trial.

Excuse defenses can be organized into three distinct categories: "involuntary actions, actions related to cognitive deficiencies, and actions related to volitional deficiencies."[4] Involuntary actions include unwilled body movements (e.g., reflex actions, convulsions, sleep walking). Cognitive deficiencies relate to the actor's ability to know certain things, such as whether the conduct in question was right or wrong. Volitional deficiencies refer to actions that are "willed" by someone or something else. For example, if Martians tell Frank to park his car in front of a fire hydrant, then Frank suffers from a volitional deficiency. The source in this case is internal (Frank's mind). Alternatively, if Bob threatens to shoot Frank if he doesn't park his car in front of the hydrant, then Frank also suffers from a volitional deficiency, but the difference is that it is external.

## Offense Modifications

Excuse and justification defenses apply to most, but not necessarily all, types of criminal liability. For example, it would be nearly impossible to claim self-defense to the crime of burglary. One would be hard-pressed to claim that burglarizing a house serves a protective function in the sense that shooting a would-be murderer does. Instead, self-defense is claimed when a person has been threatened in such a fashion that it is necessary to take protective action.

**offense modifications** A modification of a criminal offense that shields the defendant from criminal liability.

Other so-called special defenses, or **offense modifications** apply to a small handful of crime types. Consider criminal attempt (discussed further in Chapter 7). Under the Model Penal Code, criminal attempt occurs when someone takes a significant step toward committing a criminal offense. However, the Model Penal Code says that a person is not guilty of attempt if he "abandons his effort to commit the crime or prevents it from being committed."[5] This is known as abandonment, or "renunciation." Abandonment is essentially a modification to the offense that shields the defendant from liability. Someone who takes a significant step toward committing a crime has satisfied the key elements of the crime, but the abandonment "modifies" that.

---

[3]E. R. Milhizer, "Justification and Excuse: What They Were, What They Are, and What They Ought to Be," *St. John's Law Review*, Vol. 78 (2004), pp. 812–813.
[4]Ibid., p. 818.
[5]Model Penal Code Section 20.06[G].

**de minimus infraction defense** A defense that prevents conviction if the defendant's actions were so trivial or minor in relation to the intent of the criminal law.

Another example is the ***de minimus* infraction defense**. Assume Dylan stole Alex's soccer ball, but almost immediately returned it because he found his own ball. Dylan could be convicted of larceny because he arguably intended to steal the ball and went so far as to do so, but it can also be argued that the infraction was so *de minimus* (or minor) that it "did not actually cause or threaten the harm or evil sought to be prevented by the law defining the offense or did so only to an extent too trivial to warrant the condemnation of conviction."[6]

Offense modifications operate very much like failure of proof defenses. But whereas failure of proof defenses usually focus on the prosecution's failure to prove *actus reus* and *mens rea*, offense modifications usually focus on other issues, such as whether a resulting harm occurred or whether the defendant shows that the statute does not apply to him or her. Sometimes offense modifications are even spelled out in the language of the statute. Consider these hypothetical statutes:

1. Unauthorized possession of A is a crime.
2. Possession of A is a crime. If the defendant shows authorization for the possession, there is no criminal liability.[7]

With Offense 1, the prosecution will most likely need to prove that the defendant possessed A and was unauthorized to do so. The prosecution may fail to meet this burden, in which case the defendant benefits from a failure of proof defense. With Offense 2, there is a clear "modification" in the language of the statute—namely, that the defendant will escape liability if he or she can prove authorized possession.

## Nonexculpatory Defenses

**nonexculpatory defense** Defenses unrelated to the elements of the crime or the defendant's alleged fault or guilt.

**statute of limitations** The maximum amount of time allowed by law to seek prosecution for certain crimes or offenses.

**Nonexculpatory defenses**[8] are unrelated to the elements of the crime or the blameworthiness of the defendant. *Exculpatory* means "clearing or tending to clear from alleged fault or guilt."[9] So, *non*exculpatory defenses are those unrelated to the defendant's alleged fault or guilty. According to one expert, nonexculpatory defenses "reflect the proposition that society sometimes finds competing policy considerations to be weightier than its basic interest in convicting and punishing blameworthy defendants."[10] What are some examples? One is the **statute of limitations**, or the "maximum time periods during which certain actions can be brought or rights enforced."[11] Certain crimes have no statute of limitations, but of those that do, if the prosecution brings charges outside the defined period, then it does not matter whether the defendant committed the crime; he or she cannot be convicted.

[6]Model Penal Code Section 2.12(2).
[7]R. G. Singer and J. Q. LaFond, *Criminal Law: Examples and Explanations*, 4th ed. (Boston, MA: Wolters Kluwer, 2007), p. 407.
[8]P. H. Robinson, "Criminal Law Defenses: A Systematic Analysis," *Columbia Law Review*, Vol. 82 (1982), p. 1999.
[9]*Black's Law Dictionary*, 6th ed. (St. Paul, MN: West, 1990), p. 566.
[10]Milhizer, "Justification and Excuse," p. 810.
[11]*Black's Law Dictionary*, 6th ed. (St. Paul, MN: West, 1990), p. 927.

We discussed double jeopardy in Chapter 2. It is relevant here, too, in the sense that it is also a nonexculpatory defense. If a defendant is twice prosecuted for the same offense, she cannot be convicted in the second prosecution, regardless of whether she actually committed the crime.[12] Alternatively, if the defendant is not competent to stand trial, a due process requirement, but understood what he was doing at the time of the crime, he cannot be convicted. In essence, incompetency serves as a nonexculpatory defense.[13] This is not to say, however, that the prosecution couldn't wait until the defendant is competent before pressing charges.

Nonexculpatory defenses are controversial because they can result in clearly guilty criminals going free. As Eugene Milhizer notes, "Provided that all the requirements of a nonexculpatory defense are satisfied, the defense will be allowed even if society suffers a net harm from the acquittal of a defendant in a particular case."[14] This is not unlike the operation of the exclusionary rule[15] in the criminal procedure context. If police violate the Fourth Amendment and seize evidence during an unwarranted search, the evidence will be inadmissible at trial and it may be impossible for the prosecution to meet its burden. In such a case, the defendant could well go free. See Figure 4.1 for a summary of the discussion thus far.

**Figure 4.1**

Types of Defenses

| Defense Type | What it Means |
| --- | --- |
| Failure of Proof | Prosecution fails to meet its burden of proving the elements (*actus reus* and/or *mens rea*) of the underlying offense. |
| Justification | Defendant accepts responsibility for the act he or she is charged with, but argues it was permissible under the circumstances. |
| Excuse | Defendant admits that what he or she did was wrong, but claims that he or she should not be held responsible for the crime. |
| Offense Modification | Similar to failure of proof, but either alters the charge to something less serious or the statute fails to criminalize the defendant's action. |
| Nonexculpatory Defenses | Defenses that do not clear the defendant of guilt (e.g., the statute of limitations, double jeopardy). |

---

[12]See, e.g., *United States* v. *DiFrancesco*, 449 U.S. 117 (1980), pp. 127–131; *Green* v. *United States*, 355 U.S. 184 (1957), pp. 187–188.
[13]*Pate* v. *Robinson*, 383 U.S. 375 (1966), pp. 386–387.
[14]Milhizer, "Justification and Excuse," p. 811.
[15]*Weeks* v. *United States*, 232 U.S. 383 (1914); Mapp v. *Ohio*, 367 U.S. 643 (1961).

# Perfect and Imperfect Defenses

**perfect defenses**
Defenses that result in the defendant being acquitted of the crime.

Some defenses are best viewed as **perfect defenses**. A perfect defense resul acquittal of the defendant. For example, if the defendant was justified in committing a particular crime, he or she will almost always be acquitted. This often happens with the "law enforcement" defense, which we will consider later in this chapter; police officers who justifiably kill will escape criminal conviction.

**imperfect defenses**
Defenses that result in the defendant being convicted of a lesser crime, but do not result in an acquittal.

Contrast this with an **imperfect defense**. With an imperfect defense, the defendant will be found guilty, but of a lesser crime. Earlier in this chapter, in the Failure of Proof section, we presented the hypothetical of Fred shooting John. If Fred did not intend to kill John, but nevertheless killed him, Fred's defense would be imperfect; he would most likely escape a first-degree murder conviction, but he would also likely be found guilty of some lesser homicide offense such as voluntary manslaughter.

Consider this example of a real—and successful—imperfect defense, from the state of California: Brian Robinson lived with his parents and his cousin, Charles Lambert. Late one night, as Robinson was coming home, he observed Randle emerging from Lambert's car with car stereo equipment. Robinson confronted Randle, saying he was going to "beat your ass." Randle pulled a .25-caliber pistol from his pocket and fired it several times, but Robinson was not hit. Randle and his cousin, Byron, who had helped him break into Lambert's car, fled on foot. Robinson woke Lambert and the two gave chase. They caught up to the Byron, but Randle eluded them. Robinson then began beating Byron with his fists. He recovered the stolen stereo equipment and then continued beating Byron. As he was doing so, Randle returned, shot, and killed Robinson.

Randle later testified that he fired his gun to make Robinson stop beating his cousin, meaning he committed manslaughter, not murder. The trial court did not allow the jury to consider the possibility of an imperfect defense, and Robinson was found guilty of second-degree murder. The Court of Appeal reversed and the California Supreme Court affirmed, holding that the jury should have been able to convict on manslaughter if it felt Robinson's argument had merit.[16] In other words, the jury should have been allowed to consider the imperfect "defense of others."

It is difficult, if not impossible, to know what percentage of successful defenses are of the perfect versus imperfect variety. This much can be said, however: Of those defendants who successfully claim a defense, a significant percentage do not "go free." Instead, they often find themselves convicted, just of lesser crimes.

# Reasons for Justification Defenses

We now shift our attention to justification defenses. Before getting into the specific varieties of them, however, it is important to further consider why they exist in the first place. What are the reasons for justification defenses? There are three main ones: public benefit, superior interest, and moral rights.

---

[16]People v. *Randle*, 111 P.3d 987 (2005).

# Public Benefit

**public benefit theory**
A theory underlying justification defenses based on the idea that the allegedly criminal action benefits society.

Certain otherwise criminal acts are beneficial to society. A law enforcement officer who shoots and kills a dangerous criminal is arguably *helping* the public by sparing it from further victimization. Some justification defenses are thus based on a **public benefit theory**. But there is a limitation to this public benefit. As Joshua Dressler has observed, "The benefit to society is not incidental to some self-interested goal of the actor; it is the underlying motivation for the actor's conduct."[17] In our police officer example, the rationale for "justifying" his conduct is not that he takes delight in killing criminals, but rather that he is motivated to *help society*.

More than one justification defense has the public benefit as its supporting rationale. As we will see later, there are situations in which an ordinary citizen may feel compelled to act in the public interest by, say, taking a life to protect one or more other people. Such actions won't always be justifiable, but they can be depending on the circumstances.

# Superior Interest

**superior interest theory**
A theory underlying justification defenses based on the idea that a superior interest justifies criminal conduct in some situations.

Some justification defenses are also supported by a **superior interest theory**. Simply, if there is a superior interest that justifies criminal conduct, the "criminality" of said conduct will be overlooked. Dressler cites the example of a woman who trespasses by entering another person's home in order to avoid a tornado.[18] The superior interest in this instance is the preservation of human life; clearly a human life is more valuable than someone's privacy interest.

# Moral Rights

**moral rights theory**
A theory underlying justification defenses based on the idea that an innocent person has the moral right to act for his or her own benefit in certain situations.

In some instances, otherwise criminal conduct is justified under a **moral rights theory**. If, for example, Julia shoots and kills Heather because Heather first tries to stab Julia, arguably Julia has a moral right to defend herself because of Heather's initial advance. This theory focuses on the threat that a criminal's conduct poses to an otherwise innocent person.

It is difficult to say, in this situation, that Julia's life is any more or less valuable than Heather's, which is why a superior interest view does not work well. Likewise, while there may be a public benefit to Julia killing someone like Heather, note that Julia's actions do not fit with the key limitation of public benefit theory we highlighted above: that for public benefit to occur, the actor (Julia, in this case) must have the public interest in mind when committing the crime. Arguably Julia's actions were based on her interest in preserving her own life, not helping the community. A "moral rights" theory of justification thus acts as a default, or base condition. That is, if a defendant successfully asserts a justification defense, and if there is no superior interest, and if there is no public benefit, then the otherwise criminal act is justified on moral rights grounds.

---

[17]J. Dressler, *Understanding Criminal Law*, 5th ed. (Newark, NJ: Lexis Nexis, 2009), p. 209.
[18]Ibid., p. 211.

**YOUR DECISION**

1. An intruder broke into Gregory Mason's home at 3:00 a.m. on March 15, 2010, with the intent to steal his expensive and rare coin collection. Asleep upstairs when he heard the noises in the middle of the night, Gregory, armed with a baseball bat, proceeded to beat the intruder nearly to death. He was charged with the crime of aggravated battery and is awaiting trial. Gregory is considering what options, if any, he has as a defense to the crime. If you are Gregory's defense lawyer, what type of defense would you suggest and why?

2. Brian Jones was driving under the influence of alcohol and ran into a group of pedestrians walking down the sidewalk in New York City, killing two of them. Brian feels terrible about the incident, but insists it was an "accident" and that he did not intend to harm anyone. The prosecution is charging Brian with first-degree murder, a crime that requires that the defendant act with willful, deliberate, and premeditated action. Brian believes the prosecution will have difficulty proving the *mens rea* portion of its case. What possible defense, if any, can Brian claim?

## Summary

- If the prosecution fails to meet its burden of proving the various elements of an underlying offense beyond a reasonable doubt, then the result is essentially a failure of proof defense.

- With justification defenses, the defendant accepts responsibility for the act he or she is charged with, but argues that the act was permissible under the circumstances.

- With excuse defenses, the defendant admits that what he or she did was wrong but claims that he or she should not be held responsible for the crime.

- Offense modifications operate very much like failure of proof defenses. But whereas failure of proof defenses usually focus on the prosecution's failure to prove *actus reus* and *mens rea*, offense modifications usually focus on other issues, such as whether a resulting harm occurred.

- Nonexculpatory defenses are those unrelated to the defendant's alleged fault or guilty.

- A perfect defense results in the acquittal of the defendant.

- With an imperfect defense, the defendant will be found guilty, but of a lesser crime.

- There are three main reasons for justification defenses: public benefit, superior interest, and moral rights.

- Certain otherwise criminal acts are beneficial to society.

- If there is a superior interest that justifies criminal conduct, the "criminality" of said conduct will be overlooked.

- Moral rights theory focuses on the threat a criminal's conduct poses to an otherwise innocent person.

# SELF-DEFENSE AND DEFENSE OF OTHERS

### Learning Objectives

- **Summarize the defense of self-defense.**
- **Identify recent developments have complicated the law of self-defense.**

## CORE CONCEPTS

**self-defense** A justification defense in which the defendant is permitted to act in order to prevent imminent death or bodily harm.

**Self-defense** is one of the more widely known criminal defenses. Self-defense is legal, in one form or another, in every state. And while courts have grappled with its exact meaning, they have yet to chip away at it significantly. Indeed, the right of a person to defend oneself was recently invigorated in the Supreme Court's controversial decision in *District of Columbia* v. *Heller*,[19] where the Court held that the U.S. Constitution's Second Amendment guarantees individuals the right to possess firearms, and to use such firearms for self-defense, among other activities. Similar rights are spelled out in nearly every state's constitution, underscoring the prominence of self-defense in the American system of criminal law.[20]

## Elements of Self-Defense

The claim of self-defense was first recognized under common law. The rule was that a nonaggressor was justified in using force against another if he or she reasonably believed that such force was necessary to prevent the unlawful use of force by an aggressor.[21] By extension, *deadly force* was authorized only if the unlawful force used by the aggressor was also of the deadly variety. Modern-day self-defense retains most of its common law origins, but with some twists and turns. There are four general requirements for a successful modern-day claim of self-defense: an unprovoked attack, imminent danger, absence of alternatives (also called "necessity"), and proportionality.

Before we get to each of these requirements, there is a particularly confusing aspect of self-defense that we must first address. Self-defense requires both a subjective and objective component. The subjective component is the *defendant's* belief that he or she is justified in using deadly force. The objective component is concerned with whether a *reasonable person* would belief the defendant's actions were justified under the circumstances. Self-defense will be available only when these two underlying "beliefs" are in place. Why? Consider this example: If Mary interpreted Steve's advance

[19]*District of Columbia* v. *Heller*, 554 U.S. 570 (2008).
[20]E. Volokh, "State Constitutional Rights of Self-Defense and Defense of Property," *Texas Review of Law and Politics*, Vol. 11(2007), p. 400.
[21]See, e.g., *State* v. *Gheen*, 41 S.W. 3d 598 (Mo. Ct. App. 2001), p. 606.

as a threat, when it was not, and killed him, Mary might otherwise be held liable for his death. However, if a reasonable person feels Mary did the right thing (e.g., she couldn't have known, perhaps in the heat of the moment, that Steve's advance was not threatening), then it makes sense that Mary escape criminal conviction. But just who is a "reasonable person"? Juries are usually called upon to make the determination, and many factors come into play. One court offered this clarification:

> A determination of reasonableness [of self-defense] must be based on the "circumstances" facing a defendant or his "situation." Such terms encompass more than the physical movements of the potential assailant. These terms include any relevant knowledge the defendant had about that person. They also necessarily bring in the physical attributes of all persons involved, including the defendant. Furthermore, the defendant's circumstances encompass any prior experiences he had which could provide a reasonable basis for a belief that another person's intentions were to injure or rob him or that the use of deadly force was necessary under the circumstances.[22]

## Unprovoked Attack

Self-defense is only available in the case of an unprovoked attack. So, for example, if Bob attacks Sandy, but Sandy fights back, causing Bob to kill Sandy in self-defense, Bob will not succeed with a self-defense claim because he is the initial aggressor. He set the wheels in motion and thus should not escape criminal liability for actions that would not have occurred but for his initial attack. As one court eloquently put it, "[T]he law of self-defense is designed to afford protection to one who is beset by an aggressor and confronted by a necessity not of his own making."[23]

It is not always easy to identify the initial aggressor, and it is not always clear what types of behaviors constitute aggressive actions. Consider the definition of aggressor offered in *United States* v. *Peterson*—namely, any person whose "affirmative unlawful act [is] reasonably calculated to produce an affray foreboding injurious or fatal consequences."[24] Then consider the case of *State* v. *Corchado*.[25] Corchado asked an acquaintance of his, Ventura, whether Ventura had been "fooling around" with Corchado's wife, with whom he had been separated for several years. Ventura responded with a "mean smile," whereupon Corchado slapped Ventura across the face, prompting him to draw a gun on Corchado. Corchado then drew his own gun and shot and killed Ventura. The question is, "Was Corchado the aggressor?" Given the definition we just presented, the answer is not so simple. Surely the slap was not an "affirmative unlawful act reasonably calculated to produce an affray foreboding injurious or fatal consequences." The court in this case granted Corchado a new trial, so the moral of the story is that a certain amount of aggression on both sides can still result in a successful claim of self-defense.[26]

There is one key exception to the general rule that an aggressor cannot later claim self-defense. Simply, if the aggressor *withdraws* in some fashion and later uses

---

[22]*People* v. *Goetz*, 497 N.E.2d 41 (N.Y. 1986), p. 52.
[23]*Bangs* v. *State*, 608 P.2d 1 (Alaska 1980), p. 5.
[24]*United States* v. *Peterson*, 483 F.2d 1222 (D.C. Cir. 1973), p. 1233.
[25]*State* v. *Corchado*, 453 A.2d 427 (Conn. 1982).
[26]See also *State* v. *Jones*, 665 A.2d 910 (Conn. App. Ct. 1995), pp. 913–914.

Self-defense is permissible usually only in cases of unprovoked attacks–and when danger is imminent. Use of force must be necessary and basically a last resort.

Thomas Sbampato/Photolibrary

force in self-defense, he or she may escape criminal liability. As Dressler puts it, "The initial aggressor in a conflict may purge himself of that status and regain the right of self-defense."[27] In order to succeed, however, the aggressor must not only withdraw but also communicate this fact, either "expressly or impliedly," to the intended victim.[28] Here is a simple example: Assume Trey points a 9mm pistol at David, but that David responds by pointing a .44 magnum at Trey. Seeing that he is outgunned, Trey says, "Okay, you win," and sets his gun down. If David then chambers a round, Trey may be able to claim self-defense if he is able quickly grab his pistol and shoot David. This assumes, of course, that the other self-defense requirements are in place. For example, both Trey *and* a reasonable person would have to believe that the chambering of a round represented a sufficient threat to life such that Trey was entitled to respond with deadly force.

## Imminent Danger

A successful claim of self-defense can only be made in the face of an imminent threat. This was a requirement at common law and one that has carried forward to present day with little to no alterations.[29] A threat is considered imminent if it will occur "at the moment of . . . danger."[30] If a threat has subsided, then self-defense cannot be claimed.

The imminent danger requirement is sometimes likened to "necessity," the idea that force is *necessary* in order to protect one from a threat. In many situations involving an immediate threat, force is necessary, and self-defense can be reasonably claimed. If, again, David chambers a round in his .44 magnum, Trey may feel that quick action is necessary to save his life. But what if necessity and imminent danger don't match up? In other words, what if one precedes the other? Could it be necessary to use force to *prevent* an imminent attack? Some scholars certainly think so. According to Stephen Morse, "If death or serious bodily harm in the relatively near future is a virtual certainty *and* the future attack cannot be adequately defended against when it is imminent *and* if there really are *no* reasonable alternatives, traditional self-defense . . . ought to justify the pre-emptive strike."[31]

---

[27]Dressler, *Understanding Criminal Law*, p. 227.
[28]Ibid.
[29]*Ha v. State*, 892 P.2d 184 (Alaska Ct. App. 1995), p. 191.
[30]*Sydnor v. State*, 776 A.2d 669 (Md. Ct. App. 2001), p. 675.
[31]S. J. Morse, "The 'New Syndrome Excuse Syndrome,'" *Criminal Justice Ethics*, Vol. 14 (1995), p. 3.

## Absence of Alternatives

Self-defense is typically justified when there are no alternatives. Generally speaking, if the person threatened has the option of retreat or otherwise not using force in kind, that is the option that should be pursued. In *State v. Garrison*,[32] for example, the defendant disarmed a drunken man who was arguing with the defendant's sister. The drunken man then armed himself with a knife, made a threatening advance toward the defendant, at which point the defendant shot the man and killed him. An appeals court upheld his manslaughter conviction. Why? If the defendant could disarm his victim of a gun the first time, why was he so threatened by a knife the second time?

What if the would-be victim can retreat instead of use force in kind? Should he or she be required to do so? Self-defense is typically "measured against necessity,"[33] meaning that if force is not necessary, it shouldn't be used. And if there is so much as a shadow of a doubt in the defender's mind as to whether force is justified, he or she may do well to retreat, if retreat is possible, simply to avoid the possible legal ramifications that can follow even the most justifiable of self-defense actions. That said, the law in this area is complex and contradictory—and continually evolving. Most jurisdictions do not require retreat, and many have gone so far as to enact so-called **stand your ground laws**. Florida's law, enacted in 2005, says:

> A person who is not engaged in an unlawful activity and who is attacked in any . . . place where he has a right to be has no duty to retreat and has the right to stand his or her ground and meet force with force, including deadly force if he or she reasonably believes it is necessary to prevent death or great bodily harm to himself or another or to prevent the commission of a forcible felony.[34]

Some jurisdictions disagree with either the "no retreat" rule or stand your ground laws. This minority view is that all human life deserves protection and that force shouldn't be used simply because it can be. For example, Maryland courts have long required that it is the "duty of the defendant to retreat or avoid danger if such means were within his power and consistent with his safety,"[35] as have courts in other states.[36] Of the few jurisdictions that maintain a retreat requirement, they only require it when the nonaggressor can retreat to a place of *complete* safety: "Self-defense has not, by statute nor by judicial opinion, been distorted, by an unreasonable requirement of the duty to retreat, into self-destruction."[37]

## Proportionality

Subject to a few exceptions, for self-defense to apply, the nonaggressor must use no more force than is necessary to repel the aggressor. For example, if Margie (the defendant) is 5 feet 2 inches and weighs 110 pounds, and Mike (the aggressor) is 6 feet 3 inches tall and weighs 250 pounds, it may be "necessary" for Margie to use deadly

**stand your ground rule**
A legal principle that does not require a person to retreat if that person is the victim of an unprovoked attack.

---

[32]*State v. Garrison*, 525 A.2d 498 (Conn. 1987).
[33]*State v. Abbott*, 174 A.2d 881 (N.J. 1961), p. 884.
[34]Fla. Stat. 776.013(3) (2008).
[35]*Bruce v. State*, 218 Md. 87 (1958), pp. 96–97.
[36]See, e.g., *People v. Riddle*, 649 N.W.2d 30 (Mich. 2002), p. 34.
[37]*State v. Gardner*, 104 N.W. 971 (Minn. 1905), p. 975.

force to repel Mike, even if Mike makes nothing more than an advance coupled with a threat to "tear Margie a new one." If the roles had been reversed, however, and Margie is the aggressor, then Mike would be hard-pressed to claim self-defense in the event he pulled a gun and fatally shot Margie.

Similar facts were observed in *State v. Wanrow*,[38] a case where the defendant was a small woman on crutches who shot and killed an unarmed drunk man who allegedly threatened to molest her child who was asleep a few feet away. Interestingly, Washington Supreme Court overturned the woman's conviction, partly because the jury was not allowed to hear a version of the argument that "women suffer from a conspicuous lack of access to training in and the means of developing those skills necessary to effectively repel a male assailant without resorting to the use of deadly weapons."[39] The court held that the trial judge should have instructed jurors of this "sex discrimination" because, if the judge had, they may have been inclined to sanction the woman's apparent overreaction.

## The Model Penal Code Approach

The Model Penal Code sanctions the use of (nondeadly) force in "self-protection" when "the actor believes that such force is immediately necessary for the purpose of protecting himself against the use of unlawful force by such other person on the present occasion."[40] And "unless the actor believes that such force is necessary to protect himself against death, serious bodily injury, kidnapping or sexual intercourse compelled by force or threat,"[41] deadly force is not authorized. The Code names a number of limitations that further restrict these rules, but they are mostly beyond the scope of this text.

See the accompanying Court Decision for more on self-defense. In it we take a look at the case of *Quaggin* v. *State*, where an elderly man killed an unarmed juvenile who entered his home uninvited.

**COURT DECISION**

*Quaggin* v. *State*
752 So.2d 19 (Fla. App. 2000)

**Background:** Quaggin was convicted of manslaughter in Circuit Court, Volusia County. The District Court of Appeals reversed and remanded, holding that the jury instructions were confusing and misleading.

**PER CURIAM.**

Stanley Quaggin appeals his manslaughter conviction and sentence of fifteen years in prison followed by five years of probation. We agree with Quaggin that the cumulative effect of several errors requires reversal for a new trial.

Mid-afternoon on March 16, 1997, fourteen-year-old Eric Brooks was shot and killed by seventy-six-year-old Quaggin in Quaggin's DeLand home. Eric and a friend,

---

[38]*State v. Wanrow*, 559 P.2d 548 (Wash. 1976).
[39]Ibid., p. 239.
[40]Model Penal Code Section 3.04(1).
[41]Model Penal Code Section 3.04(2)(b).

ten-year-old Jon Eidelbach, had been playing nearby and ventured onto Quaggin's property, eventually entering Quaggin's home through a sliding glass door. Quaggin was sitting in a chair in the room entered by the boys and he stood up and shot Eric, allegedly in self-defense or in the belief that Eric was a burglar.

By all accounts, Quaggin's property—both inside and out—is cluttered with piles of junk. The land around Quaggin's house contains several trailers, old parade floats (which Quaggin built), and other items. According to Jon, he and Eric were playing outdoors while his father worked at a nearby warehouse. They found some wood on Quaggin's property which they were interested in using to build a fort in the woods. They did not take the wood; rather, they assumed someone lived there and wanted to ask the owner if they could have the wood. The boys entered a few of the trailers on the property—without knocking first—and picked up a cooler bag, some comic books, and some Pez candy dispensers, planning to ask the owner for permission to take these items. ***They reached some dirty sliding glass doors and saw a light on inside; according to Jon, the light made them believe even more strongly that someone might be there. One of them opened the sliding glass doors—again, without knocking—and they went inside.

***Next, Jon testified, "A guy jumped up and he says, 'what [the] hell are you doing here,' and like maybe one second pas[sed], and he shot him. He didn't give him time to respond." Quaggin was standing over by a chair on the other side of the pile; Jon could see him once he stood up but not while he had been seated. Jon denied that either he or Eric tried to "go at" the gun or Quaggin. They did not climb on the pile or say anything back after hearing Quaggin's words; there was no time for that. After Eric was shot, he fell backward and Jon started crying. Quaggin told him to climb over the pile and put his hands on top of his head, and Jon complied. Quaggin told Jon to get the telephone, and Jon did so. Quaggin then called 911 and summoned an ambulance. Eric was pronounced dead at the scene.

***Quaggin explained that when the boys first came into the house he "couldn't determine who they were, but I saw two bodies, is all I can tell you. Two bodies." Quaggin confirmed that "basically, someone came up to [his] place, opened [his] unlocked door, and walked into [his] home." He explained that he pulled the hammer back "[b]ecause I see that the one fella, I told him to stop, and he was continuing to come toward me. . . . And I just told him to stop. In fact, I told him to stop, I don't know, three, four times."

***Quaggin explained that his home had been broken into once previously, in 1987 when he was in Alaska. He bought the gun after that incident, "for the purpose of protection. I'm all by myself. You know. And an older gentlem [a]n. I mean, what can I do?" A sheriff's investigator confirmed at trial that a police report was on file reflecting a burglary of the residence in 1987 when Quaggin was in Alaska.

On appeal, Quaggin contends, and we agree, that the instructions to the jury were confusing and that the prosecutor misstated the law to the jury. The jury was instructed as follows on justifiable use of deadly force:

> An issue in this case is whether the defendant acted in self-defense. It is a defense to the offense with which Mr. Quaggin is charged if the death of Eric Brooks resulted from the justifiable use of force likely to cause death or great bodily harm.

The use of force likely to cause death or great bodily harm is justifiable only if the defendant reasonably believes that the force is necessary to prevent imminent death or great bodily harm to himself while resisting:

1. another's attempt to murder him, or
2. any attempt to commit a burglary of any dwelling house occupied by him.

A person is justified in using force likely to cause death or great bodily harm if he reasonably believes that such is necessary to prevent

1. imminent death or great bodily harm to himself or another, or
2. the imminent commission of a burglary.

This instruction tracks the language of the standard instruction on justifiable use of deadly force. The court also instructed the jury on retreat in the home:

If the defendant was attacked in his own home or on his own premises, he had no duty to retreat and had the lawful right to stand his ground and *meet force with force*, even to the extent of using force likely to cause death or great bodily harm, if it was necessary to prevent death or great bodily harm to himself or the commission of a burglary of his dwelling (emphasis added).

This language also appears in the standard instruction on justifiable use of deadly force. Quaggin urges that the inclusion of the "meet force with force" language-to which he objected below is erroneous as to defense of burglary because "[t]he law of Florida does not require a homeowner to wait until a burglar actually uses deadly force before the homeowner uses deadly force," but rather "[a] homeowner may use deadly force, if reasonable, to stop the commission of a burglary."

\*\*\*Quaggin is correct that although the court gave standard instructions on justifiable use of force, the manner in which the instructions were given was confusing and misleading. The court did not point out to the jury that self-defense in the home and defense of burglary are separate, though similar, defenses. The "meet force with force" language—even though it comes from a standard instruction—is misleading under the facts of this case, at least without an explanation of the two defenses. The giving of an instruction regarding the reasonable appearance of danger does not cure the error.

\*\*\*REVERSED and REMANDED for a new trial.

## Case Analysis

1. What are the elements of self-defense? Does Mr. Quaggin fulfill all of the requirements?
2. Did Mr. Quaggin use excessive force under the circumstances?
3. Why does the court grant Mr. Quaggin a new trial?

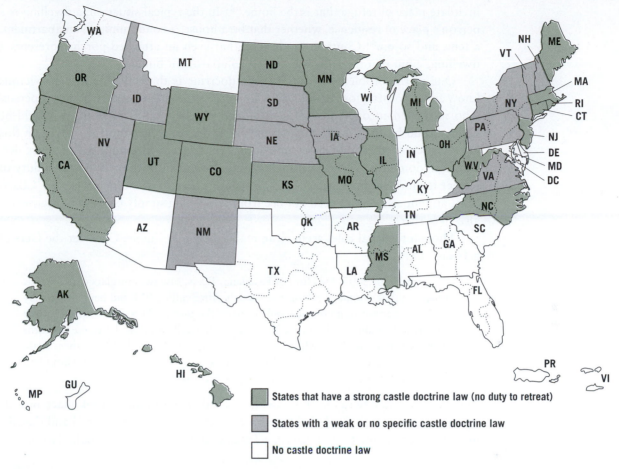

**Figure 4.2**
Castle Doctrine by State
*Sources:* D. P. Boots, J. Bihari, and E. Elliott, "The State of the Castle: An Overview of Recent Trends in State Castle Doctrine Legislation and Public Policy," *Criminal Justice Review*, Vol. 34 (2009), pp. 515–535; http://en.wikipedia.org/wiki/Castle_doctrine (accessed September 25, 2010).

## Self-Defense Complications

A number of recent developments have complicated the law of self-defense. Many states retain "castle doctrine" laws that give people great latitude to take self-defense actions within their homes. Criminal defenses such as battered woman syndrome seem, on their face, counter to traditional self-defense rationales. And finally, what is permissible in terms of self-defense against an unlawful arrest?

## The "Castle Doctrine"

**castle doctrine**
A nonaggressor is not required to retreat from his or her home if attacked.

A number of states (see Figure 4.2), even those in which retreat is the preferable action to take when someone is threatened, recognize the so-called **castle doctrine**. Simply, the castle doctrine provides that a nonaggressor is not required to retreat from his or her own dwelling.[42] The logic is that "one should not be driven from the

---

[42]D. P. Boots, J. Bihari, and E. Elliott, "The State of the Castle: An Overview of Recent Trends in State Castle Doctrine Legislation and Public Policy," *Criminal Justice Review*, Vol. 34 (2009), pp. 515–535.

inviolate place of refuge that is the home."[43] In the typical situation, a dwelling is a person's place of residence, whether that be a house, a condominium, an apartment, a tent, and so on.[44] Courts have decided that even an attached porch represents a dwelling,[45] but that the common area in an apartment building does not.[46]

One of the problems with the castle doctrine is that killers and their victims know one another most of the time. This raises the question of whether a person who is related to or acquainted with—and maybe even lives with—a would-be killer should be able to fall back on the castle doctrine. Most of the activity in this area has revolved around domestic abuse. Courts are increasingly giving more deference to domestic violence victims, arguing, for example, that "imposing a duty to retreat from the home may adversely impact victims of domestic violence."[47] Basically, an innocent victim need not flee from a dwelling simply because the aggressor also lives there.[48]

Though the legal rules seem clear, reality is not so simple. Consider the facts of a Texas case:

> In November of 2007, Joe Horn of Pasadena, Texas, saw two burglars crawling out of his neighbor's home in a Houston suburb. After calling 911 and being begged by the dispatcher not to go outside and confront the thieves, Horn responded that the new castle law allowed him to kill burglars; after telling her to hold, the operator heard two shotgun blasts. Mr. Horn shot each man in the back, killing them both. Both men were unemployed illegal immigrants from Columbia, one of whom had been deported from the U.S. 8 years prior for a cocaine offense.[49]

There are two key twists in this case, the fact that the shooting took place outside (though Texas law allows lethal force to protect a neighbor's property) and that the men were shot in the back. Even so, a Texas grand jury refused to indict Horn.

## Battered Woman Syndrome

Female victims of domestic violence who kill their partners often raise a battered woman syndrome defense. The typical situation is one in which the woman kills her partner in the heat of a fight or argument.[50] Sometimes such killings are clearly carried out in self-defense, in which case there is no need for a creative or novel claim other than straightforward self-defense. But in many situations the traditional self-defense approach does not work because, for example, the woman may shoot her husband for beating her, raising proportionality concerns. Should she then be convicted of homicide? Perhaps not. In order to address situations like this, female defendants have sought to introduce evidence of prior abuse in order to justify the actions.

---

[43]*People* v. *Aiken*, 828 N.E.2d 74 (N.Y. 2005), p. 77.
[44]*State* v. *Marsh*, 593 N.E.2d 35 (Ohio Ct. App. 1990).
[45]*People* v. *Canales*, 624 N.W.2d 439 (Mich. Ct. App. 2002).
[46]*People* v. *Hernandez*, 774 N.E.2d 198 (N.Y. 2002).
[47]*Weiand* v. *State*, 732 So.2d 1044 (Fla. 1999), p. 1052.
[48]See, e.g., *State* v. *Glowacki*, 630 HN.W.2d 392 (Minn. 2001), p. 400.
[49]Boots, Bihari, and Elliott, "The State of the Castle," *Criminal Justice Review*, Vol. 34 (2009), p. 529.
[50]H. Maguigan, "Battered Women and Self-Defense: Myths and Misconceptions in Current Reform Proposals," *University of Pennsylvania Law Review*, Vol. 140 (1991): 379, pp. 394–397.

In a minority of cases, female abuse victims kill their abusers while the abusers are asleep, passed out, or during periods of claim.[51] These situations are more complicated because they *really* run afoul of traditional self-defense concepts. Most notably, there is no imminent danger posed from an abuser who is asleep. But does this mean abuse victims must wait until their lives are threatened in order to take action? This is a tough question to answer. Courts often allow the defendant to introduce evidence of prior abuse, and some even permit expert witnesses to testify about battered woman syndrome, but there are no clear rules in this area. What's more, the case law is contradictory and confusing. Some courts have permitted juries to consider the possibility of self-defense in nonconfrontational killings.[52] Others have not.[53]

In terms of likely verdicts, victims of domestic abuse are more likely to succeed with traditional self-defense claims in confrontational killings than they are with battered woman syndrome claims in *non*confrontational killings. For example, in *State* v. *Norman*,[54] the North Carolina Supreme Court refused to sanction Judy Norman's decision to kill her abusing husband while he was asleep:

> The evidence in this case did not tend to show that the defendant reasonably believed that she was confronted by a threat of imminent death or great bodily harm . . . no harm was "imminent" or about to happen to the defendant when she shot her husband. The uncontroverted evidence was that her husband had been asleep for some time when she walked to her mother's house, returned with the pistol, fixed the pistol after it jammed and then shot her husband three times in the back of the head. The defendant was not faced with an instantaneous choice between killing her husband or being killed or seriously injured. Instead, . . . the defendant had ample time and opportunity to resort to other means of preventing further abuse by her husband. There was no action underway by the decedent from which the jury could have found that the defendant had reasonable grounds to believe either that a felonious assault was imminent or that it might result in her death or great bodily injury. Additionally, no such action by the decedent had been underway immediately prior to his falling asleep.[55]

## Resisting Unlawful Arrest

Another self-defense complication concerns the issue of whether someone can resist an unlawful arrest with force. At common law, the victim of an unlawful arrest could use as much force as necessary to resist an illegal arrest, but not deadly force.[56] If deadly force was used, what would have otherwise been murder was de-escalated to manslaughter.[57] The reason for allowing such force was that a person who was wrongfully arrested stood little chance of getting released from jail in the short term, such as via bail. The victims of wrongful arrest languished in unpleasant facilities until their trial dates.

---

[51]See, e.g., *State* v. *Norman*, 378 S.E.2d 8 (N.C. 1989).
[52]See, e.g., *State* v. *Leidholm*, 334 N.W.2d 811 (N.D. 1982).
[53]See, e.g., *State v. Stewart*, 763 P.2d 572 (Kan. 1988).
[54]*State v. Norman*, 378 S.E.2d 8 (N.C. 1989).
[55]Ibid., pp. 18–19.
[56]*People v. Curtis*, 450 P.2d 33 (Cal. 1969), p. 35.
[57]*Davis* v. *State*, 102 A.2d 816 (Md. 1954), pp. 820–821.

Just what is an unlawful arrest? There are two main types. One occurs when an officer of the law uses excessive force to effectuate the arrest. An officer who uses excessive force is, in one sense, an aggressor, entitling the would-be arrestee to respond in kind to some extent. Another type of unlawful arrest is one unsupported by proper legal justification, namely, probable cause. By definition, an arrest not supported by probable cause violates the U.S. Constitution's Fourth Amendment and is thus unlawful. Unfortunately, probable cause is a rather amorphous concept, making it difficult to identify specific situations in which it is absent.

Some states have abolished self-defense claims in this area. Courts have also increasingly denied self-defense claims in nonexcessive force resisting-arrest cases.[58] In the event that an officer uses excessive force to effect an unlawful arrest, resistance is still permissible. The Washington state Supreme Court clarified the matter thusly:

> [A]lthough a person who is being unlawfully arrested has a right . . . to use reasonable and proportional force to resist an attempt to inflict injury on him or her during the course of an arrest, that person may not use force against the arresting officers if he or she is faced only with a loss of freedom.[59]

# Defense of Others

The criminal law also recognizes a **defense of others** claim. It is essentially an extension of the defense of self-defense we just introduced. The rule is that a person is justified using force to protect another from the unlawful use of force by an aggressor.[60] Under the Model Penal Code, a defense of others claim will succeed when three conditions are met:

a. the actor would be justified under Section 3.04 in using such force to protect himself against the injury he believes to be threatened to the person whom he seeks to protect; and

b. under the circumstances as the actor believes them to be, the person whom he seeks to protect would be justified in using such protective force; and

c. the actor believes that his intervention is necessary for the protection of such other person.[61]

And while retreat is encouraged, if not required, in certain self-defense situations, the Model Penal Code adopts no such requirement in defense of other cases: A person who uses force to protect another is under no obligation to retreat—or to encourage the would-be victim to retreat—unless either would guarantee the would-be victim's complete safety.[62] Also, there is no requirement to retreat "in the other's dwelling or place of work to any greater extent than in [her] own."[63]

---

[58]See, e.g., *State* v. *Wright*, 162 S.E.2d 56 (N.C. Ct. App. 1968); *State* v. *Valentine*, 132 Wn.2d 1 (Wash. 1997).
[59]*State* v. *Valentine*, 935 P.2d 1294 (Wash. 1997), p. 21.
[60]*Commonwealth* v. *Martin*, 341 N.E.2d 885 (Mass. 1976).
[61]Model Penal Code Section 3.05(1).
[62]Ibid.
[63]Ibid.

The typical defense of others claim involves a third party intervening on behalf of a crime victim who cannot defend him- or herself. Recently, however, we have seen some atypical arguments. For example, in *State* v. *Aguillard*,[64] abortion protestors argued that they were entitled to break the law under a defense of others theory because the unborn were unable to protect themselves. The court rejected the argument:

> The "defense of others" specifically limits the use of force or violence in protection of others to situations where the person attacked would have been justified in using such force or violence to protect himself. In view of *Roe v. Wade* and the provisions of the Louisiana abortion statute, defense of others as justification for the defendants' otherwise criminal conduct is not available in these cases. Since abortion is legal in Louisiana, the defendants had no legal right to protect the unborn by means not even available to the unborn themselves.[65]

See the accompanying Court Decision for more on the defense of others. In it we take a look at the case of *People* v. *Kurr*, where a mother argued that the defense of others also applied to the protection of unborn children.

## COURT DECISION

*People* v. *Kurr*
654 N.W.2d 651 (Mich. App. 2002)

**Background:** Jaclyn Louise Kurr was convicted of voluntary manslaughter in the Circuit Court of Kalamazoo County. The Michigan Court of appeals held that defense of others extends to a mother protecting her unborn fetus and that failure to provide a jury instruction on the matter violated the defendant's constitutional rights. Reversed and remanded.

### METER, P.J.

Defendant, who killed her boyfriend, Antonio Pena, with a knife, appeals as of right from her conviction by a jury of voluntary manslaughter, M.C.L. § 750.321. The trial court sentenced her as a fourth-offense habitual offender, M.C.L. § 769.12, to five to twenty years' imprisonment. Defendant argues on appeal that she should have been allowed a jury instruction regarding the defense of others because the jurors could have concluded that she killed Pena while defending her unborn children. We agree that a defense of others jury instruction was appropriate here and therefore reverse defendant's conviction and remand this case for a new trial.

Defendant stabbed Pena on October 9, 1999. According to a Kalamazoo police officer, defendant told him that she and Pena had argued that day over Pena's cocaine use. Defendant told the officer that Pena subsequently punched her two times in the stomach and that she warned Pena not to hit her because she was carrying his babies. Defendant stated that when Pena came toward her again, she stabbed him in the chest. He died as a result of the stab wound.

---

[64]*State* v. *Aguillard*, 567 So.2d 674 (La. 1990).
[65]Ibid., p. 676.

\*\*\*At trial, defendant presented evidence of Pena's assaultive nature. Apparently, he had hit defendant on other occasions, causing her at one point to seek treatment at a hospital and stay in a domestic violence shelter. The parties also presented testimony regarding defendant's alleged pregnancy. A nurse employed with the Kalamazoo County Sheriff's Department testified that defendant had a negative pregnancy test on November 9, 1999. However, another nurse employed by the Kalamazoo County Jail testified that defendant had a positive pregnancy test on October 25, 1999, and defendant and her cellmate testified that a tissue-like discharge had appeared on defendant's sanitary napkin during the first week of November.

At the conclusion of the trial, defendant requested a jury instruction on the defense of others. See CJI2d 7.21, which states, in part, that "[a] person has the right to use force or even take a life to defend someone else under certain circumstances." Despite its earlier ruling, the trial court disallowed a defense of others instruction, noting that (1) the fetus or fetuses would have been only sixteen or seventeen weeks in gestation at the time of the stabbing and (2) according to a physician's trial testimony, a fetus under twenty-two weeks old is nonviable, i.e., it is not capable of surviving outside the mother's womb. The trial court concluded that in order for defendant to assert a defense of others theory, there had "to be a living human being existing independent of [defendant]. . . ." It stated: "[E]ven under the evidence in this case, under 22 weeks, there are no others. And, that's my theory." The trial court did allow a self-defense jury instruction.

Defendant now argues that because the trial court did not instruct the jury on the defense of others theory, she was denied her constitutional right to present a defense. In order to determine whether the court should indeed have given the defense of others instruction, we must initially decide the purely legal question whether a nonviable fetus constitutes an "other" in the context of this defense. With certain restrictions, we conclude that it does.

"In Michigan, the killing of another person in self-defense is justifiable homicide if the defendant honestly and reasonably believes that his life is in imminent danger or that there is a threat of serious bodily harm." *People v. Heflin,* 434 Mich. 482, 502, 456 N.W.2d 10 (1990). Deadly force may also be used "to repel an imminent forcible sexual penetration." *People v. Barker,* 437 Mich. 161, 163, 468 N.W.2d 492 (1991). Case law in Michigan also allows a person to use deadly force in defense of another. Traditionally, the "defense of others" concept applied solely to those persons with whom the defendant had a special relationship, such as a wife or brother. As recognized by CJI2d 7.21, however, the defense now makes no distinction between strangers and relatives with regard to its application.

We conclude that in this state, the defense should also extend to the protection of a fetus, viable or nonviable, from an assault against the mother, and we base this conclusion primarily on the fetal protection act adopted by the Legislature in 1998. This act punishes individuals who harm or kill fetuses or embryos under various circumstances. M.C.L. § 750.90a and 750.90b set forth penalties for harming a fetus or embryo during an intentional assault against a pregnant woman. M.C.L. § 750.90a punishes an individual for causing a miscarriage or stillbirth with malicious intent toward the fetus or embryo or for causing a miscarriage or stillbirth while acting "in wanton or willful disregard of the likelihood that the natural tendency of [his] conduct is to cause a miscarriage or stillbirth or great bodily harm to the embryo or fetus." M.C.L. § 750.90b punishes an individual for harming or killing a fetus or embryo during an intentional assault against a pregnant woman without regard to the individual's intent or recklessness concerning the fetus or embryo. M.C.L. § 750.90c punishes an individual for harming or killing a fetus or embryo during a grossly negligent act against a pregnant woman, again without regard to the individual's state of mind concerning the fetus or embryo.

\* \* \*Because the act reflects a public policy to protect even an embryo from unlawful assaultive or negligent conduct, we conclude that the defense of others concept does extend to the protection of a nonviable fetus from an assault against the mother.

We emphasize, however, that the defense is available *solely* in the context of an assault against the mother. Indeed, the Legislature has *not* extended the protection of the criminal laws to embryos existing outside a woman's body, i.e., frozen embryos stored for future use, and we therefore *do not* extend the applicability of the defense of others theory to situations involving these embryos.

\* \* \*We conclude that the failure to give a defense of others jury instruction deprived defendant of her due process right to present a defense. The prosecutor argues that the instructions as given were sufficient because they included a self-defense theory, which the jury rejected, and because the court allowed defendant to present testimony concerning her pregnancy in order to justify her decision to defend herself. This argument is disingenuous. Indeed, in light of the punches to defendant's stomach, the jury could have rejected defendant's self-defense theory while at the same time finding that defendant killed Pena in defense of her unborn children. There was sufficient evidence presented from which the jury could have concluded that defendant was indeed pregnant at the time of the incident. As noted, jury instructions must not exclude consideration of material issues, defenses, and theories for which there is supporting evidence. Because the jury instructions essentially excluded consideration of defendant's viable defense of others theory, a new trial is warranted.

We emphasize that our decision today is a narrow one. We are obviously aware of the raging debate occurring in this country regarding the point at which a fetus becomes a person entitled to *all* the protections of the state and federal constitutions. This issue, however, is not raised by the parties, is not pertinent to the resolution of the instant case, and does not drive our ruling today. Indeed, the issue today is straightforward: Is a nonviable fetus entitled to the protection of the laws of the state of Michigan to the extent that an individual, typically the mother, may defend the fetus during an assault against the mother? We conclude that an individual may indeed defend a fetus from such an assault and may even use deadly force if she honestly and reasonably believes the fetus to be in danger of imminent death or great bodily harm. Any other result would be anomalous, given the express policy of this state as declared by the Legislature in the fetal protection act. Because the trial court did not instruct the jury regarding the defense of others theory as requested by defendant, we reverse defendant's conviction and remand this case for a new trial.

Reversed and remanded.

## Case Analysis

1. Explain the court's holding regarding the defense of others.
2. Does the defendant also have an argument for self-defense?
3. Is the gestational age and viability of the unborn fetus relevant to the defense of others argument?

---

**YOUR DECISION**

1. Patrick O'Sullivan was an invited guest at the home of his friend, Todd Smith. Along with a group of friends, the two were playing pool, drinking beer, and watching an NFL football game. As Patrick was walking to his car to head home for the evening, he heard a fight break out in the house. As Patrick reentered the house, Todd threw kerosene on him and threatened to light him on fire. Patrick pulled out his gun and fatally shot Todd three times in the chest. Did Patrick have a duty to retreat before using force in self-defense?

2. Lily Monroe was married to John Monroe for 15 years. During that time, John consistently abused Lily both psychologically and physically. Lily was hospitalized on six different occasions as a result of John's abuse. John typically kept a loaded weapon on him at all times and Lily lived in constant fear. One evening after John had punched Lily in the face and forced her to have sexual intercourse with him, Lily decided she had had enough. Just 10 minutes after the rape occurred, as John was sitting on the couch watching a basketball game, Lily fatally shot him in the back of the head. Is Lily entitled to self-defense?

## Summary

- There are four general requirements for a successful modern-day claim of self-defense: an unprovoked attack, imminent danger, absence of alternatives, and proportionality.

- Most jurisdictions do not require retreat, and many have gone so far as to enact so-called stand your ground laws.

- The Model Penal Code sanctions use of (nondeadly) force in "self-protection" when "the actor believes that such force is immediately necessary for the purpose of protecting himself against the use of unlawful force by such other person on the present occasion." Deadly force is only authorized in limited circumstances.

- Castle doctrine laws, in the states that have them, provide that a nonaggressor is not required to retreat from his or her own dwelling before being able to use force in self-defense.

- Battered woman syndrome is a justification defense that arises mainly in domestic abuse situations.

- Battered woman syndrome rarely succeeds as a defense when the abuser is killed when he poses no immediate danger (e.g., is passed out).

- At common law, the victim of an unlawful arrest could use as much force as necessary to resist an illegal arrest, but not deadly force.
- Today, it is generally unlawful to resist arrest in nonexcessive force cases, even if the arrest itself is unlawful.
- In the event an officer uses excessive force to effect an unlawful arrest, resistance is still permissible.
- The defense of others rule holds that a person is justified using force to protect another from the unlawful use of force by an aggressor.

# MODULE 4.3 · DEFENSE OF PROPERTY AND HABITATION

### Learning Objectives

- **Distinguish between defense of habitation and defense of property.**
- **Compare and contrast "make my day" laws and the castle doctrine.**

**CORE CONCEPTS**

The old saying that "A man's home is his castle" forms the foundation for defense of property. As the court in one classic case observed,

> The house of everyone is to him his castle and fortress, as well for his defense against injury and violence, as for his repose; and although the life of a man is a thing precious and favored in law . . . if thieves come to a man's house to rob him, or murder, and the owner or his servants kill any of the thieves in defense of himself and his house, it is not felony and he shall lose nothing.[66]

Property includes not just habitation, but anything a person can claim ownership to. We will discuss each in a separate subsection because, though they overlap to some extent, there are important differences in terms of what people can do to protect their property and protect themselves in their places of habitation.

## Defense of Property

In general, a person is entitled to use *nondeadly* force to protect his or her possession of property. No more force may be used than is necessary to defend one's possessory interest in property. Also, other options should often be considered first. For example, it is advisable, if it is possible, to ask the would-be dispossessor to desist.[67]

[66]*State v. Mitcheson*, 560 P.2d 1120 (Utah 1977), p. 1122.
[67]See, e.g., *State v. Elliot*, 11 N.H. 540 (1841), pp. 544–545.

Deadly force cannot be used in defense of property. Why? Because sanctioning as much would put property interests ahead of human life. One court offered this reasoning:

> When it is said that a man may rightfully use as much force as is necessary for the protection of his person and property, it should be recollected that this rule is subject to this most important modification, that he shall not, except in extreme cases, endanger human life or do great bodily harm. It is not every right of person, and still less of property, that can lawfully be asserted, or every wrong that may rightfully be redressed by extreme remedies. There is a recklessness—a wanton disregard of humanity and social duty in taking or endeavoring to take, the life of a fellow-being, in order to save one's self from a comparatively slight wrong, which is essentially wicked, and the law abhors. You may not kill, because you cannot otherwise effect your object, although the object sought to be effected is right.[68]

Even if deadly force is the *only* option available, it cannot be used in defense of property.[69] However, deadly force may be justifiable if a defense-of-property situation evolves into a self-defense or defense of others situations. For example, assume Tammy catches Keith in the act of stealing her lawnmower and yells, "Get out of here, that's not yours!" Then assume Keith pulls out a knife and runs toward Tammy. She would likely be able to claim self-defense if she drew her gun and shot Keith. In this situation, however, she is no longer defending the lawnmower, but rather herself.

## Threatening Deadly Force

What if, in defense of your property, you simply threaten to use deadly force against the would-be dispossessor? The Supreme Court of Virginia offered an answer to this question in 2000.[70] John Douglas Alexander was charged with attempted murder after brandishing a weapon when Michael Eustler (an agent of the company that held the lien on Alexander's vehicle) repossessed Alexander's vehicle. Alexander claimed he was defending his property and was thus entitled to brandish a gun in an effort to deter, but the court disagreed, saying that "[t]he threat to use deadly force by brandishing a deadly weapon has long been considered an assault."[71] Alexander was convicted of assault.

## Defense of Habitation

People are given considerably more latitude to protect their places of habitation—even with deadly force. At common law, people were permitted to use deadly force whenever it was necessary to prevent someone from unlawfully entering the dwelling.[72] The defense could be invoked even if the intruder was unarmed and posed no threat to the

---

[68]*State* v. *Morgan*, 25 N.C. 186 (N.C. 2000), p. 193.
[69]*People* v. *Ceballos*, 526 P.2d 241 (Cal. 1974), p. 249.
[70]*Commonwealth* v. *Alexander*, 260 Va. 238 (Va. 2000).
[71]Ibid., p. 241.
[72]*State* v. *Reid*, 210 N.E.2d 142 (Ohio Ct. Ap. 1965).

dweller. As time went on, restrictions were imposed governing the defense of habitation. One approach is to limit the use of deadly force to situations in which the intruder not only enters unlawfully but also intends to injure or harm an occupant, or commit a felony therein.[73] Some jurisdictions have restricted defense of habitation even further, limiting it to situations in which either the dweller's life is threatened or a *forcible* felony, not just any felony, is likely to be committed.[74] Forcible felonies include such offenses as "murder, robbery, burglary, rape or arson."[75]

Most defense of habitation statutes are aimed at giving people the authority to *prevent* unlawful access to their dwellings. But what if the intruder has already gained access? For example, assume you wake up to find a burglar already in your house. Can you use deadly force? It would seem so, but the courts are divided. Some states do not permit deadly force in this instance—for defense of habitation.[76] Only if the situation evolves into one in which self-defense can be claimed is deadly force authorized. In contrast, some states permit deadly force for defense of habitation after the intruder has accessed the property. Illinois allows such force "to prevent or terminate" another's unlawful entry.[77] The word *terminate* is important, as it suggests the unauthorized intruder has already entered the property.

## "Make My Day" Laws

**make my day laws**
State laws that provide homeowners with considerable latitude to use force to defend their dwelling from unauthorized intruders.

Needless to say, the law surrounding defense of habitation is somewhat muddy. The rules depend on where you live. Even the statutes within specific jurisdictions are not always entirely clear. To clear up the confusion, some states have enacted so-called **make my day laws**, named after the Clint Eastwood's character, Dirty Harry Callahan, in the 1983 film *Sudden Impact*. These laws, which are similar in character to the "stand your ground" and "castle doctrine" laws discussed earlier in this chapter, give considerable latitude to people whose dwelling is entered by an unauthorized intruder. Colorado has perhaps the most "generous" statute of this sort. Its law provides:

1. The general assembly hereby recognizes that the citizens of Colorado have a right to expect absolute safety within their own homes.
2. . . . any occupant of a dwelling is justified in using any degree of physical force, including deadly physical force, against another person when that other person has made an unlawful entry into the dwelling, and when the occupant has a reasonable belief that such other person has committed a crime in the dwelling in addition to the uninvited entry, or is committing or intends to commit a crime against a person or property in addition to the uninvited entry, and when the occupant reasonably believes that such other person might use any physical force, no matter how slight, against any occupant.
3. Any occupant of a dwelling using physical force, including *deadly physical force*, in accordance with the provisions of subsection (2) of this section shall be immune from criminal prosecution for the use of such force.

---

[73]See, e.g., *State v. Pendleton*, 567 N.W.2d 265 (Minn. 1997).
[74]*Crawford v. State*, 190 A.2d 538 (Md. 1963), p. 542.
[75]Ibid.
[76]See, e.g., *State v. Brookshire*, 353 S.W.2d 681 (Mo. 1962).
[77]See N.C. Gen. Stat. Section 14-51.1 (2004); also see *People v. Stombaugh*, 284 N.E.2d 640 (Ill. 1992).

4. Any occupant of a dwelling using physical force, including deadly physical force, in accordance with the provisions of subsection (2) of this section shall be immune from any civil liability for injuries or death resulting from the use of such force.[78]

Note that Colorado's make my day law is not unlike Florida's stand your ground law discussed earlier in the self-defense section. The difference is that make my day laws are premised on a defense of habitation theory, not a self-defense theory. Note the "uninvited entry" language in Colorado's statute, whereas Florida's stand your ground law referenced protection from "death or great bodily harm."

## Spring Guns and Booby Traps

Many unauthorized entries occur in uninhabited dwellings. What, then, can a person do to protect her property while she is away? Certain standard steps, such as installation of a home security system, can be taken. But what about more extreme measures? For example, what if Caty lets her pet cobra have run of the house while she is away at work? If the snake bites an intruder, will Caty be able to claim defense of property? Probably not. This is a twist on a variety of spring gun cases. A spring gun is a gun that is set up to fire as someone attempts unlawful entry into a dwelling. In the simplest arrangement, the gun will be affixed to some sort of base and pointed toward an entry point, most likely a door. The trigger will be rigged to fire as soon as the door is opened. In general, people are not authorized to use spring guns or any other mechanical device of the sort because of the risks they pose.[79]

The most often-cited spring gun case is *People* v. *Ceballos*.[80] Don Ceballos was found guilty of assault with a deadly weapon after he aimed a .22-caliber pistol at his garage door from the inside and set it to fire if the door opened several inches. A 16-year-old boy forced open the lock on the outside of the garage door and gained entry, only to be shot in the face by the Ceballos' spring gun. A California appellate court affirmed his conviction, as did the Supreme Court of California, which offered the following in support of its decision:

> Allowing persons, at their own risk, to employ deadly mechanical devices imperils the lives of children, firemen and policemen acting within the scope of their employment, and others. Where the actor is present, there is always the possibility he will realize that deadly force is not necessary, but deadly mechanical devices are without mercy or discretion. Such devices "are silent instrumentalities of death. They deal death and destruction to the innocent as well as the criminal intruder without the slightest warning. The taking of human life [or infliction of great bodily injury] by such means is brutally savage and inhuman."[81]

It is important to note that no one was home. Had the home been occupied, then the situation would have been different. Most likely, a self-defense or defense of habitation issues would have arose.

---

[78]Col. Rev. Stat. Section 18-1-704.5.
[79]*People* v. *Ceballos*, 526 P.2d 241 (Cal. 1974), p. 244.
[80]Ibid.
[81]Ibid, p. 244; quoting *State* v. *Plumlee*, 149 So. 425 (La 1933), p. 430.

# The Model Penal Code Approach

The Model Penal Code allows *nondeadly* force in defense of property when the actor believes such force is *immediately necessary* to

1. prevent or terminate an unlawful entry or other trespass upon land or a trespass against or the unlawful carrying away of tangible, movable property . . ., or

2. to effect an entry or re-entry upon land or to retake tangible movable property, provided that the actor believes that he or the person by whose authority he acts . . . is entitled to possession.[82]

To retake property, the force used must be immediate or on "fresh pursuit after such dispossession." As long as the actor "believes that the person against whom he uses force has no claim of right to the possession of the property," the Model Penal Code gives property owners considerable latitude to not only defend their property, but also go and get it back. They are not allowed to trespass on the property of the dispossessor, however, unless not doing so would pose an "exceptional hardship." The Code also names some specific situations in which nondeadly force is prohibited, even when the aforementioned conditions are in place.[83]

As for deadly force, the Model Penal Code prohibits it in defense of property, subject to two exceptions. First, deadly force is authorized against an intruder if the actor believes the intruder is seeking to dispossess him of his dwelling, the intruder has no claim of access to the property, and the force is immediately necessary.[84] Second, deadly force is authorized if "the person against whom the force is used is attempting to commit or consummate arson, burglary, robbery, or other felonious theft or property destruction"[85] and provided that the intruder has used or threatened deadly force and that the use of nondeadly force as an alternative would pose significant risk to the person whose property is targeted. This gives considerable latitude to those who would claim defense of property after using deadly force against an unauthorized intruder. Why? If a robber points a toy gun at his intended victim, and the victim knows it's a toy, the victim would nevertheless be permitted to use deadly force to prevent the robber from "consummating" or completing his crime.

**YOUR DECISION**

1. Woody loaned his neighbor, Jed, $5,000 to buy a new John Deere tractor. On payday, Jed went to the local bar to pay Woody back for his generosity. Woody was nowhere to be found, so Jed left the cash with a mutual friend, Luke. Unfortunately, Luke decided to take the $5,000 and spend it on beer, women, and gambling. Furious about his lost money, Woody threatened to break Luke's legs if he didn't return the $5,000 as soon as possible. Woody was arrested for extortion. Can he use the defense of property to avoid a conviction?

---

[82]Model Penal Code Section 3.06(1)(b).
[83]See, e.g., Model Penal Code Section 3.06(3)(a)(iii).
[84]Ibid., Section 3.06(3)(d)(i).
[85]Ibid., Section 3.06(3)(d)(ii).

2. Jimmy Daniels lives in an isolated corner of Colorado. With the nearest police station over 100 miles away, Jimmy always has a loaded shotgun next to his bedside for protection. One evening, Jimmy hears noises in his backyard. He sees two teenagers attempting to break into a barn, which is approximately 50 yards from his house, where he stores his classic cars. Jimmy runs out into his backyard and shoots and kills both teenagers. Can Jimmy use the Colorado "Make My Day" law? Why or why not?

## Summary

- In general, a person is entitled to use *nondeadly* force to protect his or her possession of property. No more force may be used than is necessary to defend one's possessory interest in property. Deadly force cannot be used in defense of property.
- People are given considerably more latitude to protect their places of habitation—even with deadly force.
- Some states have enacted so-called make my day laws that sanction deadly force in protection of habitation.
- The difference between the castle doctrine and make my day laws is that the latter are premised on a defense of habitation theory, not a self-defense theory.
- In general, people are not authorized to use spring guns or any other mechanical device of the sort in defense of property or habitation situations.

**MODULE**

## 4.4  LAW ENFORCEMENT

### *Learning Objective*
- **Explain the law enforcement defense.**

**CORE CONCEPTS**

**law enforcement defense**
Defense available to police or other authorized agents for actions committed in the course of law enforcement.

The **law enforcement defense** extends only to those people tasked with and legally authorized to enforce laws. More often than not, those people are police officers or their equivalents. In some limited situations private persons may be authorized to enforce the law—and thus benefit from a law enforcement defense if they succeed in doing so. For example, the common law authorizes people to make "citizen arrests" for certain crimes committed in their presence. In such instances, the arresting citizen may be charged with false imprisonment, but if he can convince a court that the arrest was justified under the circumstances, he will likely escape criminal liability.

Citizen enforcement activities have been somewhat curtailed over the years. Today, the right of citizens to use deadly force for crime prevention purposes—or to effect and arrest—is limited to forcible and otherwise "atrocious" felonies.[86] Why? Lawmakers are justifiably (no pun intended) concerned with "uncontrolled vigilantism and anarchistic actions . . . [and] the danger of death or injury of innocent persons at the hands of untrained volunteers using firearms."[87] More latitude is given to citizens with respect to using nondeadly force, but the law varies from place to place. Our concern here is mostly with the law enforcement defense as it is extended to sworn peace officers, federal, state, and local.

The law enforcement defense is different from other justification defenses. In self-defense situations, for example, the defendant goes on trial and claims self-defense at trial—prosecutors often default to criminal charges. In contrast, law enforcement officials who use nondeadly or deadly force rarely go on trial. When an officer discharges her gun, an internal departmental investigation most likely takes place. Only in cases where it is fairly clear the officer was "in the wrong" will criminal charges be filed. Much of the discussion surrounding the law enforcement defense, then, hinges on the constitutionality of the officer's conduct. Two key Supreme Court decisions offer guidance. They are discussed in the next two subsections.

## Nondeadly Force

Law enforcement officials are authorized to use nondeadly force to prevent a crime, stop a crime while it is being committed, or make an arrest. The Supreme Court's 1989 decision in *Graham* v. *Connor*[88] set the standard for evaluating nondeadly force claims. The Court held that

> all claims that law enforcement officers have used excessive force—deadly or not—in the course of an arrest, investigatory stop, or other "seizure" of a free citizen should be analyzed under the Fourth Amendment and its "reasonableness" standard.

The Court also said that whether deadly force has been used appropriately should be judged from the perspective of a reasonable officer on the scene and not with the benefit of 20/20 hindsight. The justices wrote, "The calculus of reasonableness must embody allowance for the fact that police officers are often forced to make split-second judgments—in circumstances that are tense, uncertain, and rapidly evolving—about the amount of force that is necessary in a particular situation."[89]

In helping to decide what a reasonable police officer would do, courts need to consider three factors: the severity of the crime; whether the suspect poses a threat; and whether the suspect is resisting and/or attempting to flee the scene. Generally, if the crime in question is a serious one, and the suspect is dangerous or resists arrest, the suspect will have difficulty prevailing with an excessive force claim.

---

[86]See, e.g., *Laney* v. *State*, 361 S.E.2d 841 (Ga. Ct. App. 1987); *Holmes* v. *State*, 543 S.E.2d 688 (Ga. 2001).
[87]*Commonwealth* v. *Klein*, 363 N.E.2d 1313 (Mass. 1977), pp. 1317–1318.
[88]*Graham* v. *Connor*, 490 U.S. 386, 396–397 (1989).
[89]Ibid.

When arresting suspects, police officers must take care to ensure that force is not used inappropriately. Laws, court decisions, and agency policy spell out use of force standards.

Jack Dagley Photography/ Shutterstock.com

# Deadly Force

The 1985 U.S. Supreme Court case of *Tennessee* v. *Garner*[90] specified the conditions under which deadly force could be used in the apprehension of suspected felons. Edward Garner, a 15-year-old suspected burglar, was shot to death by Memphis police after he refused their order to halt and attempted to climb over a chain-link fence. In an action initiated by Garner's father, who claimed that his son's constitutional rights had been violated, the Court held that the use of deadly force by the police to prevent the escape of a fleeing felon could be justified only where the suspect could reasonably be thought to represent a significant threat of serious injury or death to the public or to the officer and where deadly force is necessary to effect the arrest. In reaching its decision, the Court declared that "[t]he use of deadly force to prevent the escape of *all* felony suspects, whatever the circumstances, is constitutionally unreasonable."[91]

More specifically, the U.S. Supreme Court ruled that deadly force may be used when two criteria are present: (1) It is necessary to prevent the suspect's escape, and (2) the officer has probable cause to believe the suspect poses a serious threat of death or serious physical injury to other people or police officers. Three justices dissented, noting that the statute struck down by the majority "assist[s] the police in apprehending suspected perpetrators of serious crimes and provide[s] notice that a lawful police order to stop and submit to arrest may not be ignored with impunity."[92] In any case, to further grasp the reach of *Garner*, it is important to consider the notion of what kind of offender poses a "serious threat." Courts will generally consider present and/or past dangerousness.

---

[90]*Tennessee* v. *Garner*, 471 U.S. 1 (1985).
[91]Ibid., p. 11.
[92]Ibid., p. 28.

## Present Dangerousness

According to Victor Kappeler, "[a] dangerous suspect is, generally, an armed suspect who can inflict serious physical harm."[93] Accordingly, suspects who are armed with a deadly weapon, be it a gun, knife, or other device, can safely be considered dangerous. Moreover, the weapon must be capable of inflicting death or serious bodily harm. Fingernail clippers, for example, cannot be considered a deadly weapon.

It is not enough that the suspect be merely armed for deadly force to be justifiably used. In addition, the danger posed by the suspect must be *immediate*. If, for example, the suspect is armed with a gun, the gun must be pointed at a police officer or some other individual. Deadly force may not be considered justified if the suspect's hand is not raised into the shooting position. In one illustrative case, one of the federal district courts concluded that the police used deadly force inappropriately when

> Hegarty repeatedly asked the officers to leave, but she neither threatened them nor did she fire any shots while the officers were present. In fact, the officers decided to enter Hegarty's home forcibly only after it appeared that she had put down her rifle. Hegarty did not threaten injury to herself at any time, nor were there other individuals in danger.[94]

## Past Dangerousness

A suspect can also pose a serious threat based on his or her past conduct—that is, based on the nature of the crime in question. It is easier to defend deadly force against suspects who have committed murder, armed robbery, and similar offenses, in contrast to less serious offenses such as burglary or motor vehicle theft. These less serious offenses, in general, do not enhance the police authority to use deadly force.

It should be emphasized that only a handful of courts have permitted deadly force based solely on past dangerousness, and the U.S. Supreme Court has never sanctioned such action. In fact, a federal circuit court of appeals has held that the use of deadly force to apprehend a suspect charged with a serious crime is unconstitutional.[95] For example, if a suspect committed robbery but was then confronted by the police and, following their orders, raised his hands, he could not then be shot.

Finally, if police are going to defend deadly force based on past dangerousness, then the serious offense that the suspect is alleged to have committed must have been committed in close temporal proximity to the deadly force. In other words, officers should avoid deadly force if too much time elapsed between the crime and the deadly force. For example, if a police officer used deadly force based solely on the fact that a suspect committed homicide several months ago, the officer's actions will probably be considered unconstitutional. This is especially true if other methods besides the use of deadly force could be used to apprehend the suspect.

---

[93]V. E. Kappeler, *Critical Issues in Police Civil Liability*, 3rd ed. (Prospect Heights, IL: Waveland, 2001), p. 72.
[94]*Hegarty* v. *Somerset County*, 848 F. Supp. 257 (1994), p. 257.
[95]*Hemphill* v. *Schott*, 141 F.3d 412 (1998).

**Figure 4.3**
Federal Deadly Force
Policy

*Defense of life.* Agents may use deadly force only when necessary—that is, only when they have probable cause to believe that the subject poses an imminent danger of death or serious physical injury to the agent or to others.

*Fleeing subject.* Deadly force may be used to prevent the escape of a fleeing subject if there is probable cause to believe that the subject has committed a felony involving the infliction or threatened infliction of serious physical injury or death and that the subject's escape would pose an imminent danger of death or serious physical injury to the agents or to others.

*Verbal warnings.* If feasible, and if doing so would not increase the danger to the agent or to others, a verbal warning to submit to the authority of the agent should be given prior to the use of deadly force.

*Warning shots.* Agents may not fire warning shots.

*Vehicles.* Agents may not fire weapons solely to disable moving vehicles. Weapons may be fired at the driver or other occupant of a moving motor vehicle only when the agent has probable cause to believe that the subject poses an imminent danger of death or serious physical injury to the agent or to others and when the use of deadly force does not create a danger to the public that outweighs the likely benefits of its use.

*Source:* John C. Hall, "FBI Training on the New Federal Deadly Force Policy," *FBI Law Enforcement Bulletin* (April 1996), pp. 25–32.

## Federal Policy

In 1995, following investigations into the actions of federal agents at the deadly siege of the Branch Davidian compound at Waco, Texas, and the deaths associated with a 1992 FBI assault on antigovernment separatists in Ruby Ridge, Idaho, the federal government announced that it was adopting an "imminent danger" standard for the use of deadly force by federal agents. The imminent danger standard restricts the use of deadly force to those situations in which the lives of agents or others are in danger. When the new standard was announced, federal agencies were criticized for taking so long to adopt them. The federal deadly force policy, as adopted by the FBI, contains five specific elements.[96] They appear in Figure 4.3.

## Model Penal Code

The Model Penal Code gives peace officers the usual authority to use deadly and nondeadly force to prevent crime and make arrests.[97] Considerably less latitude is afforded to ordinary citizens. The Code allows an ordinary citizen to use force to prevent another person from (a) committing suicide, (b) inflicting serious harm on himself, (c) committing a "crime involving or threatening bodily injury, damage to or

---

[96]John C. Hall, "FBI Training on the New Federal Deadly Force Policy," *FBI Law Enforcement Bulletin* (April 1996), pp. 25–32.
[97]Model Penal Code Section 3.07.

loss of property, or (d) breaching the peace.[98] Force is also authorized to make an arrest. So, a citizen can use force to make an arrest—or assist a peace officer in making an arrest—provided that the force is immediately necessary or helps prevent the suspect's escape, and provided that the arrestee is notified, if possible, of the purpose of the arrest.

Ordinary citizens are not authorized to use deadly force, unless (a) the citizen "is authorized to act as a peace officer or is assisting a person whom he believes to be authorized to act as a peace officer," (b) the crime in question is a felony, (c) there is no "substantial risk of injury to innocent persons" and "the crime for which the arrest is made involved conduct including the use or threatened use of deadly force" or "there is a substantial risk that the person to be arrested will cause death or serious bodily injury if his apprehension is delayed."[99]

**YOUR DECISION**

1. Paul Matthews was a private security guard at the Quick-E-Mart grocery store in Compton, California. One afternoon while Paul was on duty, two armed men entered the store and demanded money from the cashier. Armed only with pepper spray, Paul was initially paralyzed with fear and unable to respond. As the criminals were fleeing from the store, however, they also decided to take Paul's new iPad. Fearing the criminals would escape with his iPad before the police arrived, Paul chased after the gunmen, sprayed them with pepper spray, wrestled one of the guns away, and shot both men. Can Paul use a law enforcement defense?

2. Officer John Smithers was a rookie police officer on his first night shift in a notoriously bad part of town. Officer Smithers witnessed what he believed to be a group of youths burglarizing a home. He saw three teenage boys carrying a large flat screen television from an apartment building at 2:00 a.m. Officer Smithers approached the group and yelled, "Stop! Police!" The youths dropped the television and began to run. Officer Smithers fired two warning shots in the direction of the teenagers. As he was not a great shot in the dark, one shot accidentally struck a fleeing teenager in the leg. Has Officer Smithers violated any laws? Is he entitled to the law enforcement defense?

## Summary

- The law enforcement defense extends only those people tasked with and legally authorized to enforce laws. More often than not, those people are police officers or their equivalents.

- Today, the right of citizens to use deadly force for crime prevention purposes—or to effect and arrest—is limited to forcible and otherwise "atrocious" felonies.

- Law enforcement officials are authorized to use nondeadly force to prevent a crime, stop a crime while it is being committed, or make an arrest.

[98]Ibid., Section 3.07(5).
[99]Ibid., Section 3.07(2)(b).

- The Supreme Court's 1989 decision in *Graham* v. *Connor* set the standard for evaluating nondeadly force claims.
- The 1985 U.S. Supreme Court case of *Tennessee* v. *Garner* prohibited the use of deadly force against unarmed fleeing felons.

# MODULE

# 4.5     NECESSITY AND CONSENT

### *Learning Objectives*
- **Describe the necessity defense.**
- **Explain the defense of consent.**

## CORE CONCEPTS

**necessity or choice of evils defense** A justification defense in which the defendant commits a crime out of necessity or to avoid a greater evil.

**consent** A justification defense in which the victim voluntarily agrees to physical contact with the defendant, such as in the case of rape.

Two additional justification defenses are necessity and consent. The **necessity** defense, also called the **choice of evils** defense, justifies certain types of criminal activity when it cannot be avoided. The defense of **consent** involves the victim consenting to physical contact or activity with the defendant.

## Necessity

In general, for a defense of necessity to succeed, five conditions must be in place:

1. a threat of
2. imminent injury to [a] person or property
3. for which there are no (reasonable) alternatives except the commission of the crime;
4. the defendant's acts must prevent an equal or more serious harm; [and]
5. the defendant must not have created the conditions of his own [doing].[100]

A defense of necessity will likely succeed, for example, if a person drives on a suspended license, a relatively minor crime, to take a sick loved one to the hospital.[101] Note that the choice here is not a choice between *crimes*, as failure to take a loved one to the hospital is not necessarily criminal (although it could be, especially if there is a degree of negligence on the part of the loved one). Likewise, a woman who forges a check in order to obtain food out of economic necessity does not commit a crime if she goes without food. Yet some courts have noted that "economic necessity alone cannot support a choice of crime,"[102] so whether the defense will succeed depends heavily on the circumstances of the case.

---

[100]Singer and LaFond, *Criminal Law: Examples and Explanations*, p. 429.
[101]*State* v. *Baker*, 579 A.2d 479 (Vt. 1990).
[102]*People* v. *Fontes*, 89 P.3d 484 (Colo. App. 2003).

## Necessity and Homicide

Can homicide be justified on necessity grounds? In the movie *Outbreak*, starring Dustin Hoffman and Morgan Freeman, many residents of a small town were infected with a virulent strain of the Ebola virus. Military officials authorized a bomb drop that would have wiped out the town, thus ensuring the virus could not spread. Though the bombing was not ultimately carried out, assume that it had. Would the killing of a few have been justified on the grounds that millions, if not billions, of lives could have been saved? This may seem like the stuff of Hollywood, but similar dilemmas have arisen in some classic cases.

For example, in the 1884 case of *Regina* v. *Dudley and Stephens*,[103] three men and a boy were stranded at sea in a lifeboat. After the boy became ill from drinking seawater, and after assuming they would not be saved any time soon, the men killed the boy to eat his flesh so they could survive. Four days later, they were saved. They raised a defense of necessity, but they were convicted of murder and sentenced to death; however, their sentences were ultimately reduced to six months' imprisonment. In another classic case, 14 passengers were thrown out of a lifeboat because it began to sink.[104] The survivors were prosecuted for murder, but ultimately convicted of manslaughter. Again, the necessity defense failed (at least as a perfect defense).

See the accompanying Court Decision for more on the defense of necessity. In it, we take a look at the case of *Commonwealth* v. *Leno*, decided in 1993.

## COURT DECISION

*Commonwealth v. Harry W. Leno, Jr., et al.*
616 N.E.2d 453 (Mass. 1993)

**Background:** Defendants were convicted of unauthorized possession and distribution of instruments to administer controlled substances in the District Court of Essex County. On direct appeal, the Supreme Court of Massachusetts held that defendants were not entitled a jury instruction on the defense of necessity.

Massachusetts is one of ten States that prohibit distribution of hypodermic needles without a prescription. G.L. c. 94C, §§ 27, 38 (1990 ed.). In the face of those statutes the defendants operated a needle exchange program in an effort to combat the spread of acquired immunodeficiency syndrome (AIDS). As a result, the defendants were charged with and convicted of (1) unauthorized possession of instruments to administer controlled substances, and (2) unlawful distribution of an instrument to administer controlled substances, in violation of G.L. c. 94C, § 27 (1990 ed.). On appeal, the defendants challenge the judge's refusal to instruct the jury on the defense of necessity. We allowed the defendants' application for direct appellate review. We affirm.

We set forth the relevant facts. In June, 1991, the defendants were arrested and charged with sixty-five counts of unauthorized possession of hypodermic needles

---

[103] *Regina* v. *Dudley and Stephens*, 14 Q.B.D. 273 (1884).
[104] *United States* v. *Holmes*, 26 F.Cas. 360 (C.C.E.D. Pa. 1842).

and fifty-two counts of unauthorized possession of syringes. Each defendant also was charged with one count of distributing an instrument for the administration of a controlled substance. The defendants told the police they were exchanging clean syringes and needles for dirty, possibly contaminated, ones to prevent the spread of AIDS.

\*\*\*The two defendants legally purchased new sterile needles over-the-counter in Vermont. The defendants were at a specific location on Union Street in Lynn from 5 P.M. to 7 P.M. every Wednesday evening in 1991 until they were arrested June 19. They accepted dirty needles in exchange for clean needles; they exchanged between 150 and 200 needles each night, for fifty to sixty people. The defendants did not charge for the service or for the materials.

\*\*\*Kathleen Gallagher, director of the AIDS surveillance program of the Massachusetts Department of Public Health, testified that AIDS is a very serious epidemic in Massachusetts and elsewhere, that the AIDS fatality rate is "essentially 100%," that so far more than 5,000 people in Massachusetts were diagnosed as having AIDS, and that many more are infected by HIV but are still asymptomatic. In 1991, 31% of new AIDS cases were intravenous drug users. When sexual partners and children were included, 38% of AIDS cases were associated with intravenous drug use. Fifty percent of Massachusetts women with AIDS contracted the disease through intravenous drug use.

\*\*\**Discussion.* The defendants do not deny that they violated the provisions of the statutes restricting the possession and distribution of hypodermic needles; rather, they contend that the judge's refusal to instruct the jury on the defense of necessity was error. We disagree.

"[T]he application of the defense [of necessity] is limited to the following circumstances: (1) the defendant is faced with a clear and imminent danger, not one which is debatable or speculative; (2) the defendant can reasonably expect that his [or her] action will be effective as the direct cause of abating the danger; (3) there is [no] legal alternative which will be effective in abating the danger; and (4) the Legislature has not acted to preclude the defense by a clear and deliberate choice regarding the values at issue." *Commonwealth v. Schuchardt,* 408 Mass. 347, 349 (1990). "A defendant is entitled to an instruction on necessity 'only if there is evidence that would warrant a reasonable doubt whether [the defendants' actions were] justified as a choice between evils.'" *Schuchardt, supra* 408 Mass. at 349. We have emphasized that a person asserting the necessity defense must demonstrate that the danger motivating his or her unlawful conduct is imminent, and that he or she acted out of necessity at all times that he or she engaged in the unlawful conduct. The analysis of whether a danger is imminent does not call for a comparison of competing harms.

The defense of justification by necessity is not applicable unless a person is "faced with a clear and imminent danger, not one which is debatable or speculative." *Commonwealth v. Schuchardt, supra* 408 Mass. at 349. "[T]he 'competing harms' defense exonerates one who commits a crime under the 'pressure of circumstances'. . . ." *Commonwealth v. Hutchins, supra* 410 Mass. at 730.

The prevention of possible future harm does not excuse a current systematic violation of the law in anticipation of the eventual over-all benefit to the public. The defendants did not show that the danger they sought to avoid was clear and imminent, rather than debatable or speculative. The defense of necessity "[does] not deal with nonimminent or debatable harms . . . [it is inapplicable when] the hazards are long term, [and] the danger is not imminent." *Brugmann, supra* at 378, 433 N.E.2d 457. That some States prohibit the distribution of hypodermic needles without a prescription, and others do not, merely indicates that the best course to take to address the long-term hazard of the spread of AIDS remains a matter of debate.

The defendants' argument is that, in their view, the prescription requirement for possession and distribution of hypodermic needles and syringes is both ineffective and dangerous. The Legislature, however, has determined that it wants to control the distribution of drug-related paraphernalia and their use in the consumption of illicit drugs. That public policy is entitled to deference by courts. Whether a statute is wise or effective is not within the province of courts. "It is not for this court to judge the wisdom of legislation or to seek to rewrite the clear intention expressed by the statute." *Mellor v. Berman*, 390 Mass. 275, 283 (1983). "Our deference to legislative judgments reflects neither an abdication of nor unwillingness to perform the judicial role; but rather a recognition of the separation of powers and the 'undesirability of the judiciary substituting its notions of correct policy for that of a popularly elected Legislature.'" *Lammi, supra* 386 Mass. at 300, 435 N.E.2d 360.

Citizens who disagree with the Legislature's determination of policy are not without remedies. "[T]he popular initiative is coextensive with the Legislature's law-making power under Part II, c. 1, § 1. . . ." *Paisner v. Attorney Gen.*, 390 Mass. 593, 601 (1983). Thus, the defendants did not meet the requirement that there be no legal alternative to abate the danger.

The defendants argue that the increasing number of AIDS cases constitutes a societal problem of great proportions, and that their actions were an effective means of reducing the magnitude of that problem; they assert that their possession, transportation and distribution of hypodermic needles eventually will produce an over-all reduction in the spread of HIV and in the future incidence of AIDS. The defendants' argument raises the issue of jury nullification, not the defense of necessity. We decline to require an instruction on jury nullification. "We recognize that jurors may return verdicts which do not comport with the judge's instructions. We do not accept the premise that jurors have a right to nullify the law on which they are instructed by the judge, or that the judge must inform them of their power.

*Judgments affirmed.*

LIACOS, Chief Justice (concurring).

I agree with the court that the judge was not required to instruct the jury on the defense of necessity. I write separately for two reasons.

First, I reiterate my concern (not implicated by the facts of this case) that evidence of necessity not be excluded by a motion in limine once a defendant has made a sufficient offer of proof. Even though a defendant ultimately may not be entitled to an instruction on the necessity defense, the presentation of evidence regarding necessity allows the jury to fulfil their vital functions of "temper[ing] the application of strict rules of law by bringing the common sense judgment of a group of laymen to the case [and] stand[ing] as a check on arbitrary enforcement of the law" (footnote omitted). *Commonwealth v. Hood, supra* at 597, 452 N.E.2d 188 (Liacos, C.J., concurring).

Second, although the harm at issue here is "nonimminent" and "debatable" for purposes of the defense of necessity, the overwhelming and uncontroverted expert evidence presented at trial describing the effectiveness of needle exchange programs in curbing the spread of AIDS will, I hope, indicate to the Legislature the importance of joining the vast majority of jurisdictions that have decriminalized possession and distribution of hypodermic syringes. In the words of Dean Roscoe Pound: "Law must be stable, and yet it cannot stand still." R. Pound, Interpretations of Legal History 1 (1923).

## Case Analysis

1. The defendants are alleging a right to the necessity or choice of evils defense. What are the two "evils" at issue in this case?

2. What was the majority's holding in the case?

3. Explain Chief Justice Liacos's concurrence.

## Model Penal Code

The Model Penal Code recognizes a "choice of evils" defense.[105] Criminal conduct will be justified if

1. The offender believes the crime is necessary to avoid harm to himself or others,

2. The harm to be avoided is greater than the harm committed by the crime, and

3. There is no legislative language that excludes such conduct.[106]

The first two requirements are straightforward. The third one requires some clarification. It simply means that the defense will not be available if the law explicitly prohibits the necessity-based criminal conduct. For example, assume a car is involved in a hit-and-run and that the passenger is severely injured. Instead of waiting at the scene (with the other driver) for police to arrive, as the law requires, the first driver leaves for the hospital so the passenger can get treatment. This would seem a justifiable act of necessity, but if the law explicitly requires drivers to stay at the scene of the accident *and* they cannot leave under any circumstances, even to seek treatment for an injured passenger, then the Model Penal Code would not afford the first driver a necessity defense.

---

[105]Model Penal Code Section 3.02(1).
[106]Ibid.

By participating in organized sports, the players consent to certain contact between players.

Matthew Jacques/Shutterstock.com

## Consent

The defendant's actions may be justified in certain circumstances if the victim consented to the activity or physical contact. Consent *may* serve as justification in four situations:

1. No serious injury results.

2. The injury happens in a sporting event.

3. The consenting party benefits from the conduct in question (e.g., a doctor performs surgery on a consenting patient).

4. The conduct is sexual.[107]

Importantly, consent can serve as a justification defense for these actions, but only if it is:

1. Given by someone who is legally competent to give consent (i.e., of proper age),

2. Fully understood (e.g., the person giving consent does not suffer from a mental disease or defect), and

3. Voluntary (not induced by force or deception).

Courts are hesitant to excuse criminal conduct with a successful consent defense. For example, in *State* v. *Hiott*,[108] Richard Hiott was convicted of third-degree assault after his friend, Jose, was hit in the eye while the two were shooting BB guns at each other. Hiott claimed that Jose consented, that the two were shooting guns at each other voluntarily, and that they were engaged in a legitimate game. An appellate court disagreed, holding that "[s]hooting BB guns at each other is not a generally accepted game or athletic contest; the activity has no generally accepted rules; and the activity is not characterized by the common use of protective devices or clothing."[109]

---

[107]G. Fletcher, *Rethinking Criminal Law* (Boston, MA: Little, Brown, 1978), p. 770.
[108]*State* v. *Hiott*, 987 P.2d 135 (Wash. App. 1999).
[109]Ibid.

1. Kathy and Mark set off in late fall on a romantic camping trip on the Appalachian Trail. Mark, however, was not very skilled at camping and forgot to pack any type of tent or sleeping bag. As night fell, the two began to fear they would freeze to death without shelter. They stumbled upon a small cabin and broke a window to gain entry. Once inside, they started a fire, helped themselves to a few cans of SPAM and beans, and drank a bottle of fine aged scotch they found in the pantry. A neighbor noticed the smoke from the chimney and called the police. Mark and Kathy were charged with trespassing. Are they entitled to the choice of evils defense?

2. Every week Michael played in a game of intramural football with his college friends as his team's quarterback. One afternoon while playing in the intramural championship game, a particularly aggressive linebacker named Ray picked Michael off the ground and threw him violently onto the turf. As a result of the encounter, Keith fumbled the ball and he suffered a severe concussion. The referee flagged Ray with a penalty for his conduct. The police are also considering charging Ray with battery. You are Ray's lawyer. In response to the potential charges, Ray has simply stated, "That's football." Is Ray entitled to any defenses? Why or why not?

## Summary

- The necessity defense, also called the choice of evils defense, justifies certain types of criminal activity when it cannot be avoided.

- For a defense of necessity to succeed, five conditions must be in place: "(1) a threat of (2) imminent injury to [a] person or property (3) for which there are no (reasonable) alternatives except the commission of the crime; (4) the defendant's acts must prevent an equal or more serious harm; [and] (5) the defendant must not have created the conditions of his own [doing]."[110]

- Claims of necessity generally fail in cases of homicide.

---

[110]Singer and LaFond, *Criminal Law: Examples and Explanations*, p. 429.

# Chapter Review

MODULE **4.1**

## JUSTIFICATION DEFENSES IN CONTEXT

### Learning Objectives

- Distinguish among failure of proof, justification, and excuse defenses.
- Explain the differences between nonexculpatory defenses and offense modifications.
- Explain the difference between a perfect defense and an imperfect defense.
- Identify three reasons for justification defenses.

### Review Questions

1. What is the difference between a justification defense and an excuse defense?
2. How does failure of proof differ from justification and excuse defenses?
3. What is the difference between a perfect and an imperfect defense?
4. Why are justification defenses available?

### Key Terms

failure of proof defense
affirmative defense
justification defenses
excuse defenses
offense modifications
de minimus infraction defense
nonexculpatory defense

statute of limitations
perfect defenses
imperfect defenses
public benefit theory
superior interest theory
moral rights theory

MODULE **4.2**

## SELF-DEFENSE AND DEFENSE OF OTHERS

### Learning Objectives

- Summarize the defense of self-defense.
- Identify recent developments that have complicated the law of self-defense.

### Review Questions

1. What are the four elements of self-defense?
2. What is the castle doctrine? How is it relevant in the self-defense context?
3. What conditions must be in place for a battered woman syndrome defense to succeed?
4. Is it lawful to use force to resist an arrest? Under what circumstances?

### Key Terms

self-defense
stand your ground rule
castle doctrine
defense of others

MODULE **4.3**

## DEFENSE OF PROPERTY AND HABITATION

### Learning Objectives

- Distinguish between defense of habitation and defense of property.
- Compare and contrast "make my day" laws and the castle doctrine.

### Review Questions

1. How does defense of habitation differ from defense of property?
2. What are "make my day" laws? How do they differ from castle doctrine laws?
3. Is it ever legal to rig up a spring gun or a booby trap to prevent someone from breaking and entering?

### Key Terms

make my day laws

MODULE **4.4**

## LAW ENFORCEMENT

### Learning Objective

- Explain the law enforcement defense.

### Review Questions

1. What is the law enforcement defense and who can claim it?
2. Can an ordinary citizen use force and claim a law enforcement defense? If so, when? What about *deadly* force?

### Key Terms

law enforcement defense

MODULE **4.5**

## NECESSITY AND CONSENT

### Learning Objectives

- Describe the necessity defense.
- Explain the defense of consent.

### Review Questions

1. What is necessity?
2. When can a necessity defense be successfully claimed?
3. Can necessity ever justify homicide? Why or why not?
4. When is the defense of consent not available?

### Key Terms

necessity or choice of evils defense
consent

# Chapter Synthesis Questions

1. Which is more favorable, an excuse defense or a justification defense? Why?

2. What is your opinion of the castle doctrine? Explain.

3. Are people in the United States given enough latitude to be able to protect themselves and their property with force? Why or why not?

4. What justification is most important and why? If they are equally important, defend your answer with specifics.

5. Provide two examples of necessity and explain why they are justified.

# 5

# EXCUSE DEFENSES

*Learning Objectives*

MODULE **5.1** **EXCUSE DEFENSES AND DURESS**
- **Explain the reasons for excuse defenses.**
- **Summarize the conditions of the defense of duress.**

MODULE **5.2** **INTOXICATION**
- **Describe the intoxication defense.**

MODULE **5.3** **ENTRAPMENT**
- **Summarize what constitutes entrapment.**
- **Explain how entrapment relates to due process.**

MODULE **5.4** **AGE**
- **Summarize defenses based on age immaturity.**
- **Summarize methods by which some courts treat juveniles as adults.**

MODULE **5.5** **INSANITY**
- **Distinguish insanity from competency to stand trial and diminished capacity.**
- **Describe the insanity defense and the controversy surrounding it.**
- **Explain the effect of a successful insanity defense.**

MODULE **5.6** **CREATIVE EXCUSES**
- **Distinguish among and offer examples of physiological, psychological, and sociological excuse defenses.**

# EXCUSE DEFENSES AND DURESS

### *Learning Objectives*

- **Explain the reasons for excuse defenses.**
- **Summarize the conditions of the defense of duress.**

**CORE CONCEPTS**

In Chapter 4, we introduced justification defenses, those in which the offender accepts responsibility, but argues that the commission of a crime was appropriate under the circumstances. Here we turn such thinking on its head. With excuse defenses, the offender argues that there was something "wrong" with him or her at the time of the crime. A defendant who asserts an excuse defense makes one of three claims: the action was involuntary, the action was the product of a cognitive deficiency (such as insanity), or the action resulted from a volitional deficiency, meaning that an outside force compelled the action.

Excuse defenses, while controversial, are essential. Consider the case of Daryl Renard Atkins who, armed with a handgun, abducted a man, robbed him of the money he was carrying, drove him to an ATM machine and forced him to withdraw cash at gunpoint, and then took him to an isolated location and shot him eight times, killing him. Most people would agree Atkins should have been held accountable for these cruel actions. Indeed, he was convicted of capital murder and sentenced to death. Case closed, right? Not so fast. It turns out Atkins had a full-scale IQ of 59. So struck it was by Atkins's case, the Supreme Court ruled that it would be cruel and unusual punishment to execute someone like him who is "mildly mentally retarded."[1] Atkins was not set free, but the Court's decision reaffirmed the important role that mental state plays in the criminal-law context.

## Reasons for Excuse Defenses

There are three main reasons for excuse defenses.[2] The first is concerned with deterrence. Namely, if a person cannot be deterred, what is the point of punishing him or her? Returning to the earlier Atkins's case, would it have been sensible to execute him if he could not "appreciate" his actions? More generally, if a person cannot grasp that what he or she did is wrong (not because of ignorance, but because of some deficiency), then no amount of criminal law or punishment will be capable of stopping that person. This requires weighing two competing sets of interests, those of society in catching and punishing lawbreakers and those of the undeterrable actor. In some cases, the pain inflicted on the undeterrable actor may deserve more weight than society's concern with catching criminals.

---

[1] *Atkins* v. *Virginia*, 536 U.S. 304 (2002).
[2] J. Dressler, *Understanding Criminal Law*, 5th ed. (San Francisco: Lexis-Nexis, 2009), pp. 211–214.

Another reason for excuse defenses is a lack of causation. Recall that causation is a core requirement in certain criminal offenses (particularly result crimes). If a defendant's conduct is *caused* by factors beyond her control, does it make sense to punish her for it? Perhaps you saw the first *Saw* movie. Jigsaw, the villain, rigged a "reverse bear trap" that would have killed the intended victim, Amanda, if she did not unlock it in time. The key, unfortunately, was in the stomach of a man lying on the floor nearby. Desperate, Amanda violently cut open the man's stomach, retrieved the key, freed herself from the trap, and presumably killed the man in the process. Would it have been fair to hold Amanda criminally responsible for his death? Almost certainly not. An argument could be made that Jigsaw forced her hand, leaving her no choice but to commit a homicide in order to save her own life.

A third reason for excuse defenses lies in the area of moral blameworthiness. Simply, if the offender is not a "bad character," one who *deserves* punishment for his actions, then the actions should be excused. In most situations, we simply infer character from one's actions; criminals are bad and should be punished. But as is clear by now, offenders are not created equal. Some simply cannot understand or appreciate what they do, meaning their character is "innocent" on some level. Consider the toddler who bites or hits his sister. Should he be charged with assault? Of course not. The child's "innocence" precludes a finding that he formulated the intent to hurt his sibling.

# Duress

**duress** An excuse defense applicable when the defendant is forced to commit a crime by threat or force.

**Duress** is defined as compulsion by threat or force. Returning to the *Saw* example in the previous section, Amanda was arguably under duress because, had she not freed herself from the trap, she would have died—and violently. Her duress would have excused her from criminal liability. Thomas Hobbes put it this way:

> If a man, by the terror of present death, be compelled to do a fact against the law, he is totally excused, because no law can oblige a man to abandon his own preservation. And supposing such a law were obligatory, yet a man would reason thus: *If I do it not, I die presently; if I do it, I die afterwards; therefore by doing it, there is time of life gained. . . .*[3]

## Duress versus Necessity

Duress is distinct from necessity, the latter of which was introduced in the last chapter. A necessity defense is raised in cases when the defendant argues that she chose between the lesser of two evils. Duress basically takes the "choice" out of the equation; the defendant argues that she was *forced* by a coercer to engage in an unlawful act.

Another way to understand the difference between the two concerns of *who* should be held responsible. In a necessity situation, there is no blameworthy actor if it turns out the defendant's choice was one society is prepared to accept. If Larry broke into John's isolated cabin in order to avoid freezing to death, no one other than Larry could potentially be held liable. If Larry did the right thing under the circumstances (the greater evil being death from freezing), then *no one* will be held

---

[3]Thomas Hobbes, *Leviathan*, (New York: Penguin Classics, 1651/1982), Pt. II, ch. 27.

to answer for his actions. In a duress situation, however, there is of
actor who forced the defendant's hand. Returning once again to th
that person was Jigsaw, the villain.

# Elements of the Defense

The elements of a duress defense depend on the crime in question. For all *nonhomicide*
offenses, there are five general elements:

1. The defendant "acted under the compulsion or threat of imminent infliction of
   death or great bodily injury";

2. the defendant "reasonably believed that death or great bodily harm would have
   been inflicted upon him [or another] had he not acted as he did";

3. the compulsion or coercion was "imminent and impending and of such a nature
   as to induce a well-grounded apprehension of death or serious bodily harm if the
   act is not done";

4. there was "no reasonably opportunity to escape the compulsion without committing the crime"; and

5. the defendant must not have put him- or herself in a situation where it was
   "probable that he would have been subjected to compulsion or threat."[4]

Each of these requires a little clarification. First, for a duress defense to succeed, the
threat must come from another human being. The duress defense will not be available if the defendant claims an animal, an inanimate object, or anything else coerced him or her to commit a crime. So what if Barbara commits criminal trespass
by driving her vehicle into another person's carport in order to avoid impending
hail damage? She will not be able to claim duress, but she could almost certainly
claim necessity (see previous chapter).

Second, the threat must be directed at either the defendant or a member of his or
her family. It is *possible* that the defense could extend to other individuals, but such
cases are few and far between.[5] The typical duress situation is one in which the defendant fears for his or her life—or that of a family member, such as a child.

Third, it is important that the threat involve death or great bodily harm, not some
lesser degree of force. For example, if Larry threatened to fire Dave if Dave does not
dump hazardous waste down the drain, the duress defense will not be available.[6]

Fourth, to say the threat is "imminent and impending" means that it must be
operating on the actor *at the time of the crime.* This does not mean, however, that the
threat and the crime take place at the same exact moment in time. The only requirement is that the threat be operating on the defendant's mind at the time of the crime.

Fifth, the possibility of escape should not be taken lightly. Consider *State* v.
*Crawford,*[7] a case involving a drug-addicted defendant who asserted a duress

---

[4]*State* v. *Crawford*, 861 P.2d 791 (Kan. 1993), p. 797; see also *People* v. *Merhige*, 180 N.W. 418 (Mich.
  1920), p. 422.
[5]See, e.g., *United States* v. *Haney*, 287 F.3d 1266 (10th Cir. 2002).
[6]See, e.g., *People* v. *Ricker*, 262 N.E.2d 456 (Ill. 1970).
[7]*State* v. *Crawford*, Ibid.

defense after allegedly committing various crimes at the direction of his dealer (in order to pay his debts). The dealer was not present at the time the defendant committed the crime. An appeals court affirmed the defendant's conviction because it felt there was reasonable opportunity for the defendant to escape because he was out of sight of his dealer when he committed his crimes.

Finally, if the defendant puts himself in the situation and later claims duress, it is likely he will not succeed. Say, for example, that Leroy joins a white supremacist gang. The gang leader orders him to kill an African American as part of his initiation. After being told he will be killed if he doesn't comply, Leroy identifies a target, kills the individual, and promptly gets caught and prosecuted for murder. Leroy will not likely succeed with a duress claim because it was his decision to join the gang in the first place.

## Duress and Homicide

Duress is generally not a defense to intentional killing. Some states expressly forbid the defense in this context; some others treat it as an imperfect defense that could lead to a manslaughter conviction rather than a murder conviction. Why restrict the duress defense in this way? Why is it not an outright excuse? After all, if it is possible to claim duress in a situation where a victim was ordered to rob a bank or be killed, why would it be impermissible for the same victim to claim duress if he was ordered to take someone else's life? A California case, *People* v. *Anderson*,[8] offers at least one answer. Two men were charged with murder for killing a suspected child molester by beating her over the head with a rock. One of the men testified at trial that the other ordered him to retrieve a large rock or the other man would have "beat the shit out of him."[9] The man complied and, on appeal, claimed that he was under duress, fearing for his life because of his partner's threat. The California Supreme Court did not agree, stating,

> [W]hen confronted with an apparent kill-an-innocent-person-or-be-killed situation, a person can always choose to resist. As a practical matter, death will rarely, if ever, inevitably result from a choice not to kill.[10]

Some states, like we pointed out, recognize that duress can reduce culpability. For example, in *Wentworth* v. *State*,[11] Delores Taylor and her husband, David Wentworth, visited the home of another man, James Mosley. After having a few drinks, David accused James of having an adulterous affair with his wife Delores. At his request, Delores helped her husband find a gun and ammunition, which were located in the house. Delores then went outside and started the car once David said he was going to take both her and James for a ride. She even helped wipe fingerprints from surfaces she and her husband had touched. Soon, however, she developed second thoughts and fled to a neighbor's house. James's body was found the next day. Both husband and wife were prosecuted for murder, but Delores argued that she was

---

[8]*People* v. *Anderson*, 50 P.3d 368 (Cal. 2002).
[9]Ibid., p. 370.
[10]Ibid., p. 371.
[11]*Wentworth* v. *State*, 349 A.2d 421 (Md. Ct. Spec. App. 1975).

under duress at the time she helped her husband and that he was "very paranoiac and was in another fit of rage" right before the killing. Even so, she was convicted of second-degree murder. She later appealed, arguing that her condition of duress could not have supported a murder conviction. The court agreed, reversed her conviction, and remanded the case for a new trial. This indicated that a manslaughter conviction may have been more appropriate under the circumstances.[12]

## Complications for Duress

There are two specific areas where the defense of duress blurs together with one or more other defenses (usually necessity or self-defense). One is in the area of prison escapes. It is not completely clear whether an inmate who escapes does so out of necessity or because of duress. Likewise, battered woman syndrome has served as the basis for a number of self-defense claims, but abuse victims who commit crimes—and even kill—may do so partly because of duress.

### Prison Escapes

Throughout history, more than a few prison inmates have attempted to escape confinement. Escape, as it should be, is a criminal act.[13] Those who succeed and get caught often wind up sent back to prison and convicted with escape. A claim of duress, however, might preclude a conviction for escape.[14] How? What argument would an escapee raise? In one case, an escapee who was about to be transferred to another prison argued that a fellow inmate told him he would be killed on arrival at the new prison.[15] In another case, a man escaped and later claimed he feared for his life because a fellow inmate threatened him with a knife and attempted to force him to engage in homosexual activities.[16]

The problem with these arguments is that they involve elements of necessity *and* duress. On the one hand, an inmate may argue that it was *necessary* to escape in order to avoid being hurt (it was a "lesser of two evils" choice). Unfortunately, as we discussed in the previous chapter, necessity is a defense available in limited contexts and may not be able to support a defense in an escape case if the threatened conduct was not sufficiently serious. On the other hand, an escapee could argue that breaking out of prison was a direct result of being threatened, but no one *ordered* the inmate to escape, making a duress defense rather difficult. There is division in the courts over whether duress or necessity is appropriate in these cases. For example, one court held that necessity was the proper claim in one escape case where the defendant left a penitentiary without authorization and later claimed that he feared further homosexual assault and possible death.[17] Yet *duress* was the proper defense in an-

---

[12]Ibid., p. 428.
[13]The federal statute is 18 U.S.C.S. Section 751(a).
[14]See, e.g., *State* v. *Reese*, 272 N.W.2d 863 (Iowa 1978); *Spakes* v. *State*, 913 S.W.2d 597 (Tex. Crim. App. 1996); *State* v. *Tuttle*, 730 P.2d 630 (Utah 1986).
[15]*Lacey* v. *State*, 54 P.3d 304 (Alaska Ct. App. 2002).
[16]*People* v. *Unger*, 362 N.E.2d 319 (Ill. 1977).
[17]*State* v. *Reese*, 272 N.W.2d 863 (Iowa 1978).

other case, this one involving an inmate whose life was threatened by other inmates who vowed he would be killed if he returned to a main corridor.[18]

So which is it? Duress or necessity? The law is not clear, unfortunately. Answers vary depending on the court and particularly the *state* in question. Some have argued that both defenses should be available. According to Joshua Dressler,

> There is no reason why a jurisdiction would fit all prison escape cases within just one defense category . . . why should an inmate always be forced to prove that the escape was the lesser of two evils? An inmate should be permitted to raise a duress claim instead of, or in conjunction with, the necessity claim.[19]

When all is said and done, whether the defense is duress or necessity may be immaterial. The point is that it is *possible* to escape an escape conviction (again, no pun intended) if an inmate was sufficiently fearful. However, in order to succeed with either a duress or necessity defense in this conduct, it is usually required that the escapee turn him- or herself promptly after leaving prison. For the defense to succeed, the escapee must, according to the U.S. Supreme Court, make "a bona fide effort to surrender or return to custody as soon as the claimed duress or necessity has lost its coercive force."[20] Moreover, "[v]ague and necessarily self-serving statements of defendants or witnesses as to future good intentions or ambiguous conduct do not support a" claim of duress or necessity.[21] The case in question dealt with inmates who had been on the run for more than a month.

## The Return of Battered Woman Syndrome

In Chapter 4, we discussed the possibility that battered woman syndrome can form the basis of a self-defense claim. Battered woman syndrome has also come up in the duress context. Unfortunately, it is exceedingly difficult for a battered woman to be excused from criminal liability if, say, she kills her husband yet can also escape. In other words, if escape is an option, then the woman should avail herself of it.

What if duress forms the basis of a claim that an abused woman's husband forced her to commit other crimes? In one case, Judith Ann Neelley kidnapped for her abusive husband a 13-year-old girl by the name of Lisa Ann Millican. After Judith's husband raped and abused the girl, Judith killed her. She was convicted and sentenced to death. An appellate court affirmed the decision.[22] A contrasting case is *Dunn* v. *Roberts*,[23] a case involving a woman who went on a murderous rampage with her abusive husband and later asserted a battered woman syndrome defense. She was initially convicted, but a federal appeals court overturned her conviction and remanded the case for a new trial because she was not afforded the opportunity at trial to have an expert witness testify in support of her claim.

---

[18]*State* v. *Tuttle*, 730 P.2d 630 (Utah 1986).
[19]Dressler, *Understanding Criminal Law*, p. 315.
[20]*United States* v. *Bailey*, 444 U.S. 394 (1980), p. 415.
[21]Ibid.
[22]*Neelley* v. *State*, 642 So. 2d 494 (Ala. Crim. App. 1993).
[23]*Dunn* v. *Roberts*, 963 F.2d 308 (10th Cir. 1992).

## Model Penal Code

The Model Penal Code recognizes duress as a defense:

> It is an affirmative defense that the actor engaged in the conduct charged to consti-
> tute an offense because he was coerced to do so by the use of, or a threat to use,
> unlawful force against his person or the person of another, that a person of reason-
> able firmness in his situation would have been unable to resist.[24]

The defense is not available, however, if the actor recklessly or negligently places
him- or herself in the situation. The Model Penal Code does not recognize a stand-
alone battered woman defense, but if a "woman who acted on command of her
husband" will be excused from criminal liability if "she acted under such coercion as
would establish a [traditional duress defense]."[25]

**YOUR
DECISION**

1. Johnny Franco was involved with part of the Italian Mafia for the majority of his
youth and often handled illegal drug deals for the family. The local police department convinced Johnny to become an undercover informant and help them arrest
leading members of the Mafia. Johnny was scheduled to be the prosecution's star
witness at the criminal trials of the Mafia bosses. However, the family became
aware that Johnny was a "snitch" and began to threaten him. Scared for his life,
Johnny took the stand in the courtroom and lied about the family's involvement in
illegal drug dealing. Without its star witness, the prosecution was forced to drop
the charges against the Mafia bosses. Johnny is now being charged with perjury. Is
he entitled to the defense of duress? Why or why not?

2. Robert Greene is currently serving a life sentence for murder at a maximum security prison. Robert sent three threatening letters to Judge William Smart, the judge
who presided over his trial. One of the letters contained a white powdery substance
similar in appearance to anthrax. Robert claimed that the letters were the only way
he could draw attention to himself and the abusive and inhumane prison conditions. He also believed the prison guards were slowly poisoning him through his
food. Robert is attempting to use the defense of duress. Does he meet all five of the
required elements?

## Summary

- Excuse defenses, while controversial, are essential.
- There are three main reasons for excuse defenses: possible lack of deterrence,
possible lack of causation, and possible lack of moral blameworthiness.
- Duress is defined as compulsion by threat or force.
- A necessity defense is raised in cases when the defendant argues that she chose
between the lesser of two evils.

---

[24]Model Penal Code Section 2.09.
[25]Ibid.

- Duress basically takes the "choice" out of the equation; the defendant argues that she was *forced* by a coercer to engage in an unlawful act.

- For all *nonhomicide* offenses, there are five general elements of duress: (1) The defendant "acted under the compulsion or threat of imminent infliction of death or great bodily injury"; (2) the defendant "reasonably believed that death or great bodily harm would have been inflicted upon him [or another] had he not acted as he did"; (3) the compulsion or coercion was "imminent and impending and of such a nature as to induce a well-grounded apprehension of death or serious bodily harm if the act is not done"; (4) there was "no reasonably opportunity to escape the compulsion without committing the crime"; and (5) the defendant must not have put him- or herself in a situation where it was "probable that he would have been subjected to compulsion or threat."

- Some states expressly forbid a duress defense in homicide cases; some others treat it as an imperfect defense that could lead to a manslaughter conviction rather than a murder conviction.

- Duress blurs together with necessity in the case of prison escapes.

- Duress blurs together with self-defense in battered woman syndrome cases.

---

**MODULE**

**5.2**

# INTOXICATION

### *Learning Objective*

- **Describe the intoxication defense.**

## CORE CONCEPTS

**intoxication** An excuse defense applicable only if the intoxication through alcohol, drugs, or other substances is involuntary.

**Intoxication** is formally defined as a "disturbance of mental or physical capacities resulting from the introduction of any substance into the body."[26] Note that this definition does not distinguish between alcohol and other drugs. Indeed, it is possible to become intoxicated from a substance that is neither alcohol nor a drug (e.g., paint), but we are—and most cases have been—concerned with alcohol- or drug-induced intoxication. That said, most of the popular intoxication cases referenced in criminal-law books focus on alcohol intoxication.

Intoxication is important in criminal law because it affects judgment. It is well known that controlled substances impair decision-making capabilities. For example, a person who is under the influence of alcohol may not be able to form the requisite *mens rea* to commit a crime (the person may act impulsively). And even if an intoxicated person *can* form intent, that person may not act the same way in a sober state.

---

[26]*People v. Low*, 732 P.2d 622 (Colo. 1987), p. 627.

Whether and how intoxication serves as a defense to criminal liability hinges on several factors. First, and most importantly, it is critical to determine whether the intoxication was voluntary or involuntary. A person who *voluntarily* becomes intoxicated will have a considerably harder time having his or her conduct "excused." Another factor is the role intoxication plays in the commission of a crime. Did it just negate *mens rea* or did it so affect the defendant to the extent he or she "blacked out" and did not even commit a voluntary act? Yet another factor is the type of offense. A strict liability crime, you will recall, requires no *mens rea*, so an intoxication defense may be impossible. In contrast, specific intent offenses are such that the defendant's intoxication can be rather important.

## How Intoxication Overlaps with Other Defenses

Before we look at these issues in more detail, it is important to note that intoxication has a tendency to overlap with other defenses. Insanity, which we touch on later in this chapter, closely parallels intoxication. The argument can be made that an intoxicated person is "insane," if only temporarily. The argument can also be made that the habitual use of intoxicants over a long period can permanently alter an accused's mental state. To the extent that this occurs, a traditional insanity defense may be a reasonable choice. Some would say, however, that long-term addiction is more blameworthy than short-term abuse:

> There is no principled basis to distinguish between the short-term and long-term effects of voluntary intoxication by punishing the first and excusing the second. If anything, the moral blameworthiness would seem to be even greater with respect to the long-term effects of many, repeated instances of voluntary intoxication occurring over an extended period of time.[27]

Intoxication also overlaps with the concept of mistake, which we introduced in Chapter 3. For example, in one case, a drunken man mistakenly concluded that a woman consented to engage in sexual intercourse with him.[28] She did not and he was convicted of rape.

## Voluntary Intoxication

In general, a person who voluntarily ingests an intoxicant will not succeed with a defense of intoxication. The reason is obvious: Why should a person who *chooses* to get drunk or stoned then be excused for actions committed in his or her altered state? Even if a person voluntarily uses one substance and finds out later that it was laced or mixed with another, the defense will not succeed. See the accompanying Court Decision for more on voluntary intoxication. In it we take a look at *State* v. *McClenton*, where a man voluntarily smoked a marijuana cigarette that was unbeknownst to him laced with phencyclidine (PCP).

---

[27]*Bieber* v. *People*, 856 P.2d 811 (Colo. 1993), p. 817.
[28]*Regina* v. *Cogan*, Q.B. 217 (1976).

**COURT DECISION**

*State* v. *McClenton,*
781 N.W.2d 181 (Minn. App. 2010)

**Background:** Roosevelt McClenton was convicted of first-degree aggravated robbery and fifth-degree possession of a controlled substance in the District Court of Hennepin County. Defendant appealed. The Court of Appeals of Minnesota affirmed.

\*\*\*Facts

Around 7:15 p.m. on October 30, 2007, T.G. was walking down Portland Avenue South in Minneapolis. At the corner of Portland Avenue and 24th Street, a man, later identified as appellant Roosevelt McClenton, approached T.G. and asked him for money in an aggressive and hostile manner. According to T.G., appellant looked "like he was on drugs" and was "very unstable." T.G. told appellant that he did not have any money. However, appellant "kept on pressing [him]" and told T.G. "he was going to kick [his] ass," so T.G. reached into his pocket and gave appellant a $20 bill. Appellant persisted and T.G. gave him another $20 bill and some $1 bills. After T.G. handed over the money, appellant punched him in the head. T.G. fell to the ground.

\*\*\*Minneapolis police officers Kenneth Awalt and Christopher Humphrey responded to the scene first. Officer Awalt observed appellant lying on the grass on the corner of Portland and 24th. Appellant was not wearing a shirt and his pants were down around his thigh area. Appellant got up off the ground and was shaking his arms, ranting and raving, and "saying biblical homages." Appellant refused to comply with the officers' orders to get down on the ground. \*\*\* Officer Werner observed the other officers attempt to mace appellant to no avail. Appellant wandered onto Portland Avenue into traffic. Officer Werner subsequently tased appellant.

Appellant, still struggling and speaking incomprehensibly, was loaded into an ambulance. Inside the ambulance, a paramedic observed appellant "spitting and turning his head a lot." Next to the side of appellant's mouth, she saw a baggie containing a substance she believed to be crack cocaine. The substance was later identified as crack cocaine.

Appellant was charged with first-degree aggravated robbery in violation of Minn. Stat. § 609.245, subd. 1. Prior to trial, defense counsel gave notice of appellant's intent to rely upon the defenses of "Mental Illness or Deficiency" and "Intoxication." \*\*\*The district court noted that while the psychologist found appellant was in a "drug-induced psychosis" at the time of the alleged offense, the psychologist "did not give an opinion" on whether appellant had a viable mental-illness defense "because she believed that a psychosis caused by a *voluntary* injection of drugs doesn't qualify for a mental-illness defense." Based on appellant's assertion of an *involuntary*-intoxication defense, the district court requested an updated opinion.

However, on May 12, 2008, the district court issued an order requiring appellant to "make an offer of proof constituting prima facie evidence that an involuntary-intoxication defense exists in this case" before an updated Rule 20.02 evaluation would be ordered. In the accompanying memorandum, the district court stated:

On May 5, 2008, defense counsel proffered to the Court that the drug-induced psychosis from which Defendant was suffering at the time of the offense was caused by involuntary intoxication. Specifically, defense counsel proffered that in addition to the Defendant's use of cocaine during the days leading up to the date of offense; the Defendant also smoked marijuana which, the Defendant believes, was "laced" with an unknown substance. According to defense counsel, the Defendant will assert at trial that the psychosis from which he was suffering at the time of the crime was caused by an unanticipated reaction to the drugs he ingested.

The district court observed that the availability of an involuntary-intoxication defense based on the voluntary ingestion of an illegal street drug appears to be an issue of first impression in Minnesota and noted that other jurisdictions have "uniformly" rejected the defense "even if, unknown to the defendant, the illegal drug was 'laced' with another substance which caused the defendant to have an unanticipated reaction."

\*\*\*A jury trial was held and appellant was found guilty of first-degree aggravated robbery and fifth-degree possession. \*\*\*Appellant was sentenced to 180 months in prison, an upward departure from the 111-month presumptive sentence. This appeal follows.

### Analysis

\*\*\*Generally, when a defendant relies upon the use of alcohol or drugs as a defense, "mental illness caused by *voluntary* intoxication is not a defense." Appellant asserts, however, that he was involuntarily intoxicated at the time of the offenses because, unbeknownst to him, the marijuana he smoked was laced with phencyclidine (PCP). In order to prevail in asserting the defense of involuntary intoxication, appellant must show that: (1) he "was unaware that because of a particular susceptibility to it the substance would have a grossly excessive intoxicating effect" or "was innocently mistaken as to the nature of the substance taken"; (2) the "intoxication was caused by the intoxicating substance in question and not by some other intoxicant"; and (3) he was temporarily mentally ill at the time of the offenses.

\*\*\*As the district court observed, the issue of whether involuntary intoxication exists when a person voluntarily uses an illegal controlled substance unknowingly laced with some other illegal controlled substance which causes an unanticipated reaction is an issue of first impression for Minnesota state courts.

Minnesota law places the burden on the defendant to make a prima facie showing of mental illness or deficiency before the defense will be allowed. The extent of the record regarding appellant's showing to the district court is contained in the May 12 order: "Specifically, defense counsel proffered that in addition to the Defendant's use of cocaine during the days leading up to the date of offense; the Defendant also smoked marijuana which, the Defendant believes, was 'laced' with an unknown substance." The district court concluded that, before it would order an updated Rule 20.02 examination, this offer of proof was required because "a bare assertion by a defendant that he or she smoked marijuana that must have been laced with something is likely insufficient to constitute prima facie evidence of that defense." Appellant argues that this was erroneous and shows weighing of the evidence. Appellant asserts that the defense was not based upon a "bare assertion," but was based upon a fact witness who would testify to appellant's drug use, tests revealing the presence of PCP in appellant's blood, and expert testimony concerning the effects of PCP.

\*\*\*[W]e do not believe that the defense of involuntary intoxication is available to appellant under the facts of this case.

We initially observe that marijuana is a controlled substance in Minnesota. Minn. Stat. §§ 152.01, subd. 9 (defining "marijuana"), .02, subd. 2(3) (classifying marijuana as a Schedule I controlled substance) (2006). Additionally, we agree with the California appellate court's observation in *People v. Velez* that

> [i]t is common knowledge that unlawful street drugs do not come with warranties of purity or quality associated with lawfully acquired drugs such as alcohol. Thus, unlike alcohol, unlawful street drugs are frequently not the substance they purport to be or are contaminated with other substances not apparent to the naked eye.

175 Cal.App.3d 785, 221 Cal.Rptr. 631, 637 (1985); *see* Minn.Stat. § 152.01, subd. 9a (2006) (defining a controlled-substance "mixture" as "a preparation, compound, mixture, or substance containing a controlled substance, regardless of purity").

\*\*\*As the state points out, appellant cannot claim that he was pathologically intoxicated because such intoxication occurs when a person, unaware of a particular susceptibility to a substance, experiences a grossly excessive intoxication as a result of using that substance. Appellant does not claim that he was particularly susceptible to marijuana; appellant asserts that he became involuntarily intoxicated because of the effects of the PCP. Appellant did not knowingly consume PCP and, therefore, could not have been pathologically intoxicated as such intoxication results when a substance is knowingly ingested and the result from *that* substance was unexpected due to an unknown susceptibility. Moreover, by voluntarily consuming an illegal drug, appellant cannot claim that he was innocently mistaken as to the nature of the drug. To hold otherwise would effectively permit an involuntary-intoxication defense for individuals who use less "pure" drugs. While our supreme court has not yet addressed the issue, we do not believe it would find such logic persuasive. A person in appellant's position simply cannot argue involuntary intoxication because, by voluntarily choosing to smoke marijuana, any resulting intoxication (whatever that may have been) was likewise voluntary. Accordingly, we hold that a defendant who voluntarily smokes marijuana, which unbeknownst to him is laced with some other controlled substance, is not entitled to an involuntary-intoxication defense based on the resultant effects of the combined substances.

\*\*\*Affirmed.

## Case Analysis

1. What is McClenton's main argument for asserting the defense of intoxication?

2. Which defense is more appropriate for McClenton, voluntary or involuntary intoxication?

3. Was it fair for McClenton to assume that the illegal drugs he purchased were "pure"? Why or why not?

But wait, can someone then succeed with a voluntary intoxication defense if the substance used is alcohol? After all, one expects a certain amount of "purity" in a legally acquired product. Unfortunately, even voluntary alcohol intoxication almost never serves as a defense to criminal liability. We say *almost never* because a defendant can argue that intoxication weakened or eliminated the *mens rea* component of a specific intent offense. Say, for example, that an intoxicated man is arrested and charged with the specific intent offense of assault with intent to rape. He might be able to make a case that he did not *intend* to rape because of his intoxicated condition.[29] If the offense in question is of the general intent variety, then such an argument will not be permitted.[30]

Even allowing the mere argument that intoxication negates *mens rea*, however, is objectionable to some. As Supreme Court justice Antonin Scalia once remarked,

> Disallowing consideration of voluntary intoxication has the effect of increasing the punishment for all unlawful acts . . . and thereby deters drunkenness or irresponsible behavior while drunk. The rule also serves as a specific deterrent, ensuring that those who prove incapable of controlling violent impulses while voluntarily intoxicated go to prison.[31]

In the same case, Justice Sandra Day O'Connor argued, in dissent, that "where a subjective mental state [is] an element of the crime to be proved, the defense must be permitted to show, by reference to intoxication, the absence of that element."[32] But the majority in the same case upheld a Montana statute that expressly barred the introduction of intoxication evidence to disprove *mens rea*.[33] As part of its decision, the Court said, rather controversially, that "[t]he Due Process Clause does not bar States from making changes in their criminal law that have the effect of making it easier for the prosecution to obtain convictions."[34]

This case notwithstanding, some states permit evidence of intoxication, particularly in homicide cases, but only insofar as such evidence could reduce—not excuse—culpability. Intoxication *could* reduce, for example, what would otherwise be a first-degree murder conviction to one for second-degree murder (we look at these distinctions more carefully in Chapter 8).[35]

## Involuntary Intoxication

A person is involuntarily intoxicated if he or she cannot be blamed for the intoxicated state. The court in *City of Minneapolis* v. *Altimus*[36] identified four circumstances in which a person is said to be involuntarily intoxicated:

1. The person is coerced to ingest an intoxicant.
2. The person accidentally ingests an intoxicant.

---

[29]See, e.g., *State* v. *Dwyer*, 757 A.2d 597 (Conn. Ct. App. 2000).
[30]See, e.g., *United States* v. *Sewell*, 252 F.3d 647 (2nd Cir. 2001).
[31]*Montana* v. *Egelhoff*, 518 U.S. 37 (1996), pp. 49–50.
[32]Ibid., p. 70.
[33]*Montana* v. *Egelhoff*, 518 U.S. 37 (1996).
[34]Ibid., p. 55.
[35]See, e.g., *State* v. *Ludlow*, 883 P.2d 1144 (Kan. 1994).
[36]*City of Minneapolis* v. *Altimus*, 238 N.W.2d 851 (Minn. 1976).

A person whose soda is drugged, as shown in this picture, would likely be considered involuntarily intoxicated.

Laurens Parsons Photography/Shutterstock.com

3. The person becomes unexpectedly intoxicated from a prescribed medication.

4. The person suffers from "pathological intoxication," a "temporary psychotic reaction, often manifested by violence, which is triggered by consumption of alcohol by a person with a pre-disposing mental or physical condition."[37]

If a criminal defendant meets one of these conditions, he or she will be able to assert an involuntary intoxication defense and, if successful, will be entitled to full acquittal. The first three conditions are relatively straightforward; the fourth, however, is a bit complicated. To illustrate, in one case the defendant argued that he suffered from "undifferentiated schizophrenic disorder," which caused him to have adverse reactions to alcohol.[38] According to experts who testified on his behalf, "This condition lowers the tolerance level to alcohol so that not only does intoxication occur more readily but the results of intoxication are far more drastic than would normally be the case. Among such drastic reactions which may result from consumption of a relatively small amount of alcohol are confusion, amnesia, loss of perception to reality, and violent conduct."[39]

One exception to the rule that involuntary intoxication can serve as a defense lies in the realm of strict liability crimes. In *State v. Miller*,[40] the defendant drank coffee that, unbeknownst to him, was spiked with alcohol. He was subsequently convicted of driving under the influence of alcohol, a strict liability offense. The Oregon Supreme Court upheld his conviction, noting that because the crime required no proof of a culpable mental state, the defendant could not claim involuntary intoxication.

## Model Penal Code

The Model Penal Code distinguishes between three types of intoxication—"self-induced intoxication," "intoxication that is not self-induced," and "pathological

---

[37]Lawrence P. Tiffany and Mary Tiffany, "Nosologic Objections to the Criminal Defense of Pathological Intoxication: What Do the Doubters Doubt," *International Journal of Law and Psychiatry*, Vol. 13 (1990), p. 49.

[38]*Kane v. United States*, 399 F.2d 730 (9th Cir. 1968).

[39]Ibid., p. 735.

[40]*State v. Miller*, 788 P.2d 974 (Or. 1990).

intoxication"—the last of which is defined as "intoxication grossly excessive in degree, given the amount of the intoxicant, to which the actor does not know he is susceptible."[41]

The Code treats pathological intoxication and intoxication that is not self-induced as affirmative defenses, provided that "the actor at the time of his conduct lacks substantial capacity either to appreciate its criminality . . . or to conform his conduct to the requirements of law."[42] As for self-induced intoxication, the Model Penal Code permits its introduction into evidence if it negates an element of the underlying offense. The Model Penal Code is thus more "generous" with the treatment of intoxication as an excuse to liability than some of the other cases and statutes discussed earlier in this section. As a final note, if the crime with which a person is charged contains "recklessness" as one of its elements and the defendant, because of self-induced intoxication, "is unaware of a risk of which he would have been aware had he been sober, such unawareness is immaterial."[43] In other words, when charged with a crime of recklessness, a defendant who was voluntarily intoxicated at the time of crime cannot claim he was unaware of the risks his conduct posed.

## YOUR DECISION

1. Scott Murphy is a freshman in college and recently decided to pledge the fraternity Chi Gamma Omega. As a "pledge" of the fraternity, Scott is forced to participate in a number of initiation activities in order to become a brother of Chi Gamma Omega. Specifically, one night Scott was held down on the ground while other brothers poured shots of vodka into his mouth. Severely intoxicated by the initiation ritual, later that evening Scott broke into a female student's dorm room and sexually assaulted her. Scott is claiming he mistakenly believed he was entering the room of his girlfriend. Is Scott entitled to the defense of involuntary intoxication? Why or why not?

2. Jodi Sugarman is an 18-year-old high school senior and scholar athlete. One Saturday night she attended a house party where alcohol was being served to underage minors. Jodi was hoping to participate in the Olympic trials for swimming and chose not to consume any alcohol during the party. She did, however, take what she believed was a breath mint from a fellow classmate and consumed it. Unbeknownst to Jodi, the "mint" was actually laced with cocaine. Under the influence of the cocaine, Jodi entered into a physical altercation with another student and killed her. Jodi is being charged with first-degree murder. Is she entitled to the defense of intoxication? Voluntary or involuntary?

## Summary

- An intoxicated person may also be "insane," if only temporarily.
- Intoxication also overlaps with the defense of "mistake." For example, an intoxicated offender may assume sex is consensual when it is not.

---

[41]Model Penal Code Section 2.08.
[42]Ibid.
[43]Ibid.

- In general, a person who voluntarily ingests an intoxicant will not succeed with a defense of intoxication.
- Some states permit evidence of intoxication, particularly in homicide cases, but only insofar as it could reduce—not excuse—culpability.
- A person is involuntarily intoxicated if he or she cannot be blamed for the intoxicated states.
- A successful involuntary intoxication defense will result in full acquittal.

# ENTRAPMENT

### *Learning Objectives*

- **Summarize what constitutes entrapment.**
- **Explain how entrapment relates to due process.**

## CORE CONCEPTS

**entrapment** An excuse defense applicable if the government is found to have manufactured or initiated a crime that would not have otherwise occurred.

The **entrapment** defense straddles the lines between criminal law and criminal procedure. It is a defense in the criminal-law sense, but it is one of the only defenses that calls into question law enforcement's role in the instigation of crime. Hence, it is almost always brought up in the realm of criminal procedure. Even so, entrapment is an affirmative defense, which means it can easily be raised at trial. It is also an excuse defense, which is why it fits in this chapter.

## Nature of the Defense

The entrapment defense is based on the belief that someone should not be convicted of a crime that the government instigated. In its simplest form, the entrapment defense arises when government officials "plant the seeds" of criminal intent. That is, if a person commits a crime that he or she otherwise would not have committed but for the government's conduct, that person will probably succeed with an entrapment defense.

The first Supreme Court case recognizing the entrapment defense was *Sorrells* v. *United States*.[44] In that case, Chief Justice Hughes stated, "We are unable to conclude that . . . [the] . . . processes of detection or enforcement should be abused by the instigation by government officials of an act on the part of persons otherwise innocent in order to lure them to its commission and to punish them."[45] This reasoning underlies the treatment of the entrapment defense in U.S. courts to this day. The Court further stated,

> The appropriate object of this permitted activity, frequently essential to the enforcement of the law, is to reveal the criminal design; to expose the illicit traffic,

---

[44]*Sorrells* v. *United States*, 287 U.S. 435 (1932).
[45]Ibid., p. 448

the prohibited publication, the fraudulent use of the mails, the illegal conspiracy, or other offenses, and thus to disclose the would-be violators of the law. A different question is presented when the criminal design originates with the officials of the Government, and they implant in the mind of an innocent person the disposition to commit the alleged offense and induce its commission in order that they may prosecute.[46]

Despite its apparent simplicity, the entrapment defense has been a contentious one. In particular, there has been some disagreement in the courts over the relevance of the offender's predisposition and how far the government can go to lure a person into criminal activity. When an entrapment decision is based on the offender's predisposition, this is known as a *subjective inquiry*. By contrast, a focus on the government conduct presumably responsible for someone's decision to commit a crime is known as an *objective inquiry*.

The Model Penal Code takes an objective approach with regard to the entrapment defense: If the government "employ[ed] methods of persuasion or inducement which create a substantial risk that such an offense will be committed by persons other than those who are ready to commit it,"[47] then the defense is available regardless of the offender's initial willingness to offend.

The Supreme Court, however, has opted to focus on the subjective predisposition of the offender instead the government's role in instigating the crime in question.[48] In *Sorrells*, discussed earlier, the defendant was charged with violating the National Prohibition Act.[49] After two unsuccessful attempts, a law enforcement agent convinced the defendant to sell him whiskey. Chief Justice Hughes noted that "artifice and stratagem" are permissible methods of catching criminals, so entrapment did not occur. Instead, it was the defendant's predisposition to offend that was important.

In *Sherman* v. *United States*,[50] the Supreme Court reached the opposite conclusion but still adhered to the subjective test that focuses on offender predisposition. In that case, a government informant met the defendant at a doctor's office, where both were being treated for narcotics addiction. After repeated requests by the informant, the defendant provided him with illegal narcotics. The Supreme Court reversed the defendant's conviction, noting that entrapment was "patently clear" as a matter of law. Even so, the Court also pointed out that it is difficult to judge the conduct of an informant without knowing how predisposed the offender was to act before the crime was committed.

In *United States* v. *Russell*,[51] the Court continued to focus on the defendant's subjective predisposition. In *Russell*, a narcotics agent posed as a narcotics manufacturer and offered the defendant a difficult-to-obtain ingredient used to manufacture a drug. The defendant accepted and was convicted. Justice Rehnquist, author of the

---

[46]Ibid., pp. 441–442.
[47]American Law Institute, *Model Penal Code* 2.13(1)(b)(1985).
[48]See, e.g., *Hampton* v. *United States*, 425 U.S. 484 (1976).
[49]Recall that during the Prohibition era, from 1920 to 1933, it was illegal to produce and sell alcohol in the United States.
[50]*Sherman* v. *United States*, 356 U.S. 369 (1958).
[51]*United States* v. *Russell*, 411 U.S. 423 (1973).

majority opinion, observed that there was sufficient predisposition on the part of the defendant, so the entrapment defense did not apply.

In *Hampton* v. *United States*,[52] the Supreme Court once again focused on the defendant's predisposition. In that case, the defendant was convicted of distributing heroin supplied to the defendant by a government informant. The Court stated that "[i]f the police engage in illegal activity in concert with a defendant beyond the scope of their duties the remedy lies, not in freeing the equally culpable defendant, but in prosecuting the police under the applicable provisions of state or federal law."[53] In other words, it is the defendant's predisposition that matters in the context of the entrapment defense, not the government's conduct.

To suggest that the Supreme Court has ignored the role of government conduct is not entirely true. In a concurring opinion cited in *Hampton*, justices Powell and Blackmun argued that government behavior that "shocks the conscience" could conceivably violate due process. In their words, "[T]here is certainly a limit to allowing governmental involvement in crime. . . . It would be unthinkable . . . to permit government agents to instigate robberies and beatings merely to gather evidence to convict other members of a gang of hoodlums."[54] To summarize, offender predisposition has received more attention than government conduct when deciding on whether an entrapment defense should be successful.

## Entrapment and Due Process

The Supreme Court has yet to affirmatively recognize a defense to government entrapment based on due process, but some lower courts have. Generally, if government officials use violence, supply contraband that is wholly unobtainable, or engage in a criminal enterprise, then the defendant in such a case will often succeed with the entrapment defense based on a due process argument.

In an actual case,[55] Drug Enforcement Agency (DEA) agents sought out a convicted felon, Kubica, and offered to reduce the severity of his sentence if he agreed to cooperate with them. At the request of the DEA, Kubica contacted another man, Neville, and suggested that they set up a lab to manufacture "speed." Neville agreed, and the government supplied Kubica with glassware and a difficult-to-obtain ingredient used in the manufacture of speed. The government also made arrangements for purchasing the chemicals and even supplied an isolated farmhouse to serve as the laboratory. The laboratory was set up at the farmhouse and operated for one week. The men produced approximately six pounds of methamphetamine hydrochloride (i.e., speed). Kubica was completely in charge of the entire laboratory. At the end of the first week of lab operations, Neville left the farmhouse with the drugs in a suitcase. Kubica notified the DEA agents, who arrested Neville driving down the road.

---

[52]*Hampton* v. *United States*, 425 U.S. 484 (1976).
[53]Ibid., p. 490.
[54]Ibid., p. 493, n. 4
[55]*United States* v. *Twigg*, 588 F.2d 373 (3rd Cir. 1978).

A search of the car revealed, in addition to the suitcase containing six pounds of methamphetamine hydrochloride, a Lysol can containing cocaine and more speed. Neville was arrested, charged, and convicted. He appealed his conviction not on entrapment grounds but by arguing that the government's outrageous conduct had violated the due process clause of the Fourteenth Amendment. A federal appeals court agreed with his argument, concluding that the conduct in question reached a "demonstrable level of outrageousness."

**YOUR DECISION**

1. Jack Oberman is a pharmacist at a local drug store and has never engaged in any form of illegal activity. Local police officers received reports that the drug store was filling illegal prescriptions for OxyContin, a strong painkiller often sold on the streets. An undercover officer approached Jack on five separate occasions claiming that he had a daughter suffering from a terminal illness who was in severe pain and discomfort. The undercover officer claimed he could not afford medical treatment and asked Jack to illegally provide him with OxyContin for his daughter. Jack refused on the first four occasions, but finally consented after hearing the horrific stories of the young girl's suffering. Jack handed the undercover officer 10 OxyContin pills and was subsequently arrested. Is he entitled to the defense of entrapment? Would he be successful under both the objective and subjective tests?

2. Judy Smith is an undercover police office in a large metropolitan city. Her assignment is to dress in revealing clothing and stand on a street corner in an area of town known for prostitution. Bucky James approaches Officer Smith and begins a conversation simply by saying, "Hello." Officer Smith tells Bucky, "Two hundred dollars buys you anything you want tonight. Just hand over the cash and the party begins." Bucky hands Officer Smith $200 in cash and is immediately arrested. At his trial, Bucky wants to use the defense of entrapment. Was Bucky "entrapped" by Officer Smith?

## Summary

- The entrapment defense straddles the lines between criminal law and criminal procedure. It is a defense in the criminal-law sense, but it is one of the only defenses that calls into question law enforcement's role in the instigation of a crime.
- The entrapment defense is based on the belief that someone should not be convicted of a crime that the government instigated.
- In its simplest form, the entrapment defense arises when government officials "plant the seeds" of criminal intent.
- Generally, if government officials use violence, supply contraband that is wholly unobtainable, or engage in a criminal enterprise, then the defendant in such a case will often escape conviction via a due process argument—rather than an affirmative defense.

MODULE

# 5.4    AGE

## Learning Objectives

- **Summarize defenses based on age immaturity.**
- **Summarize methods by which some courts treat juveniles as adults.**

## CORE CONCEPTS

People who are below a certain age threshold cannot form, according to the law, the requisite intent to be convicted of a crime. Age thus serves to excuse criminal conduct in certain situations. Indeed, it may bar prosecution altogether.

The common law put children into three categories based on their capacity to commit crimes[56]:

1. Children under age 7 had no criminal capacity
2. Children 7–14 had no criminal capacity, but this was a presumption that could be overcome.
3. Children over 14 had the same capacity to offend as adults.

Today, these exact categories have been abandoned to some extent, but there are exceptions. In general, children under the age of 18 (i.e., juveniles) are charged and adjudicated in the juvenile justice system. Those over 18 are prosecuted and tried in the adult system. Under the federal Juvenile Delinquency Act, a juvenile is a person who has not yet turned 18 years of age.[57] And while most states have followed the federal lead, several treat 17-, 16-, and even 15-year-olds as adults.[58]

The Model Penal Code provides a defense of "immaturity" and requires that no one under the age of 16 can be convicted of a crime.[59] Further, children who were 16 or 17 at the time of their crimes can be tried in either juvenile or adult court. Presumably those who were 18 years or older at the time of their crime are prosecuted as adults.

See the accompanying Court Decision for more on the defense of age. In it we take a look at *State* v. *Guevara*, where a 10-year-old girl is charged with threatening to detonate a bomb at school.

---

[56]R. G. Singer and J. Q. La Fond, *Criminal Law: Examples and Explanations*, 4th ed. (New York: Wolters Kluwer, 2007), pp. 495–496.
[57]18 U.S.C., Section 5031.
[58]For more details, see the "Shifting Conceptions of Age" section later in this chapter.
[59]Model Penal Code Section 4.10.

Minors who break the law can sometimes use age as a defense to criminal liability.

Benis Arapovic/ Shutterstock.com

## COURT DECISION

*State* v. *Guevara,*
155 Wash. App. 1007 (Wash. Ct. App. 2010)

**Background:** Esmeralda Guevera, age 10, was convicted of threatening to bomb or injury property. The trial court concluded that despite her age Esmeralda had the capacity to commit a crime. She appealed and the Court of Appeals of Washington, Division 3 affirmed the conviction.

\*\*\*Facts

Ten-year-old Esmeralda Guevara wrote a note on a stall in the girls' bathroom at a school in College Place, Washington, on the afternoon of Monday, November 5, 2007. The note read, "[B]omb set 20 mins were [*sic*] going to die." School administrators evacuated and closed the school to allow a bomb squad to search. The squad was unable to locate a bomb.

Late that evening, Esmeralda either woke up shortly after going to sleep or was restless before going to bed. She started crying and said, "I did it. I did it." Esmeralda's mother, Zenaida Guevara, asked Esmeralda what she did. Esmeralda said she wrote the note on the bathroom stall. She told her mother she had been teased about her teeth and about being fat. Zenaida explained to Esmeralda that the matter was "really serious" and that they must call the police.

Police Officer Carol Ferraro went to the Guevara home. She arrived shortly after midnight. Both Zenaida and Esmeralda were crying when the officer arrived. Esmeralda explained to Officer Ferraro that she had written the note about the bomb. She said that she had written the message with a pink marker and then had thrown the marker in a bathroom wastebasket. She also shared that she had been feeling sad because of problems at home.

\*\*\*Officer Ferraro took Esmeralda to juvenile detention, where the officer took a written statement from Esmeralda. The statement read:

> On Monday I was feeling very sad because there is problems at my house. Like my Dad is in Jail and my sister is at College and my grandpa is sick so I wrote Bomb threat in a pink Sharpie at 2:35 p.m. and the school was evacuated and saved. At 11:50 My mom called the police and told them I had information about the bomb threat a[*sic*] I told them I did it. So the police took me to J.J.C.

This is the messege [*sic*] that I wrote[,]

> bomb
>
> set for 20 mins
>
> were [*sic*] all going to die.

The State charged Esmeralda with one count of threat to bomb or injure property. After a contested capacity hearing, the juvenile court ruled that Esmeralda had the capacity to understand the wrongfulness of her actions and could be prosecuted for the crime. Esmeralda then pleaded guilty to the crime charged. At sentencing, the court entered an order of deferred disposition and sentenced Esmeralda to a 12-month term of community supervision.

### \*\*\*Determination of Child's Capacity

Esmeralda contends that the court impermissibly relied exclusively on Esmeralda's after-the-fact statements to police to conclude that she had the capacity to understand the seriousness of this crime. She notes that she made the statements after her mother had told her that her actions were "really serious" and after the police came to her house close to midnight, arrested her because of the "seriousness" of her actions, and booked her into a juvenile detention facility.

The State responds that the court properly considered and relied on Esmeralda's statements to police because her after-the-fact acknowledgements of wrongdoing were not the only evidence rebutting the presumption of incapacity. The State says other evidence supports that Esmeralda understood the wrongfulness of her actions. Esmeralda hid evidence of her crime by acting in secret in the stall of a restroom, by disposing of the pink Sharpie marker she used to write the note, and by keeping the information to herself until her conscience got the better of her. Esmeralda further acknowledged her wrongful behavior when she cried to her mother, when Officer Ferraro arrived at the house, and when she demonstrated remorse in "her demeanor and her actions" at the detention center. She also contemplated that the school would send everyone home once they discovered the note.

A statutory presumption that children between 8 and 11 years old lack capacity to commit a crime applies in juvenile proceedings. RCW 9A.04.050. To rebut this presumption, the State must convince the trial judge that the child had sufficient capacity to understand the act and to know that it was wrong.

The court decides whether the State has rebutted the incapacity presumption by considering the following factors:

> (1) the nature of the crime, (2) the child's age and maturity, (3) whether the child evidenced a desire for secrecy, (4) whether the child told the victim (if any) not to tell, (5) prior conduct similar to that charged, (6) any consequences that attached to that prior conduct, and (7) whether the child had made an acknowledgment that the behavior is wrong and could lead to detention.

*State v. Ramer,* 151 Wash.2d 106, 114-15 (2004).

***The State, then, need not show, and the court need not find, that Esmeralda understood that her act would be punishable under the law. "The focus is on 'whether the child appreciated the quality of his or her acts at the time the act was committed,' rather than whether the child understood the legal consequences of the act. *Ramer,* 151 Wash.2d at 114 (quoting *State v. T.E.H.,* 91 Wash.App. 908, 913 (1998)).

We review this juvenile court's determination that Esmeralda had capacity to commit the crime here by examining the record to determine whether the State produced substantial evidence to rebut the presumption of incapacity. Significantly, our inquiry is whether the State *produced* sufficient evidence to meet its burden of proof and, necessarily then, we do not pass on whether the State's showing was *persuasive*. The burden of persuasion is a matter for the trier of fact (here the juvenile court judge) to resolve.

The juvenile court judge here considered and made appropriate findings on the seven factors outlined in *Ramer:*

> **Factor 1:** The alleged crime is a Class B Felony and a serious offense. The language used threatens that people will die in a short passage of time. Considering the violent nature of our society, the recent history of violence in schools and the worldwide use by terrorists of bombs, school officials and law enforcement officers are supersensitive to threats of this nature.

> **Factor 2:** The child, at the time of the incident, was approximately 10.5 years old. The child's appearance in court, her mother's testimony about the child and her activities and Officer Schneidmiller's testimony about his involvement with the child leads the Court to conclude Esmeralda is of at least average or above average maturity for a 10 year old. Officer Ferraro's testimony that she communicated well and talked to her directly support a maturity finding.

> **Factor 3:** The child did not tell anyone about her behavior that afternoon, or even early evening, when she was picked up by her mother after school was cancelled and when they returned to find the parent-teacher conferences were cancelled. She was secretive at that time.

> **Factor 4:** There was no individual victim.

> **Factor 5:** There is no history of prior similar conduct.

> **Factor 6:** There were no prior consequences.

> **Factor 7:** The child, when she told her mother later that evening, after awakening from nightmares, that she had written the threat, was at a minimum indirectly acknowledging the wrongfulness of her behavior. She also cried during the police interview.

Esmeralda argues that the record does not support the court's finding that she acknowledged the wrongfulness of her behavior. She also argues that even if supported by substantial evidence, the court's finding itself is insufficient to support the court's conclusion that she had the capacity to commit the crime. Esmeralda argues that she acknowledged the wrongfulness of her act only after she had been told by her mother and the police in the middle of the night that the act was very serious and warranted arrest. And she contends this is insufficient.

***We conclude that this evidence supports the juvenile court judge's finding and that finding supports the conclusion that Esmeralda had the capacity to understand the wrongfulness of her actions.

***We affirm the conviction.

### Case Analysis

1. Under Washington state law, when can a minor be charged and convicted of a crime?

2. What factors did the court use to determine if Esmeralda had the "capacity" to commit a crime?

3. What type of punishment is appropriate for Esmeralda based on her age and the crime she committed?

## Treating Juveniles as Adults

Juvenile courts have always had mechanisms in place for transferring, or waiving, juveniles to adult court. Whether a juvenile can be transferred to adult court varies by state. There are three main mechanisms for treating juveniles as adults: legislative exclusion, waivers, and concurrent jurisdiction. See Figure 5.1 for an overview.

### Legislative Exclusion

**legislative exclusion**
A statutory requirement that certain juveniles be treated as adults in the criminal justice system.

**Legislative exclusion** (also called *statutory exclusion*) refers to the fact that a statute excludes, or bars, a juvenile from being tried as a juvenile. In other words, legislative exclusion requires that certain juveniles be treated as adults; for example, Mississippi excludes all felonies committed by 17-year-olds,[60] whereas Arizona excludes any felony committed by a juvenile as young as 15 years old.[61]

### Waiver

**juvenile waiver** Trying juveniles as adults in the criminal justice system or waiving them into adult court.

The term **juvenile waiver** refers to trying juveniles as adults, or waiving them to adult court. Waivers have been around for some time, and they have been used on occasion

---

[60]Available at http://www.ncjj.org/stateprofiles/overviews/transfer4.asp (accessed 2/29/2008).
[61]Ibid.

**Most states have multiple ways to impose adult sanctions on offenders of juvenile age**

| State | Discretionary | Presumptive | Mandatory | Concurrent jurisdiction | Statutory exclusion | Reverse waiver | Once an adult/ always an adult | Blended sentencing Juvenile | Blended sentencing Criminal |
|---|---|---|---|---|---|---|---|---|---|
| Number of states | 45 | 15 | 15 | 15 | 29 | 25 | 34 | 15 | 17 |
| Alabama | ■ | | | | ■ | | ■ | | |
| Alaska | ■ | ■ | | | ■ | | | ■ | |
| Arizona | ■ | | | ■ | ■ | ■ | ■ | | |
| Arkansas | ■ | | | ■ | | ■ | ■ | ■ | ■ |
| California | ■ | ■ | | ■ | ■ | ■ | ■ | | ■ |
| Colorado | ■ | ■ | | ■ | | ■ | ■ | ■ | ■ |
| Connecticut | | | ■ | | | | ■ | ■ | |
| Delaware | ■ | | ■ | | ■ | | ■ | | |
| Dist. of Columbia | ■ | ■ | | ■ | | | | | |
| Florida | ■ | | | ■ | ■ | ■ | ■ | | ■ |
| Georgia | ■ | | ■ | ■ | ■ | ■ | | | |
| Hawaii | ■ | | | | | | ■ | | |
| Idaho | ■ | | | | ■ | | | | ■ |
| Illinois | ■ | ■ | ■ | | ■ | ■ | ■ | ■ | ■ |
| Indiana | ■ | | ■ | | ■ | | | | ■ |
| Iowa | ■ | | | ■ | | ■ | ■ | | ■ |
| Kansas | ■ | ■ | | | | | ■ | ■ | |
| Kentucky | ■ | | ■ | | | ■ | | | ■ |
| Louisiana | ■ | | ■ | ■ | ■ | | | | |
| Maine | ■ | ■ | | | | | ■ | | |
| Maryland | ■ | | | | ■ | ■ | ■ | | |
| Massachusetts | | | | | ■ | | | ■ | ■ |
| Michigan | ■ | | | ■ | | | ■ | ■ | ■ |
| Minnesota | ■ | ■ | | | | | ■ | ■ | ■ |
| Mississippi | ■ | | | ■ | ■ | | | | |
| Missouri | ■ | | | | | | ■ | | |
| Montana | | | | ■ | ■ | ■ | | | |
| Nebraska | | | | ■ | | ■ | | | ■ |
| Nevada | ■ | ■ | | | ■ | ■ | ■ | | |
| New Hampshire | ■ | ■ | | | | | ■ | | |
| New Jersey | ■ | ■ | ■ | | | | | | |
| New Mexico | | | | | ■ | | | ■ | ■ |
| New York | | | | | ■ | ■ | | | |
| North Carolina | ■ | | ■ | | | | ■ | | |
| North Dakota | ■ | ■ | ■ | | | | ■ | | |
| Ohio | ■ | | ■ | | | | | | |
| Oklahoma | ■ | | | ■ | ■ | ■ | ■ | | ■ |
| Oregon | ■ | | | | ■ | ■ | ■ | | |
| Pennsylvania | ■ | ■ | | | ■ | ■ | ■ | | |
| Rhode Island | ■ | ■ | ■ | | | | ■ | ■ | |
| South Carolina | ■ | | ■ | | ■ | | | | |
| South Dakota | ■ | | | | ■ | | ■ | | |
| Tennessee | ■ | | | | | ■ | ■ | | |
| Texas | ■ | | | | | | ■ | ■ | |
| Utah | ■ | ■ | | | ■ | | ■ | | |
| Vermont | ■ | | | ■ | ■ | ■ | | ■ | |
| Virginia | ■ | | ■ | ■ | | ■ | ■ | | ■ |
| Washington | ■ | | | | ■ | | | | |
| West Virginia | ■ | | ■ | | | | | | ■ |
| Wisconsin | ■ | | | | ■ | ■ | ■ | | ■ |
| Wyoming | ■ | | | ■ | | ■ | | | |

■ In states with a combination of provisions for transferring juveniles to criminal court, the exclusion, mandatory waiver, or concurrent jurisdiction provisions generally target the oldest juveniles and/or those charged with the most serious offenses, whereas younger juveniles and/or those charged with relatively less serious offenses may be eligible for discretionary waiver.

Note: Table information is as of the end of the 2004 legislative session.
Source: Authors' adaptation of Griffin's National overviews. *State juvenile justice profiles.*

**Figure 5.1**
State Legal Arrangements Governing Treatment of Juveniles as Adults

*Source*: H. N. Snyder and M. Sickmund, *Juvenile Offenders and Victims:2006 National Report* (Washington, DC: U.S. Department of Justice, Office of Justice Programs, Office of Juvenile Justice and Delinquency Prevention, 2006), Chap. 4, p. 111.

when a juvenile commits a particularly harsh crime and there is a desire to charge him or her in the adult justice system. Recent changes have made it easier to try juveniles as adult offenders, a significant departure from the original intent of having a separate juvenile justice system. There are three main types of waivers used with juveniles:

**discretionary waiver** The discretion of the juvenile court judge to waive jurisdiction over a criminal case so that the minor can be tried as an adult.

1. **Discretionary waiver.** A **discretionary waiver**, as defined by several states, "gives juvenile court judges discretion to waive jurisdiction in individual cases involving minors, so as to allow prosecution in adult criminal courts. Terminology varies from State to State—some call the process a "certification," "bindover," or "remand" for criminal prosecution, for example, or a "transfer" or "decline" rather than a waiver proceeding—but all transfer mechanisms in this category have the effect of authorizing but not requiring juvenile courts to designate appropriate cases for adult prosecution."[62]

**presumptive waiver** Waiver of a juvenile defendant from juvenile to adult court is presumed appropriate based on the age, offense, or other factors.

2. **Presumptive waiver.** Several state statutes designate a category of cases called **presumptive waiver**, in which waiver to criminal court is presumed appropriate. "In such cases, the juvenile rather than the State bears the burden of proof in the waiver hearing; if a juvenile meeting age, offense, or other statutory criteria triggering the presumption fails to make an adequate argument against transfer, the juvenile court must send the case to criminal court."[63]

**mandatory waiver** Waiver of a juvenile defendant from juvenile to adult court is mandatory based on the age, offense, or other factors.

3. **Mandatory waiver.** Several states use a **mandatory waiver** "in cases that meet certain age, offense, or other criteria. In these States, proceedings against the juvenile are initiated in juvenile court. However, the juvenile court has no role other than to confirm that the statutory requirements for mandatory waiver are met. Once it has done so, the juvenile court must send the case to a court of criminal jurisdiction."[64]

**reverse waiver** Waiver of a juvenile defendant from adult court to juvenile court for adjudication.

In a twist on these approaches to waiver, some states have a **reverse waiver**, which requires that certain cases initiated in adult court be sent to the juvenile court for an adjudicatory hearing.[65] In yet another twist, some state waiver laws have "once an adult, always an adult" provisions, requiring that once a juvenile is waived to adult court, all other offenses that juvenile commits are to be tried in adult court.[66]

## Concurrent Jurisdiction

**concurrent jurisdiction** Two courts, namely an adult and juvenile court, both have jurisdiction over a particular case. The prosecutor makes the decision regarding which court to initiate criminal proceedings.

**Concurrent jurisdiction** means that certain cases can be tried in both juvenile and adult court, and the prosecutor makes a decision as to where the case should be tried. Concurrent jurisdiction sometimes occurs outside of the juvenile justice context, as well. For example, if both a federal and state court could try the same offense, it is said that each has concurrent jurisdiction.

[62]P. Griffin, P. Torbet, and L. Szymanski, *Trying Juveniles as Adults: An Analysis of State Transfer Provisions* (Washington, DC: U.S. Department of Justice, 1998). Available at http://ojjdp.ncjrs.org/pubs/tryingjuvasadult/transfer.html (accessed August 4, 2009).
[63]Ibid.
[64]Ibid.
[65]H. N. Snyder and M. Sickmund, *Juvenile Offenders and Victims:2006 National Report* (Washington, DC: U.S. Department of Justice, Office of Justice Programs, Office of Juvenile Justice and Delinquency Prevention, 2006), Chap. 4, p. 111.
[66]Ibid.

**YOUR DECISION**

1. William Morris is 88 years old and still holds a valid driver's license. Although he does not suffer from any serious illnesses, William does have trouble with his vision and is beginning to show mild signs of dementia. One afternoon on his way back from the grocery store, William lost control of his vehicle and killed two innocent pedestrians. William is being charged with vehicular homicide and wants to assert the defense of age. Is he entitled to the defense? Why or why not?

2. Chuck Jacobson is 14 years old and lives in a tough inner city neighborhood where drugs and criminal activities are rampant. He is a below-average student in school with only a second-grade reading level. His teachers and family members also find him to be emotionally immature for his age. Chuck, however, has been an active member of a street gang since the age of 11. Chuck has been arrested on multiple occasions for assault, burglary, and drug possession. Recently he has been charged with the illegal possession of a firearm. Chuck is attempting to assert the defense of age. Is he entitled to the defense? Is it possible to charge Chuck as an adult instead of a juvenile?

## Summary

- People who are below a certain age threshold cannot form, according to the law, the requisite intent to be convicted of a crime.

- In general, children under the age of 18 (i.e., juveniles) are charged and adjudicated in the juvenile justice system. Those over 18 are prosecuted and tried in the adult system.

- Despite these generalities, several states treat 17-, 16-, and even 15-year-olds as adults.

- Juvenile courts have always had mechanisms in place for transferring, or waiving, juveniles to adult court.

- There are three main mechanisms for treating juveniles as adults: legislative exclusion, waivers, and concurrent jurisdiction.

## MODULE 5.5

# INSANITY

### *Learning Objectives*

- **Distinguish insanity from competency to stand trial and diminished capacity.**
- **Describe the insanity defense and the controversy surrounding it.**
- **Explain the effect of a successful insanity defense.**

**CORE CONCEPTS**

Hollywood loves to give the impression that crafty criminals routinely escape conviction by pleading insanity. Perhaps you recall the movie *Primal Fear*, starring Edward Norton and Richard Gere. Norton played an abused altar boy who found himself charged with a priest's murder. He successfully feigned a split personality, which led to a mistrial and his confinement in a mental hospital. Though he did not "go free," he did escape conviction. And though his confinement to a mental hospital was somewhat realistic, it is exceedingly difficult for all but accomplished actors to feign insanity. As we will see, the tests to prove insanity set the bar rather high. Also, the defense itself is rarely raised, which moviemakers fail to tell us.

## Competency to Stand Trial versus the Insanity Defense

The insanity defense is distinct from competency to stand trial. The latter deals with the defendant's ability to understand what is happening at trial, during pretrial hearings, and the like. The specific test to make such a determination is whether the defendant "has sufficient present ability to consult with his lawyer with a reasonable degree of rational understanding—and whether he has a rational as well as factual understanding of the proceedings against him."[67] The burden of proving incompetence falls on the defendant.[68] The *insanity defense*, in contrast, deals with the defendant's competence at the time he or she committed the crime.

The defendant's competence to stand trial is usually considered in a separate pretrial hearing. This was the rule announced in *Pate* v. *Robinson*,[69] a case dealing with an Illinois trial judge's decision not to hold a hearing on the question of the defendant's mental condition, even though he had a long history of mental problems. The Supreme Court held that a hearing was necessary, noting that "[the Illinois court's] reasoning offers no justification for ignoring the uncontradicted testimony of Robinson's [the defendant's] history of pronounced irrational behavior. While Robinson's demeanor at trial might be relevant to the ultimate decision as to his [present] sanity, it cannot be relied upon to dispense with a hearing on that very issue."[70]

What happens to the defendant if he or she is declared incompetent to stand trial? Usually, the defendant will be hospitalized until his or her competency is restored, if it ever is. However, in *Jackson* v. *Indiana*,[71] the Supreme Court held that there are constitutional limitations on how long a defendant can be hospitalized for the purpose of restoring competency. That case dealt with a 27-year-old deaf-mute individual with the mental level of a preschooler, who was being hospitalized until

---

[67]*Dusky* v. *United States*, 362 U.S. 402 (1960).
[68]*Medina* v. *California*, 505 U.S. 437 (1992).
[69]*Pate* v. *Robinson*, 383 U.S. 375 (1966).
[70]Ibid., p. 385.
[71]*Jackson* v. *Indiana*, 406 U.S. 715 (1972).

the staff determined him sane. The Court concluded that it was likely the defendant's condition would *never* improve. Thus, the Court said,

> We hold . . . that a person charged by a State with a criminal offense who is committed [to an institution] solely on account of his incapacity to proceed to trial cannot be held more than the reasonable period of time necessary to determine whether there is a substantial probability that he will attain that capacity in the foreseeable future. If it is determined that this is not the case, then the State must either institute the customary civil commitment proceeding that would be required to commit indefinitely any other citizen, or release the defendant.[72]

## Insanity versus Diminished Capacity

**diminished capacity** A failure of proof defense based on the defendant's inability to form the required criminal intent because of a medical disease or defect. It is a unique defense that is not equivalent to the insanity defense.

Insanity is not the same as **diminished capacity**, the latter of which is a failure of proof defense (see outset of Chapter 4). By this we mean the defendant is permitted in most cases to introduce evidence that he or she suffered from a mental condition such that intent, or the *mens rea*, to commit the crime was lacking. Very importantly, this is independent of an insanity defense. Not all states permit the defense to present such an argument, but several do.[73] The Model Penal Code adopts the same approach, stating, "Evidence that the defendant suffered from a mental disease or defect is admissible whenever it is relevant to prove that the defendant did or did not have a state of mind that is an element of the offense."[74] The logic for permitting evidence of diminished capacity was explained by the Colorado Supreme Court in *Hendershott* v. *People*:

> Once we accept the basic principles that an accused is presumed innocent and that he cannot be adjudicated guilty unless the prosecution proves beyond a reasonable doubt the existence of the mental state required for the crime charged, it defies both logic and fundamental fairness to prohibit a defendant from presenting reliable and relevant evidence that, due to a mental impairment beyond his conscious control, he lacked the capacity to entertain the very culpability which is indispensible to his criminal responsibility in the first instance.[75]

## Diminished Capacity and Partial Responsibility

The Model Penal Code also provides that when the defendant faces the possibility of a death sentence, evidence showing that the defendant lacked the capacity to appreciate the wrongfulness of his actions can be introduced at the sentence phase.[76] This is known as **partial responsibility** and, to the extent that a defendant can claim as much (few states recognize this defense), it will have a tendency to reduce a death sentence to a prison sentence. One court drew the distinction between partial insanity and either diminished capacity or insanity in this way:

**partial responsibility** A defense that reduces a death sentence to a prison term if the defendant lacked the mental ability to appreciate the wrongfulness of his contact.

> A defendant pleading diminished responsibility does not seek relief from punishment by justification or excuse, but seeks to be punished for a lesser offense

---

[72]Ibid., p. 738.
[73]Dressler, *Understanding Criminal Law*, p. 369.
[74]Model Penal Code Section 4.02(1).
[75]*Hendershott* v. *People*, 653 P.2d 385 (Colo. 1982), pp. 393–394.
[76]Model Penal Code Section 4.02(2).

which he generally admits committing. In contrast, diminished capacity focuses on a defendant's capacity to commit a specific intent crime, and, if established, does not excuse punishment, but results in punishment instead for the general intent crime defendant was capable of committing. Evidence to demonstrate such a lack of specific intent is not equivalent to evidence to establish diminished responsibility.[77]

## Insanity Tests

**insanity** An excuse defense to a criminal charge based on the defendant's mental condition at the time of the crime.

*Black's Law Dictionary* defines **insanity** as "a condition which renders the affected person unfit to enjoy liberty of action because of the unreliability of his behavior with concomitant danger to himself and others."[78] Unfortunately, it gets much more complex from here. For example, the insanity defense is a *legal* concept, so just because someone may be medically diagnosed as insane, he or she may not succeed with an insanity defense. Also, the courts use multiple tests to determine whether a person was insane at the time of the crime. Here we introduce five of the them: (1) the *M'Naghten* test, (2) the "irresistible impulse" test, (3) the Model Penal Code test, (4) the product test, and (5) the federal test. States can choose their own tests, combine two or more tests to suit their needs, or even have no insanity defense at all (see Figure 5.2).

### The *M'Naghten* Test

**M'Naghten test** An insanity test that focuses on the defendant's ability to appreciate the wrongfulness of his or her conduct based on a mental disease or defect.

In 1843, Daniel M'Naghten attempted to assassinate then-British Prime Minister Robert Peel. M'Naghten actually fired at Peel's secretary, Edward Drummond, and killed him. Realizing that M'Naghten was not of sound mind, the House of Lords asked a panel of judges to offer guidance in cases when a defendant pleads insanity, which M'Naghten did. In *M'Naghten's Case*,[79] it was decided that in order to prove insanity, it must be clearly proved that, at the time of the crime, "the party accused was labouring [*sic*] under such a defect of reason, from disease of the mind, as not to know the nature and quality of the act he was doing; or, if he did know it, that he did not know he was doing what was wrong."[80] This has come to be known as the **M'Naghten test**. According to recent data, 17 states and the federal government use this test.[81]

While the *M'Naghten* test has survived time's test, it is not without problems. First, it fails to distinguish between levels of insanity; either a person is insane or she is not. In reality, there are *levels* of insanity. Second, critics have called the test antiquated because even though a person may know something is wrong, he or she may do it anyway because of something like a volitional deficiency, an inability to control movement.[82]

---

[77]*State v. Phipps*, 883 S.W. 2d 138 (1994), p. 144.
[78]*Black's Law Dictionary*, 6th ed. (St. Paul, MN: West, 1990), p. 794.
[79]*M'Naghten's Case*, 8 Eng. Rep. 718 (1843).
[80]Ibid.
[81]*Clark* v. *Arizona*, 548 U.S. 735 (2006), pp. 750–751.
[82]See, e.g., *United States* v. *Pollard*, 171 F.Supp. 474 (E.D. Mich. 1959).

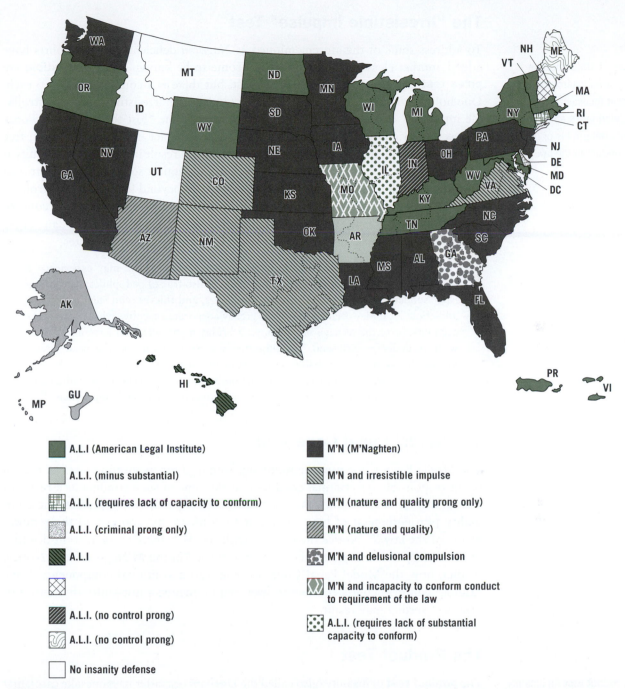

**Figure 5.2**

Insanity Tests by State

*Source*: D. B. Rottman and S. M. Strickland, *State Court Organization, 2004* (Washington, DC: Bureau of Justice Statistics, 2006), pp. 199–201. Available at: http://bjs.ojp.usdoj.gov/content/pub/pdf/sco04.pdf (accessed April 25, 2011).

Third, some of the terms that make up the test are confusing. An example is "know." What does it mean for an offender to "know" whether what he or she was doing was wrong? Does "know" mean the offender was aware of what he was doing? Or does it mean something more, like did the offender *appreciate* the gravity of what he did?

## The "Irresistible Impulse" Test

**irresistible impulse test** An insanity test that focuses on the defendant's ability to conform his or her conduct to the law.

To address some of the aforementioned *M'Naghten* deficiencies, some courts have added another element to the test. It has come to be known as the **irresistible impulse test**. There are variations on the test, but there is a common theme to each. One holds that a person is insane if she "acted from an irresistible and uncontrollable impulse."[83] Another treats a person as insane if she "lost the *power to choose* between the right and wrong, and to avoid doing the act in question, as [her] free agency was at the time destroyed."[84] Yet another will result in a finding of insanity if the defendant's will "has been otherwise than voluntarily so completely destroyed that [his or her] actions are not subject to it, but are beyond [his or her] control.[85]

The irresistible impulse test is not without its critics, either. The main concern people have with it is the impression that it excuses people who offend out an "urge" to do so. University of Florida law professor Christopher Slobogin writes,

> [T]he psychotic individual who hears voices telling him to kill may experience a powerful urge to commit crime. But that claim is also true of pedophiles, repeat rapists, "sudden" or serial murderers and assaulters, and thieves who steal to feed an addiction. . . . It may even be true of the greedy corporate executive who manipulates accounts, or of the teenage boy who, on a Friday night, wants to have intercourse with an underage girlfriend. The subjectively experienced urges of a person with mental illness are not probably greater than the urges of people we would never think of excusing. . . . If there is a distinction between the psychotic individual and the others mentioned above, it is based in cognitive, not volitional, impairment.[86]

## The Model Penal Code Test

The Model Penal Code uses the following language for its insanity test: "A person is not responsible for criminal conduct if at the time of such conduct as a result of mental disease or defect he lacks substantial capacity either to appreciate the criminality [wrongfulness] of his conduct or to conform his conduct to the requirements of the law."[87] Notice the overlap with the *M'Naghten* test. Also notice that the word *appreciate* replaces the word *know* used in the *M'Naghten* test. Notice, further, how the Model Penal Code test contains a volitional component; if one cannot "conform" one's conduct to legal requirements, a not guilty (by reason of insanity) verdict may result.

## The Product Test

**product test** An insanity test that determines whether the criminal activity is the product of a mental disease or defect.

The **product test** of insanity (also called the *Durham* test, after its namesake case), first developed in New Hampshire, provides that "an accused is not criminally responsible

---

[83]*Commonwealth* v. *Rogers*, 48 Mass. 500 (1844), p. 502.
[84]*Parsons* v. *State*, 81 Ala. 577 (1886).
[85]*Davis* v. *United States*, 165 U.S. 373 (1897), p. 378.
[86]C. Slobogin, "The Integrationist Alternative to the Insanity Defense: Reflections on the Exculpatory Scope of Mental Illness in the Wake of the Andrea Yates Trial," *American Journal of Criminal Law*, Vol. 30 (2003), p. 322.
[87]Model Penal Code Section 4.01(1)

if his unlawful act was the product of mental disease or defect."[88] *Disease* refers to "a condition which is considered capable of either improving or deteriorating."[89] A defect is "a condition which is not considered capable of either improving or deteriorating and which may be either congenital, or the result of injury, or the residual effect of a physical or mental disease."[90] Under this test, the jury was asked to determine whether defendant suffered from a mental disease or defect and, if so, whether the mental disease or defect caused the defendant to commit the crime.

The product test is more general than some of the other tests introduced earlier because it leaves open the definition of "mental disease or defect." Critics, however, feel that the general nature of the test requires too much reliance on expert testimony to prove either mental disease or defect. Experts for the defense and prosecution make a case for and against insanity, respectively, and then jurors are forced to weigh their testimony and decide who to believe (or who is most persuasive). To this day, the product test is retained only by New Hampshire. For a time it was used in the District of Columbia, but it no longer is.[91]

## The Federal Test

Federal law treats insanity as a defense. Here is the specific statutory language:

> It is an affirmative defense to a prosecution under any Federal statute that, at the time of the commission of the acts constituting the offense, the defendant, as a result of a severe mental disease or defect, was unable to appreciate the nature and quality or the wrongfulness of his acts. Mental disease or defect does not otherwise constitute a defense.[92]

This definition of insanity also parallels some of others introduced earlier. For example, it retains the Model Penal Code's "appreciate" language. However, it adds the word *severe* to the equation, possibly making it more difficult for a federal defendant to succeed with an insanity defense.

## The Real Effect of a Successful Insanity Defense

Not only are insanity defenses rarely invoked, but they rarely succeed. Moreover, even when they do succeed, they rarely result in an offender "going free." On one level, it is odd to even treat insanity as an excuse defense. It does not so much *excuse* criminal conduct as it does punish, or at least confine, someone with a lengthy term of confinement in a facility, just not a prison. As one team of researchers put it, "[T]he insanity defense is not a defense, it is a device for triggering indeterminate restraint."[93]

---

[88]*Durham* v. *United States*, 214 F.2d 862 (D.C. Cir. 1954) pp. 874–875; see *State* v. *Pike*, 49 N.H. 399 (1870), for the original.
[89]Ibid., p. 875.
[90]Ibid.
[91]*United States* v. *Brawner*, 471 F.2d 969 (D.C. Cir. 1972).
[92]18 U.S.C. Section 17(a).
[93]J. Goldstein and J. Katz, "Abolish the 'Insanity Defense'—Why Not?" *Yale Law Journal*, Vol. 72 (1963), p. 868.

Typically, a person who is found not guilty by reason of insanity (NGRI) is confined to an institution where that person can presumably be treated. Once an NGRI verdict is read, it is presumed that the person suffers from enough of a mental illness that instant confinement is necessary. In other words, there is no need for another hearing to make this determination.[94] Yet in some jurisdictions an individual found NGRI will be temporarily confined so experts can determine whether indefinite detention is warranted. Under federal law, for example, a postverdict commitment hearing must be held within a certain period of time.[95] In either case, if the convicted individual is mentally ill or a danger to herself or others (or both), she can be confined until which point she no longer is. The term of confinement is basically indefinite and is intended to last long enough to ensure the individual is fit for release.

Once a person found NGRI is successfully treated, release is considered. The mechanisms for release vary from one jurisdiction to the next, however. In some jurisdictions, the court that ordered the individual's commitment makes the determination. In others, the individual must petition for release, either to a court or a body charged with making such decisions. The burden of proof falls on the committed individual and varies, too, from one jurisdiction to the next.

## The Move toward Abolition

Since its inception, the insanity defense has met with a certain measure of opposition. Some critics oppose the insanity defense because of inaccurate media representations of how it works. However, researchers have observed that many people, even legal experts, "dramatically and grossly overestimate both the frequency and the success rate of the insanity plea."[96] Others raise more calculated arguments, claiming, for example, that the very presence of such a defense may encourage some individuals who, in terms of mental illness are "on the fence," to offend. Such individuals would have a hard time raising a successful insanity defense.

Despite arguments in favor of the insanity defense, abolitionists have worked hard to remove it from the long list of criminal defenses. Prompted by the attempted assassination of Ronald Reagan in the 1980s, four states—Idaho, Kansas, Montana, and Utah—promptly abolished the defense.[97] These states permit the defendant to introduce evidence to rebut the prosecutor's argument that the defendant possessed the requisite mental state to commit the crime, but there is no express insanity defense recognized in their laws. And the Supreme Court, it seems, has no problem with this. In *Clark* v. *Arizona*, for example, it remarked, "We have never held that the Constitution mandates an insanity defense."[98]

---

[94]*Jones* v. *United States*, 463 U.S. 354 (1983).
[95]18 U.S.C. Section 4243(c).
[96]J. Rodriguez, L. Lewinn, and M. Perlin, "The Insanity Defense Under Siege: Legislative Assaults and Legal Rejoinders," *Rutgers Law Journal*, Vol. 14 (1983), p. 401.
[97]Dressler, *Understanding Criminal Law*, pp. 363–364.
[98]*Clark* v. *Arizona*, 548 U.S. 735 (2006), p. 752, n. 20.

# Guilty but Mentally Ill

**guilty but mentally ill**
A verdict, short of finding insanity, in which the criminal defendant is mentally ill at the time of the crime.

A greater number of states have taken a more measured approach by, instead of abolishing the insanity defense, creating a **guilty but mentally ill** (GBMI; some states also use "guilty but insane," or GBI—see Figure 5.3) verdict. The intent of GBMI is to address some of the (perceived) deficiencies associated with a traditional insanity defense. For example, a successful insanity defense followed by successful treatment can result in release. While this may be the intent of the insanity defense, some people resist to releasing even those who were insane at the time of

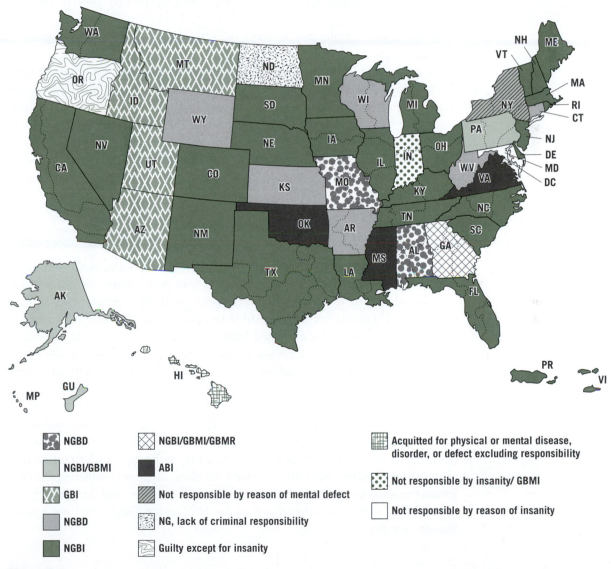

**Figure 5.3**
Insanity Verdicts
*Source*: D. B. Rottman and S. M. Strickland, *State Court Organization, 2004* (Washington, DC: Bureau of Justice Statistics, 2006), pp. 199–201. Available at: http://bjs.ojp.usdoj.gov/content/pub/pdf/sco04.pdf (accessed September 25, 2010).

their crimes. Returning to the attempted Reagan assassination, every attempt to grant outright release to John Hinckely, Jr., the man found not guilty by reason of insanity for making an attempt on the president's life, has been met with considerable resistance.[99]

Of the more than 20 states that have taken this approach, only two of them have abolished the insanity defense.[100] In GBMI states, jurors can choose between four verdicts rather than the usual three: guilty, not guilty, not guilty by reason of insanity, and guilty but mentally ill. In general, the GBMI verdict is reserved for individuals who are deemed (1) guilty of the crime, (2) sane at the time of the crime, and (3) "mentally ill" at the time of trial. An individual who is adjudicated GBMI will likely be sent to prison, but will also most likely receive treatment while there.

A problem with "guilty but mentally ill" is that it adds a layer of complexity to an already complex area of law. "Mentally ill" is not necessarily the same as "insanity," so how is a jury to distinguish between the two? Likewise, supporters of GBMI claim that the defense offers treatment to prisoners, but prisons can already offer treatment to mentally ill offenders, regardless of whether such a verdict is in place. Yet another problem is that the verdict generally is not possible unless the defendant first raises an insanity defense. Critics claim that this leads to more insanity pleas—and, by extension, more acquittals.[101] This has prompted at least one expert to call the verdict "an ill-conceived and ineffective overreaction to the problems associated with the insanity defense."[102]

## YOUR DECISION

1. Lorena Bobbit was married to an abusive husband, John, who was having affairs with multiple women. One evening, John came home extremely drunk and forced Lorena to have sexual intercourse with him. After being raped by her husband, Lorena felt an irresistible impulse to injure John. While he slept, she cut off his penis with a kitchen knife and then drove away. At her trial for assaulting John, Lorena plead not guilty by reason of insanity. Is she entitled to the insanity defense? Which of the insanity tests is most likely to apply to Lorena's situation?

2. John Sugarman killed his mother with a direct gunshot to the head. At trial, John attempted to raise the defense of insanity. The following information was discovered at trial: (a) John's expert psychiatrist diagnosed him with schizophrenia; (b) John claims he heard "voices" in his head from the devil ordering him to kill his mother; (c) John used a silencer on his weapon, (d) after completing the crime, John attempted to dump the body in a river; and (e) John told the police he "did a bad thing." In a jurisdiction that uses the *M'Naghten* test, is John not guilty by reason of insanity?

---

[99]See, e.g., http://www.cnn.com/2009/CRIME/06/17/john.hinckley/index.html (accessed May 25, 2010).
[100]Dressler, *Understanding Criminal Law*, p. 365.
[101]See, e.g., C. Slobogin, "The Guilty But Mentally Ill Verdict: An Idea Whose Time Should Not Have Come," *George Washington Law Review*, Vol. 53 (1985), p. 516.
[102]Ibid., p. 527.

# Summary

- *Black's Law Dictionary* defines insanity as "a condition which renders the affected person unfit to enjoy liberty of action because of the unreliability of his behavior with concomitant danger to himself and others."[103]

- The insanity defense is distinct from competency to stand trial. The latter deals with the defendant's ability to understand what is happening at trial (as well as at pretrial hearings, etc.). The specific test to make such a determination is whether the defendant "has sufficient present ability to consult with his lawyer with a reasonable degree of rational understanding—and whether he has a rational as well as factual understanding of the proceedings against him."[104]

- Insanity is not the same as diminished capacity, the latter of which is a failure of proof defense.

- Under the *M'Naghten* test, a defendant may escape liability if he "was labouring [*sic*] under such a defect of reason, from disease of the mind, as not to know the nature and quality of the act he was doing; or, if he did know it, that he did not know he was doing what was wrong."[105]

- According to the irresistible impulse test, person is insane if she "acted from an irresistible and uncontrollable impulse."

- The Model Penal Code test is as follows: "A person is not responsible for criminal conduct if at the time of such conduct as a result of mental disease or defect he lacks substantial capacity either to appreciate the criminality [wrongfulness] of his conduct or to conform his conduct to the requirements of the law."[106]

- The product test of insanity, recognized only in New Hampshire, provides that "an accused is not criminally responsible if his unlawful act was the product of mental disease or defect."[107]

- Federal law provides an affirmative defense of insanity that emphasizes a "mental disease or defect."

- Not only are insanity defenses rarely invoked, but they rarely succeed. Moreover, even when they do succeed, they rarely result in an offender "going free."

- Typically, a person who is found not guilty by reason of insanity (NGRI) is confined to an institution where that person can presumably be treated.

- Abolitionists have worked hard to remove insanity from the long list of criminal defenses.

- A greater number of states have taken a more measured approach by, instead of abolishing the insanity defense, creating a guilty but mentally ill (GBMI) verdict.

---

[103] *Black's Law Dictionary*, p. 794.
[104] *Dusky v. United States*, p. 402.
[105] *Clark v. Arizona*, pp. 750–751.
[106] *Durham v. United States*, pp. 874–875.
[107] Ibid., p. 875.

# CREATIVE EXCUSES

### Learning Objective

- **Distinguish among and offer examples of physiological, psychological, and sociological excuse defenses.**

**CORE CONCEPTS**

The excuse defenses we already introduced are, for better or worse, fairly unsurprising and predictable. They are the "garden variety" excuses raised in countless criminal trials over many generations. Here we shift our attention to a variety of creative and relatively novel excuse defenses. Some have been recognized as stand-alone defenses; others are just arguments raised in the context of more traditional defenses, such as insanity. We organize them into three categories: excuses based on physiology, excuses based on psychology, and sociological excuses. Together, they are sometimes called "syndrome defenses."

## Excuses Based on Physiology

Since Ceaseare Lombroso claimed he could predict a person's criminal tendency based on the shape of the head, criminologists have been looking for biological explanations for illegal behavior. At various points in history, biological explanations have fallen in and out of favor, but certain authorities have always been interested in whether some people are born predisposed to crime. It is not surprising, then, that some defenses to criminal liability pick up on this line of thinking.

One excuse based on physiology concerns the presence of an extra Y chromosome. Each fetus has two sex chromosomes. An X combined with an X yields a female. An X combined with a Y yields a male. Some males, however, are born with an extra Y chromosome. The thinking is that this extra Y chromosome makes the individual "hypermasculine" and even more disposed to crime than a male already is (recall that men, in general, are more likely to commit crime than women). Since no man can control his genetic makeup and since an extra Y chromosome may be a factor contributing to his criminal tendencies, shouldn't he be at least partially excused for any resulting criminal activity? In theory, perhaps, but the courts have answered with a resounding "no." Interestingly, the **XYY chromosome defect** is the only physiological or creative defense that has reached the appellate level in the United States (and thereby has been reported and published so we can read the courts' logic for rejecting the defense). Multiple courts have rejected it, basing their decisions on the fact that there is no consensus with respect to the possibility of a "genetic criminal."[108]

**XYY chromosome defect**
A criminal defense based on the presence of an extra Y chromosome and hypermasculinity.

---

[108]See, e.g., *People* v. *Tanner*, 91 Cal. Rptr. 656 (Cal. Ct. App. 1970); *Millard* v. *Maryland*, 261 A.2d 227 (Md. Ct. Spec. App. 1970); *People* v. *Yuki*, 372 N.Y.S.2d 313 (Sup. Ct. 1975).

**premenstrual dysphoric disorder (PMDD)** A medical condition creating extreme mental and emotional symptoms prior to menstruation that could potentially be used as a criminal defense to a crime.

Premenstrual syndrome (PMS) has also served as the basis for an excuse defense against criminal liability.[109] While many women experience cramps, nausea, and other discomforts during menstruation, some experience severe agony and sometimes even become violent. In 1994, the American Psychiatric Association (APA) added an extreme version of PMS, **premenstrual dysphoric disorder (PMDD)**, to the list of depressive disorders in its *Diagnostic and Statistical Manual*, 4th edition (DMS-IV).[110] In light of these issues, it is not surprising that some female defendants have claimed that PMS or PMDD was responsible for their violent criminal behavior. The defense has been raised on multiple occasions in U.S. courts,[111] and despite the fact that it has yet to reach the appellate level, the defense has nevertheless succeeded. In June 1991, a Virginia court accepted the first criminal defense based on PMS.[112] Perhaps as many courts have rejected the defense, too.[113]

Though XYY and PMS defenses have garnered the most attention, a few other physiological excuse defenses are coming into the limelight. Examples include hypoglycemia, Alzheimer's disease, neurotoxic damage, and even testosterone overload.[114] It is unclear to what extent such defenses will gain a foothold.

## Excuses Based on Psychology

Every criminal act contains a psychological element—namely *mens rea*. Many of the criminal defenses we have introduced already attempt to negate that element of intent. Some, however, go even further by raising creative claims of psychological causation and defense. One example is brainwashing. Singer and LaFond recount the story of Patty Hearst, heiress to the Hearst newspaper fortune:

> Ms. Hearst was kidnapped by a militant group of terrorists in California, who demanded that her father take certain social measures (such as distributing free food to thousands of hungry poor people in several California cities). Months later, Ms. Hearst appeared, dressed in black and carrying a machine gun, assisting the terrorists in robbing a California bank. She was arrested about a year later in San Francisco. When booked, she gave her name as Tanya, and her occupation as "revolutionary."[115]

At her trial, Hearst argued it was "Tanya," not she, who robbed the bank. She claimed the militants brainwashed her during captivity, indoctrinating her into their belief system. While the trial judge permitted the brainwashing argument,

---

[109]Colloquium, "Premenstrual Syndrome: The Debate Surrounding Criminal Defense," *Maryland Law Review*, Vol. 54 (1995), pp. 571–600.

[110]Ibid., p. 571.

[111]L. Taylor and K. Dalton, "Premenstrual Syndrome: A New Criminal Defense?" *California Western Law Review*, Vol. 19 (1983), pp. 269 and 276-77.

[112]M. Kasindorf, "Allowing Hormones to Take the Rap: Does the PMS Defense Help or Hinder Women?" *Newsday*, June 16, 1991, at 17.

[113]See, e.g., *Commonwealth* v. *Grass*, 595 A.2d 789 (1991), p. 792.

[114]See Singer and La Fond, *Criminal Law: Examples and Explanations*, p. 533.

[115]Ibid., p. 534.

Post-traumatic stress disorder can potentially be a defense to a crime. Soldiers who served in combat zones have used the PTSD defense.

Maksym Dragunov/Shutterstock.com

the jury did not buy it. Hearst was convicted and sentenced to 35 years in prison. Her sentence was later commuted to 7 years—and commuted even further by then-President Jimmy Carter some years later. She was released on February 1, 1979, having served just 22 months.[116]

Some defendants have also claimed that a "mob mentality" was responsible for their criminal acts. In one incident, Damien Williams, an African American and Los Angeles resident, joined a group of rioters who lashed out in response to the acquittal of several white police officers who were accused of beating Rodney King. The mob stopped a truck, pulled the white driver, Reginald Denny, from the cab, and began beating him (a video clip was broadcast across the country). Williams proceeded to hit Denny with a brick, severely injuring him. He survived, but Williams was arrested and charged with several crimes, including attempted murder. At his trial, Williams argued that he was "swept up" in the heat of the moment and had no intentions to hurt the innocent driver. The jury acquitted him of the most serious charges, but found him guilty of several misdemeanors.

Some defendants have also claimed that **post-traumatic stress disorder (PTSD)** led them to commit a crime. For example, in 2009, a Santa Clara County, California, jury found a former Army captain who was diagnosed with PTSD not guilty by reason of insanity for robbing a pharmacy of drugs at gunpoint.[117]

**post-traumatic stress disorder (PTSD)** A potential defense to a crime based on psychological trauma that the defendant suffered after experiencing a traumatic event.

---

[116]K. Dell and R. Myers, "The 10 Most Notorious Presidential Pardons," *Time*, http://www.time.com/time/2007/presidential_pardons/9.html (accessed May 27, 2010).

[117]See http://www.military.com/news/article/ptsd-tied-to-ex-gis-insanity-defense.html (accessed June 1, 2010).

# Sociological Excuses

**urban psychosis** A criminal defense based on the defendant's traumatic upbringing in a violent area.

**urban survival syndrome** A criminal defense based on the heightened sense of fear that the defendant experiences from being raised in a high-crime urban neighborhood.

Many a defendant has also claimed that his or her background or surroundings contributed to a decision to break the law. One such defense is **urban psychosis**, a condition analogous to PTSD that results from a "traumatic childhood in a violent inner-city home and neighborhood."[118] A few defendants have asserted this defense, but it appears the most success they have had is in being convicted of lesser charges. Some defendants have also raised an **urban survival syndrome** defense. Though similar to urban psychosis, this defense suggests that crime results from heightened sense of fear and danger that results from living in a high-crime urban environment.

Still other defendants have blamed television intoxication for their actions. In one case, 15-year-old Ronny Zamora and an accomplice broke into the home of an elderly neighbor. When the neighbor returned home, Zamora shot and killed her. At trial, his attorney claimed that he "had become involuntarily subliminally intoxicated by violent television programming."[119] Though the defense was couched in terms of insanity, it did not succeed. Zamora was sentenced to life imprisonment for murder.[120] He appealed on multiple occasions, and he and his family even sued three major television networks, but all these attempts failed. Zamora is not alone; others who have blamed television for their crimes have failed with the defense.[121] Efforts to blame violent conduct on watching too much pornography and listening to violent and/or "gangsta rap" music have also failed.[122]

See the accompanying Court Decision for more on sociologically based defenses. In it we take a look at *United States* v. *Nguyen*, where a defendant attempts to use his Vietnamese culture as a defense to a crime.

---

## COURT DECISION

*United States* v. *Le*
2009 WL 2947370 (E.D.Va. 2009)

**Background:** The defendant, Phuoung Nguyen Le, was charged with Mailing Threatening Communications to Congressman Bobby Scott. Le originally pled guilty to the charge, but later made a motion to withdraw his guilty plea due to legal innocence. The district court granted Le's motion.

This matter is before the Court on the defendant's MOTION TO WITHDRAW PLEA DUE TO LEGAL INNOCENCE. For the reasons set forth below, the motion will be granted.

---

[118]P. J. Falk, "Novel Theories of Criminal Defense Based upon the Toxicity of the Social Environment: Urban Psychosis, Television Intoxication, and Black Rage," *North Carolina Law Review*, Vol. 74 (1996), p. 738.
[119]Ibid., p. 742.
[120]*Zamora v. State* (Dade County Cir. Ct. 1977), aff'd, 361 So. 2d 776 (Fla. Dist. Ct. App. 1978), cert denied, 372 So. 2d 472 (Fla. 1979).
[121]See, e.g., *State v. Molina*, No. 84-2314B (11th Judicial Dist., Fla. 1984); *State v. Quillen*, No. S87-08-0118, 1989 Del. Super. LEXIS 129 (Mar. 28, 1989).
[122]Falk, "Novel Theories of CriminalDefense," pp. 746–748.

### Background

**A. Factual History:** The parties, by and large, do not dispute the material facts. The Defendant, Phuong Le, is a 49-year-old who lived in Vietnam until 1991, at which time he relocated to a Malaysian refugee camp with his family following his release from prison. Le had been imprisoned for "political reasons." Le and his family, including his first wife, moved to the United States in 1998, when they were granted refugee status. Le became a naturalized citizen in 2004 and divorced his wife in the same year. During several trips to Vietnam throughout the period of 2004 to 2007, the Defendant met and married his current wife, My Nga Ly.

Ms. Ly applied for a visa to visit the United States, but her application was denied. Le requested information about the denial from Congressman Bobby Scott; Scott obtained a letter from Charles Bennett, the Consular Chief in Vietnam, which stated that Ly's application had been denied because there was no evidence of a "*bona fide* relationship" between her and Le.

Upset by this news, Le sent a letter to Congressman Scott that made references to the Virginia Tech shootings of 2007, threatened to decapitate Bennett, and indicated that Le planned to commit suicide. The letter was also smeared with Le's blood. Le states that his letter was not intended to threaten, but rather to insult, and somewhat belatedly, has blamed his lack of understanding of English language and a difference in cultures for the misunderstanding.

**B. Procedural History:** Le was charged with a violation of 18 U.S.C. § 876, Mailing Threatening Communications, in a one count Indictment on December 15, 2008. Le pled guilty to that charge on February 4, 2009; and the guilty plea was taken by a Magistrate Judge, who issued a report and recommendation that the Court accept Le's guilty plea on the same day.

\*\*\*A sentencing hearing was held for Le on April 24, 2009, at which time Le, and his counsel, indicated that Le might seek to withdraw his guilty plea.

### \*\*\*Discussion

\*\*\* Le argues that the statute under which he was charged, 18 U.S.C. § 876(c), requires that the perpetrator mail a communication knowing that the content of the communication was a threat. \*\*\* Le argues that, because he was linguistically and culturally incapable of understanding that his communication was threatening, he could not have possessed the required *mens rea*. Le proffers expert testimony to support his factual claims. The United States argues that no *mens rea* requirement is attached to the "threat" element of § 876.

The relevant statute provides:

> [w]hoever knowingly . . . deposits or causes to be delivered . . . any communication with or without a name or designating mark subscribed thereto, addressed to any other person and containing any threat to kidnap any person or any threat to injure the person of the addressee or of another

is guilty of a crime. 18 U.S.C. § 876. The Fourth Circuit has stated that § 876 creates a specific intent crime, but only insofar as the act of mailing is concerned. However, the court of Appeals also has held that "the defendant must have a general intent to threaten the recipient at the time of the mailing." *United States v. Maxton*, 940 F.2d 103, 106 (4th Cir. 1991). This general intent "can be gleaned from the very nature of the words used in the communication; extrinsic evidence to prove an intent to threaten should only be necessary when the threatening nature of the communication is ambiguous." Id. The communication must also encompass a "true threat"—a communication that a "reasonable recipient who is familiar with the context of the letter would interpret [ ] as a threat of injury." *Worrell*, 313 F.3d at 874.

\*\*\*There can be no reasonable dispute that a letter smeared with blood that contains a threat to decapitate another individual, a reference to a notorious massacre, and a threat to commit suicide is a "true threat" under the objective standard set forth by *Maxton*. Le has not argued that he did not knowingly place that communication in the mail. Therefore, the remaining question in assessing whether there is a credible showing of innocence is his mental state respecting the threat contained in the letter which he admittedly sent.

\*\*\*However, Le has offered evidence in support of his motion in the form of expert testimony that, in Le's culture and in his language, the communication would not be threatening. This kind of evidence is generally regarded as being potentially relevant to the issue of *mens rea* in a criminal proceeding.

Dr. Leung, Le's expert, offers conclusions about the subjective meanings of Le's words as they were communicated in the letter. \*\*\*Amidst a flurry of conclusions of questionable relevance and admissibility, Dr. Leung makes three salient statements. First, Dr. Leung states that the phrase "cut his head off," as idiomatically used in Vietnamese, expresses an insult rather than an actual threat. Second, Dr. Leung states that Le's act of smearing the letter with blood is a Vietnamese tradition called "letting blood," which has the effect of vouching for the truthfulness of the content of the document. These points support Le's argument that he had no general intent to threaten and/or knowledge that his letter contained a threat and, thereby, they support Le's claim of actual innocence.

Finally, Dr. Leung opines that Le, due to his limited grasp on the English language and American culture, would not have realized that those statements and actions could lead to another individual feeling threatened. That testimony may not be admissible in that form but Dr. Leung likely would be permitted to testify to the closely-related proposition that the difference in language and culture would lead a Vietnamese not to appreciate that the English language used could constitute a threat. If that is what Dr. Leung intends to convey, it likely would be admissible and, if it is admitted, would be further evidence probative of Le's asserted innocence.

Of course there is significant contrary evidence. Dr. Leung does not explain how the stated intent to decapitate and smearing of the blood should be read in the context of the references to the Virginia Tech massacre and Le's threat of suicide. These are undoubtedly violent images, and frame the remainder of the letter in a more threatening tone. Therefore, Dr. Leung's conclusions about Le's subjective meaning are thrown into doubt by the presence of that unexplained context.

Furthermore, Le had been in the country for over ten years at the time the letter was sent, and had significant contacts with the English-speaking justice system and English-speaking authorities. The likelihood that Le would misunderstand the threatening nature of the content and style of his communication is reasonably called into doubt by his long experience in America and with English speakers.

Taken as a whole, the record shows that Le has made a non-frivolous showing of legal innocence. That evidence is not particularly strong, but it creates factual issues which, if resolved in Le's favor by a jury, could result in acquittal. The second Moore factor, therefore, weighs in his favor.

### ***Conclusion

For the foregoing reasons, ***Le has shown a fair and just reason for withdrawing his guilty plea, notwithstanding that the record reflects a fully complete and satisfactory Rule 11 colloquy. This is one of those few cases that circumstances not made known to the Magistrate Judge dispel the presumption created by an adequate colloquy. On this record, it is fair and just to permit Le to withdraw his guilty plea. Counsel have been so informed by a telephone conference and the case will be set for trial.

It is so ORDERED.

## Case Analysis

1. Why does Le want to withdraw his guilty plea? What is his legal argument?
2. Do you think a defendant's cultural background should be relevant in determining guilt or innocence?
3. What did the court ultimately rule in regards to Le's motion?

---

**black rage** A criminal defense based on the defendant's past experience with racism that caused him or her to break the law.

Of the creative sociological excuses for criminal activity, **black rage** has been raised in perhaps the most cases,[123] although it is difficult to tell how often it has succeeded. Again, most trial court decisions are not published, meaning they cannot be uncovered by researchers. We are left to look at appellate decisions, which of course represent the tip of the proverbial iceberg. There are different variations of the black rage defense, but the common theme is that a defendant's experience with racism prompts him or her to break the law. "Experience" could be a perception of prolonged racism or simply a single racially motivated incident. In either case, the defendant claims that his or her mental state was "affected" by racism.

The black rage defense goes as far back as 1846 to the case of *Freeman* v. *People*. Freeman, accused of killing four white people, claimed that mistreatment by white society rendered him insane. The jury rejected his claim.[124] One such case went all the way to the Supreme Court. In *Fisher* v. *United States*,[125] the defendant was charged with murdering a white woman who uttered a racial epithet. While the Court upheld his conviction, it signaled the presence of a defense that does not fit neatly into traditional categories of insanity and diminished capacity.[126]

---

[123]Ibid.
[124]*Freeman* v. *People*, 4 Denio 9 (N.Y. Sup. Ct. 1847).
[125]*Fisher* v. *United States*, 328 U.S. 463 (1946).
[126]For more cases invoking the black rage argument, see Falk, "Novel Theories of Criminal Defense," pp. 748–758.

**YOUR
DECISION**

1. Fumiko Kimura is a Japanese immigrant living in the United States. Fumiko discovers that her husband is having an affair and decides to commit suicide with her two young children. The concept is referred to as *oyako shinju*" in Japan, and while discouraged is a part of Japanese cultural history. Fumiko drowns her 6-month-old daughter and 4-year-old son, but survives. She is charged with two counts of murder. Fumiko would like to use a "cultural defense" since she would be shown leniency if the incident occurred in Japan. Is Fumiko entitled to any type of cultural defense?

2. Anthony Cooper is a Vietnam War veteran who served as a Marine for 25 years before retirement. While in Vietnam, Anthony was exposed to Agent Orange and witnessed the killing of many individuals. Anthony himself was responsible for countless enemy casualties. One evening while drinking in a local bar, Anthony is verbally harassed by a group of young college students. In response, Anthony suddenly "snaps" and kills one of the young men with his bare hands by breaking his neck. Anthony is charged with first-degree murder. Does anything have a defense based on post-traumatic stress disorder (PTSD)? What about his exposure to Agent Orange?

## Summary

- There are three categories of creative excuse defenses: excuses based on physiology, excuses based on psychology, and sociological excuses.

- Examples of creative physiological excuse defenses include the XYY chromosome defect, premenstrual syndrome, and premenstrual dysphoric disorder.

- Examples of creative psychological excuse defenses include brainwashing and mob mentality.

- Examples of creative excuse defenses based on sociological factors include urban psychosis, urban survival syndrome, television intoxication, and black rage.

# Chapter Review

**EXCUSE DEFENSES AND DURESS**

*Learning Objectives*

- Explain the reasons for excuse defenses.
- Summarize the conditions of the defense of duress.

*Review Questions*

1. Of the various reasons for excuse defenses, which is most important?
2. Of the five elements for a duress defense, which do you think is more important (if any) than the rest?
3. Why can a duress defense rarely succeed in homicide cases? Should the courts and state legislatures relax their treatment of duress in homicide cases? Why or why not?
4. Should an inmate who escapes prison and claims necessity and duress be forced to choose one defense over the other? Why or why not?
5. Should battered woman syndrome formulate the basis of a duress defense? Why or why not?

*Key Term*

duress

**INTOXICATION**

*Learning Objective*

- Describe the intoxication defense.

*Review Questions*

1. Should an intoxicated person be considered insane? Why or why not? What about a person who has been abusing alcohol for 20+ years?
2. Under what circumstances could voluntary intoxication serve as a defense? If none, should it result in conviction of a lesser crime? Why or why not?
3. Try to think of a situation in which involuntary intoxication may *not* result in a successful defense.

*Key Term*

intoxication

**ENTRAPMENT**

*Learning Objectives*

- Summarize what constitutes entrapment.
- Explain how entrapment relates to due process.

### Review Questions

1. Describe a situation in which entrapment may occur.

2. Which should be given more weight, the defendant's subjective intent or the government's conduct?

3. Do you believe the DEA, in the case discussed above, went too far in getting someone to commit a crime? Why or why not?

### Key Term

entrapment

## MODULE 5.4    AGE

### Learning Objectives

· Summarize defenses based on age immaturity.

· Summarize methods by which some courts treat juveniles as adults.

### Review Questions

1. What, in your opinion, is the appropriate age that a person should be tried in adult court?

2. Can you conceive of a situation in which a 12-year-old could be waived to adult court? Why or why not?

3. The juvenile justice system is looking more and more like the adult system. Is this for better or worse? Why?

### Key Terms

legislative exclusion
juvenile waiver
discretionary waiver
presumptive waiver
mandatory waiver
reverse waiver
concurrent jurisdiction

## MODULE 5.5    INSANITY

### Learning Objectives

· Distinguish insanity from competency to stand trial and diminished capacity.

· Describe the insanity defense and the controversy surrounding it.

· Explain the effect of a successful insanity defense.

### Review Questions

1. In your opinion, what insanity test is best and why?

2. Should the insanity defense be abolished? Why or why not?

3. What are your thoughts concerning the GBMI verdict? Should it be allowed? Why or why not?

*Key Terms*

diminished capacity
partial responsibility
insanity
*M'Naghten* test
irresistible impulse test
product test
guilty but mentally ill

## MODULE 5.6   CREATIVE EXCUSES

*Learning Objective*

· Distinguish among and offer examples of physiological, psychological, and
  sociological excuse defenses.

*Review Questions*

1.  Should PMS serve as an excuse to criminal liability? Why or why not?

2.  Should brainwashing serve as an excuse? Why or why not?

3.  Is "black rage" a legitimate excuse defense? Why or why not?

*Key Terms*

XYY chromosome defect
premenstrual dysphoric disorder (PMDD)
post-traumatic stress disorder (PTSD)
urban psychosis
urban survival syndrome
black rage

# Chapter Synthesizing Questions

1.  What excuse defense is most difficult to prove? Why?

2.  What excuse defense, in your view, is the most controversial? Defend your answer.

3.  Is the intoxication defense too strict? Why or why not?

4.  At what age is it appropriate to treat juveniles as adults?

5.  Should the insanity defense be available? Why or why not?

6.  Creative excuse defenses are getting increasingly popular. Is this beneficial? Why
    or why not?

# 6

# COMPLICITY AND VICARIOUS LIABILITY

*Learning Objectives*

**MODULE 6.1  INTRODUCTION TO ACCOMPLICE LIABILITY**

- Distinguish between complicity and conspiracy.
- Identify the parties to crime, including principals, accomplices, and accessories.

**MODULE 6.2  THE ELEMENTS OF COMPLICITY**

- Explain the elements of complicity.
- Explain the elements of accessory liability.

**MODULE 6.3  COMPLICITY ISSUES, LIMITATIONS, AND DEFENSES**

- Discuss some of the issues that make complicity law complicated.
- Summarize the limitations of and defenses to accomplice liability.
- Explain the Model Penal Code approach to accomplice liability.

**MODULE 6.4  VICARIOUS LIABILITY**

- Explain the concept of vicarious liability.

MODULE

# 6.1

# INTRODUCTION TO ACCOMPLICE LIABILITY

### Learning Objectives

- **Distinguish between complicity and conspiracy.**
- **Identify the parties to crime, including principals, accomplices, and accessories.**

**CORE CONCEPTS**

**complicity** Involvement in a crime as an accomplice.

**accomplice** An individual who aids before or during the commission of a crime.

**derivative liability** When the defendant derives or obtains his criminal liability from the primary offender.

This chapter marks the beginning of a new section in which we examine how the criminal law handles situations involving multiple offenders and incomplete (i.e., inchoate) crimes. This chapter covers two main topics: complicity, better known as accomplice liability, and vicarious liability. Vicarious liability refers to the transfer of *mens rea* and *actus reas* to another individual or organization.

While we have begun a new section of the book, its content is not unlike that included in the first five chapters. How is this so? To this point we have yet to get into specific definitions of distinct crime types. For example, we have not yet defined homicide and discussed its various levels. Likewise, a burglary definition is still lacking. The chapters in this section, like the ones before it, offer foundational information necessary for understanding when and how a criminal conviction is possible. We are still setting the foundation for an in-depth examination of specific crime types.

**Complicity** is defined as "a state of being an accomplice."[1] What, then, is an accomplice? An **accomplice** is "one who knowingly, voluntarily and with common intent unites with the principal offender in the commission of a crime."[2] In the typical criminal scenarios we have presented thus far throughout the book, there has been one offender and one victim. With accomplice liability, our concern is with multiple offenders. Basically, if person B assists person A in the commission of a crime, then both can be held criminally liable. This is the essence of accomplice liability.

Complicity is a form of **derivative liability**, meaning that a second offender *derives* his or her liability from the primary individual with whom he or she associates.[3] Also, accomplice liability is generally limited to felonies. There are some exceptions, but most jurisdictions limit accomplice liability to the most serious offenses.

## Common Law Parties to a Crime

The common law used four different terms to describe the parties to a crime involving two or more offenders: principal in the first degree, principal in the second degree, accessory before the fact, and accessory after the fact. While courts continue to

---

[1]*Black's Law Dictionary*, 6th ed. (St. Paul, MN: West, 1990), p. 285.
[2]Ibid., p. 17.
[3]See, e.g., *People* v. *Perez*, 113 P.3d 100 (Cal. 2005), p. 104.

refer to each in some of their modern-day decisions (and some statutes even use such language), the four-category approach has been basically abandoned in favor of a simpler scheme that we consider in the next section.

## Principal in the First Degree

The **principal in the first degree** is the primary offender. More formally, the principal in the first degree is "one who actually commits a crime, either by his own hand, or by an inanimate agency, or by an innocent instrumentality."[4] A person who "pulls the trigger," for example, is a principal in the first degree. In other words, such an individual is "the criminal actor."[5]

Some of the terms in our definition require clarification. It is fairly clear what it means for an individual to offend "by his own hand." Clubbing someone over the head, shooting a person, and the like fit the bill. But what is "inanimate agency?" A booby trap is an example of inanimate agency. The principal in the first degree could set it, forget it, and yet still be guilty of a crime if it does what it is supposed to do. As for "innocent instrumentality," it is possible that an offender could dupe another person into committing a crime for which the latter has no *mens rea*. That individual would be exculpated, but the primary offender would be found guilty. Or assume, for example, that an adult convinces a child to commit a crime. Since the child cannot form the required criminal intent, she will not be guilty of a crime, but the adult who was pulling the strings will.[6]

## Principal in the Second Degree

The **principal in the second degree** is someone who intentionally assists the principal in the first degree with the commission of a crime and who is actually or constructively present at the time of the crime. The individual is "actually present" if that person is in close physical proximity to the principal in the first degree. For example, if Larry followed Keith into the bank that Keith robbed, with the intention of helping Keith carry bags of loot away, then Larry was "actually present." In contrast, if Larry sat in a "getaway car" and was prepared to quickly shuttle Keith away from the crime scene, then Larry was "constructively present."

## Accessory before the Fact

If someone solicits, encourages, or commands another to offend, then he is an **accessory before the fact**. Coercion cannot be used, however, because then the accessory before the fact would become the principal in the first degree, and the person who commits the act will be considered an innocent instrumentality. An example will clarify this point. Suppose Rocco, the local mob boss, orders a hit on a rival boss, Gino, in the next town over. His trusted hit man, Marco, does the deed. In this case, Rocco is an accessory before the fact because he ordered Marco to commit murder.

---

[4]*State* v. *Ward*, 284 Md. 189 (Md. Ct. App. 1978), p. 197.
[5]*State* v. *Burney*, 82 P.3d 164 (Or. App. 2003), p. 166.
[6]See, e.g., *Queen* v. *Manley*, 1 Cox Crim. Cas. 104 (1844).

Marco was arguably not "coerced" because he was the mob's hit man and presumably killed people on previous occasions. Suppose, in contrast, that Jim kidnaps and threatens to kill Tom's wife, Lynne, if Tom does not rob an armored truck. Tom, being coerced, is an innocent instrumentality. He could not be held criminally liable because he did not possess the required *mens rea* to commit the crime. Jim would then become a principal in the first degree, not an accessory before the fact.

## Accessory after the Fact

**accessory after the fact**
Under common law, a person who helps the principal after the criminal event takes place.

An **accessory after the fact** is a person who helps the principal after the criminal event takes place. For example, in one case, after causing a fatal traffic accident, the driver and his passenger fled the scene and were assisted by friends in dismantling the car so it could not be detected. Despite their efforts, the car was discovered and linked to the fatal accident. The friends were charged as accessories after the fact.[7] In another case, the passenger in a vehicle that was fleeing from the police threw full beer cans at the pursuing patrol car. He was charged as an accomplice for assisting with the driver's attempted escape.[8]

An accessory after the fact is often one who is involved in "aiding and abetting" a principal.[9] If Ted provides a place for Travis, who has recently murdered someone, to stay for the night, Ted may have been "aiding and abetting" in Travis's efforts to avoid apprehension. Under common law, Ted would have been subject to accomplice liability, but he probably would not have been punished as harshly as Travis. This is no longer the case. For example, federal law now provides that whoever "aids, abets, counsels, commands, induces, or procures [a crime's] commission . . . is punishable as a principal."[10] This means not that Ted would be punished as harshly as Travis.

## Parties to a Crime Today

Why did the common law recognize four parties to a crime? At common law, all felons were subject to the death penalty. The stakes were thus much higher than they are in the case of some modern-day felonies, which is why there were distinctions between principals and accessories. The distinction spared accessories from the execution that principals may have faced, but this created problems. Under common law, no accessory could be tried or convicted until the principal was both tried and convicted. What if, for example, the principal died? The accomplice would have escaped conviction. Once it was realized that some otherwise guilty accomplices were escaping conviction, the distinctions were largely abandoned. Because of these problems, today there are two main parties to a crime: accomplices and accessories. There are some exceptions to the general rules we list below, but they are not the norm. See Figure 6.1 for a summary of the parties to a crime today compared to common law parties.

[7]*People v. Cunningham*, 201 Mich. App. 720 (1993).
[8]*People v. Branch*, 202 Mich. App. 550 (1993).
[9]See, e.g., *People v. Robinson*, 715 N.W.2d 44 (Mich. 2006).
[10]18 U.S.C. 2(a).

**Figure 6.1**
Parties to a Crime: Then
and Now

| Common Law Parties to a Crime | Parties to a Crime Today |
|---|---|
| Principal in the first degree | Accomplice |
| Principal in the second degree | Accessory |
| Accessory before the fact | |
| Accessory after the fact | |

## Accomplices

An accomplice, as we defined it earlier, is "one who knowingly, voluntarily and with common intent unites with the principal offender in the commission of a crime"[11] Anyone, other than the primary offender, who participates *before and during* the commission of a crime is thus an accomplice. Colorado's complicity statute offers an example:

> A person is legally accountable as principal for the behavior of another constituting a criminal offense if, with the intent to promote or facilitate the commission of the offense, he or she aids, abets, advises, or encourages the other person in planning or committing the offense.[12]

## Accessories

**accessory** Modern term to describe someone who participates after the crime is already committed.

An **accessory** is typically a participant in a crime *after* it is committed. Again, there are some exceptions, but many states define accessories as such. Continuing with our Colorado example, an "accessory to a crime" is defined in this way:

> A person is an accessory to a crime if, with intent to hinder, delay, or prevent the discovery, detection, apprehension, prosecution, conviction, or punishment of another for the commission of a crime, he renders assistance to such person."[13]

Importantly, whereas the accomplice is usually charged with the underlying crime (e.g., murder or robbery), an accessory is generally charged with a less serious crime (potentially even a misdemeanor). Being an accomplice to murder can mean life in prison, while being an accessory can lead to a relatively minor punishment.

**YOUR
DECISION**

1. Fred is extremely jealous that Justin was selected to be the varsity quarterback on the Happy Valley High School football team. He meets with his friends, Brian and Dan, after school one day to plan "revenge." Brian actively encourages Fred to kill Justin using a gun with a silencer. Brian even helps acquire the gun from his grandfather's basement. On the night of the shooting, only Dan accompanies Fred

---

[11]*Black's Law Dictionary*, p. 17.
[12]Colorado Revised Statutes 18-1-603 (2009).
[13]Colorado Revised Statutes 18-8-105 (2009).

to Justin's home to carry out the killing. Dan serves as a lookout while Fred shoots and kills Justin in his kitchen. Using the traditional common law terms for complicity, identify the appropriate role, if any, for Fred, Brian, and Dan in the murder.

2. Don kidnapped his 7-year old daughter, Brittany, after the family court refused to give him legal visitation rights. Don and Brittany are on the run and need a place to hide from authorities. Don arrives unannounced at the home of his childhood friend, Joe, and begs for help. Joe agrees to let Don and Brittany stay at his home for as long as necessary and does not notify the police. Using today's definitions for complicity, is Joe an accomplice or an accessory? Why or why not?

## Summary

- Complicity and accomplice liability are one in the same.
- An accomplice is "one who knowingly, voluntarily, and with common intent unites with the principal offender in the commission of a crime."[14]
- Complicity is not the same as conspiracy. Conspiracy is an inchoate (i.e., incomplete) crime. Complicity occurs when two or more offenders work together and actually commit a criminal act.
- The common law used four different terms to describe the parties to a crime involving two or more offenders: principal in the first degree, principal in the second degree, accessory before the fact, and accessory after the fact.
- The principal in the first degree is the primary offender.
- The principal in the second degree is someone who intentionally assists the principal in the first degree with the commission of a crime and who is actually or constructively present at the time of the crime.
- If someone solicits, encourages, or commands another to offend, then he is an accessory before the fact.
- An accessory after the fact is a person who helps the principal after the criminal event takes place.
- Today there are two main parties to a crime: accomplices and accessories.

# THE ELEMENTS OF COMPLICITY

### *Learning Objectives*

- **Explain the elements of complicity.**
- **Explain the elements of accessory liability.**

---

[14]*Black's Law Dictionary*, p. 17.

**CORE CONCEPTS**

The *actus reus* and *mens rea* for accomplice and accessory liability are distinct, so we will treat each one separately. We begin with the elements of accomplice liability, which require the most discussion. We wrap up with the elements of accessory liability.

## Accomplice *Actus Reus*

The *actus reus* for accomplice liability is, at its most basic level, assistance. That is, a person who *assists* a principal in the commission of a crime has satisfied the *actus reus* of accomplice/accessory liability. According to Joshua Dressler, there are three means by which assistance is typically provided: "(1) assistance by physical conduct; (2) assistance by psychological influence; and (3) assistance by omission (assuming in this latter case that the omitter has a duty to act)."[15]

### Physical Conduct

Assistance by physical conduct is straightforward. For example, in *Hensel* v. *State*,[16] the defendant, Hensel, aided in the commission of a felony by providing dynamite and fuses that were used to blow up a storage bunker. According to the court, for accomplice liability to attach, the *actus reus* component requires that the defendant "aid, abet, assist, or facilitate the commission of the particular substantive crime for which the state seeks to hold the defendant liable as an accomplice."[17] Hensel indeed satisfied this requirement because, in the words of the court, he "provided the co-defendants with capped and fused dynamite knowing that they would return to the premises previously burglarized, plant the dynamite inside the bunkers, and explode the buildings."[18]

In another case, physical assistance came in the form of "casing" the crime scene in advance of a robbery. *Actus reus* was present because the defendant had been driving around with two other individuals while they planned a robbery. Moreover, "[t]he defendant was well aware of the potential for danger, yet remained with the group of would-be robbers in spite of his awareness, even though he had several opportunities to remove himself from the plan before the robbery was committed. For example, while defendant's cohorts argued about where to find the bullets for the rifle, he went into the store which he knew was to be robbed, but never attempted to abort the robbery by warning the owner."[19]

In yet another case, 14-year-old Mario Wall accompanied a man who had a shotgun into Elizabeth Turner's apartment to retrieve guns that she allegedly kept stored there. When Turner refused to tell them where the guns were, Wall's codefendant became upset. He told Wall to close the window and lock the door, presumably

---

[15]J. Dressler, *Understanding Criminal Law*, 5th ed. (San Francisco, CA: Lexis-Nexis, 2009), p. 473.
[16]*Hensel* v. *State*, 604 P.2d 222 (Alaska 1979).
[17]Ibid., p. 238.
[18]Ibid., p. 239.
[19]*State* v. *Arillo*, 553 A.2d 281 (N.H. 1988), p. 298.

so Turner (and a friend who was also present) could not escape. He then shot Turner in the chest. She later died. He also shot Turner's friend in the arm. She survived. Wall was convicted of criminal homicide, even though he did not pull the trigger. An appellate court upheld his conviction because he "clearly and directly aided his co-defendant's criminal conduct."[20]

## Psychological Influence

What is psychological influence? It generally requires a certain amount of coaxing, encouraging, persuading, or soliciting. Mere presence at the scene of the crime is not enough.[21] For example, here are the facts from a case in which Carl Pace appealed his conviction of being an accomplice in a robbery:

> [A]ppellant, his wife and two infant children were in a car driving from South Bend to LaPorte. Eugene Rootes was riding with them. The appellant was driving with his wife and one child in the front seat. Rootes and appellant's other child were in the back seat. While in South Bend, appellant after asking his wife for permission stopped to pick up a hitchhiker, Mr. Reppert, who sat next to Rootes in the back seat with one of appellant's infant children. Later Rootes pulled a knife and took Reppert's wallet. After driving further, Reppert got out of the car, Rootes then took his watch. The appellant said nothing during the entire period and they continued driving to LaPorte. This is all of the evidence presented by the record which would have any bearing on the crime charged, i.e., accessory before the fact of robbery by placing in fear.[22]

The court decided that Pace was not an accomplice because "[w]hile he was driving the car, nothing was said nor did he act in any manner to indicate his approval or countenance of the robbery."[23] He passively acquiesced to the robbery and, therefore, could not be considered an accomplice.

Contrast the *Pace* case with one in which a woman, Constance Doody, was having arguments with her mother and, on more than one occasion, expressed a desire to have the woman killed. At one point, when Constance was with her husband, Michael, in their pickup truck, Michael opened the glove box and showed her a box of bullets. Constance reportedly said, "I won't give you any problem." When Michael subsequently killed her mother, Constance, along with Michael, was charged with murder under a theory of accomplice liability. An appellate court affirmed her conviction.[24] This case is interesting because Constance's conduct fell in the vast gray area between mere presence and outright encouragement. Constance was not present at the murder, nor did she expressly encourage or order her husband to kill her mother. However, she did seem to know what was going to happen and indicated that she would not get in the way. According to the court, her statement in the truck "could be reasonably found by the trial court to imply an assurance to Michael that she would not interfere with his plans and that she approved of the proposed crime."[25]

---

[20]*Commonwealth* v. *Hatchin*, 709 A.2d 405 (Pa. Super. Ct. 1998).
[21]See, e.g., *State* v. *Vaillancourt*, 453 A.2d 1327 (N.H. 1982).
[22]*Pace* v. *State*, 224 N.E.2d 312 (Ind. 1967), p. 313.
[23]Ibid., p. 314.
[24]*State* v. *Doody*, 434 A.2d 523 (Me. 1981).
[25]Ibid., p. 530.

At its most basic level, accomplice liability occurs when one person assists another in the commission of a crime.

BananaStock/thinkstock.com

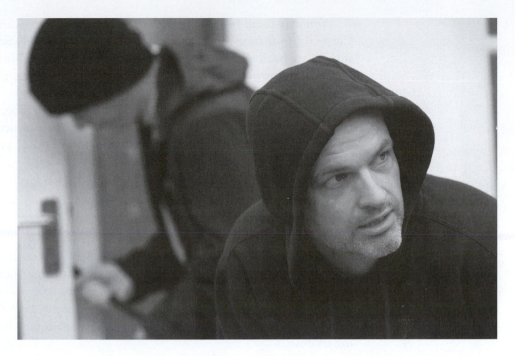

## Omission

The *actus reus* of accomplice liability can also be satisfied by way of an omission. Recall from Chapter 3 that an omission can contribute to criminal liability, but only in certain circumstances. In the case of accomplice liability, an omission will only result in conviction if the omitter has a duty to intervene. For example, in *State* v. *Walden*,[26] a mother stood by and did not attempt to intervene (or call for help) while her child was being assaulted. She was convicted as an accomplice because a North Carolina statute requires that parents have an "affirmative duty" to protect their children. In a related case, a mother knew that two men who lived with her repeatedly raped and sexually assaulted her two daughters. The court noted that there was "no doubt" that the woman was aware of what was happening and did nothing to intervene or stop it.[27]

To illustrate the *lack* of a duty to intervene, consider the infamous 1983 gang rape of a young woman in Big Dan's bar in New Bedford, Massachusetts.[28] Several bar patrons witnessed the incident, but not one of them reported it. No one cheered on the rapists or encouraged them, but none intervened and none called the police. They just stood idly by and watched. As disturbing as that may sound, not one individual who witnessed the rapes had a *legal duty to act*. As such, none of them could be held criminally liable as accomplices to the rapes.

---

[26]*State* v. *Walden*, 293 S.E.2d 780 (N.C. 1982).
[27]*Hutcheson* v. *State*, 213 S.W.3d 25 (Ark. App. 2005).
[28]For a detailed explanation of the events, see L. S. Chancer, "New Bedford, Massachusetts, March 6, 1983–March 22, 1984: The 'Before and After' of a Group Rape," *Gender and Society*, Vol. 1 (1987), pp. 239–260.

You may recall from Chapter 3 some reference to so-called Bad Samaritan laws. Currently, four states have such laws,[29] but Massachusetts is not one of them. Had such a law been in place, then perhaps the bystanders could have been held liable; however, they would then be held liable not as accomplices to the rapes, but simply as people who failed to intervene when they should have.

So if assistance is physical, psychological, or by omission, just how much of it is necessary? Once it is clear that an individual assisted a principal in the commission of a crime, it does not matter how much assistance that person provided.[30] Any amount of assistance will suffice.

## Accomplice *Mens Rea*

The *mens rea* requirement for accomplice liability is a little more tedious than the *mens rea* requirement for other crimes. For ordinary criminal liability, there is one type of *mens rea* (e.g., intent, knowledge). For accomplice liability, there are *two* levels of *mens rea*. First, there must be some degree of intent or desire to aid the primary offender. Second, there must also intent to commit the underlying offense.[31]

Consider the case of *State* v. *Harrison*.[32] Harrison drove two friends, Thompson and Carter, to a commuter parking lot, where they stole a vehicle. Thompson and Carter attempted to rob a gas station attendant, but when unsuccessful, fled the crime scene and were later arrested. Harrison was also arrested and charged as an accessory to the robbery, even though he did not participate in the actual crime. He was convicted, but appealed his conviction, arguing that the judge's instructions to the jury were flawed. The judge instructed jurors as follows:

> The State does not have to offer evidence to prove that a man charged with a crime actually had a guilty intent. This is because a person is presumed to have intended to do the act which he did do. Accordingly, until some credible evidence comes into the case tending to prove that because in the light of the circumstances as he honestly and in good faith believed them to be, the act which he did would appear to be lawful, or because the act was an accident, until such credible evidence appears in the case, the State may rest upon the presumption that the accused intended to commit an act which he did commit. Until such evidence appears in the case, the jury must presume that the accused intended to commit such acts as the jury finds he did commit, and accordingly find that the requisite guilty intent was present if it is shown that the accused, [*sic*] done by the accused, was unlawful.[33]

Harrison further argued that this instruction put the burden on *him* to prove that he did or did not intend to see the robbery completed. As you will recall from earlier

---

[29]K. Levy, "Killing, Letting Die, and the Case for Mildly Punishing Bad Samaritanism," *Georgia Law Review*, Vol. 44 (2010), pp. 607–695.

[30]See, e.g., *State* v. *Noriega*, 928 P.2d 706 (Ariz. Ct. App. 1996); *Commonwealth* v. *Murphy*, 844 A.2d 1228 (Pa. 2004), p. 1234.

[31]*State* v. *Harrison*, 425 A.2d 111 (Conn. 1979), p. 113.

[32]Ibid.

[33]Ibid., pp. 112–113.

chapters, however, this burden should fall on the prosecution. The Supreme Court of Connecticut agreed. Harrison's argument was successful and he was given a new trial.

Harrison's case dealt with the crime of robbery, for which intent to commit the crime was a specific element. But what if the *mens rea* requirement for the underlying offense involves something less than outright intent, such as recklessness or negligence? How does this affect the *mens rea* calculation for accomplice liability? *State v. Foster*,[34] another Connecticut case, offers an answer. Foster, who was convicted of being an accessory (ordinarily he would have been considered an accomplice, but some courts use both terms interchangeably) to criminally negligent homicide, argued in his appeal that there was no such crime because he could not *intend for an unintended death to occur* (negligent homicide, by way of preview, is a homicide that generally can be foreseen). While his argument was certainly plausible, the Connecticut Supreme Court disagreed:

> Contrary to the defendant's assertions, . . . liability does not require that a defendant act with the conscious objective to cause the result described by a statute . . . [The defendant] may be liable in aiding another if he acts intentionally, knowingly, recklessly or with criminal negligence toward the result, depending on the mental state required by the substantive crime. When a crime requires that a person act with criminal negligence, [the defendant] is liable if he acts 'with respect to a result or to a circumstance described by a statute defining an offense when he fails to perceive a substantial and unjustifiable risk that such result will occur or that such circumstance exists'."[35]

In other words, it is necessary to look at the specific statute to determine the *mens rea* for accomplice liability. Thus, an all-encompassing definition of accomplice *mens rea* is as follows:

1. The intent to assist the primary party to engage in the conduct that forms the basis of the offense; and

2. The mental state required for commission of the offense, as provided in the definition of the substantive crime.[36]

This means, first, that the accomplice must intend to assist. Second, assuming she intends to assist, then criminal liability will attach as long as her mental state meets with what the statute requires. If the statutory *mens rea* is defined in terms of negligence, then she will be held liable as an accomplice if she acted negligently. Similarly, if the statutory *mens rea* was defined in terms of knowledge, then she will be considered an accomplice if she acted with knowledge.

What if, to make matters a little more complicated, the accomplice *seems* to intend for the primary offender's crime to occur, but does not *really* intend for it to occur? *Wilson v. People*,[37] a classic case, offers an answer. Wilson accused Pierce of stealing his watch. The two eventually stopped arguing, but Wilson remained convinced that Pierce was guilty. Later, they agreed to break into a drug store. After

---

[34]*State v. Foster*, 202 Conn. 520 (Conn. 1987).
[35]Ibid., pp. 529–531.
[36]Dressler, *Understanding Criminal Law*, p. 478.
[37]*Wilson v. People*, 87 P.2d 5 (Colo. 1989).

Wilson boosted Pierce up so he could break a window and enter the store, he left and called the police. For unknown reasons, he returned to the drug store and received several bottles of stolen liquor from Pierce as he passed them out the window. The police arrived and arrested both men. Wilson was convicted as an accomplice, but his conviction was overturned by the Colorado Supreme Court, which placed significant emphasis on Wilson's call to the police. While he certainly had the intent to assist Pierce in the theft, the court felt he did not have the intent to permanently deprive the drug store owner of his property.

In an analogous case from some years earlier,[38] Price accompanied two acquaintances, Moran and Lindohl, on a robbery. Price's gun, however, was not loaded because unbeknownst to the other two men, he had supposedly talked to both a constable and a justice of the peace about the planned crime the day before it was committed. He reported that his intent was to foil the crime and ensure that Moran and Lindohl were caught. The court recounted the events as follows:

> the undisputed facts, as appears from the foregoing, are, that the accused, on the day of the attempted robbery, went deliberately to a constable of the town in which he lived and told him all about the contemplated crime, giving the true names of the parties, and telling him when and where it was to take place, and the name of the intended victim; that the attempt was made at the very time and place, and by the parties, stated by him, and that on the following morning he, in like manner, went to a justice of the peace and told him all about what had been done, and furnished him with the true names of the parties implicated, by means of which, on the same day, they were brought to trial, and were subsequently convicted of the crime. That a sane person, really guilty of committing so grave a crime as the one imputed to the accused, would thus act, is so inconsistent with all human experience as not to warrant the conviction of any one under the circumstances shown.[39]

Price was initially convicted, but his conviction was overturned. Again, he intended to help his codefendants, but the some *mens rea* component (mental state required for the commission of the crime of robbery) was lacking. To summarize, then, "the accomplice must not only have the purpose that someone else engage in the conduct which constitutes the particular crime charged, . . . but the accomplice must also share in the same intent which is required for the substantive offense."[40]

Before concluding our look at *mens rea* in the complicity context, one more issue bears discussion. Assume Craig helps Victor plan a "home invasion" robbery. The two pick the residence of an elderly widow, Sandy, and proceed to commit the crime. Victor kicks in the front door, armed, and finds Sandy sitting in the living room. He points the gun at her and demands that she give him all her cash and jewels. Craig sits in the car outside serving as a lookout, ready to drive away at a moment's notice. As Victor has the gun trained on Sandy, Jim steps out from a nearby corridor and surprises Victor who, startled, shoots and kills him. Victor then panics, binds and gags Sandy, and locks her in a closet while he quickly ransacks the house and exits. The two men flee the scene empty-handed. At the risk of putting the cart before the

---

[38]*Price* v. *People*, 109 Ill. 109 (Ill. 1884).
[39]Ibid., pp. 115–116.
[40]*State v. Williams*, 718 A.2d 721 (Super Ct. of N.J. Law Div. 1998), p. 723.

horse (we will look at specific crime types starting in Chapter 8), there are three crimes here: robbery, murder, and kidnapping. Clearly Craig could be considered an accomplice to the robbery, but what about the murder and kidnapping? The answer, which has common law origins and is still in use in many jurisdictions today is as follows:

> a person encouraging or facilitating the commission of a crime could be held criminally liable not only for that crime, but for any other offense that was a "natural and probable consequence" of the crime aided and abetted.[41]

**natural and probable consequences doctrine**
An individual encouraging or assisting a crime can be liable not only for the original crime, but for any other offenses that are the natural and probable consequences of the original crime.

This has come to be known as the **natural and probable consequences doctrine**. In our example, the resultant murder and kidnapping were natural and probable consequences of the home invasion robbery. Craig would likely be considered an accomplice in all three crimes because it is not uncommon for home invasion robberies to result in other (and potentially more serious) criminal acts.

Contrast the Craig and Victor example with *People* v. *Butts*,[42] an actual California case in which Butts encouraged Otwell to assault a third man, Barnard. Butts did not know, however, that Otwell would use a knife and kill, rather than assault, Barnard. The court ruled that the killing was not a natural and probable consequence of an assault.

See Figure 6.2 for a summary of accomplice liability presented in flowchart format.

**Figure 6.2**
Accomplice Liability (Complicity)

---

[41]*People* v. *Prettyman*, 926 P.2d 1013 (Cal. 1996), p. 1019.
[42]*People* v. *Butts*, 236 Cal. App. 2d 817 (Court App. Ca. 1965).

## Accessory *Actus Reus*

Recall from earlier that an accomplice most often assists before and during the crime, while the accessory typically helps after the fact. Being an accessory is not quite as serious as being an accomplice, as one who assists after the crime may engage in behaviors that are far more innocuous than helping with commission of the crime. Thus, it is common for accessories to felonies to only be convicted of a misdemeanor rather than a felony. Also, accessory liability is often limited to felonies; many states do not regard it possible for someone to act as an accessory in a misdemeanor crime. With those points made, the *actus reus* for accessorial liability happens when the accessory personally aids the person who committed the crime (e.g., by providing a place to "hide out"). For example, federal law defines the *actus reus* for an accessory after the fact as one who "receives, relieves, comforts or assists the offender. . . ."[43]

See the accompanying Court Decision for more on criminal liability as an accessory. In it we take a look at the case of *State* v. *Chism*, where the defendant was charged as an accessory after the fact to murder.

---

**COURT DECISION**

*State* v. *Chism*
436 So.2d 464 (La. 1983)

**Background:** Brian Chism was convicted of being an accessory after the fact in District Court, Caddo Parish and sentenced to three years in prison, with three and a half years suspended sentence. Chism appealed and the Supreme Court of Louisiana affirmed the conviction but vacated the sentence and remanded.

***On the evening of August 26, 1981 in Shreveport, Tony Duke gave the defendant, Brian Chism, a ride in his automobile. Brian Chism was impersonating a female, and Duke was apparently unaware of Chism's disguise. After a brief visit at a friend's house the two stopped to pick up some beer at the residence of Chism's grandmother. Chism's one-legged uncle, Ira Lloyd, joined them, and the three continued on their way, drinking as Duke drove the automobile. When Duke expressed a desire to have sexual relations with Chism, Lloyd announced that he wanted to find his ex-wife Gloria for the same purpose. Shortly after midnight, the trio arrived at the St. Vincent Avenue Church of Christ and persuaded Gloria Lloyd to come outside. As Ira Lloyd stood outside the car attempting to persuade Gloria to come with them, Chism and Duke hugged and kissed on the front seat as Duke sat behind the steering wheel.

Gloria and Ira Lloyd got into an argument, and Ira stabbed Gloria with a knife several times in the stomach and once in the neck. Gloria's shouts attracted the attention of two neighbors, who unsuccessfully tried to prevent Ira from pushing Gloria into the front seat of the car alongside Chism and Duke. Ira Lloyd climbed into the front seat also, and Duke drove off. One of the bystanders testified that she could not be sure but she thought she saw Brian's foot on the accelerator as the car left.

---

[43]18 U.S.C. Section 3.

Lloyd ordered Duke to drive to Willow Point, near Cross Lake. When they arrived Chism and Duke, under Lloyd's direction, removed Gloria from the vehicle and placed her on some high grass on the side of the roadway, near a wood line. Ira was unable to help the two because his wooden leg had come off. Afterwards, as Lloyd requested, the two drove off, leaving Gloria with him.

There was no evidence that Chism or Duke protested, resisted or attempted to avoid the actions which Lloyd ordered them to take. Although Lloyd was armed with a knife, there was no evidence that he threatened either of his companions with harm.

Duke proceeded to drop Chism off at a friend's house, where he changed to male clothing. He placed the blood-stained women's clothes in a trash bin. Afterward, Chism went with his mother to the police station at 1:15 a.m. He gave the police a complete statement, and took the officers to the place where Gloria had been left with Ira Lloyd. The police found Gloria's body in some tall grass several feet from that spot. An autopsy indicated that stab wounds had caused her death. Chism's discarded clothing disappeared before the police arrived at the trash bin.

An accessory after the fact is any person, who, after the commission of a felony, shall harbor, conceal, or aid the offender, knowing or having reasonable ground to believe that he has committed the felony, and with the intent that he may avoid or escape from arrest, trial, conviction, or punishment. La.R.S. 14:25.

\*\*\* Defendant appealed from his conviction and sentence and argues that the evidence was not sufficient to support the judgment. Consequently, in reviewing the defendant's assigned error, we must determine whether, after viewing the evidence in the light most favorable to the prosecution, any rational trier of fact could have found beyond a reasonable doubt that (a) a completed felony had been committed by Ira Lloyd before Brian Chism rendered him the assistance described below; (b) Chism knew or had reasonable grounds to know of the commission of the felony by Lloyd, and (c) Chism gave aid to Lloyd personally under circumstances that indicate either that he actively desired that the felon avoid or escape arrest, trial conviction, or punishment or that he believed that one of these consequences was substantially certain to result from his assistance.

There was clearly enough evidence to justify the finding that a felony had been completed before any assistance was rendered to Lloyd by the defendant. The record vividly demonstrates that Lloyd fatally stabbed his ex-wife before she was transported to Willow point and left in the high grass near a wood line. Thus, Lloyd committed the felonies of attempted murder, aggravated battery, and simple kidnapping, before Chism aided him in any way. \*\*\*

The evidence overwhelmingly indicates that Chism had reasonable grounds to believe that Lloyd had committed a felony before any assistance was rendered. In his confessions and his testimony Chism indicates that the victim was bleeding profusely when Lloyd pushed her into the vehicle, that she was limp and moaned as they drove to Willow Point, and that he knew Lloyd had inflicted her wounds with a knife. The Louisiana offense of accessory after the fact deviates somewhat from the original common law offense in that it does not require that the defendant actually know that a completed felony has occurred. Rather, it incorporates an objective standard by requiring only that the defendant render aid "knowing or having reasonable grounds to believe" that a felony has been committed.

The closest question presented is whether any reasonable trier of fact could have found beyond a reasonable doubt that Chism assisted Lloyd under circumstances that indicate that either Chism actively desired that Lloyd would avoid or escape arrest, trial, conviction, or punishment, or that Chism believed that one of these consequences was substantially certain to result from his assistance. After carefully reviewing the record, we conclude that the prosecution satisfied its burden of producing the required quantity of evidence.

\*\*\*In this case we conclude that the evidence is sufficient to support an ultimate finding that the reasonable findings and inferences permitted by the evidence exclude every reasonable hypothesis of innocence. Despite evidence supporting some contrary inferences, a trier of fact reasonably could have found that Chism acted with at least a general intent to help Lloyd avoid arrest because: (1) Chism did not protest or attempt to leave the car when his uncle, Lloyd, shoved the mortally wounded victim inside; (2) he did not attempt to persuade Duke, his would-be lover, exit out the driver's side of the car and flee from his uncle, whom he knew to be one-legged and armed only with a knife; (3) he did not take any of these actions at any point during the considerable ride to Willow Point; (4) at their destination, he docilely complied with Lloyd's directions to remove the victim from the car and leave Lloyd with her, despite the fact that Lloyd made no threats and that his wooden leg had become detached; (5) after leaving Lloyd with the dying victim, he made no immediate effort to report the victim's whereabouts or to obtain emergency medical treatment for her; (6) before going home or reporting the victim's dire condition he went to a friend's house, changed clothing and discarded his own in a trash bin from which the police were unable to recover them as evidence; (7) he went home without reporting the victim's condition or location; (8) and he went to the police station to report the crime only after arriving home and discussing the matter with his mother.

The defendant asserted in his statement given to the police and during trial, that he helped to remove the victim from the car and to carry her to the edge of the bushes because he feared that his uncle would use the knife on him. The defense of justification can be claimed in any crime, except murder, when it is committed through the compulsion of threats by another of death or great bodily harm and the offender reasonably believes the person making the threats is present and would immediately carry out the threats if the crime were not committed. However, Chism did not testify that Lloyd threatened him with death, bodily harm or anything. Moreover, fear as a motivation to help his uncle is inconsistent with some of Chism's actions after he left his uncle. Consequently, we conclude that despite Chism's testimony the trier of fact could have reasonably found that he acted voluntarily and not out of fear when he aided Lloyd and that he did so under circumstances indicating that he believed that it was substantially certain to follow from his assistance that Lloyd would avoid arrest, trial, conviction, or punishment.

\*\*\*Therefore, we affirm the defendant's conviction. We note, however, that the sentence imposed by the trial judge is illegal. The judge imposed a sentence of three years. He suspended two and one-half of years of the term. The trial judge has no authority to suspend *part* of a sentence in a felony case. The correct sentence would have been a suspension of all three years of the term, with a six-month term as a condition of two years probation. We therefore vacate the defendant's sentence and remand the case for resentencing.

CONVICTION AFFIRMED; SENTENCE VACATED; REMANDED.

### Case Analysis

1. Specifically, what crime did the State of Louisiana charge Brian Chism with?

2. List all of the facts that support Chism's conviction as an accessory after the fact.

3. Could Chism have alleged any type of legal defense to his charge? Why or why not?

## Accessory *Mens Rea*

There are two parts to the *mens rea* of accessorial liability. First, the accessory must have known that a crime was committed. Second, the individual must have aided the principal for the purpose of hindering arrest and prosecution. To again use a federal law example, an accessory after the fact satisfies the first *mens rea* requirement by "knowing that an offense against the United States has been committed."[44] The second requirement is satisfied if the accessory provides assistance "in order to hinder or prevent [the principal's] apprehension."[45]

See Figure 6.3 for a summary of accessorial liability presented in flowchart format.

**YOUR DECISION**

1. Jamie O'Connor is a second-grade teacher in a rural area. She notices that one of her students, Bobby, consistently comes to school with bruises and cuts. When Jamie asked Bobby about the injuries, he stated, "My daddy hits me a lot." Not wanting to interfere in family business, Jamie does nothing. Two weeks later Bobby is beaten to death by this father. Can the prosecution charge Jamie as an accomplice to murder? Why or why not?

2. Joe discovers that his wife is having an affair after 20 years of marriage. Distraught, he goes to a local bar one evening to drink away his sorrows with a few friends. During the evening Joe announces a plan to kill his wife and her lover. His friend Brian responds, "Sounds like a great idea. She deserves to die for what she did." Two days later, Joe fatally shoots his wife and her companion. Can Brian be charged as an accomplice? Why or why not?

[44]Ibid.
[45]Ibid.

**Figure 6.3**
Accessorial Liability

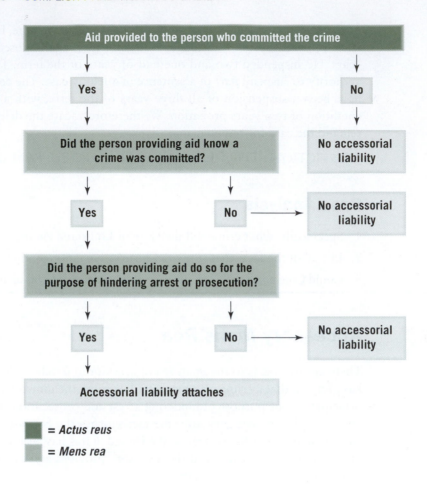

## Summary

- The *actus reus* for complicity is, at its most basic level, assistance.
- There are three means by which assistance is typically provided: (1) assistance by physical conduct; (2) assistance by psychological influence; and (3) assistance by omission (assuming in this latter case that the omitter has a duty to act).
- For accomplice liability, there are *two* levels of *mens rea*.
- First, there must be some degree of intent or desire to aid the primary offender.
- Second, there must also intent to commit the underlying offense.
- An accomplice most often assists before and during the crime, while the accessory typically helps after the fact.
- The *actus reus* for accessorial liability happens when the accessory personally aids the person who committed the crime (e.g., by providing a place to "hide out").
- There are two parts to the *mens rea* of accessorial liability. First, the accessory must have known that a crime was committed. Second, the individual must have aided the principal for the purpose of hindering arrest and prosecution.

# 6.3

# COMPLICITY ISSUES, LIMITATIONS, AND DEFENSES

### *Learning Objectives*

- **Discuss some of the issues that make complicity law complicated.**
- **Summarize the limitations of and defenses to accomplice liability.**
- **Explain the Model Penal Code approach to accomplice liability.**

**CORE CONCEPTS**

Complicity law is somewhat difficult to grasp because it involves multiple offenders. Likewise, the elements of accomplice liability make it a little more difficult to grasp than the types of criminal liability we introduced in earlier chapters. For example, as we just showed, there is more than one dimension to *mens rea*. What's more, the *actus reus* of accomplice liability can also take on more than one form. In this module we begin by looking at issues that pose complications for complicity. Toward the end, we shift our attention to limitations and defenses. We wrap up with a review of the Model Penal Code's language concerning complicity.

## Issues

Five issues complicate complicity law: (1) nonproxyable offenses; (2) the pretending principal; (3) the meaning of intent; (4) what happens if the primary party is acquitted; and (5) whether an accomplice can be "more guilty" than the primary party. Each is briefly reviewed in the following sections.

## Nonproxyable Offenses

**nonproxyable offense** A crime that can only be committed by a specific person or class of individuals.

According to Dressler, a **nonproxyable offense** "is one that, by definition, can only be perpetrated by a designated person or class of persons."[46] Such offenses introduce complications in the case of multiple offenders. For example, in *People* v. *Enfeld*,[47] a woman fraudulently induced a public official into issuing a false certificate, a crime that only a public official can commit. Because the official was fraudulently induced to commit the crime, criminal liability did not attach. Nor did it attach to the woman who obtained the false certificate! Why? She could not be an accomplice to a crime that only a public official could commit.

---

[46]Dressler, *Understanding Criminal Law*, p. 469.
[47]*People* v. *Enfeld*, 518 N.Y.S.2d 536 (Sup. Ct. 1987).

In another case, a male security guard was convicted of rape because he coerced a young couple into having intercourse.[48] His conviction was overturned, however, because he successfully argued that "one element of rape is penetration of the female sexual organ by the sexual organ of the principal of the first degree."[49]

Some courts have taken a different approach, deciding that accomplices to such nonproxyable offenses should nevertheless be held liable for their actions. For example, in *People* v. *Hernandez*,[50] a woman, armed with a rifle, forced her husband to have intercourse with another woman. She was convicted of rape and appealed, but the reviewing court rejected her appeal, stating,

> It would be unreasonable to hold a woman immune from prosecution for rape committed by a man under her "threats or menaces sufficient to show that [he] had reasonable cause to and did believe [that his life] would be endangered if [he] refused." . . . If such were the law it would create a crime without a punishable perpetrator.[51]

In yet another case, this one involving perjury (i.e., lying under oath), a woman caused a man to (without his knowledge) testify falsely at trial.[52] Traditionally, only the person who lies under oath can be convicted of perjury, making it a nonproxyable offense, but the woman in this case was convicted of perjury. An appeals court upheld her conviction, noting that even though she was not under oath, she caused an innocent party to unwittingly present false testimony.

## The Pretending Principal

In the *mens rea* discussion earlier, we presented two cases in which an accomplice *feigned* involvement as such. What if we turn things around a bit and consider a case in which the *principal* pretends to work, with criminal intent, along with another individual to commit a crime? In a classic case,[53] two men, A and B, agreed to burglarize C's store. Unknown to A, B was C's relative and before the burglary was to take place, but after the agreement was made, B obtained permission from C to enter the store so that A could be captured "in the act." On the night of the crime, A helped B enter the store through a window. B then passed goods out the window to A. As they were leaving the scene, A was arrested and convicted of burglary. His conviction was overturned, however, because B did not technically burglarize the store; he had permission from the owner. In other words, A's criminal liability could not derive from B's because B did not commit a crime.

Contrast this decision with *Vaden* v. *State*,[54] a case in which two hunting guides aided undercover agents in illegal hunting and fishing activities. The Alaska

[48]*Dusenbery* v. *Commonwealth*, 263 S.E.2d 392 (Va. 1980).
[49]Ibid., p. 394.
[50]*People* v. *Hernandez*, 18 Cal. App. 3d 651 (Ct. App. 1971).
[51]Ibid., p. 657.
[52]*United States* v. *Walser*, 3 F.3d 380 (11th Cir. 1993).
[53]*State* v. *Hayes*, 16 S.W. 514 (Mo. 1891).
[54]*Vaden* v. *State*, 768 P.2d 1102 (Alaska 1989).

Supreme Court upheld the convictions against both guides, in part, because agents' actions were not justified—even though they were never prosecuted for their actions:

> We are not persuaded by [defendants'] argument that the charges in this case be dismissed solely because the government agents engaged in illegal hunting and fishing activity . . . the correct remedy when police go outside the scope of their duties is to "prosecute the police," not "free the equally culpable defendant."[55]

## The Meaning of Intent

In our *mens rea* discussion earlier it was noted that accomplice liability attaches when (1) there is intent to assist the primary party and (2) there is intent to commit the underlying offense. But what exactly does *intent* mean? Does intent mean deliberate purpose to commit the act? Or could it mean something less, such as simple knowledge? These are important questions. Consider *United States* v. *Giovannetti*,[56] a case in which a man, Janis, rented one of his houses to some people who conducted illegal gambling activities within it, using it as a "wireroom." At Janis's trial, the judge gave jurors the so-called **ostrich instruction**, which read as follows:

**ostrich instruction** A jury instruction regarding the *mens rea* of accomplice liability that allows the jury to infer knowledge on the part of the defendant from indifference to finding the truth.

> You may infer knowledge from a combination of suspicion and indifference to the truth. If you find that a person had a strong suspicion that things were not what they seemed or that someone had withheld some important facts, yet shut his eyes for fear that he would learn, you may conclude that he acted knowingly.[57]

This is called the ostrich instruction because had Janis "stuck his head in the sand" and acted in a deliberately ignorant fashion, then he would be hard-pressed to argue that he had no knowledge of what was occurring at his property.[58] The trial jury convicted Janis, concluding that he acted like an ostrich insofar as he was a gambler who had supposedly conversed with others as though he knew what was happening on his property.

The Seventh Circuit, however, disagreed, holding that more than just knowledge—or efforts to avoid such knowledge—was necessary. To be held criminally liable as an accomplice, Janis would have needed to "in some sort associate himself with the venture, that he participate in it as in something that he wishes to bring about, that he seek by his action to make it succeed."[59] As another court put it, a person cannot be considered an accomplice unless he "share[s] the criminal intent of the principal; there must be a community of purpose in the unlawful undertaking."[60] To summarize, then, the *intent* for accomplice liability is something much higher than mere knowledge.

---

[55]Ibid.
[56]*United States* v. *Giovannetti*, 919 F.2d 1223 (7th Cir. 1990).
[57]Ibid., p. 1226.
[58]See, e.g., *United States* v. *Craig*, 178 F.3d 891 (7th Cir. 1999), p. 896.
[59]Citing *United States* v. *Peoni*, 100 F.2d 401 (2nd Cir. 1938), p. 402.
[60]*State* v. *Duran*, 526 P.2d 188 (N.M. Ct. App. 1974), p. 189.

Even though two people commit a crime together, they may be treated differently by the courts depending on the circumstances.
© Flirt/SuperStock

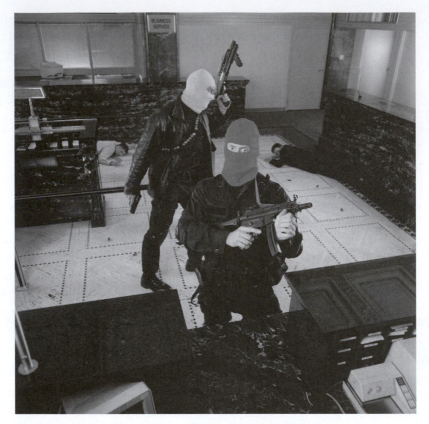

## What If the Primary Party Is Acquitted?

As you know by now, there are many means by which a person can be acquitted. Suppose, then, that the primary party is acquitted. What will become of the accomplice? Should he or she also be acquitted? These questions have come up in a number of cases. For example, in *United States* v. *Lopez*,[61] Ronald McIntosh escaped prison and landed a helicopter at another prison, flying off with one Samantha Lopez. Lopez successfully asserted a necessity defense, claiming that she faced repeated threats in prison (see Chapter 5's prison escape discussion). McIntosh asserted a similar defense, but did not succeed. An appellate court affirmed his conviction because he was unable to prove that he pursued and exhausted all legal alternatives to go about having Lopez removed from prison.

The *Lopez* case dealt with an affirmative defense (necessity). What if, instead, the primary offender escapes conviction because the prosecution cannot prove *mens rea*? Should an accomplice then go free? *Regina* v. *Cogan and Leak*,[62] a classic case, offers some answers. In that case, Leak convinced Cogan to have intercourse with Leak's wife by falsely telling him she consented. Cogan was acquitted of rape because he lacked the *mens rea* (i.e., he thought she consented). Leak was convicted as

---

[61]*United States* v. *Lopez*, 662 F.Supp. 1083 (N.D. Cal. 1987).
[62]*Regina* v. *Cogan and Leak*, 1 Q.B. 217 (Eng. 1976).

an accomplice to the rape. His appeal was unsuccessful, as it should have been. As one source put it, "courts will not allow individuals to hide behind their own legal incapacity to commit a crime if they use others to accomplish it."[63]

## Can an Accomplice Be "More Guilty" than the Principal?

Earlier we pointed out the common law rule that no accessory could be tried or convicted until the principal was both tried and convicted. Again, this rule has been abandoned, as it should have been, but it raises a potential problem. Can an accomplice be more guilty than a principal? In other words, must both the accomplice and the principal be convicted of the same offense? Or, alternatively, can the accomplice be convicted of a more serious offense than the principal? To this latter question, the answer is yes.

In *Regina* v. *Richards*,[64] a wife hired two men to beat her husband severely enough that he would be hospitalized. However, they merely roughed him up. Interestingly, the court held that the wife could not be convicted of a more serious crime than the men who roughed up her husband.

A number of courts take a different approach today, paving the way for greater accomplice culpability. For example, in *People* v. *McCoy*,[65] the California Supreme Court ruled that an accomplice to murder can be found guilty of a more serious form of homicide than the primary offender. For example, if the accomplice premeditates the killing, while the principal does not, a more serious conviction is warranted for the accomplice (the distinctions among levels of homicide, again, will be covered in the next chapter). The court in that case offered up the following hypothetical in support of its decision:

[A]ssume someone, let us call him Iago, falsely tells another person, whom we will call Othello, that Othello's wife, Desdemona, was having an affair, hoping that Othello would kill her in a fit of jealousy. Othello does so without Iago's further involvement. In that case, depending on the exact circumstances of the killing, Othello might be guilty of manslaughter, rather than murder, on a heat of passion theory. Othello's guilt of manslaughter, however, should not limit Iago's guilt if his own culpability were greater. Iago should be liable for his own acts as well Othello's, which he induced and encouraged. But Iago's criminal liability, as Othello's, would be based on his own personal mens rea. If, as our hypothetical suggests, Iago acted with malice, he would be guilty of murder even if Othello, who did the actual killing, was not.[66]

## Limitations and Defenses

There are a few situations in which accomplice liability is a legal impossibility. Likewise, an accomplice can assert any number of defenses, including those introduced in the preceding chapters. To these we can add another, namely abandonment.

---

[63]R. G. Singer and J. Q. La Fond, *Criminal Law: Examples and Explanations*, 4th ed. (New York: Wolters Kluwer, 2007), p. 387.
[64]*Regina* v. *Richards*, Q.B. 776 (1974).
[65]*People* v. *McCoy*, 24 P.3d 1210 (Cal. 2001).
[66]Ibid., pp. 1216–1217.

## Abandonment

One who assists in the commission of a criminal act may choose to withdraw from the collaborative effort or otherwise abandon his or her intent to participate in the crime. To succeed, however, the individual must notify the principal and neutralize the effects of any assistance offered to that point. For example, if someone provides a weapon for the principal to use in the crime, he must get it back. As an alternative, had that person's assistance gone only so far as an expression, then he must neutralize its effect. A statement along the lines of "Let's burglarize that house" could be neutralized by a statement to the effect that "Let's not, I changed my mind."

Importantly, it is not enough for one who offers assistance before the commission of a crime to turn heel and leave as the crime is about to be committed. Again, there must be a bona fide effort to stop the crime or neutralize the assistance already provided. For example, in *State* v. *Thomas*,[67] a man, Thomas, expressed his desire to two acquaintances to "shoot the police." When one of them pulled a gun on an officer, Thomas left. The officer was shot and killed. Thomas was convicted of aiding and abetting in the murder, and he appealed unsuccessfully. The reviewing court held:

> Defendant's own testimony at trial, taken at face value, indicates that he simply left the roof when he saw Jennette take out his gun. Nothing in his testimony suggests that he communicated to Jennette that he was leaving or that he disapproved of the contemplated act, or that he otherwise sought to actively withdraw the support to the proposed event which his presence on the roof supplied. According to defendant, he merely left the scene within minutes before the shooting occurred. As a matter of law, such a spontaneous, unannounced withdrawal, without more, only briefly before the commission of the offense which had been previously encouraged by defendant's presence or other support, is insufficient to insulate the defendant from criminal liability as an aider and abettor.[68]

See the accompanying Court Decision for more on the defense of abandonment. In it we take a look at *State* v. *Formella*, where a high school student attempted to "abandon" his plan to help steal a math test.

---

## COURT DECISION

*State* v. *Formella*
960 A.2d 722 (N.H. 2008)

**Background:** Paul Formella was convicted as an accomplice for the theft of a mathematics exam in the District Court, Lebanon County. The Supreme Court of New Hampshire affirmed the conviction.

\*\*\*The relevant facts are not in dispute. On the afternoon of Wednesday, June 13, 2007, the defendant, then a junior at Hanover High School, and two friends, were studying at the Howe Library near the school. \*\*\*Upon entering the school, they encountered another group of students who said they intended to steal mathematics

---

[67]*State* v. *Thomas*, 356 A.2d 433 (N.J. Super. Ct. App. Div. 1976).
[68]Ibid., p. 445.

exams from the third floor. The defendant and his companions were asked to serve as lookouts during the theft, which they agreed to do. They were instructed to yell something like "did you get your math book?" up to the third floor as a code to alert the thieves if someone was coming.

The defendant and his friends then proceeded to their second-floor lockers. The defendant testified that on their way to their lockers they looked around to "confirm or dispel" whether anyone was there. Once the defendant and his friends had retrieved their books, they "were all feeling like this was the wrong thing to do," and decided to head back down to the first floor to wait for the other group. On their way down the stairs, they encountered some janitors who told them that they ought to leave the school. The defendant and his friends left the school building, but waited in the parking lot for approximately five to ten minutes for the other group. Eventually, the other students exited the school with the stolen examinations and all of the students shared the exam questions.

The next week, someone informed the dean of students that some students had stolen the exams. The police were called, and in connection with their investigation they interviewed the defendant, who admitted his involvement in the theft. He was later charged with criminal liability for conduct of another. Following his conviction, the defendant appealed to this court.

On appeal, the defendant . . . contends that the trial court erred in failing to make findings of fact relative to the timing of his withdrawal from the theft and the completion of the theft because, he argues, without such findings the trial court could not properly apply RSA 626:8.

***RSA 626:8 provides, in relevant part, that an individual is criminally liable for the conduct of another when he acts as an accomplice in the commission of an offense. A person is an accomplice when with the purpose of promoting or facilitating the commission of an offense, he aids or agrees or attempts to aid another person in planning or committing the offense. RSA 626:8 further provides, however, that a person is not an accomplice if he "terminates his complicity prior to the commission of the offense and wholly deprives it of effectiveness in the commission of the offense or gives timely warning to the law enforcement authorities or otherwise makes proper effort to prevent the commission of the offense." RSA 626:8, VI(c).

The defendant does not dispute that he became an accomplice in the first instance when he agreed to act as a lookout. Accordingly, we are concerned only with whether the defendant's later acts terminated his liability as an accomplice. We note that the defendant does not contend that he gave timely warning to law enforcement or otherwise made "proper effort" to prevent the offense. Thus, under RSA 626:8, VI(c) the defendant was not an accomplice if: (1) he terminated his complicity in the crime; (2) his termination occurred prior to the commission of the offense; and (3) he wholly deprived his complicity of effectiveness in the commission of the offense.

***RSA 626:8, like much of our criminal law, is based upon the Model Penal Code. Accordingly, we look to the Model Penal Code and its commentaries for guidance. RSA 626:8 tracks the provisions of section 2.06 of the Model Penal Code. Comment 9(c) to section 2.06 addresses situations where liability may be averted if the accomplice's complicity is terminated prior to the commission of the crime. The comment notes that the actions sufficient to deprive the prior complicity of effectiveness vary with the type of accessorial behavior. Relevant to the analysis here, the comment states that if "complicity inhered in request or encouragement, countermanding disapproval may suffice to nullify its influence, providing it is heard in time to allow reconsideration by those planning to commit the crime." The comments thus indicate that in order to deprive the prior complicity of effectiveness, one who has encouraged the commission of an offense may avoid liability by terminating his or her role in the commission of the crime *and* by making his or her disapproval known to the principals sufficiently in advance of the commission of the crime to allow them time to reconsider as well.

While there appears to be a paucity of authority on the issue, the view that an accomplice must make some affirmative act, such as an overt expression of disapproval to the principals, accords with that of other jurisdictions with statutes mirroring the provisions of the Model Penal Code. Additionally, the relevant authorities weigh in favor of requiring any withdrawal to be communicated far enough in advance to allow the others involved in the crime to follow suit. This is not to say that the terminating accomplice must actually prevent the crime from occurring. Instead, he need only make some act demonstrating to the principals of the crime that he has withdrawn, and he must do so in a manner, and at such a time, that the principals could do likewise. We agree with the rationale of these authorities.

With the above understanding, we turn to the defendant's specific claims of error. According to the defendant, the trial court erred in failing to make findings of fact regarding the time the defendant terminated his complicity, and the time the theft occurred because without such findings the trial court could not properly apply the statute. Here, the trial court credited the defendant's claim that he did, in fact, terminate his complicity. Thus, he contends, it was critical to know when he withdrew and when the crime was committed, so that it could be determined whether he withdrew at a time sufficient to satisfy the statute. We disagree.

The relevant portion of the statute is phrased in the conjunctive. For a person not to be an accomplice he must terminate his complicity prior to the commission of the offense *and* wholly deprive that complicity of its effectiveness. Even assuming the defendant terminated his complicity prior to the commission of the offense, he did not wholly deprive his complicity of its effectiveness.

As stated above, to extricate himself from accomplice liability, the defendant needed to make an affirmative act, such as communicating his withdrawal to the principals. Here, the defendant made no such act. The defendant testified that he and his companions simply left the scene. He did not communicate his withdrawal, discourage the principals from acting, inform the custodians, or do any other thing which would deprive his complicity of effectiveness. In fact, the principals remained unaware of his exit. Thus, the defendant did not do that which was necessary to undo his complicity.

The defendant contends that because he had been acting as a lookout, leaving the scene so as to no longer be "looking out" deprived his complicity of its effectiveness, and, therefore, findings regarding the timing of the offense were required. We disagree. While at the point he left the scene he was no longer an effective lookout, the defendant did nothing to counter his prior complicity. According to the defendant, the principals had requested aid in committing the offense, he agreed to provide it, and he agreed to warn the principals if anyone approached, thus encouraging the act. Further, upon reaching the second floor the defendant looked around to "confirm or dispel" whether anyone was around who might have apprehended the thieves or otherwise spoiled the crime. Thus, it was the complicity of agreeing to aid the primary actors and then actually aiding them that needed to be undone; silently withdrawing from the scene did not, in any way, undermine the encouragement the defendant had provided. As there was no evidence that the defendant had wholly deprived his complicity of its effectiveness, it was not error for the trial court to refuse to make findings on the timing of the offense because such findings would not have altered the result.

\*\*\**Affirmed.*

## Case Analysis

1. Do you think that the defendant was an "accomplice" to the crime? Why or why not?
2. What is the defendant's legal argument on appeal?
3. Did the defendant effectively "abandon" his criminal plan?

## Immunity from Conviction

Accomplice liability is not possible when one the parties to a crime is supposed to be protected by the applicable statute. The best example is statutory rape. Statutory rape laws make it a crime to have sexual intercourse with a minor. So assuming Clint, an 18-year-old, has sex with his 17-year-old girlfriend (and assuming the jurisdiction in which they are located treats 17-year-olds as juveniles), he has committed statutory rape. His girlfriend was a party to the crime, but she was also protected by the statutory rape law. Thus, she cannot be considered an accomplice to her own rape. If she were to be considered an accomplice, it would undermine the purpose of the law.

Consider *In re Meagan R.*,[69] a case involving a minor female who, along with her boyfriend, broke into a neighbor's house and used the bed for intercourse. The juvenile court entered a finding that Meagan committed burglary. Interestingly, the burglary conviction was not based on any intent on her part to burglarize the home. Rather, it was based on the theory that Meagan entered the house with intent to aid and abet in her own statutory rape. The reasoning behind this approach was not laid out in the case, but an appeals court nevertheless reversed the conviction, stating,

> [A]lthough we grant Meagan was not the member of a protected class with regard to the burglary offense of which she was convicted, she was the intended and protected victim of the predicate felony used by the court to support the burglary finding. As

---

[69]*In re Meagan R.*, 42 Cal. App. 4th 17 (Ct. App. 1996).

such, she cannot harbor the culpable state of mind necessary to commit the burglary, because under any theory she cannot commit the crime of her own statutory rape. Consequently, the burglary true finding must be reversed.[70]

Next, consider an adultery case, *In re Cooper*.[71] An unmarried woman was charged with aiding and abetting in a married man's adulterous relationship. The case was decided in 1912 and concerned a California statute that made it a felony for two married persons to live together in a state of cohabitation and adultery. The woman could not be considered an accomplice to the crime of adultery because she was not married. Nor did the California Supreme Court agree with the state's argument that she would be considered the principal in the crime, as her conduct was neither criminal nor punishable by any statute—even though what she did may have been morally wrong.

## The Model Penal Code and Complicity

The Model Penal Code does not use the common law terms *accessory* or *principal*. It simply defines an accomplice as one who "solicits" another to commit the offense, "aids or agrees or attempts" to aid another in the commission of the offense, or fails to perform a legal duty to prevent the offense.[72] As to the *mens rea* of complicity, the Model Penal Code provides the following:

> When causing a particular result is an element of an offense, an accomplice in the conduct causing such result is an accomplice in the commission of that offense if he acts with the kind of culpability, if any, with respect to that result that is sufficient for the commission of the offense.[73]

This is just a fancy way of saying that the accomplice's *mens rea* must match the *mens rea* of the underlying offense. The Model Penal Code's other complicity provisions closely resemble those we have already discussed above. For example, a person cannot be considered an accomplice if he abandons his complicity prior to the offense by warning authorities. Similarly, to be an accomplice according to the Model Penal Code, one must act with the "purpose of promoting or facilitating the commission of an offense."[74] Mere knowledge that illegal activity is about to take—or is taking—place is insufficient.

**YOUR DECISION**

1. Late one Saturday evening, Joe and Mark decide to burglarize their neighbor's house. The pair plans to hop the fence and break in through the back sliding glass door. As they are about to jump over the fence they notice a very large Rottweiler in the back yard barking loudly. They also notice the next door neighbor watching them from her kitchen window and she appears to be dialing "911"

---

[70]Ibid., pp. 21–22.
[71]*In re Cooper*, 162 Cal. 81 (1912).
[72]Model Penal Code Section 2.06(3).
[73]Model Penal Code Section 2.06(4).
[74]Model Penal Code Section 2.06(3)(a).

on her telephone. The police arrest Joe and Mark. As their defense counsel, what defense, if any, can you raise? Why or why not?

2. Samantha has been physically and emotionally assaulted by her husband, Robbie, for over fifteen years. She finally decides to kill Robbie and puts poison in his meat-loaf one evening. She then calls her neighbor, Jodie, and asks for help disposing of the body. Jodie helps Samantha put Robbie's body in her minivan, drive it to the lake, and dump it in the water. At trial, the evidence of the physical abuse Samantha suffered during her marriage overwhelms the jury. They engage in jury nullification and acquit Samantha. You are the prosecutor and you must decide how to handle the case against Jodie. What, if anything, can Jodie be tried with? How, if at all, will Samantha's acquittal impact Jodie's trial?

## Summary

- Complicity cannot occur in the case of nonproxyable offenses, those that can only be committed by one individual or group.

- If the principal pretends to work, with criminal intent, along with another individual to commit a crime, he or she most likely will not be held liable.

- The *intent* for accomplice liability is something much higher than mere knowledge.

- If the principal is acquitted, an accomplice can still be held criminally liable.

- It is possible for an accomplice to be found guilty of a more serious offense than that committed by the primary offender.

- There are a few situations in which accomplice liability is a legal impossibility.

- One who abandons his or her intent to participate in the crime may not be considered an accomplice. To succeed, however, the individual must notify the principal and neutralize the effects of any assistance offered to that point.

- Accomplice liability is not possible when one of the parties to a crime is supposed to be protected by the applicable statute. The crime of statutory rape serves as an example.

- The Model Penal Code does not use the common law terms *accessory* or *principal*.

- It simply defines an accomplice as one who "solicits" another to commit the offense, "aids or agrees or attempts" to aid another in the commission of the offense, or fails to perform a legal duty to prevent the offense.

- The accomplice's *mens rea* must match the *mens rea* of the underlying offense.

MODULE

# 6.4

## VICARIOUS LIABILITY

### *Learning Objective*
- **Explain the concept of vicarious liability.**

**CORE CONCEPTS**

**vicarious liability**
Criminal liability for the
acts of another person.

With accomplice liability, as we mentioned earlier, the accomplice *derives* his or her liability from a primary offender. In other words, complicity is impossible without two or more people who act with criminal purpose. **Vicarious liability** occurs when one person is held liable for the actions of another—and perhaps when the former person has no idea what the latter person is up to.

Formally defined, vicarious liability is "[t]he imposition of liability on one person for the actionable conduct of another, based solely on a relationship between the two persons."[75] So while vicarious liability involves two or more parties, there are two conditions that make it different from accomplice liability: (1) it takes only one party's actions to trigger liability and (2) liability *transfers* from one of them to the other. For example, an employee may do something that is prohibited by law, but the *employer* will be held responsible for it.

It goes against most everything you have learned so far to hold one person responsible for the actions of another. After all, one of the key requirements of a criminal act is *mens rea*, the offender's mental state. Is it fair to hold, say, a business owner responsible if one of her employees commits a crime and she has absolutely no knowledge or awareness of it? Probably not, but just because liability can shift to another does not mean that other party is always innocent or ignorant. And sometimes, even if the other party *is* "innocent," liability can attach. The logic for this was laid out way back in 1787, in *Phile* v. *Ship Anna*:

> The law never punishes a man criminally but for his own act, yet it frequently punishes him in his pocket, for the act of another. Thus, if a wife commits an offence, the husband is not liable to the penalties; but if she obtains the property of another by any means not felonious, he must make the payment and amends.[76]

Modern-day vicarious liability works in a similar fashion.

There are many forms and theories of vicarious liability. Some are criminal; some are civil. In this section we will introduce two of the more common forms: corporate vicarious liability and individual vicarious liability. Our focus is largely on criminal liability because, after all, this is a book on criminal law. However, in some situations it is helpful to briefly consider developments in the realm of civil law, as they have implications for vicarious criminal liability.

**corporate vicarious liability** Liability of a corporation for the actions of its agents and employees.

***respondeat superior*** An employer is liable for the actions of its agents and employees while in the course of employment.

## Corporate Vicarious Liability

**Corporate vicarious liability** refers to the liability of a corporation, no matter its size, for the criminal conduct of its employees. Its origins can be traced to the medieval doctrine of ***respondeat superior***, Latin for "Let the master answer." Under *respondeat superior*, the master could be held to answer for the action of his agent. A number of nineteenth-century English court decisions also formed the basis for corporate vicarious criminal liability. However, the turning point in American history was the U.S. Supreme Court's decision in *New York Central &*

---

[75]*Black's Law Dictionary*, p. 1566.
[76]*Phile* v. *Ship Anna*, 1 U.S. 197 (1 Dall. 1787), p. 207.

*Hudson River Railroad* v. *United States*.[77] At issue was whether a corporation could be held criminally liable for the issuance of illegal rebates by its agents and officers. The Court held, in part, that "We see no valid objection in law, and every reason in public policy, why the corporation which profits by the transaction, and can only act through its agents and officers, shall be held punishable."[78] In a subsequent case, a steamship corporation was convicted of illegal dumping.[79] In the court's words, the corporation "failed to prevent the commission of a forbidden act."[80]

The general rule today is that a corporation is criminally liable for the actions of its agents when (1) those agents act in the official scope of their employment for (2) the benefit of the corporation. As one court put it, "An agent's knowledge is imputed to the corporation where the agent is acting within the scope of his authority and where the knowledge relates to matters within the scope of authority."[81] Needless to say, then, if an employee exploits his or her position for personal gain (such as by stealing inventory and selling it on the side), the corporation will most likely not be held liable.

The second requirement, that the employee be acting with the corporation's interests at heart, is less clear. As one team of experts put it, it "is not necessary that the employee be primarily concerned with benefiting the corporation, because courts recognize that many employees act primarily for their own personal gain."[82] In fact, some corporations have been held criminally liable for the actions of low-ranking employees who may have little to no knowledge about the parent company's structure or motives.[83] And corporations have even been held criminally liable for their subordinates' actions after putting into place policies and procedures intended to prevent misconduct![84]

How exactly is a corporation prosecuted, convicted, and punished? In the typical criminal context, the defendant is a human being, someone who can be fined or confined. A corporation, however, is a legal entity, not a person. Obviously something that does not exist in a physical form cannot be incarcerated. It would be more than a little difficult to take an office building and everyone in it and put it in prison! The form of punishment for corporations whose employees' actions forms the basis of vicarious liability, then, is a fine. At the federal level, the amount of the fine depends on the victim's loss and/or the company's gain multiplied by some factor set in the U.S. Sentencing Guidelines.[85]

See the accompanying Court Decision for more on corporate vicarious liability. In it we examine the case of *U.S.* v. *Ionia Management*, where a corporation is criminally charged for its employees illegal dumping of oil waste.

---

[77]*New York Central & Hudson River Railroad* v. *United States*, 212 U.S. 481 (1909).
[78]Ibid., p. 495.
[79]*Dollar S.S. Co.* v. *United States*, 101 F.2d 638 (9th Cir. 1939).
[80]Ibid., p. 640.
[81]*In re Hellenic, Inc.*, 965 F.2d 311 (7th Cir. 1992).
[82]K. Drew and K. A. Clark, "Corporate Criminal Liability," *American Criminal Law Review*, Vol. 42 (2005), p. 282.
[83]See, e.g., A. Weissmann and D. Newman, "Rethinking Criminal Corporate Liability," *Indiana Law Journal*, Vol. 82 (2007), 411–451, n. 37.
[84]Ibid.
[85]Drew and Clark, "Corporate Criminal Liability," p. 287.

**COURT DECISION**

*United States* v. *Ionia Management*
526 F.Supp.2d 319 (D. Conn. 2007)

**Background:** Defendant Ionia Management was convicted in the District Court of Connecticut of illegally discharging oil waste from its vessel the M/T Kriton and falsifying records. After the conviction, defendant brought a post-trial motion for a new trial before the District Court judge. The court denied the motion.

On September 6, 2007, at the conclusion of a jury trial, Defendant Ionia Management S.A. ("Ionia") was convicted on eighteen counts: thirteen counts of violating the Act to Prevent Pollution from Ships ("APPS") and associated regulations, 33 U.S.C. § 1908(a); three counts of falsifying records in connection with a federal investigation in violation of 18 U.S.C. § 1519; one count of obstructing justice in violation of 18 U.S.C. § 1505; and one count of conspiring to commit these offenses in violation of 18 U.S.C. § 371.

### ***Vicarious criminal liability

Ionia argues that the guilty verdict should be set aside because the jury failed to apply proper principles of agency: "the government failed to introduce sufficient evidence to establish that Ionia could be held vicariously liable for the acts of its employees and agents." Specifically, Ionia relies on the testimony of four members of the M/T Kriton's crew "that Ionia had a strict policy against the improper discharge of oily waste and bilge water, and they were each trained and promised to abide by this policy. Thus, any illegal activities undertaken by these crewmembers were not within the scope of their employment or for the actual benefit of Ionia." In addition, Defendant contends that the Government failed to prove that the crew's illegal conduct provided any actual benefit to Ionia. The Government, disputing Ionia's conception of agency, responds that the evidence was sufficient to impose vicarious criminal liability on Ionia.

### 1. Legal principles

The issue of how to properly define corporate criminal liability was the subject of much discussion by the parties in preparation for and during the trial. . . . Ionia argued that there could be no vicarious liability if the corporation had neither specifically authorized its agents to commit the criminal acts nor reaped an actual benefit as a result of the agents' conduct.

In the Second Circuit, "[i]t is settled law that a corporation may be held criminally responsible for [criminal] violations committed by its employees or agents acting within the scope of their authority." *United States v. Twentieth Century Fox Film Corp.*, 882 F.2d 656, 660 (2d Cir.1989). In an earlier, classic formulation, the court explained:

> The corporate defendant makes a separate contention that the guilt of its salesman is not to be attributed to it. But the Supreme Court has long ago determined that the corporation may be held criminally liable for the acts of an agent within the scope of his employment . . . and the state and lower federal courts have been consistent in their application of that doctrine.

*United States v. George F. Fish, Inc.,* 154 F.2d 798, 801 (2d Cir.1946). Whether an agent is acting within the scope of his employment can then be measured by whether he or she is acting with authority and with an intent to benefit the employer.

An agent need not have conferred an actual benefit, however; it is sufficient that there was an intent, at least in part, to benefit the employer. The panel in *J.C.B. Super Markets* addressed the flaw in Ionia's position that there must be an actual benefit, rejecting the argument that "the respondeat superior principle is not applicable where the agent is advancing his own rather than the corporation's interest." 530 F.2d at 1122. To this the court responded:

> The suggestion that the employee's wrongful act did not advance the interests of the employer and therefore should not be imputed to it entirely overlooks the basic concept of respondeat superior. Presumably no tortious act by an agent redounds to the benefit of the principal where the latter is held responsible for the damage which results. Yet if this reasoning were followed no principal would ever be liable.

*Id.*

*** As to the relationship between an employer's official policies, informal instructions, illegal conduct, and the imputation of vicarious liability, Judge Sand has offered a useful instruction:

> If you find that the agent was acting within the scope of his employment, the fact that the agent's act was illegal, contrary to his employer's instructions, or against the corporation's policies will not relieve the corporation of responsibility for it. However, you may consider the fact that the agent disobeyed instructions or violated company policy in determining whether the agent intended to benefit the corporation, or was acting within this authority.

1 Leonard B. Sand, et al., *Modern Federal Jury Instructions-Criminal* ¶ 2.01, Instr. 2-7 (2007).

### 2. The jury charge

Applying these guiding principles, the Court's charge to the jury included the following general instruction about vicarious criminal liability:

> As a legal entity, a corporation can only act vicariously through its agents; that is, through its directors, officers, and employees or other persons authorized to act for it. A corporation may be held criminally liable for the acts of its agent done on behalf of and for the benefit of the corporation, and directly related to the performance of the duties the employee has authority to perform.

***Following this instruction, the Court elaborated on the meaning and scope of agency in the criminal context:

> ***An act or omission that was specifically authorized by the corporation would be within the scope of the agent's employment. Even if the act or omission was not specifically authorized, it may still be within the scope of an agent's employment if (1) the agent acted for the benefit of the corporation and (2) the agent was acting within his authority. It is not necessary that the Government

prove that the corporation was actually benefitted, only that the agent intended it would be.

If you find that the agent was acting within the scope of his employment, the fact that the agent's act was illegal, contrary to his employer's instructions, or against the corporation's policies will not necessarily relieve the corporation of responsibility for the agent's act. You may consider whether the agent disobeyed instructions or violated company policy in determining whether the agent intended to benefit the corporation, and/or was acting within his authority.

In determining whether an agent was acting for the benefit of the corporation, you are instructed that the Government need not prove that the agent was only concerned with benefitting the corporation. It is sufficient if one of the agent's purposes was to benefit the corporation.***

### 3. Discussion

Ionia's position is that the actions of the Kriton's crew cannot be imputed to the company because they were acting illegally and violating company environmental policy without authorization. Moreover, Ionia contends that there was no actual benefit to be gained from illegally discharging oil waste, for the vessel's pollution prevention equipment obviated the need to make illegal discharges or shoreline disposals.

First, the Government introduced evidence that the putative agents of Ionia were acting under direct orders from their superiors. According to Second Engineer Edgardo Mercurio, Chief Engineer Efstratios Tsigonakis specifically instructed him not to use the oily water separator and to pump the oily waste overboard without utilizing the oil pollution prevention equipment; Tsigonakis and Mercurio then directed the engine room crew to connect the bypass hose and dispose of the waste directly into the ocean.

***The jury could reasonably have concluded that the crew participated in the pump-outs and records falsification with the intention of, for example, (1) following orders and maintaining the chain of command aboard the Kriton; (2) saving Ionia the time and expense of properly maintaining and using the oil pollution prevention equipment; and (3) enabling the Kriton to continue to dock at U.S. ports despite having false records.

Finally, that Ionia had official policies prohibiting the conduct by the crew which formed the basis for this prosecution does not change the conclusion that imposing vicarious criminal liability was proper. As the Court explained in instructing the jury, the existence of contrary company policies is not by itself a defense to criminal liability; whether Ionia had an official position on the course of conduct undertaken by its agents is merely one factor to be considered by the jury when assessing whether to impose vicarious liability. In this case, reasonable jurors could have concluded that, notwithstanding company policies, training, and general instructions, the actions of the Kriton's crew attributable to Ionia were actions by agents of Ionia performed within the scope of their employment.

***Applying the agency principles described above to the facts of this case, a rational trier of fact could have found Ionia guilty beyond a reasonable doubt through the acts of its employees, and there is no basis for granting a new trial in the interest of justice. Insofar as Ionia's Motion for a Judgment of Acquittal, or in the Alternative, a New Trial rests on the jury's misapplication of agency principles, it is denied.

## Case Analysis

1. Explain how a corporation can be criminally responsible for the acts of its employees.
2. Is it relevant that Ionia had an official policy against dumping polluted oil of its ships? Why or why not?
3. What type of punishment is appropriate for a corporation?
4. Should the individual employees involved in the illegal dumping also be criminally charged? Why or why not?

## Deferred Prosecution Agreements

Since the 2001 demise of energy giant Enron, much has changed in the realm of corporate vicarious liability. Instead of jumping straight to criminal prosecutions, the government often enters into so-called deferred prosecution agreements. In exchange for facing criminal prosecution, corporations are given an opportunity to "correct their ways" before the criminal law is used. This often occurs with close monitoring by federal officials in the U.S. Justice Department. Corporations appear quite willing to enter into these agreements:

> The willingness of corporations to enter into such deferred prosecution agreements is due in large measure to the vastly disproportionate power of the two sides. Prosecutors have enormous leverage due to the doctrine of vicarious liability. A single low-level employee's criminal conduct can be sufficient to trigger criminal liability on the part of the corporation.[86]

If a company rejects the government's offer for deferred prosecution, it can have dire consequences. You may recall that Arthur Anderson, one of the "big five" accounting firms, went under in 2002, in part because it handled much of the auditing for Enron. The company was given the opportunity to enter into a deferred prosecution agreement, but it rejected the offer. It was indicted and convicted of various crimes, including obstruction of justice. And while the conviction was later overturned,[87] the company has yet to return to normal operations.

## Civil Law Developments

In the civil arena, numerous restrictions have been put in place that make it increasingly unlikely that corporations will be held liable for their employees' behaviors. We discuss two such restrictions: (1) limitations on

The Enron Corporate Logo
Courtesy of Newscom

---

[86]Ibid., pp. 425–426.
[87]*Arthur Anderson, LLP v. United States*, 544 U.S. 696 (2005).

corporate liability in Title VII (shorthand for Title VII of the Civil Rights Act of 1964, which prohibits employer discrimination on the basis of race, color, religion, sex, or national origin) sexual harassment cases and (2) limitations on corporate punitive damages in vicarious criminal liability case. While these developments have occurred as a result of civil cases, they have interesting implications for corporate criminal liability.

In *Faragher* v. *City of Boca Raton*,[88] the Supreme Court dealt with a Title VII question of whether a city was responsible for sexual harassment by its supervisory lifeguards. The city argued that it had an antisexual harassment policy in place and thus could not be held civilly liable for the actions of one of its employees. The Supreme Court sided with the city because the female subordinate lifeguard who alleged sexual harassment did not argue that any adverse action was taken against her (known as "quid pro quo" harassment). The practical result of the Court's decision is that cities are shielded to some extent from vicarious *civil* liability for employee sexual harassment so long as they have in place policies intended to discourage such behavior.[89] Why do we care? Recall from the previous section that no such rule exists for criminal liability. To this day, corporations can be held *criminally* liable for the actions of their subordinates even if they have policies in place intended to prevent such misconduct! Why is civil law so much more restrictive? This discrepancy will need to be resolved some day.

The Supreme Court has also placed restrictions on punitive damages (a dollar amount intended to "punish" those at fault) that corporations can be required to pay in civil vicarious liability cases. In *Kolstad* v. *American Dental Association*,[90] Carole Kolstad sued the American Dental Association, alleging that she was passed over for promotion because of sexual harassment. The Court held that "in the punitive damages context, an employer may not be vicariously liable for the discriminatory employment decisions of managerial agents where these decisions are contrary to the employer's 'good-faith efforts to comply with Title VII.'"[91] Since the defendant had enacted policies intended to prevent employment discrimination, it was basically immune from punitive damages. This decision was significant because it placed limits on how much companies can be forced to pay as punishment for the actions of their subordinates. No such restriction has been put in place in the criminal context, where the sky remains the limit as far as what companies can be forced to pay.

## Individual Vicarious Liability

With individual vicarious liability, one person (instead of a corporation) is held liable for another's behavior. For example, in some states, parents can be held criminally liable for their kids' illegal activities. So-called principals can also be held liable for the actions of their agents (an "agent" is one who acts on behalf of a principal).

---

[88]*Faragher* v. *City of Boca Raton*, 524 U.S. 775 (1998).
[89]See also *Burlington Industries, Inc.* v. *Ellerth*, 524 U.S. 742 (1998).
[90]*Kolstad* v. *American Dental Association*, 527 U.S. 526 (1999).
[91]Ibid., p. 545.

# Parental Liability for a Child's Behavior

There are two main types of statutes used to hold parents accountable for the actions of their children. First, every state penalizes "contributing to the delinquency of a minor."[92] Known as CDM statutes, these can be used against basically anyone who contributes to a child's delinquency, not just parents.

By 1997, some 17 states had enacted laws aimed specifically at the parents of children. The common thread running throughout the laws is that they punish parents *failing* to intervene. An example is New York's "endangering the welfare of a child" statute. It provides the following:

> A person is guilty of endangering the welfare of a child when:
>
> 1. He knowingly acts in a manner likely to be injurious to the physical, mental or moral welfare of a child less than seventeen years old or directs or authorizes such child to engage in an occupation involving a substantial risk of danger to his life or health; or
> 2. Being a parent, guardian or other person legally charged with the care or custody of a child less than eighteen years old, he fails or refuses to exercise reasonable diligence in the control of such child to prevent him from becoming an "abused child," a "neglected child," a "juvenile delinquent" or a "person in need of supervision,. . . ."
>
> Endangering the welfare of a child is a class A misdemeanor.[93]

To illustrate the reach of parental responsibility laws, consider the story of Alex Provenzino, a Detroit teenager who started getting into trouble when he began associating with older kids. He was first arrested for burglarizing his family's church. Later, he was arrested for assaulting his father. Three months later, he was arrested for a string of residential burglaries. His last arrest occurred after police found marijuana and a stolen handgun on his nightstand. A year later, Alex's parents were found guilty of a misdemeanor for failing to prevent their son from committing the burglaries. Theirs was the first case tried under the St. Clair Shores parental responsibility law. The law required that parents were:

1. To keep illegal drugs or illegal firearms out of the home and legal firearms locked in places that are inaccessible to the minor.

2. To know the Curfew Ordinance of the City of St. Clair Shores, and to require the minor to observe the Curfew ordinance. . . .

3. To require the minor to attend regular school sessions and to forbid the minor to be absent from class without parental or school permission.

4. To arrange proper supervision for the minor when the parent must be absent.

5. To take the necessary precautions to prevent the minor from maliciously or willfully destroying real, personal, or mixed property which belongs to the City of St. Clair Shores, or is located in the City of St. Clair Shores.

6. To forbid the minor from keeping stolen property, illegally possessing firearms or illegal drugs, or associating with known juvenile delinquents, and to seek help

---

[92]P. K. Graham, "Parental Responsibility Laws: Let the Punishment Fit the Crime," *Loyola Law Review*, Vol. 33 (2000), pp. 1719 and 1729–1739. Should be 1719-1754, p. 1731
[93]N.Y. Penal Law 260.10.

from appropriate governmental authorities or private agencies in handling or controlling the minor, when necessary.[94]

The parents were ordered to pay $2,200 in fines and court costs plus $13,000 per year for their son's care in a youth detention home. An appeals court later overturned the verdict on a technicality,[95] but the case thrust the issue of parental responsibility laws into the limelight and is analogous to many other such cases.

## Principal–Agent Liability

Principal-agent liability is also commonplace. Once again, a principal is the individual who hires or is in charge of an agent; the agent acts on his or her behalf. Often the principal is the employer and the agent is the employee, but this need not always be the case. We will offer an example of each relationship. To illustrate an employer–employee relationship, in one case, an El Paso, Texas, bank hired a repossession company to recover Yvonne Sanchez's vehicle because she defaulted on her loan. Two men who were dispatched to Sanchez's home found the vehicle in the driveway. Sanchez confronted the men as they were hooking the vehicle to a tow truck. Just as the men were getting ready to tow the vehicle away, Sanchez jumped inside it, locked the doors, and refused to get out. The men then towed the vehicle away with Sanchez inside. They parked the car in a fenced lot and left Sanchez inside while a Doberman pinscher guard dog wandered about the lot. She was later rescued by her husband and police. An appeals court held that the bank had a duty to take precautions for safety and was responsible for the breach of peace committed by the repossession company agents.[96]

Let us use another Texas case to illustrate a principal–agent relationship that is not of the employer–employee variety. In *Marshall* v. *Allstate*, a 20-year-old college student, Wayne, had some friends over to his parents' house in Katy, Texas. At 10:30 P.M., his father told him to "Wrap things up." Wayne and friends ignored the request and instead went into the garage, after having been drinking, and built a large wooden cross. Then they carried it across town and set it on fire in the front yard of an African American family. The father was found vicariously liable for delegating authority over the family premises to his son (by simply saying, "Wrap things up"). The Fifth Circuit, however, reversed the trial court's decision:

> Assuming arguendo that [Wayne] was [his father's] agent for the purpose of "wrapping things up" around the [home] on the night of the cross-burning, the record is devoid of facts suggesting Wayne acted within the scope of that authority when he participated in the cross-burning. [His father's] testimony clearly demonstrates that when he told Wayne to "wrap things up," he intended for Wayne to send his friends home. Any suggestion that [the father] gave Wayne authority to construct a large wooden cross [at the father's premises], transport that cross to the home of an African-American family and set it on fire is the height of absurdity. The fact that [the father] knew or should have known of his son's difficulties with alcohol does not

---

[94]St. Clair Shores, Mich., Parental Responsibility Ordinance 20.560–20.566 (July 26, 1994).
[95]*City of St. Clair Shores* v. *Provenzino*, No. 96-1483 AR (County of Macomb Cir. Ct. 1997).
[96]*MBank El Paso* v. *Sanchez*, 836 S.W.2d 151 (Tex. 1992).

alter this analysis; that [the father] may have been negligent in delegating authority over his property to an untrustworthy son does not serve to expand the scope of authority given to encompass unimaginable criminal conduct wholly unrelated to the task assigned.[97]

Not unlike corporations, then, individual principals can be liable (criminally and civilly) for the actions of their agents. And whether the principal is an employer or just an ordinary person is largely immaterial.

**YOUR DECISION**

1. Judy Smart is a 17-year-old high school junior. One Saturday night she is drinking beer with a number of her high school friends in the basement of her home. Judy's parents, Bob and Mary Smart, are home at the time. They did not buy the beer that the underage minors are consuming, but they are aware of the party in their basement. Bob and Mary Smart do nothing to stop the party. On the way home, one intoxicated minor is killed when she drives her car into a ditch. Can Bob and Mary Smart be charged with a crime? Why or why not?

2. Jimmy owns a local liquor store that sells beer, wine, and hard liquor. He hired Gina to work the evening shift as a cashier. Jimmy repeatedly reminded Gina to make sure she asked for identification of anyone who looked to be younger then 30 years old. Gina, however, never carded her customers in order to boost her sales. She was ultimately caught by the police one evening selling a bottle of Jack Daniels to an 18-year-old high school student. Can Jimmy be charged with a crime as a result of Gina's actions? Why or why not?

## Summary

- Vicarious liability occurs when one person is held liable for the actions of another—and perhaps when the former person has no idea what the latter person is up to.

- There are two conditions that make vicarious liability different from accomplice liability: (1) it takes only one party's actions to trigger liability and (2) liability *transfers* from one of them to the other.

- Corporate vicarious liability refers to the liability of a corporation, no matter its size, for the criminal conduct of its employees.

- The general rule today is that a corporation is criminally liable for the actions of its agents when (1) those agents act in the official scope of their employment for (2) the benefit of the corporation.

- With individual vicarious liability, one person (instead of a corporation) is held liable for another's behavior. For example, in some states, parents can be held criminally liable for their kids' illegal activities.

---

[97]*Ross v. Marshall*, 426 F.3d 745 (5th Cir. Tex. 2005), p. 764.

# Chapter Review

## INTRODUCTION TO ACCOMPLICE LIABILITY

### Learning Objectives

- Distinguish between complicity and conspiracy.
- Identify the parties to crime, including principals, accomplices, and accessories.

### Review Questions

1. Explain how conspiracy differs from complicity.
2. Compare and contrast common law and modern-day parties to a crime.

### Key Terms

complicity
accomplice
derivative liability
principal in the first degree
principal in the second degree
accessory before the fact
accessory after the fact
accessory

## THE ELEMENTS OF COMPLICITY

### Learning Objectives

- Explain the elements of complicity.
- Explain the elements of accessory liability.

### Review Questions

1. Compare and contrast three means by which assistance is provided in the complicity context.
2. Explain the two levels of *mens rea* for purposes of a complicity.
3. How do the elements of accessory liability differ from the elements of accomplice liability?

### Key Term

natural and probable consequences doctrine

## COMPLICITY ISSUES, LIMITATIONS, AND DEFENSES

### Learning Objectives

- Discuss some of the issues that make complicity law complicated.
- Summarize the limitations of and defenses to accomplice liability.
- Explain the Model Penal Code approach to accomplice liability.

*Review Questions*

1. What is a nonproxyable offense? Explain.
2. Offer an example of a principal being acquitted and an accomplice being found guilty.
3. Identify two limitations on accomplice liability.
4. Summarize the Model Penal Code's approach to accomplice liability.

*Key Terms*

nonproxyable offense
ostrich instruction

MODULE **6.4**

**VICARIOUS LIABILITY**

*Learning Objective*

- Explain the concept of vicarious liability.

*Review Questions*

1. Compare and contrast vicarious and accomplice liability.
2. Compare and contrast the two main varieties of vicarious liability.

*Key Terms*

vicarious liability
corporate vicarious liability
*respondeat superior*

# Chapter Synthesizing Questions

1. Compare and contrast modern complicity law with the common law approach.
2. Identify and describe two factors that complicate complicity.
3. Explain the defenses to complicity.
4. Compare and contrast complicity and vicarious liability. Why are both presented in the same chapter?

# 7

# INCHOATE CRIMES

*Learning Objectives*

MODULE **7.1** **INTRODUCTION TO INCHOATE CRIMES: ATTEMPT**
- **Explain the concept of inchoate crimes.**
- **Explain the relationship of attempt to the substantive offense.**
- **Summarize what constitutes attempt.**
- **Summarize the defenses to charges of attempt.**

MODULE **7.2** **CONSPIRACY AND SOLICITATION**
- **Identify the elements and complications of conspiracy.**
- **Describe the defenses to conspiracy.**
- **Describe solicitation.**
- **Distinguish solicitation from other inchoate crimes.**

# INTRODUCTION TO INCHOATE CRIMES: ATTEMPT

### Learning Objectives
- **Explain the concept of inchoate crimes.**
- **Explain the relationship of attempt to the substantive offense.**
- **Summarize what constitutes attempt.**
- **Summarize the defenses to charges of attempt.**

## CORE CONCEPTS

**inchoate crime** A crime that has not been completed. The three inchoate offenses are **attempt**, **conspiracy**, and **solicitation**.

An **inchoate crime** is one that is "partial; unfinished; begun, but not completed."[1] Inchoate crimes are also considered "incipient," meaning they often lead to one or more other crimes. Yet even though they are not technically completed, inchoate crimes are crimes in themselves. In other words, a person can be convicted of an inchoate crime even if he does not actually complete the crime he intended to commit. One who *attempts* a robbery can be found guilty of attempted robbery. Likewise, one who attempts to kill another can be found guilty of attempted murder.

Why punish people for uncompleted crimes? There are several reasons:

- Untold numbers of crimes are started or set in motion, but never completed. But just because they are not completed, should we turn a blind eye?

- It would be unfair to let an otherwise guilty person go free simply because she failed to complete the intended crime.

- Penalizing "incomplete" crime allows the criminal justice system to be more preventive; without being able to prosecute certain offenders for what they *plan* or *try* to do, we would be forced to wait around until the damage was already done.

This module introduces the crime of attempt. The next module introduces conspiracy and solicitation. While attempt, conspiracy, and solicitation get most of the attention as far as inchoate crimes go, there are other crimes that we introduce in later chapters that can also be considered inchoate. Assault (Chapter 9) is a good example. Assault is a widely misunderstood offense because uninformed observers liken it to a physical attack. Assault, however, is anything but physical. It is *attempted* or *threatened* battery, the latter consisting of unlawful touching. Viewed this way, assault is an inchoate crime—at least some of the time. There are people who are content merely to threaten others, but often the objective is physical harm. When that is the case, assault is the incipient offense to battery. Other examples were called out by the Maryland Supreme Court in *Dabney* v. *State*:

> Even many venerable and serious crimes, that have long been accepted target crimes for attempts, are to some extent sometimes inchoate. A fully consummated kidnapping, for instance, may be inchoate to a murder or a rape or an extortion. A fully

---

[1]*Black's Law Dictionary*, 6th ed. (St. Paul, MN: West, 1990), p. 761.

consummated burglary (or one of its statutory progeny) may be inchoate to a theft or to some other crime intended to be committed on the inside. An arson may be inchoate to a murder or to an insurance fraud.[2]

To avoid confusion, we will introduce these offenses in later chapters. We will limit our focus here to the stand-alone crimes of attempt, conspiracy, and solicitation.

# Attempt

**attempt** An inchoate offense in which the defendant has the specific intent to commit the underlying offense and takes some action in furtherance of that intent, but is unsuccessful in completing the crime.

**Attempt** is the "intent to commit a crime coupled with an act taken toward committing the offense."[3] There are four elements of attempt to commit a crime:

- " . . . intent to commit it,
- an overt act toward its commission,
- failure of consummation,
- and the apparent possibility of commission."[4]

The first two elements are basically the *mens rea* and *actus reus* of attempt, respectfully. We devote detailed treatment to each of them shortly. The last two elements—failure of consummation and the apparent possibility of commission—are self-explanatory. If the crime is consummated, or completed, then it is no longer just an attempt. "Apparent possibility" just refers to the possibility that the offender could have attempted the crime. If, for example, a defendant is charged with attempted burglary but was nowhere near the scene of the crime, then it is not apparent that he could have committed the offense. This is roughly analogous to an alibi defense.

## The Relationship of Attempt to the Substantive Offense

Criminal attempt is, in most instances, "an adjunct crime; it cannot exist by itself, but only in connection with another crime."[5] This does not mean the other crime (e.g., robbery) must be completed, but rather that there is no crime of attempt that is not linked to some other substantive crime. To convict a person of attempt without reference to any other offense would leave one asking, "Attempted what?" If the offender successfully completes the target offense, then he also attempted to commit it. The reverse, of course, is not true; a person who takes a step toward the commission of a substantive offense may not "get there," which is why we have the crime of attempt. To keep it simple, in most jurisdictions a "person is guilty of a criminal attempt when, with intent to commit a crime, the person engages in conduct which

---

[2]*Dabney v. State*, 858 A.2d 1084 (Md. 2004), p. 1098.
[3]*Black's Law Dictionary*, p. 127.
[4]*State v. Stewart*, 537 S.W.2d 579 (Mo. App. 1976), p. 580.
[5]*Lane v. State*, 703 A.2d 180 (Md. 1997), p. 186.

constitutes a substantial step toward the commission of that crime whether or not his intention is accomplished."[6]

In theory, a person can be guilty of both attempt and the completed crime. But as a practical matter one cannot be guilty of both. For example, if a robbery is completed, then attempt is "absorbed" by the completed robbery. More technically, the attempted robbery would be the "lesser included offense" of robbery. If a jury were to convict an offender of both, the Fifth Amendment's double jeopardy provision would be violated because it is unconstitutional to punish a person twice for the same offense. For constitutional purposes, a completed robbery is viewed as the same offense (refer to Chapter 2 for more on double jeopardy) as attempted robbery.

Jurors, however, can be given the option of convicting an offender of either robbery or attempted robbery. Assume the prosecutor fails to convince the jury that the defendant completed the robbery. In such an event, the jury could fall back on attempt and ensure that the defendant does not go free.

## The *Mens Rea* of Attempt

Because an attempt is not a completed crime, it is more difficult to prove *mens rea*. There are two parts of the *mens rea* of attempt, namely to (1) intend the act and (2) intend the result. To intend the act means to intend that act that constitutes the attempt. The defendant must intend to commit some sort of overt act toward completion of the offense. As to intending the result, the defendant must also intend for the substantive crime to occur. So, for example, if Brian intends to shoot Larry in the knee but does not intend for Larry to die, Brian has not satisfied the *mens rea* of attempted murder. Brian will likely be convicted of some other crime, however, as he certainly did something illegal (e.g., battery).

Attempt is a specific intent offense (revisit the Chapter 3 discussion on the differences between specific and general intent offenses). This is so even if the target offense is of the general intent variety. For example, "breaking and entering" is a general intent offense; it has no specific *mens rea* requirement. Nevertheless, to be found guilty of *attempted* breaking and entering, the defendant must specifically intend to break and enter. This adds yet another layer of complexity to the *mens rea* of attempt.

## Result Crimes

Recall from Chapter 3 that result crimes require actual harm. Murder is the consummate example; without a death, the crime does not occur. Consider *State* v. *Hawkins*,[7] a case in which Gregory Thomas's Chevrolet Astrovan was rear-ended by another van driven by Darnell Hawkins. As soon as his van was hit, Thomas guided it into a nearby hotel parking lot. As he parked, he heard gunshots. He looked over his shoulder and observed Hawkins walking toward him and firing a gun in his direction. As

---

[6]*Townes* v. *State*, 548 A.2d 832 (Md. 1988), p. 834.
[7]*State* v. *Hawkins*, 631 So.2d 1288 (La. Ct. App. 1994).

Hawkins neared Thomas's van, Thomas opened the driver's door and raised his hands to show that he was unarmed. Hawkins reached into the van and, with a pistol in one hand, grabbed Thomas, put the pistol to his head and stated, "I'm going to kill you, mother f***er, I'm going to kill you!" Thomas then responded, "You can't kill me. I got three children to raise and my wife is dead, so you can't kill me." Thomas then pushed away Hawkins's hand, at which point Hawkins fired past him into the van. Once he emptied his clip, he returned to his own van to reload, at which point Thomas ran into the hotel lobby to hide. Hawkins then unloaded a second clip of ammunition into Thomas's van. Hawkins was soon apprehended, prosecuted for, and convicted of attempted second-degree murder. An appeals court reversed the conviction, however, noting,

> The evidence shows that the defendant had numerous opportunities to shoot the victim, but did not. He unloaded two clips of ammunition, one of those was while in close proximity to the victim. Although the defendant initially stated that he was going to kill the victim, he then chose to shoot bullets into and around the victim's van. This was indicative of his intent to damage the victim's property, not kill the victim. . . . The defendant held the gun to the victim's head, yet did not shoot, or attempt to shoot him. After the victim pushed away the defendant's hand, the defendant fired past him into the van. Such a firing is evidence of anger, but not an intent to kill someone who is standing less than three feet away. The victim, although shaken, remained unscathed. . . . Viewing the evidence in a light most favorable to the prosecution, no rational trier of fact could conclude that the State proved the essential elements of attempted second degree murder beyond a reasonable doubt.[8]

Hawkins was then found guilty of the lesser included offense of aggravated battery. Why? The *mens rea* was lacking for attempted second-degree murder. Hawkins clearly intended to discharge his weapon. And though he announced his intent to kill Thomas, it is doubtful, as the court noted, that it was his intent to do so.

A similar issue comes up in the context of felony murder. While we will define felony murder more fully in the next chapter, it bears mentioning here that if a person dies during the commission of some nonhomicide felony (e.g., robbery), the offender will be held liable for both crimes. This raises a question: "If a person is injured but not killed during the commission of a felony, can one be found guilty of attempted felony murder?" Assume, for example, that George robs a convenience store and demands that the manager, Leroy, open the safe. Leroy swears he cannot get into the safe, so George shoots his pistol at it a few times in an effort to force it open. A bullet ricochets off the safe and hits Leroy in the stomach, causing severe injury, but not killing him. Should George be convicted of attempted felony murder? Surely not, because there is no evidence that he *intended* to kill.[9] All but two states would take this approach, but Florida and Arkansas do not. In Florida, for example, attempted felony murder occurs when a person "commits, aids or abets an intentional act that is not an essential element of the felony and that could, but does not, cause the death of another."[10]

---

[8]Ibid., p. 1290.
[9]See, e.g., *State* v. *Robinson*, 883 P.2d 764 (Kan. 1994).
[10]Fla. Stat. ch. Section 782.051(1) (2008).

What about manslaughter? Though we give manslaughter more attention in the next chapter, we have to ask here, "Can one be convicted of attempted manslaughter?" In general, manslaughter consists of either an unintentional killing or a killing that takes place in the "heat of passion." Assume, for example, that a husband and wife have consumed several drinks and entered into a heated argument. Then assume the husband kills his wife during the course of the argument. This is arguably an example of manslaughter because even though the husband kills his wife, he did so in the heat of passion. In contrast, assume a speeding motorist accidentally hits and kills a pedestrian. The motorist would also be guilty of manslaughter, but the killing was unintentional. So which offender could be held liable for *attempted* manslaughter if the victim does not die? The husband could be held liable because his actions were voluntary.[11] The motorist, however, could not be convicted of attempted manslaughter if the pedestrian did not die. Why? It is safe to assume the motorist did not *intend* for the pedestrian to die, so to hold the motorist criminally liable for attempted manslaughter would mean that someone can intend to commit an involuntary act, which is a legal impossibility. This was further explained by the Florida Supreme Court in *Taylor* v. *State*:

> [T]here may be a crime of attempted manslaughter. We reiterate, however, that a verdict for attempted manslaughter can be rendered only if there is proof that the defendant had the requisite intent to commit an unlawful act. This holding necessitates that a distinction be made between the crimes of "manslaughter by act or procurement" and "manslaughter by culpable negligence." For the latter, there can be no corresponding attempt crime. This conclusion is mandated by the fact that there can be no intent to commit an unlawful act when the underlying conduct constitutes culpable negligence. On the other hand, when the underlying conduct constitutes an act or procurement, such as an aggravated assault, there is an intent to commit the act and, thus, there exists the requisite intent to support attempted manslaughter.[12]

To summarize, the *mens rea* for attempt in the result crime context must "match up" with the result. If, in our examples, there is no killing coupled with no intent to kill, then an attempted murder or manslaughter conviction is unlikely. The same would seem to extend to other crimes. If the defendant does not *intend* the result, then he or she cannot (with the possible exception of a failed manslaughter committed in the heat of passion) be convicted of attempting it.

## Conduct Crimes

Recall from Chapter 3 that conduct crimes do not require any end result, just the conduct in question. Presumably, it would be easier to hold someone liable for an attempted conduct crime because there is no requirement that the defendant desire some end result apart from the criminal act itself. As Dressler has argued, "[T]here is no logical reason why a person should not be convicted of an attempt to commit such a conduct crime, as long as she possesses the specific intent to engage in the conduct which, if performed, constitutes the substantive offense."[13]

---

[11]See, e.g., *Cox* v. *State*, 534 A.2d 1333 (Md. 1988).
[12]*Taylor* v. *State*, 444 So.2d 931 (Fla. 1983), p. 934.
[13]J. Dressler, *Understanding Criminal Law*, 5th ed. (San Francisco, CA: Lexis-Nexis, 2009), p. 394.

## The *Actus Reus* of Attempt

There is no uniformly accepted definition of *actus reus* for the crime of attempt. There are two reasons for this. First, the *actus reus* of attempt falls somewhere between "preparation" and "perpetration."[14] But deciding where preparation ends and perpetration begins is rather difficult, especially since no one crime is the same as the next. Second, there is a greater inclination to find intent when the substantive offense is of the serious variety. For example, if a murder fails, most would agree that holding the offender accountable for attempted murder is desirable. However, if a petty theft fails, would there be much point in going to the ends of the earth to convict someone of attempting the crime? Probably not.

The courts have formulated a number of tests for gauging the presence of *actus reus* in attempt crimes. They are not unlike the tests for insanity we introduced in Chapter 6. They are complex, they overlap to some extent, and they still leave unanswered the core question at hand: What is the *actus reus* of attempt? There simply is no clear answer; the tests merely offer some guidance. Dressler calls attention to six such tests: the "last act" test, the "physical proximity" test, the "dangerous proximity" test, the "indispensable element" test, the "probable desistance" test, and the "unequivocality" test.[15] Let's us briefly consider each one.

## The "Last Act" Test

According to the "last act" test, the *actus reus* of attempt is satisfied once the defendant has committed the last act necessary to complete the target crime. This test is advantageous because it is basically "black and white." Unfortunately, however, to

In order to satisfy the *actus reus* of attempt, the defendant needs to cross the line from preparation to actually attempting to commit the crime.
Gina Sanders/
Shutterstock.com

---

[14]Ibid., p. 396.
[15]Ibid., pp. 398–402.

wait until the very last moment undermines the intent of criminalizing attempt. As one court put it, "[T]he law of attempts would be largely without function if it could not be invoked until the trigger was pulled, the blow struck, or the money seized."[16] For this reason, there is a preference to move back in time from the completed crime to some earlier act.

## The "Physical Proximity" Test

According to this test, the *actus reus* of attempt is satisfied once the offender is *nearly able* to commit the target crime. Moreover, the offender must be physically close to the intended victim, hence the test's name. A few court decisions have offered explicit definitions of physical proximity. For example, the defendant's action "must go so far that it would result, or apparently result in the actual commission of the crime it was designed to effect, if not extrinsically hindered or frustrated by extraneous circumstances."[17]

There is a problem with the physical proximity test, however. It is possible for an attempt crime to occur when the defendant is nowhere close to the victim. For example, a person could use the Internet and attempt to take money from another's account without any requirement that the first person be in close physical proximity to the victim. A similar issue came up in *Commonwealth* v. *Kelley*,[18] a case in which two men, Kelley and Phillips, tricked a third man, Robinson, into taking $400 in cash out of his own bank account. Before the cash was taken out, an observant teller let Robinson know what was happening, so the crime was never completed. Importantly, Kelley and Phillips were not at Robinson's side as he tried to withdraw the money. They were subsequently arrested and convicted of attempted larceny. Interestingly, however, an appeals court reversed the convictions, highlighting the limitations of the physical proximity test. The court noted,

> Whether Kelley and Phillips intended by some method, at some time and at some place to secure possession of a part, if not all, of the $400.00 which Robinson intended to withdraw from his account may be assumed but it is a matter of pure conjecture. Conjecture is not a substitute for evidence and a conviction based thereon must be set aside.[19]

Had a different test been relied on, one that did not require physical proximity of the offenders to the victim, a different result would have been likely.

## The "Dangerous Proximity" Test

According to this test, the *actus reus* of intent is satisfied once the individual's conduct is in "dangerous proximity to success."[20] Alternatively, an attempt is said to occur when the act "is so near to the result that the danger of success is very great."[21]

---

[16]*People* v. *Dillon*, 668 P.2d 697 (Cal. 1983), p. 703.
[17]*Commonwealth* v. *Kelley*, 58 A.2d 375 (Pa. Super. Ct. 1948), p. 377.
[18]Ibid.
[19]Ibid., p. 377.
[20]*Hyde* v. *United States*, 225 U.S. 347 (1912), p. 388.
[21]*People* v. *Rizzo*, 158 N.E. 888 (N.Y. 1927), p. 889.

The dangerous proximity test does not require physical proximity, only a high degree of likelihood that the target offense will be completed. For example, in *People* v. *Rizzo*,[22] four men, two of whom were armed, rode about in their car looking for a fifth man, Charles Rao, who was carrying $1200 in payroll cash that they intended to rob him of. Before they found Rao, two police officers were alerted to their behavior and began following them. The men never found Rao. Soon thereafter they were arrested and convicted of attempted robbery in the first degree. Applying the test, a New York appeals court reversed Rizzo's conviction and ordered a new trial. The court's logic was as follows:

> [T]hese defendants had planned to commit a crime and were looking around the city for an opportunity to commit it, but the opportunity fortunately never came. Men would not be guilty of an attempt at burglary if they had planned to break into a building and were arrested while they were hunting about the streets for the building not knowing where it was. Neither would a man be guilty of an attempt to commit murder if he armed himself and started out to find the person whom he had planned to kill but could not find him. So here these defendants were not guilty of an attempt to commit robbery in the first degree when they had not found or reached the presence of the person they intended to rob.[23]

Because the men were not in "dangerous proximity" to completing the crime, they were not guilty of attempt.

### The "Indispensible Element" Test

The "indispensible element" test looks not at proximity to crime completion, but rather at what, if anything, is *lacking* such that the crime could not be completed. For example, in *State* v. *Addor*,[24] the defendants apparently intended to manufacture illegal liquor, but they lacked a still. Since the still was an indispensible element (liquor could not be made without it), the men were not guilty of attempting to manufacture illegal liquor.

### The "Probable Desistance" Test

This test looks at the likelihood of the offender stopping once the wheels have been set in motion. The American Law Institute (which wrote the Model Penal Code) came up with this test, noting that attempt occurs when "the actor . . . reached a point where it was unlikely that he would have voluntarily desisted from his effort to commit the crime."[25] Understood differently, the probable desistance test looks at the proverbial "point of no return." If the offender reaches it, but fails to complete the target offense, attempt occurs. The Wisconsin Supreme Court put it this way: "The defendant's conduct must pass that point where most men, holding such an intention as the defendant holds, would think better of their conduct and desist."[26]

---

[22]Ibid.
[23]Ibid., pp. 889–890.
[24]*State* v. *Addor*, 110 S.E. 650 (N.C. 1922).
[25]American Law Institute, Comment to Section 5.01.
[26]*Berry v. State*, 280 N.W.2d 204 (Wis. 1979), p. 209.

Unfortunately, it is difficult for juries to draw conclusions about the offender's subjective motivations. It is rarely clear to anyone exactly what is going on in the defendant's head, making this test somewhat limited.

### The "Unequivocality" Test

Simply put, the unequivocality test (also called the *res ipsa loquiter* test, which is Latin for "The act speaks for itself") holds that attempt occurs when it is no longer ambiguous to an ordinary person what the would-be offender intends. That is, attempt occurs "when it becomes clear what the actor's intention is and when the acts done show that the perpetrator is actually putting his plan into action."[27] As with the rest of the tests, this one is also ambiguous. It may not always be clear when an individual intends to commit a crime.

### The Model Penal Code "Substantial Step" Test

We summarize the Model Penal Code's approach to attempt later in this chapter, but its "substantial step" test is relevant here. For attempt to occur, the a substantial step must be undertaken. Examples of a "substantial step" include "lying in wait," "enticing or seeking to entice" the intended victim to a particular location, and unlawfully entering a structure in which the intended crime is to occur.[28]

See the accompanying Court Decision for more on the *actus reus* of attempt. In it we take a look at the case of *State* v. *Reid*, in which the defendant is charged with attempted criminal sexual conduct with a minor for his conduct beginning in an internet chat room.

## COURT DECISION

*State* v. *Reid*
670 S.E.2d 194 (S.C. App. 2009)

**Background:** Defendant Jamey Allen Reid was convicted in Circuit Court, Oconee County of second-degree attempted criminal sexual conduct with a minor. Defendant appealed and the Court of Appeals of South Carolina affirmed.

\*\*\*Facts

On the night of January 9, 2006, Mark Patterson, a police officer for the Westminster Police Department and the Internet Crimes Against Children Task Force, conducted an undercover investigation on the internet. As part of the operation, Patterson entered a Yahoo chat room under the guise of a fourteen year old female, using the screen name "Skatergurl."

\*\*\*At some point that night, Skatergurl received a message from a person with the screen name "Fine_Ass_Seminoles_Fan," (FASF) asking her where she lived. . . . Thereafter, the following discussion occurred:

> [FASF]: Well, what you looking for? . . . Sex, Love, Relationships, Friends, What?
>
> [Skatergurl]: Laugh out loud. What's everybody looking for?

---

[27]*People* v. *Staples*, 6 Cal. App. 3d 61 (1970), p. 67.
[28]See Model Penal Code, Section 5.01(2)(a)-(d).

***[FASF]: You need some loving? I'm asking?

[Skatergurl]: I don't know. Laugh out loud.

[FASF]: I do.

[Skatergurl]: Kewl.

The conversation turned to arranging a meeting place. FASF asked when and where they could meet. Skatergurl replied they could only meet at night and suggested Westminster Middle School. Skatergurl subsequently asked:

[Skatergurl]: Whatcha wanna do?

[FASF]: Go back to my apt.—I assume. Okay?

[Skatergurl]: Do what?

***[FASF]: Watch movie, I dunno, talk. Make love.

[Skatergurl]: Make love?

[FASF]: Yes. Wanna [ ] don't mean you have to.

[Skatergurl]: You don't care I am 14?

[FASF]: No. You?

FASF suggested meeting between 2:00 and 2:15 a.m. at the middle school that night. He told Skatergurl he would arrive in a black truck or a red car and he confirmed what Skatergurl would be wearing. Just before signing out of the chat room, FASF said, "we come here and make love, okay, snuggle, kiss, whatever, okay?" He then asked, "you wanna have sex, honestly," and Skatergurl responded, "I can try."

Officer Patterson called another Westminster police officer and they stationed their vehicles near the middle school. At approximately 2:30 a.m., a red Toyota Celica pulled into the parking lot. The officers stopped the car and arrested the driver, Jamey Allen Reid.

***A jury trial was held on March 7, 2007. At the close of the State's case, Reid's counsel moved for a directed verdict of acquittal. The court denied the motion. The jury convicted Reid . . . [and] [t]he trial court sentenced Reid to twenty years for the attempted CSC with a minor second degree conviction, which was suspended upon the service of ten years with five years probation. . . . This appeal followed.

### ***Discussion

Reid first argues the trial court erred in refusing to direct a verdict of acquittal because the State failed to demonstrate Reid committed an overt act as required to prove guilt for attempted CSC with a minor second degree. We disagree.

A person is guilty of CSC with a minor in the second degree if the actor engages in sexual battery with a victim who is fourteen years or less but who is at least eleven years of age. "A person who commits the common law offense of attempt is punishable as for the principal offense." *State v. Sutton,* 340 S.C. 393, 396 n. 3 (2000). Thus, the elements of attempted CSC with a minor in the second degree are: (1) an attempt; (2) to engage in a sexual battery; (3) with a victim; (4) who is fourteen years of age or less; (5) but who is at least eleven years of age.

Generally, the mens rea of an attempt crime is one of specific intent such that the act constituting the attempt must be done with the intent to commit that particular crime. "In the context of an attempt crime, specific intent means that the defendant consciously intended the completion of acts comprising the choate offense." *State v. Nesbitt*, 346 S.C. 226, 231 (Ct.App.2001). The State must prove the defendant's specific intent was accompanied by some overt act, beyond mere preparation, in furtherance of the intent.

Courts have struggled to determine the point at which conduct moves beyond the preparatory stage to the perpetration stage. A competition amongst policy considerations exists in this realm of the law. On the one hand, there exists a policy not to punish or convict innocent persons for evil or criminal thoughts alone; on the other hand, a countervailing policy exists to allow law enforcement to prevent criminal conduct before it reaches the point of completion. South Carolina jurisprudence in the area of attempt law is sparse. Cases in South Carolina do not clearly establish any absolute guiding test for our trial courts to employ. . . .

Other state and federal courts have employed a variety of tests, some of which have been used in part or interchangeably by various courts demonstrating the difficulty in defining a universal test. These tests generally are either directed to how much has been done, or instead, how much remains to be done in furtherance of the object crime. Notwithstanding, one rule which does appear consistent throughout the country is the sequence of events need not reach the last proximate act necessary to completion, an original common law test.

Case law additionally suggests varying proximity tests. One test credited to Justice Oliver Wendell Holmes, the common law "dangerous proximity" test, focuses on whether the act comes so close or near to the object crime that the danger of success is very great. Essentially, this test focuses upon how much remains to be done before the defendant would have succeeded in his goals; often, factors such as the nearness of danger, the substantiality of harm and the apprehension felt are considered. Further, the more severe the object crime, the less close the actor must come to completing it in order to be convicted of attempt.

Similarly, the "physical proximity" test focuses upon whether the defendant's acts "may be said to be physically proximate to the intended crime." Lafave, 2 Subst. Crim. L. § 11.4. This test has been further described as focusing upon an act which amounts to the commencement of the consummation of the object crime or stands "either as the first or some subsequent step in direct movement towards the commission of the offense after preparations are made." *State v. Dowd*, 220 S.E.2d 393, 396 (1975).

Another test, the "substantial step" test, derives from the Model Penal Code and focuses upon whether the defendant has taken a substantial step that strongly corroborates his intent to commit the object crime. Model Penal Code § 5.01. Here, the court looks to what has been done as opposed to what remains to be done. Thus, the drafters of the model code noted that the scope of attempt liability would be broadened consistent with the policy of restraining dangerous persons where the firmness of criminal purpose is shown.

The *Mandujano* court, relying upon the Model Penal Code references to other formulations of various tests, indicated the following additional tests:

(c) The indispensable element test—a variation of the proximity tests which emphasizes any indispensable aspect of the criminal endeavor over which the actor has not yet acquired control.

(d) The probable desistance test—the conduct constitutes an attempt if, in the ordinary and natural course of events, without interruption from an outside source, it will result in the crime intended.

(e) The abnormal step approach—an attempt is a step toward crime which goes beyond the point where the normal citizen would think better of his conduct and desist.

(f) The res ipsa loquitur or unequivocality test—an attempt is committed when the actor's conduct manifests an intent to commit a crime.

499 F.2d at 373 n. 5.

*** As indicated, we have not found any case in South Carolina specifically indicating how far a person must go before that person may be convicted of attempt to commit a crime. However, our state supreme court has provided some guidance. . . . Although the crime of attempt was not at issue in *Quick,* the court nonetheless discussed the distinction between preparations and overt acts, making reference in part to an "attempt to commit." *Quick,* 199 S.C. at 260. The court indicated "preparation consists in devising or arranging the means or measures necessary for the commission of the crime; the attempt or overt act is the direct movement toward the commission, after the preparations are made." The court went on to articulate "'the act' is to be liberally construed, and in numerous cases it is said to be sufficient that the act go far enough toward accomplishment of the crime to amount to the commencement of its consummation." Further, the court explained, "the act need not be the last proximate step leading to the consummation of the offense."

***Reviewing the facts herein, Reid asked a person whom he thought was a fourteen year old girl if she would meet him within the hour in order to "make love . . . snuggle, kiss, whatever." Moreover, the last question Reid asked Skatergurl was, "you wanna have sex, honestly?" This evidence constituted evidence of Reid's specific intent to accomplish CSC with a minor. Having found evidence of the specific intent to commit the underlying offense, we must determine whether the State offered sufficient evidence demonstrating Reid committed some act toward the commission of the crime beyond any act or acts of preparation.

***We have not found any precedent within our State addressing this specific type of factual situation. However, a significant number of other jurisdictions confronted with this issue have concluded that the act of a defendant who travels to a pre-arranged location with the purpose of having sex with an individual whom he believes is a child is a sufficient act in furtherance of an attempted sex crime. . . . However, other jurisdictions have held merely arriving at an arranged location is insufficient to constitute a sufficient act in furtherance of a planned sex crime.

Here, based on the evidence presented, Reid completed a requisite act in furtherance of the offense of attempted CSC with a minor second degree. Reid, in preparation, arranged a time and meeting location with a person whom he thought to be a minor. Reid described the type of car he would be driving and he confirmed the description of Skatergurl's clothing. Further, Reid left the location where he was communicating with Skatergurl and committed an act beyond mere preparation in driving to and physically arriving at the prearranged location within fifteen minutes of the agreed upon time. Reid's act, for purposes of directed verdict, constituted evidence of the first or some subsequent step in a direct movement towards the commission of the offense after any act or acts of preparation.[FN7]

FN 7. *We recognize the significant number of jurisdictions adopting the substantial step test. Many of these states have done so by legislative enactment and this may be a matter worthy of legislative attention. Notwithstanding, even if the South Carolina Supreme Court were to adopt a substantial step test, we find the case herein would meet that test as demonstrated by the case law cited herein.*

Moreover, we give weight to the policy goal of stopping dangerous persons through earlier intervention by law enforcement by punishing the attempted conduct as a crime, especially in any cybermolester type cases where the conduct also clearly manifests or strongly corroborates the intent to commit such a dangerous object crime. Accordingly, the trial court did not err because the evidence was sufficient to withstand Reid's motion for a directed verdict and warranted submission of the case to the jury.

**\*\*\*AFFIRMED.**

## Case Analysis

1. List the various tests for the *actus reus* of attempt that the court discusses.
2. What test, if any, does the court seem to suggest for adoption in South Carolina?
3. What actions did the defendant commit towards completing the crime?
4. Did the defendant cross the line between preparation and attempt? Explain.

---

See Figure 7.1 for a summary of the elements of attempt in flowchart format.

# Defenses to Attempt

One who is charged with a crime of attempt can assert almost any of the defenses we introduced in Chapters 4 and 5. There are, however, two defenses that are unique to attempt: impossibility and abandonment. Both are similar to accomplice liability defenses that we discussed in the last chapter, but they operate somewhat differently in the attempt context.

## Impossibility

In some situations, it is impossible for a defendant to have committed the attempt crime in question. For example, if an adult male enters an Internet chat room and carries on a discussion with someone who he thinks is an underage female but is actually a law

**Figure 7.1**
Attempt

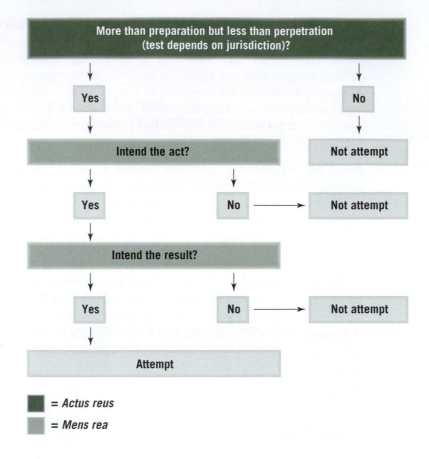

More than preparation but less than perpetration (test depends on jurisdiction)?

Yes → Intend the act? → Yes → Intend the result? → Yes → Attempt

No → Not attempt

Intend the act? No → Not attempt

Intend the result? No → Not attempt

= *Actus reus*

= *Mens rea*

enforcement officer, then he sends obscene photographs of himself to the undercover officer, can he be guilty of attempted distribution of obscene materials to a minor? The answer is not cut-and-dried, but clearly the person who received the images in our hypothetical was not a minor.[29] Such is the essence of the defense of impossibility.

The courts recognize two types of impossibility. **Factual impossibility** occurs when "extraneous circumstances unknown to the actor or beyond his control prevent consummation of the intended crime."[30] A classic example of this is when a person reaches into the pocket of another to steal a wallet, but there is no wallet in the pocket.[31] **Legal impossibility** "is said to occur where the intended acts, even if completed, would not amount to a crime."[32] Legal impossibility exists when:

1. The motive, desire and expectation is to perform an act in violation of the law;
2. There is intention to perform a physical act;
3. There is a performance of the intended physical act; and
4. The consequence resulting from the intended act does not amount to a crime.[33]

**factual impossibility**
Extraneous circumstances prevent the defendant from completing the intended crime.

**legal impossibility** A defense to the crime of attempt. The action the defendant intends to perform is not a crime, even if completed.

---

[29]See, e.g., *People v. Thousand*, 631 N.W.2d 694 (Mich. 2001).
[30]*United States* v. *Berrigan*, 482 F.2d 171 (3rd Cir. 1973), p. 188.
[31]Ibid.
[32]Ibid.
[33]Ibid.

Some examples of legal impossibility include:

1. If a married man forcibly has intercourse with a woman whom he believes to be his wife's twin sister, but who in fact is his wife, he is not guilty of rape because his intent was to have intercourse with the woman he attacked, who was in fact his wife.

2. If A takes an umbrella which he believes to belong to B, but which in fact is his own, he does not have the intent to steal, his intent being to take the umbrella he grasps in his hand, which is his own umbrella.

3. If a man, mistaking a dummy in female dress for a woman, tries to ravish it, he does not have the intent to commit rape since the ravishment of an inanimate object cannot be rape.

4. If a man mistakes a stump for his enemy and shoots at it, notwithstanding his desire and expectation to shoot his enemy, his intent is to shoot the object aimed at, which is the stump.[34]

Legal impossibility is often regarded as a defense to attempt. If, for example, a person commits an act thinking it is illegal when it is not, this is the textbook case of legal impossibility. Because there is no law criminalizing the act, it is *legally* impossible for it to occur. Thus intent for it to occur must also be an impossibility. More difficult is the situation in which the intended result is a criminal act, but the actor's actions fall short. In an early case, *Wilson* v. *State*,[35] Wilson was prosecuted for and convicted of forgery because he added a "1" to the amount on a check written to him for $2.50, making it $12.50. However, he did not alter the *writing* on the check. Under existing law at the time, he altered an "immaterial" part of the check; for forgery to have occurred, he must have also altered the written part, changing it from "Two and 50/100" to "Twelve and 50/100"—or similar. As such, his conviction was overturned.

More difficult is what Dressler calls "hybrid legal impossibility."[36] This occurs when the accused makes a factual mistake about the legal status of some detail of the crime. The classic example is when a person shoots a corpse, thinking it is alive.[37] The *factual* mistake is thinking the corpse is a living, breathing person. The *legal* mistake is basically the same, because to be convicted of homicide, the key requirement is that a "human being" be killed. In cases like this, to keep things simple, courts will default to factual instead of legal impossibility and deny the defense. The reason should be clear. In our example, a person who shoots a corpse thinking it is a living person is someone who is intent on killing another person; to clear that person of any wrongdoing would undermine efforts to criminalize attempted wrongdoing.

*Factual* impossibility, on the other hand, is generally not regarded as a defense to the crime of attempt. For example, just because an abortionist (assuming abortion is illegal in the jurisdiction in question) attempts to remove the fetus from a nonpregnant woman, should we absolve that person of all guilt? Clearly there was intent to

---

[34]Ibid., n. 35.
[35]*Wilson* v. *State*, 38 So. 46 (Miss. 1905).
[36]Dressler, *Understanding Criminal Law*, p. 408.
[37]*State* v. *Taylor*, 133 S.W.2d 336 (Mo. 1939).

commit the crime.[38] Alternatively, if a would-be killer points a gun at his intended victim, pulls the trigger, and then realizes it is not loaded, should he cleared of any wrongdoing? Probably not, as he certainly had the intent—and tried—to kill.[39] What if, however, a would-be terrorist tries to bring down a skyscraper with a fire-cracker? Would it be sensible to find him guilty of an attempt crime? According to at least one state (Minnesota), the answer is no. Minnesota recognizes a defense of **inherent impossibility**, which is a form of factual impossibility. If the actor "uses means which a reasonable person would view as completely inappropriate to the objectives sought,"[40] that person can successfully assert a factual impossibility defense. But the courts in every other state take the opposite approach, which the Nevada Supreme Court summarized in this way:

> [E]ven though the actual commission of the substantive crime is impossible because of circumstances unknown to the defendant, he is guilty of an attempt if he has the specific intent to commit the substantive offense, and under the circumstances, as he reasonably sees them, he does the acts necessary to consummate what would be the attempted crime. It is only when the results intended by the actor, if they happened as envisaged by him, would fail to consummate a crime, then and only then, would his actions fail to constitute an attempt.[41]

See the accompanying Court Decision for more on the defense of factual impossibility. In it we take a look at the case of *People* v. *Dlugash*. The central issue in the case concerns whether the victim was already dead when Defendant Dlugash shot him multiple times.

**inherent impossibility**
A defense to a crime of attempt in which the means that the defendant employs to complete the crime are completely implausible and inappropriate.

## COURT DECISION

*People* v. *Dlugash*
363 N.E.2d 1155 (N.Y. 1977)

**Background:** Melvin Dlugash was convicted of murder in Kings County. He appealed and the Supreme Court, Appellate Division, reversed and dismissed the indictment. The People appealed and the Court of Appeals of New York affirmed as modified and remitted.

The criminal law is of ancient origin, but criminal liability for attempt to commit a crime is comparatively recent. At the root of the concept of attempt liability are the very aims and purposes of penal law. The ultimate issue is whether an individual's intentions and actions, though failing to achieve a manifest and malevolent criminal purpose, constitute a danger to organized society of sufficient magnitude to warrant the imposition of criminal sanctions. Difficulties in theoretical analysis and concomitant debate over very pragmatic questions of blameworthiness appear dramatically in reference to situations where the criminal attempt failed to achieve its purpose solely because the factual or legal context in which the individual acted was not as the actor supposed them to be. Phrased somewhat differently, the concern centers on whether

---

[38]See, e.g., *State* v. *Moretti*, 244 A.2d 499 (N.J. 1968).
[39]See, e.g., *State* v. *Damms*, 100 N.W.2d 592 (Wis. 1960).
[40]*State* v. *Logan*, 656 P.2d 777 (Kan. 1983), p. 779.
[41]*Darnell* v. *State*, 92 Nev. 680 (1976), pp. 681–682.

an individual should be liable for an attempt to commit a crime when, unknown to him, it was impossible to successfully complete the crime attempted. \*\*\*We hold that, under the proof presented by the People at trial, defendant Melvin Dlugash may be held for attempted murder, though the target of the attempt may have already been slain, by the hand of another, when Dlugash made his felonious attempt.

On December 22, 1973, Michael Geller, 25 years old, was found shot to death in the bedroom of his Brooklyn apartment. The body, which had literally been riddled by bullets, was found lying face up on the floor. \*\*\*The autopsy report listed the cause of death as "(m)ultiple bullet wounds of head and chest with brain injury and massive bilateral hemothorax with penetration of (the) heart." Subsequent ballistics examination established that the four bullets recovered from the victim's head were .25 caliber bullets and that the heart-piercing bullet was of .38 caliber.

\*\*\*Defendant stated that, on the night of December 21, 1973, he, Bush and Geller had been out drinking. Bush had been staying at Geller's apartment and, during the course of the evening, Geller several times demanded that Bush pay $100 towards the rent on the apartment. According to defendant, Bush rejected these demands, telling Geller that "you better shut up or you're going to get a bullet". All three returned to Geller's apartment at approximately midnight, took seats in the bedroom, and continued to drink until sometime between 3:00 and 3:30 in the morning. When Geller again pressed his demand for rent money, Bush drew his .38 caliber pistol, aimed it at Geller and fired three times. Geller fell to the floor. After the passage of a few minutes, perhaps two, perhaps as much as five, defendant walked over to the fallen Geller, drew his .25 caliber pistol, and fired approximately five shots in the victim's head and face. Defendant contended that, by the time he fired the shots, "it looked like Mike Geller was already dead."

\*\*\*Defendant was indicted by the Grand Jury of Kings County on a single count of murder in that, acting in concert with another person actually present, he intentionally caused the death of Michael Geller. \*\*\*The defense produced but a single witness, the former Chief Medical Examiner of New York City. This expert stated that, in his view, Geller might have died of the chest wounds "very rapidly" since, in addition to the bleeding, a large bullet going through a lung and the heart would have other adverse medical effects. "Those wounds can be almost immediately or rapidly fatal or they may be delayed in there, in the time it would take for death to occur. But I would say that wounds like that which are described here as having gone through the lungs and the heart would be fatal wounds and in most cases they're rapidly fatal."

\*\*\*The jury found the defendant guilty of murder. The defendant then moved to set the verdict aside. He submitted an affidavit in which he contended that he "was absolutely, unequivocally and positively certain that Michael Geller was dead before (he) shot him." \*\*\*This motion was denied.

On appeal, the Appellate Division reversed the judgment of conviction on the law and dismissed the indictment. The court ruled that "the People failed to prove beyond a reasonable doubt that Geller had been alive at the time he was shot by defendant; defendant's conviction of murder thus cannot stand." Further, the court held that the judgment could not be modified to reflect a conviction for attempted murder because "the uncontradicted evidence is that the defendant, at the time that he fired the five shots into the body of the decedent, believed him to be dead, and * * * there is not a scintilla of evidence to contradict his assertion in that regard."

Preliminarily, we state our agreement with the Appellate Division that the evidence did not establish, beyond a reasonable doubt, that Geller was alive at the time defendant fired into his body. To sustain a homicide conviction, it must be established, beyond a reasonable doubt, that the defendant caused the death of another person. The People were required to establish that the shots fired by defendant Dlugash were a sufficiently direct cause of Geller's death. While the defendant admitted firing five shots at the victim approximately two to five minutes after Bush had fired three times, all three medical expert witnesses testified that they could not, with any degree of medical certainty, state whether the victim had been alive at the time the latter shots were fired by the defendant. Thus, the People failed to prove beyond a reasonable doubt that the victim had been alive at the time he was shot by the defendant. Whatever else it may be, it is not murder to shoot a dead body. Man dies but once.

***The most intriguing attempt cases are those where the attempt to commit a crime was unsuccessful due to mistakes of fact or law on the part of the would-be criminal. A general rule developed in most American jurisdictions that legal impossibility is a good defense but factual impossibility is not. Thus, for example, it was held that defendants who shot at a stuffed deer did not attempt to take a deer out of season, even though they believed the dummy to be a live animal. The court stated that there was no criminal attempt because it was no crime to "take" a stuffed deer, and it is no crime to attempt to do that which is legal. *State v. Guffey*, 262 S.W.2d 152 (Mo.App.). These cases are illustrative of legal impossibility. A further example is Francis Wharton's classic hypothetical involving Lady Eldon and her French lace. Lady Eldon, traveling in Europe, purchased a quantity of French lace at a high price, intending to smuggle it into England without payment of the duty. When discovered in a customs search, the lace turned out to be of English origin, of little value and not subject to duty. The traditional view is that Lady Eldon is not liable for an attempt to smuggle.

On the other hand, factual impossibility was no defense. For example, a man was held liable for attempted murder when he shot into the room in which his target usually slept and, fortuitously, the target was sleeping elsewhere in the house that night. Although one bullet struck the target's customary pillow, attainment of the criminal objective was factually impossible. *State v. Moretti*, 52 N.J. 182, presents a similar instance of factual impossibility. The defendant agreed to perform an abortion, then a criminal act, upon a female undercover police investigator who was not, in fact, pregnant. The court sustained the conviction, ruling that "when the consequences sought by a defendant are forbidden by the law as criminal, it is no defense that the defendant could not succeed in reaching his goal because of circumstances unknown to him." On the same view, it was held that men who had sexual intercourse with a woman, with the belief that she was alive and did not consent to the intercourse, could be charged for attempted rape when the woman had, in fact, died from an unrelated ailment prior to the acts of intercourse. *United States v. Thomas*, 13 U.S.C.M.A. 278.

***In the belief that neither of the two branches of the traditional impossibility arguments detracts from the offender's moral culpability. . . . a person is guilty of an attempt when, with intent to commit a crime, he engages in conduct which tends to effect the commission of such crime. It is no defense that, under the attendant circumstances, the crime was factually or legally impossible of commission, "if such crime could have been committed had the attendant circumstances been as such person believed them to be." Penal Law, s 110.10. Thus, if defendant believed the victim to be alive at the time of the shooting, it is no defense to the charge of attempted murder that the victim may have been dead.

Turning to the facts of the case before us, we believe that there is sufficient evidence in the record from which the jury could conclude that the defendant believed Geller to be alive at the time defendant fired shots into Geller's head. Defendant admitted firing five shots at a most vital part of the victim's anatomy from virtually point blank range. Although defendant contended that the victim had already been grievously wounded by another, from the defendant's admitted actions, the jury could conclude that the defendant's purpose and intention was to administer the coup de grace.

***The jury convicted the defendant of murder. Necessarily, they found that defendant intended to kill a live human being. Subsumed within this finding is the conclusion that defendant acted in the belief that Geller was alive. Thus, there is no need for additional fact findings by a jury. Although it was not established beyond a reasonable doubt that Geller was, in fact, alive, such is no defense to attempted murder since a murder would have been committed "had the attendant circumstances been as (defendant) believed them to be." Penal Law, s 110.10. The jury necessarily found that defendant believed Geller to be alive when defendant shot at him.

The Appellate Division erred in not modifying the judgment to reflect a conviction for the lesser included offense of attempted murder. An attempt to commit a murder is a lesser included offense of murder and the Appellate Division has the authority, where the trial evidence is not legally sufficient to establish the offense of which the defendant was convicted, to modify the judgment to one of conviction for a lesser included offense which is legally established by the evidence. . . . Accordingly, the order of the Appellate Division should be modified and the case remitted to the Appellate Division for its review of the facts. . . . As so modified, the order of the Appellate Division should be affirmed.

## Case Analysis

1. Explain the defendant's argument as to why he should not be criminally responsible for the victim's death.

2. What is the *mens rea* requirement of attempted murder? Do you believe that the defendant had the requisite *mens rea*?

3. What type of impossibility is at issue in this case? Explain.

## Abandonment

If a would-be offender abandons his attempt to commit a crime, should he be cleared of any wrongdoing? In general, the answer is no; most courts do not recognize a defense of abandonment in the attempt context. But there are exceptions. For example, if the defendant completely and voluntary has a change of heart, the defense may succeed. Consider the facts as explained by the court in *Pyle* v. *State*:

> At 1:15 p.m. on October 7, 1981, appellant arrived at a residence occupied by Mary McCoy and Sally Sower. Ms. McCoy was his former girlfriend. After he was invited to enter, he pulled a gun on the women. He ordered Ms. McCoy to wrap and padlock chains around herself. Thereafter, he ordered Ms. McCoy to handcuff Ms. Sowers to a bannister. He then forced Ms. McCoy into his van and drove away with her. Ms. Sowers liberated herself fifteen minutes later and called the police. Meanwhile, appellant spent the next six hours driving to Defiance, Ohio and then back to Fort Wayne, Indiana. During the trip, he repeatedly told Ms. McCoy that if the police stopped the van he would empty six bullets into her head. Eventually, a police car signaled the van to stop. Consequently, appellant exclaimed "we're caught" and proceeded to pull over to the side of the road. Subsequently, he grabbed the gun, said "good bye Mary" and shot her in the chest. He then surrendered to the police.[42]

Mary did not die, but rather suffered a serious wound. The defendant was found guilty of attempted murder. He appealed, claiming that he did not intend, at the last minute, for Mary to die and only wanted to inflict a superficial wound. The court did not buy his argument and affirmed his conviction, noting that he evidenced no "rising revulsion for the harm intended."[43] Likewise, if a would-be offender abandons his attempted crime in the face of victim resistance, he will not succeed with an abandonment defense, as it is not voluntary.[44] For an abandonment claim to succeed, then, the offender must *genuinely and completely* withdraw from his or her efforts to break the law—and convince a jury of it.

## Model Penal Code

According to the Model Penal Code, attempt occurs when a person acting with the culpability (intent) required for the target offense:

a. purposely engages in conduct that would constitute the crime if the attendant circumstances were as he believes them to be; or

b. when causing a particular result is an element of the crime, does or omits to do anything with the purpose of causing or with the belief that it will cause such result without further conduct on his part; or

c. purposely does or omits to do anything that, under the circumstances as he believes them to be, is an act or omission constituting a substantial step in a course of conduct planned to culminate in his commission of the crime.[45]

---

[42]*Pyle* v. *State*, 476 N.E.2d 124 (Ind. 1985), p. 125.
[43]Ibid., p. 126.
[44]See, e.g., *People* v. *Cross*, 466 N.W.2d 368 (Mich. Ct. App. 1991).
[45]Model Penal Code Section 5.01(1).

Subsections (a) and (b) cover *completed* attempts, whereas subsection (c) covers *incomplete* attempts. Moreover, subsection (a) covers *conduct* crimes while subsection (b) covers *result* crimes. We discussed what constitute a "substantial step" earlier when we summarized the various tests for the *actus reus* of attempt. The Model Penal Code does not recognize a defense of impossibility, but it does recognize a defense of abandonment.[46]

**YOUR DECISION**

1. Joseph is a member of the notorious Crips gang while Walter is a member of the Aryan Brotherhood. These two organizations are often engaged in violent confrontations, often motivated by racial hatred. One evening, Joseph enters an area of the city within the control of the Aryan Brotherhood and is attacked by Walter. Joseph survives the encounter but is severely beaten. Joseph suffers a broken nose, broken jaw, severe facial lacerations, and internal bleeding. The prosecutor wants to charge Walter with battery and attempted murder. Walter is challenging the attempted murder charge, claiming he only wanted "to teach Joseph a lesson" about trespassing on the Brotherhood's land and never intended to kill him. Is Walter guilty of attempted murder? Why or why not?

2. Tracie Reeves and Molly Coffman, twelve-year-old middle school students, decided they wanted to kill their homeroom teacher, Janice Geiger. The girls were planning on poisoning Ms. Geiger with rat poison, stealing her car, and driving it to the Smoky Mountains. One morning, Molly Coffman brought a packet of rat poison to school and placed in on Ms. Geiger's desk next to her coffee cup. Ms. Geiger saw the girls at her desk and asked them to return to their seats. Tracie and Molly never put the poison in Ms. Geiger's coffee cup. Tracie and Molly are charged with attempted murder in a jurisdiction that uses the Model Penal Code's "substantial step test." Are they guilty of attempted murder? Would your answer be the same in a jurisdiction that utilizes the "Last Act" test?

## Summary

- An inchoate crime is one that is partial, unfinished, or begun and not completed.
- Inchoate crimes include attempt, conspiracy, and solicitation.
- Criminal attempt is an adjunct crime, meaning it cannot exist by itself.
- There is no crime of attempt that is not linked to some other substantive crime.
- There are two parts of the *mens rea* of attempt, namely to (1) intend the act and (2) intend the result.
- Attempt is a specific intent offense.
- The *mens rea* for attempt in the result crime context must "match up" with the result. For example, if there is no intent to kill, then an attempted murder conviction is unlikely.

---

[46]Model Penal Code Section 5.01(4).

- It would be easier to hold someone liable for an attempted conduct crime because there is no requirement that the defendant desire some end result apart from the criminal act itself.

- Multiple tests are used to determine the presence of *actus reus* in the attempt context.

- According to the "last act" test, the *actus reus* of attempt is satisfied once the defendant has committed the last act necessary to complete the target crime.

- According to the "physical proximity" test, the *actus reus* of attempt is satisfied once the offender is *nearly able* to commit the target crime.

- According to the "dangerous proximity" test, the *actus reus* of intent is satisfied once the individual's conduct is in "dangerous proximity to success."

- The "indispensible element" test looks not at proximity to crime completion, but rather at what, if anything, is *lacking* such that the crime could not be completed.

- The "probable desistance" test looks at the likelihood of the offender stopping once the wheels have been set in motion.

- The "unequivocality" test holds that attempt occurs when it is no longer ambiguous what the would-be offender intends.

- The impossibility defense is available if it is factually or legally impossible for the defendant to have committed the crime.

- Abandonment is sometimes available as a defense in the attempt context. For example, if the defendant completely and voluntary has a change of heart, the defense may succeed.

MODULE

# 7.2

# CONSPIRACY AND SOLICITATION

### *Learning Objectives*
- **Identify the elements and complications of conspiracy.**
- **Describe the defenses to conspiracy.**
- **Describe solicitation.**
- **Distinguish solicitation from other inchoate crimes.**

**CORE CONCEPTS**

Conspiracy, the next inchoate crime we consider, generally refers to the act of *planning but not completing* a crime. Conspiracies often involve two or more people and thus tend to resemble some of the accomplice liability situations we introduced in Chapter 6. The key difference, again, is that conspiracies are *plans* to commit one or more specific crimes. This is why conspiracies are considered inchoate crimes. The chapter then wraps up with the introduction to solicitation, another inchoate crime in which one person seeks to have another person commit a crime on his or her behalf.

# Conspiracy

**conspiracy** An inchoate offense in which an agreement is reached to commit a crime.

Conspiracy is a type of inchoate crime, but it also closely resembles complicity because one person (or multiple people) can be held criminally liable for the actions of someone else. Under common law, a **conspiracy** was defined as an agreement between two or more persons to commit a criminal act. The common law's approach was "bilateral," in reference to the minimum requirement that two or more people be involved in the conspiracy. Thus, if one person entered into an agreement with and undercover police officer to break the law, there was no conspiracy because there were not two guilty parties. Modern statutes take a "unilateral" approach, which permits the conviction of *any* person who agrees with another to commit a crime, even if only one party to the agreement breaks the law.

**overt act** A voluntary action taken by the defendant in furtherance of the crime of conspiracy.

Under common law, nothing other than the agreement was necessary. Under modern statutes, however, it is often required that the prosecutor prove that those who entered into the agreement actually took some step in furtherance of the agreement—called an **overt act**. For example, if Susan and Margie agreed on a plan to kill Mike, this would be conspiracy under common law. If they went one step further and acquired a gun, then this is the "overt act" part of modern conspiracies. There are exceptions to the overt act requirement, however. On the one hand, the Supreme Court has held, with respect to federal drug laws, that an overt act is not necessary for a conspiracy to be completed.[47] On the other hand, some states require a "substantial act," which is more significant than an "overt act."

In a chain conspiracy, such as drug distribution, every party involved in growing, moving, distributing and selling the product are part of the conspiracy. These coca farmers in Bolivia can be the beginning of the "chain."
© George Philipas/Alamy

---

[47]*United States* v. *Shabani*, 513 U.S. 10 (1994).

## Distinguishing Complicity from Conspiracy

Students are sometimes confused as to the relationship between complicity and conspiracy. Conspiracy is an inchoate (i.e., incomplete) crime. In other words, conspiracy is an *agreement* to commit a crime, typically combined with some overt act in furtherance of that agreement.

Complicity, by way of reminder, occurs when two or more offenders work together and actually commit a criminal act. A conspiracy could evolve into complicity, but it cannot work the other way around. For example, if Fred and Susan settle on a plan to kill John and then buy the gun they hope to use, they may be found guilty of conspiracy. They, however, would not be complicit (or accomplices) in any crime because John has not been killed. If, however, Fred and Susan ultimately kill John, they would both be accomplices to murder regardless of who pulled the trigger. This is the key difference between complicity and conspiracy.

*Pinkerton* **rule** A defendant can be charged both with the crime of conspiracy and the completed offense.

The rule that complicity (and other noncomplicity) cases are distinct from conspiracy cases is known as the ***Pinkerton* rule**, from the Supreme Court's decision in *Pinkerton* v. *United States*.[48] In that case, two brothers who conspired to avoid paying taxes were convicted of both conspiracy and tax law violations. They argued that they should have been convicted of one underlying offense. The Supreme Court disagreed. Justice Douglas wrote, "It has been long and consistently recognized by the Court that the commission of the substantive offense of conspiracy to commit it are separate and distinct offenses."[49] The *Pinkerton* rule is also relevant in conspiracy cases (discussed in the next chapter) because it means that each party to a conspiracy (an agreement to commit a crime) can be held liable for any reasonably foreseeable crime committed by any co-conspirator in furtherance of the agreement.

## Advantages of Conspiracy Laws

Conspiracy laws exist primarily because criminals often act in collaboration with others. Indeed, there are special dangers associated with group criminality, especially in the realm of organized crime. As it was put in one Supreme Court case, "[T]he strength, opportunities, and resources of many is obviously more dangerous and more difficult to police than the efforts of a lone wrongdoer."[50] Also, conspiracy laws are advantageous in the same way the crime of "attempt" exists; some of the time, it is helpful for authorities to tackle crime without having to wait until the harm is done. Since a big part of conspiracy is an *agreement* to offend, such laws permit earlier intervention and the possibility of disrupting a crime before it is carried through to completion.

Conspiracy laws are also advantageous from a prosecutorial standpoint. The Sixth Amendment states that the accused has the right to trial "by an impartial jury of the state and district wherein the crime shall have been committed." Conspiracies are not necessarily limited to any single locale, so this affords prosecutors the option of choosing a venue for the trial. Also, since all parties to a conspiracy are viewed has

---

[48]*Pinkerton* v. *United States*, 328 U.S. 640 (1946).
[49]Ibid., p. 643.
[50]*Krulewitch* v. *United States*, 336 U.S. 440 (1949), pp. 448–449.

having committed the same crime, their trials can be combined into one or very few, which saves resources. But this raises problems of guilt by association. Jurors may find all defendants guilty even if just one clearly is by virtue of their association with one another. In *Krulewitch* v. *United States*, Justice Jackson said this of the guilt by association problem:

> A co-defendant in a conspiracy trial occupies an uneasy seat. There generally will be evidence of wrongdoing by somebody. It is difficult for the individual to make his own case stand on its own merits in the minds of jurors who are ready to believe that birds of a feather are flocked together.[51]

**hearsay** An out-of-court statement admitted in court for the truth of the matter asserted.

Conspiracy laws also give prosecutors the advantage of using hearsay evidence, which is typically inadmissible. **Hearsay** is a statement made by someone who is not actually testifying. Instead, the statement is conveyed via someone else who *is* testifying. It is something that is "heard," then "said"—hence the name *hearsay*. Courts prefer to go to the "horse's mouth," which is why hearsay is generally inadmissible. Yet there are many exceptions to this hearsay rule. Conspiracy is one of them. Since each co-conspirator is presumably authorized by other parties to the conspiracy to act on their behalf, hearsay is admissible. But this creates a logical problem. What if hearsay is the only type of evidence available to prove the existence of a conspiracy? Should evidence that is admissible only if a conspiracy exists be used to prove that a conspiracy exists? This has been called **bootstrapping** (a term used in many contexts to refer to a circular self-sustaining process). The Supreme Court, however, resolved it somewhat in *Bourjaily* v. *United States*,[52] where it held that jurors may indeed use hearsay evidence to decide whether a conspiracy existed. So, despite some of the pitfalls in this area, prosecutors still enjoy considerable advantages by proceeding with conspiracy (rather than individual) charges in certain cases.

**bootstrapping** A circular, self-sustaining process.

Finally, conspiracy laws offer prosecutors something of a "double whammy." Offenders can be convicted of both conspiracy to commit a crime *and* the crime itself. This, again, is known as the *Pinkerton* rule.

## The *Mens Rea* of Conspiracy

Under common law, conspiracy was a specific intent crime. Today, it is regarded in basically the same fashion. First, the defendant must intend to enter into an agreement with one or more others to commit a crime. Second, the defendant must have intended to commit the target offense. Note the similarity of conspiracy *mens rea* to complicity *mens rea*.

There is some question about what *intent* means. Is it the defendant's conscious objective to commit the target crime? Or is it sufficient if the defendant simply knows it is likely to happen? At the risk of casting too wide a net, courts typically prefer to equate intent with purpose. However, knowledge may suffice. For example, in *Direct Sales Co.* v. *United States*,[53] the defendant, a drug wholesaler, sold morphine to a

---

[51]Ibid., p. 454.
[52]*Bourjaily* v. *United States*, 483 U.S. 171 (1987).
[53]*Direct Sales Co.* v. *United States*, 319 U.S. 703 (1943).

physician in quantities 300 times higher than those that would have been required for lawful purposes. The U.S. Supreme Court affirmed his conviction. In another case, defendants who sold sugar to persons they knew were manufacturing illegal whiskey had their convictions affirmed.[54] So while the defendants in these cases may not have intended for customers to break the law, they surely knew what the buyers were doing.

## Attendant Circumstances

There is some question about whether, in a conspiracy prosecution, the government must prove that the defendants intended the circumstantial elements (if any) of the targeted crime. This came up in *United States* v. *Feola*,[55] a case in which several defendants agreed to sell heroin. They then decided to sell powdered sugar to unwitting customers in an effort to boost their profits. And they also agreed that if a buyer caught on to their scam, they would take the individuals' money by force. Unfortunately for the defendants, the buyers were undercover federal law enforcement agents and during the course of the sale, two of the defendants attacked one of the agents. The defendants were convicted of assault on a federal officer and *conspiring* to do the same. The Supreme Court affirmed the first assault charges, as both defendants had the intent to commit the assaultive act. But could their conspiracy charges be affirmed? Could they have *conspired* to assault a federal officer, not knowing that the victim was indeed an officer? The Court answered this question with a surprising "yes":

> This interpretation poses no risk of unfairness to defendants. It is no snare for the unsuspecting. Although the perpetrator of a narcotics "ripoff," such as the one involved here, may be surprised to find that his intended victim is a federal officer in civilian apparel, he nonetheless knows from the very outset that his planned course of conduct is wrongful.[56]

This case was significant because the court decided that the federal conspiracy statute did not require any higher degree of proof toward the circumstantial element (the assault, not the sale) than that required for the underlying offense. That said, the case was not decided on constitutional grounds, meaning that states are still free to set the bar higher.

## The "Corrupt Motives" Doctrine

In *People* v. *Powell*,[57] a classic case, county officials bought supplies for the poor without putting a request out for bid, in violation of the law. They took this approach knowingly and did so with the intent of saving the county money. Even so, they were charged with conspiring to commit official misconduct. Their subsequent convictions were reversed because they did not have the "corrupt motives" necessary to sustain the conviction. The court noted, "The agreement must have been entered into with an evil

---

[54]*United States* v. *Falcone*, 311 U.S. 205 (1940).
[55]*United States* v. *Feola*, 420 U.S. 671 (1975).
[56]Ibid., p. 685.
[57]*People* v. *Powell*, 63 N.Y. 88 (1875).

**corrupt motives doctrine**
A requirement in some states that defendants have a corrupt motive in order to commit the crime of conspiracy.

purpose, as distinguished from a purpose simply to do the act prohibited, in ignorance of the prohibition."[58] This **corrupt motives doctrine** is recognized in several states, though not all of them. Also, to the extent the issue of corrupt motives ever comes up, it is usually in the context of *malum prohibitum* rather than *malum in se* crimes. The latter are wrong in themselves, so "evil purpose" is inferred from the act itself.

## The *Actus Reus* of Conspiracy

The *actus reus* of conspiracy consists of two parts. First, and most importantly, there must be an agreement to commit a crime. Second, more than likely it is necessary that the parties to the conspiracy commit an "overt act" in furtherance of the agreement. Once again, common law did not require this second *actus reus* element, but modern statutes frequently do.

### The Agreement

The agreement to commit a crime between two or more people can take a number of forms. It may be an express agreement. Jim could say to John, "Let's kill Bob." It may also be an unspoken agreement. John could look at Jim, nod his head in Bob's direction, and then be present when Jim kills Bob. Indeed, John may be nowhere around and still be convicted of a crime because he gave an earlier order to Jim that he "take care of Bob." In this instance, a "conspiracy may exist even if a conspirator does not agree to commit or facilitate each and every part of the substantive offense."[59] Assume, for example, that Jim decides to hire his own "hit man" to kill Bob. Even though John is arguably not aware of this, he is a party to a conspiracy because of that simple order to "take care of Bob."

Most conspiracies are relatively secret, at least beyond the parties to the agreement. This, it would seem, could make it difficult for a prosecutor to prove the presence of a conspiracy. After all, how could a prosecutor *prove* the existence of something that no one besides the parties to the agreement know? Fortunately, the courts are quite flexible in terms of the evidence that can be used to prove the existence of an agreement to commit a crime. They have to be, as the alternative would make it exceedingly difficult to prove the presence of a conspiracy. As one court observed, "[B]ecause of the clandestine nature of a conspiracy and the foreseeable difficulty of the prosecution's burden of establishing the conspiracy by direct proof, the courts have permitted broad inferences to be drawn . . . from evidence of acts, conduct, and circumstances."[60] Hearsay, circumstantial evidence, and the like are admissible. Yet the government must also ensure that defendants' due process rights are not violated in its zeal to prove the presence of conspiratorial agreements.

An example will clarify. *United States* v. *Alvarez*,[61] dealt with Manuel Juan Alvarez, a man who was convicted of joining with three other men in a conspiracy to import 110,000 pounds of marijuana into the United States by air from Columbia.

---

[58]Ibid., p. 91.
[59]*Salinas* v. *United States*, 522 U.S. 52 (1997), p. 63.
[60]*People* v. *Persinger*, 363 N.E.2d 897 (Ill. App. Ct. 1977), p. 901.
[61]*United States* v. *Alvarez*, 610 F.2d 1250 (5th Cir. 1980), conviction affd., 625 F.2d 1196 (1980) (en banc).

He was an underling in the operation and only involved in loading and off-loading the plane used to carry the drugs. He knew why the plane left the states for Columbia and he knew about the cargo it was going to pick up. Undercover agents who agreed to purchase the drugs even asked him if he would be around to help unload the plane, to which Alvarez nodded and said, "Yes." As soon as the plane was about to leave, Alvarez and two other men were arrested and charged with conspiracy to important illegal drugs into the United States. Alvarez's conviction was reversed by the Fifth Circuit, but later affirmed, noting that

> the aggregate of the evidence is sufficient to infer that Alvarez knew that criminal activity was afoot. It must also have been obvious to him that there was conspiracy to import the contraband because prior planning and concerted action would be required to load the marijuana in Colombia, fly it into this country, and unload it upon its arrival.[62]

All it took was Alvarez's knowledge of the illegal activity to support his conspiracy conviction.

Contrast *Alvarez* with *Commonwealth* v. *Cook*.[63] In that case, two brothers, Maurice and Dennis Cook, were drinking and smoking marijuana at a housing project when they met a 17-year-old woman. The two introduced themselves, engaged in small talk, and invited the woman to walk with them to a convenience store in order to buy cigarettes. While they were walking to the store through a secluded area, the woman tripped and fell, at which point Maurice jumped on top of her, covered her mouth, and took off his belt, handing it to Dennis. Maurice then raped her—and Dennis encouraged him as he was doing so. The victim lost consciousness during the attack, later awoke after the brothers were gone, and then went to a friend's house to report the incident. Both brothers were arrested. Maurice was convicted of rape. Dennis was convicted of conspiring to rape the woman and as an accomplice to rape. An appeals court affirmed his conviction as an accomplice, as it should have, but it reversed his conspiracy conviction:

> The circumstances under which the victim and the Cooks met and socialized were not indicative of a preconceived plan between the defendant and his brother to commit a sexual assault. Rather, the meeting and subsequent engagement were consistent with a chance social encounter common between young persons. The area where the group stayed prior to setting out for the store was used frequently as a gathering spot, and there was no evidence either that the Cooks attempted to conceal from others the fact that they were with the victim or that they consciously attempted to mislead her as to their identities. . . . While openness will not automatically sanitize a conspiracy, highly visible conduct has to be considered inconsistent with the shadowy environment which usually shrouds the crime. The purpose for leaving the area was on its face innocuous and was suggested by Maurice, not the defendant. While the route chosen was arguably suspicious, the evidence established that it also was selected by Maurice, not the defendant. There was evidence that the path provided a short, reasonably direct route to a gasoline station which was nearby, well-lighted, and visible from the crest of the hill. We do not think that the events up to the time the victim fell were sufficient to establish a criminal agreement or to warrant the jury in inferring the state of facts that the Commonwealth claims to have existed.[64]

---

[62]Ibid., p. 1198.
[63]*Commonwealth* v. *Cook*, 411 N.E.2d 1326 (Mass. App. Ct. 1980).
[64]Ibid., p. 1329.

This case differed from the *Alvarez* case because of the apparently spontaneous nature of the rape; there was no preconceived plan in place.

## The Overt Act

The overt act requirement for the *mens rea* of conspiracy is relatively recent in its origins. Not every jurisdiction requires proof of an overt act, but logic for such a requirement is straightforward; it offers evidence that a conspiracy has moved beyond the "talk stage" and is actively being carried out.

There is no requirement that the overt act be illegal. Indeed, it can be perfectly legal. The example we offered at the outset of this section was purchasing a gun. Assuming there is no law against doing so (or the person is barred by law from buying a gun), there is nothing criminal about such an act. There is also no requirement that all parties to a conspiracy commit an overt act. If one party to a larger conspiracy commits the overt act, no other action is necessary.

What exactly is an overt act? In jurisdictions that require an overt act, any act will suffice. No matter how trivial the action, it will meet the overt act requirement. For example, assume Steve and Mary agree to kill Sandy. If Steve calls Sandy to see if she is home, he has committed an overt act taken in furtherance of the agreement. The phone call is far more innocuous than, say, buying a gun. Nevertheless, Steve did *something* in furtherance of the agreement, which is all it takes.

As mentioned at the outset of this section, some jurisdictions require a "substantial act" or a "substantial step" in lieu of an overt act.[65] For example, Washington State's conspiracy statute reads, in part, that "[a] person is guilty of criminal conspiracy when, with intent that conduct constituting a crime be performed, he or she agrees with one or more persons to engage in or cause the performance of such conduct, and any one of them takes a substantial step in pursuance of such agreement."[66]

Just what, then, is a *substantial step*? One court defined it as conduct that is "strongly corroborative of the actor's criminal purpose."[67] Moreover, the substantial step "need not be the last proximate act prior to the consumation of the offense."[68] This definition is clearly subjective, meaning that courts decide what constitutes a substantial step on a case-by-case basis. For example, in *State* v. *Sunderland*, the defendant, who mistakenly believed that an off-duty police officer was the person who previously threatened him, pointed a shotgun in the officer's direction and threatened to "blow [his] head off." This action constituted a substantial step in furtherance of the crime.[69] On the other hand, some jurisdictions have deemed preparatory acts, such as casing a building, substantial steps.[70] Clearly there is much room for interpretation. See Figure 7.2 for a summary of conspiracy in flowchart format.

---

[65]See, e.g., Maine Rev. Stat. Ann. tit. 17-A (West 2006), Section 151.4; Wash. Rev. Code Ann. Section 9A.28.040 (West 2006).

[66]Wash. Rev. Code Ann. Section 9A.28.040 (West 2006), Section (1).

[67]*State* v. *Brooks*, 44 Ohio St. 3d 185 (1989), p. 191.

[68]Ibid.

[69]*State* v. *Sunderland* (Dec. 19, 1985), Cuyahoga App. No. 49950, unreported. For more details, see *State* v. *Brooks*, 44 Ohio St. 3d 185 (1989).

[70]See, e.g., *United States* v. *Permenter*, 969 F.2d 911 (10th Cir. 1992).

**Figure 7.2**
Conspiracy

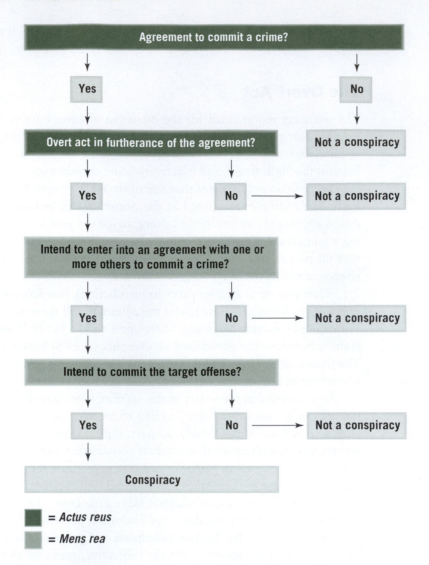

## Conspiracy Complications

No one conspiracy is the same as the next, which can make prosecuting one more than a little interesting. Conspiracies can get rather complicated because of the number of people involved, the scope of the agreement, the length of the agreement, and the purpose of the conspiracy, among other issues. In this section, we briefly touch on some of the issues (and cases involving them) that complicate the identification and prosecution of conspiracies.

### Types of Conspiracies

Two of the most difficult questions facing prosecutors are (1) who is involved in the conspiracy and (2) how many conspiracies are there? These questions are important because their answers can help prosecutors decide on the proper venue in which to try the case, whether joint trials are warranted, what offenses the parties can be liable for, and so on. On the one hand, there may be one conspiracy with multiple criminal objectives.[71] For example, three friends may agree to rob a bank each day for a week. On the other hand, there may be multiple agreements to commit a single crime. A and B might agree today to kill X two days from now. C and D may agree tomorrow to kill X the next day. There are two conspiracies, but one criminal outcome. These examples are simple, but reality can get rather tedious.

In *Kotteakos* v. *United States*,[72] 32 defendants were charged and convicted of participating in a *single* conspiracy with Simon Brown to fraudulently obtain loans. The defendants argued that they had each formed separate conspiracies with Mr. Brown. Why? Under the government's approach, each defendant could be punished for participating in 32 separate criminal acts. Under their approach, each would be punished for a single conspiracy and be spared a considerable amount of prison time. The Supreme Court sided with the defendants, concluding that although the crimes were similar, the defendants did not know one another and thus could not have conspired together to obtain the loans. Prosecutors hoped to prove that Brown's was a so-called **spoke and wheel conspiracy** (see Figure 7.3) because they viewed Brown as the hub, the spokes as each of the 32 defendants, and the rim as the connection between each spoke. The Supreme Court decided that the rim was absent because there was no connection between each defendant. Perhaps more aptly, this conspiracy should have been called a "hub and spoke" conspiracy.

Contrast *Kotteakos* with *Interstate Circuit, Inc.* v. *United States*.[73] In that case, the manager of a chain of theaters conspired with eight movie distributors to fix

**spoke and wheel conspiracy** A type of large-scale conspiracy in which one central actor (the hub) has control of all of the aspects of the conspiracy, while the other members of the conspiracy (the spokes) have control of only one aspect.

**Figure 7.3**

Example of a Spoke and Wheel Conspiracy

---

[71]*Braverman* v. *United States*, 317 U.S. 49 (1942).
[72]*Kotteakos* v. *United States*, 328 U.S. 750 (1946).
[73]*Interstate Circuit, Inc.* v. *United States*, 306 U.S. 208 (1939).

**Figure 7.4**
Example of a Chain Conspiracy

**chain conspiracy** A type
of large-scale conspiracy
in which the individuals
at one end of the
conspiracy are not aware
of the individuals at the
other end.
**wheel and chain**
**conspiracy** A type of large-
scale conspiracy that has
attributes of both the spoke
and the wheel and chain
types of conspiracies.

prices, in violation of the Sherman Antitrust Act. Each distributor was copied on the correspondence to the others, so each knew precisely what was happening. The Supreme Court upheld the convictions, concluding, "It is elementary that an unlawful conspiracy may be and often is formed without simultaneous action or *agreement* on the part of the conspirators."[74] The defendants in this case completed the wheel; the connection between each was analogous to the rim of a wheel. Each defendant was a spoke—and each of the eight spokes was connected via a rim (the awareness on the part of each what was happening).

Sometimes prosecutors are faced with a **chain conspiracy** (Figure 7.4). The hallmark of a chain conspiracy is a linear connection in time. For example, A's criminal conduct precedes B's, which precedes C's. These are typically the easiest conspiracies for prosecutors to prove. In *Blumenthal v. United States*,[75] one person sent shipments of liquor to Weiss and Goldsmith, who, in turn, agreed with three other defendants to sell liquor to various taverns at inflated prices, in violation of price cap laws. The Supreme Court affirmed the conspiracy convictions of all six defendants. It likened each one of them to links in a chain. If, for example, Weiss and Goldsmith did not participate, the chain would have been broken.

Courts have also recognized more complex **wheel and chain conspiracies**, which contain elements of both wheels and chains. *United States v. Bruno*,[76] dealt with four groups, one of which imported drugs into the country (Group 1) and sold them to middlemen (Group 2). The middlemen then distributed the drugs to two groups of retailers in New York (Group 3) and Louisiana (Group 4). Each group was regarded as a wheel yet also connected together in time via a chain (the distributors first sold to the middlemen, then the middlemen sold drugs to the retailers). The convictions were affirmed.

## The Length of the Agreement

There is always a time dimension to conspiracies, which begs the question, "How long does a conspiracy last?" Under common law, a conspiracy ended when all of its objectives were accomplished. Even today, once all the objectives are completed, the clock starts ticking on the statute of limitations, meaning that if prosecutors do not move soon enough, they will not be able to secure conspiracy convictions. This has prompted some prosecutors to get rather creative in terms of *extending* the time frame over which a conspiracy presumably runs. In *Krulewitch v. United States*,[77] a case introduced earlier on in this chapter, the government argued that the parties to a conspiracy continually sought to conceal their identities, even after the conspiracy's criminal objectives were accomplished. They then sought to introduce hearsay evidence, the out-of-court statement of one conspirator, to convict another conspirator several months after the crime. The Supreme Court decided that such evidence is inadmissible because the conspiracy terminated with the

---

[74]Ibid., p. 227, emphasis added.
[75]*Blumenthal v. United States*, 332 U.S. 539 (1947).
[76]*United States v. Bruno*, 105 F.2d 921 (2nd Cir.), revd. on other grounds, 308 U.S. 287 (1939).
[77]*Krulewitch v. United States*, 336 U.S. 440 (1949).

commission of the criminal act. There are exceptions to this rule, but they are exceedingly rare.[78] The common law rule thus remains more or less intact.

## The Purpose of the Conspiracy

Just as there can be some confusion over when a conspiracy begins and ends, or how many people or conspiracies are involved, there can be some confusion over the very purpose of a conspiracy. It is important to clear up any such confusion, as it bears directly on what punishments are available. Assume that, in one agreement, Alex and Brock decide to commit a robbery today and a burglary tomorrow. Then assume that, *as an alternative*, they agree to commit only robbery, one today and one tomorrow. Does the ordering of events in either instance bear on whether they will be convicted for conspiracy? And does it matter whether one agreement resulted in multiple and distinct criminal acts or repeated counts of the same offense? The Supreme Court offered an answer to these questions in *Braverman* v. *United States*[79]:

> [T]he precise nature and extent of the conspiracy must be determined by reference to the agreement which embraces and defines its objects. Whether the object of a single agreement is to commit one or many crimes, it is in either case that agreement which constitutes the conspiracy which the statute punishes. The one agreement cannot be taken to be several agreements and hence several conspiracies because it envisages the violation of several statutes rather than one.[80]

In other words, it is basically immaterial whether two or more people agreed to break two laws or break one law multiple times. The lynchpin is the agreement. In our examples, there was one agreement. Had Alex and Brock entered into separate agreements, then they may have been guilty of more than one conspiracy. Consider these two agreements:

**Agreement 1.** Rob a person today, burglarize a house tomorrow.

**Agreement 2.** Rob a person today, rob another person tomorrow.

Assuming Alex and Brock entered into both of these agreements *separately* and one was not an alternative to another, then each is guilty of participation in two distinct conspiracies. Needless to say, deciding whether two or more agreements were made can be difficult for prosecutors. As a result, they often place emphasis on the first agreement and treat it as the one that *implicitly* incorporated any other criminal objectives.

## Conspiracy Under the Model Penal Code

The Model Penal Code defines the crime of conspiracy in Section 5.03. First, the agreement must have been made with the "purpose of promoting or facilitating" a crime. Second, conspiracy occurs when either (a) an agreement is made to aid in the planning

---

[78]See, e.g., *State* v. *Rivenbark*, 311 Md. 147 (1987).
[79]*Braverman* v. *United States*, Ibid.
[80]Ibid., p. 53.

or commission of a crime or (b) an agreement is made that one or more of the parties will commit, solicit, or attempt the crime. Third, the Model Penal Code requires an overt act. There is also no requirement that the defendant know all the parties to the agreement. For example, if A and B conspire to commit a crime, but B has C commit the act, A can be liable for C's conduct under the Model Penal Code. The Code does limit, however, conspiracy charges to each agreement, not each criminal objective. This means that if there is one agreement that will lead to multiple crimes, the defendant can be convicted of just one conspiracy count. The Model Penal Code imposes a number of other restrictions and limitations, but they are mostly beyond the scope of this book.

See the accompanying Court Decision for more on the crime of conspiracy. In it we take a look at the case of *United States* v. *Soto* involving a drug conspiracy in New York City.

## COURT DECISION

*United States* v. *Soto*
716 F.2d 989 (2d Cir. 1983)

**Background:** Evelyn Soto was convicted of drug conspiracy in the Southern District of New York. Soto appealed and the Second Circuit Court of Appeals reversed her conviction.

\*\*\*I

The basic facts are not in dispute. At the trial the government presented the testimony of four Drug Enforcement Administration (DEA) special agents. In essence their testimony established that Soto resided in a Bronx apartment located at 2526 Bronx Park East, 5-B, which was used, in part, as a narcotics "cutting mill."

The government's chief witness was DEA Agent Fred Marrero. Agent Marrero testified that in his role as an undercover agent he met the person in charge of the cutting mill—a man known as "Cheo"—on June 29, 1982. Marrero was invited up to the Bronx apartment by Cheo where a group of six persons, including Soto, gathered in the bedroom. During Marrero's half-hour visit Soto remained in the bedroom for approximately ten to fifteen minutes. The meeting was interrupted at one point by the building superintendent who came to the apartment to speak to Cheo. As Cheo got up to leave, he commented that he (Cheo) did not allow anyone into the bedroom. At the time several handguns and drug paraphernalia were in plain view. There was no discussion or mention of either narcotics or weapons by anyone during Marrero's visit.

Following a tip from a confidential informant, DEA Agents Thomas Ward and Marrero made several arrests and seized a cache of guns and drugs at the apartment in the early morning hours of July 2, 1982. At the time of the agents' entry into the apartment, Agent Ward found Soto and her young child asleep in the bedroom. A search of that room uncovered drugs, drug paraphernalia and a weapon. A search of the rest of the apartment reaped a large quantity of drugs, drug paraphernalia, cash and more weapons. Although the apartment contained a substantial amount of contraband, it is equally clear that apartment 5-B was more than just a cutting mill—it was also a domicile for several individuals, including Soto, being furnished with couches, sleeping cots and a television set.

Two stipulations were also made part of the record. The first provided that Soto arrived in New York from Puerto Rico on or about June 8, 1982; that she resided at 2526 Bronx Park East, apartment 5-B, from June 8, through July 2; and that apartment 5-B was leased in the name of Pablo Rodriguez but, in reality, was paid for and controlled by Cheo and his wife, Nancy Medina. The second stipulation specified that ledger books found during the search of the apartment were examined by government experts for fingerprints and handwriting; that Soto's fingerprints were not identified, but those of Cheo and his wife were; and that Soto's handwriting was not identified as appearing anywhere on the ledger sheets. In this connection, Marrero testified that the ledger books contained a list of Cheo's employees and their salaries, but did not contain Soto's name.

Against this background, we address Soto's principal contention that the evidence was insufficient as a matter of law to convict her beyond a reasonable doubt.

## II

\*\*\*The most significant circumstance relied on by the government in support of the jury's finding of guilt is the fact that Soto lived in apartment 5-B for three weeks prior to her arrest. Her sustained and regular presence in that apartment, the government contends, is circumstantial evidence from which the jury could infer defendant's membership in the narcotics and firearms conspiracies.

We are constrained to disagree. While it would not be accurate to characterize Soto's presence at the apartment as merely transitory, we nevertheless consider the total circumstances of how Soto came to reside there to be highly significant. For here we have an individual newly arrived from Puerto Rico, accompanied by a child of tender years, clearly in need of shelter. To this end, as soon as she arrived in New York defendant took up residence at the 2526 Bronx Park East apartment. Although the living arrangements there may not have been ideal, there is no indication that defendant had any other alternative.

As defendant correctly observes, and as the government necessarily concedes, Soto's mere presence at the apartment, even coupled with the knowledge that a crime was being committed there, is not sufficient to establish her guilt. Evidence tending to show knowing participation in the conspiracy is also needed. Absent some showing of purposeful behavior tending to connect defendant with the acquisition, concealment, importation, use or sale of drugs or firearms, participation in the conspiracies cannot be proven by presence alone.

The government stresses that on the morning of the July 2 arrests Soto was found sleeping in the room where the drugs were cut. But this fact demonstrates nothing more than that defendant, as a mere guest or invitee, did not enjoy exclusive dominion or control over the bedroom or, for that matter, over the apartment in general. The government further submits that based on the statement by Cheo to Marrero to the effect that Cheo did not want the building superintendent in the bedroom, the inference can be drawn that Cheo trusted Soto and that, therefore, Soto must have joined the conspiracy. In our view, however, even conceding the reasonableness of such an inference, Cheo's statement at most shows that he trusted Soto, a feeling any person would quite naturally have before inviting another to share living quarters. To conclude from this that Soto had joined the conspiracy would require an inference no jury could reasonably make. The fact that Soto was considered trustworthy, given the circumstances here, is a far cry from her participation in the conspiracies.

Finally, we find misplaced the government's reliance on those cases where members of a vessel's crew were held to be participants in a drug conspiracy. There, the existence of a joint enterprise is inferable in view of the close relationship among those on board, coupled with the foreknowledge of the vessel's illicit mission given the large quantities of contraband frequently involved.

Here, by contrast, there is no comparable showing or even the slightest suggestion that Soto had knowledge of the ongoing drug mill activities before moving into the Bronx apartment. Moreover, considering the absence of her name from the list maintained by Cheo of persons he employed in the furtherance of the drug operation, the inescapable inference to be drawn from the evidence is that she never joined the conspiracy

In sum, while the evidence need not have excluded every possible hypothesis of innocence, nevertheless, "[w]here the crime charged is conspiracy, a conviction cannot be sustained unless the Government establishes beyond a reasonable doubt that the defendant had the specific intent to violate the substantive statute[s]." *United States v. Cangiano,* 491 F.2d 906, 909 (2d Cir. 1974). The government here produced no evidence whatever linking defendant to the conspiracies. Instead, we believe that on the basis of association alone, the jurors "let their imaginations run rampant."

### III

For the foregoing reasons, the judgment of the district court is reversed and remanded with direction to enter a judgment of acquittal.

## Case Analysis

1. List all of the facts that support the government's argument that Defendant Soto engaged in a drug conspiracy.
2. Is Soto's knowledge of the illegal activity in her apartment sufficient to find her guilty of any crime? Why or why not?
3. Did Soto have a legal duty to report the illegal activity? Why or why not?

# Conspiracy Defenses

There are four defenses to conspiracy. As you will recall from earlier in the chapter, two of them—abandonment and impossibility—are also defenses to attempt. The others—withdrawal and Wharton's Rule—are somewhat unique to conspiracy. We briefly look at each in the following subsections.

## Abandonment

Since the essence of conspiracy is an agreement, once the agreement is made, the proverbial horse has already left the barn. In other words, once a crime has been committed, it cannot be "undone."[81] For this reason, there is usually no abandonment defense to a conspiracy charge. This is true regardless of whether an overt act is a requirement for a conspiracy conviction. That said, abandonment *may* work as something of a defense to charges for subsequent crimes arising from a conspiratorial agreement; if one party to a conspiracy withdraws and then finds him- or herself charged with conspiracy for crimes committed after such withdrawal, then the defense may succeed.

The Model Penal Code calls this defense "renunciation."[82] For it to apply, two conditions must be met. First, the defendant must have "thwarted the success of the conspiracy." Second, the abandonment must have been "complete and voluntary." For example, if Larry is a party to a murder conspiracy with Frank and tells police that he can no longer "see it through," he may succeed with the defense if the police are able to prevent Frank (such as by arresting him) from committing the crime. If the agreement was for any other crime than murder, and if Larry's decision to contact police still did not stop the intended crime, then the clock on the statute of limitations would begin running for Larry, but not for Frank.

## Withdrawal

Withdrawal is similar to abandonment, but it is not the same. First, abandonment requires that the defendant seek to defeat the conspiracy. There is no such requirement with withdrawal. Also, the withdrawal defense is more widely available than abandonment.[83] Withdrawal is similar to abandonment, however, as it starts the clock on the statute of limitations; the statute of limitations starts at the point of withdrawal, not at some subsequent point in time if another crime is committed that the defendant did not agree to or participate in. The Model Penal Code also contains a withdrawal defense, which requires that the defendant either advise his co-conspirators that he is no longer involved in it or inform police about the conspiracy.[84]

## Impossibility

Though impossibility rarely comes up in a conspiracy context, it is a possible defense in certain contexts. Assume Jack and Jill just bought a new mattress to replace their tired, worn-out one. They notice on the side of the mattress a tag that says "Under penalty of law, this tag may not be removed." They decide to tear it off, thinking they have committed a crime. They fail to notice, however, that the tag also says, "except by the consumer." They have not committed a crime, even though they think they have. Such is the essence of impossibility—particularly *legal* impossibility.

It is also helpful to think of *factual* impossibility. Assume once again that Frank and Larry decide to commit murder. One of them buys a gun. They then agree to break into John's house in the middle of the night and shoot him. Unbeknownst to Frank and Larry, John died of a heart attack earlier that night while he was sleeping.

---

[81] *United States* v. *Rogers*, 102 F.3d 641 (1st Cir. 1996), p. 644.
[82] Model Penal Code Section 5.03(6).
[83] See, e.g., *Hyde* v. *United States*, 225 U.S. 347 (1912).
[84] Model Penal Code Section 5.03(7)(c).

Frank pulls the trigger and shoots John. It is impossible for him to murder John because John is already dead. This does not mean, however, that Frank and Larry will go free. If caught, they will likely face conspiracy charges for *attempted* murder.

## Wharton's Rule

Recall that one of the key purposes of conspiracy laws was to give authorities some extra tools to address the dangers of group criminality. Certain crimes, however, cannot be completed without two people. Adultery is one such (common law) crime; it cannot be completed without two people. A drug sale works in the same way; it requires a buyer and seller. Does it make sense to use conspiracy laws to target such crimes? In general, no, and **Wharton's Rule** offers some protection. The rule provides that a conspiracy cannot occur when two persons are required for the commission of a crime.

The intentions of Wharton's Rule are noble, but it also frustrates law enforcement. Why? Strictly applied, if two parties entered into an agreement for one to sell and the other to buy drugs, prosecutors could do nothing until the sale was attempted. Instead of being able to *prevent* the crime, the authorities would have to wait until it was nearly completed. For this reason, courts often limit Wharton's Rule to cases in which the intended crime has been completed or attempted.[85] So, in our example, both parties could be charged with conspiracy to sell drugs—even in the face of Wharton's Rule.

Wharton's Rule is also limited in other ways. First, if more than the minimum number of offenders is involved (e.g., a third person in our drug sale example), the rule will not apply. Likewise, if there are two parties to an agreement, but they are not the two parties necessary to complete the crime, then the rule does not apply. For example, if two men conspire for one of them sell drugs to a third person, then the rule does not apply because the buyer was not a party to the agreement. Finally, the Supreme Court has limited Wharton's Rule such that it is widely regarded as no more than a presumption in the absence of contrary legislative intent.[86] If, for example, a law permits a conspiracy charge in the context of a two-party crime, then the rule will be ignored.

## Solicitation

**Solicitation** occurs when a person entices, advises, incites, orders, or otherwise encourages someone else to commit a crime. There is no requirement that the crime actually be completed. Solicitation is typically limited to felonies or misdemeanors that involve either obstruction of justice or breach of peace. Under common law, solicitation was a misdemeanor. Under the Model Penal Code and many state statutes, it is a crime of the same grade and degree as the most serious crime solicited. Some states, however, still treat solicitation as less serious than the target offense.[87]

**Wharton's Rule** A conspiracy cannot occur when two persons are required for the commission of a crime.

**solicitation** An inchoate offense that occurs when a person entices, advises, incites, orders, or otherwise encourages someone else to commit a crime.

---

[85]See, e.g., *State* v. *Miller*, 929 P.2d 372 (Wash. 1997), p. 378.
[86]*Iannelli* v. *United States*, 420 U.S. 770 (1975).
[87]See, e.g., *Commonwealth* v. *Barsell*, 678 N.E.2d 143 (Mass. 1997).

## Elements of Solicitation

Under common law, solicitation was a specific intent crime, meaning that the solicitor must have intended for the "solicited" to commit a particular crime. Much the same holds true today. For example, if Leroy says to Bubba, "Wouldn't it be cool if you blew up Cletus's trailer?," he has merely *joked* about having Bubba commit a crime. He has not satisfied the *mens rea* element of solicitation. However, if Leroy offers Bubba $100 (although he is not obligated to offer money for solicitation to occur) and says, "I'll let you keep this if you blow up Cletus's trailer," then arguably he intends for a crime to be committed.

The *actus reus* of solicitation occurs when, as indicated above, another person entices, advises, incites, orders, or otherwise encourages another to commit a crime. The solicitor may *hire* someone to commit a crime, which is what we typically think of with respect to solicitation, but there is no requirement that money change hands. Also, there is no requirement that any steps be taken toward completion of the target crime. That is, there is no "overt act" requirement, as with conspiracy. A simple agreement between two people that one will commit the crime for the other suffices. This is true even if the solicited party refuses to commit the crime or *says* he or she will do so but does not really mean it.

One key limitation is that if the solicitor's message never reaches the solicited person (or if it cannot be known whether it reaches the solicited person), the *actus reus* requirement has not been satisfied. In *State* v. *Cotton*,[88] a prison inmate sent letters to his wife on the outside, soliciting various criminal activities. There was no evidence the letters actually reached his wife, so the inmate could not be convicted of solicitation. See Figure 7.5 for a summary of the crime of solicitation.

**Figure 7.5**
Solicitation

- = *Actus reus*
- = *Mens rea*

---

[88]*State* v. *Cotton*, 790 P.2d 1050 (N.M. 1990).

## Distinguishing Solicitation from Other Crimes

"[T]he essence of criminal solicitation is an attempt [by the solicitor] to induce another to commit a criminal offense."[89] Moreover, it is a requirement that the solicitor intend to hide behind the solicited, or to "work behind the scenes."[90] Anything more than that may elevate a solicitation to something more significant, such as conspiracy or attempt. With these points in mind, then, let's first make it clear that solicitation does not occur if the solicitor intends to commit the crime.

Solicitation also does not occur if one person uses another as an "innocent instrumentality" in the commission of a crime. For example, if Leroy fraudulently tells Bubba that Cletus has his lawnmower and asks Bubba to go get it for him [Leroy], then Leroy is an accomplice, not a solicitor. Why? Assuming Bubba believes Leroy and has no intent to steal the lawnmower, only to go get it for Leroy, then solicitation has not occurred. This issue was covered in the complicity section of the last chapter (Module 6–2).

Solicitation is also distinguished from conspiracy. In general, solicitation is an attempted conspiracy. It consists of an *offer*. Usually conspiracy consists of an *agreement*—as well as an overt act. But a conspiracy need not be preceded by solicitation; conspiracy can occur at any time and without the requirement that one party solicit the other to commit a crime.

Finally, distinguish solicitation from the crime of attempt. Attempt is very similar to solicitation, but the former usually requires a "slight act" following the agreement[91] or that the solicitation be "proximate" to the intended crime—that is, in close temporal proximity to it.[92] For example, if Denise pays Jennifer to kill Patrick next week, she has solicited murder, but if she pays Jennifer to kill Patrick immediately, she may be guilty of attempted murder, too. A number of courts treat attempt and solicitation as fundamentally distinct, however, holding that "no matter what acts the solicitor commits, he cannot be guilty of attempt because it is not his purpose to commit the offense personally."[93] How attempt and solicitation are related to one another thus depends on the jurisdiction in question.

See the accompanying Court Decision for more on the crime of solicitation. In it we take a look at the case of *United States* v. *White*, where the defendant is charged with soliciting a crime via his Internet Web site. The First Amendment right of freedom of speech in relation to the potential crime of solicitation is also a key factor in the case.

**COURT DECISION**

*United States* v. *White*
638 F.Supp.2d 935 (N.D. Ill. 2009)

**Background:** William White was charged with solicitation to commit a crime of violence. White moved to dismiss the indictment and the Northern District of Illinois granted his motion on First Amendment grounds.

[89]*People* v. *Herman*, 97 Cal. App. 4th 1369 (2002), p. 1381.
[90]See, e.g., *People* v. *Kauten*, 755 N.E.2d 1016 (Ill. App. Ct. 2001).
[91]See, e.g., *People* v. *Decker*, 157 P.3d 1017 (Cal. 2007), p. 1022.
[92]See, e.g., *Mettler* v. *State*, 697 N.E.2d 502 (Ind. Ct. App. 1998).
[93]American Law Institute, Comment to Section 5.02.

**Decision and Order**

LYNN ADELMAN, District Judge.

The government charged defendant William White with violating 18 U.S.C. § 373 by soliciting another person to harm the foreperson of the federal jury that convicted white supremacist leader Matthew Hale. Defendant now moves to dismiss the indictment. . . . I conclude that I must dismiss the indictment.

### ***I. Background

In 2003, a jury in the Northern District of Illinois convicted Hale of soliciting the murder of District Judge Joan Lefkow, who had presided over a civil case involving Hale's organization. Hale was sentenced to 480 months in prison.

On October 21, 2008, the government indicted defendant, alleging that on his website, Overthrow.com, he solicited or otherwise endeavored to persuade another person to harm "Juror A," the Hale jury foreperson. Specifically, the government alleged that on or about September 11, 2008, defendant displayed on the front page of his website a post entitled, "The Juror Who Convicted Matt Hale." The post read:

> Gay anti-racist [Juror A] was a juror who played a key role in convicting Matt Hale. Born [date], [he/she] lives at [address] with [his/her] gay black lover and [his/her] cat [name]. [His/Her] phone number is [phone number], cell phone [phone number], and [his/her] office is [phone number].

The post did not expressly advocate that Juror A be harmed.

The indictment further alleged that on September 12, 2008, defendant displayed on the front page of his website a post entitled: "[Juror A] Update——Since They Blocked the first photo" and stating:

> Gay anti-racist [Juror A] was a juror who played a key role in convicting Matt Hale. Born [date], [he/she] lives at [address] with [his/her] gay black lover and [his/her] cat [name]. [His/Her] phone number is [phone number], cell phone [phone number], and [his/her] office is [phone number]. Note that [University A] blocked much of [Juror A's] information after we linked to [his/her] photograph.

This post also did not expressly advocate that Juror A be harmed.

As "circumstances strongly corroborative of [defendant's] intent" that another person harm Juror A, the indictment alleged that when he posted the above statements, defendant was aware that white supremacists, Overthrow.com's target audience, sometimes committed acts of violence against non-whites, Jews, homosexuals and others perceived as acting contrary to the interests of the white race. The indictment also alleged that before he posted the above statements, defendant displayed on Overthrow.com other posts, some of which were still available, purporting to contain the home addresses of and/or other identifying information about individuals who had been criticized on the website, and that in certain of these posts, defendant expressed a desire that the individuals be harmed.

***The indictment further alleged that on February 13, 2007, defendant posted material regarding Elie Wiesel, an internationally known Holocaust survivor and author, who had been attacked on February 1, 2007 by a man named Eric Hunt. The material was entitled "Where Elie Wiesel Lives—In Case Anyone was Looking For Him," and it listed three addresses. The indictment also alleged that on February 21, 2007, defendant posted the following statement:

> Elie Wiesel should be afraid to walk out his front door but for the rightful vengeance of white working people he and his holocaust lies have exploited. . . .
>
> For decades, the Jews and the liars have used physical force, violent attacks on peaceful demonstrators and peaceful meetings, and the violent physical force of unjust and tyrannical laws to silence those who question the holocaust lie. If white people are going to undo this system, we have to be ready to adapt and use the tactics of our exploiters . . .
>
> Heil Hitler

The indictment further alleged that on or about September 25, 2008, defendant displayed a post stating: "Last year, a fan of this website kidnapped Wiesel and tried to force him to confess his books on the 'Holocaust' were knowing lies."

### ***II. Applicable Legal Standards

***The First Amendment provides that "Congress shall make no law . . . abridging the freedom of speech." In a democratic society, it is axiomatic that the Amendment's protections are not limited to the genteel, the enlightened or the tasteful. Sixty years ago, the Supreme Court explained that:

> [A] function of free speech under our system of government is to invite dispute. It may indeed best serve its high purpose when it induces a condition of unrest, creates dissatisfaction with conditions as they are, or even stirs people to anger. Speech is often provocative and challenging. It may strike at prejudices and preconceptions and have profound unsettling effects as it presses for acceptance of an idea. That is why freedom of speech, though not absolute, is nevertheless protected against censorship or punishment, unless shown likely to produce a clear and present danger of a serious substantive evil that rises far above public inconvenience, annoyance, or unrest. There is no room under our Constitution for a more restrictive view.

*Terminiello v. City of Chicago,* 337 U.S. 1, 4-5 (1949). Thus, the government may not ban speech that even "'a vast majority of its citizens believes to be false and fraught with evil consequence.'" *Virginia v. Black,* 538 U.S. 343, 358 (2003).

The Court recognizes that the Amendment's protections are not absolute and that legislative bodies may proscribe certain categories of expression. As is relevant here, such categories include advocacy of the use of force or of violation of the law "where such advocacy is directed to inciting or producing imminent lawless action and is likely to incite or produce such action," *Brandenburg v. Ohio,* 395 U.S. 444, 447 (1969), "true threats," i.e. "those statements where the speaker means to communicate a serious expression of an intent to commit an act of unlawful violence to a particular individual or group of individuals," *Black,* 538 U.S. at 359, and offers to engage in illegal transactions.

### \*\*\*III. Analysis

For the following reasons, I conclude that defendant's speech, as alleged in the indictment, is protected by the First Amendment and does not state a violation of § 373.

**A. Posts Regarding Juror A:** Defendant's posts regarding Juror A do not expressly solicit or endeavor to persuade another person to harm Juror A. Rather, they disclose personal information about Juror A and comment on his/her sexual orientation and attitude toward race. Although the posts may be reasonably read as criticizing Juror A's vote to convict Hale, nowhere in them does defendant expressly advocate that Juror A be harmed.

Scrutiny and criticism of people involved in the investigation and prosecution of crimes is protected by the First Amendment. Such scrutiny may involve disclosure of information about the people involved.

**B. Alleged Corroborating Circumstances:** In order to state an offense under § 373, the indictment must allege that defendant intentionally solicited or endeavored to persuade another person to harm Juror A, under circumstances strongly corroborative of defendant's intent that the person commit a violent crime against Juror A. As stated, defendant's posts about Juror A do not expressly solicit or endeavor to persuade another person to harm him/her. Moreover, as discussed, defendant's posts about Juror A, in themselves, are protected by the First Amendment. Thus, the corroborating circumstances alleged must, consistent with the First Amendment, transform defendant's lawful statements about Juror A into a criminal solicitation. The corroborating circumstances alleged in the indictment fail to do so.

\*\*\*In the present case, defendant's posts about Juror A are disturbing because of the possibility that others might respond to them, but the cases hold that the government may not, consistent with the First Amendment, criminalize general calls to action.

\*\*\*This Court does not intend to minimize the real fear of harm and intimidation that law enforcement-related, corrections officer-related, and court-related employees, and their families, may experience. [J]udges and court employees are common targets of threats and harassment. However, we live in a democratic society founded on fundamental constitutional principles. In this society, we do not quash fear by increasing government power, proscribing those constitutional principles, and silencing those speakers of whom the majority disapproves. Rather, as Justice Harlan eloquently explained, the First Amendment demands that we confront those speakers with superior ideas:

> The constitutional right of free expression is powerful medicine in a society as diverse and populous as ours. It is designed and intended to remove governmental restraints from the arena of public discussion, putting the decision as to what views shall be voiced largely into the hands of each of us, in the hope that use of such freedom will ultimately produce a more capable citizenry and more perfect polity and in the belief that no other approach would comport with the premise of individual dignity and choice upon which our political system rests. To many, the immediate consequence of this freedom may often appear to be only verbal tumult, discord, and even offensive utterance. These are, however, within established limits, in truth necessary side effects of the broader enduring values which

the process of open debate permits us to achieve. That the air may at times seem filled with verbal cacophony is, in this sense not a sign of weakness but of strength. We cannot lose sight of the fact that, in what otherwise might seem a trifling and annoying instance of individual distasteful abuse of a privilege, these fundamental societal values are truly implicated. *Cohen*, 403 U.S. at 24-25.

### ***IV. Conclusion

For the reasons set forth above, the allegations in the indictment are insufficient to state a violation of § 373. Defendant's posts about Juror A do not solicit violence; the alleged corroborating circumstances set forth in the indictment are insufficient to transform the posts regarding Juror A into a solicitation of violence and also fail to provide the strong corroboration necessary for a lawful prosecution under § 373 and the First Amendment. Finally, all of the relevant recent case law supports the conclusion that the indictment does not charge a punishable offense. The indictment must be dismissed.

**THEREFORE, IT IS ORDERED** that defendant's motion to dismiss is **GRANTED.**

## Case Analysis

1. Is there a limit to the First Amendment right to freedom of speech? If so, what are those limitations?

2. Did White commit the crime of solicitation? Why or why not?

3. Does the fact that the Internet was used as the method of communication in this case alter the legal issues presented? Why or why not?

## Solicitation under the Model Penal Code

In general, the Model Penal Code definition of solicitation requires that (a) a person "commands, encourages or requests" another person to engage in an illegal act with (b) the purpose to promote or facilitate it.[94] The Code treats solicitation as seriously as the target offense, and it does not limit solicitation to felonies. Even an attempted solicitation is considered solicitation under the Model Penal Code. However, the Model Penal Code does offer a defense of "renunciation." A person is not guilty of solicitation if he (a) completely and voluntarily renounces his criminal intent and (b) either persuades the other party not to offend or blocks the crime's commission.[95]

**YOUR DECISION**

1. The Bottoccellis, an Italian Mafia "family" in Chicago, are involved in a number of criminal enterprises. As part of tradition, it is generally understood that all relatives have an obligation to help the "family" whenever possible. Mario is the 18-year-old nephew of the Mafia boss. He has never discussed any illegal activity directly with his uncle or any other member of the family. One evening, however, a family member is arrested for dealing cocaine. In response, Mario bribes the arresting officer to

[94]Model Penal Code Section 5.02(1).
[95]Model Penal Code Section 5.02(3).

release his relative and dispose of the evidence against him. The prosecutor believes Mario acted in agreement with other family members and wants to charge Mario both with bribery and conspiracy to commit bribery. Is Mario guilty of conspiracy? Why or why not?

2. George, a local delivery truck driver, is distraught to learn that his wife of 20 years is having an affair with her personal trainer, Fabio. George decides to drown his sorrows in beer at the local tavern with his friends. During the course of the evening, George states in a drunken rage, "I would pay a million dollars to anyone who kills Fabio and teaches him a lesson once and for all." An off-duty police officer is also in the bar and overhears the conversation. George is arrested and charged with solicitation to commit murder. Is he guilty of solicitation? Why or why not?

# Summary

- Under common law, a conspiracy was defined as an agreement between two or more persons to commit a criminal act.

- Modern statutes take a "unilateral" approach, which permits the conviction of *any* person who agrees with another to commit a crime.

- Under common law, nothing other than the agreement was necessary.

- Under modern statutes, however, it is often required that the prosecutor prove that those who entered into the agreement actually took some step in furtherance of the agreement—called an *overt act*.

- Conspiracy is generally regarded as a specific intent crime.

- There are two parts to the *mens rea* of conspiracy. First, the defendant must intend to enter into an agreement with one or more others to commit a crime. Second, the defendant must have intend to commit the target offense.

- What is intent? The courts typically equate intent with purpose.

- The *actus reus* of conspiracy consists of two parts. First, and most importantly, there must be an agreement to commit a crime. Second, more than likely it is necessary that the parties to the conspiracy commit an "overt act" in furtherance of the agreement.

- The agreement to commit a crime between two or more people can take a number of forms. It may be an express agreement, but it need not be.

- Not every jurisdiction requires proof of an overt act, but logic for such a requirement is straightforward; it offers evidence that a conspiracy has moved beyond the "talk stage" and is actively being carried out.

- It is often difficult for prosecutors to determine is who involved in the conspiracy and how many conspiracies there are. Making such determinations is important because they can help prosecutors decide on the proper venue in which to try the case, whether joint trials are warranted, what offenses the parties can be liable for, and so on.

- It is sometimes difficult to determine when a conspiracy starts and ends.

- Just as there can be some confusion over when a conspiracy begins and ends, or how many people or conspiracies are involved, there can be some confusion over the very purpose of a conspiracy. It is important to clear up any such confusion, as it bears directly on what punishments are available.

- An abandonment defense *may* work as something of a defense to charges for subsequent crimes arising from a conspiratorial agreement; if one party to a conspiracy withdraws and then finds him- or herself charged with conspiracy for crimes committed after such withdrawal, then the defense may succeed.

- The withdrawal defense is more widely available than abandonment.

- Though impossibility rarely comes up in a conspiracy context, it is a possible defense in certain contexts.

- Wharton's Rule provides that a conspiracy cannot occur when two persons are required for the commission of a crime.

- Solicitation occurs when a person entices, advises, incites, orders, or otherwise encourages someone else to commit a crime.

- There is no requirement that the crime actually be completed.

- Solicitation is typically limited to felonies or misdemeanors that involve either obstruction of justice or breach of peace.

- Solicitation does not occur if the solicitor intends to commit the crime.

- Solicitation does not occur if one person uses another as an "innocent instrumentality" in the commission of a crime.

- Solicitation is distinguished from conspiracy. In general, solicitation is an attempted conspiracy.

- Attempt is very similar to solicitation, but the former usually requires a "slight act" (or something similar) following the agreement.

# Chapter Review

## INTRODUCTION TO INCHOATE CRIMES: ATTEMPT

### Learning Objectives

- Explain the concept of inchoate crimes.
- Explain the relationship of attempt to the substantive offense.
- Summarize what constitutes attempt.
- Summarize the defenses to charges of attempt.

### Review Questions

1. Compare and contrast attempt and the substantive offense.
2. Explain both components of the *mens rea* of attempt.
3. In your opinion, which is the best test for the *actus reus* of attempt? Defend your answer.

### Key Terms

inchoate crime
attempt
factual impossibility
legal impossibility
inherent impossibility

## CONSPIRACY AND SOLICITATION

### Learning Objectives

- Identify the elements and complications of conspiracy.
- Describe the defenses to conspiracy.
- Describe solicitation.
- Distinguish solicitation from other inchoate crimes.

### Review Questions

1. Compare and contrast conspiracy at common law and under modern-day statutes.
2. Briefly summarize the elements of conspiracy.
3. Explain the issues that pose complications for conspiracy prosecutions.
4. List and define the defenses to a conspiracy charge.
5. What is solicitation and how does it differ from conspiracy?

### Key Terms

conspiracy
overt act
*Pinkerton* rule

hearsay
bootstrapping
corrupt motives doctrine
spoke and wheel conspiracy
chain conspiracy
wheel and chain conspiracy
Wharton's Rule
solicitation

## Chapter Synthesis Questions

1. Identify and describe an inchoate crime *other than* attempt, conspiracy, or solicitation.

2. Explain the logic for targeting inchoate crimes with the criminal law.

3. Which, in your opinion, is the most serious: attempt, conspiracy, or solicitation? Defend your answer.

4. Explain Wharton's Rule.

# 8

# HOMICIDE

*Learning Objectives*

**MODULE 8.1  INTRODUCTION TO HOMICIDE**

- **Distinguish between criminal homicide and noncriminal homicide.**
- **Define *human being* for purposes of homicide law.**

**MODULE 8.2  THE ELEMENTS OF HOMICIDE**

- **Distinguish between first-degree murder and second-degree murder.**
- **Explain when the death penalty is an acceptable form of punishment for homicide.**
- **Summarize the elements of voluntary and involuntary manslaughter.**
- **Explain the Model Penal Code approach to homicide.**

**MODULE 8.3  ISSUES AND COMPLICATIONS FOR HOMICIDE**

- **Explain the felony murder rule.**
- **Identify two types of "mercy killings."**
- **Explain corporation murder.**

**MODULE**

# 8.1

# INTRODUCTION TO HOMICIDE

### Learning Objectives

- **Distinguish between criminal homicide and noncriminal homicide.**
- **Define *human being* for purposes of homicide law.**

**CORE CONCEPTS**

This chapter marks the beginning of our focus on specific crime types. We have occasionally referenced homicide (and other offenses) in previous chapters in order to make a point, but here is where we consider them in much more detail. We finally have a chance to define homicide, carefully examine the various levels of homicide, and discuss some controversies surrounding homicide, including mercy killings, assisted suicide, and felony murder. Homicide is arguably the most serious crime, which is why we first focus on it. There is no "descending order" of seriousness, however, in the crimes covered over the next several chapters.

Once this chapter wraps up, we shift our focus to so-called assaultive offenses, including rape, sexual assault, robbery, assault, battery, kidnapping, false imprisonment, and various "domestic" offenses (e.g., child abuse). Both this and Chapter 9 make up Section 4 of the book, Crimes Against Persons. Chapter 10 then takes us into a new section on crimes against property. In it, we examine property damage, property invasion (e.g., burglary), and certain types of computer crime. Chapter 11 looks at theft and analogous offenses. Section 6 of the book contains chapters on public order crimes, morality crimes, terrorism, offenses against the state, and similar crimes.

## Homicide Defined

**homicide** The killing of a human being by another human being.

The common law defined **homicide** as the killing of a human being by another human being. All homicides were punishable by death under early common law, but that gradually changed. Homicide was eventually broken by judicial decisions and statutes into two categories: murder and manslaughter. Murder, in turn, was further broken down into subcategories, particularly first-degree and second-degree murder. In general, first-degree murderers could be executed; second-degree murderers could not.

While the definition of *criminal homicide* seems straightforward on its face, there is some confusion and disagreement about what a *human being* is. Also, the term *homicide* carries a negative connotation, as it should in most cases. Yet we do not wish to give the impression that it is never permissible for one human being to kill another. It is therefore important that we distinguish criminal homicide from *non*criminal homicide. *Criminal* homicide is a subtype of homicide.

# What Is a "Human Being"?

If homicide is the killing of another human being, then naturally we have to define the term *human being*. In most homicide situations, it is a nonissue, as it is clear that the victim was a living, breathing, human being. For example, when an otherwise healthy teenager is killed, there is little doubt that he or she was a "human being" within the meaning of applicable homicide statutes. It gets messy, however, near the beginning and end of life.

## The Beginning of Life

When does life begin? Abortion proponents and opponents have been debating the answer to this question for generations. It is unlikely we can achieve any resolution here. Fortunately, for purposes of homicide, there is some resolution. The common law defined the beginning of life as occurring when a fetus was born alive.[1] This definition has been carried forward into several modern court decisions. For example, in *Keeler* v. *Superior Court*,[2] the defendant purposely kicked his pregnant former wife in the stomach. The fetus died. The court held that the fetus was not a human being.

Contrast this decision with *Commonwealth* v. *Cass*,[3] a case in which a motorist crashed into another vehicle being driven by a woman who was nearly nine months pregnant. The fetus died as a result of injuries the woman sustained and was delivered by Caesarean section. An autopsy revealed that the fetus was viable at the time of the crash. The Supreme Judicial Court of Massachusetts rejected the common law definition of human being, noting,

> We think that the better rule is that infliction of prenatal injuries resulting in the death of a viable fetus, before or after it is born, is homicide. If a person were to commit violence against a pregnant woman and destroy the fetus within her, we would not want the death of the fetus to go unpunished. We believe that our criminal law should extend its protection to viable fetuses.[4]

Most jurisdictions continue to retain the common law definition of the beginning of life, but Massachusetts and several other states have begun to treat viable fetuses as human beings. In such states, it is possible for people to be convicted of the crime of **feticide**, causing the death of a fetus. Indeed, some states have gone even further than Massachusetts. California defines a human being as a fetus that has progressed beyond the embryonic stage of seven to eight weeks.[5] According to the California Supreme Court,

**feticide** Causing the death of an unborn fetus.

> The state's interest in protecting the "potentiality of human life" includes protection of the unborn child, whether an embryo or a nonviable or viable fetus, and it protects, too, the woman's interest in her unborn child and her right to decide whether it shall be carried in utero. The interest of a criminal assailant in terminating a woman's pregnancy does not outweigh the woman's right to continue the pregnancy.[6]

---

[1]See, e.g., *Meadows* v. *State*, 722 S.W.2d 584 (Ark. 1987), p. 585.
[2]*Keeler* v. *Superior Court*, 2 Cal. 3d 619 (1970).
[3]*Commonwealth* v. *Cass*, 467 N.E.2d 1324 (Mass. 1984).
[4]Ibid., p. 1329.
[5]*People* v. *Davis*, 872 P.2d 591 (Cal. 1994).
[6]Ibid., p. 599.

According to the criminal law, life ends with brain death. A person can be kept alive on a ventilator, but until brain death occurs, he or she is still considered "alive."

Reflekta/Shutterstock.com

## The End of Life

Just as it can be difficult to decide when life begins, it can be difficult to decide when life ends. At what point is a person no longer considered a "human being"? The common law focused on whether the heart continued to beat; if someone's heart stopped beating, that person was no longer considered a human being. Today, because of medical technologies, it is possible to preserve life even if a person's heart has stopped beating on its own. Thus, most courts now define *death* in terms of "brain death." That is, a person is no longer a human being if that person is "brain dead." Some states go further and define the cessation of life in terms of "whole brain death." Some states offer a broader definition of *death* that includes cessation of circulation, respiration, and/or brain function. According to the state of Kansas, for example,

> An individual who has sustained either (1) irreversible cessation of circulatory and respiratory functions, or (2) irreversible cessation of all functions of the entire brain, including the brain stem, is dead.[7]

It may seem overly tedious to define *death* in such exact terms, but it is critically important from a homicide prosecution standpoint. And it is also important from the standpoint that all would-be killings do not necessarily result in death. Oftentimes the victim sustains serious injuries that require long-term hospitalization, but not death.

**year-and-a-day rule**
A common law rule stating that a person could not be prosecuted for homicide unless the victim died within a year and a day of the act that was responsible for the fatal injury.

The common law's **year-and-a-day rule** provided that a person could not be prosecuted for homicide unless the victim died within a year and a day of the act that was responsible for the fatal injury. The rule can be traced to medieval times when the practice of medicine was far from an exact science. Doctors were not always able to ascertain cause of death after a victim languished in a bedridden state for an extended period of time. Modern medicine, however, now affords the experts with a greater understanding of death's causes, even when death comes months or years after an injury was inflicted. For this reason, the common law year-and-a-day rule has been largely abandoned. One court called it "an outdated relic of the common law."[8] Today, most states have abandoned the rule and can prosecute killers for deaths that occur years after the crime was committed.

---

[7]Kan. Stat. Ann. Section 77-205 (2008).
[8]*Rogers v. Tennessee*, 532 U.S. 451 (2001), p. 462.

# Distinguishing Criminal from Noncriminal Homicide

*Homicide* is a legally neutral term. For it to be criminal, it must be "unjustified and unexcused." This implies that certain homicides are legally permissible, which is indeed true. Law enforcement officials can escape punishment for homicides carried out in the course of their legal duties. Likewise, ordinary citizens who kill out of self-defense (or defense of another) can escape conviction because their actions were justified.

These justification defenses, however, do not necessarily serve as bars to prosecution. Unless the case is particularly clear-cut, especially if an ordinary citizen is involved, it is possible that a homicide prosecution could result. The defendant would then need to succeed with a justification defense in order to escape conviction. The same is true of certain excuse defenses, examples being duress and insanity (see Chapter 6). Even police officers who justifiably kill do not escape scrutiny. Every police shooting is investigated internally and/or by a prosecutor's office. The "presumption of innocence," introduced early on in Chapter 1, is often anything but—especially in the case of serious crimes like homicide.

The moral of the story is that even the most justified killings are not treated in the way Hollywood would have us believe. Perhaps you are a fan of the FX series *Justified*. Deputy U.S. Marshal Raylan Givens seems to kill at least one person on every episode and, as far as viewers can tell, not one of the killings is investigated. Were a real law enforcement officer to kill so many people, that officer would be placed on indefinite leave and likely be fired.

## YOUR DECISION

1. Joey McGrady was driving under the influence of alcohol when he lost control and collided with Melissa Jacobs's car. Melissa was 35 weeks pregnant at the time of the accident. After the accident, Melissa gave birth to a baby boy, Seth, who lived only 11 hours before dying from injuries he sustained in the car crash. The prosecutor charged Joey with vehicular homicide for Seth's death. Joey argues that Seth was not "alive" at the time of the accident so he cannot be charged with homicide. Can Joey be charged with vehicular homicide? Why or why not?

2. Jill Parks was a healthy, vibrant 22-year-old college student embarking on her senior year. One evening after drinking at a local bar with her friends, Jill was crossing the street when an oncoming car suddenly hit her. Jill was not killed, but rather entered into a comatose state. At the hospital, the doctors informed Jill's parents that she would likely never recover and remain in a vegetative state for the rest of her life. Knowing Jill was an organ donor, her parents decided to allow the doctors to remove her organs and give them to other patients in need. The doctors subsequently removed Jill's organs. A later autopsy revealed that although Jill suffered a severe brain injury, she was in fact *not* brain dead at the time of the organ removal. The prosecutor is considering charging the doctors with some form of criminal homicide for Jill's death. What type of homicide, if any, would be appropriate under these circumstances? Could the parents also be charged? Why or why not?

# Summary

- *Homicide* is the killing of a human being by another human being.
- *Homicide* often carries a negative connotation, but it need not.
- A healthy, living person is a *human being*.
- There is some disagreement over the meaning of *human being* at the beginning/end of life.
- Most jurisdictions retain the common law definition of the beginning of life, namely that life begins when a fetus is born alive. There are exceptions to this definition.
- Most courts now define *death* as "brain death." A person is no longer considered alive if he or she is brain dead.
- *Homicide* is a legally neutral term.
- Successful excuse and justification defenses ensure that a person who commits homicide is not criminally liable for it.

---

**MODULE**

# 8.2    THE ELEMENTS OF HOMICIDE

*Learning Objectives*

- **Distinguish between first-degree murder and second-degree murder.**
- **Explain when the death penalty is an acceptable form of punishment for homicide.**
- **Summarize the elements of voluntary and involuntary manslaughter.**
- **Explain the Model Penal Code approach to homicide.**

---

## CORE CONCEPTS

**murder** The unlawful killing of another person with malice aforethought.

**manslaughter** The unlawful killing of another human being without malice aforethought.

*Criminal* homicides, the focus of the rest of this chapter, fall into two general categories: murder and manslaughter. The common law defined **murder** as "the killing of a human being by another human being with malice aforethought."[9] **Manslaughter** was the same as murder, but without the malice aforethought requirement. These definitions have been more or less retained over time, but now they are broken down further into different subtypes. Statutes often contain gradations, or levels of murder (first degree, second degree, etc.). Manslaughter, too, is typically broken down into subtypes.

As we go through the elements of homicide, bear in mind that most of our attention will focus on the *mens rea* of homicide rather than the *actus reus*. For homicide,

---

[9]*United States v. Wharton*, 433 F.2d 451 (D.C. Cir. 1970), p. 454.

the *actus reus* is rather simple—there must be a death. In other words, the death, rather than the killing, is the *actus reus*. What sets different types of homicide apart from one another is primarily the offender's mental state.

# Murder

**malice aforethought**
Killing another person without justification, excuse, or mitigating circumstances.

Without **malice aforethought**, a homicide is not murder. What, then, is *malice aforethought*? In general, if one person kills another person without justification, excuse, or any mitigating circumstances, that person is said to have killed with malice aforethought. There is no requirement that *aforethought* involve deliberate planning well in advance of a murder. Likewise, *malice* carries a particularly negative connotation, implying that it is someone's specific intent to kill another, but this is not a requirement. One person could decide to kill another on the spur of the moment and still display malice aforethought. *Malice aforethought* is thus a loosely defined term of art that can be manifested in a number of different ways.

Not all states grade murders by degree, but for ease of interpretation, we will do so here. There are usually two types of murder, first and second degree. The former is eligible for the death penalty under certain circumstances; the latter is not.

## First-Degree Murder

**first-degree murder** The deliberate, willful, and premeditated killing of another person.

Subject to some exceptions, **first-degree murder** is a murder that is willful, premeditated, and deliberated. The defendant *intends* for the killing to occur, *thinks* about his or her decision in advance of the killing, and *deliberates* it, perhaps thinking about the costs and benefits associated with killing another person. First-degree murder is set apart from other types of killings by the requirement that there must be *more than just intention to kill*. It is a "cold-blooded" killing, one that is arguably more "evil" than a spontaneous killing.

There is considerable variability across jurisdictions concerning the extent to which "willful," "premeditated," and "deliberate" are essential elements of first-degree murder. Some equate "deliberate" with "willful."[10] Others distinguish "deliberate" from "willful" by focusing on whether the defendant *weighed* the costs and benefits associated with a decision to kill.[11] Still others lump all three elements together, equating them with the specific intent to kill. Evidence of this latter view holds the following:

> There need be no appreciable space of time between the intention to kill and the act of killing. They may be as instantaneous as successive thoughts of mind. It is only necessary that the act of killing be preceded by a concurrence of will, deliberation, and premeditation on the part of the slayer, and, if such is the case, the killing is murder in the first degree.[12]

[10]See, e.g., *Commonwealth* v. *Carroll*, 194 A.2d 911 (Pa. 1963), p. 917.
[11]See, e.g., *People* v. *Morrin*, 187 N.W.2d 434 (Mich. Ct. App. 1971), p. 449.
[12]*Macias* v. *State*, 36 Ariz. 140 (1929), pp. 149–150.

At the risk of simplification, we can distinguish between the three terms in this way:

**Willful:** Intent to kill.

**Deliberate:** Acting with a cool mind and reflection.

**Premeditated:** A design to kill formed in the mind by the time of the killing.

Of these three terms, there is considerable disagreement over the precise meaning premeditation. While everyone can agree that premeditation is the same as thinking of something in advance, not everyone can agree on the *amount* of premeditation that is necessary—particularly the time it takes. According to one view, "[a]ny interval of time between the forming of the intent to kill and the execution of that intent, which is sufficient in duration for the accused to be fully conscious of what he intended" is sufficient.[13] According to another view, for a killing to become first-degree murder, the state must prove that "some appreciable time passed during which the consideration, planning, preparation, or determination . . . prior to the commission of the act took place."[14] Still other courts feel it is best to leave the decision to a jury:

> The law fixes upon no length of time as necessary to form the intention to kill, but leaves the existence of a fully formed intent as a fact to be determined by the jury, from all the facts and circumstances in the evidence.[15]

### Other Types of First-Degree Murder.

A number of states also define as first-degree murder certain killings that do not involve willful, premeditated, and/or deliberate action. For example, Minnesota law provides that a person is guilty of murder in the first degree if that person "causes the death of a minor while committing child abuse, when the perpetrator has engaged in a past pattern of child abuse upon a child and the death occurs under circumstances manifesting an extreme indifference to human life."[16] A first-degree murder conviction is also possible for one who "causes the death of a human being while committing, conspiring to commit, or attempting to commit a felony crime to further terrorism and the death occurs under circumstances manifesting an extreme indifference to human life."[17] A number of other actions constitute first-degree murder, too, and Minnesota is by no means alone in this regard.

### The Death Penalty.

Only certain first-degree murderers are eligible for the death penalty. Some states do not practice capital punishment and, as such, incarcerate murderers. And in those states that *do* practice capital punishment, just because someone is convicted of first-degree murder does not mean that person will be sentenced to death. The decision as to whether a first-degree murderer will be sentenced to death is usually made by a jury in a post-trial hearing. This is known as **bifurcation**. The jury will be asked to consider whether various **aggravating factors** were in place, which would call for execution. Aggravating factors are those factors that add

**bifurcation** Separating a trial into two parts. In first-degree murder cases, the defendant's guilt or innocence is decided first by the jury. Then, the penalty of life imprisonment or death is decided separately by the jury.

**aggravating circumstances** Circumstances that would lend toward a harsher penalty during sentencing.

---

[13]*State v. Guthrie*, 461 S.E.2d 163 (W. Va. 1995), pp. 182–183.
[14]*State v. Moore*, 481 N.W.2d 355 (Minn. 1992), p. 361.
[15]*Commonwealth v. Drum*, WL 7210 (1868), p. 6.
[16]Minn. Stat. Section 609.185(1).
[17]Ibid.

**mitigating circumstances**

Circumstances that would lend toward a lighter or reduced criminal penalty during sentencing.

to the seriousness or enormity of the offense. The jury will also consider whether **mitigating circumstances** existed. Mitigating circumstances serve to extenuate or reduce the degree of moral culpability.

The list of aggravating and mitigating circumstances that can make a first-degree murder eligible for the death penalty (or eligible for incarceration instead of death) varies by state. For example, here are some (though not all) of the aggravating factors that must be considered under Arizona law:

- The defendant has been convicted of another offense in the United States for which under Arizona law a sentence of life imprisonment or death was imposable.
- The defendant has been or was previously convicted of a serious offense, whether preparatory or completed. Convictions for serious offenses committed on the same occasion as the homicide, or not committed on the same occasion but consolidated for trial with the homicide, shall be treated as a serious offense under this paragraph.
- In the commission of the offense the defendant knowingly created a grave risk of death to another person or persons in addition to the person murdered during the commission of the offense.
- The defendant procured the commission of the offense by payment, or promise of payment, of anything of pecuniary value.
- The defendant committed the offense in an especially heinous, cruel or depraved manner.
- The defendant has been convicted of one or more other homicides . . . that were committed during the commission of the offense.
- The defendant was an adult at the time the offense was committed or was tried as an adult and the murdered person was under fifteen years of age, was an unborn child in the womb at any stage of its development or was seventy years of age or older.[18]

And here are some of the mitigating factors:

- The defendant's capacity to appreciate the wrongfulness of his conduct or to conform his conduct to the requirements of law was significantly impaired, but not so impaired as to constitute a defense to prosecution.
- The defendant was under unusual and substantial duress, although not such as to constitute a defense to prosecution.
- The defendant could not reasonably have foreseen that his conduct in the course of the commission of the offense for which the defendant was convicted would cause, or would create a grave risk of causing, death to another person.
- The defendant's age.[19]

To sentence a first-degree murderer to death, it is usually required that jurors (a) find at least one aggravating factor and (b) no mitigating circumstances.

See the accompanying Court Decision for more on aggravating and mitigating factors in a first-degree murder trial. In it we examine the case of *Nibert* v. *Florida*, where the Supreme Court of Florida balanced the competing factors to determine if the death penalty is the appropriate sentence for Billy Ray Nibert.

---

[18]Ariz. Rev. Stat. Section 13-703(F).
[19]Ariz. Rev. Stat. Section 13-703(G).

*Nibert* v. *Florida*
574 So.2d 1059 (Fla. 1990)

**Background:** Billy Ray Nibert was convicted of capital murder in the Circuit Court, Hillsborough County and he appealed. The Supreme Court of Florida affirmed the conviction, vacated the death sentence and remanded for resentencing. The Circuit Court again sentenced Nibert to death and he appealed. The Supreme Court of Florida vacated the death sentence and remanded for imposition of a life sentence.

\*\*\*Eugene Snavely ("Snavely"), 57, was a frequently intoxicated alcoholic and one of Nibert's drinking buddies. Snavely lived across the street from his brother, James, in Hillsborough County, Florida. James testified that on November 16, 1984, he looked through his window and saw an individual approach Snavely and enter Snavely's home with him. Forty-five minutes later, Snavely appeared at James's door, holding a knife and bleeding profusely. Medical testimony showed that Snavely had been stabbed seventeen times. Three of the stab wounds were serious enough to be lethal, and some of the wounds were defensive in nature. Snavely may have been conscious throughout the stabbing, but he would have lost consciousness within minutes. [Nibert was convicted of first-degree murder for stabbing Snavely. The issue on appeal is simply determining the appropriate sentence for the crime.]

\*\*\*Nibert's estranged wife testified that Nibert had a serious problem with alcohol, including binges that lasted for days. Those problems destroyed their marriage. "When he is sober he is the nicest person that could ever be," she said. "It's just that drinking does things to him."

Nibert's sisters testified that he was raised by an alcoholic mother and a succession of stepfathers, and that his mother forced him to start drinking alcohol at the age of eleven or twelve. His mother frequently brought home men from bars and had sex in the living room in front of the children. She asked Nibert to steal money from those men, but he refused. She beat the children with a belt or a switch nearly every day. Both sisters later required psychiatric treatment because of their childhood problems with their mother.

Dr. Sidney Merin, a clinical psychologist and neuropsychologist, said . . . that Nibert told him that on the morning of the murder, Nibert sold blood to a blood bank and bought whiskey, which he drank. Then he drank more at a tavern that afternoon, and drank beer with Snavely at Snavely's house. . . . Dr. Merin also said Nibert's mother and father were alcoholics, and that Nibert had been mentally and physically abused as a child. Drinking was encouraged from the age of twelve.

Dr. Merin concluded that Nibert committed the murder under the influence of extreme mental or emotional disturbance, and that his capacity to control his behavior was substantially impaired, although he could appreciate the criminality of his conduct. Some test results were consistent with a person of a below-average IQ. Evidence also showed that Nibert felt "a great deal" of remorse and has a "good potential for rehabilitation." A structured environment, such as a prison, is helpful for rehabilitation, Dr. Merin said, and the improvement in Nibert's test results indicates that positive changes already have taken place. There was no evidence that Nibert had a prior record of violent criminal behavior.

The state presented no evidence to challenge any of the mitigating evidence.

The jury voted seven to five to recommend the death sentence. The trial court imposed the death sentence upon finding one aggravating circumstance: that the murder was committed in an especially heinous, atrocious, or cruel manner. The trial court found no statutory mitigating circumstances, expressly rejecting the claims that Nibert lacked the capacity to conform his conduct to the requirements of the law, and that Nibert was under the influence of extreme emotional or mental disturbance. As to nonstatutory mitigation, the trial court found "possible" mitigation in that Nibert "had an abused childhood; however, at the time of the murder the Defendant was twenty-seven (27) years old and had not lived with his mother since he was eighteen (18)."

Initially, we find that the trial court did not err in concluding that the murder was heinous, atrocious, or cruel. The Court reached the same conclusion in Nibert's first appeal on the same aggravating evidence, reasoning that "[t]he victim was stabbed seventeen times. There was testimony that some of his wounds were defensive wounds and that the victim remained conscious throughout the stabbing." *Nibert,* 508 So.2d at 4.

However, we agree with Nibert's claim that the trial court should have found additional mitigating circumstances, and, in light of all the mitigating evidence, the sentence of death was disproportional when compared with other capital cases where this Court has vacated the death sentence and imposed life imprisonment.

A mitigating circumstance must be "reasonably established by the greater weight of the evidence." *Campbell* v. *State,* 571 So.2d 415 (Fla.1990). Where uncontroverted evidence of a mitigating circumstance has been presented, a reasonable quantum of competent proof is required before the circumstance can be said to have been established. Thus, when a reasonable quantum of competent, uncontroverted evidence of a mitigating circumstance is presented, the trial court must find that the mitigating circumstance has been proved. A trial court may reject a defendant's claim that a mitigating circumstance has been proved, however, provided that the record contains "competent substantial evidence to support the trial court's rejection of these mitigating circumstances." *Kight* v. *State,* 512 So.2d 922, 933 (Fla.1987).

Nibert presented a large quantum of uncontroverted mitigating evidence. First, Nibert produced uncontroverted evidence that he had been physically and psychologically abused in his youth for many years. The trial court found this to be "possible" mitigation, but dismissed the mitigation by pointing out that "at the time of the murder the Defendant was twenty-seven (27) years old and had not lived with his mother since he was eighteen (18)." We find that analysis inapposite. The fact that a defendant had suffered through more than a decade of psychological and physical abuse during the defendant's formative childhood and adolescent years is in no way diminished by the fact that the abuse finally came to an end. To accept that analysis would mean that a defendant's history as a victim of child abuse would never be accepted as a mitigating circumstance, despite well-settled law to the contrary. Nibert reasonably proved this nonstatutory mitigating circumstance, and there is no competent, substantial evidence to support the trial court's refusal to consider it.

Second, evidence showed that Nibert has felt "a great deal" of remorse and has a "good potential for rehabilitation," especially in the kind of structured prison environment where his mental condition has improved markedly since the crime occurred. We have held the potential for rehabilitation to be a valid mitigating circumstance. The trial court erred by not finding and weighing this uncontroverted mitigating circumstance.

Finally, Dr. Merin, an expert in the field of brain dysfunction, testified without equivocation that in his opinion, Nibert committed the murder under the influence of extreme mental or emotional disturbance, and that his capacity to control his behavior was substantially impaired. Dr. Merin supported those conclusions with a battery of psychological examinations conducted over a two-and-one-half-year period; with interviews of Nibert and his family; and with Dr. Merin's examination of the record evidence in this case. Moreover, there was proof that Nibert has suffered from chronic and extreme alcohol abuse since his preteen years; that he was a nice person when sober but a completely different person when drunk; that he had been drinking heavily on the day of the murder; and that, consistent with the physical evidence at the scene, he was drinking when he attacked the victim. We have held that such evidence is relevant and supportive of the mitigating circumstances of extreme mental or emotional disturbance and substantial impairment of a defendant's capacity to control his behavior.

In this instance, there was no competent, substantial evidence in the record to refute the mitigating evidence. Rather, the record shows that Nibert was a child-abused, chronic alcoholic who lacked substantial control over his behavior when he drank, and that he had been drinking heavily on the day of Snavely's murder.

We conclude that the trial court failed to properly weigh a substantial number of statutory and nonstatutory mitigating circumstances. There is no need to have the trial court reweigh the aggravating and mitigating circumstances because on this record we find that the death penalty was disproportional punishment when compared to other cases decided by this Court. . . . This case involves substantial mitigation, and we have held that substantial mitigation may make the death penalty inappropriate even when the aggravating circumstance of heinous, atrocious, or cruel has been proved.

There is no need to address other issues Nibert raises on appeal. We vacate the reimposition of the death sentence and remand for imposition of a sentence of life imprisonment.

It is so ordered.

## Case Analysis

1. List all of the aggravating and mitigating factors found in relation to Billy Ray Nibert.
2. Should voluntary alcohol and/or drug use prior to a crime count as a mitigating factor when determining the appropriate sentence? Why or why not?
3. Should a judge be able to overrule the sentencing determination of the jury? Why or why not?

## Second-Degree Murder

States that grade murders by degree generally treat any murder that is not "willful, premeditated, and deliberate" as second-degree murder. In other words, second-degree murder is the default category. For a first-degree murder conviction to be secured, the prosecutor must prove the conditions for second-degree murder *plus* the added requirements discussed in the previous section.

In those states that grade murder by degrees, two types of killings constitute murder in the second degree. One occurs when the offender intends to cause grievous bodily injury and the result is death. Another occurs when the killer acts with a "depraved heart," which then leads to the death of another person.

**Intent to Inflict Grievous Bodily Injury.**     If a person intends to inflict grievous bodily injury (sometimes called *great bodily harm*, *great bodily injury*, *serious bodily harm*, or *serious bodily injury*) to another and death results, it is second-degree murder. This begs the question, "What is 'grievous bodily injury'?" One court defined it as "such injury as is grave and not trivial, and gives rise to apprehension of danger to life, health, or limb."[20] Tennessee's statutory definition is as follows: "substantial risk of death, protracted unconsciousness, extreme physical pain, protracted or obvious disfigurement, protracted loss or substantial impairment of a function of a bodily member, organ, or mental faculty."[21] California's is more simplistic: "significant or substantial physical injury."[22] Wisconsin defines *great bodily injury* as

> bodily injury which creates a substantial risk of death, or which causes serious permanent disfigurement, or which causes a permanent or protracted loss or impairment of the function of any bodily member or organ or other serious bodily injury.[23]

None of these definitions is particularly helpful, as they fail to tell us exactly what kinds of actions can be said to amount to result in grievous or serious bodily injury. We must turn to some additional court decisions for clarification. For example, in *State* v. *Perry*,[24] a prison inmate beat and kicked another inmate and then put his belt around the other inmate's neck and began choking him. A trial court concluded that his actions resulted in serious bodily injury. In another case, the defendant kidnapped a woman, transported her across state lines, bound her, raped her, slashed her neck, and left her for dead.[25] Not surprisingly, his actions resulted in serious bodily injury. At the other end of the spectrum, were a person to slap another who then died of a heart attack, it is unlikely a court would conclude that serious bodily injury was inflicted.

It must be emphasized that this type of second-degree murder does *not require the intent to kill*, only the intent to inflict harm. If the victim then dies, a second-degree murder conviction is likely. If, on the other hand, the defendant sets out to kill the victim, then it is likely that it is first-, not second-degree, murder.

---

[20]*State* v. *Bogenreif*, 465 N.W.2d 777 (S.D. 1991), p. 780.
[21]Tenn. Code. Ann. Section 39-11-106(a)(34)(A)-(E) (2008).
[22]Cal. Penal Code Section 12022.7(f).
[23]Wis. Stat. Ann. Section 939.22(14) (West 2005).
[24]*State* v. *Perry*, 426 P.2d 415 (Ariz. Ct. App. 1967), p. 418.
[25]*United States* v. *Rodriguez*, 581 F.3d 775 (8th Cir. 2009).

**Depraved Heart Killings.**     *Depraved heart killings* are also considered second-degree murders—again, in those states that grade murder by degrees. Simply, if a person acts with a "depraved heart,"[26] "an abandoned heart," or "an abandoned and malignant heart,"[27] and death results, it is second-degree murder. Depraved heart killings are also likened to killings based on "extreme recklessness" or "extreme indifference" to human life. Regardless of the terminology used, the key is that the accused does not *intend* to kill, but that death results because of, as one court put it, "wanton and willful disregard of the likelihood that the natural tendency of [the] defendant's behavior is to cause death or great bodily harm."[28]

Let's consider a couple examples to get a sense of the meaning of *depraved heart*. In *State v. Robinson*,[29] the defendant, Robinson, hit the victim, Crowley, over the head with a golf club, killing him. Robinson was convicted of depraved heart murder and appealed, but the Kansas Supreme Court affirmed his conviction, noting that the following:

> The evidence was sufficient in this case for the jury to find that Robinson recklessly killed a person while manifesting an extreme indifference to the value of one specific human life—Crowley's life. The evidence indicated that Robinson swung a golf club at Crowley with great force, intending to hit Crowley.[30]

In Maryland, a *depraved heart murder* has been defined as a killing resulting from "the deliberate perpetration of a knowingly dangerous act with reckless and wanton unconcern and indifference as to whether anyone is harmed or not."[31] So, when Jacqueline Robinson shot her lover, Henry Garvey, in the leg, which caused the bullet to travel upward into his abdomen, where it lodged and eventually killed him, she arguably acted with a depraved heart.[32]

Throughout history, a number of depraved heart cases have turned on the issue of whether the defendant's indifference to human life be directed solely at the victim or at society at large. For example, in a classic case, *Darry v. People*,[33] the defendant beat his wife, who died as a result of the wounds she suffered. The New York Supreme Court decided that his actions did not amount to "recklessness and disregard of human life generally," which was required by statute at the time.[34] Likewise, in *Mitchell v. State*,[35] another classic case, the defendant struck another man with a stick, killing him. The Supreme Court of Alabama concluded that the universal malice required for a murder conviction was lacking. In other words, the defendant did not act with indifference to *all* life.

More recent decisions have abandoned any requirement that the defendant act with a depraved heart *generally*. Statutes have been amended, too, meaning that a person can now manifest extreme indifference to human life, even though such

[26]See, e.g., *Windham v. State*, 602 So. 2d 798 (Miss. 1992), p. 800.
[27]See, e.g., Cal. Penal Code Section 188.
[28]*People v. Goecke*, 579 N.W.2d 868 (Mich. 1998), p. 879.
[29]*State v. Robinson*, 934 P.2d 38 (Kan. 1997).
[30]Ibid., pp. 49–50.
[31]*Robinson v. State*, 307 Md. 738 (1986), p. 744.
[32]Ibid.
[33]*Darry v. People*, 10 N.Y. 120 (1854).
[34]Ibid., p. 156.
[35]*Mitchell v. State*, 60 Ala. 26 (1877).

indifference is directed toward a single person.[36] Even Sir William Blackstone's classic commentaries suggested that a depraved heart could be directed at one person:

> Also, even if upon a sudden provocation one beats another in a cruel and unusual manner, so that he dies, though he did not intend his death, yet he is guilty of murder by express malice. . . . As when a park-keeper tied a boy, that was stealing wood, to a horse's tail, and dragged him along the park; when a master corrected his servant with an iron bar, and a schoolmaster stamped on his scholar's belly; so that each of the sufferers died; these were justly held to be murders, because the correction being excessive, and such as could not proceed but from a bad heart, it was equivalent to a deliberate act of slaughter. Neither shall he be guilty of a less crime, who kills another in consequence of such a willful act, as shows him to be an enemy to all mankind in general; as going deliberately with a horse used to strike, or discharging a gun, among a multitude of people. So if a man resolves to kill the next man he meets, and does kill him, it is murder, although he knew him not; for this is universal malice.[37]

Today, courts mostly focus on the issues of a depraved heart or extreme recklessness *without regard to the target of the behavior*. So, when Sabine Davidson's poorly trained Rottweiler dogs mauled and killed 11-year-old Christopher Wilson, she acted with a depraved heart simply because of her actions leading up to the incident:

> [S]he selected powerful dogs with a potential for aggressive behavior and that she owned a number of these dogs in which she fostered aggressive behavior by failing to properly train the dogs. She ignored the advice from experts on how to properly train her dogs and their warnings of the dire results which could occur from improper training. She was told to socialize her dogs and chose not to do so. She ignores the evidence of the dogs getting out on numerous occasions and her failure to properly secure the gate. She ignored the aggressive behavior her dogs displayed toward her neighbors and their children . . . she created a profound risk and ignored foreseeable consequences that her dogs could attack or injure someone.[38]

Davidson's second-degree murder conviction was affirmed.

Or consider the case Brian Fuller, a repeat offender who was legally drunk, who led police on a high-speed chase for 17 miles before crashing into a truck, killing two of its passengers.[39] Fuller was convicted of two counts of second-degree murder. An appellate court affirmed the convictions, noting:

> Defendant here operated his automobile with a high degree of alcohol in his blood and after numerous prior driving convictions, including reckless driving, speeding and driving while his license was revoked due to his habitual offender status. During the 16.7-mile chase, defendant ran both a stop sign and a red stop light, passing stopped traffic at speeds of 90–95 m.p.h. Both passengers in the truck defendant struck died as a result of the collision. We conclude this conduct manifests a mind utterly without regard for human life and social duty, supporting a finding of malice sufficient for a conviction of second-degree murder.[40]

---

[36]See, e.g., *State* v. *Lowe*, 68 N.W. 1094 (Minn. 1896); *Hogan* v. *State*, 36 Wis. 226 (1874).
[37]4 Bl. Comm. 199-200 (1769, Facsimile ed. 1979).
[38]*State* v. *Davidson*, 987 P.2d 335 (Kan. 1999), p. 344.
[39]*State* v. *Fuller*, 531 S.E.2d 861 (N.C. Ct. App. 2000).
[40]Ibid., p. 864.

See the accompanying Court Decision for more on depraved heart murder. In it we take a look at the case of *People* v. *Roe*, where a 15-year-old plays a deadly game of Russian roulette.

## COURT DECISION

*People* v. *Roe*
542 N.E.2d 610 (N.Y. App. 1989)

**Background:** Steven Roe was convicted for second degree murder in the Westchester County Court. The Appellate Division of the Supreme Court affirmed and the defendant appealed. The Court of Appeals, which is New York's highest appellate court, affirmed the conviction.

### Opinion of the Court

HANCOCK, Judge.

In defendant's appeal from his conviction for depraved indifference murder for the shooting death of a 13-year-old boy, the sole question we address is the legal sufficiency of the evidence. Defendant, a 15 1/2 year-old high school student, deliberately loaded a mix of "live" and "dummy" shells at random into the magazine of a 12-gauge shotgun. He pumped a shell into the firing chamber not knowing whether it was a "dummy" or a "live" round. He raised the gun to his shoulder and pointed it directly at the victim, Darrin Seifert, who was standing approximately 10 feet away. As he did so, he exclaimed "Let's play Polish roulette" and asked "Who is first?". When he pulled the trigger, the gun discharged sending a "live" round into Darrin's chest. Darrin died as a result of the massive injuries.

Defendant was convicted after a bench trial and the Appellate Division unanimously affirmed, holding that the evidence was legally sufficient to establish defendant's guilt. ***On our review of the record, we conclude, as did the Appellate Division, that the proof is legally sufficient. Accordingly, there should be an affirmance.

***Before analyzing the evidence and its legal sufficiency, a brief examination of the crime of depraved indifference murder and its elements is instructive. Depraved indifference murder, like reckless manslaughter is a *nonintentional* homicide. It differs from manslaughter, however, in that it must be shown that the actor's reckless conduct is imminently dangerous and presents a grave risk of death; in manslaughter, the conduct need only present the lesser "substantial risk" of death. Whether the lesser risk sufficient for manslaughter is elevated into the very substantial risk present in murder depends upon the wantonness of defendant's acts—i.e., whether they were committed "[u]nder circumstances evincing a depraved indifference to human life" (Penal Law § 125.25[2] ). This is not a *mens rea* element which focuses "upon the subjective intent of the defendant, as it is with intentional murder (Penal Law, § 125.25, subd. 1)"; rather it involves "an objective assessment of the degree of risk presented by defendant's reckless conduct" (*People* v. *Register,* 60 N.Y.2d at 277).

***Generally, the assessment of the objective circumstances evincing the actor's "depraved indifference to human life"—i.e., those which elevate the risk to the gravity required for a murder conviction—is a qualitative judgment to be made by the trier of the facts. If there is evidence which supports the jury's determination, it is this court's obligation to uphold the verdict. Examples of conduct which have been held sufficient to justify a jury's finding of depraved indifference include: driving an automobile on a city sidewalk at excessive speeds and striking a pedestrian without applying the brakes; firing several bullets into a house; continually beating an infant over a five-day period; and playing "Russian roulette" with one "live" shell in a six-cylinder gun.

With this background, we turn to the issue before us, now more fully stated: whether, viewing the evidence in the light most favorable to the People, any rational trier of the fact could have concluded that the objective circumstances surrounding defendant's reckless conduct so elevated the gravity of the risk created as to evince the depraved indifference to human life necessary to sustain the murder conviction. A brief summary of the evidence is necessary.

\* \* \*The evidence of the objective circumstances surrounding defendant's point-blank discharge of the shotgun is, in our view, sufficient to support a finding of the very serious risk of death required for depraved indifference murder. Because the escalating factor—depraved indifference to human life—is based on an objective assessment of the circumstances surrounding the act of shooting and not the *mens rea* of the actor, the evidence stressed by the dissent concerning defendant's *mens rea*—his emotional condition in the aftermath of the killing is beside the point.

\* \* \*The comparable case here is not that of a person, uneducated in use of weapons, who, while playing with a gun that he does not know is loaded, accidentally discharges it; rather, the apt analogy is a macabre game of chance where the victim's fate—life or death—may be decreed by the flip of a coin or a roll of a die. It is no different where the odds are even that the shell pumped into the firing chamber of a 12-gauge shotgun is a "live" round, the gun is aimed at the victim standing close by, and the trigger is pulled.

The sheer enormity of the act—putting another's life at such grave peril in this fashion—is not diminished because the sponsor of the game is a youth of 15.

\* \* \*Accordingly, the order of the Appellate Division should be affirmed.

## Case Analysis

1. What elements are necessary to convict the defendant of depraved heart murder?
2. The court engages in a significant discussion of the *mens rea* requirement for depraved heart murder. Is the test subjective or objective? Explain.
3. The defendant is this case is 15-years old. Should he be treated differently because of his age? Why or why not?

# Manslaughter

Manslaughter is an unlawful homicide committed with the malice aforethought required for murder. As such, manslaughter can be voluntary and involuntary. At the risk of simplification, a voluntary manslaughter is the same as a "heat of passion" killing. An involuntary manslaughter is either a reckless or "criminally negligent" killing. We look at each of these in more detail in the following subsections.

## Voluntary Manslaughter

Under common law, a killing that was committed in the "sudden heat of passion" because of "adequate provocation" was considered less blameworthy than murder.[41] Note the three distinct elements here: (1) sudden heat of passion; (2) adequate provocation; and (3) causation, the requirement that the sudden heat of passion *resulted from* adequate provocation. Let's look at each of these in more detail.

### Sudden Heat of Passion.

The notion of heat of passion should be fairly self-explanatory. If a person acts when his or her emotions are running high, such actions are often undertaken in the heat of passion. So it goes with homicide. Blackstone put it this way:

> If upon a sudden quarrel two persons fight, and one of them kills the other, this is [voluntary] manslaughter. And, so it is, if they upon such an occasion go out and fight in a field, for this is one continued act of passion and the law pays that regard to human frailty, as not to put a hasty and a deliberate act upon the same footing with regard to guilty. So also a man be greatly provoked, as by pulling his nose, or other great indignity, and immediately kills the aggressor, though this is not excusable, since there is no absolute necessity for doing so to preserve himself, yet neither is it murder for there is no previous malice.[42]

So, the fight that erupted at the beginning of Blackstone's scenario is what prompted one party to act in the heat of passion. The killer in this instance arguably acted out of anger, but there is no requirement that "heat of passion" be likened to anger. Emotions ranging from jealousy[43] to desperation[44] can qualify.

For the heat of passion to exist, the accused must not have had time to cool off. In one classic case, the defendant killed a sodomist who victimized him some three weeks earlier while he was unconscious. An appellate court held that too much time had elapsed between the provocation and the killing to support a manslaughter conviction.[45] There are no hard and fast rules concerning the "cooling-off" period. Juries are usually tasked with making the decision.

### Adequate Provocation.

Under common law, a person was considered adequately provoked if what that person experienced or observed was sufficiently serious. Examples included assault, battery, mutual combat, witnessing a serious crime committed against someone else, and the like.[46] Actions that *did not*, according to the courts, provide adequate provocation to reduce a murder to manslaughter were insults, learning of spouse's adultery, or being a victim of minor battery, among others.[47]

As time has gone on, courts have abandoned their attempts to list all the circumstances that would be considered adequate provocation. More often than not, juries are left with making the decision. For example, it is not uncommon for

---

[41]See, e.g., *Comber v. United States*, 584 A.2d 26 (D.C. Ct. App. 1990).
[42]4 Bl. Comm. 191 (1769, Facsimile ed. 1979).
[43]See, e.g., *People v. Berry*, 556 P.2d 777 (Cal. 1976).
[44]See, e.g., *People v. Borchers*, 325 P.2d 97 (Cal. 1958).
[45]*State v. Gounagias*, 153 P. 9 (Wash. 1915).
[46]See J. Dressler, *Understanding Criminal Law*, 5th ed. (Newark, NJ: Lexis-Nexis, 2009), p. 536.
[47]Ibid.

someone to be prosecuted for murder, but the jury may be instructed that it can find the defendant guilty of manslaughter if the circumstances merit—that is, if it is confident that the crime was committed in the heat of passion and with sufficient provocation. As one court put it, if the circumstances "might render ordinary men, of fair average disposition, liable to act rashly or without due deliberation or reflection, and from passion, rather than judgment,"[48] then manslaughter is the appropriate verdict.

There is one exception to the modern rule that there is no agreed-upon list of circumstances that would be considered adequate provocation: Words alone are rarely sufficient. For example, in one case, an African-American man, Green, killed his white neighbor after the neighbor informed Green that he shot Green's dog the week earlier and that he had done so because "it was bad enough living around niggers, much less dogs."[49] The Supreme Court of Michigan declined to hear Green's appeal. We say "rarely" sufficient because there are exceptions. Minnesota, for example, defines first-degree (i.e., voluntary) manslaughter thusly:

> intentionally [causing] the death of another person in the heat of passion provided by *such words* or acts of another as would provoke a person of ordinary self-control under like circumstances, provided that the crying of a child does not constitute provocation.[50]

### Causation.
The third voluntary manslaughter requirement is, again, that adequate provocation must *cause* the heat of passion. Assume, for example, that Keith intends to kill his wife, Tammy, because, in his view, she was always "talking smack" about him behind his back. Further assume he comes home one afternoon, grabs his favorite gun, and when opening the bedroom door to find Tammy, sees her in bed with his best friend. Enraged, he kills her. Keith committed murder in this instance, not manslaughter. Why? He set out to kill Tammy in advance. Tammy's earlier words provoked him to engage in a planned killing. He was going to kill her anyway, so the fact that he observed his best friend sleeping with his wife was immaterial.

**paramour rule** A husband catching his wife in the act of adultery provides adequate provocation to reduce a charge for killing another from murder to manslaughter.

What if Keith hadn't planned to kill Tammy and instead killed her after witnessing her infidelity? Under common law, the **paramour rule** provided that a husband who caught his wife in an act of adultery had adequate provocation to kill (moving it from murder to manslaughter). Some states even sanctioned such killings. And over time the rule was modified such that wives could justifiably kill unfaithful husbands—or at least be found guilty of manslaughter rather than murder. These days, however, it is exceedingly rare for witnessing adultery to amount to adequate provocation. For example, in *Commonwealth v. Schnopps*,[51] the Supreme Judicial Court of Massachusetts upheld the first-degree murder conviction of a man who killed his wife, in part because of an affair she was having.

Also consider the case of John Patrick Dennis, who killed his estranged wife, Robin, after witnessing her in an embrace with her boyfriend, Dantz, and after

---

[48]*Maher* v. *People*, 10 Mich. 212 (1862), p. 220.
[49]*People* v. *Green*, 519 N.W.2d 853 (Mich. 1994), p. 856.
[50]Minnesota Criminal Code Section 609.20(1).
[51]*Commonwealth* v. *Schnopps*, 459 N.E.2d 98 (Mass. 1984).

learning that she was doing drugs with Dantz in view of John and Robin's son. Dennis was convicted of first-degree murder, and his conviction was later affirmed:

> Antecedent events may be relevant in determining whether the triggering event in fact produced the hot blood necessary to rebut malice—they may support or detract from that nexus—but they do not suffice to give the triggering event a legal quality it does not otherwise have. Discovering one's spouse in an embrace with a paramour will not constitute adequate provocation because at some earlier time he or she committed adultery with that paramour. That is a matter for the divorce court; it does not reduce murder to some lesser offense.[52]

**last straw rule** An unlawful killing can be reduced from murder to manslaughter if it was caused by long-standing resentment or humiliation that triggered the crime.

The appeals court in this case basically rejected the so-called **last straw rule**. According to the rule, murder may be reduced to manslaughter in light of "a smoldering resentment or pent-up rage resulting from earlier insults or humiliating events culminating in a triggering event that, by itself, might be insufficient to provoke the deadly act."[53] The court felt that even though Dennis went through some trying times, including trying to support Robin and their son even in the face of Robin's infidelity and continued drug use, his tribulations were not sufficient to clear him of a murder conviction.

## Involuntary Manslaughter

Involuntary manslaughter is typically an unintentional killing. Some states define involuntary manslaughter as a stand-alone offense. Others, like Minnesota, grade manslaughter by degree, usually defining first-degree manslaughters as voluntary and second-degree manslaughters as *in*voluntary. Regardless of the approach, there are typically two types of involuntary manslaughter: (1) criminal negligence manslaughter and (2) criminal act manslaughter.

### Criminal Negligence Manslaughter.
Involuntary criminal negligence manslaughter occurs when someone deviates substantially from the usual standard of care or behavior that we would expect of people in normal situations. It must be "so gross as to be deserving of punishment."[54] The defendant (1) creates a high degree of risk and (2) is aware that death or serious bodily injury could result, yet acts anyway.

Parental neglect is a classic example of behavior that can lead to an involuntary (criminal negligence) manslaughter conviction. An example would be a parent who ignores a child's need for food or medical care *and is unaware of the peril this places the child in*—the result is likely involuntary manslaughter.[55] On the other hand, if the parent *is* aware of the risk, then the child's death may be murder.[56]

### Criminal Act Manslaughter.
Criminal act manslaughter occurs when an unintentional death results from another *nonfelonious* criminal act. We discuss *felony* murder in the next section. Here we are interested in deaths that result during the commission of a separate offense or infraction that is less serious than a felony.

---

[52]*Dennis v. State*, 105 Md. App. 687 (1995), p. 699.
[53]Ibid., p. 689.
[54]*Hazelwood v. State*, 912 P.2d 1266 (Alaska Ct. App. 1996), p. 1279, n. 16.
[55]See, e.g., *State v. Williams*, 484 P.2d 1167 (Wash Ct. App. 1971).
[56]See, e.g., *People v. Burden*, 72 Cal. App. 3d 603 (Ct. App. 1977).

For example, some states permit this sort of manslaughter conviction if a motorist runs a stop sign and kills another individual, such as a pedestrian crossing the street.[57] Some states take a more restrictive approach and limit (involuntary) criminal act manslaughter convictions to cases involving misdemeanors (as opposed to traffic law violations). If a person hits another person in the face and the latter dies, then arguably the result is involuntary manslaughter—provided that the person doing the hitting did not *intend* for the victim to die.[58]

## Homicide Under the Model Penal Code

The Model Penal Code references three types of criminal homicide: murder, manslaughter, and negligent homicide. Assuming there is no justification or excuse and/or no mitigating circumstances, a murder occurs when someone kills another person (1) purposely or knowingly or (2) recklessly, with extreme indifference to human life.[59] This differs from some of the other definitions of murder presented thus far, as the Model Penal Code does note grade the crime into levels. Nor does the Model Penal Code's definition of murder require malice aforethought, as was the case under common law.

Manslaughter occurs when someone either (1) recklessly kills someone else or (2) kills someone else under circumstances that would constitute murder, but the crime occurs as a result of "extreme mental or emotional disturbance" and for which there is a "reasonable explanation or excuse."[60] Reckless manslaughter is the lesser included offense of reckless murder, without the extreme indifference to the value of human life. As for "extreme mental or emotional disturbance," the Model Penal Code includes in it sudden heat of passion and diminished capacity. For example, a woman who finds her husband in bed with another woman and, enraged, kills him, would arguably be guilty of manslaughter under the Model Penal Code.

Finally, negligent homicide is the least serious form of homicide under the Model Penal Code. A person is guilty of the crime if that person kills another because of a "gross deviation" from the standard of care a reasonable person would exercise.[61] Assume a driver, texting, fails to see a child in the crosswalk in a school zone, hits the child, and kills him. The driver would likely be guilty of negligent homicide under the Model Penal Code.

**YOUR DECISION**

1. Elizabeth Harris and Paul Thibodeaux lived together with four children. Paul believed he was the biological father of all four children. One afternoon, however, Elizabeth informed Paul that she once had an affair and that he was not the biological father of the 2-month-old baby girl. Devastated by the news, Paul took the infant, walked with her for about a mile, and then killed her. Paul is being charged with murder. He claims that he acted in the "heat of passion" and should only be charged with voluntary manslaughter. Is Paul guilty of murder or voluntary manslaughter? Was the provocation adequate to reduce the charges? Why or why not?

[57]See, e.g., *State* v. *Hupf*, 101 A.2d 355 (Del. 1953).
[58]*Comber v. United States*, 584 A.2d 26 (D.C. Ct. App. 1990).
[59]Model Penal Code Section 210.2(1)(a)-(b).
[60]Model Penal Code Section 210.3(1)(a)-(b).
[61]Model Penal Code Section 210.4.

2. The South River High School football team began summer practice in August 2008, under the guidance of Coach Jim Williams. The temperature reached 95 degrees as the students entered their fourth hour of intense practice. A sophomore, Billy Schultz, collapsed during the practice and was rushed to the emergency room with heat stroke. Billy died three days later from heat stroke complications. The prosecutor wants to charge Coach Williams with some form of criminal homicide for Billy's death. What form of criminal homicide would be appropriate in this circumstance, if any?

## Summary

- *Murder* is homicide with malice aforethought.
- In general, if one person kills another person without justification, excuse, or any mitigating circumstances, that person is said to have killed with malice aforethought.
- Some states do not distinguish between first- and second-degree murder.
- In general, first-degree murder is murder that is willful, premeditated, and deliberated. It is a "cold-blooded" killing, one that is arguably more "evil" than a spontaneous killing.
- Any murder that is not "willful, premeditated, and deliberate" is considered second-degree murder. See Figure 8.1 for a summary.
- One form of second-degree murder occurs when the offender intends to cause grievous bodily injury and the result is death. Another occurs when

**Figure 8.1**

Distinguishing between First- and Second-Degree Murder

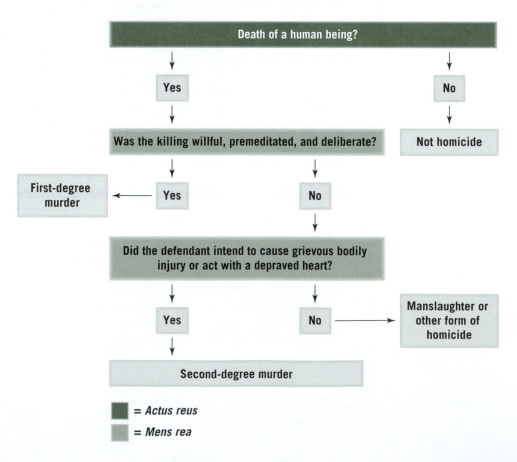

**Figure 8.2**

Distinguishing between Voluntary and Involuntary Manslaughter

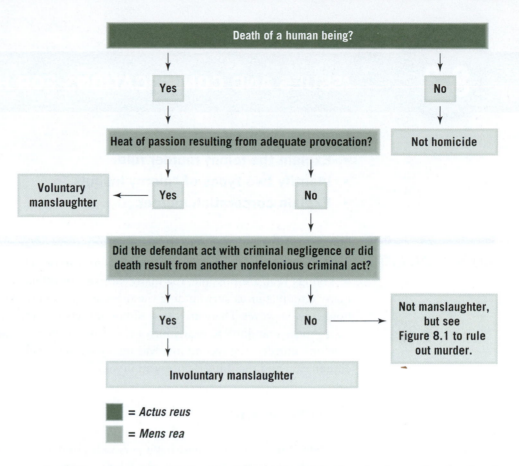

the killer acts with a "depraved heart," which then leads to the death of another person.

- Some states do not practice capital punishment and, as such, incarcerate murderers.
- The decision as to whether a first-degree murderer will be sentenced to death is usually made by a jury in a post-trial hearing.
- The death penalty may apply if aggravating factors, which add to the seriousness or enormity of the case, outweigh mitigating factors (factors that serve to extenuate or reduce the degree of moral culpability), if there even are any.
- Manslaughter is an unlawful homicide committed with the malice aforethought required for murder.
- At the risk of simplification, a voluntary manslaughter is the same as a "heat of passion" killing. Under common law, a killing committed in the "sudden heat of passion" because of "adequate provocation" was considered less blameworthy than murder (i.e., voluntary manslaughter). See Figure 8.2 for a summary.
- An involuntary manslaughter is either a reckless or "criminally negligent" killing. There are typically two types of involuntary manslaughter: (1) criminal negligence manslaughter and (2) criminal act manslaughter.
- The Model Penal Code references three types of criminal homicide: murder, manslaughter, and negligent homicide.
- The Model Penal Code does not grade homicide into degrees (e.g., first-degree murder).

# ISSUES AND COMPLICATIONS FOR HOMICIDE

### *Learning Objectives*

- **Explain the felony murder rule.**
- **Identify two types of "mercy killings."**
- **Explain corporation murder.**

**CORE CONCEPTS**

As is clear by now, homicide is a complicated offense. This owes to the many types of killings that are possible, the many motives an offender brings to the table, the many circumstances surrounding the offense, and so on. We are not yet done with homicide, however. There are three additional sets of circumstances we need to consider—ones that don't fit neatly into any of this chapter's foregoing sections. The first is felony murder; the second involves mercy killings, including assisted suicides and euthanasia; and the third is corporation murder.

## Felony Murder

**felony murder** A person is guilty of murder when a death results during that person's commission of a violent felony.

The **felony murder** rule states that a person is guilty of murder when a death results during that person's commission of a felony. Nearly every state recognizes this rule, usually limiting it to certain listed (and serious) felonies. Examples include robbery, rape, arson, and burglary.

Assume, for example, that Bob burglarizes Jim's house. During the burglary, Jim grabs a gun and confronts Bob. Bob shoots Jim. Bob would be guilty of murder, as he intentionally shot Jim. What makes the felony murder rule even stricter than this, however, is that even if Jim's death was accidental, the rule would still apply. What if Jim died from fright instead of a gunshot wound? Bob would still be liable for murder. The felony murder rule thus establishes strict liability for *any* death that occurs during the commission of a felony.

Why maintain a felony murder rule? The primary logic behind it is deterrence. According to one court, the goal of the felony murder rule is

> to deter dangerous conduct by punishing as murder a homicide resulting from dangerous conduct in the perpetration of a felony. . . . If the felonious conduct, under all of the circumstances, made death a foreseeable consequence, it is reasonable for the law to infer . . . the malice that qualifies the homicide as murder.[62]

### Felony Murder Limitations

Though the felony murder rule is far-reaching, there are limitations to it. One of them is that most states limit the rule to inherently dangerous felonies, those most

---

[62]*Fisher and Utley v. State*, 786 A.2d 706 (Md. 2001), p. 732.

likely to result in serious injury or loss of life. This includes any felony that "by its very nature, . . . cannot be committed without creating a substantial risk that someone will be killed."[63] For crimes like robbery and arson, this definition suffices. For some others, however, it may not. Thus courts will sometimes examine "the facts and the circumstances of the particular case to determine if such felony was inherently dangerous in the manner and circumstances in which it was committed."[64]

A second limitation placed on the felony murder rule is that the felony must be *independent of the homicide*. Assume Sarah negligently kills Michelle. Under most circumstances, such a killing (involuntary manslaughter) would be considered a felony. Since a death occurred here during the course of a felony (i.e., the involuntary manslaughter), then under the felony murder rule, the manslaughter would be murder. In other words, if the felony murder rule were strictly applied to situations like this, there could never be the crime of manslaughter, only murder. A harsher punishment could thus result—perhaps when it need not do so.

Or consider the case of Les who arrives home to find his wife, Julia, in bed with another man. Enraged, he shoots and kills both of them. Under most circumstances, this would be considered voluntary manslaughter. A strict application of the felony murder rule would elevate the voluntary manslaughter in this case to murder. Why? A death resulted during the commission of a felony (i.e., voluntary manslaughter). There would be no crime of voluntary manslaughter, and it is not the intent of the felony murder rule to eliminate all other forms of homicide besides just murder.

Would a prosecutor in our Les and Julia situation be forced to stick with the voluntary manslaughter charge? Perhaps not. What if the prosecutor charged Les with assault with a deadly weapon, instead of letting the felonious act of voluntary manslaughter serve to establish felony murder? Some states permit prosecutors to do this, and the practical result in our case would be a harsher punishment for Les.[65] Most states, however, do not permit felonious assault or battery to trigger the felony murder rule.[66]

So how do we determine if the felony is independent of the homicide? Here is how one court answered the question:

> [A] felony does not merge with a homicide where the act causing death was committed with a collateral and independent felonious design separate from the intent to inflict the injury that caused death.[67]

For example, if a kidnapping results in death, it will be considered distinct from homicide and the felony murder rule will apply.[68] The two offenses do not merge together into the same offense because the intent to kidnap is distinct from the intent to kill. Were the two offenses treated as the same, the felony murder rule could not serve its purpose, which is again to deter people from killing people during the commission of felonies.

The **res gestae** (Latin for "things done to commit") requirement places yet another limitation on the felony murder rule. Simply, the homicide must occur during the *res gestae* of the felony. There are three subcomponents to the *res gestae* requirement:

**res gestae** Latin term meaning "things done to commit." In regard to felony murder, the sequence of the felony from beginning to end.

---

[63]*People v. Burroughs*, 678 P.2d 894 (Cal. 1984), p. 900.
[64]*State v. Stewart*, 663 A.2d 912 (R.I. 1995), p. 919.
[65]See, e.g., *Roary v. State*, 867 A.2d 1095 (Md. 2005).
[66]See, e.g., *Barnett v. State*, 783 So. 2d 929 (Ala. Crim. App. 2000).
[67]*People v. Hansen*, 885 P.2d 1022 (Cal. 1994), p. 1029.
[68]*People v. Escobar*, 48 Cal. App. 4th 999 (Ct. App. 1996), pp. 1012-13.

1. The felony and the homicide must accompany each other in close temporal proximity. On the one hand, if the homicide occurs first and is later followed by a separate felony, the felony murder rule will not apply. The temporal ordering should be reversed. On the other hand, when the homicide occurs post-felony, the felony murder rule applies. For example, if a suspect robs a bank and kills a security guard while fleeing the scene, felony murder results. The same would hold even if a police officer, in pursuit of the suspect across urban rooftops in the dark, falls into an air shaft and dies.[69] The felony murder rule would *not* apply, however, if the fleeing suspect runs a stop sign and kills another motorist hundreds of miles from the crime scene.[70]

2. The second component of the *res gestae* requirement is that there be a *cause* between the felony and the homicide. If the later is wholly independent of the former, the felony murder rule will not apply. This is not unlike the causation requirement introduced back in Chapter 3. Consider the case of Nelson King, who, along with Mark Bailey, was flying a plane containing over 500 pounds of marijuana to a location in Virginia. The men encountered heavy cloud cover, became lost, and eventually crashed. Bailey was killed in the crash. The court in *King* v. *Commonwealth*[71] held that King was not guilty of felony murder because the crash could have occurred even if they were carrying legal cargo. In other words, the felony in this case (transporting the marijuana) did not *cause* Bailey's death.

3. The third component of the *res gestae* requirement focuses on the *who* of the killing. Simply, what if a killing occurs during the course of a felony, but at the hands of someone else? In general, the answer is that the felony murder rule "does not extend to a killing, although growing out of the commission of the felony, if directly attributable to the act of one other than the defendant or those associated with him in the unlawful enterprise." This means that if someone else other than the felon, even an adversary (such as a security guard who fires her gun at a bank robbery suspect and kills an innocent bystander), is responsible for the killing, the felony murder rule does not apply. So even though the felon sets the wheels in motion, he or she may not be properly held responsible for all harms that result from the felony he or she is responsible for. Not all courts agree with this approach. As one put it,

> [W]hen a felon's attempt to commit a forcible felony sets in motion a chain of events which were or should have been within his contemplation when the motion was initiated, he should have been responsible for any death which by direct and almost inevitable sequence results from the initial criminal act.[72]

Under this construction, it is still unclear whether a jury would find the defendant guilty of felony murder. The question is whether (to again use our security guard example) the death of an innocent at the hands of a security guard was a reasonable foreseeable consequence of the bank robbery.

---

[69]*People* v. *Matos*, 634 N.E.2d 157 (N.Y. 1994).
[70]See *Doane* v. *Commonwealth*, 237 S.E.2d 797 (Va. 1977), p. 798.
[71]*King* v. *Commonwealth*, 368 S.E.2d 704 (Va. Ct. App. 1988).
[72]*People* v. *Lowery*, 687 N.E.2d 973 (Ill. 1997), p. 976.

# Situating the Felony Murder Rule within the Context of Other Homicides

To summarize the felony murder rule and at the same time situate it within the context of other homicides, consider this observation from the District of Columbia Court of Appeals in *Comber* v. *United States*:

> One who acts with the specific intent to kill or to inflict serious bodily injury is guilty of murder. If those two states of mind are accompanied by recognized circumstances of mitigation, however, the crime is voluntary manslaughter. (It is conceivable that voluntary manslaughter liability might arise where one, acting under circumstances of mitigation, consciously disregards an extreme risk of death of serious bodily injury, but such scenarios seem highly improbable.) The other two malicious mental states also have corollaries in the involuntary manslaughter category. One who acts in conscious disregard of an extreme risk of death or serious bodily injury is guilty of murder, but if he or she is only unreasonably unaware of such a risk, the crime is involuntary manslaughter. Finally, one who kills in the course of a felony . . . is guilty of murder, but one who kills in the commission of a misdemeanor . . . is guilty of involuntary manslaughter.[73]

See the accompanying Court Decision for more on felony murder. In it we take a look at the case of *State* v. *Leech*, where a firefighter was killed while responding to a case of arson.

## COURT DECISION

*State* v. *Leech*
790 P.2d 160 (Wash. 1990)

**Background:** Clyde Leech was convicted in the Superior Court of King County of first-degree felony murder. Defendant appealed. The Court of Appeals reversed and remanded. The state sought discretionary review. The Supreme Court of Washington reversed the Court of Appeals and affirmed the conviction.

ANDERSEN, Justice

### Facts of Case

At issue in this case is whether a fire fighter's death occurred in the furtherance of an arson, thus rendering the arsonist liable for the crime of first degree felony murder.

On July 12, 1987, a fire broke out at the largely abandoned Crest apartment building in Seattle. Robert Earhart was one of nearly 70 City of Seattle fire fighters who responded to the alarm. Fire investigators suspected arson, and Clyde Dale Leech, the defendant herein, was arrested at the scene. The substantial evidence against the defendant included his having been seen leaving the Crest just minutes before smoke emerged from the vacant area he had been in.

Robert Earhart died of carbon monoxide poisoning while fighting the fire inside the Crest. When his body was found, his breathing apparatus was on the floor beside

---

[73]*Comber* v. *United States*, 584 A.2d 26 (D.C. Ct. App. 1990), p. 52.

him and the air bottle read at or near zero. Subsequent tests showed that the breathing apparatus was not defective but was simply empty.

The defendant was charged with first degree felony murder. His main defense was that the negligence of Earhart and the Seattle Fire Department, rather than the arson, was the proximate cause of Earhart's death. A safety inspector for the Washington State Department of Labor and Industries testified that if Earhart had obeyed state safety regulations and gotten a new air bottle when the alarm in his breathing apparatus sounded, his death could have been avoided. (The apparatus was designed to sound an alarm when less than 5 minutes of oxygen remained in the air bottle.)

\*\*\*The jury found the defendant guilty of first degree felony murder, which is statutorily defined in this case as a death that is caused "in the course of and in furtherance of" first degree arson.

\*\*\*The Court of Appeals held that the arson was a proximate cause of Earhart's death but also held that the death did not occur in "furtherance of" the arson. The Court of Appeals vacated the defendant's conviction of felony murder but found that the jury, by its verdict, had necessarily convicted him of the lesser included offense of first degree arson. The Court of Appeals remanded the case to the Superior Court for resentencing.

Thereupon the State sought discretionary review of the Court of Appeals decision in this court and we granted review.

**\*\*\*Issue**

Did the fire fighter's death occur in the furtherance of the arson as required by the felony murder statute?

**Decision**

CONCLUSION. A death that is caused by an arson fire before it is extinguished occurs in furtherance of the arson and renders the arsonist liable for felony murder.

The statute defining the crime of first degree felony murder provides that a person is guilty of first degree murder when

> *He commits or attempts to commit the crime of* either (1) robbery, in the first or second degree, (2) rape in the first or second degree, (3) burglary in the first degree, (4) *arson in the first degree,* or (5) kidnapping, in the first or second degree, *and; in the course of and in furtherance of such crime* or in immediate flight therefrom, *he, or another participant, causes the death of a person other than one of the participants;* . . .
> (Italics ours.) RCW 9A.32.030(1)(c) (part).

The defendant claimed before the Court of Appeals that the felony murder statute was inapplicable to his case because (1) Earhart's negligence was not a "specifically foreseeable" result of the arson; (2) the arson fire was not the proximate cause of Earhart's death; and (3) Earhart's death was not caused in the course of and in furtherance of the arson.

We agree with the Court of Appeals disposition of the defendant's first two contentions. With regard to the claim that Earhart's alleged negligence was not foreseeable, the court noted that RCW 9A.48.020 defines first degree arson as including fires that are knowingly and maliciously set which are "'manifestly dangerous to any human life, including firemen'". In addition, the court cited its holding in *State* v. *Levage,* 23 Wash.App. 33, 35 (1979):

> experience teaches that one of the certainties attendant upon a hostile fire is that firemen will be called and will come. Danger inheres in fire fighting. In setting a hostile fire, the arsonist can anticipate that firemen will be endangered.

\*\*\*It does not seem to us that human error in fighting a fire is an extraordinary occurrence. The implication of the defendant's argument is that an arsonist is entitled to have his fire fought in a perfect, risk-free manner by a fire department; this is not the law. Thus, the Court of Appeals properly rejected the contention that the defendant was not guilty of felony murder because Earhart's alleged negligence was not specifically foreseeable.

We also agree with the Court of Appeals conclusion that the arson fire proximately caused Earhart's death. We find it sufficient to simply note here that the fire fighter's alleged negligence in using his breathing apparatus was not the sole cause of his death. Since his failure to use the apparatus would not have killed him had the defendant not set the arson fire, the defendant's conduct in setting the fire was a proximate cause of Earhart's death.

We next turn to the Court of Appeals analysis regarding the defendant's third contention: whether Earhart's death was caused "in the course of and in furtherance of" the arson. The Court of Appeals held that Earhart's death clearly occurred "in the course of" the arson, *i.e.,* during the fire. It concluded, however, that the death did not occur "in furtherance of" the arson, since the defendant did not cause Earhart's death in acting to promote or advance the arson: "by the time Earhart arrived, the fire was well under way and [the defendant] had left the premises. Thus, [the defendant] did not cause Earhart's death 'in furtherance' of the arson." It is this conclusion that is at issue.

A homicide is deemed committed during the perpetration of a felony, for the purpose of felony murder, if the homicide is within the "res gestae" of the felony, *i.e.,* if there was a close proximity in terms of time and distance between the felony and the homicide.

The defendant argues (and the Court of Appeals apparently agreed) that the act of arson is complete once a fire is set and has a potential for harm and that any subsequent death caused by the still-burning fire is not sufficiently related in time to the arson to occur within the res gestae of that felony or in the furtherance thereof. According to this argument, the arsonist is not liable for felony murder unless he or she accidentally kills someone who is attempting to prevent the arsonist from starting the fire.

This argument is addressed by a leading treatise in discussing the time connection required by felony murder statutes that use phrases such as "in the furtherance of" and "in the commission of."

> Burglary is committed when the defendant breaks and enters the building with the appropriate intent; nothing further, like the caption and asportation necessary for robbery, is required for burglary. Arson is committed when the

building first catches fire; the further consumption of the building by fire adds nothing further to the arson already committed. Rape is committed upon the first penetration; further sexual activity by the defendant after this initial connection adds nothing to the crime of rape already committed.

Yet for purposes of the time connection implicit in the expression "in the commission of," the crimes of arson, burglary and rape may be considered to continue while the building burns, while the burglars search the building and while the sexual connection is maintained.

2 W. LaFave & A. Scott § 7.5, at 224-25.

***To apply the "in furtherance of" language only to the time in which an arson fire is being set is to achieve an absurd consequence, *i.e.,* a situation in which an arsonist whose fire kills will almost never be liable for murder.

We hold that because the fire fighter's death in this case occurred while the arson fire was still engaged, the death was sufficiently close in time and place to the arson to be part of the res gestae of that felony. Thus, the death of Seattle fire fighter Robert Earhart occurred "in furtherance of" the arson and the defendant was properly charged and convicted of the crime of felony murder; the Court of Appeals holding to the contrary is reversed.

***The Court of Appeals is reversed and the defendant's conviction of the crime of first degree felony murder is affirmed.

## Case Analysis

1. What is the predicate felony involved in this case? Is it always "inherently dangerous"?

2. What are the defendant's three main legal arguments regarding his felony murder conviction? How does the Supreme Court of Washington rule on each argument?

3. Do you believe the defendant was the proximate cause of the firefighter's death? Why or why not?

## Mercy Killings

**physician-assisted suicide** A patient seeks the assistance of a physician to end his or her own life.

**euthanasia** Purposeful termination of life by someone other than the patient.

Most homicide victims are unwilling; they don't *want* to die. Some individuals, however, do want to die, either because they are in extreme pain, suffering from a debilitating condition, or both. From time to time, such individuals have sought the assistance of their physicians in ending their lives, a practice known as **physician-assisted suicide**. Others have sought **euthanasia**, a purposeful termination of life by someone other than the patient.

Emotions run high on these subjects. Supporters feel people should be able to chart their own destiny and end their lives if they see fit. Others feel it is morally wrong for anyone to prematurely end his or her own life. We cannot hope to settle the debate here. What we *can* do, however, is call attention to the legal implications of these practices. Is it a violation of the criminal law for a physician to assist a patient in ending his or her life? Likewise, is euthanasia criminal? We will look at each practice separately.

## Physician-Assisted Suicide

On June 4, 1990, the American public learned that Dr. Jack Kevorkian helped Janet Adkins, a 54-year-old Alzheimer's patient, end her life.[74] He met Ms. Adkins in a van he had outfitted with a "suicide machine" that was set up to administer a lethal chemical cocktail via an intravenous line. Ms. Adkins pushed a lever that released the chemicals into her body, thus making her suicide physician assisted.

Jack Kevorkian's actions gained considerable publicity, thrusting the assisted suicide issue center stage (even though what Kevorkian did was not technically physician-assisted suicide, as we will see in the next subsection). It did so, in part, because what Kevorkian did was illegal in Michigan, but not in every state. For example, Washington State's "Death with Dignity Act," enacted in 2008, permits the practice, subject to certain restrictions.[75] It was patterned after Oregon's law that, like Washington's, came to pass by way of popular initiative (i.e., enough voter signatures were secured to put it on a statewide ballot). Washington's law contains these restrictions:

- The patient must be an adult (18 or over) resident of the state of Washington.
- The patient must be mentally competent, verified by two physicians (or referred to a mental health evaluation).
- The patient must be terminally ill with less than 6 months to live, verified by two physicians.
- The patient must make voluntary requests, without coercion, verified by two physicians.
- The patient must be informed of all other options including palliative and hospice care.
- There is a 15 day waiting period between the first oral request and a written request.
- There is a 48 hour waiting period between the written request and the writing of the prescription.
- The written request must be signed by two independent witnesses, at least one of whom is not related to the patient or employed by the health care facility.
- The patient is encouraged to discuss with family (not required because of confidentiality laws).
- The patient may change their mind at any time and rescind the request.[76]

In 1997, the Supreme Court upheld an earlier Washington statute (and a New York statute) that criminalized the practice of assisted suicide,[77] but the Court left

---

[74]See *People v. Kevorkian*, 527 N.W.2d 714 (Mich. 1994).
[75]Revised Code of Washington Section 70.245.
[76]See http://apps.leg.wa.gov/RCW/default.aspx?cite=70.245 (accessed May 6, 2011).
[77]*Washington v. Glucksberg*, 521 U.S. 702 (1997).

open the possibility that states could opt to make the practice legal, which Washington and Oregon then did. Their laws continue to survive legal scrutiny.[78] Montana joins Washington and Oregon as the only states to sanction physician-assisted suicide. The practice remains illegal in 47 states. Thus, a physician in any state besides Washington, Oregon, or Montana who assists an individual with ending his or her life could be charged with and found guilty of a homicide offense.

Over time, states have abolished their laws against suicide. While attempted suicide was a misdemeanor under common law, it no longer is. This trend suggests a certain measure of "tolerance" for the practice of suicide, which may be why some states have legalized physician-assisted suicide. Supporters view the practice as anything but homicide: "Assisted suicide is distinguished from murder by the individual's consent, the same principle that distinguishes sex from rape, exchange from theft, confession from duress, and a variety of other matters found throughout our legal system."[79]

## Euthanasia

On September 17, 1998, Jack Kevorkian administered a lethal injection to Thomas Youk, then 52, who was in the final stages of amyotrophic lateral sclerosis (ALS). Though Youk consented, he did not actually press a lever to end his life, like Ms. Adkins did. Instead, Kevorkian administered the drug. Kevorkian thus *euthanized* Mr. Youk, which is distinct from helping him commit suicide. Kevorkian was prosecuted for murder and convicted by a Michigan jury of second-degree murder. He was paroled after spending just over eight years in prison.

Euthanasia is a form of intentional homicide, but with a motivation of mercy.[80] It is homicide because, though the victim may consent to the practice, he or she has no direct or active role in the killing. As such, euthanasia is considered a form of murder, even in the three states that sanction physician-assisted suicide. As one court put it, "Murder is no less murder because the homicide is committed at the desire of the victim."[81] At most, the defendant's or victim's intentions may serve as mitigating factors, thus reducing the punishment the defendant could receive. But euthanasia remains criminal in all 50 states.

## Corporation Murder

Homicides are typically committed by one or more people against one or more other people. Can we extend this, then, to corporations? After all, corporations are made up of several people. The answer is yes, but it can be rather difficult for a prosecutor to secure a conviction.

In 1978, the Ford Motor Company recalled the then-popular Pinto following allegations that a faulty fuel tank design was responsible for some motorists' deaths.

---

[78]See, e.g., *Oregon v. Ashcroft*, 368 F.3d 1118 (9th Cir. 2004), aff'd., 546 U.S. 243 (2006).
[79]E. Rubin, "Assisted Suicide, Morality, and Law: Why Prohibiting Assisted Suicide Violates the Establishment Clause," *Vanderbilt Law Review*, Vol. 63(2010), p. 811.
[80]N. M. Gorsuch, "The Right to Assisted Suicide and Euthanasia," *Harvard Journal of Law and Public Policy*, Vol. 23 (2000), pp. 599–710.
[81]*State v. Fuller*, 278 N.W.2d 756 (Neb. 1979), p. 761.

Employers are required to use precautions to prevent their employees from harm. Otherwise they may face criminal charges.

Photodisc/Thinkstock

The recall followed allegations that Ford was aware of the flaw and initially refused to redesign the fuel tanks, opting instead to settle lawsuits because the costs involved were lower. This claim, combined with other allegations, prompted to the state of Indiana to bring reckless homicide charges against the company. In 1980, a jury returned "not guilty" verdicts on three counts that the Pinto's design flaw resulted in three women's deaths.[82] Though the verdict was a victory for the company, it signaled the possibility that a company could be held criminal liable for homicide.

In the 1980s, a Texas nursing home was prosecuted for murder when an 87-year-old woman died from apparent neglect.[83] The court granted a defense motion for a mistrial at the end of what is still the longest trial in Texas history (seven months). Even so, the case signaled the possibility that corporations, like individuals, can be criminally responsible for homicide. Such convictions are quite rare, however. Obvious questions remain. Who will be punished? A corporation, though it is made up of several people, is a legal construction, not flesh and bone. If it is not a physical being, it cannot be punished in the traditional sense (e.g., put in prison) but only through fines. Thus any resulting conviction, if not against the officers of the corporation, would be largely symbolic. No company would want a murder conviction to threaten its business!

**YOUR DECISION**

1. Dana Smith was a notorious drug dealer in a dangerous inner city neighborhood. One afternoon, Stanley Jacobs visited Dana's apartment for the purpose of buying illegal drugs. Dana sold Stanley three pills that she described as "Ecstasy." When Stanley took the pills in Dana's presence, she even offered him a beer to wash them down. Two hours later, Stanley died of a drug overdose at a local hospital. The prosecutor wants to charge Dana under the felony murder doctrine and hold her responsible for Stanley's death. Is felony murder applicable to Dana's case? Why or why not?

2. Joe and Jane Moyer were happily married for over 50 years. Tragically, in 2008 Jane was diagnosed with ALS, or Lou Gehrig's disease, and her health began to

[82]P. J. Becker, A. J. Jipson, and A. S. Bruce, "*State of Indiana* v. *Ford Motor Company* Revisited," *American Journal of Criminal Justice*, Vol. 26 (2002), pp. 181–202.
[83]*State of Texas* v. *Autumn Hills Convalescent Center, Inc.*, No. 85-CR-2625 (Dist. Ct. of Bexar Co., 187th Judicial District of Texas, March 25, 1986).

rapidly decline. Joe was heartbroken to see his wife suffer from such a terrible illness. One evening while Jane was asleep in their bedroom, Joe fatally shot her in the head. Joe claims he only killed Jane out of "mercy" to end her suffering. Can Joe be charged with some form of criminal homicide? If so, what type? Would you reach a different result in Montana, Washington, or Oregon? Why or why not?

## Summary

- The felony murder rule states that a person is guilty of murder when a death results during that person's commission of a felony.

- The felony murder rule establishes strict liability for *any* death that occurs during the commission of a felony.

- Most states limit the felony murder rule to inherently dangerous felonies, those that are most likely to result in serious injury or loss of life.

- A second limitation placed on the felony murder rule is that the felony must be *independent of the homicide*.

- The third limitation placed on the felony murder rule, the *res gestae* (Latin for "things done to commit") requirement, requires that the homicide occur during the *res gestae* of the felony.

- In physician-assisted suicide, a physician helps a person end his or her life (the person, not the physician, commits suicide).

- Euthanasia is a form of intentional homicide, with a motivation of mercy.

- Euthanasia is criminal in all 50 states; physician-assisted suicide is legal in three states (Washington, Oregon, and Montana).

- Homicides are typically committed e by one or more people against one or more other people.

- If a corporation is responsible for homicide, it can be found guilty of murder.

- Corporate murder convictions are exceptionally rare. Moreover, it is impossible to "punish" a corporation with a prison sentence.

# Chapter Review

## INTRODUCTION TO HOMICIDE

### *Learning Objectives*

· Distinguish between criminal homicide and noncriminal homicide.

· Define *human being* for purposes of homicide law.

### *Review Questions*

1. What is homicide?

2. For purposes of defining *homicide*, what exactly is a *human being*?

3. When does life begin and end? Why?

4. Explain the common law "year-and-a-day" rule.

5. *Homicide* is a legally neutral term. Why?

### *Key Terms*

homicide
feticide
year-and-a-day rule

## THE ELEMENTS OF HOMICIDE

### *Learning Objectives*

· Distinguish between first-degree murder and second-degree murder.

· Explain when the death penalty is an acceptable form of punishment for homicide.

· Summarize the elements of voluntary and involuntary manslaughter.

· Explain the Model Penal Code approach to homicide.

### *Review Questions*

1. What is murder?

2. Explain the concept of bifurcation as it relates to a first-degree murder trial.

3. In those jurisdictions that grade murder by levels, what is the difference between first- and second-degree murder?

4. When is a murder convict eligible for the death penalty and how is the decision reached?

5. What is manslaughter? What is the key difference between voluntary and involuntary manslaughter?

6. List two circumstances that would be considered "adequate provocation" to reduce a crime from murder to voluntary manslaughter.

7. How does the Model Penal Code approach to homicide differ from the approach of several states?

**Key Terms**

murder
manslaughter
malice aforethought
first-degree murder
bifurcation
aggravating circumstances
mitigating circumstances
paramour rule
last straw rule

MODULE **8.3**     **ISSUES AND COMPLICATIONS FOR HOMICIDE**

**Learning Objectives**

· Explain the felony murder rule.
· Identify two types of "mercy killings."
· Explain corporation murder.

**Review Questions**

1. What is felony murder? How does it differ from traditional murder?
2. Explain the limitations that have been placed on the felony murder rule.
3. What is the difference between physician-assisted suicide and euthanasia? Which, if either, is criminal?
4. What is corporation murder? Can a corporation be found guilty of murder?

**Key Terms**

felony murder
*res gestae*
physician-assisted suicide
euthanasia

# Chapter Synthesizing Questions

1. Should homicide be graded into levels in all states? Why or why not?
2. Only some states treat the killing of an unborn fetus as murder. Why? What approach should be taken?
3. What problems can result from strict application of the felony murder rule?
4. Why is physician-assisted suicide legal in only three states?
5. Who should be punished harsher, the person who kills an unarmed stranger or the mine corporation whose decision to cut corners leads to the deaths of 10 employees? Why do you feel this way?

# ASSAULTIVE OFFENSES

*Learning Objectives*

**MODULE 9.1 RAPE AND SEXUAL ASSAULT**
- Distinguish between rape and sexual assault.
- Summarize the nature and elements of the crime of rape.
- Summarize the laws pertaining to the crime of rape.

**MODULE 9.2 ROBBERY**
- Describe the crime of robbery.
- Distinguish armed robbery from other forms of robbery.

**MODULE 9.3 ASSAULT AND BATTERY**
- Describe the crime of assault.
- Describe the crime of battery.

**MODULE 9.4 OTHER ASSAULTIVE OFFENSES**
- Describe the crime of kidnapping.
- Describe the crime of false imprisonment.
- Define carjacking.
- Identify and define two domestic offenses.
- Differentiate between harassment and stalking.

# RAPE AND SEXUAL ASSAULT

### *Learning Objectives*
- **Distinguish between rape and sexual assault.**
- **Summarize the nature and elements of the crime of rape.**
- **Summarize the laws pertaining to the crime of rape.**

**CORE CONCEPTS**

In this chapter, we turn our attention to the wide array of what we call *assaultive offenses*. We use the term *assaultive* for two reasons. First, the term loosely refers to criminal acts that involve physical harm—or the threat of physical harm—to others. If an assaultive act results in death, then the proper course of action is to treat the crime as a homicide, adhering to the definitions we laid out in the previous chapter. Second, some states lump the offenses discussed in this chapter into a single penal code section. Texas offers an example. Its Penal Code combines rape, assault, and related offenses into a single section.

## Comparing Rape and Sexual Assault

One of the most serious assaultive offenses is rape. Sexual assaults also tend to evoke intense reactions because of their intimate and personal nature. Most of the attention will focus on rape, however, as it is arguably the most serious sex offense. Indeed, rape is often considered the second most serious criminal offense overall, just behind homicide.

**rape** Sexual intercourse without the consent of the victim.

At the risk of simplification, **rape** is "the taking of sexual intimacy with an unwilling person by force or without consent."[1] This definition is timeless, meaning that it incorporates both common law and current conceptions of rape. Early on, rape was a heterosexual crime, particularly male on female. At common law, a husband who forced his wife to engage in sexual intercourse was not guilty of rape, which is no longer the case in about half of the states.[2] Modern definitions of rape incorporate homosexual intercourse as well as forcible intercourse between married couples.

One of the reasons modern rape statutes are broader is that feminist criticisms prompted legislatures to abandon antiquated definitions of the crime that failed to account for some modern-day realities. Feminists argued, for example, that just because a man and woman are married does not mean that every act of

---

[1]R. G. Singer and J. Q. LaFond, *Criminal Law: Examples and Explanations*, 4th ed. (New York: Wolters and Kluwer, 2007, p. 219).
[2]See M. J. Anderson, "Marital Immunity, Intimate Relationships, and Improper Inferences: A New Law on Sexual Offenses by Intimates," *Hastings Law Journal*, Vol. 54 (2003), pp. 1465–1574.

sexual intercourse is voluntary. Some marriages are a loveless sham, held together only by a legal document, making a forcible sex act little different than one between strangers. Today, rape is regarded as "gender neutral" and the crime has been broadened to incorporate all forms of penetration.

At many points throughout history, rape was treated as a capital offense. As recent as the mid-1920s, several states, the District of Columbia, and the federal government authorized capital punishment for rapists. In 1977, however, the U.S. Supreme Court decided that executing rapists, particularly males who raped adult females, constituted cruel and unusual punishment, in violation of the Eighth Amendment.[3] More recently, the Court outlawed the death penalty for offenders convicted of child rape.[4] Prison terms for rapists, however, can run from several years to life.[5]

## Sexual Assault

**sexual assault** A general term that covers a range of nonconsensual sexual offenses against another person.

**Sexual assault** refers to an assault of a sexual nature. We define *assault* in detail later in this chapter (Module 3). For now, it is important to know, as we compare rape and sexual assault, that the former is a subtype of the latter. It is possible for a sexual assault to occur in the absence of intercourse. Inappropriate touching, forced kissing, indecent exposure, and a variety of other acts may constitute sexual assault. Definitions vary by jurisdiction. Because rape gets most of the attention, we limit our discussion primarily to it.

The term *sexual assault* is a bit of a misnomer. An assault does not require physical contact (see Module 3 for more details), but sexual assault is usually always likened with some form of physical contact. This is another reason why we limit our attention primarily to rape, as reconciling the meaning of *sexual assault* with a non-sexual assault can be rather difficult. Just know that some statutes use *sexual assault* to refer to a number of inappropriate actions of a sexual nature. Rape may be folded into a jurisdiction's sexual assault statute. It may also be a stand-alone offense.

# Elements of Rape

In this section we consider the elements of rape. The *mens rea* of rape is rather straightforward, as it is a general intent offense. The *actus reus* of rape can be a bit more complicated.

## The *Mens Rea* of Rape

Recall from Chapter 3 that a general intent crime is one that contains no specific *mens rea* component. In most jurisdictions, rape is a general intent offense. This means that the defendant need not possess an intention that the rape is nonconsensual.[6] The act only need *be* nonconsensual, irrespective of what the offender was thinking.

---

[3]*Coker v. Georgia*, 433 U.S. 584 (1977).
[4]*Kennedy v. Louisiana*, 554 U.S. 407 (2008).
[5]See, e.g., Mich. Comp. Laws Section 750.520b (2008), authorizing life imprisonment for rapists.
[6]See, e.g., *Commonwealth v. Grant*, 464 N.E.2d 33 (Mass. 1984), p. 36.

On the other hand, if the defendant reasonably believed that the victim consented, then he (we will use *he* most of the time for consistency, realizing of course that rape is largely gender neutral these days) cannot be guilty of rape. As one court put it, "the State must demonstrate either that [the] defendant did not actually believe that affirmative permission had been freely-given or that such a belief was unreasonable under all of the circumstances."[7] Not every jurisdiction takes this approach, however. For example, in Pennsylvania, the defendant's reasonable mistake as to the victim's lack of consent is not a defense to the crime of rape:

> The charge requested by the defendant [to inform jurors he believed the victim consented to his sexual advances] is not now and has never been the law of Pennsylvania. The crux of the offense of rape is force and lack of victim's consent. When one individual uses force or the threat thereof to have sexual relations with a person not his spouse and without the person's consent he has committed the crime of rape. If the element of the defendant's belief as to the victim's state of mind is to be established as a defense to the crime of rape, then it should be done by our legislature which has the power to define crimes and offenses. We refuse to create such a defense.[8]

This is a controversial decision—and it is not isolated. Other courts have taken a similar approach.[9] This begs some difficult questions: Is a defendant who mistakenly concludes that the victim consented to intercourse morally blameworthy? If not, should he then be found guilty of rape? As Joshua Dressler has observed, "The effect of dispensing with the reasonable-mistake-of-fact doctrine is, effectively, to convert rape, a felony carrying very severe penalties, into a strict liability offense."[10]

Even states that recognize a defendant can reasonably believe a victim consented are nervous about instructing jurors of the possibility. In California, this "reasonable mistake" instruction will not be given to jurors unless there is "substantial evidence of equivocal conduct [on the victim's part] that would have led a defendant to reasonably and in good faith believe consent existed where it did not."[11]

The Model Penal Code treats rape (in its section, Sex Offenses) as a specific intent offense, and since some state criminal codes emulate it, we cannot say that rape is *always* a general intent offense. Rape, according to the Model Penal Code, occurs when a male, acting purposely, knowingly, or recklessly, has sexual intercourse with a female under one or more of the following circumstances:

- the female is less than 10 years old
- the female is unconscious
- he compels the female to submit by force or threat of force (to her or others)
- he uses drugs or intoxicants such that the victim's ability to control her actions is compromised.[12]

---

[7]*State in the Interest of M.T.S.*, 609 A.2d 1266 (N.J. 1992), p. 1279.

[8]*Commonwealth v. Williams*, 439 A.2d 765 (Pa. Super. Ct. 1980), p. 769.

[9]See, e.g., *Commonwealth v. Ascolillo*, 541 N.E.2d 570 (Mass. 1989), p. 575; *Clifton v. Commonwealth*, 468 S.E.2d 155 (Va. Ct. App. 1996), p. 158.

[10]In the Interest of M.T.S., 609 A.2D 1266 (N.J. 1992), p. 444.

[11]*People v. Williams*, 841 P.2d 961 (Cal. 1992), p. 966.

[12]Model Penal Code, Section 213.1(1).

Note that not only does the Model Penal Code regard rape as a specific intent offense, but the crime is also not gender neutral. Perhaps more interesting still, the Code does not define as rape nonconsensual intercourse between a husband and wife who live together. Why the apparently antiquated approach to rape? The Model Penal Code was drafted in the 1950s, then adopted by the American Law Institute in 1962, well before the feminist movement and the changes it imposed on rape statutes around the country. Critics of the Model Penal Code's rape definition claim Section 213 "should be pulled and replaced."[13]

## The *Actus Reus* of Rape

The *actus reus* of rape varies somewhat, depending on whether the rape occurs in one or more of the following situations:

1. Force is used or threatened.
2. Deception is used.
3. The victim is asleep or unconscious.
4. The victim cannot give consent (e.g., is under the influence of drugs or is under age, as in the case of statutory rape).

Of these situations, forcible rape is most conventional. As such, we will devote most of our attention to it.

**Forcible Rape.**    What exactly is *forcible rape*? In general, it is rape that occurs when (1) the victim does not consent and (2) the sexual intercourse is secured by force or the threat of force. Both of these elements can be rather difficult to prove. What's more, there is a lack of agreement as to what each means. Let us begin with consent, then shift gears to force.

How is the determination made that a victim does not consent to intercourse? A verbal "no" may suffice, but for various reasons the victim may not externalize her preferences. For example, she may not want intercourse and yet fail to say as much. Should a defendant accused of rape in such a situation be guilty of the crime? Complicating the matter further is the fact that consent can be given and then withdrawn (or vice versa). What if the apparent victim consents initially and then withdraws consent once intercourse is underway? Unfortunately, there are no easy answers to questions like these[14]—and rape statutes rarely offer much clarification.

*Consent* is widely regarded as a self-evident term, but it may not be. Some courts have offered clarification by putting consent in terms of "affirmative and freely-given *permission* of the victim to the specific act of penetration [emphasis added],"[15] but even this definition is imperfect. What exactly constitutes permission? Often juries are left to decide whether consent was given, weighing the cases and testimony presented by both prosecution and defense.

---

[13]D. W. Denno, "Why the Model Penal Code's Sexual Offense Provisions Should Be Pulled and Replaced," *Ohio State Journal of Criminal Law*, Vol. 1 (2003), pp. 207–218.

[14]See, e.g., *People v. John Z.*, 60 P.3d 183 (Cal. 2003); *State v. Siering*, 644 A.2d 958 (Conn. App. 1994).

[15]*State in the Interest of M.T.S.*, 609 A.2d 1266 (N.J. 1992), p. 1277.

As for the force dimension to rape, a little historical overview is necessary. Most people recognize force (or the threat thereof) when they see it. Yet force or threatened force were not always enough, even in the absence of consent, for a prosecutor to secure a rape conviction. At common law, the victim must also have *resisted*. Interestingly, this resistance requirement has carried forward into recent history. Even today, some courts require a lack of consent, force by the perpetrator, and resistance on the victim's part.

For example, in a 1962 Tennessee case, the state's supreme court required that the victim resist "the attack in every way possible and continue such resistance until she [is] overcome by force, [is] insensible through fright, or cease[s] resistance from exhaustion, fear of death or great bodily harm."[16] Some years later, in *Rusk* v. *State*,[17] a Maryland appeals court was confronted with the question of whether a man's rape conviction should be upheld after the victim said, once he put his hands lightly around her throat, "If I do what you want, will you let me go without killing me?" The court concluded that no rape occurred because the victim failed to resist, although it later reversed the decision, holding that the jury should have made that determination: the "reasonableness of [the victim's] apprehension of fear [and, thus, her justification for not physically resisting] was plainly a question of fact for the jury to determine."[18]

In another case, *State* v. *Alston*,[19] a woman in an abusive relationship would sometimes have sex with her partner "just to accommodate" his demands. On such occasions she "would stand still and remain entirely passive while [he] undressed her and had intercourse with her." The man was eventually convicted of forcible rape after the woman said, clearly, that she did not want to have sex with him. Even so, the appellate court overturned his conviction, reasoning that there was insufficient evidence that he "used force or threats to overcome the will of the victim to resist the sexual intercourse."[20]

Much the same decision was reached in yet another case, this one involving a college student who was convicted of raping another student in her dorm room.[21] Although she said "no" several times, she did not resist after the male student locked the door, pushed her onto a bed, straddled her, and then had intercourse. The state supreme court affirmed a lower court's decision to overturn the conviction, pointing out that although consent was lacking, the victim's "testimony [was] devoid of any statement which clearly or adequately describes the use of force or the threat of force against her."[22] This decision was reach in 1992.

In recent years, courts, legislatures, and critics of traditional conceptions of rape have come to realize that the common law resistance requirement is unreasonable. Some rape victims become paralyzed with fear and thus do not physically resist. Should their rapists never be convicted? Of course not. And even if a victim resists,

---

[16]*King* v. *State*, 357 S.W.2d 42 (Tenn. 1962), p. 45.

[17]*Rusk* v. *State*, 406 A.2d 624 (Md. Ct. Spec. App. 1979), reversed, 424 A.2d 720 (Md. 1981).

[18]Ibid.

[19]*State* v. *Alston*, 312 S.E.2d 470 (N.C. 1984).

[20]Ibid.

[21]*Commonwealth* v. *Berkowitz*, 609 A.2d 1338 (Pa. Super. Ct. 1992), aff'd, 641 A.2d 1161 (Pa. 1994).

[22]Ibid., 641 A.2d, p. 1164 (Pa. 1994).

doing so can be rather dangerous. From a self-protection standpoint, there may be a compelling reason *not* to resist. In light of these realizations, a number of states have amended their rape statutes. Others have largely abandoned the resistance requirement through court decisions.

Courts have also reconceptualized force itself. Once regarded as a mostly violent act, one that causes physical harm, force is now viewed by some courts in more relaxed terms. For example, the California Supreme Court has stated that there is nothing "in the common usage definitions of the term 'force,' or in the express statutory language . . . that suggests force . . . actually means force '*substantially* different from or *substantially* greater than' the physical force normally inherent in an act of consensual sexual intercourse."[23] Another court put it this way:

> [T]he law of rape primarily guards the integrity of a woman's will and the privacy of her sexuality from an act of intercourse undertaken without her consent. Because the fundamental wrong is the violation of a woman's will and sexuality, the law of rape does not require that "force" cause physical harm. Rather, . . . 'force' plays merely a supporting evidentiary role, as necessary only to insure an act of intercourse has been undertaken against a victim's will.[24]

To summarize the *actus reus* forcible rape, then, the key *modern* ingredients are (1) a lack of consent on the victim's part and (2) sexual penetration. There is no requirement that injury result. Increasingly, there is no requirement that the victim resist in any manner (physical or verbal). Of course, there are some exceptions. And gray areas remain. For example, a key unresolved question is, "What level of consent, other than an express and verbally uttered 'yes,' suffices?"

See the accompanying Court Decision for more on consent. In it we examine the case of *People* v. *Ireland*, where the defendant is charged with raping prostitutes who initially consented to sexual intercourse for money.

## COURT DECISION

### *People* v. *Ireland*
### 114 Cal.Rptr.3d 915 (Cal. App. 2010)

**Background:** Anthony Ireland was convicted in Superior Court, Fresno County of four counts of forcible rape. Ireland was sentenced to 100 years in state prison, with four consecutive sentences of 25-years-to-life. Defendant appealed and the California Court of Appeals affirmed.

\*\*\*Facts

Each of appellant's four convictions of forcible rape involved a different victim but a similar scenario.

**Count 1: V.B.** In late October of 2007, V.B. was working as a prostitute on Motel Drive when appellant, in a four-door burgundy car, approached and asked her for a "date," which she described as an agreement to have sex for an agreed-upon amount of money. The two agreed on a price of $40. . . . They parked in a driveway near railroad tracks.

---

[23]*People* v. *Griffin*, 94 P.2d 1089 (Cal. 2004), p. 1094.
[24]*People* v. *Cicero*, 157 Cal. App. 3d (Ct. App. 1984), p. 475.

Appellant told V.B. to get into the back seat of the car, which she did. When appellant entered the back seat, V.B. felt a metal knife against her neck. V.B. began to cry and begged appellant "please don't hurt me." V.B. testified she was afraid and did not want to die. Appellant told her to be quiet and that he would not hurt her if she cooperated. V.B. was afraid that, if she resisted, appellant would cut or stab her.

Appellant then had vaginal intercourse with V.B., while holding the knife to her throat. V.B. described the knife as a big butcher knife with a seven- to nine-inch blade and a wooden handle. . . . V.B. had never met appellant prior to the incident. She did not consent to the sexual act as it happened, and she did not agree to the use of the knife when she got into the car. V.B. did not report the incident to the police at first, because she was a prostitute.

**Count 2: J.W.** In late September or early October of 2007, J.W. was working as a prostitute when appellant, in a four-door burgundy car, pulled up next to her and asked for a "date.". . . The two agreed to have sex in the car, so J.W. climbed into the back seat. . . . When he opened the back door, J.W. asked him for her money. Appellant said, "oh, oh, yeah," reached toward the waist of his pants, and pulled out a large knife with a 10-inch blade.

Appellant got into the back seat and on top of J.W. and held the knife to the side of her neck. When J.W. asked appellant what he was doing, he told her to "shut up." J.W. felt that appellant had an erection and asked him to put on a condom. He told her to put it on him. J.W. was afraid appellant might "slice [her] neck off." She asked appellant not to hurt her. She cooperated because she was fearful she might die.

Appellant held the knife to J.W.'s throat the entire time. She was very frightened and asked appellant to remove the knife from her neck. But appellant said "no" because "'you might scream.'" He told her not to scream or make any sudden movements or he would use the knife. J.W. did not scream, because she was afraid appellant might stab her in the neck.

Appellant had sex with her. After he ejaculated, he got out of the car and threw the condom on the ground. He did not pay her. J.W. never agreed to have sexual intercourse with appellant while he held a knife to her throat.

[Victim 3, A.H., and Victim 4, C.S. who was only 15-years old, had sexual intercourse under similar factual circumstances as the first two counts].

***Discussion

**1. Sufficiency of the Evidence.** Appellant argues there is insufficient evidence to convict him of any of the forcible rapes. He specifically contends that each woman consented to engage in sex acts in return for money and, although each woman objected to the use of the knife, the use of that knife did not automatically terminate the consent. He claims there was insufficient evidence to establish that each woman withdrew her consent and communicated that withdrawal of consent to appellant. We disagree.

***Lack of consent is an element of the crime of rape. Consent is defined in section 261.6 as "positive cooperation in act or attitude pursuant to an exercise of free will. The person must act freely and voluntarily and have knowledge of the nature of the act or transaction involved." CALCRIM No. 1000, as given here, instructed that "[t]o consent, a woman must act freely and voluntarily and know the nature of the act."

"Actual consent must be distinguished from submission. [A] victim's decision to submit to an attacker's sexual demands out of fear of bodily injury is not consent because the decision is not freely and voluntarily made (§ 261.6). A selection by the victim of the lesser of two evils—rape versus the violence threatened by the attacker if the victim resists—is hardly an exercise of free will." (*People* v. *Giardino* (2000) 82 Cal.App.4th 454, 460, fn. 3).

Where the woman's lack of consent was uncommunicated and could not reasonably be detected, however, the accused may not be guilty of rape. It is a defense that the accused reasonably and in good faith believed the woman engaged in the act consensually.

***Appellant's argument is that each victim gave her consent to the sex act that was committed, that his use of the knife during the act did not automatically negate that consent, and that there was insufficient evidence that any of the victims communicated a withdrawal of consent to him. Respondent [State of California], on the other hand, contends the determinative question is not whether the victims communicated a withdrawal of consent. Instead, according to respondent, appellant's use of the knife, along with his express or implied threat to harm his victims if they did not cooperate, did automatically negate their previously given consent.

We agree with respondent's analysis. There is no doubt that, at the beginning of each encounter, each victim freely consented to intercourse. But as to each of the victims, appellant communicated the express or implied threat that, if they did not continue to cooperate even after he produced the knife and held it to their throats, he would do them harm. As to the victim V.B., the testimony was that appellant told her "just to cooperate" and she "won't get hurt." When the victim J.W. asked appellant what he was doing with the knife, he told her to "'shut up.'" She did, because she was afraid he would otherwise "slice [her] neck off." He told her not to scream or make any sudden movements and he would not use the knife. When the victim A.H. reacted to appellant putting the knife to her throat by saying "no," appellant responded by instructing her to put a condom on his penis, remove her pants, and get on her knees. She complied because she thought he would otherwise kill her. To the victim C.S., appellant said "do what I say and you won't get hurt." She cooperated out of fear.

***The essence of consent is that it is given out of free will. That is why it can be withdrawn. While there exists a defense to rape based on the defendant's actual and reasonable belief that the victim does consent, we do not require that victims communicate their lack of consent. We certainly do not require that victims resist. Yet this is what appellant proposes here. At the time of the offenses, appellant told his victims to cooperate or be hurt. Now he contends they were required to express to him their lack of cooperation. That cannot be the law. When appellant used the knife and expressly or impliedly threatened his victims, and in the absence of any conduct by the victims indicating that they continued to consent, the previously given consent no longer existed, either in fact or in law.

\*\*\*From all of this evidence, it is clear that these victims did not continue to consent when appellant put the knife to their throats and that appellant knew they did not continue to consent. Thus, if they were required to communicate a withdrawal of consent, they adequately did so.

Substantial evidence supports each of the convictions of forcible rape, and we reject appellant's claim to the contrary.

## Case Analysis

1. The court acknowledges that all four victims initially consented to sexual intercourse with the defendant. Did they effectively withdraw their consent? Why or why not?

2. Should rape laws have a different standard for prostitutes? Why or why not?

3. The defendant was sentenced to 100 years in prison. Is that an appropriate sentence for his crime?

---

**Rape by Deception.**  At common law, rape by deception was not a crime. A man could use any method of trickery or deception to lure a woman into having intercourse. For example, in *Boro* v. *Superior Court*, a woman consented to sex after her doctor told her she contracted a dangerous disease that could only be cured through surgery or via intercourse with a male who was presumably injected with a serum.[25] She agreed to sex with the doctor. He was convicted of rape, but the conviction was overturned on appeal once it was clear that the "victim was aware of the nature of the act. . . ."[26] In contrast, as happened in an actual case, if a male doctor secures permission from his female patient to insert an instrument into her vagina while she is unconscious, he is guilty of rape if the instrument is his penis.[27]

**Rape When the Victim Is Asleep or Unconscious.**  What if, in a situation similar to the one we just presented, a male has intercourse with a female while she is asleep or unconscious? Typically, such an act will be considered rape, as consent is lacking. It is difficult to conceive of a situation in which a rape victim could have consented to sexual intercourse and then either fallen asleep or slipped into unconsciousness.

**Rape When the Victim Cannot Give Consent.**  A victim may be incompetent to give consent in one of three situations. First, she is drugged and therefore not thinking rationally. It does not matter whether such intoxication was self-induced or attributable to another individual. Second, consent generally cannot be given if the victim is mentally disabled. Finally, if the victim is too young, consent cannot be given. This is known as **statutory rape**. Some states use the term *rape of a child* in

**statutory rape** A strict liability crime in which the defendant has sexual intercourse with a minor under the age of consent.

---

[25]See, e.g., *Boro* v. *Superior Court*, 163 Cal. App. 3d 1224 (Ct. App. 1985).
[26]Ibid., p. 1224.
[27]*Pomeroy* v. *State*, 94 Ind. 96 (1883).

**Figure 9.1**
Rape

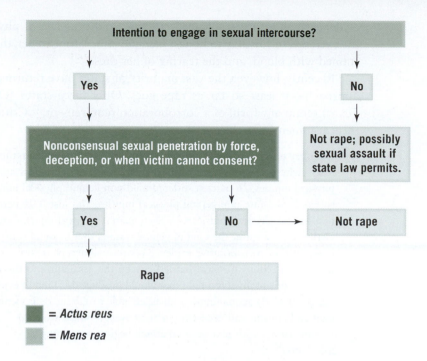

place of statutory rape. In either case, the crime occurs when the victim is legally incapable of giving consent. The age at which a victim can legally give consent varies by state.[28] Likewise, the age of the offender may enter into the equation, but whether it does varies by state as well. Finally, most states also require that the two individuals have a certain "gap" of years between their ages, usually around four years. So, for example, an 18-year-old who has sex with a 17-year-old is generally not guilty of statutory rape in most states because there is an insufficient age gap.

See Figure 9.1 for a summary of rape in flowchart format.

## Proving Rape

Recent developments in rape law have tipped the scales in favor of the prosecution. Rape prosecutions are not as difficult as they once were partly because of the disappearing corroboration requirement. Also, rape shield laws make it difficult for defense attorneys to call into question the victim's character.

### The Disappearing Corroboration Requirement

At common law, there was no requirement that a rape victim have her testimony corroborated with physical evidence. Indeed, any crime other than perjury could be proven without physical evidence.[29] This made it rather easy to convict criminal defendants. As time went on, states began to add corroboration requirements, partly out of fear that false charges would be made. Rape victims were required to show

---

[28]For an overview of statutory rape laws by state, see http://www.cga.ct.gov/2003/olrdata/jud/rpt/2003-r-0376.htm (accessed September 6, 2010).
[29]*United States* v. *Wiley*, 492 F.2d 547 (D.C. Cir. 1974).

evidence such as bruises, ripped clothing, and evidence of physical struggle—or, in the extreme, to "display to honest men the injury done to her, the blood and her dress stained with blood, and the tearing of her dress."[30]

Recently, however, the vast majority of states have returned to the common law approach—at least so far as rape goes. Only three states (Ohio, New York, and Texas) retain any form of a corroboration requirement.[31] Critics of this progression raise arguments like this:

> Contrary to popular belief. . . , non-genital, physical injury from rape is uncommon. . . . Sixty-eight percent of . . . admitted emergency room rape victims suffered no non-genital physical injuries, 26 percent suffered mild non-genital physical injuries, only 5 percent suffered moderate non-genital physical injuries, and just 0.02 percent suffered severe non-genital physical injuries. . . . Even genital physical injuries are rare as most rape victims do not suffer the kind of genital trauma that hospital staffs can detect. . . . The other type of corroborative evidence courts will accept is torn clothing or other evidence of a serious physical battle between the assailant and the victim. Most rapes, however, do not involve a fight that would produce this kind of evidence. . . . Most rapists, particularly acquaintance rapists, are able to subdue their victims with verbal coercion and pinning and need not resort to overt physical violence. . . . Some women also become frozen with fear once an attack begins, preventing physical resistance of their assailants.[32]

## Rape Shield Laws

Over the years, defense attorneys in rape prosecutions have raised a number of arguments. For example, they have argued in some instances that the victim consented to intercourse. They have also argued that the victim may have had prior consensual sexual relations with the accused, perhaps making the instant act consensual as well. And they have even gone so far as to argue that the victim was promiscuous, given to a lack of sexual discretion. While defense attorneys can and still do argue that consent existed, they are limited in the other two areas. Defense attorneys are now significantly limited in their abilities to attack the credibility of a suspected rape victim. Why? So-called **rape shield laws** have been enacted across the country.[33] They limit evidence about the victim's prior sexual history. In 1974, Michigan passed the first such law. It said,

**rape shield laws**
Statutes that restrict the admissibility of the victim's past sexual history at trial.

> Evidence of specific instances of the victim's sexual conduct, opinion evidence of the victim's sexual conduct, and reputation evidence of the victim's sexual conduct shall not be admitted . . . unless and only to the extent that the judge finds that the following proposed evidence is material to a fact at issue in the case and that its inflammatory or prejudicial nature does not outweigh its probative value: (a) Evidence of the victim's past sexual conduct with the actor, (b) Evidence of specific instances of sexual activity showing the source or origin of semen, pregnancy, or disease.[34]

---

[30]M. J. Anderson, "The Legacy of the Prompt Complaint Requirement, Corroboration Requirement, and Cautionary Instructions on Campus Sexual Assault," *Boston University Law Review*, Vol. 84 (2004), p. 947.
[31]See N.Y. Penal Law Section 130.16(2008); Tex. Crim. Proc. Ann. Section 38.07(a) (2007); Ohio Rev. Code Ann. 2907.06(B) (2004).
[32]Anderson, "The Legacy of the Prompt Complaint," pp. 978–979.
[33]For an overview of such laws, see http://www.ndaa.org/pdf/NCPCA%20Rape%20Shield%202011.pdf (accessed September 6, 2010).
[34]Mich. Comp. Laws Section 750.520j (2009).

Consider *People* v. *Wilhelm*, a case in which the defendant sought to introduce evidence that the victim (both were in a bar at the same time, although not together) exposed her breasts to two men seated at her table, allowing them to fondle her breast. The court did not allow the evidence to be presented, however, noting that "we fail to see how a woman's consensual sexual conduct with another in public indicates to third parties that the woman would engage in similar behavior with them."[35] It fell back on the rape shield statute. Critics of rape shield laws claim that they threaten the Sixth Amendment right to confrontation, which gives defendants an opportunity to confront and cross-examine their accusers and adverse who testify against them.

## YOUR DECISION

1. Julie and her girlfriends are excited to attend their first college party at a campus fraternity. Before they head out to the party, the girls decide to do a few "pregame" shots of vodka in their dorm room. When they arrive at the party, Julie also drinks several glasses of a fruity purple punch. Unbeknownst to Julie, the punch is made with 80-proof grain alcohol. Julie soon finds herself intoxicated and passes out in the bedroom of one of the fraternity brothers, Roger. Julie and Roger have an astronomy class together and have been flirting the first week of school. When Roger returns to his room at 2:00 A.M. and finds Julie in his bed, he assumes she is there to pursue a sexual relationship. Roger and Julie engage in sexual intercourse. Julie's memory of the event is very "fuzzy." She does not recall whether she said anything to Roger while they were having sex. Can Roger be charged with rape? Why or why not?

2. Jim and Brenda dated for approximately 12 months before they finally ended their tumultuous relationship. One evening 6 months into the relationship, Brenda alleges that Jim forced her to engage in sexual intercourse against her will. Brenda suffered some injuries, and Jim drove her to a local hospital for medical treatment. Brenda did not report the incident to the police at that time and in fact continued to date Jim for another 6 months. Brenda reported the incident only after the two ended their relationship. Jim claims Brenda is just "bitter" that he dumped her and is trying to ruin his reputation. Assuming what Brenda says is true, can Jim be charged with rape? Why or why not?

## Summary

- *Rape* is generally defined as the "taking of sexual intimacy with an unwilling person by force or without consent."

- Rape is usually intercourse; sexual assault is other sexual contact without consent. Rape is a subtype of sexual assault.

- Rape is a general intent offense, meaning that as long as the act is not consensual, *mens rea* has been satisfied.

---

[35] *People* v. *Wilhelm*, 476 N.W.2d 753 (Mich. Ct. App. 1991), p. 759.

- The *actus reus* of rape varies somewhat, depending on whether the rape occurs by force, deception, the victim is asleep/unconscious, or the victim cannot give consent.

- In general, forcible rape occurs when (1) the victim does not consent and (2) the sexual intercourse is secured by force or the threat of force.

- A rape victim may not be able to give consent either because she is not thinking rationally (e.g., from intoxication) or because she cannot legally give consent (called *statutory rape*).

- Recent developments in rape law have tipped the scales in favor of the prosecution.

- Most states have abandoned the requirement that rape victims corroborate their allegations with physical evidence.

- Defense attorneys are now significantly limited in their abilities to attack the credibility of a suspected rape victim because of states' enactment of so-called rape shield laws.

## MODULE 9.2 ROBBERY

### Learning Objectives
- **Describe the crime of robbery.**
- **Distinguish armed robbery from other forms of robbery.**

**CORE CONCEPTS**  Like rape, robbery is a serious crime. The Federal Bureau of Investigation (FBI) classifies it as one of four serious crimes in the Uniform Crime Reports (the others are rape, homicide, and aggravated assault). Robbery is an assaultive offense, meaning that it involves threats and the potential for physical contact. It is also a crime of theft that occurs under circumstances in which the victim is in some way forced into submission.

## Elements of Robbery

There are six traditional elements of robbery:

1. The taking
2. and carrying away
3. of the personal property

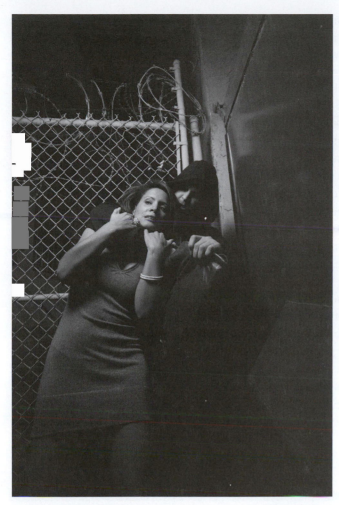

Robbery requires either the use of violence or putting the victim in fear.

© Felixcasio/Dreamstime.com

4. of another person

5. by violence or by putting the victim in fear

6. with intent to permanently deprive the owner of the property.[36]

Note that the first five parts of this definition constitute the *actus reus* of robbery; the last constitutes the *mens rea*. Not all states treat robbery as a specific intent offense, however. Let us look at each in more detail.

## The *Actus Reus* of Robbery

The "taking" element of robbery is fairly self-explanatory. Early on, however, the "taking" element of robbery had to occur in a trespassory fashion, meaning from the person or in the victim's presence. Some jurisdictions have realized that this can make it difficult to convict a person of robbery in some circumstances. Sue Titus Reid presents these scenarios in which robbery occurs, but without the trespassory element:

- A person, wishing to steal property from a farmhouse, encounters the owner in the field, knocks him unconscious, and proceeds to the house to steal.
- A person takes a victim at gunpoint and forces him to call his office and instruct an employee to remove money from the company safe and deliver it to a designated person.[37]

Note that were a trespassory taking required in either instance, a robbery would not have occurred because the crimes failed to occur in the victim's presence.

Or, as an alternative, consider this:

- . . . a bank teller receives a call from the defendant, who threatens to set off a bomb at the teller's home unless a large sum of money be delivered to a hidden location designated by the caller.[38]

Has a robbery occurred here? Again, were it not for abandoning the trespassory element of early robbery definitions, the answer would be "no."

---

[36]A. A. Moenssens, R. J. Bacigal, G. G. Ashdown, and V. E. Hench, *Criminal Law: Cases and Concepts,* 8th ed. (New York: Foundation Press, 2008), p. 756.

[37]S. T. Reid, *Criminal Law*, 8th ed. (New York: Oxford University Press, 2010), p. 177. See also NY CLS Penal, Article 160, Note (2009). From Commission Staff notes.

[38]A. A. Moenssens, R. J. Bacigal, G. G. Ashdown, and V. E. Hench, *Criminal Law: Cases and Concepts*, 8th ed. (New York: Foundation Press, 2008), p. 769.

Just as the "taking" component of robbery is fairly clear, so too is the "carrying away" part. For example, if Hank points a gun at Steve, demands that Steve hand over his wallet, and then waits patiently for police to arrive, Hank may not have committed robbery. Obviously no robber in his or her right mind would "stick around," but the point is that for robbery to formally occur, the offender must not only take the property, but also leave the scene.

Robbery is limited to *personal* property. In general, and exclusive of situations like the two we pointed out earlier, if the property sought is not in the **actual possession** or **constructive possession** of the victim and is taken, it is a crime of larceny, not robbery. Property is in a person's actual possession if he or she is holding it or it is attached to the victim in some fashion. Constructive possession means the victim has control over the property, usually because it is in close physical proximity to the victim.

While robbery is a crime against property, it is also a crime against a person—hence our decision to include it in this chapter. If there is not a person as victim, then again the crime will be larceny. For example, if Bill steals Ted's lawnmower while Ted is sleeping, he has not "robbed" Ted because Ted was not present or in any way confronted (e.g., hit and knocked unconscious) prior to the commission of the crime.

Finally, the fifth element of the *actus reus* of robbery is violence or putting the victim in fear. Obviously, since Ted was sleeping in our previous example, he was not robbed because he was not put in fear. At the other extreme, the offender who threatens a victim with a knife has arguably done enough to put the victim in fear such that the *actus reus* of robbery is satisfied.

See the accompanying Court Decision for more on the use of "force" requirement for robbery. In it we examine the case of *People* v. *Dreas*, where the defendant drugs his robbery victims.

**actual possession**
Property that is either held by the individual or attached to that individual in some fashion.

**constructive possession**
The individual has control over the property but is not physically touching it.

## COURT DECISION

*People* v. *Dreas*
153 Cal.App.3d 623 (1984)

**Background:** Saban Dreas was convicted in the Superior Court, San Francisco County of robbery, administering drugs with intent to commit a felony, burglary and two counts of auto theft. Dreas was sentenced to 10 years and 8 months in prison and appealed. The California Court of Appeals affirmed.

CALDECOTT, Presiding Justice.

The principal issue presented on this appeal is whether the administering of drugs to overcome the victim's resistance can constitute the element of force within the meaning of Penal Code section 211.

> Section 211 provides that "Robbery is the felonious taking of personal property in the possession of another, from his person or immediate presence, and against his will, accomplished by means of force or fear."

Saban Dreas appeals from a judgment of conviction, following a jury trial, of three counts of robbery, three counts of administering drugs with intent to commit a felony (§ 222), three counts of burglary and two counts of auto theft.

The facts in each of the three instances are basically the same. Appellant would patronize a bar, strike up a conversation with the victim, a patron, and suggest that they go and have coffee. They would go to the victim's home, where appellant would surreptitiously insert Lorazepam, a hypnotic sedative and tranquilizer, into the victim's coffee. After the victim was rendered unconscious, appellant would take money, valuable items of personal property (in two incidents in excess of $25,000) and in two incidents the victim's automobile.

### I. The "Force" Element of the Robbery

As stated above, appellant was found guilty of three counts of robbery. These convictions were predicated on evidence showing that in each instance appellant used Lorazepam, a tranquilizer, dissolved in hot coffee in order to drug his victims. The drug rendered the victims unconscious, overcoming their resistance to the taking of various items of personal property from their homes or persons. Appellant contends that the evidence is insufficient to sustain the robbery convictions because the use of drugs does not constitute "means of force or fear" within the meaning of section 211. We disagree.

While the issue thus presented is one of first impression in California, the legal authorities and sister state cases unanimously underline that the administering of drugs to overcoming the victim's resistance does constitute force within the purview of section 211.

Thus, Professor Perkins addressing this issue in his treatise concluded that: "Just as battery may be committed by the administration of poison, so the force used to obtain property from a person against his will may be applied internally." (Perkins & Boyce, Criminal Law (3d ed. 1982) p. 348.) Other scholars have reached identical conclusions. LeFave and Scott write: "One may commit robbery by striking his victim with fist or weapon and then, having thus rendered the victim unconscious or dazed or unwilling to risk another blow, taking property away from him. One may also render one's victim helpless by more subtle means, as by administering intoxicating liquors or drugs in order to produce a state of unconsciousness or stupefaction; to act in this way is to use force for purposes of robbery." (LeFave & Scott, Criminal Law (1972) pp. 697–698).

A case in point is *State* v. *Snyder*. In *Snyder*, appellant administered chloralhydrate to one Cooper, who was in charge of a saloon. After Cooper became unconscious, appellant took money from the cash register. The Nevada Supreme Court held that the administering of the drug constituted so-called "constructive force" which was sufficient to sustain the robbery conviction. In his concurring opinion, Chief Justice McCarran explained the matter as follows: " 'Force' is the power or energy by which resistance is overcome. . . . When, to take the personal effects of another, a blow is struck with a bludgeon, thereby paralyzing the victim's power of resistance, the taking will constitute robbery. The same effect might be produced on the victim by the physical act of administering a deadly potion. In either case resistance is involuntarily overcome. Great physical strength might be required to accomplish the result in the first instance, while a mere turning of the hand might effect the consequence in the second; force, however, is present in both. The agency through which the force operates is immaterial. The result in either case is the overcoming of resistance without the voluntary co-operation of the subject whose resistance is repressed; this is the test." *State* v. *Snyder, supra,* 172 P. at pp. 366–367.

The principles set out above rest on sound logical foundation. A showing of "force or fear" is not (and cannot be) limited to external forces such as bludgeoning the victim or displaying a lethal weapon to overcome his will and resistance. A poison or intoxicant, although internally applied, may also serve as a potent means to achieve the same goal and may also render the felonious taking of personal property a taking against the will of the victim, thereby constituting robbery.

\*\*\*The judgment is affirmed.

## Case Analysis

1. What are the elements necessary to convict the defendant of robbery?
2. Do you think the defendant used "means of force or fear" as required by the criminal statute?
3. The California Court of Appeals noted that this was a case "of first impression in California." What is the court referring to?

## The *Mens Rea* of Robbery

In general, a robbery does not occur unless, along with the *actus reus* of the offense, the offender intends to permanently deprive the owner of the property. There are exceptions. For example, some statutes contain an implicit *mens rea* component. California defines robbery in this way:

> Robbery is the felonious taking of personal property in the possession of another, from his person or immediate presence, and against his will, accomplished by means of force or fear.[39]

The *felonious taking* language captures the *mens rea* of robbery in California. Usually *felonious taking* means the taking of property with intent to deprive.

Other states treat robbery as a general intent crime. In Kansas, robbery is simply "the taking of property from the person or presence of another by force or by threat of bodily harm to any person."[40] The norm, however, is to define robbery as a specific intent offense. But whether the required intent is (a) to permanently deprive the owner of the property or (b) to force a victim to give up property depends on the law. For example, New York's statute reads, in part,

> Robbery is forcible stealing. A person forcibly steals property and commits robbery when, in the course of committing a larceny, he uses or threatens the immediate use of physical force upon another person for the *purpose* of: (1) Preventing or overcoming resistance to the taking of the property or to the retention thereof immediately

---

[39]California Penal Code, Section 211 (2010).
[40]Kan. Stat. Ann. 21-3426 (2010); also see *State* v. *Thompson*, 558 P.2d 1079 (Kan. 1976).

**Figure 9.2**
Robbery

= *Actus reus*

= *Mens rea*

after the taking; or (2) Compelling the owner of such property or another person to deliver up the property or to engage in other conduct which aids in the commission of the larceny (emphasis added).[41]

Note that the *mens rea* here is couched in terms of "purpose" and that there is no requirement imposed that the offender intend to permanently deprive.

Wisconsin's robbery statute emphasizes not just intent to commit the crime, but also the intent to steal:

Whoever, with *intent to steal*, takes property from the person or presence of the owner by either of the following means is guilty of [robbery]: (a) By using force against the person of the owner with *intent* thereby to overcome his physical resistance or physical power of resistance to the taking or carrying away of property; or (b) By threatening the imminent use of force against the person of the owner or of another who is present with *intent* thereby to compel the owner to acquiesce in the taking or carrying away of property (emphasis added).[42]

See Figure 9.2 for a summary of robbery. Since there is no "one best" definition for the *mens rea* of robbery, we use the most common—namely, the intention to permanently deprive the owner of the property.

## Armed Robbery

**armed robbery**
The defendant is in possession of a weapon while committing the crime of robbery.

A robber who uses violence and/or puts the victim in fear need not use a weapon to do so. Indeed, many robbery statutes do not reference weapons. Some, however, do and thus define a more serious offense of **armed robbery**. In Illinois, for example,

[41]N.Y. Penal Law 160.00 (2010)
[42]Wis. Stat. Ann. 943.32 (2010).

armed robbery requires that the offense be committed "while armed with a dangerous weapon."[43] Note the term *while*. It is not necessary that the weapon actually be *used* during commission of the offense.[44]

What qualifies as a deadly weapon? There are no easy answers. For example, what if a robbery suspect was carrying an unloaded pistol? Does doing so elevate the crime from robbery to armed robbery? According to a New York appeals court, the answer is "yes," partly because even an unloaded pistol can be used to bludgeon someone.[45] What about a toy gun? At least one court has decided that a toy gun, even one with a blocked barrel, can sustain a charge of robbery with a firearm.[46] Other jurisdictions have taken exception, especially if the gun in question is made out of lightweight plastic and could not be used as a bludgeon. To help other courts draw the line between deadly and nondeadly weapons, the Illinois Supreme Court adopted this fact-oriented test:

> [M]any objects, including guns, can be dangerous and cause serious injury, even when used in a fashion for which they were not intended. Most, if not all, unloaded real guns and many toy guns, because of their size and weight, could be used in deadly fashion as bludgeons. Since the robbery victim could be quite badly hurt or even killed by such weapons if used in that fashion, it seems to us they can properly be classified as dangerous weapons although they were not in fact used in that manner during the commission of the particular offense. It suffices that the potential for such use is present; the victim need not provoke its actual use in such manner.[47]

Some jurisdictions treat robbery with a firearm as two separate offenses, meaning that a person can be convicted of (a) robbery and (b) use of a firearm in the commission of a robbery. The latter crime is defined thusly:

> It shall be unlawful for any person to use or attempt to use any pistol, shotgun, rifle, or other firearm or display such weapon in a threatening manner while committing or attempting to commit murder, rape, forcible sodomy, inanimate or animate object sexual penetration . . . *robbery*, carjacking, burglary, malicious wounding . . ., or abduction.[48]

**YOUR DECISION**

1. Josh is an excellent pickpocket and manages to make a living lifting wallets from executives on Wall Street. Josh is generally so good that his victims do not even realize their wallets are being stolen right out of their back pockets. One afternoon, however, Josh's luck runs out. He accidentally trips and bumps into one his victims while trying to get the wallet. The victim realizes what is happening, knocks Josh to the ground, and calls the police. Can Josh be charged with robbery? Why or why not? Can Josh also be charged with robbery for the other jobs he completed where the victims were unaware of the encounter?

2. Joe and Janine are walking home from dinner and a movie one evening when Lucas suddenly pops out from behind a dumpster, points a gun at the couple, and

---

[43]Ill. Rev. Stats., Ch. 38, Section 18-2 (2010).
[44]See, e.g., *Commonwealth* v. *Blackburn*, 237 N.E.2d 35 (1968).
[45]*People* v. *Roden*, 235 N.E.2d 776 (1968).
[46]*Johnson* v. *Commonwealth*, 163 S.E.2d 570 (1968).
[47]*People* v. *Skelton*, 414 N.E.2d 455 (1980), p. 458.
[48]Virginia Code Section 18.2-53.1 (2004).

demands they turn over all of their belongings. Joe tries to wrestle away the gun, but both Joe and Janine are fatally wounded. Only after the couple dies from their gunshot wounds does Lucas take their money and jewelry. In addition to criminal homicide, can Lucas be charged with robbery? Why or why not? What if Lucas did not return until the next day to recover the belongings from the bodies? Would that be considered robbery?

## Summary

* Robbery consists of (1) the taking (2) and carrying away (3) of the personal property (4) of another person (5) by violence or by putting the victim in fear (6) with intent to permanently deprive the owner of the property.

* At common law, the "taking" element of robbery must have been trespassory.

* Robbery is limited to *personal* property. If the property sought is not in the actual possession or constructive possession of the victim and is taken, it is a crime of larceny, not robbery.

* In general, a robbery does not occur unless, along with the *actus reus* of the offense, the offender intends to permanently deprive the owner of the property. There are exceptions.

* A robber who uses violence and/or puts the victim in fear need not use a weapon to do so.

* In addition to criminalizing robbery, some states also define a more serious offense of armed robbery.

* Armed robbery occurs when the offender commits robbery while armed with a dangerous weapon.

---

MODULE

# 9.3   ASSAULT AND BATTERY

### Learning Objectives
* **Describe the crime of assault.**
* **Describe the crime of battery.**

**CORE CONCEPTS**

**assault** The threat of bodily harm to another person without physical contact.

*Assault* and *battery* are among the most misused terms in criminal law. The mistake people typically make is to describe **assault** in terms of physical contact. Battery involves contact; assault falls just short of physical contact. We begin with battery, as it is difficult to understand assault without first understanding the meaning of battery.

# Battery

**battery** Unlawful offensive touching of another without consent.

**Battery** is unlawful touching, typically with injury. It occurs when one person makes violent physical contact with another person who does not consent to the contact. Not every statute requires injury, however. In addition, some courts have expanded the definition of *battery* and include actions that fall short of even physical contact. For example, if the law permits, it could be considered battery to spit in another person's face.[49]

## Elements of Battery

Criminal statutes do not always spell out the *mens rea* of battery. For example, California defines the crime as nothing more than "willful and unlawful use of force or violence upon another."[50] In Florida, battery occurs when a person "actually and intentionally touches or strikes another person against the will of the other; or intentionally causes bodily harm to another person."[51] States that distinguish between *levels* of intent (e.g., negligence vs. recklessness), for battery usually do so if they grade the offense by seriousness (e.g., first degree, second degree; felony, misdemeanor).

As for *actus reus*, as we mentioned earlier, battery is commonly associated with physical injury. This means that in some states battery does not occur unless there is physical injury. Yet in other states, such Florida, all that is required is a "touch" or a "strike." Likewise, the California statute we quoted in the previous paragraph also falls short of requiring physical injury. Battery is summarized in Figure 9.3.

**Figure 9.3**
Battery

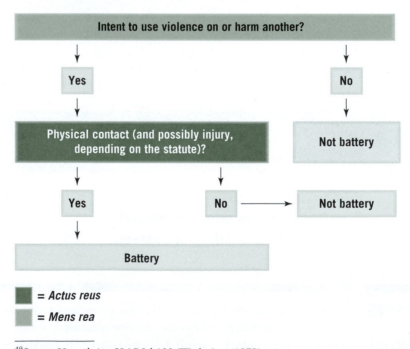

---

[49]*State* v. *Humphries*, 586 P.2d 130 (Wash. App. 1978).
[50]Cal. Penal Code Section 240 (2010).
[51]Fla. Stat. Section 784.03 (2010).

Many states go so far as to identify specific actions that are *not* considered battery. For example, Virginia law provides that various named school officials do not commit battery in any of the following instances while acting in their official capacities:

(i) incidental, minor or reasonable physical contact or other actions designed to maintain order and control; (ii) reasonable and necessary force to quell a disturbance or remove a student from the scene of a disturbance that threatens physical injury to persons or damage to property; (iii) reasonable and necessary force to prevent a student from inflicting physical harm on himself; (iv) reasonable and necessary force for self-defense or the defense of others; or (v) reasonable and necessary force to obtain possession of weapons or other dangerous objects or controlled substances or associated paraphernalia that are upon the person of the student or within his control.[52]

## Battery Classifications

It is relatively uncommon for states to maintain just one battery statute. Instead, the norm is to criminalize various types of battery, each with their own distinct elements. This accommodates the reality that there is no one "most common" type of battery, nor is there an ideal universal definition for the crime.

Some states define *battery* in terms of levels. Separate statutes may distinguish between, for example, simple battery and aggravated battery. To illustrate, aggravated battery occurs in Florida when the offender

[i]ntentionally or knowingly causes great bodily harm, permanent disability, or permanent disfigurement; . . . uses a deadly weapon; [or] . . . if the person who was the victim of the battery was pregnant at the time of the offense and the offender knew or should have known that the victim was pregnant.[53]

In contrast, simple battery may be conduct that falls short of aggravated battery. Or it may be noninjurious yet nonconsensual insulting or harmful contact.

Other states reserve separate battery statutes for particular types of conduct, ranging from sexual battery to elder abuse. Florida is a state that does this—and also distinguishes between levels of battery (felony and aggravated). It reserves separate battery statutes for the following types of conduct, and several others:

- Domestic battery by strangulation
- Battery of law enforcement officers, firefighters, emergency medical care providers, public transit employees or agents, or other specified officers
- Battery on sexually violent predator detention or commitment facility staff
- Battery on a juvenile probation officer
- Battery on health services personnel
- Battery on persons 65 years of age or older
- Battery on code inspectors
- Child battery.[54]

---

[52]V.A. Code Section 18.2-57(F) (2010).
[53]Fla. Stat. Section 784.045 (2010).
[54]Fla. Stat. Section 784 (2010).

## Battery without Assault

Battery is usually regarded as a consummated assault. Yet there is no ironclad requirement that a battery be preceded by an assault.[55] And while we have not yet formally defined assault, suffice it to say for now that assault requires a measure of anticipation on the victim's part. So, if an irate student clubs an unsuspecting professor in the head from behind while she is writing on the whiteboard, the student has committed a battery without assault. Alternatively, assume Evan is at a fraternity party and thinks it would be neat to drop the glass "punch" bowl out a second-story window, above the sidewalk to the front door, just to hear it smash on the ground. If he drops the bowl and it hits a visitor in the head, he has committed battery with no assault. Whether this would happen is up for debate, but it illustrates a key point: assault and battery are not necessarily tied together, nor are they one in the same offense.

# Assault

**threatened battery assault** A type of assault in which the criminal intentionally places another person in fear of an imminent battery.

**attempted battery assault** A type of assault in which the criminal attempts to commit the crime of battery but is unsuccessful.

Under common law, there were two kinds of assault: **threatened battery assault** and **attempted battery assault**. Threatened battery assault occurred when one person intentionally placed another person in anticipation of imminent battery.[56] Attempted battery assault occurred when one person attempted to commit the crime of battery with the intent to injure another. It is noteworthy that in an attempted battery assault, the victim did not need to be aware of the attempted battery. An attempted battery assault focused exclusively on the overt actions of the defendant.

Some states do not distinguish these two types of assault. Others do not distinguish between assault and battery, either. Washington is one such state. It lumps all actions that would be considered assault and/or battery into a single category of assaults.[57] This likely contributes to some of the confusion concerning the use of the terms *assault* and *battery*.

## Elements of Assault

The *mens rea* of threatened battery assault is the intention to cause another person to fear imminent battery. The *actus reus* is translating intent into action. For example, if one person aggressively lunges in the direction of another with the intention of scaring him or her, but stops short of physical contact, a threatened battery assault has occurred—so long as the victim is aware of the threat or reasonably fears imminent battery. In contrast, an attempted battery assault does not require that the victim be aware of the threat. Instead, the defendant must have the criminal intent to commit battery. For example, if the same victim was facing away from the offender and did not know about the aggressive lunge, then the result is attempted battery assault.

---

[55]A. Reed, "Omission to Act Can Amount to an Assault or Battery," *Journal of Criminal Law*, Vol. 68 (2004), pp. 459–462.
[56]See, e.g., *Carter* v. *Commonwealth*, 594 S.E.2d 284 (Va. Ct. App. 2004), p. 288.
[57]See Rev. Code Wash. Chapter 9A.36 (2010).

**Figure 9.4**
Assault

= *Actus reus*

= *Mens rea*

Prosecutions for assault (without battery) are relatively rare because of the absence of contact or injury. Why? The victimization is merely psychological. When an assault is carried through to completion and then results in battery, a prosecution is more likely because of the potential for physical injury. Assault is summarized in Figure 9.4.

See the accompanying Court Decision for more on using a deadly weapon in the commission of an assault and battery. In it we examine the case of *Commonwealth* v. *Fettes*, where the Appeals Court of Massachusetts examines whether a pit bull terrier can be a deadly weapon.

**COURT DECISION**

*Commonwealth* v. *Fettes*
835 N.E.2d 639 (Mass. App. 2005)

**Background:** Christopher Fettes was convicted of assault and battery by means of a dangerous weapon. He appealed and the Appeals Court of Massachusetts affirmed.

Convicted of assault and battery by means of a dangerous weapon, an eight month old pit bull terrier, on a person sixty years or older, the defendant argues that it was error to deny his motion for a required finding of not guilty made at the close of the Commonwealth's case and renewed at the close of all the evidence. We affirm the judgment.

**1. The Commonwealth's evidence.** We relate the evidence in the light most favorable to the Commonwealth. On the day of the incident, the sixty-six year old victim went to an apartment building that she owned. Her purpose was to collect rents due her. There she saw a man, later identified from an array of photographs as the defendant (identification was not a live issue at trial), descending an exterior staircase of the building. The defendant was accompanied by a dog on a leash that was wrapped around his hand "very tightly by his side." As the victim and the defendant stood several feet apart from each other, she asked him whether he resided in the building. The defendant responded that he did not. At this time, the dog was standing by the defendant and was calm and well-behaved. The victim, admittedly "upset," then accused the defendant of allowing the dog to leave his droppings on the flat roof and yard of her building. The defendant then became agitated and denied that his dog was responsible for the alleged droppings.

As the victim then began to walk away from the defendant and the dog, she heard him speak a "short phrase" to the dog "[i]n a stern voice," and saw him partially release or unravel the leash while still holding it. As the defendant did so, the dog immediately lunged at the victim and bit her hand. The victim and the defendant, with his dog in tow, then fled the scene. The victim received medical attention (stitches, antibiotics, and tetanus and rabies shots) for the wound that caused her nerve damage.

**2. Discussion.** A dog can be a dangerous weapon. "A dangerous weapon is 'any instrument or instrumentality so constructed or so used as to be likely to produce death or great bodily harm.' *Commonwealth v. Farrell*, 322 Mass. 606, 614-615 (1948). There can be little doubt that a dog . . . used for the purpose of intimidation or attack falls within this definition." *Commonwealth v. Tarrant*, 2 Mass.App.Ct. 483, 486 (1974). The defendant does not argue to the contrary. Rather, he claims that he was entitled to a required finding of not guilty because the Commonwealth failed to show that the dog had been trained to attack, what the "stern words" used by the defendant were, or that the dog had been manipulated by the defendant to attack the victim. In short, he argues that the Commonwealth failed to show that the dog did not act of its own volition or that its actions were brought about through his reckless conduct.

We conclude that the Commonwealth's evidence was sufficient to allow the jury reasonably to infer that once the conversation between the defendant and the victim turned from casual to confrontational, the defendant either deliberately provoked the dog to attack the victim, or acted recklessly when he intentionally released his grip on the leash. The evidence presented by the defendant neither weakened nor otherwise diminished the Commonwealth's case. Rather, the evidence he presented, that the dog was not violent, that he slackened his grip on the dog's leash for the sole purpose of giving his dog enough slack to walk, and that he arranged to have an intermediary deliver a rabies certificate to the hospital where the victim was being treated, went to matters to be considered by the jury in resolving questions of fact.

*Judgment affirmed.*

## Case Analysis

1. How is the term *dangerous weapon* defined by the court? Do you agree that a dog can be considered a dangerous weapon?

2. In this case, the dog is a pit bull terrier. Should the breed of dog be relevant in determining if it is a dangerous weapon? For example, can a five-pound Chihuahua also be considered a dangerous weapon?

## Levels of Assault

Assaults are often lumped into two categories: simple and aggravated. For example, New Jersey defines simple assault as follows:

> A person commits a simple assault if he/she attempts to cause or purposely, knowingly or recklessly causes bodily injury to another.[58]

Note that this definition includes both the traditional definition of *assault* (an incomplete battery) and *battery*, or physical contact. Vermont takes a similar approach, defining simple assault in these terms:

> a. A person is guilty of simple assault if he or she:
>   1. attempts to cause or purposely, knowingly or recklessly causes bodily injury to another; or
>   2. negligently causes bodily injury to another with a deadly weapon; or
>   3. attempts by physical menace to put another in fear of imminent serious bodily injury.[59]

Note that (1) contains the traditional definition of *assault* and that (2) contains actual physical contact.

If the victim suffers serious bodily injury, the crime is more likely *aggravated assault*. The crime is aggravated in the sense that the victim is seriously injured or because the circumstances surrounding the assault demand that it be treated more harshly than a simple assault. The District of Columbia defines *aggravated assault* in this way:

> a. A person commits the offense of aggravated assault if:
>   1. By any means, that person knowingly or purposely causes serious bodily injury to another person; or
>   2. Under circumstances manifesting extreme indifference to human life, that person intentionally or knowingly engages in conduct which creates a grave risk of serious bodily injury to another person, and thereby causes serious bodily injury.[60]

The Model Penal Code also identifies the crime of reckless assault, distinct from either simple or aggravated assault: "A person commits a misdemeanor if he recklessly engages in conduct which places or may place another person in danger of death or serious bodily injury."[61]

---

[58]N.J.S.A. 2C:12-1a(1) (2010).
[59]13 V.S.A. Section 1023 (2010).
[60]D.C. Code, Title 22, Section 22-404.01 (2010).
[61]Model Penal Code, Section 211.2.

Some states opt to criminalize various *degrees* of assault. For example, Alaska recognizes four separate degrees of assault. *First-degree assault* is defined as follows:

a. A person commits the crime of assault in the first degree if
 1. that person recklessly causes serious physical injury to another by means of a dangerous instrument;
 2. with intent to cause serious physical injury to another, the person causes serious physical injury to any person;
 3. the person knowingly engages in conduct that results in serious physical injury to another under circumstances manifesting extreme indifference to the value of human life; or
 4. that person recklessly causes serious physical injury to another by repeated assaults using a dangerous instrument, even if each assault individually does not cause serious physical injury.[62]

On the other hand, *fourth-degree assault* occurs when

a. [a] person commits the crime of assault in the fourth degree if
 1. that person recklessly causes physical injury to another person;
 2. with criminal negligence that person causes physical injury to another person by means of a dangerous instrument; or
 3. by words or other conduct that person recklessly places another person in fear of imminent physical injury.[63]

**YOUR DECISION**

1. Zach Schultz is the hottest new celebrity in Hollywood, starring in several successful films. One evening while Zach is on a dinner date, he is surrounded by paparazzi trying to get a photo for the weekly tabloids. Zach repeatedly asks the paparazzi to back off, but they continue to get more aggressive. Finally, Zach pushes a photographer, grabs his camera, and smashes it to the ground. You are the prosecutor in Los Angeles County. Can you charge Zach with battery or another crime? Explain.
2. Juliette is the top equestrian in the state and is out riding her horse, Biscuit, in preparation for an upcoming competition. Sarah is second best equestrian in the state and really wants Juliette to "break a leg" so she cannot compete in the state championships. While Juliette is riding, Sarah swings a large tree branch and hits Biscuit right in the chest. Juliette is not hit by the branch, but she is violently thrown off the horse and suffers several broken bones. Can Sarah be charged with battery? Why or why not?

## Summary

- Battery is unlawful touching, typically with injury.
- Whether battery is a general or specific intent offense varies by state.
- Though the *actus reus* of battery usually requires injury, not all states impose this requirement.

[62]Alaska Stat. 11.41.200 (2010).
[63]Alaska Stat. 11.41.230 (2010).

- The norm in most states is to criminalize various types of battery, each with their own distinct elements.
- Battery is usually regarded as a consummated assault, yet there is no ironclad requirement that a battery be preceded by an assault
- An assault occurs when one person intentionally places another person in anticipation of imminent battery.
- Assault is often viewed as attempted battery.
- The *mens rea* of traditional assault is the intention to cause another person to fear imminent battery.
- The *actus reus* is translating intent into action.
- Assaults are often lumped into two categories: simple and aggravated. Aggravated assaults, which are counted in the FBI's crime index, are the most serious.

---

**MODULE 9.4**

# OTHER ASSAULTIVE OFFENSES

### *Learning Objectives*
- **Describe the crime of kidnapping.**
- **Describe the crime of false imprisonment.**
- **Define carjacking.**
- **Identify and define two domestic offenses.**
- **Differentiate between harassment and stalking.**

---

**CORE CONCEPTS**

As assaultive crimes, rape, robbery, assault, and battery get the lion's share of the attention. Yet there are many other such offenses that often get overlooked because crime statistics do not always tell us much about them. Examples include kidnapping, false imprisonment, carjacking, child abuse, domestic violence, harassment, and stalking. The FBI's crime index does not count any of these offenses, but it is difficult to argue that they are any less serious than the rest. We look at each in this section not because they are fundamentally similar to one another (they are not), but because they all contain an assaultive component.

**kidnapping** The unlawful taking and carrying away of another person with the intent to deprive that person of his or her liberty.

## Kidnapping

*Kidnapping* is a bit of a misnomer, as there is no requirement that a "kid" be targeted. **Kidnapping** refers to the unlawful taking and carrying away of another person with the intent to deprive that person of his or her liberty. The *actus reus* is thus the

**asportation** In regard to the crime of kidnapping, the taking and carrying away of another person.

seizing and carrying away (also called **asportation**) of another person. Although in many kidnapping cases the victim is often taken far away from the scene of the abduction, there is no specific distance requirement. In one case, the *actus reus* of kidnapping was satisfied once the victim was forced into a car just 22 feet away.[64] And although kidnappers sometimes demand ransoms, there is no requirement that any such demands be made to satisfy *actus reus*.

As for the *mens rea*, kidnapping statutes often require specific intent, such as intent to confine, restrain, or otherwise hold the victim in secret. Nevada's kidnapping statute illustrates the specific intent of kidnapping (although it does not *require* such intent):

1. A person who willfully seizes, confines, inveigles, entices, decoys, abducts, conceals, kidnaps or carries away a person by any means whatsoever with the *intent to hold or detain*, or who holds or detains, the person for ransom, or reward, or for the purpose of committing sexual assault, extortion or robbery upon or from the person, or for the purpose of killing the person or inflicting substantial bodily harm upon the person, or to exact from relatives, friends, or any other person any money or valuable thing for the return or disposition of the kidnapped person, and a person who leads, takes, entices, or carries away or detains any minor with the intent to keep, imprison, or confine the minor from his or her parents, guardians, or any other person having lawful custody of the minor, or with the intent to hold the minor to unlawful service, or perpetrate upon the person of the minor any unlawful act is guilty of kidnapping in the first degree . . . .

2. A person who willfully and without authority of law seizes, inveigles, takes, carries away or kidnaps another person with the intent to keep the person secretly imprisoned within the State, or for the purpose of conveying the person out of the State without authority of law, or in any manner held to service or detained against the person's will, is guilty of kidnapping in the second degree.[65]

Note the all-encompassing nature of Nevada's statute. It covers a wide range of motives for kidnapping. Also note the difference between first- and second-degree kidnapping. Second-degree kidnapping is more concerned with the act itself, whereas a first-degree kidnapping conviction is reserved for abductions with more nefarious motives.

## False Imprisonment

**false imprisonment** The unlawful detention or restraint of another person.

**False imprisonment** is similar to kidnapping, but is usually regarded as less serious because it lacks the "carrying away" element. It has been defined as forcing a person "to remain where he does not wish to remain."[66] For comparison's sake, let us once again consider the state of Nevada. There, *false imprisonment* is defined as "an unlawful violation of the personal liberty of another, and consists [of] confinement or detention without sufficient legal authority."[67] This definition contains no specific intent requirement, hence there is not much to the *mens rea*. The *actus reus* is also equally clear—confinement or detention of another without proper authority.

---

[64]*People v. Chessman*, 238 P.2d 1001 (Cal. 1951).
[65]Nev. Rev. Stat. 200.310 (2010).
[66]*McKendree v. Christy*, 172 N.E.2d 380 (1961).
[67]Nev. Rev. Stat. 200.460 (2010).

Some states call false imprisonment "unlawful restraint." And some states also require specific intent. Consider Texas' relatively concise statute: "A person commits an offense if he intentionally or knowingly restrains another person."[68] Note the requirement that the conduct be "intentional" or "knowing." This statute seems a bit far-reaching, however. What if a police officer wishes to apprehend a suspect? What if a private party wants to make a citizen's arrest? In either case, the same statute states, "It is no offense to detain or move another under this section when it is for the purpose of effecting a lawful arrest or detaining an individual lawfully arrested."[69]

See the accompanying Court Decision for more on false imprisonment. In it we examine the case of *Dewald* v. *State*, where the defendant is a bounty hunter charged with criminal confinement.

## COURT DECISION

### *Dewald* v. *State*
### 898 N.W.2d 488 (Ind. App. 2009)

**Background:** Bart Dewald was convicted in Superior Court, Elkhart County of two counts of felony criminal confinement (another term for false imprisonment). Defendant appealed and the Indiana Court of Appeals affirmed the conviction.

**Facts and Procedural History**

In June 2006, Dewald and Constantine Nichols were both bail bondsmen and fugitive recovery agents in Indiana. In the course of his work as a bail bondsman, Dewald posted a bond for an individual named Evelyn Mitchell. Mitchell owned a 2001 Chrysler Town and Country minivan that looked green or blue, depending upon lighting conditions.

On June 14, 2006, Dewald received a tip that Mitchell planned to flee from Indiana. He called Nichols to ask for assistance in locating and apprehending Mitchell. . . . Nichols drove toward Mitchell's parents' residence, while Dewald drove to Mitchell's house.

While Dewald watched Mitchell's house, a light-colored minivan pulled up to the house, dropped off a child, and then drove away. Dewald called Nichols to alert him that "a van had just stopped at the residence and took off at a high rate of speed. And he thought that he was going to follow, because he suspected that, possibly, . . . [Mitchell] was in that van; he wasn't sure." Nichols joined Dewald in pursuit of the minivan. He passed the minivan, while Dewald followed it closely. Once in front of the minivan, Nichols braked, forcing the minivan, which had been traveling thirty-five to forty miles per hour, to quickly brake and stop. Nichols' vehicle was several feet in front of the stopped minivan, and Dewald pulled up in his vehicle about two feet behind the minivan. This prevented the driver of the minivan from pulling away.

Dewald and Nichols exited their vehicles and walked to the front of the minivan. Dewald stood on the driver's side, while Nichols stood on the passenger's side. They

---

[68]Texas Penal Code Section 20.02 (2010).
[69]Ibid.

encountered two women, neither of whom was Mitchell, sitting in the front seat. In fact, the minivan belonged to Oaklawn Psychiatric Center, and the two women inside of the minivan were child therapists employed by Oaklawn. The therapists, Sara Trovatore and Marilyn Draper, were transporting children to and from therapy sessions in the minivan, and they had just dropped off a child at Mitchell's residence. When Dewald and Nichols stopped them, Trovatore and Draper still had one child patient in the minivan.

Dewald and Nichols began questioning Trovatore and Draper about Mitchell's whereabouts. Trovatore informed the men that she did not know where Mitchell was. However, Dewald and Nichols continued questioning the women. Dewald asked Trovatore to call Mitchell and to tell her that something bad had happened to her son and that she needed to come home. Trovatore refused to do so. Eventually, Dewald and Nichols commented that they were wasting their time and left. The entire incident lasted between five and ten minutes. Later, Draper reported the incident to her supervisor at Oaklawn, and Trovatore reported the incident to police.

The State charged Dewald with two counts of Class D felony criminal confinement. Ind.Code § 35-42-3-3(a). After a jury trial, Dewald was convicted as charged. The trial court entered judgment of conviction on both counts and, after a sentencing hearing, sentenced Dewald to concurrent terms of one-and-one-half years. Dewald now appeals his convictions.

### Discussion and Decision

**\*\*\*I. Confinement:** In order to convict Dewald of Class D felony criminal confinement, the State had to prove that he "knowingly or intentionally:...confine[d] another person without the other person's consent[.]" I.C. § 35-42-3-3(a). Dewald argues that the State presented insufficient evidence to prove that he confined Trovatore and Draper. His argument has three components. First, he contends that the evidence does not show that Trovatore and Draper were unable to leave during their encounter with Dewald and Nichols. [Finally], he contends that confining the women was not illegal because he had the authority, as a bail bondsman, to detain them in order to effectively perform his job.

To "confine" means "to substantially interfere with the liberty of a person." Ind. Code § 35-42-3-1. Here, evidence was presented that Nichols passed the minivan driven by Trovatore and braked suddenly, forcing the minivan, which had been traveling thirty-five to forty miles per hour, to quickly brake and stop. Nichols' stopped vehicle was two to five feet in front of the stopped minivan. Dewald stopped his vehicle about two feet behind the minivan. This prevented Trovatore and Draper from pulling away. Dewald and Nichols then approached the minivan and questioned Trovatore and Draper. Regarding her inability to drive away in the minivan during this encounter, Trovatore testified:

Q. And at that point in time, could you have moved the vehicle you were in?

A. No.

Q. Why not?

A. We wouldn't have been able to—we wouldn't have had enough room to get turned to get out without hitting one of the vehicles.

Dewald's contention that because there was "enough room for Nichols to walk between the front bumper of the Oaklawn van and the back bumper of his vehicle" the women were not confined is merely a request that we reweigh the evidence, which we will not do. The evidence is sufficient to show that Trovatore and Draper were confined.

\*\*\*Nonetheless, Dewald further argues that the State failed to prove that he unlawfully confined Trovatore and Draper because he had the authority, as a bail bondsman, to detain them. Dewald cites *Mishler v. State,* 660 N.E.2d 343 (Ind. Ct.App.1996), in support of his claim that bail bondsmen enjoy a special position in society allowing them to detain members of the public. In *Mishler,* bail bondsmen went to a defendant's mother's home, aware that the defendant did not live there, and forcefully entered the home in order to search for the defendant. Rejecting the bail bondsmen's argument that they were authorized to enter the home forcibly in search of the defendant, we recognized a bail agent's common law and statutory rights to apprehend a defendant. *Mishler,* 660 N.E.2d at 345. We held, however, that the rights associated with this "special position" are limited to the apprehension of the defendant, concluding that where a bondsman forcibly enters the dwelling of a third party, the bondsman is liable under the criminal laws of Indiana. Further, we agreed with the line of reasoning employed in a decision from the Minnesota Court of Appeals, which affirmed a bail bondsman's burglary convictions and provided in part:

> "The contractual authority of a bondsman does not provide justification to infringe on third party rights. The surety-principal contract generally authorizes the bail bondsman, or his agent, to exercise jurisdiction and control over the principal during the period for which the bond is executed. *However, this contractual authority does not include the authority to infringe upon the rights of persons who are not parties to the contract.*"

*Id.* at 346.

\*\*\*Detaining third parties, no matter how briefly, infringes upon their rights. We decline Dewald's invitation to expand the law pertaining to the authority of bail bondsmen to permit bondsmen to conduct investigatory stops of third parties.

**II. Mens Rea.** Next, Dewald argues that the evidence fails to show that he acted "knowingly." He contends that the State failed to disprove that he believed that he acted within his authority in detaining Trovatore and Draper. For this reason, he argues, he did not knowingly commit criminal confinement.

Dewald's contention that he believed that he acted lawfully when he stopped Trovatore and Draper and that he therefore did not commit the crime of confinement "knowingly" is unavailing. "A person engages in conduct 'knowingly' if, when he engages in the conduct, he is aware of a high probability that he is doing so." Ind. Code § 35-42-2-2(b). Even if we take Dewald at his word that he fully believed that he was permitted by law to detain third parties when trying to locate his bail customers (which he had no reason under *Mishler* to believe), it is well-settled that ignorance of the law is no excuse for criminal behavior. Instead, the relevant inquiry is whether Dewald was aware of the high probability that he "substantially interfere[d] with the liberty" of Trovatore and Draper. I.C. § 35-42-3-1.

The evidence reflects that he was. Trovatore and Draper were forced to stop their employer's minivan after Nichols suddenly braked and stopped in front of them. With Nichols' vehicle only two to five feet in front of the stopped minivan, Dewald pulled up and parked his vehicle only two feet behind the minivan. This deprived Trovatore and Draper of enough space between the vehicles to drive away. Dewald then participated in questioning the women while they sat inside their boxed-in vehicle. The evidence is sufficient to prove that he confined Trovatore and Draper knowingly.

### Conclusion

The evidence is sufficient to support Dewald's two convictions for Class D felony criminal confinement. Further, we decline Dewald's request that we expand the authority of bail bondsmen to permit them to detain third parties for investigatory purposes. The judgment of the trial court is affirmed.

## Case Analysis

1. State the elements necessary to convict the defendant of criminal confinement, also known as false imprisonment.

2. Do you believe the occupants of the vehicle were "confined" under the legal defendant provided by the court?

3. Should bounty hunters have the legal authority to detain potential suspects? Why or why not?

## Carjacking

**carjacking** Intentionally taking another person's occupied motor vehicle with the use of a deadly weapon, force, and/or intimidation.

**Carjacking**, another assaultive offense, combines elements of robbery with the motivation to take a person's vehicle. The *actus reus* usually contains two elements: (1) taking of another person's occupied motor vehicle (2) by use of a deadly weapon and/or force or intimidation. Carjacking is a specific intent offense, meaning that the offender must intend for the crime to occur—or at least know that it is occurring. In Tennessee, carjacking is defined as

> the intentional or knowing taking of a motor vehicle from the possession of another by use of: (1) a deadly weapon; or (2) force or intimidation.[70]

One of the key requirements for carjacking is taking possession from another. In other words, carjacking does not occur unless the offender takes possession of the vehicle from someone else (presumably its owner or someone legally authorized to drive it). Were it not for the presence of a victim, carjacking would be relegated to theft.

---

[70]Tenn. Code Ann. Section 39-13-402 (2010).

Victims of domestic violence are sometimes reluctant to report the crime to police.

Warren Goldswain/Shutterstock.com

**domestic violence** Assault, battery, or other abusive conduct committed against a family member or intimate partner.

**wobbler** A criminal offense that can be charged as either a felony or misdemeanor depending on the circumstances.

# Domestic Offenses

Domestic violence and child abuse are both considered "domestic" offenses, as they typically occur in the home. Both, however, need not be standalone offenses, as traditional assault and statutes can be used to prosecute abusive intimate partners and adults to abuse child victims.

According to the National Center for Victims of Crime, **domestic violence** is defined as the "willful intimidation, assault, battery, sexual assault or other abusive behavior perpetrated by one family member, household member, or intimate partner against another."[71] California criminalizes domestic violence in two sections of its penal code. The felony domestic battery statute provides the following:

> Any person who willfully inflicts upon a person who is his or her spouse, former spouse, cohabitant, former cohabitant, or the mother or father of his or her child, corporal injury resulting in a traumatic condition, is guilty of a felony.[72]

California treats as a misdemeanor battery that which "is committed against a spouse, a person with whom the defendant is cohabiting, a person who is the parent of the defendant's child, former spouse, fiancé, or fiancée, or a person with whom the defendant currently has, or has previously had, a dating or engagement relationship."[73] Note the overlapping language between both statutes. What's a prosecutor to do? As defined in California, domestic violence is known as a **wobbler**, meaning that it is an offense that can be charged as either a felony or a misdemeanor depending on the circumstances.

To get a sense of the elements of domestic violence, look again at California's felony statute. The *mens rea* is straightforward—willful infliction of corporal injury. As for the *actus reus*, there is no requirement that physical injury result, only a "traumatic condition." Also note that California's statute is rather all-encompassing in terms of the relationships it covers. Domestic violence is not limited to spousal relationships, but also to many other current and former domestic relationships.

---

[71]http://www.ncvc.org/ncvc/main.aspx?dbName=DocumentViewer&DocumentID=32347#1 (accessed September 13, 2010).
[72]Cal. Penal Code Section 273.5 (2010).
[73]Cal. Penal Code Section 243(e)(1) (2010).

State child abuse statutes are worded similarly. For example, Florida law defines the crime as follows:

> any willful act or threatened act that results in any physical, mental, or sexual injury or harm that causes or is likely to cause the child's physical, mental, or emotional health to be significantly impaired. Abuse of a child includes acts or omissions. Corporal discipline of a child by a parent or legal custodian for disciplinary purposes does not in itself constitute abuse when it does not result in harm to the child.[74]

Other states retain a variety of child abuse statutes, covering a wide range of abusive actions, including not just physical abuse, but also neglect, child exploitation, emotional abuse, parental substance abuse, and abandonment. The federal Child Abuse Prevention and Treatment Act (CAPTA) spells out minimum standards that, in order to receive financial assistance, states must incorporate into their child abuse laws. According to CAPTA, **child abuse** is defined as "Any recent act or failure to act on the part of a parent or caretakers, which results in death, serious physical or emotional harm, sexual abuse, or exploitation, or an act or failure to act which presents an imminent risk of serious harm."[75]

**child abuse** The physical, sexual, or emotional abuse of a child through voluntary action or failure to act.

Domestic violence is an important offense not just because of its gravity, but because many states have enacted "mandatory arrest" laws intended to hold perpetrators accountable. This brings more and more cases before the courts, making domestic violence all the more serious and important.

# Harassment and Stalking

Harassment and stalking are closely related assaultive offenses. According to federal law, **harassment** is defined as "a course of conduct directed at a specific person that causes substantial emotional distress in such person and serves no legitimate purpose."[76] **Stalking** is defined in almost the same way, but it usually adds an element of *following* the victim in some form or fashion. For example, in addition to criminalizing other types of stalking-related activities, Kansas law prohibits "[f]ollowing, approaching or confronting the targeted person or a member of such person's immediate family."[77]

**harassment** Systematic conduct that intentionally annoys, threatens, and/or intimidates another person.

**stalking** Intentionally frightening another person by following, harassing, and/or terrorizing.

Note that under this definition, *harassment*, as we have defined it, and *stalking* are basically one in the same; one who harasses and does not necessarily *follow* a victim can be prosecuted as a stalker in Kansas. See the accompanying Court Decision for more on stalking. In it we examine the case of *United States* v. *Infante* in which a college student was charged with interstate stalking.

---

[74]Fla. Stat. Section 39.01(2) (2010).
[75]42 U.S.C.A. Section 5106g(2) (2003).
[76]18 U.S.C.A. Section 1514(c)(1) (2010).
[77]K.S.A. Section 21-3438 (2010).

**COURT DECISION**

U.S. v. *Infante*
2010 WL 1268140 (D. Ariz. 2010)

**Background:** Ricardo Infante was charged with interstate stalking. After the preliminary hearing, Infante requested dismissal of the complaint. The District Court of Arizona dismissed the complaint for lack of probable cause.

**Order**

LAWRENCE O. ANDERSON, United States Magistrate Judge.

> *Whenever a man does a thoroughly stupid thing, it is always from the noblest motives.*

This matter is before the Court on Defendant's Request for Dismissal of Complaint, Discharge of Defendant pursuant to Fed.R.Crim.P. 5.1(f). Defendant argues that the Government has not established probable cause that Defendant committed the crime of Interstate Stalking in violation of 18 U.S.C. § 2261A. The Court has reviewed the parties' briefing on the issue. The Court finds insufficient evidence was presented at the March 12, 2010 preliminary hearing to hold all Defendant to answer to the Western District of New York for trial on the crime charged.

**I. Background:** The Government alleges that on or about February through February 10, 2010, Defendant committed the crime of Interstate Stalking in violation of 18 U.S.C. § 2261A. . . . In June 2009, L.B., the alleged victim, met Defendant at Arizona State University. They attended the same course, which included a three week trip to Russia which they both attended. L.B. and Defendant had coffee one time, and L.B. determined she was not interested in him. L.B. returned home to New Jersey after the conclusion of the course at A.S.U.

While in New Jersey, on August 28, 2009, Defendant contacted L.B. via her internet Facebook account. In September 2009, L.B. returned to the University of Rochester, located in Rochester, New York. On February 6, 2010, Defendant sent L.B. an e-mail and several others between February 6 and 8, 2010. In one e-mail, Defendant stated that he had a "powerful longing" for L.B. He also stated, in a text message, that he wanted L.B.'s forgiveness for having been "a jerk, a masochist and even a criminal all this time. . . ."

On February 8, 2010, L.B. received two phone messages from Defendant in which he said he was in Rochester and wanted to see her. On February 8, 2010, L.B. received an e-mail from the University of Rochester Common Connection, advising her that a florist had flowers for her to pick up. L.B. called the florist and learned that the flowers were from Defendant. On February 11, 2010, the flower shop advised Investigator Lafferty that Defendant personally came into the shop on February 5, 2010 and ordered the flowers for L.B.

On February 9, 2010,. . . Defendant stated that he flew to Rochester on February 4, 2010 and went to the University of Rochester's campus trying to find L.B. Defendant explained how he tried to contact L.B. through e-mails, phone messages, through Professor Laura Givens, and through flowers and gifts. He indicated that he saw L.B. during his weekend in Rochester, including one occasion in the library. He stated that he did not get any closer to her than 10 to 15 feet, and did not want to make eye contact with her. L.B. told the police that she suffered substantial emotional distress as a result of Defendant traveling to Rochester and trying to contact her.

***Interstate Stalking, 18 U.S.C. § 18 U.S.C. § 2261A**

Title 18 U.S.C. § 2261A provides, in relevant part, that:

> Whoever—(1) travels in interstate . . . commerce . . .with the intent to kill, injure, harass, or intimidate or to place under surveillance with intent to kill, injure, harass or intimidate another person, and in the course of, or as a result of, such travel places that person in reasonable fear of the death, or serious bodily injury to, or causes substantial emotional distress to that person, a member of the immediate family . . . of that person, or the spouse or intimate partner of that person . . . shall be punished as provided in section 2261(b).

Section 2261A has three elements: (1) interstate travel occurred; (2) a defendant's intent was to injure or harass another person; and (3) the person defendant intended to harass or injure was placed in reasonable fear of death or serious bodily injury to herself or a member of her family as a result of that travel. Defendant does not dispute the first and third elements. Rather, Defendant argues that the Government has not established probable cause that his interstate travel was done with the "intent to harass" or with the "intent to place under surveillance with the intent to harass," the alleged victim, L.B.

*Mens Rea* **of Intent to Harass.** The Interstate Stalking Statute does not clearly articulate the state of mind required to satisfy the "intent to harass" element of the offense. Defendant argues that the legislative history indicates that the Government "must establish that the defendant's state of mind was of a purposeful intent to create a severe adverse reaction in the victim." Relying on *Washington v. Davis*, 426 U.S. 229, 252 (1976), the Government argues that the general rule in criminal cases is that intent will be inferred from objective evidence of what actually happened rather than evidence describing the subjective state of mind of the actor. The Government further argues that circumstantial evidence establishes that Defendant's purpose for traveling to Rochester was to harass L.B.

***Based on the foregoing, the [court] concludes that the "intent-to-harass" element of the Interstate Stalking Statute, 18 U.S.C. § 2261A, requires that a defendant act with the purpose to harass.

***Defendant's alleged acts here show that he was trying to get a second romantic chance with L.B. and earn her forgiveness. Although he did travel to Rochester to locate L.B. to "woo" her back, he never sent her any threatening messages before or after his travels, did not try to contact her in person on the one occasion he thought he saw her on campus. Defendant simply tried to send her flowers and small gifts, typical gestures of affection, that were left for L.B. at a flower shop for her to pick up. No evidence was presented at the preliminary hearing that after he returned from Rochester to Arizona, Defendant had any further direct or indirect contact with L.B.

***From the express language used by Congress in adopting 18 U.S.C. § 2261A, the issue is not whether the Government presented sufficient evidence that a reasonable person would find Defendant's conduct constituted harassment of L.B.; rather, the issue is whether the Government presented sufficient evidence to show that Defendant's conduct was done with "the intent and purpose" to harass L.B. The Court finds that "a person of ordinary prudence and caution [would not] conscientiously entertain a reasonable belief" that Defendant's travel and conduct in Rochester, New York was with "the intent and purpose" to harass L.B. *Coleman,* 477 F.2d at 1202.

In conclusion, the Complaint should be dismissed...because the Government has failed to establish probable cause exists that Defendant had the requisite intent to harass, a necessary element to the federal Interstate Stalking Statute, 18 U.S.C. 2261A.

## Case Analysis

1. What are the elements necessary to convict a defendant under the federal stalking statute, 18 U.S.C. 2261A?

2. What is defendant's legal argument? Do you think the defendant acted with the "intent to harass" L.B.?

3. This case resolved the defendant's motion to dismiss the complaint. What happens to the defendant after this case was decided?

Until recently, harassment and stalking took place either in the physical world or via written correspondence. With the integration of computers and the Internet into our daily lives, both crimes have moved into cyberspace. And while some states have been slow to respond to this development, others have already acted. For example, California recently amended its stalking law such that **cyberstalking**, or stalking via any electronic communication device, is now criminal. Stalking is now defined as

**cyberstalking** Committing the crime of stalking through electronic communication.

> a verbal or written threat, including that performed through the use of an electronic communication device, or a threat implied by a pattern of conduct or a combination of verbal, written, or electronically communicated statements and conduct made with the intent to place the person that is the target of the threat in reasonable fear for his or her safety or the safety of his or her family and made with the apparent ability to carry out the threat so as to cause the person who is the target of the threat to reasonably fear for his or her safety or the safety of his or her family. It is not necessary to prove that the defendant had the intent to actually carry out the threat.[78]

Cyberstalking is no less serious than traditional stalking. As a U.S. Justice Department report observed:

> The fact that cyberstalking does not involve physical contact may create the misperception that it is more benign than physical stalking. This is not necessarily true. As the Internet becomes an ever more integral part of our personal and professional lives, stalkers can take advantage of the ease of communications as well as increased access to personal information. In addition, the ease of use and non-confrontational, impersonal, and sometimes anonymous nature of Internet communications may remove disincentives to cyberstalking. Put another way, whereas a potential stalker may be unwilling or unable to confront a victim in person or on the telephone, he or she may have little hesitation sending harassing or threatening electronic communications to a victim. Finally, as with physical stalking, online harassment and threats may be a prelude to more serious behavior, including physical violence.[79]

---

[78]Cal. Penal Code Section 646.9(g) (2010).
[79]U.S. Department of Justice, *1999 Report on Cyberstalking: A New Challenge for Law Enforcement and Industry* (Washington, DC: U.S. Department of Justice, 1999). Available at: http://www.justice.gov/criminal/cybercrime/cyberstalking.htm (accessed October 5, 2010).

**Figure 9.5**

Comparison of Offline and Online Stalking

*Source:* U.S. Department of Justice, *1999 Report on Cyberstalking: A New Challenge for Law Enforcement and Industry* (Washington, DC: U.S. Department of Justice, 1999). Available at: http://www.justice.gov/criminal/cybercrime/cyberstalking.htm (accessed October 5, 2010).

**Major Similarities**

Majority of cases involve stalking by former intimates, although stranger stalking occurs in the real world and in cyberspace.

Most victims are women; most stalkers are men.

Stalkers are generally motivated by the desire to control the victim.

**Major Differences**

Offline stalking generally requires the perpetrator and the victim to be located in the same geographic area; cyberstalkers may be located across the street or across the country.

Electronic communications technologies make it much easier for a cyberstalker to encourage third parties to harass and/or threaten a victim (e.g., impersonating the victim and posting inflammatory messages to bulletin boards and in chat rooms, causing viewers of that message to send threatening messages back to the victim "author").

Electronic communications technologies also lower the barriers to harassment and threats; a cyberstalker does not need to physically confront the victim.

Cyberstalking also shares several characteristics with traditional stalking. Many stalkers, whether they are offline or online, are motivated by the same objectives, such as the desire to exert control over their victims.[80] Evidence also shows that majority of stalkers, whether offline or online, are males targeting female victims.[81] Finally, in many cases, the victims had prior relationships with the offenders.[82] See Figure 9.5 for a further comparison of traditional/offline stalking and cyberstalking.

## YOUR DECISION

1. Joey Bricker is a screenwriter for a famous Hollywood production company. Joey was thrilled to learn that one of the films he worked on, *Spiderman vs. the Hulk*, was nominated for an Academy Award. Joey and his wife Samantha arrived at the red carpet, ready to socialize with all the famous celebrities. Just as they began walking toward an entertainment news station for an interview, however, security guards at the Oscars ushered them off the red carpet to a small detention room. Joey and Samantha were held in the room for six hours and interrogated about how they managed to make their way onto the red carpet. Joey and Samantha contacted the police and would like to press charges. Can the Oscar security guards be charged with a crime? Why or why not?

2. Edward was devastated when Brittany ended their two-year relationship. Desperate for a way to win her back, Edward created a fictitious Facebook account under a different name. Brittany accepted the friend request unaware of Edward's disguise.

---

[80]Ibid.

[81]Ibid.

[82]Ibid.

Edward sent Brittany approximately 25 messages a day via this Facebook account. He even posted compromising photos and videos of Brittany he had obtained while they were dating. Brittany has contacted the police and would like to press charges for stalking. Can Edward be charged with stalking? Why or why not?

## Summary

- *Kidnapping* refers to the unlawful taking and carrying away of another person with the intent to deprive that person of his or her liberty.

- The *actus reus* of kidnapping is the seizing and carrying away of another person. Kidnapping statutes often require specific intent, such as intent to confine, restrain, or otherwise hold the victim in secret.

- False imprisonment is similar to kidnapping, but is usually regarded as less serious.

- *False imprisonment* has been defined as forcing a person "to remain where he does not wish to remain."

- Carjacking, another assaultive offense, combines elements of robbery with the motivation to take a person's vehicle.

- The *actus reus* of carjacking usually contains two elements: (1) taking of another person's occupied motor vehicle (2) by use of a deadly weapon and/or force or intimidation.

- In terms of *mens rea*, carjacking is a specific intent offense, meaning that the offender must intend for the crime to occur—or at least know that it is occurring.

- *Domestic violence* is defined as the "willful intimidation, assault, battery, sexual assault or other abusive behavior perpetrated by one family member, household member, or intimate partner against another."[83]

- *Child abuse* is defined as "Any recent act or failure to act on the part of a parent or caretakers, which results in death, serious physical or emotional harm, sexual abuse, or exploitation, or an act or failure to act which presents an imminent risk of serious harm."[84]

- Harassment and stalking are closely related assaultive offenses.

- According to federal law, *harassment* is defined as "a course of conduct directed at a specific person that causes substantial emotional distress in such person and serves no legitimate purpose."[85]

- *Stalking* is defined in much the same way as *harassment*, but it usually adds an element of *following* the victim in some form or fashion.

---

[83]http://www.ncvc.org/ncvc/main.aspx?dbName=DocumentViewer&DocumentID=32347#1.
[84]42 U.S.C.A. Section 5106g(2).
[85]18 U.S.C.A. Section 1514(c)(1).

# Chapter Review

MODULE **9.1**

## RAPE AND SEXUAL ASSAULT

### Learning Objectives

· Distinguish between rape and sexual assault.

· Summarize the nature and elements of the crime of rape.

· Summarize the laws pertaining to the crime of rape.

### Review Questions

1. How does sexual assault compare to rape?

2. Explain the *mens rea* of rape.

3. In what ways does the *actus reus* of rape vary?

4. Explain forcible rape and compare it to other types of rape.

5. What legislative developments have affected a prosecutor's ability to prove rape in court? Explain.

### Key Terms

rape
sexual assault
statutory rape
rape shield laws

MODULE **9.2**

## ROBBERY

### Learning Objectives

· Describe the crime of robbery.

· Distinguish armed robbery from other forms of robbery.

### Review Questions

1. Explain the five parts of the *actus reus* of robbery.

2. What is the *mens rea* of robbery?

3. Why do some states treat armed robbery different than other forms of robbery?

### Key Terms

actual possession
construction possession
armed robbery

MODULE **9.3**

## ASSAULT AND BATTERY

### Learning Objectives

· Describe the crime of assault.

· Describe the crime of battery.

*Review Questions*

1. What is battery and how does it differ from assault?

2. Should assault and battery be defined separately in the penal code? Why or why not?

3. Can a person be a victim of battery without an assault? If so, explain.

*Key Terms*

battery
threatened battery assault
attempted battery assault

---

MODULE **9.4**

**OTHER ASSAULTIVE OFFENSES**

*Learning Objectives*

- Describe the crime of kidnapping.

- Describe the crime of false imprisonment.

- Define carjacking.

- Identify and define two domestic offenses.

- Differentiate between harassment and stalking.

*Review Questions*

1. The term *kidnapping* is a misnomer. Why?

2. Explain *asportation*.

3. Compare and contrast kidnapping and false imprisonment.

4. Carjacking combines elements of what two offenses?

5. Distinguish between domestic violence and child abuse.

6. Compare and contrast harassment and stalking.

*Key Terms*

kidnapping
asportation
false imprisonment
carjacking
domestic violence
child abuse
wobbler
harassment
stalking
cyberstalking

# Chapter Synthesizing Questions

1. How are rape and sexual assault similar? How are they different?
2. Compare and contrast robbery and battery.
3. Compare and contrast rape and domestic violence.
4. Assault and battery are often lumped together in the same sentence. Why?
5. Which assaultive offense is most serious and why?
6. Look through your state's penal or criminal code and identify two assaultive offenses not presented in this chapter. How are they similar or different?

# 10

# PROPERTY DAMAGE AND INVASION

*Learning Objectives*

**MODULE 10.1  PROPERTY DAMAGE**
- Describe the crime of arson.
- Explain the elements of criminal mischief.
- Explain the elements of vandalism.

**MODULE 10.2  PROPERTY INVASION**
- Summarize the elements of trespassing.
- Explain how trespassing statutes have been used to target illegal immigration.
- Describe the crime of burglary.

**MODULE 10.3  PROPERTY DAMAGE AND INVASION WITH COMPUTERS**
- Define and explain cybercrime.
- Identify laws aimed at controlling property invasion and damage with a computer.

# PROPERTY DAMAGE

### Learning Objectives
- **Describe the crime of arson.**
- **Explain the elements of criminal mischief.**
- **Explain the elements of vandalism.**

**CORE CONCEPTS**

This chapter is the first in a new section focusing on crimes against property. In this chapter, we look at the most serious property crimes—namely, arson and burglary, both of which are reported in the FBI's crime index (arson became a reportable offense only some years after the launch of the Uniform Crime Reports, in 1978). We also look at the lesser known, but also fairly serious property crimes of criminal mischief, vandalism, and property damage/invasion with computers. In Chapter 11, we turn our attention to theft and analogous offenses (e.g., embezzlement, forgery).

This module focuses on crimes that cause property *damage*. Arson is the most serious such offense, followed somewhat distantly by criminal mischief and vandalism. While criminal mischief and vandalism are chiefly concerned with damage to property, arson can be damaging in terms of human life, not just property damage. For example, the intentional burning of an occupied dwelling that leads to loss of life could result not just in an arson prosecution, but also one for homicide.

## Arson

**arson** Intentionally setting a fire to burn a structure or other physical property.

**Arson** is defined, generally, as intentionally setting a fire. It is the leading cause of fires in the United States and results in hundreds of deaths and thousands of injuries.[1] William Blackstone, in his *Commentaries on the Laws of England*, once called it an "offense of very great malignity, and much more serious than simple theft." Why?

> Because, first, it is an offence against that right, of habitation, which is acquired by the law of nature as well as the laws of society. Next, because of the terror and confusion that necessarily attends it. And, lastly, because in simple theft the thing stolen only changes its master, but still remains in essence for the benefit of the public, whereas by burning the very substance is absolutely destroyed.[2]

---

[1]United States Fire Administration, *Topical Fire Research Series*, http://www.usfa.dhs.gov/downloads/pdf/tfrs/v1i8-508.pdf (accessed September 16, 2010).
[2]W. Blackstone, *Commentaries on the Laws of England, IV* (Oxford: Clarendon Press, 1769), p. 220.

## Arson at Common Law

At common law, arson was limited to dwellings, requiring four elements:

1. The malicious
2. burning
3. of a dwelling
4. of another.[3]

*Malicious* did not need to mean intent per se, only the creation of great risk that something would burn. So, for example, a person who, on a hot, windy day, was burning scrap lumber next to an area full of dry brush and set the surrounding forest on fire created a great risk of fire, but did not *intend* for the damage to occur.

At common law, any burning of a dwelling sufficed for an arson conviction. There was no requirement that the property be totally destroyed, only that it be burned (as opposed to, say, discolored by smoke) to some degree. Yet arson was limited strictly to dwellings, defined as any structure used as a residence on either a permanent or part-time basis. Not limited to homes, arson could have occurred if any outbuilding, barn, or similar structure was burned, so long as it was used as a residence in some form or fashion.

The fourth common law element of arson limited the crime to the burning of *others'* property. It was not possible, therefore, to commit arson against one's own property. This was true even if a tenant set fire to his or her landlord's property. Even setting fire to one's own property for the purpose of collecting insurance money did not constitute common law arson.

## Modern-Day Arson

Arson laws have undergone substantial changes over the years, in response to the dual realities that (1) a person can maliciously burn much more than a single dwelling, causing extensive damage and perhaps loss of life, and (2) insurance companies could not possibly stay in business if their insured could burn their homes with little fear of reprisal.

Arson (like some other crimes, including kidnapping) can be either a federal or state crime. Federal law provides, by way of summary, that it is a crime to "maliciously damage, by means of fire, any building used in interstate or foreign commerce or in any activity affecting interstate or foreign commerce."[4] To use a simple example, if a disgruntled former Wal-Mart employee decided to set a distribution warehouse on fire, that employee would be subjected to federal prosecution because doing so would likely affect the company's ability to ship products around the country. However, in a 2000 case, the U.S. Supreme Court decided that the federal arson statute, codified as 18 U.S.C. Section 844(i), cannot be used to prosecute an individual for burning an owner-occupied property that is not used for commercial purposes.[5]

State arson laws are typically reserved for prosecution of arsonists who do not fall within the federal law's interstate commerce limitation. Let us look closely at the *actus reus* and *mens rea* of state-level arson.

---

[3]A. A. Moenssens, R. J. Bacigal, G. G. Ashdown, and V. E. Hench, *Criminal Law: Cases and Comments*, 8th ed. (New York: Foundation Press, 2008), pp. 790–791.
[4]*Jones* v. *United States*, 529 U.S. 848 (2000), p. 850.
[5]Ibid.

**Actus Reus.**    The *actus reus* of modern-day arson is, typically, damage by fire or explosion. The meaning of *fire* and *explosion* are relatively straightforward, but *damage* is less clear. Everything from total destruction to visible charring satisfies the *actus reus* of arson.

What if there is no charring, just smoke damage or some soot left on the floor? This question arose in *Williams* v. *State*,[6] a case in which Tonyia Williams, a New Year's party guest, started a fire in the basement of the house she was visiting, after an argument. She was unsuccessful in setting the house on fire, but she managed to cause a measure of smoke and soot damage. She was convicted of arson, but argued that because there was no charring, she should not have been convicted. An appeals court disagreed, stating that "the smoke damage and the soot on the basement wall were enough to support a conviction for arson."[7] The Indiana statute used to support Williams's conviction provided, in part, that a person is guilty of arson if he or she "knowingly or intentionally *damages* . . . a dwelling of another person without his [or her] consent" (emphasis added).[8] The appeals court decided that a looser interpretation of *damage* was warranted than that which the common law suggested. In other words, the court disagreed with the common law definition of damage, namely,

> any charring of the wood of a building, so that the fiber of the wood was destroyed, was enough to constitute a sufficient burning to complete the crime of arson.[9]

The Model Penal Code avoids use of the word *damage*. Section 220.1 defines the *actus reus* of arson as, simply, starting a fire or causing an explosion. The Model Penal Code also defines as criminal the less serious offenses of "reckless burning or exploding" and "failure to control or report dangerous fire."

**Mens Rea.**    The *mens rea* of arson varies by statute, but typically requires an element of intent or knowledge. The Indiana statute quoted earlier used both terms. Some states get very specific with their *mens rea* requirement. For example, the Texas arson statute reads, in part:

> A person commits an offense if the person starts a fire, regardless of whether the fire continues after ignition, or causes an explosion with intent to destroy or damage:
> 1. any vegetation, fence, or structure on open-space land; or
> 2. any building, habitation, or vehicle:
>     A. knowing that it is within the limits of an incorporated city or town;
>     B. knowing that it is insured against damage or destruction;
>     C. knowing that it is subject to a mortgage or other security interest;
>     D. knowing that it is located on property belonging to another;
>     E. knowing that it has located within it property belonging to another; or
>     F. when the person is reckless about whether the burning or explosion will endanger the life of some individual or the safety of the property of another.[10]

Note that the *mens rea* in this statute appears in two places. First, the statute is limited to fires or explosions with which there is *intent* to destroy or damage. Second,

---

[6] *Williams* v. *State*, 600 N.E.2d 962 (Ind. App. 1992).
[7] Ibid., p. 965.
[8] Ibid., p. 964.
[9] Ibid.
[10] Texas Penal Code Section 28.02 (2010).

**Figure 10.1**
Arson

= *Actus reus*

= *Mens rea*

elements A–F contain further *mens rea* requirements. Based on this statute, if Chad intends to burn an open field yet does not know it is part of an incorporated city or town (and further demonstrates no knowledge pertaining to B–E and does not act recklessly), he would not be guilty of arson under Texas law. One would be hard-pressed to come up with a real-life example of such a situation, however.

The *mens rea* of arson under the Model Penal Code is "purpose." Specifically, arson occurs if a person starts a fire or causes an explosion "*with the purpose of*" either "destroying a building or occupied structure of another"; or "destroying or damaging any property, whether his own or another's, to collect insurance for such loss."[11] See Figure 10.1 for a summary of arson in flowchart format.

## Degrees of Arson

Some states classify arson into degrees. In New York, there are five degrees of arson, ranging from least to most serious:

- A person is guilty of arson in the *fifth degree* when he or she intentionally damages property of another without consent of the owner by intentionally starting a fire or causing an explosion.
- A person is guilty of arson in the *fourth degree* when he recklessly damages a building or motor vehicle by intentionally starting a fire or causing an explosion.
- A person is guilty of arson in the *third degree* when he intentionally damages a building or motor vehicle by starting a fire or causing an explosion.
- A person is guilty of arson in the *second degree* when he intentionally damages a building or motor vehicle by starting a fire, and when (a) another person who is not a participant in the crime is present in such building or motor vehicle at the time, and (b) the defendant knows that fact or the circumstances are such as to render the presence of such a person therein a reasonable possibility.[12]

[11]Model Penal Code Section 11.1(1).
[12]N.Y. Penal Law Sections 150.01-150.15 (2010).

New York reserves *first-degree* arson convictions for fires and explosions (a) caused by incendiary devices and/or (b) that harm people, are committed with one or more people present (or there is a "reasonable possibility" that one or more people is present), or are committed for financial gain.[13] For example, if Bill decides to burn his house down because he cannot sell it in a flatlined real estate market, he would be guilty of first-degree arson in New York, a felony.

See the accompanying Court Decision for more on arson. In it we examine the case of *State* v. *Pigott*, where the defendant is charged with first-degree arson in North Carolina.

## COURT DECISION

*State* v. *Pigott*
415 S.E.2d 555 (N.C. 1992)

**Background:** Henry Levi Pigott was convicted of first-degree murder, armed robbery, first-degree arson, and first-degree kidnapping in the Superior Court, Brunswick County. Defendant appealed. In regards to the arson charge, the Supreme Court of North Carolina affirmed. The case was remanded for a new sentencing hearing in regards to a sentencing error.

* * *Evidence presented by the State, including a voluntary statement by defendant, tended to show that, shortly after midnight, 25 September 1988, defendant visited his employer, Darwin Freeman, who lived in an apartment adjoining the office of his lumber business. Defendant asked Freeman for a fifty-dollar loan, but was refused. Defendant left but soon returned with a gun. Defendant forced Freeman to lie on the floor, bound his hands with the sash from his robe, and ransacked the apartment and office for money. Defendant subsequently bound Freeman's feet to his hands and shot him in the head. After looking around for more money, defendant located some kerosene with which he doused rags and furnishings, which he then ignited. Defendant left again and later returned with his girlfriend and some gasoline to Freeman's apartment, where he poured the gasoline throughout the bedroom and kitchen, ignited it and left. Freeman's body was discovered in the burning building shortly before 4:00 a.m. A pathologist who performed the autopsy testified that cause of death was probably the gunshot wound to the head although carbon monoxide was found in sufficient quantities in the bloodstream to have caused death. The pathologist testified that the level of carbon monoxide in the bloodstream indicated that Freeman had been alive and breathed fumes from the fire for some time. He admitted that some carbon monoxide could have entered Freeman's body through reflexive inhalation.

* * *Defendant . . . contends the trial court erred in denying defendant's timely motion to dismiss the charge of first-degree arson. Defendant argues the State failed to produce sufficient evidence to establish the building was occupied by a living person when the arson occurred.

---

[13]Ibid., Section 150.20 (2010).

\*\*\*The common law definition of arson, in force in this state, is " 'the willful and malicious burning of the dwelling house of another person.' " Because "the main purpose of common law arson is to protect against danger to those persons who might be in the dwelling house which is burned," the codification of this offense for punishment purposes distinguishes between a dwelling house that is occupied and one that is not:

> There shall be two degrees of arson as defined at the common law. If the dwelling burned was occupied at the time of the burning, the offense is arson in the first degree and is punishable as a Class C felony. If the dwelling burned was unoccupied at the time of the burning, the offense is arson in the second degree and is punishable as a Class D felony.

N.C.G.S. § 14-58 (1986). The crime of arson is consummated by the burning of any part of the house; and a burning occurs when there is charring, that is, when wood is reduced to coal and its identity changed, but not when it is merely scorched or discolored by the heat.

The State's evidence in support of the offense of first-degree arson tended to show as follows:

> Defendant recounted in his pretrial statement offered against him at trial that he had poured kerosene throughout the building and had "lit a fire in the bedroom area of the building." When defendant left, the victim was "still alive and breathing." Defendant told one witness that the building had not burned when doused with kerosene, so he got his girlfriend "to go back with him to get some gas." Defendant returned with a gallon of gasoline, poured it in the bedroom and kitchen area of the building, ignited it, and left. Investigators discovered burned areas on part of the porch roof and around the window and door frame in addition to burned furnishings. The pathologist who examined the victim's body testified that it contained a potentially lethal fifty percent saturation of carbon monoxide, caused by smoke inhalation. The pathologist concluded the victim had been alive while the fire was burning and generating carbon monoxide because of the significant quantity inhaled.

We hold this evidence supports the elements of first-degree arson. From it a jury could reasonably infer that the victim, while living, inhaled quantities of smoke containing carbon monoxide from the same fire that caused the charring of the window and door frames. If a reasonable inference of defendant's guilt can be drawn from evidence that is not merely speculative, but real and substantial, "then it is the jury's decision whether such evidence convinces them beyond a reasonable doubt of defendant's guilt." We conclude the trial court did not err in denying defendant's motion to dismiss the charge of first-degree arson.

## Case Analysis

1. Explain the two different degrees of arson in North Carolina.

2. What is defendant's legal argument regarding his arson conviction?

3. What is the definition of *burning* under North Carolina law?

# Criminal Mischief

**criminal mischief**
Intentionally damaging or destroying another's property.

**Criminal mischief**, once called *malicious mischief*, consists of intentionally damaging or destroying property. So long as it does not involve intentional burning or exploding, almost any form of damage, defacement, or destruction of property qualifies as criminal mischief. We will shift attention to vandalism in the next section, but for now know that some states criminalize under their "mischief" statutes conduct that would be considered vandalism, were a vandalism law on the books. Likewise, some state criminal mischief statutes cover conduct that could be considered arson. And depending on the offender's motivations, some states even maintain malicious *harassment* statutes, often reserved for conduct that does not necessarily lead to damage, but nonetheless amounts to harassment of the target.

## Elements of Criminal Mischief

The *actus reus* of criminal mischief is usually satisfied by one or more of several behaviors. In Ohio, for example, the following actions constitute the *actus reus* of criminal mischief:

1. Defacement, damage, or destruction to property
2. "[R]eleasing a substance that is harmful or offensive to persons exposed or that tends to cause public alarm"
3. Tampering with boundary markers, monuments, or survey stations
4. Tampering with any safety device
5. Setting fire to personal property outside and apart from any building or structure
6. Impairing the function of a computer or computer system[14]

Texas criminalizes much of the same conduct, but its criminal mischief statute also covers actions that could be considered vandalism: any "markings, including inscriptions, slogans, drawings, or paintings, on the tangible property of the owner."[15]

The *mens rea* of criminal mischief typically requires some level of intent. According to the Model Penal Code, criminal mischief includes damage to the tangible property of another person that is done "purposely, recklessly, or by negligence."[16] Some states use similar language; others do not. Texas requires "intent" or "knowledge."[17] The Ohio statute quoted above requires either knowledge or purpose depending on the specific conduct in question.

Former JetBlue flight attendant Steven Slater, who, in August 2010, allegedly "flipped out," opened a landed airplane's door, and exited it by way of an inflatable evacuation slide, was charged with criminal mischief for his actions—and also reckless endangerment. According to one article, "Cops must have been scratching their heads to come up with the charges,"[18] as there are not too many statutes that target such actions.

---

[14] Ohio Rev. Code Section 2909.07 (2010).
[15] Texas Penal Code Section 28.03(a)(3) (2010).
[16] Model Penal Code Section 220.3.
[17] Texas Penal Code Section 28.03(a)(3) (2010).
[18] J. Molloy, "Slater Does What We All Dream of Doing," *New York Daily News*, http://tinyurl.com/237gtyw (accessed September 17, 2010).

## Criminal Mischief without Damage

What if otherwise mischievous behavior fails to cause damage, but is nonetheless offensive or emotionally damaging? In some states, prosecutors may not press charges because no statute covers the conduct in question. In other states, laws have been enacted to address such limitations. Consider the Supreme Court's decision in *Virginia* v. *Black*,[19] a case addressing the constitutionality of Virginia's cross-burning statute. Two men were convicted, under Virginia's cross-burning statute, of burning crosses with intent to intimidate. They argued that the law was unconstitutional and violated their First Amendment rights to freely express themselves. The U.S. Supreme Court disagreed, however, siding with the state of Virginia:

> The First Amendment permits a state to outlaw cross-burnings done with the intent to intimidate because burning a cross is a particularly virulent form of intimidation. Instead of prohibiting all intimidating messages, a state may choose to regulate this subset of intimidating messages in light of cross-burning's long and pernicious history as a signal of impending violence. Thus, just as a state may regulate only that obscenity which is the most obscene due to its prurient content, so too may a state choose to prohibit only those forms of intimidation that are most likely to inspire fear of bodily harm. A ban on cross-burning carried out with the intent to intimidate is proscribable under the First Amendment.[20]

The state enacted the cross-burning statute partly because its criminal mischief statute would not otherwise permit prosecution of individuals who engage in mischievous conduct (in this case cross burning) but fail to cause physical damage.

Graffiti constitutes a type of vandalism and can affect neighborhood quality of life.

Galina Barskaya/
Shutterstock.com

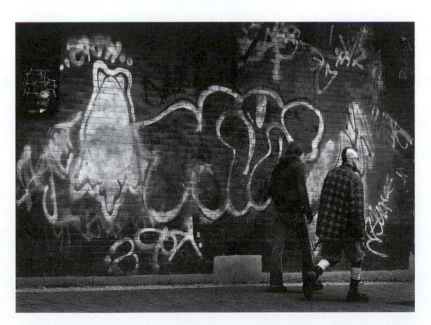

---

[19]*Virginia* v. *Black*, 538 U.S. 343 (2003).
[20]Ibid.

# Vandalism

**vandalism** Sometimes considered a form of *criminal mischief,* willful or malicious acts intended to damage property.

**Vandalism,** sometimes considered a form of criminal or malicious mischief, is usually defined as willful or malicious acts intended to damage property. This definition is quite similar to our earlier definition of criminal mischief, however. Whether it is a stand-alone offense depends on the laws of each state. For example, Pennsylvania includes within its criminal mischief statute "defacing or damaging property with graffiti."[21] At the other extreme, California maintains a vandalism statute, providing that:

> (a) Every person who maliciously commits any of the following acts with respect to any real or personal property not his or her own, in cases other than those specified by state law, is guilty of vandalism: (1) Defaces with graffiti or other inscribed material. (2) Damages. (3) Destroys.[22]

Tennessee takes yet another approach. Its *vandalism* statute includes actions that would be considered criminal mischief. Its law provides that "[a]ny person who knowingly causes damage to or the destruction of any real or personal property of another or of the state, the United States, any county, city, or town knowing that the person does not have the owner's consent is guilty of an offense under this section."[23] The offenses range from a misdemeanor to a serious felony (8–30 years in prison) depending on the monetary value assigned to the property damage.[24]

*Vandalism* is also frequently defined as such at the county or municipal level, usually in reference to graffiti and similar markings. For example, San Diego's municipal code makes it illegal to write graffiti on any building, fence, or structure, without the property owner's express permission.[25] A number of cities also criminalize the mere *possession* of graffiti-related tools. To illustrate, in Oklahoma City, "[n]o person under the age of 18 years may possess an aerosol spray paint container or broad-tipped indelible marker on any public property unless accompanied by a parent, guardian, employer, teacher, or other adult in any similar relationship and such possession is for a lawful purpose."[26]

## YOUR DECISION

1. Just days before graduation, Jeremy Bates learns he failed his chemistry final and will not be graduating from high school. Determined to get "revenge," he plans to burn down the school. Jeremy's high school is constructed entirely of cinder block and cement and contains no wood or other flammable items, however, and since Jeremy did not do well in chemistry, he does not realize that cinder block and cement will not burn. He starts a small fire with twigs in the corner of his science classroom, but obviously the wall and floor do not catch on fire. A small black residue remains on the wall and floor. Can Jeremy be charged with arson? Why or why not? Are there any other possible crimes to charge Jeremy with?

2. Stephanie, an amateur painter, lives in a rough inner city neighborhood with decaying buildings and littered streets. Stephanie decides she wants to "beautify"

---

[21]42 Pa. Cons. Stat Section 3302 (2010).
[22]Cal. Penal Code Section 594 (2010).
[23]Tenn. Code Ann. Section 39-14-408 (2010).
[24]Ibid.
[25]San Diego Municipal Code Section 95.0127(c)(1),(2), (1992).
[26]Oklahoma City Mun. Code Section 35-201 (2010).

the neighborhood and make it a more pleasant place to live. One evening, she takes her painting supplies and creates a large mural of rainbows and flowers on the side of an abandoned tattoo parlor. Stephanie does not own the tattoo parlor. The next morning the police see Stephanie's "work." Can Stephanie be charged with a crime? If so, which crime or crimes?

## Summary

- There were four common law elements of arson: (1) malicious (2) burning (3) of a dwelling (4) of another.

- The common law definition of *arson* was restrictive, mainly because it limited the crime to dwellings.

- At common law, setting fire to one's own property was not considered arson.

- The *actus reus* of arson today is damage by fire or explosion.

- Smoke damage, without visible charring, may satisfy the *actus reus* of arson.

- The *mens rea* of arson varies by statute, but typically requires intent or knowledge.

- Criminal mischief was called "malicious mischief" under common law.

- The *actus reus* of criminal mischief depends on the law in question, but usually consists of defacement, damage, or destruction of property.

- The *mens rea* of criminal mischief requires some level of intent, anything from "purpose" to simple "knowledge."

- The *actus reus* of vandalism is similar to that for criminal mischief, typically the damage to or defacement of property.

- The *mens rea* of vandalism is also similar to that for criminal mischief and arson: some degree of intent or knowledge.

MODULE

# 10.2  PROPERTY INVASION

### *Learning Objectives*
- **Summarize the elements of trespassing.**
- **Explain how trespassing statutes have been used to target illegal immigration.**
- **Describe the crime of burglary.**

**CORE CONCEPTS**   Property invasion crimes are those during which the offender enters the private property of another individual. The two main property invasion crimes are trespassing and burglary. Trespassing is concerned primarily with illegal entry onto private property. Burglary combines trespassing with the intent to commit a felony.

# Trespassing

**trespassing** Physical entry onto another person's property without consent.

The criminal law definition of **trespassing** is, simply, entry onto private property without the owner's consent. Odds are you have seen a "No Trespassing" sign at some time in your life. More often than not, property owners post such signs in an effort to protect their privacy, often without regard to whether the act of trespassing is criminal. But depending on the jurisdiction in question, trespassing may be a criminal offense.

Trespassing statutes offer prosecutors an alternative to criminal mischief or burglary statutes. We define *burglary* in the next subsection, but for now it bears mentioning that if there is no intent to commit a felony (typically theft), burglary does not occur. Likewise, if a person's conduct does not amount to mischief, but that person nevertheless enters private land without permission, a trespassing conviction is possible.

## Elements of Trespassing

The *actus reus* of trespassing is satisfied when a person either enters or remains on another's private property without permission. Trespassing is sometimes considered a general intent offense. In Texas, for example, it is defined as follows:

> a. A person commits an offense if the person enters or remains on or in property of another, including residential land, agricultural land, a recreational vehicle park, a building, or an aircraft or other vehicle, without effective consent and the person:
> 1. had notice that the entry was forbidden; or
> 2. received notice to depart but failed to do so.[27]

There are a few noteworthy elements in this statute. First, note that trespassing in Texas is a general intent offense. There is no specific *mens rea* that the prosecutor is required to prove. If a person is given notice that entry is forbidden and enters anyway, then the *mens rea* is presumed. Second, note that trespassing extends to more than just real property. Finally, to find a person guilty of trespassing, it must be shown that he or she was given notice that entry was forbidden. According to Texas law, notice can include signs, fencing, and both oral and written communications. So, for example, if Ernest yells to Cletus, "Get off my land!" and Cletus fails to do so, he could be guilty of criminal trespass. Trespassing is considered a misdemeanor in Texas.

In Ohio, criminal trespass is considered a specific intent offense. The state defines criminal trespass thusly:

> A. No person, without privilege to do so, shall do any of the following:
> 1. Knowingly enter or remain on the land or premises of another;
> 2. Knowingly enter or remain on the land or premises of another, the use of which is lawfully restricted to certain persons, purposes, modes, or hours, when the offender knows the offender is in violation of any such restriction or is reckless in that regard;

---

[27]Texas Penal Code Section 30.05(a) (2010).

**Figure 10.2**
Trespassing

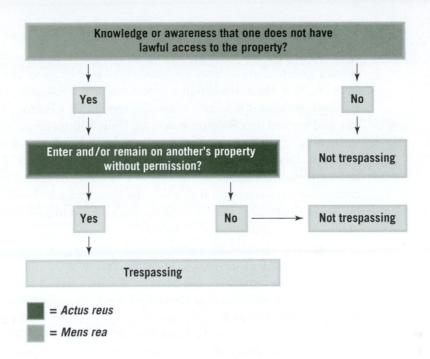

3. Recklessly enter or remain on the land or premises of another, as to which notice against unauthorized access or presence is given by actual communication to the offender, or in a manner prescribed by law, or by posting in a manner reasonably calculated to come to the attention of potential intruders, or by fencing or other enclosure manifestly designed to restrict access;

4. Being on the land or premises of another, negligently fail or refuse to leave upon being notified by signage posted in a conspicuous place or otherwise being notified to do so by the owner or occupant, or the agent or servant of either.[28]

Note the use of the terms *knowingly*, *recklessly*, and *negligently* in this statute. To secure a trespassing conviction, prosecutors must prove the specific intent required for the criminal conduct being alleged (see Figure 10.2).

Both the Texas and Ohio statutes refer, generally, to others' private property. Some states add to their trespass statutes very specific types of property on which people cannot enter without permission—or outside of normal operating hours. For example, Maine's criminal trespass statute provides, in part, that a "person is guilty of criminal trespass if, knowing that that person is not licensed or privileged to do so, that person"[29]:

Enters or remains in a cemetery or burial ground at any time between 1/2 hour after sunset and 1/2 hour before sunrise the following day, unless that person enters or remains during hours in which visitors are permitted to enter or remain by municipal ordinance or, in the case of a privately owned and operated cemetery, by posting.[30]

---

[28]Ohio Rev. Code Section 2911.21 (2010).
[29]Maine Rev. Stat. 17-A Section 402(1) (2010).
[30]Ibid., Section 402(1)(F).

## Creative Use of Trespassing Statutes

At least one jurisdiction has used its state criminal trespassing statute to target a very specific group of individuals: undocumented immigrants.[31] In April of 2005, a New Ipswich, New Hampshire, police officer stopped a motorist. The driver, Jorge Mora Ramirez, produced a forged Massachusetts driver's license. The officer questioned him and learned that Ramirez was in the United States illegally. Ramirez was arrested for operating a vehicle without a license and taken into custody. The New Ipswich police contacted Immigration and Customs Enforcement (ICE) to advise them they had an illegal immigrant in custody. ICE declined to take Ramirez into its custody, citing scarce resources. At that point, the New Ipswich Sheriff, W. Garrett Chamberlain, consulted with a local prosecutor. Both agreed to prosecute Ramirez under New Hampshire's criminal trespass statute.

The New Hampshire statute defined criminal trespass as follows: "[a] person is guilty of criminal trespass if, knowing that he is not licensed or privileged to do so, he enters or remains in any place."[32] Chamberlain and the prosecutor reasoned that because Ramirez was in the United States illegally, he was also in New Hampshire illegally. A sheriff in the neighboring town of Hudson then used the same theory to detain 10 more illegal immigrants. Ramirez and the other detainees challenged the trespassing charges, arguing that New Hampshire law was preempted by the federal Immigration and Nationality Act (Article VI of the U.S. Constitution makes U.S. law the supreme law of the land). Prosecutors countered and argued that since the federal government did not want to take custody of the defendants, they were entitled to fall back on state law. A district court sided with the defendants. And while the case was unsuccessful, it does not bind the courts in other states. Moreover, the case has gathered plenty of attention in other states, suggesting that perhaps other cases are on the horizon.[33] Critics of the trespassing approach to illegal immigration do raise meritorious arguments, however. As one of them put it,

> [F]ederal law occupies the field of sanctioning unlawful presence in the United States. The Immigration and Nationality Act creates a pervasive regulatory scheme, mixing civil and criminal penalties, for punishing illegal entry and presence in the United States. That being the case, the states are not free to add to the slate of penalties provided for by Congress. Second, allowing states to sanction illegal immigrants for trespass would undermine federal objectives by creating a non-uniform system of immigration enforcement, and is therefore invalid under the doctrine of conflict preemption. State officials may be frustrated by federal enforcement efforts, but frustration alone cannot justify state action outside the bounds of what the Constitution and our federal system permit.[34]

---

[31]Much of this discussion draws from M. R. Boland, Jr., "No Trespassing: The States, the Supremacy Clause, and the Use of Criminal Trespass Laws to Fight Illegal Immigration," *Penn State Law Review*, Vol. 111 (2006), pp. 481–503.

[32]N.H. Rev. Stat. Section 635:2 (2004).

[33]P. Belluck, "Town Uses Trespass Law to Fight Illegal Immigrants," *New York Times*, July 13, 2005, http://www.nytimes.com/2005/07/13/national/13immigrants.html (accessed September 20, 2010).

[34]Boland, "No Trespassing," pp. 502–503.

# Burglary

**burglary** Breaking and entering into the dwelling or structure of another with the intent to commit a felony inside.

**Burglary**, like criminal trespassing, is concerned with property invasion. It is different from trespassing, however, because burglary typically adds to the invasion the *intent to commit a felony*.

Burglary is often viewed—inaccurately, mind you—as a crime of theft from a dwelling. A person who breaks into the home of another and steals the television is often described as a "burglar." Importantly, there is *no* requirement that a theft take place for the entry to become burglary. Even if no property is taken, a burglary may occur.

Burglary has long been considered a serious crime. This offense, along with homicide, rape, aggravated assault, and other serious crimes, is reported in the FBI's crime index, reinforcing its serious nature. As far back as 1769, Sir William Blackstone commented on the gravity of the offense:

> Burglary . . . has always been looked upon as a very heinous offense, not only because of the abundant terror that it naturally carries with it, but also as it is a forcible invasion and disturbance of that right of habitation, which every individual might acquire in a state of nature. . . . And the law of England has so particular and tender regard to the immunity of a man's house, that it styles it a castle and will never suffer it to be violated.[35]

## Common Law Burglary

At common law, burglary elements were as follows:

1. Breaking and entering
2. Of the dwelling of another
3. During the nighttime
4. With intent to commit a felony inside

Breaking and entering is akin to trespassing. *Breaking* meant forcible entry, but simple *entering* also sufficed, say if the front door was unlocked. Also, like trespassing, "breaking and entering" assumes the person doing it does not have the owner's consent. Next, common law burglary was limited to dwellings—particularly "others'" dwellings. This meant (and still means today) that a person could not burglarize his or her own dwelling. Next, *burglary* was defined at common law as a crime that was committed at night. Finally, common law burglary required that the intent to commit a felony was in place at the time of the breaking and entering. So, if a person forcibly entered the dwelling of another at night but had no intent to commit a felony inside, a burglary did not occur.

## Burglary Today

Modern burglary statutes retain most of the common law elements, but the nighttime requirement has been largely abandoned. Since burglaries are largely crimes of opportunity, they often occur during the daytime when people are not home, so it is sensible to relax the nighttime requirement. Several states have also eased up on both

---

[35]Blackstone, *Commentaries on the Laws of England*, p. 223.

the "dwelling" and "intent to commit a felony" requirements. With respect to the former, many structures besides dwellings can now be burglarized. Likewise, many statutes permit burglary convictions if the defendant intends to commit a "crime," which of course includes felonies *and* misdemeanors. Pennsylvania's burglary statute captures several of these changes:

> A person is guilty of burglary if he enters a building or occupied structure, or separately secured or occupied portion thereof, with intent to commit a crime therein, unless the premises are at the time open to the public or the actor is licensed or privileged to enter.[36]

Note how the statute contains no nighttime requirement. Also note that it is not limited to intent to commit a "felony." Any crime suffices. The Pennsylvania statute *does* retain at least one common law element: the occupied dwelling requirement. Other states have extended the definition of burglary to much more than occupied structures. California's burglary statute offers one such example:

> Every person who enters any house, room, apartment, tenement, shop, warehouse, store, mull, barn, stable, outhouse or other building, tent, vessel, . . . floating home, . . . railroad car, locked or sealed cargo container, . . . trailer coach, . . . any house care, . . . inhabited camper, . . . aircraft, . . . or mine or any underground portion thereof, with intent to commit grand or petit larceny or any felony is guilty of burglary.[37]

This statute is very specific about the types of properties that can be burglarized. Also note, however, that its intent requirement is more restrictive than Pennsylvania's. Petit (or petty) larceny is the only misdemeanor that one can intend to commit and still have the unlawful entry amount to burglary. For example, if a person forcibly entered a railroad car for the purpose of marking it up with graffiti (a misdemeanor in most states), that person could not be found guilty of burglary.

The Model Penal Code definition of burglary is perhaps the most concise. To paraphrase, a burglary occurs if a person enters a building or occupied structure with the purpose to commit a crime inside.[38] Also, if the premises are open to the public, then entry does not constitute burglary.

### *Actus Reus* of Burglary.

Burglary statutes are fairly specific in terms of the properties they seek to protect. Likewise, it is quite clear what constitutes entrance without permission. Some confusion surrounds the definition of *breaking*, however. And since the typical burglary that comes to mind is one premised on forcible entry, it behooves us to give this important term a little more thought. What exactly is *breaking*?

On the one hand, smashing a window in with a crowbar clearly constitutes breaking. But what if the defendant merely scales a fence? Does that constitute breaking? It depends on what the burglary statute requires. In a Nebraska case, the defendant scaled a fence and stole transmission parts from a secured storage yard.[39] He was convicted of burglary, but later appealed, arguing that he did not forcibly enter the property, which the Nebraska burglary statute required. The statute defined *burglary* in this way:

---

[36]18 Pa. Cons. Stat Section 3502(a)(b) (2010).
[37]California Penal Code Section 459 (2010).
[38]Model Penal Code Section 221.1.
[39]*State* v. *McDowell*, 522 N.W.2d 738 (Neb. 1994).

A person commits burglary if such person willfully, maliciously, and *forcibly* breaks and enters any real estate or any improvements erected thereon with intent to commit any felony or with intent to steal property of any value [emphasis added].[40]

McDowell, the appellant, argued that climbing a fence is not the same as forcible entry. The Nebraska Supreme Court agreed:

> Although it undoubtedly took McDowell some measure of force to climb or jump the fence in the instant case, no obstruction was removed. McDowell merely entered through the open space above the fence. Thus, as a matter of law there was no breaking, and therefore no burglary. McDowell's motion to dismiss should have been sustained with respect to the charge of burglary. McDowell's conviction for burglary is therefore, reversed.[41]

Just because McDowell's burglary conviction was reversed does not mean he went free. In all likelihood, he was convicted of a less serious larceny-related offense.

So breaking a window is forcible entry. Climbing a fence, at least in Nebraska, is not. What about the middle ground, say opening a closed, though unlocked, door? In case law from the same state, courts have repeatedly held that there is no requirement that a door be locked for a burglary conviction to stand: "The opening of a closed door to enter a building is 'breaking' within the definition of burglary."[42] If the door is both unlocked *and* open, then entrance through it is not considered breaking.[43] Note, again, that these decisions arose from Nebraska cases. Other states may take a more strict approach, while still others' approach may be more relaxed. For example, California's burglary statute (see earlier) does not contain any mention of "forcible"—thus the meaning of the term is something of a nonissue in that state.

Some statutes, and the Model Penal Code, extend the *actus reus* of burglary to the practice of **surreptitious remaining**. This occurs when a person has lawful access the property, but then remains until that person no longer does, and intends to commit a crime. Hiding in a department store bathroom until it closes with intent to steal merchandise is an example of behavior that would constitute surreptitious remaining.

See the accompanying Court Decision for more on the *actus reus* of burglary. In it we examine the case of *Ferrara* v. *State*, where the defendant is charged with burglary even though he did not physically enter the victim's home.

**surreptitious remaining**
A person has lawful access the property, but then remains until he or she no longer does, and intends to commit a crime.

# COURT DECISION

*Ferrara* v. *State*
19 So.3d 1033 (Fla. App. 2009)

**Background:** Jeremy Ferrara was convicted of burglary of a dwelling in the Circuit Court, Hernando County. Ferrara appealed and the District Court of Appeals of Florida affirmed.

Jeremy Ferrara ["Ferrara"] appeals his conviction of burglary of a dwelling for stealing a screen door and attempting to steal copper tubing from the air conditioning

[40]Neb. Rev. Stat. Ann. Section 28-507 (2010).
[41]*State* v. *McDowell*, 522 N.W.2d 738, p. 744.
[42]*State* v. *Sutton*, 368 N.W.2d 492 (Neb. 1985), p. 495.
[43]See, e.g., *Hayward* v. *State*, 149 N.W. 105 (1914).

unit of a vacant residence. He mainly contends that he cannot be convicted of burglary of a dwelling because he did not enter the structure. We affirm.

On October 19, 2007, between 5 and 6 a.m., Ralph Philbin, an employee of the St. Petersburg Times, was standing outside the Times building when he noticed a dark colored car pull into the carport of the unoccupied property across the street. The employee then heard a loud noise, and he called 911. The car remained at the dwelling for about five minutes and then it departed.

In response to the dispatch of a burglary in progress, Detective Brian Mott approached the residence. As he was approaching, he saw a dark colored pick-up truck departing. The truck accelerated to seventy-five miles per hour, then made an abrupt u-turn and stopped. The driver fled on foot. A search of the vehicle revealed Ferrara's identification and a screen door in the bed of the truck.

Meanwhile, Deputy Jill Morrell . . . heard a hissing sound, which she determined to be the sound of Freon escaping from an outdoor air conditioner situated underneath the roof of an attached carport. The air conditioner had been pulled away from the house and the copper wiring had been cut. She then went around to the front of the house and found that a screen door appeared to have been removed from its hinges. She did not find any other signs of forced entry.

Ferrara contends that the trial court erred in denying his motion for judgment of acquittal on the burglary of a dwelling charge because the evidence was insufficient to support a conviction for burglary of a dwelling. Specifically, he contends that the State failed to prove that a burglary of a dwelling occurred with regard to either the screen door or the copper tubing from the air conditioner because neither involved an entry into the house, an attached porch, or the curtilage.

To prove a burglary of a dwelling, the State needs to prove that a defendant entered a dwelling with the intent to commit an offense therein. Section 810.011(2), Florida Statutes (2008), defines "dwelling" as: "a building or conveyance of any kind, *including any attached porch,* whether such building or conveyance is temporary or permanent, mobile or immobile, which has a roof over it and is designed to be occupied by people lodging therein at night, *together with the curtilage thereof.* . . ." (Emphasis added). The standard jury instructions define "dwelling" as "a building or conveyance of any kind, including any attached porch, whether such building or conveyance is temporary or permanent, mobile or immobile, which has a roof over it and is designed to be occupied by people lodging therein at night, together with the enclosed space of ground and outbuildings immediately surrounding it." It also provides that the entry necessary "need not be the whole body of the defendant. It is sufficient if the defendant extends any part of the body far enough into the [structure] to commit [burglary]."

Ferrara contends that, because the property was not enclosed, going to the front door of the house and removing the screen door did not constitute entry into a dwelling under the burglary statute. In *Weber* v. *State,* the defendant was convicted of burglary of a dwelling for stealing a ceiling fan lying on a cement slab. The slab adjoined the rear of the apartment, had a roof over it and was supported by posts. This Court held that the slab from which the fan was stolen qualified as an attached porch pursuant to section 810.011(2), Florida Statutes. Here, similar to *Weber,* Ferrara had to enter a covered porch at the front of the residence to steal the door. The front porch is part of the dwelling as defined under section 810.011(2), Florida Statutes. By entering the attached porch to steal the screen door, Ferrara committed a burglary.

Ferrara also asserts that he is entitled to a judgment of acquittal with regard to the copper tubing attached to the outside air conditioner because the carport where the air conditioner is located is neither an "attached porch," nor within the curtilage of the home.... In *Burston,* the Second District Court of Appeal determined that an attached carport, similar to the carport in this case, constituted part of the curtilage of the dwelling. There, the defendant was charged with burglary of a dwelling for stealing a lawnmower from a carport. The carport was contiguous to the home and consisted of a cement slab, a roof that was flush with the roof of the dwelling, and four aluminum poles supporting the roof. The carport, no longer used for storing vehicles, shared a wall with the dwelling and the kitchen door opened onto the carport.

[W]e hold that a carport attached to a dwelling is a burglarizable part of the dwelling. Ferrara's conviction was proper.

AFFIRMED.

## Case Analysis

1. Which specific element of burglary is the defendant contesting in this case?

2. The court refers to the term *curtilage* in regards to its analysis. What is *curtilage* and how is it relevant to the defendant's case?

3. Do you agree with the court's conclusion regarding both the screen door and the copper tubing? Why or why not?

---

***Mens Rea* of Burglary.**   Burglary is a specific intent offense because of the requirement that the prosecution prove the defendant's (a) intent of breaking, entering, or remaining, and (b) the intent to commit a crime once inside. Without such intent, there is no burglary. Again, burglary does not require that the intended crime (usually theft) be completed. All that is needed is intent. For example, if Dan breaks into Joe's house with the intent of stealing Joe's hunting rifle, but can't find it, he has still committed burglary even though he did not complete the crime.

If burglary can include this type of "attempted" theft, then what constitutes attempted burglary? Assume that Dan has a hard time breaking into Joe's house. Further assume that with a large crowbar, he tries for all he's worth to force open Joe's front door. And, finally, assume a police officer observes his actions and makes an arrest. Dan's actions in this situation amount to attempted burglary because he never successfully entered the property. See Figure 10.3 for a summary of burglary in flowchart format.

## Degrees of Burglary

State burglary statutes also vary in terms of how they treat burglaries. Usually first-degree burglary, if such a crime exists, is reserved for defendants who are armed or who hurt or threaten to hurt the occupants of the targeted structure (some states call this *aggravated burglary*—in addition to or instead of first-degree burglary). Alabama defines first-degree burglary thusly:

**Figure 10.3**
Burglary

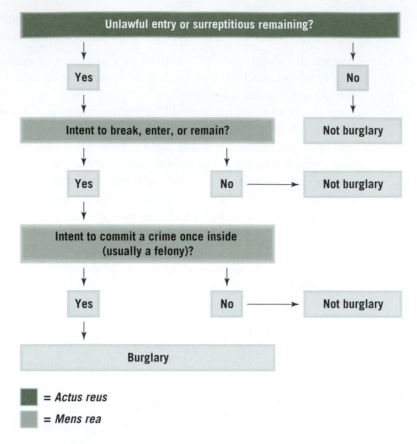

= *Actus reus*

= *Mens rea*

a. A person commits the crime of burglary in the first degree if he or she knowingly and unlawfully enters or remains unlawfully in a dwelling with intent to commit a crime therein, and, if, in effecting entry or while in dwelling or in immediate flight therefrom, the person or another participant in the crime:
   1. Is armed with explosives; or
   2. Causes physical injury to any person who is not a participant in the crime; or
   3. In effecting entry, is armed with a deadly weapon or dangerous instrument or, while in the dwelling or immediate flight from the dwelling, uses or threatens the immediate use of a deadly weapon or dangerous instrument against another person. . . .[44]

At the other extreme, third-degree burglary is the least serious, occurring when one "knowingly enters or remains unlawfully in a building with intent to commit a crime therein."[45]

**YOUR DECISION**

1. Joey's family owns several acres of property in the Pocono Mountains. Joey often hunts, hikes, and rides snowmobiles throughout the family property. One snowy afternoon, Joey rides his snowmobile onto the neighbor's property. If Joey is unaware the he crossed onto his neighbor's property, can he be guilty of trespassing? What if an old "No Trespassing" sign was nailed to a tree?

[44]Al. Code Section 13A-7-5 (2010).
[45]Al. Code Section 13A-7-7 (2010).

2. One afternoon Dan notices that his neighbor's front door is wide open and no one appears to be home. Dan enters the front door to make sure that everything is all right inside. After he enters the foyer, however, Dan sees that the deliveryman left a brand new PlayStation 3, still in the box. Dan decides to take the box for himself, hoping that the neighbors will blame the missing PlayStation on a delivery error. Has Dan committed burglary? Why or why not?

## Summary

- The *actus reus* of trespassing is entering or remaining on another person's property without permission.

- The *mens rea* of trespassing varies by statute, but in states with general intent trespassing laws, *mens rea* is presumed so long as the trespasser is given *notice* that access is not authorized. "Notice" can include signs, fencing, and oral or written communication.

- Prosecutors in New Hampshire attempted to use their state's trespassing statute to target undocumented immigrants.

- The logic behind the New Hampshire prosecution was that if the immigrants were in the country illegally, they were also in the state illegally.

- The New Hampshire trespassing statute was worded very generally, defining *trespassing* as entering or remaining in "any place" without permission.

- Burglary is not a crime of theft, contrary to popular belief.

- Common law burglary required (1) breaking and entering (2) of the dwelling of another (3) during the nighttime (4) with intent to commit a felony inside.

- Modern-day burglary has relaxed the second, third, and fourth common law elements.

- The *actus reus* of burglary occurs via "breaking" (which can include opening a closed yet unlocked door) or surreptitious remaining.

- Burglary is a specific intent offense, meaning that the prosecution must prove intent to commit a crime (usually a felony) inside.

MODULE

# 10.3 PROPERTY DAMAGE AND INVASION WITH COMPUTERS

*Learning Objectives*
- **Define and explain cybercrime.**
- **Identify laws aimed at controlling property invasion and damage with a computer.**

Computer crime, or **cybercrime**, refers to any crime committed with the assistance of an electronic device, primarily a computer, but also smart phones and other devices. For our purposes, cybercrime falls into two separate yet closely related categories. The first is theft. Thieves use computers to steal a wide range of information from unsuspecting victims, ranging from ordinary citizens to powerful corporations. Computers are also used for the purpose of property invasion and destruction. Often criminals will try to gain access to sensitive data systems so they can then steal information, which is why both types of activity are interrelated. Sometimes, however, they seek to gain access merely for the purpose of causing havoc and either overloading or shutting down valuable computer systems. Property damage and invasion are the focus of this module. We look at theft, including intellectual property theft and identity theft, in the next chapter's larceny module.

It is difficult for the criminal law to "keep up" with technology. Before cybercrime statutes were enacted, prosecutors were forced to charge under traditional statutes, which posed difficulties. For example, if a traditional theft statute required the "carrying away" of items, how would that apply in the case of theft via computer? Unfortunately, criminals often continue to stay one step ahead of legislators, making it a continued struggle for prosecutors to target high-tech criminal activity.

# Cybercrime

Most of us are at least somewhat familiar with computer crime through receipt of spam e-mail messages containing everything from appeals that we update our accounts (often in banks we are not customers of!) to requests that we become fiduciaries of some important person's fortune. Cybercrime can include everything from flagrant attacks through the use of viruses, Trojan horses, software piracy, and surreptitious installation of malware programs, to those annoying phishing e-mail messages that seek to acquire our personal information. Criminals often go further by posing as other individuals in an effort to obtain passwords and other privileged information, in a practice known as **social engineering**.

> This involves persuading administrators or telephonists to give details of passwords or other things by pretending to be staff, suppliers or trusted individuals—even police officers. They could be even masquerading as a computer repair man to get access to the premises.[46]

Kevin Mitnick, who was once the FBI's most wanted hacker, agrees. In an interview after his release from prison, Mitnick said that

> malicious hackers don't need to use stealth computer techniques to break into a network. . . . Often they just trick someone into giving them passwords and other information. . . . People are the weakest link. . . . You can have the best technology,

---

[46]P. Turunen, "Hack Attack: How You Might Be a Target," CNN.com, April 12, 2002. Web posted at http://archives.cnn.com/2002/TECH/ptech/04/12/hack.dangers/index.html (accessed June 27, 2007).

firewalls, intrusion-detection systems, biometric devices . . . and somebody can call an unsuspecting employee . . . [and] they [get] everything.[47]

These and other computer crimes have taken on a transnational flavor, thus tying them in to some of the other problems we have discussed elsewhere in this chapter. Also, terrorists are increasingly exploiting computer technology to do everything from raising money through credit card fraud to communicating with each other.

While these problems are most difficult for law enforcement officials to effectively target, these officials have certainly not been left behind. Technological advances have helped law enforcement, as well:

> Law enforcement access to high-technology investigative tools has produced enormous amounts of information on crimes and suspects, and the use of innovating investigative tools like DNA fingerprinting, keystroke captures, laser and night vision technologies, digital imaging, and thermography are beginning to shape many of the practical aspects of the twenty-first-century criminal justice system.[48]

Figure 10.4 contains a list of specific cybercrimes, mostly those consisting of hacking, fraud, and Internet-related crime. It also presents a list of the federal agencies most likely to investigate such acts.

## The Jurisdiction Problem

*Jurisdiction* refers to the state's power to hear a criminal case and render a verdict. For example, if you commit a murder entirely in Texas, you cannot be prosecuted for the crime in Pennsylvania. Crimes committed *without* the assistance of computers usually have clear jurisdictional boundaries. This is at least true for the traditional types of serious crime with which we are most familiar—homicide, rape, robbery, and so on. Certain offenses, such as kidnapping, can cross jurisdictional boundaries, adding a interstate flavor and therefore complicating prosecution. Questions of cybercrime jurisdiction, however, can cause one's head to spin. Consider this scenario:

> A Web site in Germany caters to the adult market, and has done so happily for three years. Then, out of the blue, it finds itself indicted in Singapore because of spreading pornographic material in Singapore, even though the company has never done business with someone from Singapore. To make things worse, the Web site owners are ordered to appear in court in Belgium, because some of the adult pictures are considered to be of 17-year old minors, constituting the crime of child pornography (which, in Belgium, entails persons under 18 years of age; in Germany, the age limit is 14). The business is perfectly legal in Germany, but since it uses the Internet to conduct its business, it finds itself confronted with the criminal laws of all countries connected to the Internet—that is, all countries of the world.[49]

---

[47]E. Abreu, "Kevin Mitnick Bares All," *Industry Standard*. Web posted at http://www.networkworld.com/news/2000/0928mitnick.html (accessed June 27, 2007).

[48]F. Schmalleger, *Criminal Justice Today: An Introductory Text for the 21st Century*, 9th ed. (Upper Saddle River, NJ: Prentice-Hall, 2006), p. 712.

[49]S. W. Brenner and B. Koops, "Approaches to Cybercrime Jurisdiction," *Journal of High Tech Law*, Vol. 4 (2004), p. 3.

**Figure 10.4**
Primary Types of
Computer Crime and
Federal Agencies
Tasked with
Investigation

*Source:* http://www.cybercrime.
gov/reporting.htm#cc
(accessed September 27,
2010).

| Type of Crime | Appropriate Federal Investigative Law Enforcement Agencies |
|---|---|
| Computer Intrusion (i.e., hacking) | • FBI local office<br>• U.S. Secret Service<br>• Internet Crime Complaint Center |
| Password Trafficking | • FBI local office<br>• U.S. Secret Service<br>• Internet Crime Complaint Center |
| Counterfeiting of Currency | • U.S. Secret Service<br>• FBI local office |
| Child Pornography or Exploitation | • If imported, U.S. Immigration and Customs Enforcement<br>• Internet Crime Complaint Center |
| Child Exploitation and Internet Fraud Matters That Have a Mail Nexus | • U.S. Postal Inspection Service<br>• Internet Crime Complaint Center |
| Internet Fraud and SPAM | • FBI local office<br>• U.S. Secret Service (Financial Crimes Division)<br>• Federal Trade Commission (online complaint)<br>• if securities fraud or investment-related SPAM e-mails, Securities and Exchange Commission (online complaint)<br>• The Internet Crime Complaint Center |
| Internet Harassment | • FBI local office |
| Internet Bomb Threats | • FBI local office<br>• ATF local office |
| Trafficking in Explosive or Incendiary Devices or Firearms over the Internet | • FBI local office<br>• ATF local office |

Clearly, a number of jurisdictional questions can arise. This is an area of continual development in the law, too. In the United States alone, there is a bewildering array of federal and state legislation that can be used to target cybercriminals. In general, however, if the federal government (or its interests) is the victim, federal prosecution is in order. If a state is the victim, then a state prosecution will likely occur. And if the victim is an individual, then depending on the conduct in question, the prosecution may occur at either the state or the federal level.

Federal cybercrime law continues to evolve and change with the times, but most of it is found in the so-called **Computer Fraud and Abuse Act (CFAA)**.[50] The types of actions criminalized in the CFAA as well as the penalties provided appear in Figure 10.5. State laws also continue to change as the needs arise.

**Computer Fraud and Abuse Act (CFAA)**
Federal legislation that criminalizes various types of cybercrime.

[50]18 U.S.C. Section 1030 (2010).

| Offense | Section | Sentence* |
|---|---|---|
| Obtaining National Security Information | (a)(1) | 10 (20) years |
| Compromising the Confidentiality of a Computer | (a)(2) | 1 or 5 |
| Trespassing in a Government Computer | (a)(3) | 1 (10) |
| Accessing a Computer to Defraud & Obtain Value | (a)(4) | 5 (10) |
| Knowing Transmission and Intentional Damage | (a)(5)(A)(i) | 10 (20 or life) |
| Intentional Access and Reckless Damage | (a)(5)(A)(ii) | 5 (20) |
| Intentional Access and Damage | (a)(5)(A)(iii) | 1 (10) |
| Trafficking in Passwords | (a)(6) | 1 (10) |
| Extortion Involving Threats to Damage Computer | (a)(7) | 5 (10) |

*The maximum prison sentences for second convictions are noted in parentheses.

**Figure 10.5**
Summary of CFAA Provisions

*Source:* S. Eltringham, Ed., *Prosecuting Computer Crimes* (Washington, DC: United States Department of Justice, Computer Crime and Intellectual Property Section, 2007). Available at: http://www.justice.gov/criminal/cybercrime/ccmanual/ (accessed September 27, 2010), p. 2.

See the accompanying Court Decision for more on the CFAA. In it, we examine the case of *United States* v. *Phillips*, where a computer science student attacks his own university's computer system.

## COURT DECISION

*United States* v. *Phillips*
477 F.3d 215 (5th Cir. 2007)

**Background:** Christopher Andrew Phillips was convicted in Western District of Texas for violating the Computer Fraud and Abuse Act (CFAA). Phillips appealed and the Fifth Circuit Court of Appeal affirmed.

***I. Background**

Phillips entered the University of Texas at Austin ("UT") in 2001 and was admitted to the Department of Computer Sciences in 2003. Like all incoming UT students, Phillips signed UT's "acceptable use" computer policy, in which he agreed not to perform port scans using his university computer account. Nonetheless, only a few weeks after matriculating, Phillips began using various programs designed to scan computer networks and steal encrypted data and passwords. He succeeded in infiltrating hundreds of computers, including machines belonging to other UT students, private businesses, U.S. Government agencies, and the British Armed Services webserver. In a matter of months, Phillips amassed a veritable informational goldmine by stealing and cataloguing a wide variety of personal and proprietary data, such as credit card numbers, bank account information, student financial aid statements, birth records, passwords, and Social Security numbers.

The scans, however, were soon discovered by UT's Information Security Office ("ISO"), which informed Phillips on three separate occasions that his computer had been detected portscanning hundreds of thousands of external computers for vulnerabilities. Despite several instructions to stop, Phillips continued to scan and infiltrate computers within and without the UT system, daily adding to his database of stolen information.

At around the time ISO issued its first warning in early 2002, Phillips designed a computer program expressly for the purpose of hacking into the UT system via a portal known as the "TXClass Learning Central: A Complete Training Resource for UT Faculty and Staff." TXClass was a "secure" server operated by UT and used by faculty and staff as a resource for enrollment in professional education courses. Authorized users gained access to their TXClass accounts by typing their Social Security numbers in a field on the TXClass website's log-on page. Phillips exploited the vulnerability inherent in this log-on protocol by transmitting a "brute-force attack" program, which automatically transmitted to the website as many as six Social Security numbers per second, at least some of which would correspond to those of authorized TXClass users.

### ***II. Discussion

**A. Sufficiency of the Evidence.** Phillips asserts that the Government failed to produce sufficient evidence that he "intentionally access[ed] a protected computer without authorization" under § 1030(a)(5)(A)(ii). . . . Phillips's insufficiency argument takes two parts: that the Government failed to prove (1) he gained access to the TXClass website without authorization and (2) he did so intentionally.

With regard to his authorization, the CFAA does not define the term, but it does clearly differentiate between unauthorized users and those who "exceed[ ] authorized access." Several subsections of the CFAA apply exclusively to users who lack access authorization altogether. In conditioning the nature of the intrusion in part on the level of authorization a computer user possesses, Congress distinguished between "insiders, who are authorized to access a computer," and "outside hackers who break into a computer."

Courts have therefore typically analyzed the scope of a user's authorization to access a protected computer on the basis of the expected norms of intended use or the nature of the relationship established between the computer owner and the user. Applying such an intended-use analysis, in *United States* v. *Morris*, 928 F.2d 504 (2d Cir.1991), a case involving an invasive procedure that prefigured modern portscanning, the Second Circuit held that transmission of an internet worm designed "to demonstrate the inadequacies of current security measures on computer networks by exploiting . . . security defects" was sufficient to permit a jury to find unauthorized access within the meaning of § 1030(a)(5)(A). *Morris*, 928 F.2d at 505. The *Morris* court determined that conduct, like "password guessing" or finding "holes in . . . programs," that uses computer systems not "in any way related to their intended function" amounts to obtaining unauthorized access.

Phillips's brute-force attack program was not an intended use of the UT network within the understanding of any reasonable computer user and constitutes a method of obtaining unauthorized access to computerized data that he was not permitted to view or use. During cross-examination, Phillips admitted that TXClass's normal hourly hit volume did not exceed a few hundred requests, but that his brute-force attack created as many as 40,000. He also monitored the UT system during the multiple crashes his program caused, and backed up the numerical ranges of the Social Security numbers after the crashes so as not to omit any potential matches. Phillips intentionally and meticulously executed both his intrusion into TXClass and the extraction of a sizable quantity of confidential personal data. There was no lack of evidence to find him guilty of intentional unauthorized access.

Phillips makes a subsidiary argument that because the TXClass website was a public application, he, like any internet user, was a *de facto* authorized user. In essence, Phillips contends that his theft of other people's data from TXClass merely exceeded the preexisting generic authorization that he maintained as a user of the World Wide Web, and he cannot be considered an unauthorized user under § 1030(a)(5)(A)(ii).

This argument misconstrues the nature of obtaining "access" to an internet application and the CFAA's use of the term "authorization." While it is true that any internet user can insert the appropriate URL into a web browser and thereby view the "TXClass Administrative Training System" log-in web page, a user cannot gain access to the TXClass application itself without a valid Social Security number password to which UT has affirmatively granted authorization. Neither Phillips, nor members of the public, obtain such authorization from UT merely by viewing a log-in page, or clicking a hypertext link. Instead, courts have recognized that authorized access typically arises only out of a contractual or agency relationship. While Phillips was authorized to use his UT email account and engage in other activities defined by UT's acceptable computer use policy, he was never authorized to access TXClass. The method of access he used makes this fact even more plain. In short, the government produced sufficient evidence at trial to support Phillips's conviction under § 1030(a)(5)(A)(ii).

### ***III. Conclusion

For the foregoing reasons, the conviction and sentence are AFFIRMED.

## Case Analysis

1. The defendant is accused of "portscanning" in the case. The court described that process as "a technique used by computer hackers by which an individual sends requests via a worm or other program to various networked computer ports in an effort to ascertain whether particular machines have vulnerabilities that would leave them susceptible to external intrusion."

2. What is the defendant's legal argument in the appeal?

3. Should a defendant in these types of case be forced to pay restitution to the damaged parties?

## Property Invasion with Computers

**hacking** Breaking into computer systems with the intent to alter or modify settings.

**Hacking** is the term used to describe breaking into computer systems, often with the intention to alter or modify settings. Hacking fits well within this chapter because it is similar in character to trespassing, criminal mischief, and vandalism. It is also similar to burglary if the offender is motivated to commit a more serious crime once he or she gains access. Every state has its own hacking, or "unauthorized access," law.[51] For example, New York's "computer trespass" statute reads as follows:

A person is guilty of computer trespass when he or she knowingly uses, causes to be used, or accesses a computer, computer service, or computer network without authorization and:
1. he or she does so with an intent to commit or attempt to commit or further the commission of any felony; or
2. he or she thereby knowingly gains access to computer material.[52]

Note that there are two *mens rea* elements: knowledge that the individual is not authorized to access the data and either (1) intent to commit a crime once access is gained or (2) knowledge that the material sought is accessed. The *actus reus* is, simply, unauthorized access. New York also criminalizes a number of other access offenses, including unauthorized use, tampering, and unlawful duplication.

Some state laws, such as California's,[53] are considerably more elaborate and cannot be reprinted here because of space constraints. Other state laws are rather brief, yet encompass a wide range of actions. Texas's "breach of computer security" statute provides that "[a] person commits an offense if the person knowingly accesses a computer, computer network, or computer system without the effective consent of the owner."[54] Other state laws criminalize both access *and* tampering. We look at a few in the following section.

## Property Damage with Computers

Cybercriminals sometimes access protected computer systems just to say they can do it. Other times their intentions are more insidious. They may seek to corrupt data; disrupt equipment; threaten system reliability; disseminate viruses, worms, or malware; launch botnets (software running on a collection of compromised computers); steal sensitive information; and otherwise cause widespread havoc. In the worst case, terrorists may seek to use computers to launch attacks against their enemies.

Just as states have laws aimed at preventing hacking, they also have laws that prohibit tampering with computer systems. For example, Arizona's "computer tampering" law criminalizes not just unauthorized access, but also various forms of tampering and/or destruction once the offender gains access. The law reads, in part,

A person who acts without authority or who exceeds authorization of use commits computer tampering by:
1. Accessing, altering, damaging or destroying any computer, computer system or network, or any part of a computer, computer system or network, with the intent to devise or execute any scheme or artifice to defraud or deceive, or to control property or services by means of false or fraudulent pretenses, representations or promises.

---

[51]For a state-by-state comparison, see http://www.ncsl.org/default.aspx?tabid=13494 (accessed September 27, 2010).
[52]N.Y. Penal Law Section 156.10 (2010).
[53]Cal. Penal Code Section 502 (2010.
[54]Texas Penal Code Section 33.02 (2010).

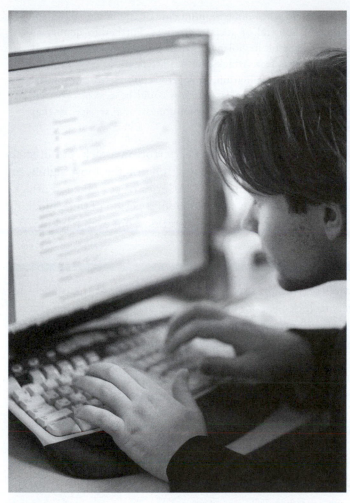

Computers can be used for a number of illicit purposes, including property damage, theft, and cyberterrorism.

Perov Stanislav/Shutterstock.com

2. Knowingly altering, damaging, deleting or destroying computer programs or data.

3. Knowingly introducing a computer contaminant into any computer, computer system or network.

4. Recklessly disrupting or causing the disruption of computer, computer system or network services or denying or causing the denial of computer or network services to any authorized user of a computer, computer system or network.

5. Recklessly using a computer, computer system or network to engage in a scheme or course of conduct that is directed at another person and that seriously alarms, torments, threatens or terrorizes the person. . . .

6. Preventing a computer user from exiting a site, computer system or network-connected location in order to compel the user's computer to continue communicating with, connecting to or displaying the content of the service, site or system.

7. Knowingly obtaining any information that is required by law to be kept confidential or any records that are not public records by accessing any computer, computer system or network that is operated by this state, a political subdivision of this state or a medical institution. . . .

8. Knowingly accessing any computer, computer system or network or any computer software, program or data that is contained in a computer, computer system or network.[55]

Note how this statute criminalizes a variety of actions aimed at causing damage to computers, computer systems, networks, and the like. Also note that the *mens rea* varies by the conduct alleged.

## Cyberterrorism

**cyberterrorism** A politically motivated attack using computers or other technology.

Of considerable concern these days is the threat of **cyberterrorism**. Defined as "politically motivated hacking operations intended to cause grave harm such as loss of life or severe economic damage,"[56] cyberterrorism combines elements of cybercrime and traditional terrorism. Computer security expert Dorothy Denning described the threat in this way:

> Cyberterrorism is the convergence of terrorism and cyberspace. It is generally understood to mean unlawful attacks and threats of attack against computers, networks,

---

[55]Ariz. Rev. Stat. Ann. Section 13-2316 (2010).

[56]D. Denning, "Activism, Hacktivism, and Cyberterrorism: The Internet as a Tool for Influencing Foreign Policy," in J. Arquilla and D. Ronfeldt, eds., *Networks and Netwars* (Santa Monica, CA: Rand, 2001), p. 241.

and the information stored therein when done to intimidate or coerce a government or its people in furtherance of political or social objectives. Further, to qualify as cyberterrorism, an attack should result in violence against persons or property, or at least cause enough harm to generate fear. Attacks that lead to death or bodily injury, explosions, plane crashes, water contamination, or severe economic loss would be examples. Serious attacks against critical infrastructures could be acts of cyberterrorism, depending on their impact. Attacks that disrupt nonessential services or that are mainly a costly nuisance would not.[57]

The United States has yet to see a large-scale cyberterrorism attack, but officials are still acknowledging the threat. As of this writing, one of the most significant attacks on record occurred in Estonia during 2007. A series of coordinated attacks caused a series of governmental Web sites to shut down for a period of time, blocking legitimate users and crippling not just government operations, but even banking.[58]

**YOUR DECISION**

1. Larry and Jeff are always playing practical jokes on each other at the office. One afternoon, Larry forgets to lock his computer while he goes to lunch. Jeff decides to log on to Larry's e-mail without permission and distribute a picture of child pornography to the entire office. Assume that the distribution of child pornography is a felony. Is Jeff guilty of any type of cybercrime? If so, which type?
2. Mark is a self-appointed computer science expert. He decides one day to challenge himself and see if he can hack into the United States Department of Defense Web site "just for kicks." Mark has no intention of stealing information or damaging the system. He just wants to prove to himself that he has the skill and ability to crack into such a secure computer system. Mark is finally successful, and does nothing with the information except to brag to his friends on Facebook. Has Mark committed a crime? If so, which one?

## Summary

- Cybercrime refers to any crime committed with the assistance of a computer.
- Cybercrime often falls into two categories: theft and property damage/destruction.
- Hackers use computers for property invasion, which is similar to trespassing, criminal mischief, and vandalism.
- Hacking is also similar to burglary if the offender is motivated by the intent to steal.
- Computers are also used to cause property damage. For example, offenders may seek to corrupt data; disrupt equipment; threaten system reliability; disseminate viruses, worms, or malware; launch botnets; and steal sensitive information, among other actions.

[57]D. Denning, "Cyberterrorism," Testimony before the Special Oversight Panel of Terrorism, Committee on Armed Services, U.S. House of Representatives, May 23, 2000. Available at: http://www.cs.georgetown.edu/~denning/infosec/cyberterror.html (accessed September 28, 2010).
[58]C. Wilson, *Botnets, Cybercrime, and Cyberterrorism: Vulnerabilities and Policy Issues for Congress* (Washington, DC: Congressional Research Service, 2008), p. 6.

# Chapter Review

MODULE **10.1**

## PROPERTY DAMAGE

### *Learning Objectives*

- Describe the crime of arson.
- Explain the elements of criminal mischief.
- Explain the elements of vandalism.

### *Review Questions*

1. Compare and contrast common law arson with modern-day arson.
2. Can criminal mischief occur without damage? If so, how?
3. Compare and contrast vandalism and criminal mischief.

### *Key Terms*

arson
criminal mischief
vandalism

MODULE **10.2**

## PROPERTY INVASION

### *Learning Objectives*

- Summarize the elements of trespassing.
- Explain how trespassing statutes have been used to target illegal immigration.
- Describe the crime of burglary.

### *Review Questions*

1. A trespassing prosecution may be a "fallback" to other alternatives. Explain how.
2. Should the crime of trespassing have a more specific *mens rea* requirement? Why or why not?
3. What is your opinion of the appellate court's decision in the New Hampshire trespassing/illegal immigration case?
4. Compare and contrast burglary and trespassing.

### *Key Terms*

trespassing
burglary
surreptitious remaining

MODULE **10.3**

## PROPERTY DAMAGE AND INVASION WITH COMPUTERS

### *Learning Objectives*

- Define and explain cybercrime.
- Identify laws aimed at controlling property invasion and damage with a computer.

### Review Questions

1. Which should we be more concerned with: traditional property damage and invasion, or property damage and invasion with computers?

2. Explain social engineering.

3. Compare and contrast cybercrime and cyberterrorism.

4. In what way are cybercrime prosecutions compromised by jurisdictional problems?

### Key Terms

cybercrime
social engineering
Computer Fraud and Abuse Act (CFAA)
hacking
cyberterrorism

# Chapter Synthesizing Questions

1. What common thread runs through all the offenses in this chapter?

2. Compare and contrast trespassing and burglary.

3. Should officials be more or less concerned than they are with cybercrime and cyberterrorism? Explain your answer.

4. What could be done, if anything, to clear up the jurisdictional problems surrounding cybercrime prosecutions?

5. Look up a hacking or computer tampering statute (from a state other than those whose laws served as examples in this chapter). Identify the *mens rea* and the *actus reus*.

# 11

# THEFT AND ANALOGOUS OFFENSES

*Learning Objectives*

**MODULE 11.1 LARCENY**

- Identify the elements of larceny.
- Summarize the legal issues/complications that can come up during a larceny prosecution.

**MODULE 11.2 RECEIVING STOLEN PROPERTY, EXTORTION, AND EMBEZZLEMENT**

- Describe the crime of receiving stolen property.
- Describe the crime of extortion.
- Describe the crime of embezzlement.

**MODULE 11.3 FALSE PRETENSES, FORGERY/UTTERING, AND EMERGING THEFT OFFENSES**

- Summarize the elements of false pretenses and forgery/uttering.
- Compare and contrast identity theft and theft of intellectual property.
- Explain the reasons for the consolidation of theft crimes.

# LARCENY

## Learning Objectives

- **Identify the elements of larceny.**
- **Summarize the legal issues/complications that can come up during a larceny prosecution.**

## CORE CONCEPTS

**larceny** The trespassory taking and carrying away of the person property of another with the intent to permanently deprive the owner of possession.

In this chapter, we turn our attention to theft, which includes larceny, embezzlement, false pretenses, and similar crimes. What we all know and recognize as *theft* is formally called **larceny**, the focus of this first module. Common law larceny consisted of four distinct elements:

1. The trespassory taking
2. and carrying away
3. of the personal property of another
4. with intent to permanently deprive the owner/possessor of the property.[1]

Note that the first three elements identified the *actus reus* of larceny and the fourth identified the *mens rea*. Also note that, as defined, larceny was a conduct crime, not a result crime. In other words, the offense was complete once a person took and carried away another's personal property. There was no requirement that the dispossessor (the person taking the property) put the property to his or her own use.

The common law distinguished between petit (petty) and grand larceny. The former involved theft of items beneath a certain value; the latter involved theft of items *above* a certain value. At common law, the amount that turned petty to grand larceny was "twelvepence," which equals less than ten cents in today's dollars.[2] Today, the cut-off point is somewhere in the neighborhood of $1,000, meaning that theft of items valued less than that is considered petty.

At common law, grand theft was punishable by death. Today, no theft conviction provides for capital punishment. Instead, grand theft is a felony and petty theft is a misdemeanor. That said, don't think for a moment that theft penalties are always light. California's three-strikes law provides for life in prison in the case of grand theft, provided the convicted individual has two "strikeable" felonies on his or her record beforehand.[3] Offenders have literally received life sentences for stealing items such as golf clubs.[4]

---

[1]See, e.g., *Lee* v. *State*, 474 A.2d 537 (Md. Ct. Spec. App. 1984), p. 539.
[2]J. Dressler, *Understanding Criminal Law*, 5th ed. (Newark, NJ: Lexis-Nexis, 2009), p. 555.
[3]F. E. Zimring, G. Hawkins, and S. Kamin, *Punishment and Democracy: Three Strikes and You're Out in California* (New York: Oxford University Press, 2001).
[4]See *Ewing* v. *California*, 538 U.S. 11 (2003).

# Elements of Larceny

Punishments for larceny have changed over time; however, the common law elements of the crime have remained more or less intact. We begin with the *actus reus*, then turn our attention to the *mens rea*.

## Actus Reus

There are four elements to the *actus reus* of larceny. They are

1. Trespass
2. Taking
3. Carrying away
4. Personal property

**Trespass.**    Common law larceny required a "trespass." As noted in one early decision, "[t]here can be no larceny without a trespass, and there can be no trespass unless the property was in the possession of the one from whom it is charged to have been stolen."[5] The term *trespass*, however, took on a different meaning, distinct from the *crime* of trespassing. The trespass element of larceny stems from the Latin phrase *trespass be bonis asportatis*, which referred to a tort in which one party interfered with another's lawful possession of a chattel (i.e., movable personal property). The trespass of larceny was thus akin to taking possession of another's property. This remains true today.

Common law larceny also required that the trespass involved an element of stealth. The doctrine of *caveat emptor* (i.e., "Let the buyer beware") applied, meaning that one who defrauded another of his or her property was not considered a thief. This, as you probably know by now, has changed with the times.[6] Indeed, as we will see later in this chapter, there are specific offenses aimed directly at those who would defraud people of their property.

**Taking.**    The trespass element of larceny is straightforward enough, as we have seen. The *taking* element, however, is much more complicated. What does *taking* mean? What types of actions amount to "taking" another's property? There are a number of possible complications that make it difficult to arrive at any best answers to these questions.

In general, *taking* refers to the removing the property from the *possession* of another. This means that we have to define *possession*. The robbery section of Chapter 9 briefly distinguished between two types of possession: actual and constructive. To refresh your memory, property is in a person's actual possession if that person is holding it or it is attached to the victim in some fashion. In contrast, constructive possession means the owner has control over the property, usually because it is in close physical proximity to him or her, but also because the owner may have given

---

[5]*People* v. *Hoban*, 88 N.E. 806 (Ill. 1909), p. 807.
[6]The wheels were set in motion as early as 1779. See *King* v. *Pear*, 168 Eng. Rep. 208 (1779).

custody (defined presently) of the property to someone else. As Dressler has observed, "[a]ll non-abandoned property is in the actual or constructive possession of some party at all times."[7]

Possession also has to be distinguished from custody. One who has property in his or her custody has control over it. However, just because one has custody over property does not mean the property is in that individual's possession. For example, a jewelry merchant who hands a ring to a customer who then tries it on transfers the custody of the ring *and* no longer has actual possession of it.[8] However, the merchant *does* retain constructive possession of the ring. Should the customer leave with the ring and not pay for it, larceny occurs.

Also consider the case of an employer who lends a company vehicle to an employee. The employee takes custody of the vehicle, but constructive possession remains with the owner. Thus, if the employee likes the vehicle and decides to keep it, he has committed larceny because he interfered with the employer's constructive possession of the vehicle.[9] Why do we care about these details? Again, larceny is a crime in which property is taken from the *possession* of another, not the custody of another. This distinction rarely comes up in practice, but it is still important. To summarize, taking is synonymous with dispossessing someone of property. In other words, one who removes property from the possession of another "takes" it.

### Carrying Away (Asportation).

The carrying way (or asportation) of property is another essential—and time-honored—element of larceny. Significant movement is not necessary, however. For example, a shoplifter who has apparel in her possession and is moving toward the exit commits larceny, even though she has not yet "carried away" the property from the premises.[10]

It bears mentioning, however, that not all movement constitutes "carrying away." Assume a defendant removed a box from a high shelf and set it on the floor in order to steal the contents. Such action constitutes attempted larceny, but not larceny itself. Why? Because the purpose of moving the box was to make the contents more accessible; it was not the same as carrying it away.[11] Given the fine line between both types of movement, the Model Penal Code does not require proof of "carrying away."[12] Theft occurs simply if one person "unlawfully takes another's property."[13]

### Personal Property of Another.

Personal property is distinct from real property, the latter of which is typically land. Since land cannot be picked up and carried away, it cannot be stolen—at least under a common law definition of larceny. The only ways to take possession of land are either to evict the owner from the property or obtain title to the land. Both actions, if illegal, are remedied by means other than larceny prosecution (there are legal means for taking land, such as eminent domain).

---

[7]Dressler, *Understanding Criminal Law*, p. 557.
[8]See, e.g., *Chisser's Case*, 83 Eng. Rep. 142 (1678).
[9]See, e.g., Dressler, *Understanding Criminal Law*, p. 558.
[10]See, e.g., *People* v. *Olivo*, 420 N.E.2d 40 (N.Y. 1981), p. 44.
[11]See, e.g., *Cherry's Case*, 168 Eng. Rep. 221 (1781).
[12]Model Penal Code Section 223.2(1).
[13]Ibid.

Even certain items *attached* to real property are considered the same as real property and thus cannot be stolen.[14] If items attached to real property are then removed, they become personal property and thus can be stolen. For example, if a Christmas tree farmer's trees are cut down without his permission and removed from the property, larceny has occurred.

What, then, is *personal property*? At the risk of simplification, *personal property* is anything other than real property that is also tangible (intangible property, such as intellectual property, is often covered in other statutes—see discussion later in this chapter). There were times in history when certain types of property that we would consider personal today were not. For example, at common law domesticated dogs were not considered personal property.[15] That has since changed. Modern larceny laws extend to nearly "anything of value."[16] Some even protect real property.[17]

In closing, larceny is also limited to the taking of *another's* property. *Another's property* is defined as "property in which any person other than the actor has an interest."[18] Basically, a person cannot steal his or her own property.

As mentioned earlier, the value of the stolen property is directly related to whether the defendant will be charged with a felony or a misdemeanor. Consequently, a number of courts consider the "value" of the property to constitute an additional element of certain types of larceny. See the accompanying Court Decision for more on this issue. In it we examine the case of *Foreman* v. *United States*, where the court is confronted with determining the value of an iPod and its downloaded contents.

---

**COURT DECISION**

*Foreman* v. *United States*
988 A.2d 505 (D.C. App. 2010)

**Background:** John Foreman was convicted of first-degree theft in the Superior Court. Foreman appealed and District of Columbia Court of Appeals reversed and remanded.

Appellant was charged with, among other things, armed robbery and possession of a firearm during a crime of violence, both arising from an incident in which, according to the indictment, he forcibly took an iPod from Marcus Curry while brandishing a handgun. The jury acquitted him of these charges but returned a guilty verdict on first-degree theft and hung on unarmed robbery, both of which had been submitted to it as lesser-included offenses of the armed robbery.

We hold that the evidence was insufficient to permit appellant's conviction of first-degree theft, because the government presented no evidence from which a rational juror could infer that the combined value of the stolen iPod and its contents exceeded $250. Although the proof requirement for theft in the first degree that "the value of the property obtained" was "$250 or more" appears in a penalty statute, § 22-3212(a), not in the definition of "theft," § 22-3211, our decisions leave no

---

[14]See, e.g., *Parker* v. *State*, 352 So. 2d 1386 (Ala. Crim. App. 1977).
[15]Dressler, *Understanding Criminal Law*, p. 563.
[16]Model Penal Code Section 223.0(6).
[17]Ibid.
[18]Model Penal Code Section 223.0(7).

doubt that the issue of value distinguishing first degree (or felony) theft from second degree (or misdemeanor) theft, implicates an element of the offense and must be submitted to the trier of fact. Our cases have further established that, "when the proof [at trial] indicates a value nearing [the] minimum" separating felony from misdemeanor theft, "such proof may need to be offered with greater precision" than when the issue is not a close one.

\*\*\*Here, the government's proof of value exceeding the statutory amount of $250 was insufficient to rule out a verdict based on "surmise or conjecture." Perhaps understandably, in a case where the parties disagreed most strongly on whether appellant had forcibly assaulted (*i.e.,* robbed) Curry, and if so whether he had used a firearm, the evidence on the value of the iPod consisted of sparse testimony by Curry and his mother unelucidated by other evidence. Marcus Curry stated that his mother had bought the iPod for him in December 2006 as a Christmas gift (*i.e.,* some four months before the April 12, 2007 theft), and that he believed she had paid $300 for it. But Mrs. Curry corrected this by stating that she had paid "about $250" for the iPod, though with "tax and shipping it came up to about $300." Marcus Curry further testified that he had "movies and pictures of [himself] and [his] friends and . . . family" on the iPod, and had downloaded "about four hundred or more" songs onto the device. While he had "had to pay" to put the movies on the iPod, "some of [the] songs" were "free downloaded songs" and "some of them you had to pay for." That was the sum of the value evidence presented to the jury.

Value in this context means the "fair market value" of the property, defined as the "price at which a willing seller and a willing buyer will trade." *Williams v. United States,* 376 A.2d 442, 444 (D.C.1977). Significantly, the determination of market value starts with the "base price" and excludes "ancillary" costs such as shipping and handling, as well as taxes. Thus, we set aside Mrs. Curry's mention of the amounts in excess of $250 that she paid for the iPod, which left the value of the device at the time of purchase at exactly the statutory dividing line. Our decisions have also made clear, however, that electronic products of this nature have a tendency to depreciate rapidly as technology changes and old versions are replaced. Thus, since no contrary evidence was presented that iPods retain the market value reflected in their purchase price, only speculation allowed the jury to infer that Curry's device, by itself, was still worth $250 some four months after it was bought.

The government appears to agree up to this point, because it places nearly all of its reliance on the presumed market value of the movies and songs that Curry downloaded onto the iPod. The word "presumed" here is key, however, because Curry did not state or estimate—as he was not asked—how much he had paid for the downloads, individually or altogether; he offered no opinion on what such items generally cost; and indeed, as to the "four hundred or more" songs, he did not say how many he had paid for at all rather than downloading them "free." The absence of independent proof of the usual cost of iPod downloads might not be fatal, since "[t]he market value of a chattel . . . may be established by the testimony of its non-expert owner," *Zellers,* 682 A.2d at 1120; but Curry's testimony merely that he had paid *something* for an undetermined portion of his songs and for his movies did not allow an inference beyond a reasonable doubt that the iPod *and* its contents were worth more than the depreciated value of the device alone, which had cost the bare statutory minimum when purchased.

*FN3. Appellant points also to the fact that Curry did not identify the names or artists of any of the songs and movies on the iPod, relying on this court's observation in Zellers, 682 A.2d at 1121, that "the value of any . . . musical recording depends in large part on what is recorded. . . .[A] CD containing a collection of arias sung by Enrico Caruso. . . may be of greater value than an album of musical ephemera sung by yesterday's rock star du jour." Of course, depending on the relevant market place, the opposite of this conclusion may also be true, and because it is not obvious to us what an identification of Curry's songs would have contributed to the issue of value, we leave that point aside.*

This conclusion does not change when we factor in a jury's acknowledged right to bring its own experiences to bear on the evaluation of evidence. There may well be circumstances where the intrinsic value of an object (say, a new high-priced automobile) is so much a part of common knowledge that no further proof of value exceeding $250 is needed. But that is not this case, given Curry's admission that he had paid nothing for "some" of the songs. Permitting jurors here to rely on their own experience of what iPod downloads cost would not be a proper drawing of inferences "from the facts . . . proven in light of [their] own experience"; rather, it would substitute for a failure of proof on the point.

Consequently, appellant's conviction for theft in the first degree must be vacated for insufficient evidence. He asks us to remand with directions for the trial court to enter judgment on the lesser included offense of theft in the second degree, but the record does not tell us—nor could the parties at oral argument—whether the charge of robbery on which the jury hung is still pending and so subject to retrial. We leave these matters to be determined on remand.

*Reversed and remanded with directions to enter judgment of acquittal on theft in the first degree.*

## Case Analysis

1. List the elements of first-degree theft in the District of Columbia, as outlined by the case.
2. What is the defendant's legal argument? Do you agree with his position?
3. Should certain downloaded songs or videos be considered more "valuable" than others when evaluating a larceny or theft case?

## Mens Rea

The *mens rea* of larceny requires intent to permanently deprive the owner/possessor of the property. More simply, it is *intent to steal*. Assume you test drive a vehicle at your local car dealership. If the salesperson lets you take the vehicle for a drive and you elect to keep it permanently, without paying for it, you commit larceny. If, instead, you keep it for a little longer than the usual test drive, just to

**Figure 11.1**
Larceny

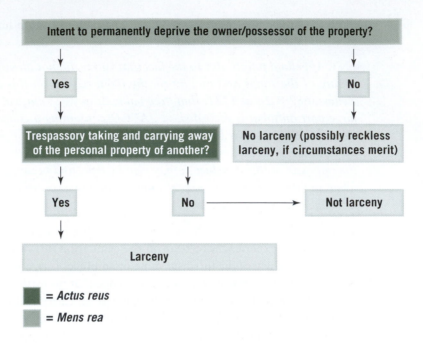

take it for a "joy ride," then larceny has *not* occurred. This underscores the intent element of larceny. Again, there must be intent to permanently deprive the owner/possessor of the property.

What if the property in question is perishable? Perhaps Bill made off with Sarah's tasty-looking (and uncooked) rib eye steaks. If he gets distracted, fails to cook them, and the meat goes bad, is Bill guilty of larceny? As long as Bill's action was sufficient to "appropriate a major portion of its economic value," then the answer is "yes."[19] Since a rotten piece of meat would be worth less than a still-fresh one, then Bill has committed theft, so it is quite possible to be guilty of stealing perishable items.

Another issue that arises in the *mens rea* of larceny is whether the accused seeks to gain from the theft. In general, there is no requirement that the accused seek to gain from the theft. If the accused intends to deprive a woman of her priceless artwork by throwing it on a bonfire, then larceny still occurs. Figure 11.1 summarizes the elements of larceny discussed in this and previous subsections.

**Reckless Larceny.**   Some statutes provide for a larceny conviction if the accused recklessly puts the property at risk of permanent loss. Assume Ray took Jim's car (without Jim's permission) for a joy ride. Further assume Ray stopped for a sandwich in a high-crime area and left the car parked out of view with the windows down and keys in the ignition. Ray lacks intent to permanently deprive Jim of the car, but if the car is stolen, then arguably Ray has recklessly put Jim's property at risk of permanent lost. In theory, he could be convicted of larceny simply because of his reckless actions.

---

[19]American Law Institute, Comment to Section 223.3, p. 175.

What if a department store "customer" removes a shirt from a clothing rack, takes it to the counter, claims it is his, and seeks a refund? Assuming he is successful, do his actions constitute larceny? There is no apparent intent to permanently deprive the store of the shirt, so traditional larceny *mens rea* does not apply. Even so, courts have decided—as they should—that this type of action constitutes larceny.[20] In *People* v. *Davis*, the case on which this example is based, an observant security guard was alerted to the defendant's actions, which brought the case to light. The California Supreme Court noted that although the defendant may not have intended to permanently deprive the store of the shirt (his argument was that he only had the shirt in his possession long enough to get a refund), he might as well have:

> [A]s a practical matter, the risk that such a taking will be permanent is not a mere theoretical possibility; rather, by taking an item from a store display with the intent to demand a refund a defendant creates a substantial risk of permanent loss. . . . This is so because if the defendant's attempt to obtain a refund for the item fails for any reason, he has a powerful incentive to keep the item in order to avoid drawing attention to the theft. A person who has taken an item from a store display and has claimed the right to "return" it at a sales counter, but has been rebuffed because, for example, he has no receipt, will not be inclined to run the risk of confirming the suspicions of the sales clerk or store security personnel by putting the item back in the display.[21]

## Larceny Issues and Complications

Larceny is very common, accounting for approximately two-thirds of all property crimes.[22] The vast majority of larcenies are simple cases of theft with few complications and surprises. Even so, there are some "twists and turns" the make a number of larcenies complicated from a legal perspective. We consider several of those complications in this section.

### Concurrence

Chapter 3 introduced concurrence, or the requirement that *actus reus* and *mens rea* occur contemporaneously. Concurrence is especially relevant in certain larceny cases, particularly when one person sets out to *borrow* another's property. Say, for example, that Robert grabs a golf ball out of Jim's bag with the intent of returning it after the round, but then decides he likes its "feel" and keeps it. Has Robert committed larceny? The problem in this example is that Robert lacked intent to steal at the time he took the ball. He only formed the requisite intent later. Common law courts dealt with this complication by forming the doctrine of *continuing trespass*, which meant the original taking was trespassory even if the intent to permanently deprive the owner of the property was not in place from the outset.[23]

---

[20]See, e.g., *People* v. *Davis*, 965 P.2d 1165 (Cal. 1998).
[21]Ibid., p. 1175.
[22]Federal Bureau of Investigation, *Uniform Crime Reports, 2009*, http://www.fbi.gov/about-us/cjis/ucr/crime-in-the-u.s/2009 (accessed October 19, 2010).
[23]See, e.g., *State* v. *Somerville*, 21 Me. 14 (1842), p. 19.

## Finders, Keepers

Everyone has heard the old adage, "Finders keepers, losers weepers." What if one person loses property, only to have it found and kept by someone else? Does such action constitute larceny? On the one hand, it would seem that keeping what is found is not trespassory. On the other hand, just because someone loses his or her property doesn't mean he or she no longer has an interest in it.

The general rule in the finders–keepers situation is this: If the owner of the lost property retains constructive possession of the property and the finder keeps it, larceny occurs. Constructive possession is determined if there is some clue as to the ownership of the lost item. For example, if Paul loses his wedding ring, only to have it found and kept by Bob, Bob will be guilty of larceny if he ignores the inscription on the band listing Paul's full name and phone number. The courts have also held that a reasonable clue to ownership exists if the finder "has reasonable ground to believe, from the nature of the property, or the circumstances under which it is found, that if he. . . deals honestly with it, the owner will appear or be ascertained."[24]

If there is no indication to whom the property belongs and no one steps forward to claim it, then a finder who keeps it will likely not be found guilty of theft. At the end of the day, however, intent is paramount. Even if there is no identifying information on lost property and there is no obvious attempt by the owner to get it back, the finder will be guilty of larceny if he or she sets out, at the instant the property is found, to keep it permanently. The real-world problem here is of course inferring intent. Prosecution for such action would be all but impossible, because how could a prosecutor prove that someone who found lost property was intent on stealing it at the moment it was found?

## Claim of Right

**claim of right** A good-faith belief that the individual has a right to possess the property.

Assume Max and Jay work together on a construction site. At the end of the day, Max takes home Jay's circular saw, convinced it is his own (he has one that looks just like it). In formal legal terms, Max has exercised a **claim of right** (a good faith belief that he has a right to possess the property). But has Max committed larceny? After all, he lacked the requisite intent to steal needed to support a larceny conviction. Max has *not* committed larceny because he did not intend to trespassorily deprive Jay of his saw.[25]

What if, when walking back to his car at the end of the day, Max observed the saw that he thought was his sitting on the front seat of Jay's locked pickup truck? Could he *forcibly* enter Jay's truck to retrieve the saw? In reality, he probably would not. (Why not just ask Jay to unlock the truck?) In theory, he could, but he would most likely be guilty of larceny. Why? Max's first course of action should be to seek return of the property, not default to forcibly entering the vehicle. Even so, some courts have sanctioned the use of force to secure the return of what one person believes, in good faith, is his or her property. Consider *People* v. *Tufunga*,[26] a case in which a man gave his ex-wife $200 to pay a bill she owed, but when he learned that

---

[24]*Brooks* v. *State*, 35 Ohio St. 46 (1878), p. 50.
[25]See, e.g., *People* v. *Tufunga*, 987 P.2d 168 (Cal. 1999), p. 174.
[26]*People* v. *Tufunga*, 987 P.2d 168 (Cal. 1999).

she was not going to use the money for that purpose, he forcibly took the money back. The California Supreme Court reversed his robbery conviction, noting:

> A good faith claim of right to title or ownership of specific property taken from another can negate the element of felonious taking (taking accomplished with intent to steal) necessary to establish theft . . . or robbery. . . . At common law, claim of right was recognized as a defense to the crime of larceny because it was deemed to negate the *animus furandi*—or felonious intent to steal—of that offense. Because robbery was viewed as simply an aggravated form of larceny, it was likewise subject to the same claim-of-right defense. By adopting the identical phrase "felonious taking" as used in the common law with regard to both offenses, the Legislature intended to incorporate the same meanings attached to those phrases at common law. Theft is a lesser included offense of robbery, which includes the additional element of force or fear, and robbery is a species of aggravated larceny. A conclusion that a claim of right, for policy reasons, should no longer be recognized as a defense to robbery—even where the defendant took back specific property to which he or she has lawful title or a bona fide claim of ownership—would mean such a defendant could be convicted of robbery based on theft of his or her own property, a proposition that would stand in patent conflict with both the commonsense notion that someone cannot steal one's own property, and the corollary rule that theft, the taking of the personal property of another, is a lesser included offense at the core of every robbery.[27]

## Unwilling Sale

What if Bonnie takes Lynne's rare guitar with intent to permanently deprive Lynne of it, but leaves Lynne an envelope full of cash equal to the market value of the instrument? Bonnie intended to commit larceny, but she did *not* intend to deprive Lynne of the guitar's value. What should a court decide? The simple answer is that Bonnie committed larceny because the property was not for sale.

What if, in contrast, the guitar was for sale, but Bonnie decided not to sell it to Lynne out of concern that she would not take good care of it? The answer is less than clear. Consider *Jupiter v. State*,[28] a case in which a liquor store clerk would not sell beer to Jupiter because he appeared intoxicated. Jupiter later returned to the store with a shotgun, paid for the beer, and left with it. He was convicted of robbery and later appealed. The Court of Appeals for Maryland affirmed his conviction, noting:

> Yates (the store clerk) was prohibited by law from selling to intoxicated persons. . . . There is evidence that Jupiter was, in the words of the statute, "visibly under the influence" of alcohol. Yates told Jupiter that he could not sell him beer, and he told him why. Hence the evidence clearly was sufficient to support jury findings that Jupiter knew that he did not have a right to purchase beer, that he intended to take it in any event, and that he took it away with the intent permanently to deprive the owner of it. Ordinarily those findings sufficiently support an ultimate finding of an intent to steal.[29]

---

[27]Ibid., p. 175.
[28]See, e.g., *Jupiter v. State*, 616 A.2d 412 (Md. 1992).
[29]Ibid., p. 414.

## Stealing Stolen or Illegal Property

Can someone steal stolen or illegal property? In other words, if one person cannot legally claim possession to a particular type of property, can theft of that property constitute larceny? Surprisingly, the answer to both questions is "yes." It is larceny to steal stolen property from another thief.[30] It is also larceny to steal contraband from someone else.[31] These rules are surprising, because they suggest the criminal justice system, some of the time, likes to look out for criminals. The concern is that not defining as criminal theft between other thieves or criminals would lead to a free-for-all. In a Prohibition case, the Supreme Court of Pennsylvania once said this concerning the matter:

> To establish the rule that the owner of liquor, illegally held, had no property right therein, would lead to a condition of terror and bloodshed among rival bootleggers far worse than we have known.[32]

A quick glance south of the U.S. border makes it clear that even the best intentions may be widely ignored; there is no shortage of violence in Mexico between rival drug cartels seeking control of lucrative drug smuggling routes.

**YOUR DECISION**

1. Michael Janson is a local police officer. One evening, Janson pulled over George McCain for making an illegal lane change without a signal. Janson insisted that George exit the vehicle and searched him. Throughout the interaction, George believed the officer was following proper police protocol. It was later discovered, however, that during the search Officer Janson removed George's wallet from his back pocket without his knowledge. Did Officer Janson commit larceny? Why or why not?

2. Carrie is addicted to heroin and will do anything to feed her addiction. She decides to take her husband's Rolex watch and sell it at the local pawnshop for cash. The Rolex watch was purchased with funds from a joint checking account shared by Carrie and her husband. Has Carrie committed larceny? Why or why not?

## Summary

- *Common law larceny* was defined as the trespassory taking and carrying away of the personal property of another with intent to permanently deprive the owner/possessor of the property.

- In general, the "taking" element of larceny refers to removing the property from the *possession* of another person.

- For the "carrying away" (asportation) element of larceny to occur, there is no requirement that the movement be significant.

---

[30]See, e.g., *People v. Otis*, 139 N.E. 562 (N.Y. 1923).
[31]Ibid.
[32]*Commonwealth v. Crow*, 154 A. 283 (Pa. 1931), p. 286.

- The Model Penal Code does not require "carrying away" in its definition of larceny.
- Larceny applies primarily to personal property, not real property. Personal property is anything other than real property that is also tangible.
- The *mens rea* of larceny, "intent to permanently deprive the owner/possessor of the property," is the same as intent to steal.
- Some statutes provide for a larceny conviction if the accused recklessly puts the property at risk of permanent loss.
- Concurrence of *actus reus* and *mens rea* are very important in the larceny context.
- If the owner of lost property retains constructive possession of it and the finder of that property keeps it, larceny occurs. Constructive possession is determined if there is some clue as to the ownership of the lost item.
- A good-faith "claim of right," or a belief that one has a right to possess particular property, negates the *mens rea* element of larceny.
- A forced sale amounts to larceny.
- It is larceny to steal stolen property from another thief. It is also larceny to steal contraband from someone else.

MODULE

# 11.2   RECEIVING STOLEN PROPERTY, EXTORTION, AND EMBEZZLEMENT

### *Learning Objectives*

- **Describe the crime of receiving stolen property.**
- **Describe the crime of extortion.**
- **Describe the crime of embezzlement.**

**CORE CONCEPTS**    Closely tied to larceny are the crimes of receiving stolen property (not to be confused with *stealing* stolen property), extortion, and embezzlement. The following sections elaborate on each.

## Receiving Stolen Property

It is a crime for a person to receive stolen property, even if that person did not actually steal the property. Why criminalize the receipt of stolen property? It removes any possible benefit a person stands to gain a result of another person's theft. To prove receiving stolen property, the prosecution typically needs to show that the defendant knowingly received the property, the property was stolen, and the defendant knew

Purchasing products that "appear" to be stolen raises the potential for a receiving stolen property offense.

Peter Rayner/Axiom Photographic/Newscom

the property had been stolen or believed it was. For example, New Jersey's receiving stolen property statute reads:

> A person is guilty of theft if he knowingly receives (or brings into this State) movable property of another knowing that it has been stolen, or believing that it has probably been stolen.[33]

Kentucky's statute is similar, but slightly more elaborate:

> A person is guilty of receiving stolen property when he receives, retains, or disposes of movable property of another knowing that it has been stolen, or having reason to believe that it has been stolen, unless the property is received, retained, or disposed of with intent to restore it to the owner.[34]

What if the defendant received stolen property, but only to return it to its rightful owner? He or she would not be convicted of the crime, as a receiving stolen property conviction requires an implied intent to keep the property. Also, most states do not require proof that the defendant knew the property was stolen. Knowledge is often inferred, but some states, such as Texas, require proof that the defendant knew the property was stolen.[35] Finally, the crime of receiving stolen property is usually treated as a misdemeanor.

## Extortion

**extortion** Also known as *blackmail*; taking property from another with threats of future harm.

**Extortion**, or blackmail, consists of taking another's property by threats of future harm. The key is *future* harm, otherwise extortion would be the same as robbery. A California appellate court distinguished between robbery and extortion thusly:

> The crime of extortion is related to and sometimes difficult to distinguish from the crime of robbery. . . . Both crimes have their roots in the common law crime of larceny. Both crimes share the element of an acquisition by means of force or fear. One distinction

[33]N.J.S.A. Section 2C:10-7a (2010).
[34]K.R.S. Section 514.110 (2010).
[35]See, e.g., *Sonnier* v. *State*, 849 S.W.2d 828 (Tex. App. 1992).

**Figure 11.2**
Extortion

between robbery and extortion is that with robbery, property is taken from another by force or fear against the victim's will, while with extortion, property is taken from another by force or fear with the victim's consent. The two crimes, however, have other distinctions. Robbery requires a "felonious taking," which means a specific intent to permanently deprive the victim of the property. Robbery also requires the property to be taken from the victim's "person or immediate presence. . . . Extortion does not require proof of either of these elements. Extortion does, however, require the specific intent of inducing the victim to consent to part with his or her property.[36]

Assume Susan knows that Jackie has a secret that could disgrace Jackie if it were revealed. If Susan demands money from Jackie in exchange for her silence, this is a classic instance of extortion. Extortion is a consensual crime, meaning that Jackie would have to consent (but not in the truest sense of the term) to pay Susan. If she did not consent and Susan still received the money, then she would most likely go about getting it via traditional larceny.

The *mens rea* of extortion is usually the general intent to take someone else's property by threats of harm or damage. The *actus reus* is actually doing so. Oregon's "theft by extortion" statute reveals each of these, including the many possible threats (also see Figure 11.2 for a summary):

1. A person commits theft by extortion when the person compels or induces another to deliver property to the person or to a third person by instilling in the other a fear that, if the property is not so delivered, the actor or a third person will in the future:
   a. Cause physical injury to some person;
   b. Cause damage to property;
   c. Engage in other conduct constituting a crime;
   d. Accuse some person of a crime or cause criminal charges to be instituted against the person;

---

[36]*People v. Torres*, 33 Cal. App. 4th 37 (1995), p. 50.

e. Expose a secret or publicize an asserted fact, whether true or false, tending to subject some person to hatred, contempt or ridicule;

f. Cause or continue a strike, boycott or other collective action injurious to some person's business, except that such conduct is not considered extortion when the property is demanded or received for the benefit of the group in whose interest the actor purports to act;

g. Testify or provide information or withhold testimony or information with respect to another's legal claim or defense;

h. Use or abuse the position as a public servant by performing some act within or related to official duties, or by failing or refusing to perform an official duty, in such manner as to affect some person adversely; or

i. Inflict any other harm that would not benefit the actor.[37]

# Embezzlement

**embezzlement** Someone in lawful possession of property retains or converts the property for his or her own use with the intent to steal or defraud the rightful owner.

**Embezzlement** is one of a few crimes that was not defined as such at common law; it is a relatively recent creation, partly because of what happened in the famous 1799 *Bazeley* case.[38] Bazeley, a bank teller, took a customer's deposit and pocketed it, rather than put it in the till. Bazeley was acquitted of larceny because he took possession of the money, which was given to him voluntarily by the customer. Moreover, the bank never had possession of the money because Bazeley never put it in the till. Even though it seems he committed larceny, he did not in the truest sense. Why? It was never in his employer's possession, much less its custody. Once it was realized that people (typically employees) could act dishonestly like this *and* escape larceny convictions, statutes were enacted to deal with the problem. For example, one early statute read:

[I]f any servant or clerk, or any person employed . . . by virtue of such employment receive or take into his possession any money, goods, bond, bill, note, banker's draft, or other valuable security, or effects, for or in the name or on the account of his master or masters, or employer or employers, and shall fraudulently embezzle, secrete, or make away with the same, or any part thereof . . . [he] shall be deemed to have feloniously stolen the same.[39]

Modern-day embezzlement statutes are quite similar. Arizona's embezzlement statute reads as follows:

Any bailee of any money, goods or property, who converts it to his or her own use, with the intent to steal it or to defraud the owner or owners thereof and any agent, manager or clerk of any person, corporation, association or partnership, or any person with whom any money, property or effects have been deposited or entrusted, who uses or appropriates the money, property or effects or any part thereof in any manner or for any other purpose than that for which they were deposited or entrusted, is guilty of embezzlement, and shall be punished in the manner prescribed by law for the stealing or larceny of property of the kind and name of the money, goods, property or effects so taken, converted, stolen, used or appropriated.[40]

[37]O.R.S. Section 164.075 (2009).
[38]*King* v. *Bazeley*, 168 Eng. Rep. 517 (1799).
[39]39 Geo. III, C. 85 (1799).
[40]A.R.S. Section 205.300 (2010).

The *mens rea* of this statute is straightforward: "intent to steal it or to defraud...." The *actus reus*, however, is a bit more complicated. Why? Embezzlement statutes have to cover every conceivable type of action by which a **bailee** (one to whom goods are entrusted) could benefit by *converting* the property of a **bailor** (the one, usually an employer, who entrusts the bailee with property). We define *converting* below, when we compare embezzlement to larceny.

Embezzlement is often regarded as a white-collar crime. **White-collar crime** is a term used to describe "various types of unlawful, nonviolent conduct committed by corporations and individuals including theft or fraud and other violations of trust committed in the course of the offender's occupation (e.g., embezzlement, commercial bribery, racketeering, anti-trust violations, price-fixing, stock manipulation, insider trading, and the like."[41] Embezzlement is typically an individual—as opposed to corporate—crime, meaning that no more than one person's actions are necessary to complete the offense.

See the accompanying Court Decision for more on the crime of embezzlement. In it we examine the case of *George* v. *Commonwealth of Virginia*, where an employer is accused of embezzling tax funds.

**bailee** Person to whom goods or property are entrusted.

**bailor** The individual, usually an employer, who entrust the bailee with his or her property.

**white-collar crime** Various crimes typically committed by corporate executive or other employees in the course of their employment.

## COURT DECISION

*George* v. *Commonwealth of Virginia*
655 S.E.2d 43 (Va. App. 2008)

**Background:** Francis Habo George was convicted of four counts of embezzlement in Circuit Court, Page County. George appealed and the Court of Appeals of Virginia affirmed.

\*\*\*From 1996 to 2004, appellant, a physician, owned and operated a medical practice in Luray, Virginia. During the period from 2001 to 2004, appellant employed a number of individuals at the medical practice, including office staff, nursing assistants, nurse practitioners, and a pediatrician. Appellant withheld funds from his employees' salaries representing state income taxes owed to the Commonwealth. Appellant maintained the withheld funds in the same bank account he used to pay both his personal expenses and those of the medical practice. Despite withholding the funds from his employees' paychecks, appellant failed to file quarterly withholding tax returns required by Virginia state law, nor did he remit the withheld funds to the Commonwealth. At times during 2001-2004, the amount of cash reflected as the available balance in appellant's bank account fell below the total amount of funds withheld from his employees to pay the state income taxes owed to the Commonwealth.

### I.

Appellant was convicted of violating Code § 18.2-111 by embezzling money belonging to the Commonwealth.... Appellant next argues that the Commonwealth's evidence was insufficient to prove him guilty of violating Code § 18.2-111, which provides:

If any person wrongfully and fraudulently use, dispose of, conceal or embezzle any money, bill, note, check, order, draft, bond, receipt, bill of lading or any

[41]*Black's Law Dictionary*, 6th ed. (St. Paul, MN: West, 1990), p. 1596.

other personal property, tangible or intangible, which he shall have received for another or for his employer, principal or bailor, or by virtue of his office, trust, or employment, or which shall have been entrusted or delivered to him by another or by any court, corporation or company, he shall be guilty of embezzlement.

To sustain a conviction of embezzlement,

the Commonwealth must prove that the accused wrongfully appropriated to his or her own benefit property entrusted or delivered to the accused with the intent to deprive the owner thereof. Although the Commonwealth need not establish the existence of a formal fiduciary relationship, it must prove that the defendant was entrusted with the property of another.

*Rooney v. Commonwealth*, 27 Va.App. 634, 644 (1998).

Appellant contends the evidence was insufficient to prove embezzlement because the funds he withheld from his employees' paychecks were not owned or entrusted to him by the Commonwealth. The money in appellant's bank account contained fees paid to him and his business for medical services rendered, as well as the withheld funds. Appellant argues that because the withheld funds amounted to nothing more than a debt he owed the Commonwealth, he did not commit embezzlement.

We have recognized that "[a] debtor-creditor relationship is an insufficient basis upon which to premise an embezzlement charge and conviction." *Dove v. Commonwealth*, 41 Va.App. 571, 579 (2003). Where one uses money owed to another by virtue of a business relationship, that fact, standing alone, is insufficient to prove embezzlement.

However, while appellant at all relevant times remained responsible for paying the Commonwealth the funds he had withheld from his employees' paychecks, the Commonwealth was not merely his creditor. By operation of statute, the funds appellant retained for withholding taxes were maintained in his possession in trust for the Commonwealth. Code § 58.1-474 provides:

Every employer who fails to withhold or pay to the Tax Commissioner any sums required by this article to be withheld and paid shall be personally and individually liable therefor. *Any sum or sums withheld in accordance with the provisions of this article shall be deemed to be held in trust for the Commonwealth.*

Just as in Code § 58.1-474 regarding withholding taxes, the General Assembly has imposed a trust for the Commonwealth's benefit upon other categories of taxes collected by a third party on behalf of a governmental entity. The failure to remit such taxes to the governmental entity can constitute embezzlement.

Despite the obligations of the fiduciary relationship created by Code § 58.1-474, appellant neither remitted the withheld funds to the Commonwealth nor maintained them for its benefit. In fact, appellant continued to use the money as though it were his own. "A person entrusted with possession of another's personalty who converts such property to his own use or benefit is guilty of the statutory offense of embezzlement." *Smith v. Commonwealth*, 222 Va. 646, 649 (1981).

The evidence established that appellant used for his own benefit funds he held in trust for the Commonwealth and thus, he was guilty of embezzlement. Accordingly, the trial court did not err in denying appellant's motion to set aside the convictions.

\*\*\**Affirmed.*

## Case Analysis

1. Under Virginia law, what are the elements necessary to convict the defendant of embezzlement?

2. Is the defendant simply "in debt" to the Commonwealth of Virginia for unpaid taxes? Why or why not?

3. Do you agree with the court's ruling? Or do you believe the defendant is guilty of a different crime?

## Distinguishing between Embezzlement and Larceny

Consider the following hypothetical examples:

1. An ex-employee breaks into the electronics store where she once worked and steals three DVD players.

2. An employee who works in the appliance section of a "big-box" electronic store takes home from another department, with intent to keep it, a DVD player.

3. The same employee opens a shipment of DVD players, sets aside three for herself (and later takes them home with intent to keep them), falsifies the packing slip and other records of the shipment, and never tells anyone that the shipment was short three DVD players.

In which scenario, if any, did the employee commit embezzlement? The answer requires that we consider the differences between embezzlement and other property crimes, particularly larceny.

Embezzlement differs from larceny in two key respects. First, "[i]n embezzlement, the property comes lawfully into the possession of the taker and is fraudulently or unlawfully appropriated by him; in larceny, there is a trespass in the unlawful taking of the property."[42] The property comes into the taker's lawful possession usually because he or she is entrusted with it. For example, an employee who takes money from his employer's "petty cash" drawer comes into possession of it lawfully (by virtue of being an employee with access to it).

Second, embezzlement requires conversion, which is basically involves some degree of serious interference in the property (e.g., converting it to his or her own use)—above and beyond what could ordinarily be required for larceny. Formally defined,

---

[42]*State v. Smith*, 98 P.2d 647 (Wash. 1939), p. 648.

**Figure 11.3**
Embezzlement

conversion is "[a]ny unauthorized act which deprives an owner of his property permanently or for an indefinite time."[43] Examples of such acts include altering records and failing to disclose information, among many others.

Returning to our hypothetical examples, who is guilty of embezzlement? The answer is person number three. Person one committed burglary. Person two committed mere larceny. Person three, however, was (a) trusted with the property *and* (b) converted it to her own use, a classic example of embezzlement. This example dealt with an employee–employer relationship. We should point out that embezzlement can occur in the absence of an employer–employee relationship. A company executive could embezzle funds from his or her own corporation! Likewise, embezzlement may be conducted for the benefit of one or more other people besides the defendant. See Figure 11.3 for a summary of embezzlement.

**conversion** An unauthorized act that deprives an owner of his property.

**YOUR DECISION**

1. Joey offers to sell Melissa the latest version of a popular gaming system for only $25 cash, although in the store it generally costs over $200. The deal seems too good to be true and Melissa assumes that the gaming system is stolen. If Melissa purchases the item, is she guilty of receiving stolen property? What if Joey tells Melissa that the gaming system "fell off the back of a truck." Does that change Melissa's potential liability? Why or why not?

2. This exercise is based on a real case. Jim and his girlfriend Tammy were pulled over by a police officer while speeding at 100 mph down the highway. After stopping the car, the officer noticed it was filled with marijuana smoke. The police officer threatened the couple with arrest unless Tammy agreed to have sexual relations with him. Desperate to stay out of jail, Tammy agreed and had sexual intercourse with the police officer. What crime, if any, did the police officer commit?

---

[43]*Black's Law Dictionary*, p. 332.

## Summary

- It is a crime for a person to receive stolen property, even if that person did not actually steal the property.

- One who receives stolen property, but only to return the property to its rightful owner, does not commit a crime.

- Extortion (also called "blackmail") consists of taking another person's property by threats of future harm. The key difference between extortion and robbery is the former's threat of *future* harm.

- Embezzlement occurs when, with intent to steal or defraud, a person in lawful possession of the property deprives an owner of his or her property for a permanent or indefinite period of time (i.e., conversion).

- Embezzlement is different than larceny because (1) the property comes lawfully into the possession of the taker and (2) conversion is required.

---

<table>
<tr><td>MODULE<br>**11.3**</td><td>**FALSE PRETENSES, FORGERY/UTTERING,<br>AND EMERGING THEFT OFFENSES**</td></tr>
</table>

### *Learning Objectives*

- **Summarize the elements of false pretenses and forgery/uttering.**
- **Compare and contrast identity theft and theft of intellectual property.**
- **Explain the reasons for the consolidation of theft crimes.**

**CORE CONCEPTS**    Closely related to the crime of larceny are false pretenses, forgery/uttering, and a number of emerging theft offenses, including identity theft and theft of intellectual property. This module focuses on each. It wraps up with a quick look at efforts to "consolidate" theft offenses. Given the complexity of larceny law, a number of jurisdictions have combined numerous theft offenses (usually larceny, embezzlement, and false pretenses) into a single statute, which makes it easier for the prosecution to make its case.

## False Pretenses

**false pretenses**
Obtaining the property of another through fraud or deception.

**False pretenses** is shorthand for "*obtaining property* by false pretenses" or, more simply, "deception." Obtaining property by false pretenses is different from embezzlement because the embezzler obtains the property lawfully at first, only to fraudulently convert it to his or her use later. In the crime of false pretenses, however, the victim *willingly* gives the property to the criminal. False pretenses also differs from larceny because it requires the additional elements of deception and false representation.[44]

Some jurisdictions criminalize "larceny by trick," a crime distinct from false pretenses. In the famous *Pear's Case*,[45] a man fraudulently rented another man's horse, intending all along to steal the animal. Because the two entered into a rental agreement, there were no false pretenses. Likewise, consider *Hufstetler* v. *State*,[46] a case in which a man went to a gas station; the attendant filled his tank, and then the man drove away without paying. An appeals court determined his actions amounted to larceny by trick, not false pretenses. These cases may leave you wondering, what, then, are the elements of false pretenses? Let's look at them.

## Elements of False Pretenses

False pretenses is knowingly obtaining the property of another by deception with the intent to defraud. The *core* element of false pretenses is false representation, or deception. Such deception can be manifested verbally, in writing, or even by conduct. An example of the latter occurred when one person obtained property from another by donning Oxford apparel, giving the (false) impression he was a student at the famous college.[47] In contrast, a person's *failure to disclose* important information (unless there is a legal obligation to do so) will not amount to false representation.

To get more specific, for something to amount to false representation, it must satisfy three criteria. First, it must in fact be false. If it is not false, there are no false pretenses. Second, opinions, even if expressed with intent to defraud another person, do not constitute false representation.[48] For example, if a car salesperson says "this is the best machine on four wheels" and it is not, it is not a case of false pretenses. Third, false pretenses applies to current, not future, conduct. That is, false pretenses are not the same as "false promises." A false promise would be a homebuyer's promise to repay a mortgage, only to stop making payments at some point in the future (even if the borrower's original plan was to stop making payments the first place).

The *mens rea* of false pretenses is straightforward. It must be shown that the defendant intended to use the false information to secure property that he or she did not otherwise have a right to. This means that even if someone lies to obtain property to which she is entitled, there are no false pretenses.

To summarize, consider North Carolina's "obtaining property by false pretenses" statute. It succinctly captures both the *actus reus* and *mens rea* of the offense:

> If any person shall knowingly and designedly by means of any kind of false pretense whatsoever, whether the false pretense is of a past or subsisting fact or of a future fulfillment or event, obtain or attempt to obtain from any person within this State any money, goods, property, services, chose in action, or other thing of value with intent to cheat or defraud any person of such money, goods, property, services, chose in action or other thing of value, such person shall be guilty of a felony.[49]

---

[44]See e.g., *Bell* v. *United States*, 462 U.S. 356 (1983), p. 359.
[45]*King* v. *Pear*, 168 Eng. Rep. 208 (1779).
[46]*Hufstetler* v. *State*, 63 So. 2d 730 (Ala. Ct. App. 1953).
[47]*Rex* v. *Barnard*, 173 Eng. Rep. 342 (1837).
[48]See, e.g., *Regina* v. *Bryan*, 7 Cox. Crim. Cas. 312 (1857).
[49]N.C. Gen. Stat. Section 14-100 (2010).

Although North Carolina treats false pretenses as a felony, not all jurisdictions do. Such actions amounted to a misdemeanor at common law.

# Forgery/Uttering

**forgery** Materially altering a document with the intent to defraud.

**uttering** Passing a forged document to another with the intent to defraud.

**Forgery** is defined as "the false making or the material altering of a document with the intent to defraud."[50] **Uttering** refers to the act of passing a forged document on to someone else. Both are considered crimes. Obviously, however, the crime of forgery may well go undetected until someone actually attempts to use the forged document. Examples of forgery and uttering include

- Signing someone else's name on a legal document.
- Printing counterfeit tickets for a sporting event.
- Altering the amount of a check.
- Altering grades on a college transcript.

## Elements of Forgery/Uttering

Many states have opted to criminalize forgery and uttering via a single statute. Arizona is one such state. Its forgery statute provides the following:

> A. A person commits forgery if, with intent to defraud, the person:
> 1. Falsely makes, completes or alters a written instrument; or
> 2. Knowingly possesses a forged instrument; or
> 3. Offers or presents, whether accepted or not, a forged instrument or one which contains false information.[51]

Note that the *mens rea* is "intent to defraud." Also note that the *actus reus* varies depending on the conduct in question. The "offers or presents" language is the uttering component of the statute. See Figure 11.4 for a summary.

Other jurisdictions have taken more elaborate measures to target forgery and uttering, having enacted separate statutes for a variety of specific offenses. For example, in West Virginia, there are eight statutes aimed at currency-related forgery alone.[52] This is not surprising given the scope of the counterfeit currency problem. All states and the federal government[53] maintain statutes aimed at discouraging counterfeiting as well. Much the same applies to misuse of credit cards, falsification of checks, and so on.

The criminal law is intensely interested in discouraging forgery and uttering of financial instruments and documents, and defendants can get rather creative (or desperate) in their attempts to escape conviction under the applicable statutes. In one case, the defendant was convicted of counterfeiting currency under a federal statute providing that "[w]hoever, with intent to defraud, passes, utters, publishes, or sells, or attempts to pass, utter, publish, or sell, or with like intent brings into the United States or keeps in possession or conceals any falsely made, forged, counterfeited, or

---

[50]*Black's Law Dictionary*, p. 650.
[51]Ariz. Rev. Stat. Section 13-2002 (2010).
[52]West Va. Code Sections 61-4-1-61-4-8 (2010).
[53]18 U.S.C. Section 471 (2010).

**Figure 11.4**
Forgery/Uttering

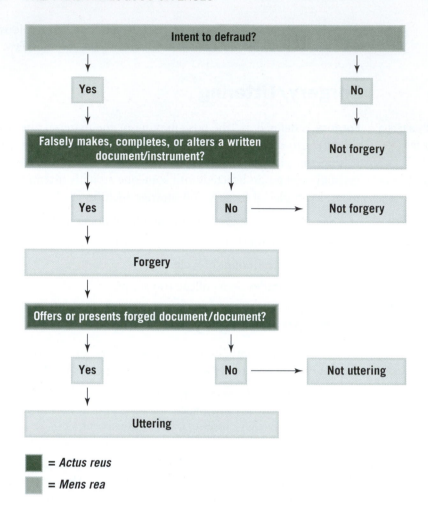

altered obligation or other security of the United States, shall be fined under this title or imprisoned...."[54] In an attempt to reverse his conviction, the defendant argued that counterfeited $50 bill he passed to a store clerk was "not of an appearance calculated to deceive an unsuspecting person of ordinary observation and care"[55] and therefore that he was wrongfully convicted. The court disagreed, noting that the bill was a

> falsely made and altered obligation of the United States because it was composed of parts of three genuine bills which had been fastened together with transparent tape. When folded with the right half of the obverse side showing, it has the appearance of a good $50 bill. . . . Although the workmanship on the bill was crude, it was of such character that under favorable circumstances it could be uttered and accepted as genuine. Those circumstances are presented in the peculiar facts of this case and are sufficient to establish a violation of the statute.[56]

**e-mail spoofing** Altering an e-mail address so that it appears to come from a person other than the sender.

Recently, forgery has move into cyberspace, particularly via **e-mail spoofing**, or "forging" key parts of an email address to give the impression that a message comes

---

[54]18 U.S.C. Section 472 (2010).
[55]*United States* v. *Drumright*, 534 F.2d 1383 (10th Cir. 1976), p. 1385.
[56]Ibid., pp. 1385–1386.

from one person when in fact it comes from another.[57] This is often done as a means of shielding the identity of someone who sends "spam" e-mail. It is also done to trick recipients into divulging sensitive information. The recipient of such a spoof may get an

- e-mail claiming to be from a system administrator requesting users to change their passwords to a specified string and threatening to suspend their account if they do not comply.
- e-mail claiming to be from a person in authority requesting users to send them a copy of a password file or other sensitive information.[58]

States have been slow to criminalize e-mail spoofing. Some have enacted antispam statutes aimed at deterring this high-tech form of forgery, but as of this writing, the majority of them have not.[59]

See the accompanying Court Decision for more on the crime of forgery. In it we examine the case of *State* v. *Stallings*, where a prisoner attempts to "forge" his way to freedom.

## COURT DECISION

*State* v. *Stallings*
158 S.W.3d 310 (Missouri App. 2005)

**Background:** Rickey Stallings was convicted of forgery in the Circuit Court, Cole County and sentenced to ten years in prison. Stallings appealed and the Missouri Court of Appeals affirmed his conviction.

***Factual and Procedural History**

In April 2002, Stallings was incarcerated at the Algoa Correctional Center, having served thirteen years of his twenty-three year sentence for various felony offenses. He worked as a clerk in the prison's library.

On April 22, 2002, an office assistant in the Algoa records department opened a manila envelope that came from the message center, a room where mail was sorted for delivery to various departments in the prison. The unsealed envelope appeared to have been sent through inter-agency mail from the Fulton Reception and Diagnostic Center. Among the documents in the envelope was a four-page order, purportedly from the St. Louis County Circuit Court, stating that Stallings' prison sentence had been reduced to thirteen years. Upon review of the order, Algoa records officer Teresa Adams became suspicious that it was not authentic. Adams noticed the order had no original signatures and the court clerk's certification on the last page did not include an embossed seal.

Subsequent investigation revealed there was no order in Stallings' court file to amend or otherwise reduce his prison sentence. The order that arrived in the Algoa records department was determined to be a forgery, with a photocopied signature of the sentencing judge and a photocopied certification seal. The document was sent to the

---

[57]See, e.g., S. Austria, "Forgery in Cyberspace: The Spoof Could Be on You!," *Pittsburgh Journal of Technology Law and Policy*, Vol. 4 (2004), p. 2.
[58]U.S. Computer Emergency Readiness Team, *Home Network Security*. Available at: http://www.cert.org/tech_tips/email_spoofing.html (accessed July 22, 2011).
[59]Austria, "Forgery in Cyberspace," p. 2.

Missouri State Highway Patrol laboratory for fingerprint testing. Four of Stallings' thumbprints were found on pages of the forged document.

Stallings was charged with one count of forgery. At the jury trial, the State presented evidence that Stallings, as a clerk, had access to electronic typewriters and a copy machine in the prison library. Library clerks also were permitted to enter the message center without supervision. A Highway Patrol official identified Stallings' fingerprints on the counterfeit document. A prison official testified that although outgoing inmate mail was generally checked for contraband and inappropriate content an envelope marked as "legal mail" would not be opened unless it was suspected of containing contraband.

### \*\*\*Sufficiency of the Evidence

In his first point on appeal, Stallings contends the trial court erred in entering the judgment of conviction because the evidence was insufficient to prove he committed forgery under Section 570.090. Our review of this point is limited to determining whether the jury had substantial evidence from which to find the defendant guilty beyond a reasonable doubt.

\*\*\*Stallings was charged with committing a forgery in violation of Section 570.090, which provides in relevant part:

1. A person commits the crime of forgery if, with the purpose to defraud, he
   (1) Makes, completes, alters or authenticates any writing so that it purports to have been made by another or at another time or place or in a numbered sequence other than was in fact the case or with different terms or by authority of one who did not give such authority; or . . .
   (4) Uses as genuine, or possesses for the purpose of using as genuine, or transfers with the knowledge or belief that it will be used as genuine, any writing or other thing which the actor knows has been made or altered in the manner described in this section.

Stallings argues the evidence was insufficient to find that he *transferred* a forged writing, as required in Section 570.090.1(4). The term "transfer" is not defined in the statute. Stallings contends the applicable dictionary definition of "transfer" is "to make over or negotiate the possession or control of (a right, title, or property) by a legal process usu[ally] for consideration." He relies on *State v. Conaway,* 824 S.W.2d 50, 53 (Mo.App.1991), wherein the court applied this definition and held the evidence was sufficient to support a forgery conviction because a "transfer" took place when the defendant negotiated fraudulently-endorsed checks by depositing them into his bank account. Stallings argues that *Conaway* indicates the "clear legislative intent [of § 570.090.1(4) ] to use the term 'transfer' in its financial sense." Because there was no evidence that he negotiated a financial instrument, Stallings contends the State failed to prove the element of transfer.

When a statutory term is undefined, we must apply its common sense, dictionary meaning, in the absence of an indication of specialized use. The common meaning of "transfer" is not limited to the negotiation of financial documents; *Webster's* dictionary also defines the term as "to cause to pass from one person or place to another: transmit." Similarly, Black's Law Dictionary offers several definitions of "transfer," including "[t]o convey or remove from one place or one person to another; to pass or hand from one to another[.]" This use of the term was apparent in *State v. Pride*, 1 S.W.3d 494, 499–501 (Mo.App.1999), where we found the defendant demonstrated the requisite intent to commit forgery by *faxing* fraudulent copies of a cashier's check and a certificate of insurance.

Forgery is a crime that can be committed by transferring a fraudulent writing in several ways. In *Pride*, the defendant's "transfer" was the transmission of a facsimile, whereas in *Conaway* it was the depositing of a check. The applicable common sense meaning of the term depends on the factual situation. In light of the circumstances here, the State sought to apply the term as used in *Pride*, by proving that Stallings transferred the fraudulent court order by placing it in the prison mail system. The State's theory was a reasonable application of the dictionary definition of "transfer" as the conveyance or removal of an object from one place to another.

We also find that the evidence at trial supported the State's theory. Prison officials testified that Stallings had access to typewriters and a copy machine, which would have equipped him to prepare the court order. The fingerprint evidence provided direct proof that Stallings handled and had knowledge of the counterfeit document. Testimony further established that, as a library clerk, Stallings had unsupervised access to Algoa's message center, from which the envelope containing the fraudulent order was dispatched to the records department. Stallings also had a reason to perpetrate the crime, in that he had served thirteen years of his twenty-three year sentence, and the falsified court document would have cleared the way for his immediate release from prison.

Based on this evidence, the element of "transfer" was circumstantially established by proof that Stallings had the means, opportunity, and motive to commit the forgery. There was substantial evidence from which the jury could reasonably infer that Stallings prepared the forged document and then used the prison mail system to transfer it from the message center to the records department. Accordingly, the evidence was sufficient to support the determination that Stallings was guilty of forgery beyond a reasonable doubt. Point I is denied.

\*\*\*The judgment of the trial court is affirmed.

## Case Analysis

1. Which element of forgery is the defendant attacking with his legal argument?
2. Explain the court's statutory analysis of Section 570.090.
3. How did the prior precedent of *Conway* and *Pride* impact the court's decision?

## Identity Theft

Recent data show that almost 8 million households in the United States experienced at least one form of identity theft in the past year.[60] From year to year, the number continues to grow. **Identity theft** (sometimes called "identity fraud")

**identity theft** Utilizing personal information of another person to commit fraud or deception.

[60]L. Langton and K. Baum, *Identity Theft Reported by Households, 2007—Statistical Tables* (Washington, DC: U.S. Department of Justice, 2010).

**Figure 11.5**

Common Forms of
Identity Theft

*Account Fraud:* There are two basic forms of account fraud: the misuse of a victim's existing account, and the opening of a new account in the victim's name.

*Blocking:* Refers to a victim's right under §605B of the Fair Credit Reporting Act to prevent information that is the result of identity theft from appearing on her credit report.

*Criminal Identity Theft:* Criminal identity theft occurs when someone uses the victim's name and information as his own during an investigation, issuance of a ticket, or arrest by law enforcement.

*Employment Identity Theft:* Some identity thieves use a victim's Social Security number for employment. Identity thieves might use another person's identity if they have a criminal record that might prevent their being hired, or if they do not have legal status to work in this country.

*Medical Identity Theft:* In cases of medical identity theft, thieves use a victim's name and possibly insurance information to obtain medical services or goods. The victim is then saddled with proving she is not responsible for costly medical bills, or may find that the thief has exhausted the victim's insurance coverage.

*Synthetic Identity Theft:* Each of the types of identity theft listed above involves the thief impersonating the victim to obtain benefits. In some cases, the thief does not steal the victim's entire identity, but rather uses only the victim's Social Security number, in combination with another person's name and birth date, to create a new, fictitious identity.

*Tax Fraud:* In this type of fraud, an identity thief files a tax return in the victim's name in order to receive a refund or other payment, such as a stimulus check. If the thief files for the refund before the victim, the IRS may deny the victim's rightful refund or stimulus check.

*Source:* President's Task Force on Identity Theft, *Guide for Assisting Identity Theft Victims,* http://www.idtheft.gov/probono/index.html (accessed October 29, 2010).

occurs "when someone uses or attempts to use the sensitive personal information of another person to commit fraud."[61] Common varieties of identity theft appear in Figure 11.5.

Identity theft is both a federal and state crime. Federal law provides, in part, that it is a felony to "knowingly transfer, possess or use, without lawful authority, a means of identification of another person with the intent to commit, or to aid or abet, any unlawful activity that constitutes a violation of Federal law, or that constitutes a felony under any applicable State or local law."[62] State laws vary in their intent and scope.[63] Some states maintain single identity theft/fraud statutes. Others criminalize identity theft/fraud through a wide range of statutes.

---

[61]President's Task Force on Identity Theft, *Guide for Assisting Identity Theft Victims,* http://www.idtheft. gov/probono/index.html (accessed October 29, 2010).

[62]18 U.S.C.A. Section 1028 (2010).

[63]For a list of the many state statutes, see http://www.ncsl.org/?tabid=12538 (accessed October 29, 2010).

Still others fit identity theft into their larceny statutes. As an example, Maryland law provides the following:

> (c) A person may not knowingly and willfully assume the identity of another:
> (1) to avoid identification, apprehension, or prosecution for a crime; or
> (2) with fraudulent intent to:
> (i) get a benefit, credit, good, service, or other thing of value; or
> (ii) avoid the payment of debt or other legal obligation.[64]

Note that the *mens rea* in this statute is "knowingly and willfully." The *actus reus* varies according to the defendant's intent. A recent Supreme Court case, *Flores-Figueroa* v. *United States*,[65] calls attention to the importance of *mens rea* in the identity theft context. In that case, a man presented to his employer counterfeit Social Security and alien registration cards, both of which contained numbers that had been assigned to other people. He was convicted in a federal district court of aggravated identity theft. The Eight Circuit affirmed, but the U.S. Supreme Court reversed, noting that the government had failed to prove, as applicable federal law[66] required, that the defendant "knowingly" assumed the identity of someone else. The Court's reasoning is rather informative:

> [I]n the classic case of identity theft, intent is generally not difficult to prove. For example, where a defendant has used another person's identification information to get access to that person's bank account, the Government can prove knowledge with little difficulty. The same is true when the defendant has gone through someone else's trash to find discarded credit card and bank statements, or pretends to be from the victim's bank and requests personal identifying information. Indeed, the examples of identity theft in the legislative history (dumpster diving, computer hacking, and the like) are all examples of the types of classic identity theft where intent should be relatively easy to prove, and there will be no practical enforcement problem. For another thing, to the extent that Congress may have been concerned about criminalizing the conduct of a broader class of individuals, the concerns about practical enforceability are insufficient to outweigh the clarity of the text. . . . But had Congress placed conclusive weight upon practical enforcement, the statute would likely not read the way it now reads. Instead, Congress used the word "knowingly" followed by a list of offense elements. And we cannot find indications in statements of its purpose or in the practical problems of enforcement sufficient to overcome the ordinary meaning, in English or through ordinary interpretive practice, of the words that it wrote.[67]

## Theft of Intellectual Property

**intellectual property**
Intangible property that can be protected under federal law, such as copyrights, patents, and trademarks.

**Intellectual property** is a blanket term describing the many varieties of products attributable to human intellect. Examples include copyrights, patents, trademarks, and trade secrets. Since intellectual property can be quite valuable, it is no surprise that thieves target them. Patent infringement, copyright infringement, trademark counterfeiting, theft of trade secrets, and other crimes have become quite common and difficult to prevent and control.

---

[64]Md. Code Section 8-301 (2010).
[65]*Flores-Figueroa* v. *United States*, 129 S.Ct. 1886 (2009).
[66]18 U.S.C. Section 1028(A)(a)(1).
[67]*Flores-Figueroa* v. *United States*, pp. 18–19.

Copyright Symbol
© Fabinus08 | Dreamstime.com

"Copyrights" refer to the legal protection afforded to an author's original works. Examples include the lyrics of a popular song, books, and poetry. Federal law is the primary mechanism used for criminal prosecution of copyright infringement. The applicable statute reads:

> Any person who willfully infringes a copyright shall be punished as provided under section 2319 of title 18, if the infringement was committed—
>
> A. for purposes of commercial advantage or private financial gain;
> B. by the reproduction or distribution, including by electronic means, during any 180-day period, of 1 or more copies or phonorecords of 1 or more copyrighted works, which have a total retail value of more than $1,000; or
> C. by the distribution of a work being prepared for commercial distribution, by making it available on a computer network accessible to members of the public, if such person knew or should have known that the work was intended for commercial distribution.[68]

For example, if a student bought a copy of this textbook, made 100 copies of it, and sold it to friends for a cheap price, he or she would be violating federal law (note the "All Rights Reserved" provision in the book's opening pages).

A patent is a grant of right, from the federal government, to exclude others from producing or using a discovery or invention. Most inventions and discoveries that are not of an obvious nature apply for patent protection from the United States Patent and Trademark Office. The patent holder then benefits financially from marketing the product. Without patent law, there would be little incentive to invent, as competitors would take away sales from the inventor and possibly undercut the inventor in terms of price. Patent infringements are usually dealt with via civil process; however, the federal Patent Act provides for criminal prosecution in certain instances (beyond the scope of this book).

Trademarks, the distinctive words, phrases, and symbols used to identify products, are also protected intellectual property. The Trademark Counterfeiting Act of 1984 provides that the following:

> Whoever intentionally traffics or attempts to traffic in goods or services and knowingly uses a counterfeit mark on or in connection with such goods or services shall, if an individual, be fined not more than $2,000,000 or imprisoned not more than 10 years, or both, and, if a person other than an individual, be fined not more than $5,000,000.[69]

Generally, trademark infringement occurs when a competitor uses a phrase or symbol that is likely to cause confusion among consumers regarding the product. For example, if I sold counterfeit purses on the streets of New York City using the famous symbol of Louis Vuitton, I would be violating the Counterfeiting Act.

Finally, trade secrets are protected intellectual property. Examples include "all forms and types of financial, business, scientific, technical, economic, or engineering information . . . whether tangible or intangible, and whether or how stored, compiled, or memorialized physically, electronically, graphically, photographically, or in writing."[70] A customer list is a classic example of a trade secret, since it often takes businesses years to compile such sensitive and potentially lucrative information. In order

---

[68]18 U.S.C. Section 506(a) (2010).
[69]18 U.S.C. Section 2320 (2010).
[70]18 U.S.C. Section 1839(3) (2010).

for something to be legally considered a trade secret, however, the company must make reasonable efforts to keep that information private and secure from public view. Business is competitive, so there is often an incentive for one company to learn of another's secrets for the purpose of making it more profitable. Federal law criminalizes such activity, including even *attempting* to steal trade secrets.[71]

# Consolidation of Theft Offenses

As time has gone on, theft law has become rather complicated. A number of states have dozens of theft-related statutes. To ease the burden on prosecutors, states have increasingly begun to consolidate their theft statutes into one all-encompassing law. Some have patterned their laws after the Model Penal Code's "theft" statute. The Model Penal Code's theft provision does not require "taking" or "asportation."[72] Nor does it require intent to permanently deprive. Trespass is not needed, either. And "anything of value, including real estate, tangible or intangible personal property, contract rights, choses-in-action [a form of intangible personal property] and other interests in or claims to wealth, admission or transportation tickets, captured or domestic animals, food and drink, electric or other power" are all possible targets of theft.[73] Theft, however, can be accomplished by a number of means under the Model Penal Code, including larceny, embezzlement, and false pretenses. California offers perhaps the most consolidated of all theft statutes, which reads in relevant part:

> Every person who shall feloniously steal, take, carry, lead, or drive away the personal property of another, or who shall fraudulently appropriate property which has been entrusted to him or her, or who shall knowingly and designedly, by any false or fraudulent representation or pretense, defraud any other person of money, labor or real or personal property, or who causes or procures others to report falsely of his or her wealth or mercantile character and by thus imposing upon any person, obtains credit and thereby fraudulently gets or obtains possession of money, or property or obtains the labor or service of another, is guilty of theft. . . .[74]

Note the many different types of conduct referenced in this excerpt. California has not abolished all its other theft statutes, however, which has led to some confusion.[75] Nevertheless, the Penal Code section quoted earlier at least illustrates how a legislature can lump various theft-related offenses into a single statute.

**YOUR DECISION**

1. In the days following Hurricane Katrina, Steven Matthews established the Web site http://www.redcross-usa.org. Steven had no official affiliation with the Red Cross and was attempting to obtain donations from unwitting citizens following the natural disaster. In order to secure the online donations for himself, Steven

---

[71] 18 U.S.C. Section 1832 (2010).
[72] Model Penal Code Section 223.
[73] Ibid.
[74] Cal. Penal Code Section 484.
[75] See, e.g., S. A. Moore, "Nevada's Comprehensive Theft Statute: Consolidation or Confusion?," *Nevada Law Journal*, Vol. 8 (2008), pp. 672–697.

created a number of PayPal accounts using the names, e-mail addresses and other personal information of third parties he obtained illegally. What crimes, if any, has Steven committed? Are any intellectual property rights implicated in this case?

2. Phil Smith is a general contractor. Harry and Sally Jones hired Phil to finish their basement and willingly provided him with a $10,000 deposit. Phil described his expertise in basement finishing and the Jones' believed Phil would finish their basement within the next three to six months. Over a year later, Phil has not yet begun work on their basement. The Jones' would like to pursue any criminal charges available. Has Phil Smith committed a crime? If so, which one?

## Summary

- *False pretenses* is shorthand for "obtaining property by deception." It is distinct from larceny because of deception and/or false representation.

- False pretenses is not the same as larceny by trick.

- For something to amount to false representation, it must (1) be false, (2) not constitute and opinion, and (3) apply to current, not future conduct.

- The *mens rea* of false pretenses requires a showing that the defendant intended to use the false information to secure property that he or she did not otherwise have the right to.

- Forgery is the false making or material altering of a document with intent to defraud. Uttering refers to passing a forged document.

- E-mail spoofing is a form of forgery.

- Identity theft occurs when someone uses or attempts to use sensitive personal information of another person with intent to defraud.

- *Intellectual property* is a blanket term describing the many varieties of products attributable to human intellect. Examples include copyrights, patents, trademarks, and trade secrets, among many others. Theft of intellectual property is a crime.

- Given the complexity of theft laws (and the many varieties of theft), several states have increasingly begun to consolidate their theft statutes into one all-encompassing law.

# Chapter Review

MODULE **11.1**

## LARCENY

### Learning Objectives

- Identify the elements of larceny.
- Summarize the legal issues/complications that can come up during a larceny prosecution.

### Review Questions

1. Compare and contrast modern larceny with common law larceny.
2. Distinguish between custody and possession and explain why both are relevant in the larceny context.
3. Compare reckless larceny to ordinary larceny.
4. What is the criminal law rule for "Finders keepers, losers weepers"?
5. Should it be a crime for someone to steal stolen property? Why or why not?

### Key Terms

larceny
claim of right

MODULE **11.2**

## RECEIVING STOLEN PROPERTY, EXTORTION, AND EMBEZZLEMENT

### Learning Objectives

- Describe the crime of receiving stolen property.
- Describe the crime of extortion.
- Describe the crime of embezzlement.

### Review Questions

1. Describe a situation in which someone who receives stolen property is not guilty of a crime.
2. Compare and contrast extortion and robbery.
3. Compare and contrast larceny and embezzlement.

### Key Terms

extortion
embezzlement
bailee
bailor
white-collar crime
conversion

MODULE **11.3** **FALSE PRETENSES, FORGERY/UTTERING, AND EMERGING THEFT OFFENSES**

### Learning Objectives

· Summarize the elements of false pretenses and forgery/uttering.

· Compare and contrast identity theft and theft of intellectual property.

· Explain the reasons for the consolidation of theft crimes.

### Review Questions

1. Compare and contrast false pretenses and larceny by trick.

2. What are the elements of a "false representation"?

3. Compare and contrast forgery and uttering.

4. Discuss some common forms of identity theft.

5. Define intellectual property.

6. What, in your opinion, are the pros and cons of theft law consolidation?

### Key Terms

false pretenses
forgery
uttering
e-mail spoofing
identity theft
intellectual property

## Chapter Synthesis Questions

1. Which theft offense is most serious? Defend your answer.

2. Which emerging theft offense discussed in this chapter is most serious? Why?

3. Draft a consolidated theft statute that combines at least three distinct crimes covered in this chapter.

# 12

# PUBLIC ORDER, MORALITY, AND VICE CRIMES

## *Learning Objectives*

**MODULE 12.1 GROUP CRIMINALITY AND OFFENSES AGAINST PUBLIC ORDER**

- Describe the crimes of riot and unlawful assembly.
- Summarize legislative approaches to criminalizing gang activity.
- Describe six offenses against public order.

**MODULE 12.2 VICE CRIMES AND DRUG OFFENSES**

- Describe prostitution and its legal status across the United States.
- Summarize the legal status of gambling.
- Distinguish between alcohol and drug offenses.

**MODULE 12.3 CRIMES AGAINST DECENCY AND/OR MORALITY**

- Summarize government efforts throughout history to criminalize immorality.
- Describe modern-day crimes against decency and/or morality.
- Summarize the means by which the criminal law controls profanity.

# GROUP CRIMINALITY AND OFFENSES AGAINST PUBLIC ORDER

### Learning Objectives

- **Describe the crimes of riot and unlawful assembly.**
- **Summarize legislative approaches to criminalizing gang activity.**
- **Describe six offenses against public order.**

**CORE CONCEPTS**

In this chapter we present a variety of what we call "public order," "morality," and "vice" crimes. They are also called "quality-of-life crimes" since they impact the quality of life of residents living in the neighborhoods where these offenses are committed. For example, a neighborhood filled with homeless individuals begging for money (the crimes of "vagrancy" and "panhandling") would have, according to most people, a lower quality of life than a neighborhood without homelessness. While quality-of-life crimes are still significant, the public and the law often regard them as "less serious" than the violent offenses, such as murder, rape, or robbery.

Offenses against public order can be committed by both individuals and groups. Riots, unlawful assembly, certain gang activity, resisting arrest, disorderly conduct, and other offenses fall into this category. Vice crimes include prostitution, gambling, and pornography/obscenity. Drug offenses focus on alcohol and other controlled substances. Finally, crimes against decency and morality cover a range of conduct, including incest, indecent exposure, bigamy, polygamy, and profanity.

This chapter does not cover every conceivable offense with a public order, morality, or vice dimension to it, but it certainly covers the more major ones. It is also important to note that some of the offenses we cover in one category could well fit in another. For example, we dedicate a specific section to alcohol and drug crimes, but many people feel the consumption of either is immoral. We begin with group criminality and offenses against public order.

## Group Criminality

**riot** A group of three or more people involved in a public disturbance of the peace.

Chapter 6 introduced complicity and vicarious liability. With complicity, an accomplice *derives* his or her criminal liability from a primary offender. With vicarious liability, one person is held liable for the actions of another based on their relationship. Both offense types require the involvement (whether knowing or not) of more than one person. Group criminality is similar in the sense that it involves more than one person. However, we distinguish this section's subject matter from complicity and vicarious liability because *many* offenders may be involved. Forms of group criminality that involve multiple offenders include **riot**, unlawful assembly, and certain types of gang activity. Though each necessarily requires multiple offenders, it is individuals who are held criminally liable for such actions (perhaps many will be prosecuted together).

## Riot

According to the Federal Anti-Riot Act of 1968,

> the term "riot" means a public disturbance involving (1) an act or acts of violence by one or more persons part of an assemblage of three or more persons, which act or acts shall constitute a clear and present danger of, or shall result in, damage or injury to the property of any other person or to the person of any other individual or (2) a threat or threats of the commission of an act or acts of violence by one or more persons part of an assemblage of three or more persons having, individually or collectively, the ability of immediate execution of such threat or threats, where the performance of the threatened act or acts of violence would constitute a clear and present danger of, or would result in, damage or injury to the property of any other person or to the person of any other individual.[1]

Various dimensions of rioting are criminalized at both the federal and state level. At the federal level, one who incites, encourages, participates in, and/or carries on a riot may be guilty of an offense—provided there is an interstate or foreign commerce dimension to the activities. For example, if a person mailed letters to other people in several states, encouraging them to riot against the government, that person's actions would violate federal law.

States have similar statutes that prohibit rioting within their jurisdictions. Oregon's riot statute provides that "a person commits the crime of riot if while participating with five or more other persons the person engages in tumultuous and violent conduct and thereby intentionally or recklessly creates a grave risk of causing public alarm."[2] Note that, as defined in Oregon, rioting is a specific intent offense, requiring either intentional or reckless action on the part of the defendant. The *actus reus* requires proof of three elements:

1. Five or more people who
2. Engage in tumultuous or violent conduct [and]
3. Create a grave risk of public alarm.[3]

On their face, these elements may seem easy enough to prove. However, Oregon's law has been challenged more than once (albeit unsuccessfully) on the grounds that it is unconstitutionally vague.[4]

## Unlawful Assembly

**unlawful assembly** A group of people publicly gather unlawfully or for an illegal purpose.

Riot closely parallels **unlawful assembly**, as each occurs when a group consisting of a certain number of people assemble unlawfully—or for an unlawful purpose. Both are distinct, however. The classic example of unlawful assembly is a protest. When a protest turns violent, then riot often occurs.

---

[1]18 U.S.C. Section 2102(a) (2010).
[2]Or. Rev. Stat. Section 166.015 (2010).
[3]Ibid.
[4]See, e.g., *State* v. *Chakerian*, 938 P.2d 756 (Or. 1997).

**rout** An unlawfully assembled groups takes a significant step toward rioting.

Some states also define a crime of **rout**, which occurs when an unlawfully assembled groups takes a significant step toward rioting. California's Penal Code provides that "[w]henever two or more persons, assembled and acting together, make any attempt or advance toward the commission of an act which would be a riot if actually committed, such an assembly is rout."[5] In other words, a riot is the culmination of both unlawful assembly and rout. Most states do not define *rout* as a crime and instead combine activities that would be considered rout with either their riot or unlawful assembly statutes.

Returning to unlawful assembly in particular, let us briefly examine Minnesota's statute. It provides the following:

When three or more persons assemble, each participant is guilty of unlawful assembly, which is a misdemeanor, if the assembly is:

1. With intent to commit any unlawful act by force; or
2. With intent to carry out any purpose in such manner as will disturb or threaten the public peace; or
3. Without unlawful purpose, but the participants so conduct themselves in a disorderly manner as to disturb or threaten the public peace.[6]

As defined, unlawful assembly is a specific intent offense. The *actus reus* requires proof of either elements 1, 2, or 3. Note that element 3 seems to cover actions that would ordinarily be considered rout, were such actions criminalized under a separate statute.

## Gang Activity

By definition, gang activity occurs in groups. And while gang affiliates who commit crimes are often prosecuted individually, a number of states—as well as the District of Columbia—have enacted statutes aimed at targeting gang assembly, participation, and membership.[7] The District of Columbia's controversial statute, which is undergoing challenge as of this writing, reads in part as follows:

a. (1) It is unlawful for a person to solicit, invite, recruit, encourage, or otherwise cause, or attempt to cause, another individual to become a member of, remain in, or actively participate in what the person knows to be a criminal street gang. . . .
b. (1) It is unlawful for any person who is a member of or actively participates in a criminal street gang to knowingly and willfully participate in any felony or violent misdemeanor committed for the benefit of, at the direction of, or in association with any other member or participant of that criminal street gang.[8]

A *criminal street gang* is defined as any association or group of six or more persons that either requires, as a condition of membership, the commission of a crime of violence or, as part of its purpose or frequent activities, violates the criminal laws of the District. The statute was written such that not only would the individual perpetrator be held liable for his or her criminal actions, but other members of the gang would, too.

---

[5]Cal. Penal Code Section 406 (2010).
[6]Minn. Code Section 609.705 (2005).
[7]For an overview, see http://www.nationalgangcenter.gov/Legislation (accessed November 4, 2010).
[8]D.C. Code Section 22-951 (2007).

Some states have also created "gang-free zones," making it a criminal offense for gang members to frequent particular locations, such as playgrounds, shopping malls, movie theaters, and schools.[9] And antigang legislation is by no means limited to assembly issues. Laws have been enacted to tackle every conceivable dimension of the gang problem. Judges have issued injunctions, barring known gang members from associating with one another. Most such approaches, unfortunately, are beyond the scope of this text.[10]

# Offenses against Public Order

A number of offenses are tied together by the theme that they threaten public order in some fashion. Within the category of crimes against public order are certain quality-of-life crimes, including vagrancy and loitering. Some offenses considered later in this chapter, such as public intoxication, could also be said to threaten public order or quality of life, but we introduce those crimes alongside other very similar ones. The list of offenses discussed in this section is by no means exhaustive, but most people can agree that resisting arrest, disorderly conduct, breach of peace, vagrancy, loitering, and panhandling do their share to threaten public order. We consider each of these in no particular order of seriousness.

## Resisting Arrest

It is a crime to resist a lawful arrest. To permit otherwise would seriously compromise law enforcement's effectiveness. At common law, it was not considered criminal to resist an *unlawful* arrest.[11] These days, however, it is generally unlawful to resist *any* kind of arrest.[12] New York's resisting arrest statute is illustrative:

> A person may not use physical force to resist an arrest, whether authorized or unauthorized, which is being effected or attempted by a police officer or peace officer when it would reasonably appear that the latter is a police officer or a peace officer.[13]

If the arresting officer uses excessive force to effect an otherwise lawful arrest, then the intended arrestee may usually use physical force in kind, but of a concern for protecting himself or herself, not just for the sake of resisting. As the Oregon Supreme Court argued,

> [I]f an officer making an arrest uses excessive force, the permissible use of physical force by the arrestee is limited to the use of such force as is reasonably necessary under the circumstances for self-defense against the excessive force being used by the arresting officer.[14]

---

[9]See, e.g., Tx. Penal Code Section 71.028 (2010).

[10]Again, see http://www.nationalgangcenter.gov/Legislation (accessed November 4, 2010).

[11]See, e.g., *United States* v. *Heliczer*, 373 F.2d 241 (2nd Cir. 1967). Also see Chapter 4's Resisting Unlawful Arrest section.

[12]See, e.g., *Miller* v. *State*, 462 P.2d 421 (Alaska 1969).

[13]N.Y. Penal Law Section 35.27.

[14]*State* v. *Wright*, 799 P.2d 642 (Or. 1990), p. 645.

If the arrest is unsupported by probable cause and excessive force is not used, resistance is typically criminal. Why? Probable cause is a bit of an amorphous concept. It would unreasonable to let ordinary citizens decide when it is and is not present. Also, if an arrestee decides probable cause is absent and therefore resists, the possibility of injury to him- or herself is greatly increased. A "don't-resist" rule protects against needless injury and/or loss of life.

## Disorderly Conduct

**disorderly conduct** An individual causes a public disturbance, harm, or annoyance.

**Disorderly conduct** is roughly equivalent to an individual version of riot or unlawful assembly. According to the Model Penal Code, a person commits disorderly conduct if, "with purpose to cause public inconvenience, annoyance or alarm, or recklessly creating a risk thereof, he:

a. engages in fighting or threatening, or in violent or tumultuous behavior; or

b. makes unreasonable noise or offensively coarse utterance, gesture or display, or addresses abusive language to any person present; or

c. creates a hazardous or physically offensive condition by any act which serves no legitimate purpose of the actor."[15]

State laws are relatively similar. For example, the Indiana Code provides that "(a) A person who recklessly, knowingly, or intentionally: (1) engages in fighting or in tumultuous conduct; (2) makes unreasonable noise and continues to do so after being asked to stop; or (3) disrupts a lawful assembly of persons . . ."[16] commits disorderly conduct. Also note the similarities in this statute and the above Model Penal Code excerpt to the rioting and unlawful assembly statutes introduced previously. The main difference between rioting, unlawful assembly, and disorderly conduct is that the latter focuses on "a person," as opposed to a group.

The key to a disorderly conduct conviction is *disorder*. A person who peacefully protests will not be guilty of the crime. For example, in a classic civil rights case, *Edwards* v. *South Carolina*,[17] the U.S. Supreme Court reviewed the convictions of several individuals who participated in a protest against the state's racial segregation laws. They gave speeches, sang songs, and clapped and stamped their feet, but they were no more disorderly than this. The Supreme Court concluded:

> These petitioners were convicted of an offense as to be, in the words of the South Carolina Supreme Court, "not susceptible of exact definition." And they were convicted upon evidence which showed no more than that the opinions which they were peaceably expressing were sufficiently opposed to the views of the majority of the community to attract a crowd and necessitate police protection. The Fourteenth Amendment does not permit a State to make criminal the peaceful expression of unpopular views.[18]

In a similar case, the protestors blocked the driveway at a local jail, but their disorderly conduct convictions were upheld. The Supreme Court held, "The State, no less

---

[15]Model Penal Code Section 250.2.
[16]Ind. Code Ann. Section 35-45-1-3 (2010).
[17]*Edwards* v. *South Carolina*, 372 U.S. 229 (1963).
[18]Ibid., p. 237.

than a private owner of property, has power to preserve the property under its control for the use to which it is lawfully dedicated."[19]

The First Amendment rights to freedom of speech and assembly are also implicated in protest cases. See the accompanying Court Decision for more on unlawful assembly and disorderly conduct. In it we examine the case of *Phelps-Roper* v. *Nixon*, which involves the highly publicized church group that protested at the funerals of U.S. soldiers.

## COURT DECISION

### *Phelps-Roper* v. *Nixon*
### 545 F.3d 685 (8th Cir. 2008)

**Background:** Shirley Phelps-Roper brought a civil lawsuit challenging the validity of a Missouri statute. Phelps-Roper claimed the statutes violate her First Amendment rights and requested a preliminary injunction to stop enforcement of the statute while legal proceedings were pending. The Western District of Missouri denied the motion for a preliminary injunction. The Eighth Circuit Court of Appeals reversed and granted the preliminary injunction.

\*\*\*Phelps-Roper is a member of the Westboro Baptist Church (WBC) in Topeka, Kansas. Phelps alleges members of her church believe God is punishing America for what WBC considers the sin of homosexuality by killing Americans, including soldiers. As part of her religious duties, she believes she must protest and picket at certain funerals, including the funerals of United States soldiers, to publish the church's religious message: that God's promise of love and heaven for those who obey him in this life is counterbalanced by God's wrath and hell for those who do not. Phelps believes funerals are the only place where her religious message can be delivered in a timely and relevant manner.

On August 5, 2005, Phelps-Roper and other WBC members held a picket and protest near the location of the funeral of Army Spc. Edward Lee Myers in St. Joseph, Missouri. In direct response to the protest, Missouri enacted section 578.501, which criminalizes picketing "in front or about" a funeral location or procession, and section 578.502, which criminalizes picketing within 300 feet of a funeral location or procession, in the event section 578.501 is declared unconstitutional. Section 578.501 states, in pertinent part:

1. This section shall be known as "Spc. Edward Lee Myers' Law."
2. It shall be unlawful for any person to engage in picketing or other protest activities in front of or about any location at which a funeral is held, within one hour prior to the commencement of any funeral, and until one hour following the cessation of any funeral. Each day on which a violation occurs shall constitute a separate offense. Violation of this section is a class B misdemeanor, unless committed by a person who has previously pled guilty to or been found guilty of a violation of this section, in which case the violation is a class A misdemeanor.

---

[19]*Adderley v. Florida*, 385 U.S. 39 (1966), p. 47.

3. For the purposes of this section, "funeral" means the ceremonies, processions and memorial services held in connection with the burial or cremation of the dead.

Mo.Rev.Stat. § 578.501.

Phelps-Roper brought suit under 42 U.S.C. § 1983 alleging these laws invade her First Amendment rights. She seeks: (1) entry of a declaratory judgment finding sections 578.501 and 578.502 unconstitutional; (2) issuance of a preliminary and permanent injunction enjoining enforcement of sections 578.501 and 578.502.

\* \* \* Peaceful picketing is an expressive activity protected by the First Amendment. It is well-settled law that a "loss of First Amendment freedoms, for even minimal periods of time, unquestionably constitutes irreparable injury." If Phelps-Roper can establish a sufficient likelihood of success on the merits of her First Amendment claim, she will also have established irreparable harm as the result of the deprivation.

\* \* \*A content-neutral time, place and manner regulation may be imposed in a public forum if it: (1) serves a significant government interest; (2) is narrowly tailored; and (3) leaves open ample alternative channels of communication.

## A

The district court found the state has a significant interest in preserving and protecting the sanctity and dignity of memorial and funeral services, as well as protecting the privacy of family and friends of the deceased during a time of mourning and distress. The Supreme Court has not addressed this issue, but has recognized the state's interest in protecting citizens from unwanted communications while in their homes, and when otherwise "captive." One other circuit court, which recently analyzed the constitutionality of similar funeral protest statutes, has . . . acknowledged the state has an interest in protecting mourners, which were found to be a captive audience, from unwanted speech during a burial or funeral.

We note our own opinion in *Olmer v. Lincoln,* 192 F.3d 1176, 1178 (8th Cir.1999), which affirmed a preliminary injunction enjoining the enforcement of an ordinance that "restrict[ed] to certain areas the 'focused picketing' of churches and other religious premises thirty minutes before, during, and thirty minutes after any scheduled religious activity" because it violated the First Amendment. In *Olmer,* we held the government has no compelling interest in protecting an individual from unwanted speech outside of the residential context. We stated:

> As the Supreme Court said in *Frisby,* 'the home is different,' and, in our view, unique. Allowing other locations, even churches, to claim the same level of constitutionally protected privacy would, we think, permit government to prohibit too much speech and other communication. We recognize that lines have to be drawn, and we choose to draw the line in such a way as to give the maximum possible protection to speech, which is protected by the express words of the Constitution.

Because of our holding in *Olmer,* we conclude Phelps-Roper is likely to prove any interest the state has in protecting funeral mourners from unwanted speech is outweighed by the First Amendment right to free speech.

**B**

For a statute to be narrowly tailored, it must not burden substantially more speech than necessary to further the state's legitimate interests. An overbroad statute may be challenged on its face even though a more narrowly drawn statute would be valid as applied to the party in the case before it. To prevail, a plaintiff must show the challenged law either "could never be applied in a valid manner" or it is "written so broadly that [it] may inhibit the constitutionally protected speech of third parties."

\*\*\*Section 578.501 does not limit itself to activity that targets, disrupts, or is otherwise related to the funeral, memorial service or procession. While the Sixth Circuit concluded a similar ordinance was limited to activity that was directed at a funeral or burial service, the statute involved in that case defined "other protest activities" to include "any action that is *disruptive or undertaken to disrupt or disturb a funeral or burial service*." *Phelps-Roper,* 539 F.3d at 368. Because the Missouri statute does not contain any such provisions, Phelps-Roper is likely to prove the statute does not limit its coverage to activity that targets or disrupts a funeral or burial service.

We conclude there is enough likelihood Phelps-Roper will be able to prove section 578.501 is not narrowly tailored or is facially overbroad to the point she is likely to prevail on the merits of her claim.

**C**

The remaining requirement the state must satisfy to defend its time, place and manner restrictions is such restrictions must leave open ample alternative channels for communication of the information. As the Supreme Court has stated, "one is not to have the exercise of his liberty of expression in appropriate places abridged on the plea that it may be exercised in some other place." *Schneider v. New Jersey,* 308 U.S. 147, 151-52 (1939).

The Eighth Circuit has found other anti-picketing regulations did not leave open ample alternative channels for communication of the information. When addressing whether a permanent injunction should issue in *Kirkeby,* the Court reasoned:

> [P]laintiffs wish to express an opinion about an individual to that individual and others, and they wish to direct their message at that individual. . . . Therefore, allowing them to picket in the town square or even the next block does not satisfy the second *Ward* requirement [of leaving open ample alternative channels for communication]. These time limits do not give the plaintiffs enough opportunity to direct their intended message at their intended recipients.

By analogy, Phelps-Roper presents a viable argument that those who protest or picket at or near a military funeral wish to reach an audience that can only be addressed at such occasion and to convey to and through such an audience a particular message. She is likely to prevail in proving section 578.501 fails to afford open, ample and adequate alternative channels for the dissemination of her particular message.

**IV**

Because we conclude Phelps-Roper has demonstrated a likelihood of prevailing on the merits of her claim, we find she will suffer irreparable injury if the preliminary injunction is not issued. The injunction will not cause substantial harm to others, and the public is served by the preservation of constitutional rights. The district court abused its discretion when it concluded the balance of harms weighed toward denying the motion for a preliminary injunction based on its erroneous determination as to Phelps-Roper being unlikely to succeed on the merits. . . . We hold only that Phelps-Roper is entitled to a preliminary injunction while the constitutionality of section 578.501 is thoroughly reviewed. The contrary judgment of the district court is reversed.

## Case Analysis

1. This is a civil case in which the plaintiff is asking for a preliminary injunction. Explain what a preliminary injunction is and how it relates to the case.

2. Identify the three-part test the Eighth Circuit is using to evaluate the First Amendment issues raised in this case.

3. In 2010, the Spc. Edward Lee Myers' Law addressed in this case was declared unconstitutional by the Western District of Missouri (see *Phelps-Roper* v. *Koster*, 2010 WL 3257796, 2010 U.S. Dist. LEXIS 83518). Do you agree that the law is unconstitutional? Why or why not?

## Breach of Peace

**breach of peace** An unlawful act that disturbs the peace or harmony of the neighborhood.

**Breach of peace**, or more formally, "breaching the peace," occurs in a number of ways. For example, in Connecticut, a breach of the peace in the *first degree* occurs when someone, "with intent to cause inconvenience, annoyance or alarm, or recklessly creating a risk thereof, such person places a nonfunctional limitation of an explosive or incendiary device or an imitation of a hazardous substance in a public place or in a place or manner likely to be discovered by another person."[20] A *second-degree* breach of the peace occurs when a person, "with intent to cause inconvenience, annoyance or alarm, or recklessly creating a risk thereof:

1. Engages in fighting or in violent, tumultuous or threatening behavior in a public place; or

2. assaults or strikes another; or

3. threatens to commit any crime against another person or such other person's property; or

4. publicly exhibits, distributes, posts up or advertises any offensive, indecent or abusive matter concerning any person; or

5. in a public place, uses abusive or obscene language or makes an obscene gesture; or

6. creates a public and hazardous or physically offensive condition by any act which such person is not licensed or privileged to do."[21]

---

[20]Conn. Code Section 53a-180aa (2005).
[21]Ibid., Section 53a-181.

Some of these behaviors overlap with rioting and disorderly conduct, yet Connecticut criminalizes those behaviors under separate statutes. Breach of peace therefore acts, in some jurisdictions, as a "catch-all" statute that targets a variety of disruptive behaviors that do not always fit neatly into the categories of riot, unlawful assembly, and disorderly conduct.

Note that, in Connecticut, fighting is a form of breaching the peace. Many states adopt this approach of criminalizing fighting under a disorderly conduct or breach of peace statute. Others retain stand-alone fighting statutes, especially for cases in which weapons may be used. Consider Mississippi's statute:

> If any person shall be guilty of fighting in any city, town, village, or other public place, and shall in such fight use any rifle, shotgun, sword, sword-cane, pistol, dirk, bowie-knife, dirk-knife, or any other deadly weapon, or if any person shall be second or aid in such fight, the person so offending shall be fined not less than three hundred dollars, and shall be imprisoned not less than three months; and if any person shall be killed in such fight, the person so killing the other may be prosecuted and convicted as in other cases of murder.[22]

## Vagrancy, Loitering, and Panhandling

**vagrancy** Moving about with no visible means of financial support.

**loitering** The act of lingering aimlessly with no apparent purpose.

**panhandling** Public begging for food or money.

**Vagrancy** refers to moving about with no visible means of financial support. Essentially, vagrancy laws can be viewed as criminalizing homelessness. **Loitering** is the act of lingering aimlessly or "hanging out" with no apparent purpose. Loitering statutes are often geared at groups of teenagers or young adults who tend to "hang out" on a particular street corner or area of the city. Finally, **panhandling** is the same as begging. All three of these activities can have a dramatic effect on the "quality of life" of a particular neighborhood. Each action has been criminalized at various points in history and for various reasons, but defining them with precision has proven quite difficult. Vagrancy and loitering laws in particular have been subjected to constitutional challenge on multiple occasions (also see the "Void for Vagueness" discussion back in Chapter 2).

Laws criminalizing vagrancy, or homelessness, raise constitutional concerns.
BananaStock/Thinkstock

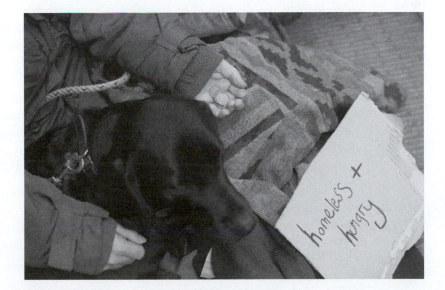

---

[22]Miss. Code Section 97-39-11 (2010).

Consider *Papachristou* v. *City of Jacksonville*,[23] a case in which the Supreme Court declared unconstitutional a municipal ordinance that targeted "vagrants" and "rogues and vagabonds, or dissolute persons who go about begging . . . common drunkards, lewd, wanton and lascivious persons, . . . persons wandering or strolling around from place to place without any lawful purpose or object, habitual loafers, [and] disorderly persons."[24] The Court concluded that the ordinance provided "no standards governing the exercise of . . . discretion" and thereby "permit[ted] and encourage[d] an arbitrary and discriminatory enforcement of the law" and resulted "in a regime in which the poor and the unpopular are permitted to 'stand on the sidewalk...only at the whim of any police officer.'"[25]

In a more recent case, *Kolender* v. *Lawson*,[26] the Supreme Court struck down another statute that made a misdemeanant of any person "[w]ho loiters or wanders upon the streets or from place to place without apparent reason or business and who refuses to identify himself and to account for his presence when requested by any peace officer to do so, if the surrounding circumstances are such as to indicate to a reasonable man that the public safety demands such identification."[27] The Court ruled that the statute was too vague because it "vests virtually complete discretion in the hands of the police to determine whether the suspect has satisfied the statute and must be permitted to go on his way in the absence of probable cause to arrest."[28]

Even after *Kolender*, a number of jurisdictions have attempted to devise sufficiently specific loitering statutes. For example, the city of Chicago passed a statute providing that "whenever a police officer observes a person whom he reasonably believes to be a criminal street gang member loitering in any public place with one or more other persons, he shall order all such persons to disperse and remove themselves from the area." Loitering was defined as "to remain in any one place with no apparent purpose." Despite the more specific language of this statute, however, the Supreme Court also struck it down, declaring that the statute was unconstitutionally vague.[29] The majority believed that the statute still gave police too much discretion to decide which people could be classified as gang members. The Court suggested it may have upheld the statute if it had applied to gang members or to those with "an apparently harmful purpose or effect," but instead, that statute applied to "everyone in the city who may remain in one place with one suspected gang member as long as their purpose is not apparent to an officer observing them."[30]

States still retain vagrancy, loitering, and panhandling statutes, but they remain controversial because of definitional problems and the possibility of unequal enforcement by police officials. Statutes that withstand constitutional scrutiny are those that criminalize a person's *actions*, not that person's status. Even statutes that criminalize actions can prove flawed, however. The city of Akron, Ohio, once made

[23]*Papachristou v. City of Jacksonville*, 405 U.S. 156 (1972).
[24]Ibid., p. 157, n. 1.
[25]Ibid., p. 170.
[26]*Kolender v. Lawson*, 461 U.S. 352 (1983).
[27]Ibid., p. 354, n. 1.
[28]Ibid., p. 358.
[29]*Chicago v. Morales*, 527 U.S. 41 (1999).
[30]Ibid.

it an offense to loiter "for the purpose of engaging in drug-related activity."[31] The ordinance listed several factors that police officers should consider in making that determination, including "looking like a drug user."[32] The ordinance was overturned because of its vague character.

Panhandling also potentially implicates the constitutional right to free speech under the First Amendment. Imagine you are walking down the street of a major metropolitan city. You see one individual with a sign that reads "The End of the World is Near" and he yells words or warnings as you walk by. Generally, his speech would be protected under the First Amendment right to freedom of speech. What if, on the same street corner, you also see a man with a sign that reads, "Starving. Need money for food," and as you walk by he asks you repeatedly for any spare change. Potentially, this second man has committed the crime of panhandling. Shouldn't his "speech" also be protected by the First Amendment? The Supreme Court explained that states are permitted to regulate the time, place, and manner of speech to support governmental interests as long as they do not regulate the content of your speech (see Chapter 2 for further discussion).[33]

---

**YOUR DECISION**

1. A large group of young women, referred to as the Daughters of Anarchy, are standing on the corner of Main Street in front of the state capital. They are known in the area as a sort of female motorcycle gang. Their purpose is to protest a new law requiring motorcycle riders to wear helmets. They do not have a permit for the protest. Some members of the group are screaming profanity at lawmakers as they pass by. Other members are aggressively asking individuals on the street for monetary donations for their cause. Still others start a fight with a rival organization, Daughters of Peace. List all of the possible crimes, if any, committed by the Daughters of Anarchy.

2. The state legislature passes the following law: "It shall be illegal for any person to engage in aggressive panhandling in the evening within 100 feet of any major tourist attraction." You are a local civil rights attorney who represents a group of concerned homeless people who live in the area. These individuals rely on public begging for food and basic needs. What constitutional arguments, if any, can you make regarding this law?

## Summary

- Forms of group criminality that involve multiple offenders include riot, unlawful assembly, and certain types of gang activity.
- Various dimensions of rioting are criminalized at both the federal and state level. At the federal level, one who incites, encourages, participates in, and/or carries on a riot may be guilty of an offense—provided there is an interstate or foreign

---

[31]See *Akron v. Rowland*, 618 N.E.2d 138 (Ohio 1993).
[32]Ibid.
[33]*R.A.V. v. City of St. Paul*, 505 U.S. 377 (1992).

commerce dimension to the activities. States have similar statutes that prohibit rioting within their jurisdictions.

- The classic example of unlawful assembly is a protest. When a protest turns violent, then riot often occurs.

- Some states also define a crime of *rout*, which occurs when an unlawfully assembled groups takes a significant step toward rioting.

- A number of states—as well as the District of Columbia—have enacted statutes aimed at targeting gang assembly, participation, and membership.

- Some of the common offenses that threaten public order are resisting arrest, disorderly conduct, breach of peace, vagrancy, loitering, and panhandling.

- It is a crime to resist a lawful arrest. Today, it is usually a crime to resist both lawful *and* unlawful arrest.

- Disorderly conduct is roughly equivalent to an individual version of riot or unlawful assembly.

- Breach of peace occurs in a number of ways depending on state law. Examples include causing an inconvenience, creating a risk of harm to others, and even fighting.

- Vagrancy refers, generally, to moving about with no visible means of financial support. Loitering is the act of lingering aimlessly or "hanging out" with no apparent purpose. Finally, panhandling is the same as begging.

---

**MODULE**

# 12.2

# VICE CRIMES AND DRUG OFFENSES

## Learning Objectives

- **Describe prostitution and its legal status across the United States.**
- **Summarize the legal status of gambling.**
- **Distinguish between alcohol and drug offenses.**

---

## CORE CONCEPTS

**vice** Immoral conduct, practices, or habits.

**Vice** is loosely defined as immoral conduct, practices, or habits. Several of the crimes presented in this chapter could fit within that definition, but the most universally recognized crimes of vice are prostitution, gambling, and pornography/obscenity. Crimes involving drugs and alcohol are often said to fall into the category of vice as well. The following sections look at each of these offenses.

Vice crimes are controversial because they are often based on moral considerations rather than objective harms. They are also referred to as "victimless crimes" since they lack the traditional victim seen in crimes like rape, murder, or robbery. It is often said, for example, that gambling, though criminal in many jurisdictions, does not cause harm in the sense that conventional street crimes do. Why, then, is it criminalized? For better or worse, the criminal law will continue to be premised to some extent on morals, beliefs, and values. Justice Byron White once remarked that "the law . . . is constantly based on notions of morality, and if all laws representing essentially moral choices are to be invalidated. . . ., the courts will be very busy indeed."[34]

# Prostitution

**prostitution** Performing or agreeing to perform a sexual act for hire.

Often called "the world's oldest profession," **prostitution** is defined as performing or agreeing to perform a sexual act for hire. It is criminalized in all states except Nevada, where a limited number of rural counties license legal brothels. Prostitution remains illegal in Las Vegas and other metropolitan areas throughout the state.

In addition to criminalizing prostitution itself, every state does the same with solicitation, the act of securing a prostitute's (or a suspected prostitute's) agreement to participate in a sex act. Texas's prostitution law illustrates:

a. A person commits an offense if he knowingly:
1. offers to engage, agrees to engage, or engages in sexual conduct for a fee; or
2. solicits another in a public place to engage with him in sexual conduct for hire.[35]

The *mens rea* of prostitution is "knowingly." The *actus reus* is either the act itself or any effort to get to that point.

States also criminalize a number of activities related to prostitution, including

- Promotion of prostitution,
- Compelling prostitution,
- Child prostitution,
- Running or residing in a house of prostitution, and/or
- Receiving earning as or from a prostitute.

See the accompanying Court Decision for more on criminalizing the acts of the pimp or panderer. In it we examine the case of *Helms* v. *State*, in which a man running an escort service claims he had no idea prostitution was occurring.

---

**COURT
DECISION**

*Helms* v. *State*
38 So.3d 182 (Fla. App. 2010)

**Background:** James Helms was convicted in Circuit Court, Duval County of deriving support from the proceeds of prostitution and transporting another individual for the purposes of prostitution. Defendant appealed and the District Court of Appeal of Florida affirmed.

---

[34]*Bowers* v. *Hardwick*, 478 U.S. 186 (1986), p. 196.
[35]Tx. Penal Code Section 43.02 (2009).

Facts

At trial, the evidence showed defendant managed an escort service which advertised on the internet. An undercover officer testified he scheduled a meeting with one of defendant's escorts based on a series of these advertisements, each of which were introduced into evidence. The officer testified that the cost of the escort's time was $250 per hour, and that they arranged to meet at an apartment commonly used by law enforcement for undercover operations. The officer stated that on the day of the meeting, defendant arrived at the apartment with the escort and accepted the money.

At this point, an audiotape of the officer's interaction with defendant and the escort was introduced over objection. The audiotape was played for the jury and revealed that defendant asked for the $250, then left the apartment after receiving the money. Over the audiotape, the officer then asked if the escort would engage in sexual activity. She agreed, prompting other officers, who had been monitoring the situation, to enter the apartment and arrest her. Defendant was arrested separately.

Throughout the trial, defendant denied that he knew or had reasonable cause to believe prostitution would occur when he left the apartment. To support this assertion, he testified each of the escorts working for him had signed a contract forbidding prostitution. He pointed out that each of the advertisements in evidence contained a disclaimer with slight variations of the following:

> [m]oney exchanged is for time, companionship, and legal services such as nude modeling, erotic dancing, body rub, etc. Anything else that may occur is between two consenting adults and has not been promised or contracted for!

Defendant testified the advertisements featured scantily-clad women not to imply prostitution would occur, but simply because such images attracted clients, as is the case with many businesses catering to men. Regarding this particular case, defendant emphasized to the jury that he was not privy to any conversations regarding sexual activity while he was in the apartment.

Ultimately, the jury rejected defendant's claims and explanations and found him guilty as charged. This appeal followed.

*A defendant's state of mind, or intent, is an element that the jury must infer from the evidence.*

\*\*\*An element of both of the charges for which defendant was convicted required the State to prove he knew or had reasonable cause to believe prostitution might occur. Section 796.05(1) states it shall be unlawful for any person "with reasonable belief or knowing another person is engaged in prostitution" to derive support from the earnings of such prostitution. Section 796.07(2)(d) prohibits any person from transporting another "with knowledge or reasonable cause to believe that the purpose of such [ ] transporting is prostitution." The statute goes on to define "prostitution" as "the giving or receiving of the body for sexual activity for hire but excludes sexual activity between spouses." § 796.07(1)(a), Fla. Stat. The State offered direct evidence that defendant took the $250 through the testimony of the undercover officer. This is direct evidence the jury could accept to establish prostitution, and was obviously material to both offenses.

\*\*\*The only real question for the jury in this case was defendant's state of mind. Whether the evidence sufficiently demonstrates a state of mind or establishes a specific intent is considered a question of fact for the jury to decide. Accordingly, if the jury could reasonably infer from the evidence presented at trial that defendant knew or had reason to believe the escort would engage in prostitution, the question must be left for the jury to decide. Several points can be made to illustrate how the evidence here clearly supported such an inference.

First, the internet advertisements strongly implied sexual activity would occur if the escort was hired. The advertisements, which were listed under the heading of "erotic services" on Craigslist and featured pictures of a scantily-clad woman, described the escort as "5'5, 120 lbs. with a sexy toned body, perky 36-Cs, and a face like an angel!" One of the advertisements stated "Your Ultimate Pleasure and Pure Satisfaction Is My Goal!! I may be young and new, but I know how to please a man!"

Second, the very disclaimers that defendant relies on for his defense could be accepted by the jury as further evidence of guilt. Although the disclaimers stated the escort service was not for prostitution, the jury was not required to accept them at face value. Given the substance of the advertisements, it would be rational for a juror to infer that the disclaimers were bogus. The jury could reasonably infer the disclaimers were either an attempt to emphasize that the escort service's primary purpose was prostitution or designed to be used as a defense if defendant was ever arrested.

Third, the jury may have used the evidence of defendant's actions preceding his arrest to infer guilty knowledge on defendant's part. Defendant admitted to driving the escort to an apartment to meet with an adult male neither of them knew. This adult male wanted to pay $250 per hour for the escort's "companionship" after seeing the advertisements. The escorting was to occur only within the apartment. Defendant testified he took the money, then left the escort alone in the apartment with the unknown male.

Viewing the conduct in conjunction with the substance of the advertisements, and drawing all reasonable inferences in favor of the State, as we are compelled to do, we conclude a rational trier of fact could reasonably infer that defendant knew or had "reasonable cause to believe" the escort would engage in prostitution.

Finally, if we adopted defendant's argument, it would have bizarre consequences. Defendant argues a jury, as a matter of law, could not conclude he knew or had reasonable cause to believe prostitution would occur because his advertisements contained a disclaimer and each escort signed a contract forbidding prostitution. In essence, defendant argues his self-serving statements and actions must be accepted by the jury, along with each inference he would like to be drawn. If this were the law, any defendant, by planning ahead, could avoid a conviction for any crime requiring proof of a certain state of mind. The burglar could buy an advertisement in the local paper declaring he "would never enter a home with the intent of committing a crime therein." The would-be murderer, with a little planning, could post on the internet that although he planned to hurt the victim, he had "absolutely no premeditated intent to kill."

These examples point out the folly of arguing that self-serving statements denying intent will, as a matter of law, prevent conviction. Here, the only hope defendant had for an acquittal was that the jury would find his disclaimers, contracts, and denials persuasive. They didn't. The denial of the motion for judgment of acquittal must be affirmed.

## Case Analysis

1. According to the criminal statute, what *mens rea* is required to convict the defendant?

2. The case makes almost no mention of the prostitute involved in the undercover operation. If she was a healthy, consenting adult, should that impact the defendant's case? Why or why not?

3. Every phone book in America has "escort services" listed. Are all of these companies committing a crime? Does America tend to "ignore" the prostitution issue?

---

# Gambling

**gambling** Making a bet involving monetary risk.

**Gambling**, the act of making a bet involving monetary risk, is criminalized in some form or fashion in nearly every state. Even so, people routinely gamble, even if it is illegal where they live. This is especially true for social gambling, or gambling in which no one individual profits by hosting the game.

Gambling laws are extraordinarily diverse and complex.[36] In Nevada, for example, gambling laws are relaxed, although the business of gambling is closely regulated by the state. At the extreme, some states ban nearly every conceivable form of gambling. To boot, Indian reservations often run casinos, which they are often entitled to do.

Gambling laws vary significantly by state.
©Blair_witch | Dreamstime.com

---

[36]See, e.g., http://www.gambling-law-us.com (accessed November 8, 2010).

Idaho offers an interesting example of a restrictive gambling law. The state defines gambling rather thoroughly as

> risking any money, credit, deposit or other thing of value for gain contingent in whole or in part upon lot, chance, the operation of a gambling device or the happening or outcome of an event, including a sporting event, the operation of casino gambling including, but not limited to, blackjack, craps, roulette, poker, bacarrat [baccarat] or keno . . . .[37]

Idaho law then provides the following:

1. A person is guilty of gambling if he:
   a. Participates in gambling; or
   b. Knowingly permits any gambling to be played, conducted or dealt upon or in any real or personal property owned, rented, or under the control of the actor, whether in whole or in part.
2. Gambling is a misdemeanor.[38]

Note that the *mens rea* is either general or specific, depending on the conduct alleged. The *actus reus* is rather uncomplicated. Even social gambling is illegal in Idaho. According to one review of state law, about half of all states sanction social gambling, so Idaho is not exactly in the minority.[39]

# Pornography and Obscenity

The criminal law places a number of restrictions on pornography and obscenity. Before we can consider such restrictions, however, it is necessary to define both pornography and obscenity.

## Definitions

**pornography** The depiction of sexual acts or behaviors intending to arouse sexual excitement.

**obscenity** Appealing to the prurient interest while lacking in scientific, artistic, or political merit.

What is pornographic? What is obscene? Answers to these questions have proven rather difficult to arrive at. At the risk of simplification, **pornography** is a form of **obscenity**. There is no requirement that obscenity be of a sexual nature. Anything foul, disgusting, or repulsive could be considered obscene. Most of the time, however, pornography and obscenity are used interchangeably to describe materials of a sexual or erotic nature.

Several decades ago, in *Roth* v. *United States*,[40] the Supreme Court announced that the test for identifying obscenity was "whether to the average person applying contemporary standards, the dominant theme of the material taken as a whole, appeals to the prurient interest."[41] *Prurient* refers, typically, to causing lust, desire, or sexual longing. Not long after that, Justice Potter Stewart famously remarked of obscenity that "I know it when I see it," but needless to say, he stopped short of a specific definition.[42]

---

[37]Idaho Stat. Section 18-3801.
[38]Idaho Stat. Section 18-3802.
[39]See, e.g., http://www.gambling-law-us.com (accessed November 8, 2010).
[40]*Roth* v. *United States*, 354 U.S. 476 (1957).
[41]Ibid., p. 489.
[42]*Jacobellis* v. *Ohio*, 378 U.S. 184 (1964), p. 197.

In *Miller* v. *California*,[43] the Supreme Court refined its test, emphasizing that juries can make their judgments on what constitutes obscenity based on local standards.

> [B]asic guidelines for the trier of fact must be: (1) whether "the average person, applying contemporary community standards," would find that the work, taken as a whole, appeals to the prurient interest; (b) whether the work depicts or describes, in a patently offensive way, sexual conduct specifically defined by the applicable state law; and (c) whether the work, taken as a whole, lacks serious literary, artistic, political, or scientific value.[44]

The Court interpreted "patently offensive" to mean "representations or descriptions of ultimate sexual acts, normal or perverted, actual or simulated. . . ., representations or descriptions of masturbation, excretory functions, and lewd exhibition of genitals."[45] Notice that Supreme Court essentially creates a special exception for items viewed as having "artistic value." For example, a play conducted entirely by nude actors would not be considered obscene under the *Miller* test.

In a later decision as to whether the popular 1970s movie *Carnal Knowledge* depicted obscenity under the *Miller* test, the Court offered further clarification, noting that the movie was not a "portrayal of hard core sexual conduct for its own sake, and for the ensuing commercial gain."[46] The "sexual conduct for its own sake" language sets the bar somewhat high; not just any depiction or description of a sex act will be considered obscene.

Though the Supreme Court defined obscenity, states are not obligated to follow its lead—at least as far as their pornography definitions go. Some have adopted rather relaxed obscenity standards. Others have gone the opposite route. An example of the former is the Oregon Supreme Court's interpretation that "any person can write, print, read, say, show or sell anything to a consenting adult even though that expression may be generally or universally condemned as 'obscene.'"[47]

## Child Pornography

**child pornography**
Pornography that depicts actual minors in sexually explicit situations.

In *New York* v. *Ferber*,[48] the Supreme Court unanimously decided that **child pornography** is not protected by the First Amendment. In upholding a New York law that prohibited people from distributing materials depicting children engaged in sexual activity, the Court offered the following in defense of its position:

> (1) [T]he legislative judgment that the use of children as subjects of pornographic materials is harmful to the physiological, emotional, and mental health of the child, easily passes muster under the First Amendment; (2) the standard of *Miller v. California* . . . ., for determining what is legally obscene is not a satisfactory solution to the child pornography problem; (3) the advertising and selling of child pornography provide an economic motive for and are thus an integral part of the production of such materials, an activity illegal throughout the Nation; (4) the value of

---

[43]*Miller* v. *California*, 413 U.S. 15 (1973).
[44]Ibid., p. 24.
[45]Ibid., p. 25.
[46]*Jenkins* v. *Georgia*, 418 U.S. 153 (1974), p. 161.
[47]*State* v. *Henry*, 732 P.2d 9 (Or. 1987), p. 18.
[48]*New York* v. *Ferber*, 458 U.S. 747 (1982).

permitting live performances and photographic reproductions of children engaged in lewd exhibitions is exceedingly modest, if not *de minimis*; and (5) . . . [w]hen a definable class of material, such as that covered by the New York statute, bears so heavily and pervasively on the welfare of children engaged in its production, the balance of competing interests is clearly struck, and it is permissible to consider these materials as without the First Amendment's protection.[49]

## Obscenity on the Internet

Were pornography and obscenity limited to verbal or print media, criminalization and enforcement would be difficult. The Internet, however, makes both nearly impossible. The government's effort to limit depictions of obscenity on the World Wide Web serves as a prime example. In *Reno* v. *American Civil Liberties Union*,[50] the Supreme Court struck down part of the Communications Decency Act of 1996 (CDA) that prohibited the knowing transmission of obscene material to people under the age of 18. The provided, in part, the following:

> Whoever knowingly and with knowledge of the character of the material, in interstate or foreign commerce by means of the World Wide Web, makes any communication for commercial purposes that is available to any minor and that includes any material that is harmful to minors shall be fined not more than $50,000, imprisoned not more than 6 months, or both.[51]

In 1998, Congress reacted by passing the Child Online Protection Act (COPA). In 2007, a federal judge struck down COPA, finding it unconstitutionally vague.[52] Not long after, the U.S. Court of Appeals for the Third Circuit upheld the judge's decision.[53] The U.S. Supreme Court then denied review, effectively ending COPA.[54]

In 2003, the so-called PROTECT Act (which stands for Prosecutorial Remedies and Other Tools to end the Exploitation of Children Today) passed.[55] Of particular relevance to the subject of Internet obscenity, the law prohibits "pandering" (i.e., offering or requesting to transfer, sell, or trade) child pornography. Moreover, it prohibits pandering "any material or purported material in a manner that reflects the belief, or that is intended to cause another to believe" that the material is illegal child pornography. In *United States* v. *Williams*,[56] the Supreme Court upheld the law, holding that there is no First Amendment protection for offers to engage in illegal behavior, nor is there protection for "the collateral speech that introduces such material into the child-pornography distribution network."[57] Williams, the man at the center of the case, used an Internet chat room to exchange child pornography with a Secret Service agent who posed as a person receptive to swapping images.

[49]Ibid., pp. 756–764.
[50]*Reno* v. *American Civil Liberties Union*, 521 U.S. 844 (1997).
[51]47 U.S.C. Section 231.
[52]*American Civil Liberties Union* v. *Gonzales*, 478 F.Supp.2d 775 (E.D. Pa. 2007).
[53]*American Civil Liberties Union* v. *Mukasey*,
[54]129 S.Ct. 1032 (2009).
[55]Pub. L. 108-21.
[56]*United States* v. *Williams*, 553 U.S. 285 (2008).
[57]Ibid.

Though pandering can be accomplished by other means than the Internet, the law—and the Supreme Court's decision—bode well for the government's efforts to regulate online obscenity. Even so, there is the problem of hosting such material in other countries. The Internet knows no geographic boundaries. This makes it especially difficult to prosecute a person who resides in—and sends material from—somewhere outside the United States.

## State Obscenity Laws

Every state maintains a number of obscenity-related laws. Some grade the offense into levels, as New York does:

- A person is guilty of obscenity in the *third degree* when, knowing its content and character, he: 1. Promotes, or possesses with intent to promote, any obscene material; or 2. Produces, presents or directs an obscene performance or participates in a portion thereof which is obscene or which contributes to its obscenity . . . .
- A person is guilty of obscenity in the *second degree* when he commits the crime of obscenity in the third degree . . . and has been previously convicted of obscenity in the third degree . . . .
- A person is guilty of obscenity in the *first degree* when, knowing its content and character, he wholesale promotes or possesses with intent to wholesale promote, any obscene material . . . .[58]

State obscenity laws, like their federal counterparts, have not escaped constitutional challenge. This is an area of continued legislative evolution. States continue to struggle to enact statutes that do not violate First Amendment protections.

## Sexting

**sexting** Transmitting sexually explicit images to another person via e-mail or cellular phone.

The increased use of cellular phones and other technological devices have led to the creation of a potentially new crime, **sexting**. A person is "sexting" if he or she transmits sexually explicit images to another person via a cellular phone or e-mail account. Among consenting adults, the practice would not violate any established criminal laws. When juveniles are involved, however, the practice can potentially rise to the level of child pornography. States are now struggling with how to charge defendants for these crimes. See the accompanying Court Decision for more on the crime of sexting. In it we examine the case of *State* v. *Canal*, where an 18-year-old man sends sexually explicit images to a 14-year-old high school student.

## COURT DECISION

*State* v. *Canal*
773 N.W.2d 528 (Iowa 2009)

**Background:** Jorge Canal was convicted in the District Court, Dallas County of knowingly disseminating obscene material to a minor. The Court of Appeals affirmed. Defendant appealed again and the Supreme Court of Iowa affirmed.

---

[58]N.Y. Penal Law Sections 235.05-235.07.

This case involves sexting among teenagers. "Sexting" is the practice of sending nude photographs via text message. In this appeal, we must determine whether sufficient evidence supported the defendant's conviction for knowingly disseminating obscene material to a minor in violation of Iowa Code section 728.2 (2005) .... Because the evidence was sufficient to support his conviction ... we affirm the decision of the court of appeals and the judgment of the district court.

## I. Background Facts and Proceedings.

On May 15, 2005, C.E., a fourteen-year-old female attending high school, received two photographs via e-mail from Jorge Canal. Canal was eighteen years of age and attended the same school when this incident occurred. One of the photographs was of Canal's erect penis; the other was a photograph of his face. A text message attached to the photograph of his face said, "I love you."

C.E. and Canal were friends and had known each other for roughly a year before Canal sent the photograph of his erect penis .... C.E. testified the photograph was sent only as a joke because some of her friends were doing it. She further testified that she did not ask for the photograph as a means to excite any feelings. Finally, C.E. testified that she asked for a photograph of Canal's penis, but not his erect penis.

C.E.'s mother, who checked her daughter's e-mail and internet use, found the photographs and forwarded them to her husband. C.E.'s father then showed the photographs to a police officer. ... The State charged Canal with violating Iowa Code section 728.2, for knowingly disseminating obscene material to a minor.

The case was tried to a jury. The jury found Canal guilty of knowingly disseminating obscene material to a minor. The court imposed a deferred judgment, a civil penalty of $250, and probation with the department of corrections for one year. The court also instructed Canal that he must register as a sex offender and ordered that an evaluation take place to determine if treatment was necessary as a condition of his probation. Canal received notification of the requirement to register as a sex offender on April 6, 2006.

***Canal did not object to the instructions given to the jury at trial. Therefore, the jury instructions become the law of the case for purposes of our review of the record for sufficiency of the evidence. Instruction number thirteen was the marshalling instruction. It stated the elements of knowingly disseminating obscene material to a minor as follows:

1. On or about the 15th day of May, 2005, the defendant knowingly disseminated or exhibited obscene material to C.E.

2. C.E. was then under the age of eighteen.

3. The defendant was not the parent or guardian of C.E.

Jury instruction number eighteen defined "obscene material" as

any material depicting or describing the genitals, sex acts, masturbation, excretory functions or sadomasochistic abuse which the average person, taking the material as a whole and applying contemporary community standards with respect to what is suitable material for minors, would find appeals to the prurient interest and is patently offensive; and the material, taken as a whole, lacks serious literary, scientific, political, or artistic value.

The same instruction defined "prurient interest" as "a shameful or morbid interest in nudity, sex, or excretion." Finally, regarding "community standards," instruction eighteen stated:

> In determining the community standards, you are entitled to draw on your own knowledge of the views of the average person in the community or the vicinity from which you come to make your determination, within the parameters of the definitions you have been given.

Canal's sole contention regarding the sufficiency of the evidence is that the material he sent to C.E. was not obscene. The jury instruction defining obscenity incorporates the Supreme Court's definition of obscenity, but adds the phrase "with respect to what is suitable material for minors." In other words, the jury instruction recognizes that the obscenity test as to minors is different from the test as to adults. . . .

However, minors are still "entitled to a significant measure of First Amendment protection and only in relatively narrow and well-defined circumstances may government bar public dissemination of protected materials to them." In *Erznoznik*, the Court found that "all nudity cannot be deemed obscene even as to minors." There, the ordinance outlawed anyone from exhibiting movies where a human male or female bare buttocks, female bare breasts, or human bare pubic area was shown, if visible from a public street. Despite holding this ordinance invalid, the Court still stated it would not "deprecate the legitimate interests asserted by the city."

Finally, the instructions, as given, allow the jury to determine the contemporary community standards with respect to what is suitable material for minors. This instruction is consistent with the Supreme Court's pronouncement in *Miller*. Under the community standards test, jurors in different regions of the country or a state may come to different conclusions on whether the same material is obscene. This is because jurors are allowed to draw on their own knowledge of the views of the average person in the community or vicinage from which they come when determining community standards.

Applying the jury instructions as given and reviewing the evidence in the light most favorable to the State, the question we must resolve is whether, under this record, a rational juror could find Canal guilty beyond a reasonable doubt of knowingly disseminating obscene material to a minor. Canal took one photograph of his face and one photograph of his erect penis. He e-mailed the photographs to C.E. separately. He attached a text message to the photograph of his face that said, "I love you."

Although Canal argued to the jury the material he sent C.E. only appealed to a natural interest in sex, under the instructions given the jury could find, by applying its own contemporary community standards with respect to what is suitable material for minors, that the material appealed to the prurient interest, was patently offensive, and lacked serious literary, scientific, political, or artistic value. On a sufficiency-of-the-evidence review, our task is not to refind the facts. Moreover, on this record we cannot conclude, as a matter of law, the materials Canal sent to C.E. were not obscene. Therefore, even though another jury in a different community may have found this material not to be obscene, the evidence in this record was sufficient for this jury to determine, under its own community standards, that the material Canal sent to C.E. was obscene.

**\*\*\*DECISION OF COURT OF APPEALS AND JUDGMENT OF DISTRICT COURT AFFIRMED.**

## Case Analysis

1. The Supreme Court of Iowa relies on U.S. Supreme Court precedent related to obscenity in this case. Name the case and the test used for evaluating obscenity.

2. What constitutional right does this statute implicate? Does the statute violate the defendant's constitutional right?

3. Should sexting be treated the same as other types of pornography and obscenity in the eyes of the law? Why or why not?

# Alcohol Offenses

**driving under the influence (DUI)** Operating a motor vehicle with a blood or breath alcohol level over the legal limit of alcohol.

Alcohol and crime go hand in hand.[59] In some cases, however, alcohol itself is the key element of the crime. The leading stand-alone alcohol-related offenses are **driving under the influence** (DUI—also called "driving while intoxicated," or DWI); minor in possession (MIP), or consumption of alcohol by a minor; and public intoxication. The following subsections take a brief look at each.

## Driving under the Influence

According to the organization Mothers Against Drunk Driving, one person is injured every minute in an alcohol-related vehicular crash.[60] One person *dies* in an alcohol-related crash every 45 minutes.[61] Though fatalities have declined over the years (see Figure 12.1), drunk driving is a problem.

States currently maintain laws providing that a person is considered under the influence if that person operates a motor vehicle with a blood or breath alcohol level of 0.08 or above. The point at which a person reaches this level depends on the quantity consumed, the percentage of alcohol in the drink, the person's weight, and the time spent drinking.[62] Some of the penalties include fines, community service, probation, imprisonment, impoundment of the driver's vehicle, or a mixture of each.

---

[59]See, e.g., J. Yu and W. R. Williford, "Alcohol, Other Drugs, and Criminality: A Structural Analysis," *The American Journal of Drug and Alcohol Abuse*, Vol. 20 (1994), pp. 373–393.

[60]Mothers Against Drunk Driving Web site, http://www.madd.org/statistics (accessed November 9, 2010).

[61]Ibid.

[62]To calculate blood alcohol level, visit http://www.bloodalcoholcalculator.org (accessed November 9, 2010).

**Figure 12.1**

Total Fatalities in Alcohol-Related Crashes, 1982–2008
*Sources:* U.S. Department of Transportation, National Highway Traffic Safety Administration, *Traffic Safety Facts 2006* (Washington, DC: U.S. Department of Transportation, 2007), p. 32, Table 13; http://www.nrd.nhtsa.dot.gov/pubs/811172.pdf (accessed November 9, 2010).

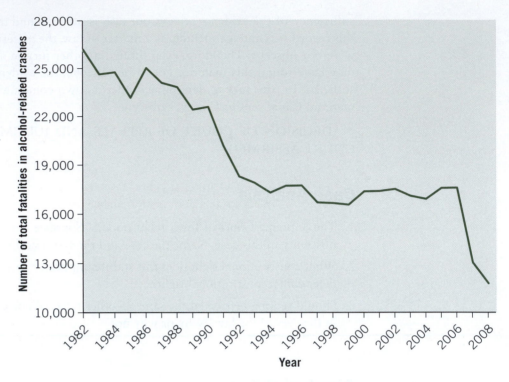

State DUI laws often encompass more than just ordinary driving and/or alcohol. For example, California's Vehicle Code sets a lower legal limit for commercial drivers and extends the law to include drug addiction:

a. It is unlawful for any person who is under the influence of any alcoholic beverage or drug, or under the combined influence of any alcoholic beverage and drug, to drive a vehicle.

b. It is unlawful for any person who has 0.08 percent or more, by weight, of alcohol in his or her blood to drive a vehicle . . . .

c. It is unlawful for any person who is addicted to the use of any drug to drive a vehicle . . . .

d. It is unlawful for any person who has 0.04 percent or more, by weight, of alcohol in his or her blood to drive a commercial motor vehicle . . . .[63]

The legal limit is often lower for juveniles, typically 0.02.[64]

DUI laws are almost always of the strict liability variety (see Chapter 3). This means, by way of review, that there is no requirement that the prosecution prove a culpable mental state, only that the driver was indeed under the influence at the time of the crime. That DUI is considered a strict liability offense reinforces how seriously it is treated.

## Consumption/Possession by Minors

All states prohibit minors (those under the age of 21) from purchasing, possessing, and/or consuming alcohol. States are free to set their own drinking ages, but federal

---

[63]California Vehicle Code Section 23152.
[64]See, e.g., *Commonwealth* v. *Howard*, 969 S.W.2d 700 (Ky. 1998).

law requires the Secretary of Transportation to withhold otherwise allocable highway funds from states that set their drinking age beneath 21.[65] None have done so, as the Supreme Court has sanctioned the use of so-called Section 158 for this purpose:

> Incident to the spending power, Congress may attach conditions on the receipt of federal funds. However, exercise of the power is subject to certain restrictions, including that it must be in pursuit of "the general welfare." Section 158 is consistent with such restriction, since the means chosen by Congress to address a dangerous situation—the interstate problem resulting from the incentive, created by differing state drinking ages, for young persons to combine drinking and driving—were reasonably calculated to advance the general welfare. Section 158 also is consistent with the spending power restrictions that, if Congress desires to condition the States' receipt of federal funds, it must do so unambiguously, enabling the States to exercise their choice knowingly, cognizant of the consequences of their participation; and that conditions on federal grants must be related to a national concern.[66]

Not only do states attempt to restrict underage drinking by setting age limits on purchase, they also put in place strict penalties for minors caught drinking (or in possession). Texas maintains one of the stricter laws:

> Minors who purchase, attempt to purchase, possess, or consume alcoholic beverages, as well as minors who are intoxicated in public or misrepresent their age to obtain alcoholic beverages, face the following consequences:
>
> - Class C misdemeanor, punishable by a fine up to $500
> - Alcohol awareness class
> - 8 to 40 hours community service
> - 30 to 180 days loss or denial of driver's license
>
> If a minor is seventeen years of age or older and the violation is the third offense, the offense is punishable by a fine of $250 to $2,000, confinement in jail for up to 180 days or both, as well as automatic driver's license suspension.
>
> A minor with previous alcohol-related convictions will have his or her driver's license suspended for one year if the minor does not attend alcohol awareness training that has been required by the judge.[67]

Despite the fact that alcohol cannot be legally purchased or consumed by those under 21 years of age, problems persist. For example, according to the Centers for Disease Control and Prevention, 42% of high school students report drinking alcohol in the previous 30 days.[68] Other surveys indicate that nearly one-third of youth between 12 and 20 drink alcohol.[69] It seems no amount of legal deterrents is doing the job. In fact, approximately 100 college presidents from some of the nation's most respected universities recently called on lawmakers to lower the drinking age in an effort to control binge drinking on their campuses.[70] Not much has changed as of this writing.

---

[65]See 23 U.S.C. Section 158.

[66]*South Dakota* v. *Dole*, 483 U.S. 203 (1987).

[67]Texas Alcoholic Beverage Commission, *Underage Drinking Laws*. Available at: http://www.tabc.state.tx.us/laws/underage_drinking_laws.asp (accessed November 9, 2010).

[68]Centers for Disease Control and Prevention, *Fact Sheets: Underage Drinking*. Available at: http://www.cdc.gov/alcohol/fact-sheets/underage-drinking.htm (accessed November 9, 2010).

[69]Ibid.

[70]J. Pope, "College Presidents Want Lower Drinking Age," *Associated Press*, http://www.usatoday.com/news/education/2008-08-18-college-drinking_N.htm (accessed December 10, 2010).

## Public Intoxication

**public intoxication**
Appearing in a public place while under the influence of alcohol or substances to a degree where the individual is likely to endanger themselves, others, or property.

**Public intoxication**, or public drunkenness, is illegal in every state. For example, Kentucky law provides that the following:

> A person is guilty of public intoxication when he appears in a public place manifestly under the influence of a controlled substance, or other intoxicating substance, excluding alcohol (unless the alcohol is present in combination with any of the above), not therapeutically administered, to the degree that he may endanger himself or other persons or property, or unreasonably annoy persons in his vicinity.[71]

Public intoxication is usually treated as a misdemeanor. One of the problems with public intoxication laws is that they sometimes ensnare people with a legitimate drinking problem who, without treatment, will be released from jail and arrested all over again. In light of this concern, some states have elected only to criminalize disorderly intoxication. Florida is one of them. Its disorderly intoxication statute provides in part:

> No person in the state shall be intoxicated and endanger the safety of another person or property, and no person in the state shall be intoxicated or drink any alcoholic beverage in a public place or in or upon any public conveyance and cause a public disturbance.[72]

Clearly this statute is aimed at targeting the *problems* associated with public drunkenness, not just drunkenness itself.

## Drug Offenses

Alcohol is more ubiquitous than other drugs, but marijuana, cocaine, heroin, methamphetamine, and the like are often regarded as more serious and deserving of criminalization. Throughout American history, a number of laws have been enacted in an effort to criminalize the sale and possession of certain drugs. The **Harrison Narcotics Tax Act** of 1914[73] was the federal government's first effort to criminalize opium and cocaine. Though the act purported to tax the production, importation, and distribution of opiates, it also created criminal penalties for those who failed to register and pay required taxes. The act permitted doctors to prescribe opiates for legitimate medical reasons, but not to satisfy patients' addiction. The Harrison Act withstood challenge in the Supreme Court,[74] and states soon went on to enact their own laws aimed at the control of opiates.

**Harrison Narcotics Tax Act**
A federal statute passed in 1914 that constituted the federal government's first effort to criminalize opium and cocaine.

During Prohibition, many people turned to marijuana as a cheap alternative to alcohol. Once Prohibition ended, states and the federal government turned their attention back to marijuana. By the late 1930s, the vast majority of states enacted laws criminalizing marijuana. In 1937, the **Marijuana Tax Act**[75] marked the federal government's first effort to control marijuana. Like the Harrison Act, it levied a tax against marijuana-related commerce, but did not criminalize it per se. This ran counter to most states' laws against marijuana, prompting the U.S. Supreme Court in 1969 to declare the Marijuana Tax Act unconstitutional.[76]

**Marijuana Tax Act** A federal statute passed in 1937 that marked the federal government's first effort to regulate marijuana.

[71]Ky. Rev. Stat. Section 525.100.
[72]Fl. Code Section 856.011.
[73]38 Stat. 785.
[74]*United States* v. *Doremus*, 249 U.S. 86 (1919).
[75]50 Stat. 551.
[76]*Leary* v. *United States*, 395 U.S. 6 (1969).

### Schedule I

- The drug or other substance has a high potential for abuse.
- The drug or other substance has no currently accepted medical use in treatment in the United States.
- There is a lack of accepted safety for use of the drug or other substance under medical supervision.
- Examples of Schedule I substances include heroin, lysergic acid diethylamide (LSD), marijuana, and methaqualone.

### Schedule II

- The drug or other substance has a high potential for abuse.
- The drug or other substance has a currently accepted medical use in treatment in the United States or a currently accepted medical use with severe restrictions.
- Abuse of the drug or other substance may lead to severe psychological or physical dependence.
- Examples of Schedule II substances include morphine, phencyclidine (PCP), cocaine, methadone, and methamphetamine.

### Schedule III

- The drug or other substance has less potential for abuse than the drugs or other substances in Schedules I and II.
- The drug or other substance has a currently accepted medical use in treatment in the United States.

- Abuse of the drug or other substance may lead to moderate or low physical dependence or high psychological dependence.
- Anabolic steroids, codeine and hydrocodone with aspirin or Tylenol®, and some barbiturates are examples of Schedule III substances.

### Schedule IV

- The drug or other substance has a low potential for abuse relative to the drugs or other substances in Schedule III.
- The drug or other substance has a currently accepted medical use in treatment in the United States.
- Abuse of the drug or other substance may lead to limited physical dependence or psychological dependence relative to the drugs or other substances in Schedule III.
- Examples of drugs included in Schedule IV are Darvon®, Talwin®, Equanil®, Valium®, and Xanax®.

### Schedule V

- The drug or other substance has a low potential for abuse relative to the drugs or other substances in Schedule IV.
- The drug or other substance has a currently accepted medical use in treatment in the United States.
- Abuse of the drug or other substances may lead to limited physical dependence or psychological dependence relative to the drugs or other substances in Schedule IV.
- Cough medicines with codeine are examples of Schedule V drugs.

**Figure 12.2**
Controlled Substances Act Drug Schedules
*Source:* Drug Enforcement Administration, *Drugs of Abuse* (Washington, DC: U.S. Department of Justice, 2005), pp. 3–4. Available at: http://www.justice.gov/dea/pubs/abuse/doa-p.pdf (accessed November 15, 2010).

**Controlled Substances Act** Federal legislation that classifies illegal narcotics into five different schedules.

During the 1960s, the United States saw a surge in drug use, prompting further legislative action. Congress responded with the Drug Abuse and Prevention Control Act of 1970.[77] Also called the **Controlled Substances Act** (CSA), this legislation classified drugs according to five different schedules (see Figure 12.2). The Drug Enforcement Administration and the Food and Drug Administration decide which drugs go in each schedule. So-called Schedule I drugs carry the highest potential for abuse and include heroin and marijuana. The CSA provides penalties for the unlawful manufacture, distribution, and dispensing of controlled substances. See Figure 12.3 for a description of the penalties, by schedule, for trafficking in

---

[77]84 Stat. 1236.

**U.S. Department of Justice**
Drug Enforcement Administration

# Federal Trafficking Penalties

| Drug Schedule | Quantity | 1st Offense | 2nd Offense | Quantity | 1st Offense | 2nd Offense |
|---|---|---|---|---|---|---|
| Methamphetamine Schedule II | 5-49 gms pure or 50-499 gms mixture | Not less than 5 yrs and not more than 40 yrs. If death or serious injury, not less than 20 or more than life. Fine of not more than $2 million if an individual, $5 million if other than an individual. | Not less than 10 yrs and not more than life. If death or serious injury, not less than life or more than life. Fine of not more than $4 million if an individual, $10 million if other than an individual. | 50 gms or more pure or 500 gms or more mixture | Not less than 10 yrs and not more than life. If death or serious injury, not less than 20 or more than life. Fine of not more than $4 million if an individual, $10 million if other than an individual. | Not less than 20 yrs and not more than life. If death or serious injury, not less than life. Fine of not more than $8 million if an individual, $20 million if other than an individual. |
| Heroin Schedule I | 100-999 gms mixture | | | 1 kg or more mixture | | |
| Cocaine Schedule II | 500-4,999 gms mixture | | | 5 gms or more mixture | | |
| Cocaine Base Schedule II | 5-49 gms mixture | | | 50 gms or more mixture | | |
| PCP Schedule II | 10-99 gms pure or 100-999 gms mixture | | | 100 gms or more pure or 1 kg or more mixture | | |
| LSD Schedule I | 1-9 gms mixture | | | 10 gms or more mixture | **3rd Offense or More** | |
| Fentanyl Schedule II | 40-399 gms mixture | | | 400 gms or more mixture | Life Imprisonment | |
| Fentanyl Analogue Schedule I | 10-99 gms mixture | | | 100 gms or more mixture | | |
| Others Schedules I & II *(Includes 1 gm or more flunitrazepam and gamma hydroxybutyric acid)* | Any | Not more than 20 yrs. If death or serious injury, not less than 20 yrs, not more than life. Fine of $1 million if an individual, $5 million if other than an individual. | Not more than 30 yrs. If death or serious injury, life. Fine of $2 million if an individual, $10 million if other than an individual. | | | |

| | | **1st Offense** | | **2nd Offense** | | |
|---|---|---|---|---|---|---|
| Others Schedules III *(Includes 30 mgs - 999 mgs flunitrazepam)* | Any | Not more than 5 yrs. Fine not more than $250,000 if an individual, $1 million if other than an individual. | | Not more than 10 yrs. Fine not more than $500,000 if an individual, $2 million if other than an individual. | | |
| Others* Schedules IV *(Includes less than 30 mgs flunitrazepam)* | Any | Not more than 3 yrs. Fine not more than $250,000 if an individual, $1 million if other than an individual. | | Not more than 6 yrs. Fine not more than $500,000 if an individual, $2 million if other than an individual. | | |
| All Schedules V | Any | Not more than 1 yr. Fine not more than $100,000 if an individual, $250,000 if other than an individual. | | Not more than 2 yrs. Fine not more than $200,000 if an individual, $500,000 if other than an individual. | | |

*Although flunitrazepam is a Schedule IV controlled substance, quantities of 30 or more milligrams of flunitrazepam are subject to greater statutory maximum penalties than the above-referenced penalties for Schedule IV controlled substances. See 21 U.S.C. §841(b)(1)(C) and (D).

**Figure 12.3**
CSA Penalties for Drug Trafficking
*Source:* Drug Enforcement Administration, *Drugs of Abuse* (Washington, DC: U.S. Department of Justice, 2005), p. 10. Available at: http://www.justice.gov/dea/pubs/abuse/doa-p.pdf (accessed November 15, 2010).

**Combat Methamphetamine Epidemic Act** Federal legislation that primarily restricts access to precursor chemicals used in the manufacture of methamphetamines, particularly ephedrine, pseudoephedrine, and phenylpropanolamine.

**Uniform Controlled Substances Act** A uniform act drafted to standardize state drug laws. States must affirmatively adopt the act in order for the provisions to becoming binding law.

controlled substances. A number of other federal laws also establish penalties for a wide range of drug-related offenses, including simple possession and even possession of drug paraphernalia.

Federal law continues to evolve as new problems emerge. For example, in 2005, Congress passed the **Combat Methamphetamine Epidemic Act** in response to the increasing realization that methamphetamine (also called "crystal meth" or "crank") was becoming a serious public health threat. The legislation primarily restricts access to precursor chemicals used in the manufacture of the drug, particularly ephedrine, pseudoephedrine, and phenylpropanolamine.

## State Drug Laws

While the CSA was being drafted, so too was the **Uniform Controlled Substances Act**. Finalized in 1972, its purpose was to achieve uniformity in state laws concerning the criminalization and scheduling of drugs. It was later revised in 1990 and 1994. In neither version was it federal law. Rather, it was similar to the Model Penal Code—a suggested legal arrangement that states were encouraged to adopt in the interest of consistency and uniformity. Indeed, all states have since adopted one of the versions of the Uniform Controlled Substances Act.

While state drug laws are mostly aligned with federal law, such is not always the case, especially when it comes to marijuana. Marijuana has been made criminal by the CSA.[78] Yet a number of states (15 as of this writing[79]) have legalized medical marijuana, permitting doctors to prescribe the drug to select patients. This creates an obvious conflict between federal and state law. Recently, California voters nearly approved an initiative providing for full-blown legalization in the Golden State. The measure was defeated, but the high percentage of voters who chose legalization signals an increasing tolerance for the likes of marijuana. President Obama and Attorney General Eric Holder announced in 2009 that they would not pursue raids of medical marijuana dispensaries,[80] but it seems, as of this writing, that they may have gone back on that promise,[81] further creating tension between state and federal law. The federal government remains committed to the continued criminalization of marijuana.[82]

State drug laws are far too detailed and complex to summarize in this limited space. A number of resources are available, however, for those who are interested in

---

[78]And the Supreme Court has refused to acknowledge a "medical necessity exception" to the CSA. See *United States v. Oakland Cannabis Buyers' Cooperative*, 532 U.S. 483 (2001). Also see *Gonzales v. Raich*, 545 U.S. 1 (2005), which permitted the federal government, under the Commerce Clause, to prohibit mere possession of marijuana, even if solely for medical use.

[79]Associated Press, "Arizona Becomes 14th State to Approve Medical Marijuana," *New York Times*, Nov. 14, 2010. Available at: http://www.nytimes.com/2010/11/15/us/politics/15arizona.html (accessed November 15, 2010).

[80]D. Johnston, "Obama Administration to Stop Raids on Medical Marijuana Dispensers," *New York Times*, March 18, 2009. Available at: http://www.nytimes.com/2009/03/19/us/19holder.html (accessed November 15, 2010).

[81]R. J. Corry, Jr., "The Audacity of Dope: Obama Breaks Medical Marijuana Promise," *The Huffington Post*, Oct. 11, 2010. Available at: http://www.huffingtonpost.com/robert-j-corry-jr/wont-get-fooled-again-oba_b_758389.html (accessed November 15, 2010).

[82]See, e.g., http://www.whitehousedrugpolicy.gov/publications/pdf/mj_legal.pdf (accessed November 15, 2010).

exploring state-by-state differences in antidrug policy. For example, the Office of National Drug Control Policy's *State and Local Resources* Web site[83] is a valuable resource, as is the Web site for the National Organization for the Reform of Marijuana Laws, which maintains an updated list of state marijuana laws.[84] State drug laws are more similar to federal law than they are different, however.

## YOUR DECISION

1. Joseph is interested in child pornography and often searches the Internet for pictures of children engaged in sexual activity. One evening, Joseph downloads a piece of "virtual child pornography," which is completely computer generated and does not involve the use of child actors. Has Joseph committed a crime? Why or why not? What if the video involved 18-year-old actors who physically appeared to be only 14 years old?

2. George is suffering from a terrible cold at work one evening. To try and combat the symptoms, he drinks an entire bottle of a nighttime cold medicine before driving home. He is pulled over by the police for driving erratically and fails a sobriety test. George assures the officer he has not been drinking, but is arrested. Is George guilty of driving under the influence? Is he guilty under the California statute described in the text? Why or why not?

## Summary

- *Vice* is loosely defined as immoral conduct, practices, or habits. That said, the most universally recognized crimes of vice are prostitution, gambling, and pornography/obscenity.

- Vice crimes are controversial because they are often based on moral considerations rather than objective harms.

- *Prostitution* is defined as performing or agreeing to perform a sexual act for hire. It is criminalized in all states, except Nevada, where a limited number of rural counties license legal brothels.

- In addition to criminalizing prostitution itself, every state does the same with solicitation, the act of securing a prostitute's (or a suspected prostitute's) agreement to participate in a sex act.

- Gambling, the act of making a bet involving monetary risk, is criminalized in some form or fashion in nearly every state.

- Social gambling, or gambling in which no one individual profits by hosting the game, is also illegal in a minority of states.

- Pornography is a form of obscenity. There is no requirement that obscenity be of a sexual nature.

---

[83]http://www.whitehousedrugpolicy.gov/statelocal/index.html (accessed November 15, 2010).
[84]See http://norml.org/index.cfm?Group_ID=4516 (accessed November 15, 2010).

- In *Roth* v. *United States*, the Supreme Court announced that the test for identifying obscenity was "whether to the average person applying contemporary standards, the dominant theme of the material taken as a whole, appeals to the prurient interest."[85]

- Today, *obscenity* is defined in terms of the "portrayal of hard core sexual conduct for its own sake, and for the ensuing commercial gain."[86]

- In *New York* v. *Ferber*, the Supreme Court unanimously decided that child pornography is not protected by the First Amendment.

- The control of pornography on the Internet has proved to be quite difficult. The Supreme Court has struck down several laws aimed at controlling Internet pornography because of their vague nature.

- Every state maintains a number of obscenity-related laws.

- The leading stand-alone alcohol-related offenses are driving under the influence (DUI—also called "driving while intoxicated," or DWI); minor in possession (MIP), or consumption of alcohol by a minor; and public intoxication.

- Throughout American history, a number of laws have been enacted in an effort to criminalize the sale and possession of certain drugs. Examples include the Harrison Narcotics Tax Act, the Marijuana Tax Act, the Drug Abuse and Prevention Control Act of 1970, and more recently the Combat Methamphetamine Epidemic Act.

- Most state drug laws parallel federal law.

**MODULE**

# 12.3

# CRIMES AGAINST DECENCY AND/OR MORALITY

### *Learning Objectives*

- **Summarize government efforts throughout history to criminalize immorality.**
- **Describe modern-day crimes against decency and/or morality.**
- **Summarize the means by which the criminal law controls profanity.**

**CORE CONCEPTS**

Some would argue that prostitution, drug use, alcohol consumption, and even gambling are immoral. In this section, however, we look at a hodgepodge of offenses that contain an element of indecency and/or immorality. The offenses that fall into this category include incest, indecent exposure, voyeurism, bigamy, and polygamy. Each of these crimes involves a sexual element (or at least has the *potential* to involve a

---

[85]See, e.g., http://www.gambling-law-us.com.
[86]*Miller v. California*, 413 U.S. 15.

sexual element, as in the case of bigamy or polygamy). To them we add another, nonsexual offense, namely profanity. Before looking at each offense in detail, some historical overview will be helpful.

## Legislating Morality throughout History

**fornication** Sexual intercourse between unmarried persons.

**adultery** Sexual intercourse between a male and a female, at least one of who is married to someone else.

**sodomy** Either oral or anal sex between humans, or sexual intercourse between humans and animals.

The criminal law traditionally prohibited a wide range of consensual sexual acts, including fornication, adultery, sodomy, and others. **Fornication**, or sexual intercourse between unmarried persons, was regarded as immoral and was punished by the ecclesiastical courts of England. The same held true for **adultery**, or sexual intercourse between a male and a female, at least one of who is married to someone else. Neither offense was considered a common law crime. Only if they were committed in the open were they treated as criminal.

**Sodomy**, usually defined as either oral or anal sex between humans or sexual intercourse between humans and animals (also called "beastiality"), *was* considered a crime under common law. Until fairly recently, most states had laws outlawing sodomy in its various forms. That has since changed, however. As recently as 2003, in *Lawrence* v. *Texas*,[87] the U.S. Supreme Court struck down one of the country's last remaining sodomy laws. As police officers responded to a weapons disturbance, they entered a man's apartment and observed him engaging in anal intercourse with another man. The two men were arrested and prosecuted under a Texas statute that criminalized "deviate sexual intercourse." The Court held:

> The present case does not involve minors. It does not involve persons who might be injured or coerced or who are situated in relationships where consent might not easily be refused. It does not involve public conduct or prostitution. It does not involve whether the government must give formal recognition to any relationship that homosexual persons seek to enter. The case does involve two adults who, with full and mutual consent from each other, engaged in sexual practices common to a homosexual lifestyle. The petitioners are entitled to respect for their private lives. The State cannot demean their existence or control their destiny by making their private sexual conduct a crime. Their right to liberty under the Due Process Clause gives them the full right to engage in their conduct without intervention of the government.[88]

Fornication, adultery, and sodomy, while perhaps frowned upon, are no longer considered criminal in most jurisdictions—or even deviant. Some states, however, still criminalize fornication and adultery.

## Incest

**incest** Sexual intercourse with certain relatives.

**Incest** refers to sexual intercourse with certain relatives. So-called "consanguineous" (i.e., close in kinship) relationships can produced deformed offspring, which is one of the primary reasons incest is taboo even today.[89] All states and the District of

---

[87]*Lawrence* v. *Texas*, 539 U.S. 558 (2003).
[88]Ibid., pp. 525–526.
[89]There are many other reasons, too. See "Inbred Obscurity: Improving Incest Laws in the Shadow of the 'Sexual Family,'" *Harvard Law Review*, Vol. 119 (2006), pp. 2464–2485.

Columbia thus prohibit incest in some form or fashion. For example, Massachusetts law provides:

> Persons within degrees of consanguinity within which marriages are prohibited or declared by law to be incestuous and void, who intermarry or have sexual intercourse with each other, or who engage in sexual activities with each other, including but not limited to, oral or anal intercourse, fellatio, cunnilingus, or other penetration of a part of a person's body, or insertion of an object into the genital or anal opening of another person's body, or the manual manipulation of the genitalia of another person's body, shall be punished by imprisonment . . . .[90]

Massachusetts's law is rather sweeping. Other states limit the reach of their incest laws. New Jersey does not punish incest if it occurs between relatives over the age of 18.[91] Ohio targets only the acts of parental figures.[92]

## Indecent Exposure and Voyeurism

**indecent exposure**
Revealing your sexual genitalia to another person.

**Indecent exposure**, sometimes called "lewd and lascivious conduct," occurs when one displays his or her "private parts" in front of others—typically with their knowledge or awareness.[93] Indecent exposure laws are typically concerned with public exposure, but this is not always necessary. For example, in *People v. Neal*,[94] a Michigan appellate court upheld the conviction of a man who displayed his erect penis to a minor victim in a private residence.

Not every part one would consider "private" falls within the scope of indecent exposure laws. *Duvallon v. District of Columbia*[95] considered the indecent exposure conviction of a woman who protested in front of the U.S. Supreme Court building, wearing a cardboard sign around her neck that covered the front of her body but not the back. Her buttocks were in full view. The court concluded:

> Ms. Duvallon's actions offend individual senses of propriety, modesty and self-respect. But this court is not asked to decide whether or not Ms. Duvallon violated notions of personal modesty or propriety. Instead we are simply called upon to apply the rule of law and decide whether she broke the law. To answer this question, we search neither our own standards of morality nor standards of dress but rather the rule of law. An examination of decisional law, treatises, and basic principles of statutory construction leads inexorably to the conclusion that public exposure of the bare buttocks is not a violation of D.C. Code § 22-1112 (a).[96]

It would seem, then, that indecent exposure statutes are intended to control display of the genitalia. Also, for indecent exposure to be criminal, it must usually be done

---

[90]Mass. Gen. Laws Ann. 272 Section 17 (2005).
[91]N.J. Stat. Ann. Section 2C:I4-2 (2005).
[92]Ohio Rev. Code Ann. Section 2907.03(A)(5) (1997).
[93]See, e.g., *State* v. *Werner*, 609 So.2d 585 (Fla. 1992); but see *State* v. *Bryan*, 130 P.3d 85 (Kan. 2006) for an opposing view.
[94]*People* v. *Neal*, 702 N.W.2d 696 (Mich. App. 2005).
[95]*Duvallon* v. *District of Columbia*, 515 A.2d 724 (D.C. App. 1986).
[96]Ibid., p. 725.

willfully and/or in an offensive manner.[97] One who experiences an embarrassing "wardrobe malfunction" will likely not be guilty of indecent exposure.

The subject of indecent exposure invariably brings up the question of nude dancing establishments. Typically nude dancing is a protected form of expression, but state and local governments are permitted to impose restrictions on what body parts can be exposed. For example, in *Barnes* v. *Glen Theatre, Inc.*,[98] the Supreme Court upheld an Indiana statute that required nightclub dancers to wear "pasties" over their breasts and G-string bottoms. A similar law was upheld in Erie, Pennsylvania.[99]

**voyeurism** The act of spying on the intimate activities of other people.

**Voyeurism** refers, in general, to the act of spying on the intimate activities of other people. So-called Peeping Tom laws (named for the legend of a man named Tom who watched Lady Godiva, an Anglo-Saxon noblewoman, ride naked through the streets of Coventry, England, in protest against taxation) criminalize voyeurism in nearly every state. Indiana defines the crime of voyeurism (or "peeping") as follows:

a. A person:
   1. who: (A) peeps; or (B) goes upon the land of another with the intent to peep; into an occupied dwelling of another person; or
   2. who peeps into an area where an occupant of the area reasonably can be expected to disrobe, including: (A) restrooms; (B) baths; (C) showers; and (D) dressing rooms; without the consent of the other person, commits voyeurism, a Class B misdemeanor.[100]

Some states fold voyeurism into other sexual deviance statutes and thus do not treat it as a stand-alone offense.

# Bigamy and Polygamy

**bigamy** Marriage between two persons when one is married to another.

**polygamy** One person being married simultaneously to several others.

**Bigamy,** or marriage between two persons when one is married to another, is illegal in all American jurisdictions. The same is true for **polygamy,** or one person being married to several others. Religious arguments have been advanced in support of both practices, but the Supreme Court has decided bigamists and polygamists enjoy no First Amendment protection for their actions. In *Reynolds* v. *United States*,[101] the Court concluded:

> Polygamy has always been odious among the northern and western nations of Europe, and, until the establishment of the Mormon Church, was almost exclusively a feature of the life of Asiatic and of African people. At common law, the second marriage was always void, and from the earliest history of England polygamy has been treated as an offence against society . . . .

---

[97]See, e.g., *People* v. *Randall*, 711 P.2d 689 (Colo. 1985).
[98]*Barnes* v. *Glen Theatre, Inc.*, 501 U.S. 560 (1991).
[99]*City of Erie* v. *Pap's A.M.*, 529 U.S. 277 (2000).
[100]Indiana Code Section 35-45-4-5
[101]*Reynolds* v. *United States*, 98 U.S. 145 (1878).

FLDS women at the YFZ Ranch express their grief following the removal of their children by Texas authorities

Chris Detrick/Rapport Press/ Newscom

> From that day to this we think it may safely be said there never has been a time in any State of the Union when polygamy has not been an offence against society, cognizable by the civil courts and punishable with more or less severity. In the face of all this evidence, it is impossible to believe that the constitutional guaranty of religious freedom was intended to prohibit legislation in respect to this most important feature of social life.

In response to the Court's decision, the Mormon church renounced polygamy, but the practice continues in some "fundamentalist" Mormon communities. Prosecutions are rare, but they do occur from time to time.[102] For example, you may recall the widely publicized 2008 raid on the polygamist YFZ (Yearning for Zion) ranch in Eldorado, Texas. Several prosecutions followed.

Bigamy and polygamy statutes vary in their language, but all are remarkably similar. Several states criminalize both acts in a single statute because polygamy is a form of bigamy, albeit with multiple partners. Consider Texas's statute:

An individual commits an offense if:

1. he is legally married and he:
   A. purports to marry or does marry a person other than his spouse in this state, or any other state or foreign country, under circumstances that would, but for the actor's prior marriage, constitute a marriage; or
   B. lives with a person other than his spouse in this state under the appearance of being married; or
2. he knows that a married person other than his spouse is married and he:
   A. purports to marry or does marry that person in this state, or any other state or foreign country, under circumstances that would, but for the person's prior marriage, constitute a marriage; or
   B. lives with that person in this state under the appearance of being married.[103]

---

[102]See, e.g., *State* v. *Green*, 99 P.3d 820 (Utah 2004).
[103]Texas Penal Code Section 25.01

# Profanity

**profanity** Foul language or curse words generally deemed offensive.

**Profanity** was sometimes prohibited in dedicated state or local statutes, but that has changed. Most states now incorporate into their disorderly conduct (and similar) statutes various prohibitions against public profanity. Why? Normal prohibitions against profanity have a tendency to run afoul of First Amendment protections. In *Cohen* v. *California*,[104] for example, the Supreme Court invalidated the "offense conduct" conviction of a man who entered a courtroom wearing a jacket with "F*** the Draft" written across the front of it. Justice Harlan wrote, "[W]hile the particular four-letter-word being litigated here is perhaps more distasteful than others of its genre, it is nevertheless often true that one man's vulgarity is another's lyric."[105]

Sanctions against the use of profanity remain for broadcasters who use it. In 2009, the Supreme Court ruled that the Federal Communications Commission (FCC) acts within its authority when it fines broadcasters for failing to shield viewers and/or listeners from profanity, especially during times when children may be watching/listening.[106] The case stemmed from a 2006 FCC decision to fine the Fox television network for violating decency rules when singer Cher used profanity during the 2002 Billboard Music Awards and actress Nicole Richie did the same in the 2003 awards.

---

**YOUR DECISION**

1. John is part of a religious group that believes a man should have multiple wives. However, since John realizes the United States criminalizes plural marriages, he only officially marries one woman at the local courthouse. While he has three other "wives," he never officially marries them in any formal ceremony. All of the women and their children live with John under one roof as a family. Since wives two, three, and four are technically considered "single mothers" in the eyes of the law, they apply for and receive food stamps, welfare, and other forms of government assistance. Have any crimes been committed by John and his family? Why or why not?

2. Judy was at the mall with her girlfriends trying on prom dresses at a local department store. Directly outside of the women's dressing rooms was a collection of large mirrors where the girls would stand to model and discuss the various dress choices. Edward, a 41-year-old man, sat outside the dressing room for over an hour watching the teenage girls model their dresses. Edward never entered the dressing room itself where the girls' actually changed clothes. Upset by his presence, the girls contact store security and Edward was ultimately arrested. Can he be charged with voyeurism? Why or why not? Apply the Indiana statute provided in the text to the scenario.

---

[104]*Cohen* v. *California*, 403 U.S. 15 (1971).
[105]Ibid., p. 25.
[106]*Federal Communications Commission* v. *Fox Television Stations, Inc.*, 129 S.Ct. 1800 (2009).

# Summary

- Crimes against decency and/or morality include incest, indecent exposure, voyeurism, bigamy, polygamy, and in some jurisdictions, profanity.

- The criminal law traditionally prohibited a wide range of consensual sexual acts, including fornication, adultery, and sodomy. These acts are no longer considered criminal.

- Incest refers to sexual intercourse with certain relatives. State incest laws vary considerably.

- Indecent exposure, sometimes called "lewd and lascivious conduct," occurs when one displays his or her "private parts" in front of others—typically with their knowledge or awareness.

- Voyeurism refers, in general, to the act of spying on the intimate activities of other people and is illegal in most jurisdictions.

- Bigamy, or marriage between two persons when one is married to another, is illegal in all American jurisdictions. The same is true for polygamy, or one person being married to several others.

- Profanity was sometimes prohibited in dedicated state or local statutes, but that has changed. Most states now incorporate into their disorderly conduct (and similar) statutes various prohibitions against public profanity.

# Chapter Review

MODULE **12.1**

## GROUP CRIMINALITY AND OFFENSES AGAINST PUBLIC ORDER

### Learning Objectives

- Describe the crimes of riot and unlawful assembly.
- Summarize legislative approaches to criminalizing gang activity.
- Describe six offenses against public order.

### Review Questions

1. Explain how group criminality differs from complicity and vicarious liability.
2. Explain the relationship between unlawful assembly, rout, and riot.
3. Compare and contrast at least three offenses against public order.

### Key Terms

riot
unlawful assembly
rout
disorderly conduct
breach of peace
vagrancy
loitering
panhandling

MODULE **12.2**

## VICE CRIMES AND DRUG OFFENSES

- Describe prostitution and its legal status across the United States.
- Summarize the legal status of gambling.
- Distinguish between alcohol and drug offenses.

### Review Questions

1. Should prostitution be illegal? Why or why not?
2. Should gambling be illegal? What about social gambling? Defend your answer.
3. Has the Supreme Court adequately defined obscenity? Why or why not?
4. Should the drinking age be raised, lowered, or kept the same? Why?

### Key Terms

vice
prostitution
gambling
pornography
obscenity
child pornography

sexting
driving under the influence (DUI)
public intoxication
Harrison Narcotics Tax Act
Marijuana Tax Act
Controlled Substances Act
Combat Methamphetamine Epidemic Act
Uniform Controlled Substances Act

MODULE **12.3**    **CRIMES AGAINST DECENCY AND/OR MORALITY**

- Summarize government efforts throughout history to legislate morality.
- Describe modern-day crimes against decency and/or morality.
- Summarize the means by which the criminal law controls profanity.

### Review Questions

1. What is your opinion of government's efforts over the years to legislate morality?

2. At what point should indecent exposure be considered criminal? Why?

3. Should swearing be illegal? Why or why not?

### Key Terms

fornication
adultery
sodomy
incest
indecent exposure
voyeurism
bigamy
polygamy
profanity

## Chapter Synthesis Questions

1. Are dedicated antigang statutes necessary? Do they go too far or not far enough? Refer to specific statutory examples.

2. It is typically illegal to resist even an *unlawful* arrest. Is this good law? Why or why not?

3. Should loitering in and of itself be criminal? Why?

4. What can be done, if anything, to regulate pornography on the Internet? Should anything be done?

5. Should medical marijuana be legal? Why or why not?

# 13

# TERRORISM AND OFFENSES AGAINST THE STATE

*Learning Objectives*

**MODULE 13.1 TERRORISM**

- **Define terrorism.**
- **Identify several types of terrorism.**
- **Explain how the criminal law controls terrorism.**

**MODULE 13.2 OTHER OFFENSES AGAINST THE STATE**

- **Distinguish among treason, sedition, and espionage.**
- **Summarize sabotage and criminal syndicalism.**
- **Explain how other criminal law statutes can be used in cases involving threats against the government.**

# TERRORISM

### Learning Objectives

- **Define terrorism.**
- **Identify several types of terrorism.**
- **Explain how the criminal law controls terrorism.**

**CORE CONCEPTS**

Terrorism is criminal activity not unlike the usual violent crimes that exist in almost all developed societies. Terrorists are murderers, exactly like the criminal who kills a victim during the course of a robbery. But terrorism also differs from the usual homicides we see all too often on the evening news because it tends to have religious and/or political motivations, is often international in scope or origin, and is carried out with what the perpetrators consider to be noble (albeit delusional) goals.

## Defining Terrorism

**terrorism** Premeditated, politically motivated violence against noncombatants.

Most of us know terrorism when we see it; the 9/11 incidents were prime examples of terrorism. Even so, there is no single definition of **terrorism**. The Foreign Relations Authorization Act defines the word in terms of four main characteristics: premeditation, political motivation, violence, and committed against noncombatants (e.g., innocent bystanders).[1] An alternative definition has been put forth by the FBI, which defines *terrorism* as

> a violent act or an act dangerous to human life in violation of the criminal laws of the United States or of any state to intimidate or coerce a government, the civilian population, or any segment thereof, in furtherance of political or social objectives.[2]

These definitions are fairly concise. An even more detailed definition, this one from the Immigration and Nationality Act, appears in Figure 13.1.

Criminologist Gwynn Nettler proposes a definition of *terrorism* that consists of six characteristics:

1. **No rules.** There are no moral constraints or standards of what is considered acceptable. In other words, anything goes.

2. **No innocents.** Terrorists do not distinguish between innocents and noninnocents, or soldiers and civilians.

---

[1]In the words of the act, "The term 'terrorism' means premeditated, political motivated violence perpetrated against noncombatant targets by subnational groups or clandestine agents." 22 U.S.C. 2656 f(d)(2).

[2]Federal Bureau of Investigation, *Counterterrorism Section, Terrorism in the United States, 1987* (Washington, DC: FBI, 1987).

3. **Economy.** The concern is with inflicting as much damage as possible but at the same time scaring even more people (e.g., kill one person, terrify 10,000 more).

4. **Publicity.** All terrorist incidents are highly publicized. Terrorists seek publicity in an effort to heighten people's fear levels, weaken economies, and so forth.

5. **Meaning.** Violent acts and the infliction of mass casualties gives meaning to terrorists' lives.

6. **No clarity.** The long-term goals of terrorism are either delusion or impossible to implement (e.g., Islamic dominance).[3]

## Types of Terrorism

**domestic terrorism**
Terrorism carried out by an individual or group based and operating within the United States in furtherance of a political or social objective.

The two main types of terrorism are domestic and international. **Domestic terrorism** is homegrown terrorism—that is, terrorism carried out by an individual or group based and operating within this country. Moreover, domestic terrorism is not directed by international sources. The most notorious example of domestic terrorism is the infamous 1995 Oklahoma City federal building bombing by Timothy McVeigh. He was not only a homegrown terrorist, but he was also not directed by any foreign source.

**Figure 13.1**
Terrorism Defined

*Source*: Immigration and Nationality Act, Public Law 82-414 [Section 212(a)(3)(B)].

[T]he term "terrorist activity" means any activity which is unlawful under the laws of the place where it is committed (or which, if it had been committed in the United States, would be unlawful under the laws of the United States or any State) and which involves any of the following:

  (I) The highjacking or sabotage of any conveyance (including an aircraft, vessel, or vehicle).

 (II) The seizing or detaining, and threatening to kill, injure, or continue to detain, another individual in order to compel a third person (including a governmental organization) to do or abstain from doing any act as an explicit or implicit condition for the release of the individual seized or detained.

(III) A violent attack upon an internationally protected person (as defined in section 1116(b)(4) of title 18, United States Code) or upon the liberty of such a person.

(IV) An assassination.

 (V) The use of any-

   (aa) biological agent, chemical agent, or nuclear weapon or device, or

   (bb) explosive, firearm, or other weapon or dangerous device (other than for mere personal monetary gain), with intent to endanger, directly or indirectly, the safety of one or more individuals or to cause substantial damage to property.

(VI) A threat, attempt, or conspiracy to do any of the foregoing.

---

[3]G. Nettler, *Killing One Another* (Cincinnati, OH: Anderson, 1982).

**international terrorism**
The unlawful use of violence by a group or individual with some connection to a foreign power or group in furtherance of a political or social objective.

**International terrorism** refers to the unlawful use of violence by a group or individual with some connection with a foreign power or group. *International terrorism* is sometimes mistakenly called *foreign terrorism*, but *foreign* refers to terrorism that takes place in another country, outside the United States. The most prominent example of international terrorism in recent years occurred at various U.S. sites on September 11, 2001. While the acts took place within our borders, they clearly had international origins.

## Other Forms of Terrorism

The typical terrorist incident is international. Although there has not been much in the way of domestic terrorism to report in recent years, other, lesser-known forms of terrorism include **cyberterrorism**, **narcoterrorism**, and **ecoterrorism**.

**cyberterrorism** The use of technology, including computers and the Internet, to carry out terroristic attacks.

**narcoterrorism** Terroristic activities that result from a collaboration between drug traffickers and traditional terrorist groups.

**ecoterrorism** Terroristic activities aimed at those perceived to be harming the environment.

In cyberterrorism, high technology (computers and the Internet) is used to carry out attacks. Barry Collin, a senior research fellow at the California-based Institute for Security and Intelligence, first coined the term in the 1980s.[4] The term was later made popular in the report by the RAND Corporation where a warning of "new terrorism" was issued.[5] The FBI subsequently developed a definition of *cyberterrorism* as "the premeditated, politically motivated attack against information, computer systems, computer programs, and data which results in violence against noncombatant targets by subnational groups or clandestine agents."[6]

There have been no major cyberterrorist incidents to report, but it is easy to imagine some possibilities. An attack against the nation's air traffic control system, for example, could wreak havoc by leading planes to collide in midair. If power grids were successfully attacked, this could threaten the storage of valuable data, although technological advances have thus far kept these threats contained.

In September 2002, the President's Critical Infrastructure Protection Board published the *National Strategy to Secure Cyberspace*[7] and, in 2003, the National Infrastructure Advisory Council was created pursuant to a presidential directive. According to its charter, "The NIAC shall draw on the expertise of its members so as to provide advice and make recommendations on the following"[8]:

a. enhancing cooperation between the public and private sectors in protecting information systems supporting critical infrastructures in key economic sectors and providing reports on the issue to the President, as appropriate;

b. enhancing cooperation between the public and private sectors in protecting critical infrastructure assets in other key economic sectors and providing reports on these issues to the President, as appropriate; and,

c. proposing and developing ways to encourage private industry to perform periodic risk assessments of critical information and telecommunications systems.[9]

---

[4]B. Collin, "The Future of Cyberterrorism," *Crime and Justice International* (March 1997), pp. 15–18.
[5]J. Arquilla and D. Ronfeldt, *The Advent of Netwar* (Santa Monica, CA: RAND Corporation, 1996).
[6]M. M. Pollitt, "Cyberterrorism: Fact or Fancy?," *Proceedings of the Twentieth National Information Systems Security Conference* (October 1997), pp. 285–289.
[7]President's Critical Infrastructure Protection Board, *The National Strategy to Secure Cyberspace* (Washington, DC: U.S. Government Printing Office, 2002).
[8]U.S. Department of Homeland Security, *Charter of the National Infrastructure Advisory Council* (Washington, DC: 2003), http://www.dhs.gov/xlibrary/assets/niac/NIAC_Charter.pdf (accessed June 20, 2007).
[9]Ibid.

*Narcoterrorism* is concerned with collaboration between drug traffickers and terrorist groups. For example, during 2005, Afghan drug lord Bashir Noorzai was arrested in New York on charges that he attempted to smuggle $50 million worth of heroin into the United States. People have also used the term *narcoterrorism* to refer to attacks by drug traffickers against their governments and law enforcement authorities. These insurgent operations, like that of the Columbia-based 19th of April Movement (M-19), make enforcement of a nation's antinarcotics laws difficult, at best. The true extent of the problem remains unknown, partly because of the clandestine nature of the illicit drug trade. Narcoterrorism also raises a number of questions, such as those posed by noted drug researcher James Inciardi:

- What is the full threat posed by narcoterrorism?
- How should narcoterrorism be dealt with?
- Is narcoterrorism a law enforcement problem or a military one?
- How might narcoterrorism be affected by changes in official U.S. policy toward drugs and drug use?
- Is the international drug trade being used as a tool by anti-U.S. and other interests to undermine Western democracies in a calculated way?[10]

According to one official's testimony before the Senate Foreign Relations Subcommittee on Terrorism, Narcotics, and International Operations, our country is ill-prepared to address the problem of narcoterrorism:

We must recognize that the rules of the crime game have changed. . . . International criminal organizations are challenging governments, permeating societies. They're running roughshod over weak institutions and exploiting gaps in the U.S. and international response. They have the upper hand at the moment and they know it.[11]

While cyberterrorism and narcoterrorism can have a strong international component, this is less true of *ecoterrorism*. According to one source, "[e]coterrorism involves extremist views on environmental issues and animal rights, and is a fringe-issue form of terrorism aimed primarily at inflicting economic damage on those seen as profiting from the destruction and exploitation of the environment."[12] One well-known ecoterrorist group goes by the name Earth Liberation Front, or ELF. There is a Web site[13] that uses ELF's name but specifically disavows any connection to the unstructured organization states that ELF has no leadership, membership, or official spokesperson. The site describes ELF as an underground movement by autonomous and anonymous individuals who use sabotage and guerilla warfare to stop what it calls the "exploitation and destruction of the natural environment."

The 1998 arson attack against the Vail, Colorado, ski resort serves as an example of ecoterrorism. On December 15, 2006, Chelsea Dawn Gerlach and Stanilas Gregory Meyerhoff pleaded guilty to setting the fire (as well as several other fires in several western states) that led to some $12 million in damages. Readers may also note the irony inherent in destroying the earth to save the earth. Even Gerlach herself

---

[10]J. A. Inciardi, "Narcoterrorism," paper presented at the annual meeting of the Academy of Criminal Justice Sciences, San Francisco, 1988, p. 8.

[11]"U.S. Government Lacks Strategy to Neutralize International Crime," *Criminal Justice International*, Vol. 10 (Sept./Oct. 1994), p. 5.

[12]http://www.drtomoconnor.com/3410/3410lect05.htm.

[13]http://www.earthliberationfront.org/elffaqs.html.

A terrorist training camp in the Middle East.

e85/e85/ZUMA Press/ Newscom

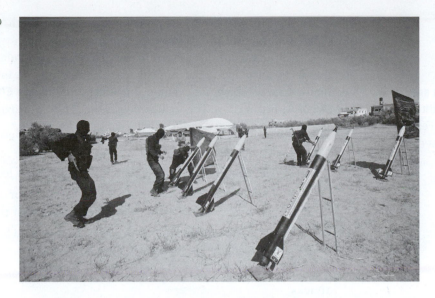

noted that the attacks that she and her colleagues in "the family" (a Eugene-based ELF cell) carried out probably did more harm than good. The ELF movement has by no means been quashed, and the group remains a significant concern to law enforcement officials.

## Controlling Terrorism

The U.S. government has adopted a so-called "4D strategy" for combating terrorism: Defeat, Deny, Diminish, and Defend.[14] *Defeat* refers to defeating terrorists and their organizations. *Deny* refers to denial of "sponsorship, support, and sanctuary" to terrorists:

> The strategy to deny sponsorship, support, and sanctuary is three-fold. First, it focuses on the responsibilities of all states to fulfill their obligations to combat terrorism both within their borders and internationally. Second, it helps target U.S. assistance to those states who are willing to combat terrorism, but may not have the means. And finally, when states prove reluctant or unwilling to meet their international obligations to deny support and sanctuary to terrorists, the United States, in cooperation with friends and allies, or if necessary, acting independently, will take appropriate steps to convince them to change their policies.[15]

*Diminish* refers to altering the underlying conditions that terrorists use to justify their attacks. U.S. efforts to resolve regional disputes, foster development, and encourage democracy fall into this category. *Defend* refers to all strategies, both in the United States and abroad, to protect our country's interests. We will see shortly how some of this work is being carried out by federal, state, and local law enforcement officials. The military, intelligence agencies, and other entities also combine

---

[14]U.S. National Security Council, *From U.S. Security to Terrorism* (Washington, DC: Executive Office of the President, 2002), p. 17.
[15]Ibid.

their efforts to round out the government's concern with defending the United States from (and preventing) future terrorist attacks.

The government has also taken many deliberate, particularly legislative, steps in addition to forming a national strategy to combat terrorism. In the wake of the 1995 Oklahoma City bombing, for example, the **Antiterrorism and Effective Death Penalty Act (AEDPA)** became law. The following lists the act's key provisions:

**Antiterrorism and Effective Death Penalty Act (AEDPA)** Federal legislation that defines specific terrorism crimes and penalties.

- Within the United States, it bans fund-raising for and financial support of international terrorist organizations.

- It provided $1 billion for enhanced fighting of terrorism by federal and local officials.

- It allowed foreign terrorist suspects to be deported or to be kept out of the United States *without* disclosure of the evidence against them.

- It sanctioned use of the death penalty against anyone who commits an international terrorist incident within the United States.

- It made it a federal crime to use the United States as a base for planning terrorist attacks.

- It required that so-called taggants, or chemical markers, be added to certain explosives during their manufacture.

- It ordered a feasibility study on marking other explosives (other than gunpowder).[16]

Readers may be more familiar with the USA PATRIOT Act. Given its breadth relative to the AEDPA, we reserved a separate section for coverage of the act. Now let's look more closely at the USA PATRIOT Act.

## The USA PATRIOT Act

On September 14, 2001, in response to the September 11 attacks on the World Trade Center, President George W. Bush declared a state of emergency, which permitted him to invoke certain presidential powers. These powers include the ability to summon reserve troops, marshal military units, and issue executive orders for the implementation of such things as military tribunals. Congress also took action to empower the Justice Department to respond to terrorism by passing the **USA PATRIOT Act** on October 26, 2001, which President Bush signed into law the following day.

**USA PATRIOT Act** Federal legislation passed in response to the September 11, 2001, terrorist attacks; the act includes expanded tools for law enforcement.

The act's full title is the Uniting and Strengthening America by Providing Appropriate Tools Required to Intercept and Obstruct Terrorism. It is a very long and complex piece of legislation, consisting of 10 parts and over 300 single-spaced pages. Given its staggering size and breadth, the act is a testament to the fact that Congress *can* move quickly when it must.

The USA PATRIOT Act made several important changes to past law and practice:

- It centralized federal law enforcement authority in the U.S. Department of Justice. For example, Section 808 of the act reassigned the authority for investigating several federal crimes of violence from law enforcement agencies such as the U.S. Secret Service and the Bureau of Alcohol, Tobacco, Firearms and Explosives to the U.S. Attorney General.

---

[16]F. Schmalleger, *Criminal Justice Today: An Introductory Text for the 21st Century*, 9th ed. (Upper Saddle River, NJ: Prentice-Hall, 2006), p. 684.

- It provided for CIA (Central Intelligence Agency) oversight of all domestic intelligence gathering. Prior to the USA PATRIOT Act, the CIA's role was primarily concerned with foreign intelligence gathering.

- It expanded the definition of the terms *terrorism* and *domestic terrorism* to include activities that: "(A) involve acts dangerous to human life that are a violation of the criminal laws of the United States or of any state; (B) appear to be intended (i) to intimidate or coerce a civilian population; (ii) to influence the policy of a government by mass destruction, assassination, or kidnapping; or (iii) to effect the conduct of a government by mass destruction, assassination, or kidnapping; and (C) occur primarily within the territorial jurisdiction of the United States."[17]

There were also several noteworthy changes in criminal procedure attributable to the USA PATRIOT Act. Before describing these changes, some background will be informative. First, the U.S. Supreme Court has held that the Fifth and Sixth Amendment rights of due process and access to jury trials apply to all "persons," not just citizens of the United States.[18] In addition, the Court has held that all undocumented aliens living inside the U.S. borders are entitled to the protections enunciated in the Bill of Rights.[19] Specifically, the Court has stated that

> the Fifth Amendment, as well as the Fourteenth Amendment, protects every one of these persons from deprivation of life, liberty, or property without due process of law. Even one whose presence in this country is unlawful, involuntary, or transitory is entitled to constitutional protection.[20]

These rights also apply to the exclusion of aliens from within the U.S. borders. That is, proceedings for the deportation of aliens must conform to constitutional requirements, especially due process.[21] In short, legal, illegal, resident, and temporary aliens have historically enjoyed the same constitutional protections as ordinary U.S. citizens. Why does all this matter? In several ways, the USA PATRIOT Act alters and even abolishes constitutional protections historically available to people under the jurisdiction of the United States, including aliens. Space constraints prevent full coverage of all the relevant changes (see Figure 13.2 for an overview of the act's main sections), but we consider some of them here.

The USA PATRIOT Act also has implications for investigative detentions. Section 412 of the act requires the U.S. attorney general to take into custody any alien whom he has "reasonable grounds to believe" is "engaged in any other activity that endangers the national security of the United States."[22] The alien can then be held for seven days, at the end of which he or she must be released, charged criminally, or deported. Importantly, if an alien is detained for purposes related to immigration, rather than suspected criminal activity, that alien can be detained indefinitely. This has been one tool in the war on terrorism; authorities can indefinitely detain illegal immigrants, which obviously raises serious due process concerns.

---

[17]USA PATRIOT Act 802, 115 Stat. at 376.
[18]*United States v. Verdugo-Urquidez*, 494 U.S. 259 (1990), pp. 264–266.
[19]*Mathews v. Diaz*, 426 U.S. 67 (1976), p. 77.
[20]Ibid.
[21]*Shaughnessy v. United States ex rel. Mezei*, 345 U.S. 206 (1953), p. 212.
[22]USA PATRIOT Act, Pub. L. No. 107-56, 412, 115 Stat. 272, 350 (2001).

**Figure 13.2**

Main Titles of the USA
PATRIOT Act

*Source:* USA PATRIOT Act,
Public Law 107-56.

| | |
|---|---|
| TITLE I | — ENHANCING DOMESTIC SECURITY AGAINST TERRORISM |
| TITLE II | — ENHANCED SURVEILLANCE PROCEDURES |
| TITLE III | — INTERNATIONAL MONEY LAUNDERING ABATEMENT AND ANTI-TERRORIST FINANCING ACT OF 2001 |
| TITLE IV | — PROTECTING THE BORDER |
| TITLE V | — REMOVING OBSTACLES TO INVESTIGATING TERRORISM |
| TITLE VI | — PROVIDING FOR VICTIMS OF TERRORISM, PUBLIC SAFETY OFFICERS, AND THEIR FAMILIES |
| TITLE VII | — INCREASED INFORMATION SHARING FOR CRITICAL INFRASTRUCTURE PROTECTION |
| TITLE VIII | — STRENGTHENING THE CRIMINAL LAWS AGAINST TERRORISM |
| TITLE IX | — IMPROVED INTELLIGENCE |
| TITLE X | — MISCELLANEOUS |

It is also worth pointing out that the USA PATRIOT Act permits the seizure of certain assets without due process protections. Specifically, Section 106 of the act increases the President's power over the property and assets of foreign persons and organizations. This portion of the USA PATRIOT Act permits the President to "confiscate any property, subject to the jurisdiction of the United States, of any foreign person, foreign organization, or foreign country that he determines has planned, authorized, aided, or engaged in such hostilities or attacks against the United States."[23] The act also allows the President to direct other agencies and individuals to use or transfer such property as he deems necessary.

The USA PATRIOT Act has also given enhanced authority to law enforcement in the name of intelligence gathering. For example, the act modified portions of the Electronic Communications Privacy Act that governs access to stored electronic communications, like e-mail correspondence and voice mail. Wiretap orders, which traditionally were difficult to secure, are now only required to intercept real-time phone communications. As another example of improved intelligence gathering, Section 206 creates so-called roving wiretap authority. This basically abandons a previous requirement that a government eavesdropper make sure the target is actually using the device being monitored. This means that if a suspected terrorist switches cell phones, the government can continue to listen.

The act also amended Title 18, Section 3103, of the U.S. Code to authorize courts to issue search warrants that delay notification of an impending search and that can be executed in the absence of the suspect. This is very different than the typical search warrant scenario, where an announcement is made before the warrant is served and the occupant is usually present during the search. These so-called sneak and peak warrants can be obtained, pursuant to the USA PATRIOT Act, if a court finds "reasonable cause" that by providing advance notification, even right before the search, an "adverse result" could occur. Several other such changes were authorized by the act, all with the common theme of giving investigative authorities broader power to investigate terrorism and related forms of criminal activity.

---

[23]USA PATRIOT Act 106, 115 Stat. at 277.

Title VIII of the act contains several provisions with relevance to criminal law. For example, it created a probation against harboring terrorists. It also eliminated the statute of limitations for certain terrorist offenses and put in place new maximum penalties for terrorist offenses. A brief synopsis of these and other pertinent criminal law provisions in the PATRIOT Act appear in Figure 13.3.

A key provision of the PATRIOT ACT, Section 2339A, makes it a felony to "provide material support or resources" to a terrorist organization. This crime, which

Amends the Federal criminal code to prohibit specific terrorist acts or otherwise destructive, disruptive, or violent acts against mass transportation vehicles, ferries, providers, employees, passengers, or operating systems.

(Sec. 802) Amends the Federal criminal code to: (1) revise the definition of "international terrorism" to include activities that appear to be intended to affect the conduct of government by mass destruction; and (2) define "domestic terrorism" as activities that occur primarily within U.S. jurisdiction, that involve criminal acts dangerous to human life, and that appear to be intended to intimidate or coerce a civilian population, to influence government policy by intimidation or coercion, or to affect government conduct by mass destruction, assassination, or kidnapping.

(Sec. 803) Prohibits harboring any person knowing or having reasonable grounds to believe that such person has committed or to be about to commit a terrorism offense.

(Sec. 804) Establishes Federal jurisdiction over crimes committed at U.S. facilities abroad.

(Sec. 805) Applies the prohibitions against providing material support for terrorism to offenses outside of the United States.

(Sec. 806) Subjects to civil forfeiture all assets, foreign or domestic, of terrorist organizations.

(Sec. 808) Expands: (1) the offenses over which the Attorney General shall have primary investigative jurisdiction under provisions governing acts of terrorism transcending national boundaries; and (2) the offenses included within the definition of the Federal crime of terrorism.

(Sec. 809) Provides that there shall be no statute of limitations for certain terrorism offenses if the commission of such an offense resulted in, or created a foreseeable risk of, death or serious bodily injury to another person.

(Sec. 810) Provides for alternative maximum penalties for specified terrorism crimes.

(Sec. 811) Makes: (1) the penalties for attempts and conspiracies the same as those for terrorism offenses; (2) the supervised release terms for offenses with terrorism predicates any term of years or life; and (3) specified terrorism crimes Racketeer Influenced and Corrupt Organizations statute predicates.

(Sec. 814) Revises prohibitions and penalties regarding fraud and related activity in connection with computers to include specified cyber-terrorism offenses.

(Sec. 816) Directs the Attorney General to establish regional computer forensic laboratories, and to support existing laboratories, to develop specified cyber-security capabilities.

(Sec. 817) Prescribes penalties for knowing possession in certain circumstances of biological agents, toxins, or delivery systems, especially by certain restricted persons.

**Figure 13.3**

Criminal Law Provisions of the PATRIOT Act

*Source*: J. A. Bullock, G. D. Haddow, D. Coppola, E. Ergin, L. Westerman, and S. Yeletaysi, *Homeland Security*, 2nd ed. (Burlington, MA: Elsevier Butterworth-Heinemann, 2006), pp. 526–576.

was originally enacted as part of the AEDPA, is designed to target individuals who provide crucial support to terrorist organizations without actually participating in their illegal activities. The constitutionality of the material support provision has been challenged in court on void for vagueness and First Amendment grounds (see Chapter 2). See the accompanying Court Decision for the U.S. Supreme Court's ruling on the constitutionality of the provision.

**COURT DECISION**

*Holder* v. *Humanitarian Law Project*
130 S.Ct. 2705 (2010)

**Background:**Plaintiffs filed suit to prevent the enforcement of the criminal statute outlawing "providing material support" to terrorist organization. The United States District Court for the Central District of California heard the case twice and entered an injunction in relation to portions of the statute as unconstitutionally vague. The Ninth Circuit Court of Appeals, who also heard the case twice, affirmed. The United States Supreme Court granted certiorari and upheld the statue as constitutional.

Chief Justice ROBERTS delivered the opinion of the Court.

Congress has prohibited the provision of "material support or resources" to certain foreign organizations that engage in terrorist activity. 18 U.S.C. § 2339B(a)(1). That prohibition is based on a finding that the specified organizations "are so tainted by their criminal conduct that any contribution to such an organization facilitates that conduct. The plaintiffs in this litigation seek to provide support to two such organizations. Plaintiffs claim that they seek to facilitate only the lawful, nonviolent purposes of those groups, and that applying the material-support law to prevent them from doing so violates the Constitution. In particular, they claim that the statute is too vague, in violation of the Fifth Amendment, and that it infringes their rights to freedom of speech and association, in violation of the First Amendment. We conclude that the material-support statute is constitutional as applied to the particular activities plaintiffs have told us they wish to pursue. We do not, however, address the resolution of more difficult cases that may arise under the statute in the future.

This litigation concerns 18 U.S.C. § 2339B, which makes it a federal crime to "knowingly provid[e] material support or resources to a foreign terrorist organization." Congress has amended the definition of "material support or resources" periodically, but at present it is defined as follows:

> "[T]he term 'material support or resources' means any property, tangible or intangible, or service, including currency or monetary instruments or financial securities, financial services, lodging, training, expert advice or assistance, safehouses, false documentation or identification, communications equipment, facilities, weapons, lethal substances, explosives, personnel (1 or more individuals who may be or include oneself), and transportation, except medicine or religious materials." § 2339A(b)(1); see also § 2339B(g)(4).

The authority to designate an entity a "foreign terrorist organization" rests with the Secretary of State. She may, in consultation with the Secretary of the Treasury and the Attorney General, so designate an organization upon finding that it is foreign, engages in "terrorist activity" or "terrorism," and thereby "threatens the security of United States nationals or the national security of the United States". . . . In 1997, the Secretary of State designated 30 groups as foreign terrorist organizations. Two of those groups are the Kurdistan Workers' Party (also known as the Partiya Karkeran Kurdistan, or PKK) and the Liberation Tigers of Tamil Eelam (LTTE). The PKK is an organization founded in 1974 with the aim of establishing an independent Kurdish state in southeastern Turkey. The LTTE is an organization founded in 1976 for the purpose of creating an independent Tamil state in Sri Lanka. The District Court in this action found that the PKK and the LTTE engage in political and humanitarian activities. The Government has presented evidence that both groups have also committed numerous terrorist attacks, some of which have harmed American citizens. . . .

In 1998, plaintiffs filed suit in federal court challenging the constitutionality of the material-support statute, § 2339B. Plaintiffs claimed that they wished to provide support for the humanitarian and political activities of the PKK and the LTTE in the form of monetary contributions, other tangible aid, legal training, and political advocacy, but that they could not do so for fear of prosecution under § 2339B. [During the 12 years of litigation regarding this issue, Congress modified the statute in order to address vagueness concerns and make the statute more specific.]

**[Vagueness Argument]**

***Under a proper analysis, plaintiffs' claims of vagueness lack merit. Plaintiffs do not argue that the material-support statute grants too much enforcement discretion to the Government. We therefore address only whether the statute "provide[s] a person of ordinary intelligence fair notice of what is prohibited."

As a general matter, the statutory terms at issue here are quite different from the sorts of terms that we have previously declared to be vague. We have in the past "struck down statutes that tied criminal culpability to whether the defendant's conduct was 'annoying' or 'indecent'—wholly subjective judgments without statutory definitions, narrowing context, or settled legal meanings." Applying the statutory terms in this action—"training," "expert advice or assistance," "service," and "personnel"— does not require similarly untethered, subjective judgments.

Congress also took care to add narrowing definitions to the material-support statute over time. These definitions increased the clarity of the statute's terms. See § 2339A(b)(2) ("'training' means instruction or teaching designed to impart a specific skill, as opposed to general knowledge"); § 2339A(b)(3) ("'expert advice or assistance' means advice or assistance derived from scientific, technical or other specialized knowledge"); § 2339B(h) (clarifying the scope of "personnel"). And the knowledge requirement of the statute further reduces any potential for vagueness, as we have held with respect to other statutes containing a similar requirement.

Of course, the scope of the material-support statute may not be clear in every application. But the dispositive point here is that the statutory terms are clear in their application to plaintiffs' proposed conduct, which means that plaintiffs' vagueness challenge must fail. . . . Most of the activities in which plaintiffs seek to engage readily fall within the scope of the terms "training" and "expert advice or assistance."

Plaintiffs want to "train members of [the] PKK on how to use humanitarian and international law to peacefully resolve disputes," and "teach PKK members how to petition various representative bodies such as the United Nations for relief." A person of ordinary intelligence would understand that instruction on resolving disputes through international law falls within the statute's definition of "training" because it imparts a "specific skill," not "general knowledge." § 2339A(b)(2). Plaintiffs' activities also fall comfortably within the scope of "expert advice or assistance": A reasonable person would recognize that teaching the PKK how to petition for humanitarian relief before the United Nations involves advice derived from, as the statute puts it, "specialized knowledge." § 2339A(b)(3).

### [First Amendment Argument]

***We next consider whether the material-support statute, as applied to plaintiffs, violates the freedom of speech guaranteed by the First Amendment. Both plaintiffs and the Government take extreme positions on this question. Plaintiffs claim that Congress has banned their "pure political speech." It has not. Under the material-support statute, plaintiffs may say anything they wish on any topic. They may speak and write freely about the PKK and LTTE, the governments of Turkey and Sri Lanka, human rights, and international law. They may advocate before the United Nations. As the Government states: "The statute does not prohibit independent advocacy or expression of any kind." Section 2339B also "does not prevent [plaintiffs] from becoming members of the PKK and LTTE or impose any sanction on them for doing so." Congress has not, therefore, sought to suppress ideas or opinions in the form of "pure political speech." Rather, Congress has prohibited "material support," which most often does not take the form of speech at all. And when it does, the statute is carefully drawn to cover only a narrow category of speech to, under the direction of, or in coordination with foreign groups that the speaker knows to be terrorist organizations.

***The Preamble to the Constitution proclaims that the people of the United States ordained and established that charter of government in part to "provide for the common defence." As Madison explained, "[s]ecurity against foreign danger is . . . an avowed and essential object of the American Union." We hold that, in regulating the particular forms of support that plaintiffs seek to provide to foreign terrorist organizations, Congress has pursued that objective consistent with the limitations of the First and Fifth Amendments.

## Case Analysis

1. The plaintiffs make two constitutional arguments regarding the validity of the statute. Identify these two arguments and the constitutional amendments involved.

2. Summarize the Supreme Court's ruling on the constitutionality of the statute.

3. Do you believe the statute infringes on the plaintiff's constitutional rights? Why or why not?

The USA PATRIOT Act was set to expire at the end of 2005. In March 2006, then-President Bush signed into law a "renewal" of the act that incorporated some changes. On the one hand, various civil liberties protections were written into the new version. Many of these addressed so-called Section 215 requests, which permit the government to access business and library records. On the other hand, the act also expanded law enforcement, especially through the Combat Methamphetamine Epidemic Act of 2005. According to the White House,

> [T]his bill introduces commonsense safeguards that will make many ingredients used in methamphetamine manufacturing more difficult to obtain in bulk and easier for law enforcement to track. For example, the bill places limits on large-scale purchases of over-the-counter drugs that are used to manufacture methamphetamines—and requires stores to keep these ingredients behind the counter or in locked display cases. It increases penalties for smuggling and selling methamphetamines.[24]

The PATRIOT Act has been amended under the Obama administration. For example, in early 2010, the President signed a one-year extension of several key provisions. The key activities President Obama reauthorized were "court-approved roving wiretaps that permit surveillance on multiple phones, . . . seizure of records and property in anti-terrorism operations, . . . [and] surveillance against a so-called lone wolf, a non-U.S. citizen engaged in terrorism who may not be part of a recognized terrorist group."[25]

## Other Terrorism Legislation

A number of other federal laws are used to prosecute terrorists. The U.S. Justice Department classifies the available statutes as follows:

> Category I cases involve violations of federal statutes that are directly related to international terrorism and that are utilized regularly in international terrorism matters. These statutes prohibit, for example, terrorist acts abroad against United States nationals, the use of weapons of mass destruction, conspiracy to murder persons overseas, providing material support to terrorists or foreign terrorist organizations, receiving military style training from foreign terrorist organizations, and bombings of public places or government facilities. . . .
>
> Category II cases include defendants charged with violating a variety of other statutes where the investigation involved an identified link to international terrorism. These Category II cases include offenses such as those involving fraud, immigration, firearms, drugs, false statements, perjury, and obstruction of justice, as well as general conspiracy charges under 18 U.S.C. § 371. Prosecuting terror-related targets using Category II offenses and others is often an effective method—and sometimes the only available method—of deterring and disrupting potential terrorist planning and support activities. . . .[26]

Figure 13.4 contains a detailed listing of example offenses in each category.

---

[24]http://www.whitehouse.gov/infocus/patriotact/.
[25]Associated Press, "Obama Signs Extension of Patriot Act," http://www.usatoday.com/news/washington/2010-02-27-Patriot-Act_N.htm (accessed January 3, 2011).
[26]http://tinyurl.com/ydoe3s8.

**Category I Offenses**

- Aircraft Sabotage (18 U.S.C. § 32)
- Animal Enterprise Terrorism (18 U.S.C. § 43)
- Crimes Against Internationally Protected Persons (18 U.S.C. § § 112, 878, 1116, l201(a)(4))
- Use of Biological, Nuclear, Chemical or Other Weapons of Mass Destruction (18 U.S.C. §§ 175, 175b, 229, 831, 2332a)
- Production, Transfer, or Possession of Variola Virus (Smallpox) (18 U.S.C. § 175c)
- Participation in Nuclear and WMD Threats to the United States (18 U.S.C. § 832)
- Conspiracy Within the United States to Murder, Kidnap, or Maim Persons or to Damage Certain Property Overseas (18 U.S.C. § 956)
- Hostage Taking (18 U.S.C. § 1203)
- Terrorist Attacks Against Mass Transportation Systems (18 U.S.C. § 1993)
- Terrorist Acts Abroad Against United States Nationals (18 U.S.C. § 2332)
- Terrorism Transcending National Boundaries (18 U.S.C. § 2332b)
- Bombings of places of public use, Government facilities, public transportation systems and infrastructure facilities (18 U.S.C. § 2332f)
- Missile Systems designed to Destroy Aircraft (18 U.S.C. § 2332g)
- Production, Transfer, or Possession of Radiological Dispersal Devices (18 U.S.C. § 2332h)
- Harboring Terrorists (18 U.S.C. § 2339)
- Providing Material Support to Terrorists (18 U.S.C. § 2339A)
- Providing Material Support to Designated Terrorist Organizations (18 U.S.C. § 2339B)
- Prohibition Against Financing of Terrorism (18 U.S.C. § 2339C)
- Receiving Military-Type Training from an FTO (18 U.S.C. § 2339D)
- Narco-Terrorism (21 U.S.C. § 1010A)
- Sabotage of Nuclear Facilities or Fuel (42 U.S.C. § 2284)
- Aircraft Piracy (49 U.S.C. § 46502)
- Violations of IEEPA (50 U.S.C. § 1705(b)) involving E.O. 12947 (Terrorists Who Threaten to Disrupt the Middle East Peace Process); E.O. 13224 (Blocking Property and Prohibiting Transactions With Persons Who Commit, Threaten to Commit, or Support Terrorism or Global Terrorism List); and E.O. 13129 (Blocking Property and Prohibiting Transactions With the Taliban)

**Category II Offenses**

- Crimes Committed Within the Special Maritime and Territorial Jurisdiction of the United States (l8 U.S.C. §§ 7, 113, 114, 115, 1111, 1112, 1201, 2111)
- Violence at International Airports (18 U.S.C. § 37)
- Arsons and Bombings (18 U.S.C. §§ 842(m), 842(n), 844(f), 844(l))
- Killings in the Course of Attack on a Federal Facility (18 U.S.C. § 930(c))
- False Statements (18 U.S.C. § 1001)
- Protection of Computers (18 U.S.C. § 1030)
- False Information and Hoaxes (18 U.S.C. § 1038)
- Genocide (18 U.S.C. § 1091)
- Destruction of Communication Lines (18 U.S.C. § 1362)
- Sea Piracy (18 U.S.C. § 1651)
- Unlicensed Money Remitter Charges (18 U.S.C. § 1960)
- Wrecking Trains (18 U.S.C. § 1992)
- Destruction of National Defense Materials, Premises, or Utilities (18 U.S.C. § 2155)
- Violence against Maritime Navigation and Maritime Fixed Platforms (18 U.S.C. §§ 2280, 2281)
- Torture (18 U.S.C. § 2340A)
- War Crimes (18 U.S.C. § 2441)
- International Traffic in Arms Regulations (22 U.S.C. § 2778, and the rules and regulations promulgated thereunder, 22 C.F.R. § 121-130)
- Crimes in the Special Aircraft Jurisdiction other than Aircraft Piracy (49 U.S.C. §§ 46503-46507)
- Destruction of Interstate Gas or Hazardous Liquid Pipeline Facilities (49 U.S.C. § 60123(b))

**Figure 13.4**

Examples of Federal Statutes Used to Prosecute Terrorists

*Source*: U.S. Justice Department, http://tinyurl.com/ydoe3s8.

**YOUR DECISION**

1. John Walker Lindh is an American citizen who was captured by the Northern Alliance on the battlefield in Afghanistan in November 2001. Known as "the American Taliban," Lindh attended a military training camp run by Harakut ul-Mujahideen in Pakistan before joining the Taliban in Afghanistan. Lindh allegedly told Taliban officials "that he was an American and that he wanted to go to the front lines to fight," and received additional military training at an al-Qaeda training camp. During his training, Lindh personally met Osama bin Laden, "who thanked him and other trainees for taking part in jihad." Lindh carried a weapon during his time fighting with the Taliban. What possible crimes has Lindh committed?

2. Judy Smith was just dumped by her boyfriend of five years, Stephen Myers. Stephen has found a new woman in his life and is about to take her on a seven-day Caribbean cruise. Judy is distraught at the thought of Stephen with another woman. She writes a letter threatening to blow up the entire cruise ship if Stephen does not take her back. Federal law enforcement learns of the threat to the cruise ship and uses the PATRIOT Act to investigate Judy. Has Judy committed a crime of terrorism? Why or why not? Should the PATRIOT Act be used to investigate this type of crime?

## Summary

- An act is terrorism if it is premeditated, politically motivated, violent, and committed against noncombatants.

- Domestic terrorism is carried out by an individual or group that is based within and operate within this country. International terrorism refers to the unlawful use of violence by a group or individual having some connection with a foreign power or group.

- Cyberterrorism uses high technology, especially computers and the Internet, to carry out terrorist attacks. Narcoterrorism involves collaboration between drug traffickers and terrorist groups. Ecoterrorism involves extremist views on environmental issues and animal rights, and is a fringe-issue form of terrorism aimed primarily at inflicting economic damage on those seen as profiting from the destruction and exploitation of the environment.

- The U.S. government has adopted a so-called 4D strategy for combating terrorism: Defeat, Deny, Diminish, and Defend.

- Legislative efforts to combat terrorism include the Antiterrorism and Effective Death Penalty Act (AEDPA), the USA PATRIOT Act, and dozens of other federal statutes.

MODULE

# 13.2

# OTHER OFFENSES AGAINST THE STATE

### Learning Objectives

- **Distinguish among treason, sedition, and espionage.**
- **Summarize sabotage and criminal syndicalism.**
- **Explain how other criminal law statutes can be used in cases involving threats against the government.**

**CORE CONCEPTS**

Terrorism is perhaps the most visible and potentially destructive crime against the state. Yet there are several other offenses against the state that sometimes receive little attention. Examples include treason, sedition, espionage, sabotage, and criminal syndicalism. This module briefly introduces each. We conclude with a brief examination of the use of traditional criminal law offenses to target threats against the state.

Both the offenses discussed in this section *and* terrorism typically involve violations of federal law. As such, most cases are prosecuted in federal court. There are some exceptions, as in the case of criminal syndicalism, but to say an offense is "against the state" is almost always the same as saying it is against the federal government. For example, you would never see a county-level treason prosecution.

## Treason

**treason** Levying war against the United States or providing aid and comfort to the enemies of the United States.

**Treason** is the only crime defined in the U.S. Constitution. Article III, Section 3 reads:

> Treason against the United States, shall consist only in levying War against them, or, in adhering to their Enemies, giving them Aid and Comfort. No Person shall be convicted of Treason unless on the Testimony of two Witnesses to the same overt Act, or on Confession in open Court.

The Constitution gave Congress the power to declare the punishment for treason, which it has since done. The U.S. Code contains the same language found in Article III of the Constitution, but also adds the punishment:

> Whoever, owing allegiance to the United States, levies war against them or adheres to their enemies, giving them aid and comfort within the United States or elsewhere, is guilty of treason and shall suffer death, or shall be imprisoned not less than five years and fined under this title but not less than $10,000; and shall be incapable of holding any office under the United States.[27]

Clearly treason is regarded as a serious offense. What, in simple terms, is *treason*? It is the betrayal of one's nation. *Black's Law Dictionary* defines the word as "[a] breach of allegiance to one's government, usually committed through levying war against such government or by giving aid or comfort to the enemy."[28] Former Supreme Court Justice Robert Jackson defined treason even more specifically in *Cramer* v. *United States*:

> [T]he crime of treason consists of two elements: adherence to the enemy; and rendering him aid and comfort. A citizen intellectually or emotionally may favor the enemy and harbor sympathies or convictions disloyal to this country's policy or interest, but so long as he commits no act of aid and comfort to the enemy, there is no treason. On the other hand, a citizen may take actions, which do aid and comfort the enemy—making a speech critical of the government or opposing its measures, profiteering, striking in defense plants or essential work, and the hundred other things which impair our cohesion and diminish our strength—but if there is no adherence to the enemy in this, if there is no intent to betray, there is no treason.[29]

---

[27]18 U.S.C. Section 2381.
[28]*Black's Law Dictionary*, 6th ed. (St. Paul, MN: West, 1990), p. 1501.
[29]*Cramer* v. *United States*, 325 U.S. 1 (1945).

**Figure 13.5**
Treason

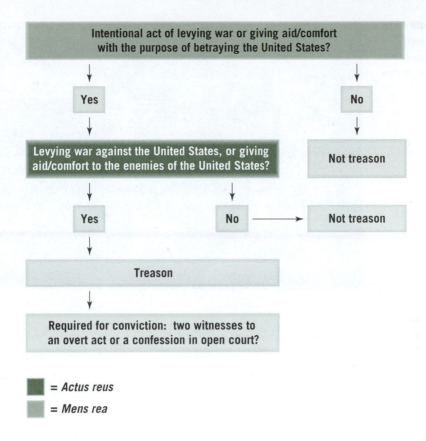

Also see Figure 13.5 for a summary of treason.

Treason is less of a concern today than it once was. The Founding Fathers realized that for the new republic to survive its formative years, the people would need to support and stand behind their government. Treason prosecutions have been exceptionally rare. Fewer than 40 individuals have been prosecuted for it since the Constitution was written.

The most recent treason indictment was against Adam Yahiye Gadahn, a U.S. citizen turned al-Qaeda operative, who remains on the FBI's "Most Wanted" list. He was the first American charged with treason since Tomoya Kawakita in 1952. Kawakita was sentenced to death for treason in connection with World War II, but President John F. Kennedy pardoned him in 1963 on the condition that he be deported to Japan for the rest of his life.[30]

# Sedition

It is also a crime—and it long has been—to incite rebellion against the government. More formally, **sedition** is

> advocating, or with knowledge of its contents knowingly publishing, selling or distributing any document which advocates, or, with knowledge of its purpose, knowingly

**sedition** Advocating the violent overthrow of the U.S. government.

---

[30]See *Kawakita v. United States*, 343 U.S. 717 (1952).

Protest does not rise to the level of sedition unless it advocates the violent overthrow of the government.

L. Kragt Bakker/
Shutterstock.com

becoming a member of any organization which advocates the overthrow or reformation of the existing form of government . . . by violence or unlawful means.[31]

Today, the government relies on the federal seditious conspiracy statute to prosecute people for sedition. Title 18 of the U.S. Code defines the crime as follows:

> If two or more persons in any State or Territory, or in any place subject to the jurisdiction of the United States, conspire to overthrow, put down, or to destroy by force the Government of the United States, or to levy war against them, or to oppose by force the authority thereof, or by force to prevent, hinder, or delay the execution of any law of the United States, or by force to seize, take, or possess any property of the United States contrary to the authority thereof, they shall each be fined under this title or imprisoned not more than twenty years, or both.[32]

In *United States* v. *Rahman et al.*,[33] a fairly recent case, the Second Circuit heard an appeal involving ten defendants who were convicted of seditious conspiracy as part of a plot to conduct urban terrorism. According to the court, "[a]mong the activities of some or all of the defendants were rendering assistance to those who bombed the World Trade Center . . ., planning to bomb bridges and tunnels in New York City, murdering Rabbi Meir Kahane, and planning to murder the President of Egypt."[34] One argument raised in the appeal is that the federal statute threatened free speech under the First Amendment. The court was not convinced, noting,

> The evidence justifying Abdel Rahman's conviction . . . showed beyond a reasonable doubt that he crossed the line. His speeches were not simply the expression of ideas; in some instances they constituted the crime of conspiracy to wage war on the United States . . . and solicitation of attack on the United States. . . .[35]

---

[31]*Black's Law Dictionary*, 6th ed. (St. Paul, MN: West, 1990), p. 1357.
[32]18 U.S.C. Section 2384.
[33]*United States* v. *Rahman et al.*, 189 F.3d 88 (2nd Cir. 1999).
[34]Ibid.
[35]Ibid.

# Espionage

**espionage** Spying for the benefit of a foreign government.

**Espionage**, or spying, occurs when one gathers, transmits, and/or "loses" defense information to injure the United States or for the benefit of a foreign power. The Espionage Act of 1917,[36] now part of the U.S. Code, criminalizes espionage and breaks it into two categories: espionage during peace[37] and espionage during war.[38] Espionage during wartime is defined as follows:

> Whoever, with intent or reason to believe that it is to be used to the injury of the United States or to the advantage of a foreign nation, communicates, delivers, or transmits, or attempts to communicate, deliver, or transmit, to any foreign government, or to any faction or party or military or naval force within a foreign country, whether recognized or unrecognized by the United States, or to any representative, officer, agent, employee, subject, or citizen thereof, either directly or indirectly, any document, writing, code book, signal book, sketch, photograph, photographic negative, blueprint, plan, map, model, note, instrument, appliance, or information relating to the national defense, shall be punished by death or by imprisonment for any term of years or for life. . . .[39]

Take note of the penalty. Espionage is an offense eligible for the death penalty (subject to certain restrictions), although the norm is to sentence offenders to lengthy prison terms. Ethel and Julius Rosenberg were, in 1953, the first (and only) civilians executed for espionage in connection with their passing of atomic bomb secrets to the Soviet Union. Executions of federal prisoners are fairly rare.[40] The military has executed approximately 160 soldiers for crimes they committed while in service to the United States, but none were for espionage. Espionage prosecutions are also fairly rare. As of this writing, officials are deciding whether to charge Julian Assange, the founder of WikiLeaks, with espionage in connection to the publication of numerous classified diplomatic cables.

In 1996, the Economic Espionage Act also made the theft of trade secrets a federal crime. We touched on this briefly in Chapter 11. See the accompanying Court Decision for an example of an individual being charged with crimes against the state. In it we examine the case of Hassan Abu-Jihaad, a former member of the U.S. Navy accused of disclosing confidential information to a potential terrorist organization.

---

**COURT DECISION**

*United States v. Abu-Jihaad*
600 F.Supp.2d 362 (D. Conn. 2009)

**Background:** Hassan Abu-Jihaad was convicted of disclosing national defense information and of providing material support to terrorists by a jury in the District Court of Connecticut. Abu-Jihaad moved for a judgment of acquittal and a new trial. The

---

[36]The Espionage Act of 1917 was upheld by the U.S. Supreme Court in *Schenck v. United States*, 249 U.S. 47 (1919).
[37]18 U.S.C. Section 794(a).
[38]18 U.S.C. Section 794(b).
[39]18 U.S.C. Section 794(a).
[40]For a list of executed federal prisoners, see http://www.bop.gov/about/history/execchart.jsp (accessed December 14, 2010).

District Court of Connecticut partially granted the motion for an acquittal and set aside the providing material support conviction. The conviction for disclosing defense information remains in effect.

**Memorandum of Decision**

MARK R. KRAVITZ, District Judge.

Following a six-day trial in March 2008, a jury convicted Defendant Hassan Abu-Jihaad on two charges: (1) disclosing national defense information to those not entitled to receive it in violation of 18 U.S.C. § 793(d); and (2) providing material support to terrorists in violation of 18 U.S.C. § 2339A and § 2. The Government alleged that in 2001, while Mr. Abu-Jihaad was serving as a U.S. Navy Signalman aboard the destroyer, the *U.S.S. Benfold,* he disclosed classified information regarding the movement of the Fifth Fleet Battle Group, which included the aircraft carrier, the *U.S.S. Constellation,* to individuals in London associated with Azzam Publications, an organization that the Government alleged supported violent Islamic jihad. According to the Government, Mr. Abu-Jihaad knew or intended that the information he disclosed would be used to kill United States nationals. By its verdict, the jury agreed with the Government's assertions. Mr. Abu-Jihaad now moves for judgment of acquittal and for a new trial.

\*\*\*The document—which was often referred to at trial as the "Battlegroup Document"—purported to predict ship movements beginning on March 15, 2001, and therefore, the information contained in the document appeared to have been provided before that date. The first page of the document began as follows:

In the coming days the United States will be deploying a large naval/marine force to the Middle East.

This will be a two group force: the Battle Group (BG) and the Amphibious Readiness Group (ARG)—these groups will be replacing the already deployed groups in the gulf. . . .

Beneath this text was a diagram labeled "Formations Through Straits," which purported to show in a two-column formation each of the components of the battlegroup. Thereafter, the document described the capabilities of each vessel in the battlegroup, led by the aircraft carrier, the *U.S.S. Constellation,* plus smaller vessels including a destroyer named the *U.S.S. Benfold.* . . . The document ended with an overall assessment of the battlegroup's vulnerabilities:

**Weakness**

They have nothing to stop a small craft with RPG etc, except their Seals' stinger missiles.

**Deploy ops in Gulf 29 April-04 October.**

**29th APRIL is more likely the day through the Straits. For the whole of March is tax-free—a moral booster. Many sailors do not like the Gulf.**

**Please destroy message.**

[The document was found on a floppy disk in the home of Babar Ahmad, who had ties with a suspected terrorist organization, Azzam Publications].

\*\*\*[FBI] Agent Bowling located eleven e-mails between Azzam [the suspected terrorist group] and Mr. Abu-Jihaad dating from August 21, 2000, through September 3, 2001. Some e-mails were to or from his military e-mail addresses (abujihah@ benfold. navy. mil and later Abujihaad H@ benfold. navy. mil), while others were from his private e-mail address (abujihaad 01@ hotmail. com). Navy personnel records confirmed that Mr. Abu-jihaad was assigned to the *Benfold* during this period of time. . . . From the contents of the e-mails between Mr. Abu-Jihaad and Azzam, it was apparent that he made known to Azzam both his identity and his status as an active member of the U.S. Navy stationed aboard a warship deployed to the Persian Gulf. The e-mails also showed that Mr. Abu-Jihaad was reading the Azzam websites and that he sent money orders to Azzam to purchase various videos that Azzam had created to support violent Islamic jihad. . . . Agent Bowling did not find the Battlegroup Document or information from the Battlegroup Document in any of the e-mails between Mr. Abu-Jihaad and Azzam. Therefore, the Government's case against Mr. Abu-Jihaad was built solely on circumstantial evidence regarding his motive and his access to information contained in the Battlegroup Document.

\*\*\*As the Court told the jury in its instructions on the law, to be found guilty of disclosing national defense information to those not entitled to receive it in violation of 18 U.S.C. § 793(d), the Government was required to prove the following essential elements:

1. *First,* that Mr. Abu-Jihaad lawfully had possession of, access to, control over, or was entrusted with information relating to the national defense.

2. *Second,* that Mr. Abu-Jihaad had reason to believe that such information could be used to the injury of the United States or to the advantage of any foreign nation.

3. *Third,* that Mr. Abu-Jihaad willfully communicated, delivered, transmitted or caused to be communicated, delivered, or transmitted such information.

4. *Fourth,* that Mr. Abu-Jihaad did so to a person not entitled to receive it.

While Mr. Abu-Jihaad's arguments for a judgment of acquittal are substantial, the Court concludes that the evidence presented on the disclosure of classified information charge was neither equal, nor nearly equal, to the evidence in support of a theory of innocence. Accordingly, the Court declines to set aside the jury's conviction on that charge.

\*\*\*Mr. Abu-Jihaad was also convicted of providing material support to terrorists in violation of 18 U.S.C. § 2339A and § 2. Section 2339A makes it a crime to provide "material support or resources . . . knowing or intending that they are to be used in preparation for, or in carrying out, a violation" of certain enumerated statutes. *Id.* "Material support or resources" are defined as follows: "currency or other financial securities, financial services, lodging, training, safehouses, false documentation or identification, communications equipment, facilities, weapons, lethal substances, explosives, *personnel,* transportation, *and other physical assets,* except medicine or religious materials." Mr. Abu-Jihaad was charged with providing "personnel" and "physical assets," knowing or intending that such support would be used in preparation for, or in carrying out, a violation of 18 U.S.C. § 2332(b)—that is, a plan to kill United States nationals. . . .

Taking the evidence in the light most favorable to the Government and fully cognizant of the deference owed to the jury, the Court does not believe that a rational juror could conclude beyond a reasonable doubt that Mr. Abu-Jihaad provided material support to Azzam in the form of a physical asset. The Court says this for two principal reasons.

First and foremost, there was no evidence whatsoever regarding how Mr. Abu-Jihaad transmitted national defense information to Azzam, what was said when the information was provided, or how he expected Azzam would distribute or transmit the information he provided. . . . Second, the Government's emphasis on what was supposedly "reasonably foreseeable" to Mr. Abu-Jihaad does not comport with the requirements of 18 U.S.C. § 2(b). . . . Therefore, "to establish a conviction through the use of section 2(b), the government must prove that the defendant had the mental state necessary to violate the underlying criminal statute and that the defendant '*wilfully caused*' another to commit the necessary act." Here, there was no evidence from which a rational jury could conclude beyond a reasonable doubt that Mr. Abu-Jihaad *willfully caused* Mr. Ahsan to violate § 2339A by copying the Battlegroup Document onto a floppy disk.

\*\*\*For the reasons stated, the Court GRANTS IN PART AND DENIES IN PART the Motion for Judgment of Acquittal.

## Case Analysis

1. Identify the two crimes the defendant is charged with and list the elements of each offense.
2. Identify how the court ruled on the defendant's motion for a judgment of acquittal for each offense.
3. The defendant's conviction was based primarily on circumstantial evidence. What evidence did the government have against the defendant? Do you believe there was sufficient evidence to convict the defendant of a crime?

## Sabotage

**sabotage** Damage to property of the United States or obstructing preparation for war or national defense.

Sabotage has a conventional meaning that need not be connected with the criminal law. The criminal offense of **sabotage**, however, is typically damage to property or obstructing preparation for war or national defense. The U.S. Code defines sabotage as follows:

> Whoever, when the United States is at war, or in times of national emergency as declared by the President or by the Congress, with intent to injure, interfere with, or obstruct the United States or any associate nation in preparing for or carrying on the war or defense activities, or, with reason to believe that his act may injure, interfere with, or obstruct the United States or any associate nation in preparing for or carrying on the war or defense activities, willfully injures, destroys, contaminates or infects, or attempts to so injure, destroy, contaminate or infect any war material, war premises, or war utilities, shall be fined under this title or imprisoned not more than thirty years, or both.[41]

---

[41] 18 U.S.C. Section 2153.

**Figure 13.6**
Criminal Syndicalism
in Utah
*Source*: Utah Code 76-8-902.

Any person who by word of mouth or writing advocates, suggests, or teaches the duty, necessity, propriety, or expediency of crime, criminal syndicalism or sabotage, or who advocates, suggests or teaches the duty, necessity, propriety, or expediency or doing any act of violence, the destruction of or damage to any property, the bodily injury to any person, or the commission of any crime or unlawful act as a means of accomplishing or effecting any industrial or political ends, change or revolution, or who prints, publishes, edits, or issues, or knowingly circulates, sells, or distributes, or publicly displays, any books, pamphlets, paper, handbill, poster, document, or written or printed matter in any form whatsoever, containing, advocating, advising, suggesting, or teaching crime, criminal syndicalism, sabotage, the doing of any act of violence, the destruction of or damage to any property, the injury to any person, or the commission of any crime or unlawful act, as a means of accomplishing, effecting, or bringing about any industrial or political ends or change, or as a means of accomplishing, effecting, or bringing about any industrial or political revolution, or who openly or at all attempts to justify by word of mouth or writing the commission or the attempt to commit sabotage, any act of violence, the destruction of or damage to any property, the injury of any person, or the commission of any crime or unlawful act, with the intent to exemplify, spread, or teach or suggest criminal syndicalism, or organizes, or helps to organize, or becomes a member of, or voluntarily assembles with, any society or assemblage of persons formed to teach or advocate, or which teaches, advocates, or suggests the doctrine of criminal syndicalism or sabotage, or the necessity, propriety, or expediency of doing any act of violence or the commission of any crime or unlawful act as a means of accomplishing or effecting any industrial or political ends, change or revolution, is guilty of a felony of the third degree.

It is also criminal, under federal law, to target certain installations, harbors, and other strategic assets.[42] In addition, it is an offense to intentionally produce defective war and national defense-related materials.[43]

# Criminal Syndicalism

**criminal syndicalism** The use of unlawful means to accomplish economic or political reform.

Syndicalism is an alternative to capitalism, typically a cooperative economic system. Though such a system has never been realized, governments (especially the United States') are naturally wary of any actions that could signal a movement in that direction. **Criminal syndicalism** is thus the use of unlawful means (sabotage, terrorism, etc.) to accomplish economic or political reform. Interestingly, there is no federal criminal syndicalism statute. Most states, however, have had them at one point or another. Utah's "advocating criminal syndicalism or sabotage" statute appears in Figure 13.6.

---

[42]Ibid., Sections 2154 and 2155.
[43]Ibid., Section 2151.

Several state syndicalism laws have been deemed unconstitutional because they run afoul of the First Amendment. For example, in *Brandenburg* v. *Ohio*,[44] the Supreme Court overturned the conviction of a Ku Klux Klan leader because of a speech he made that did not, the Court felt, incite lawless action. If not declared unconstitutional, some statutes have been severely criticized and discredited.[45] Still other state syndicalism statutes remain "on the books," but are rarely invoked.

## Targeting Threats against the State with Other Criminal Law Offenses

The foregoing introduced the common statutes invoked in response to threats against the government. Also available to prosecutors are traditional criminal law statutes—with a twist. Some we have already examined earlier in this book (e.g., conspiracy). Others we have not yet considered, but are clearly relevant when the offender's objective is to hurt or threaten the government. This section thus discusses the means by which a variety of criminal-law statutes can be made applicable in the case of conduct that threatens the government.

### Refusal to Testify Before Congress

**contempt of Congress**
A crime for refusing to testify before the U.S. Congress.

If an individual refuses to testify before the U.S. Congress, he or she can be charged with a crime known as **contempt of Congress**. Similar to a judge holding an individual in "contempt of court," the crime generally refers to failure to obey the commands of Congress. In *Barenblatt* v. *United States*,[46] the Supreme Court reviewed the contempt of Congress conviction of a man who refused to answer questions posed by a federal subcommittee of the House Committee on Un-American Activities. The committee was investigating the possible infiltration of Communist ideology into U.S. schools. Barenblatt, a former graduate student and teaching fellow at the University of Michigan, refused to answer questions as to whether he had ever been a member of the Communist Party. He refused to answer both on the grounds that doing so would incriminate him under the Fifth Amendment and that his political preferences enjoyed First Amendment protection.

The Supreme Court disagreed with his arguments, holding that "the balance between the individual and the governmental interests here at stake must be struck in favor of the latter, and, therefore, the provisions of the First Amendment were not transgressed by the Subcommittee's inquiry into petitioner's past or present membership in the Communist party."[47] In other cases, however, the Court has overturned similar convictions, suggesting that Congress needs to tread softly in this area.[48] In those cases, the questioning was deemed too far removed from the subcommittee's

---

[44]*Brandenburg* v. *Ohio*, 395 U.S. 444 (1969).
[45]See, e.g., *Dennis* v. *United States*, 341 U.S. 494 (1951), p. 507.
[46]*Barenblatt* v. *United States*, 360 U.S. 109 (1959).
[47]Ibid., p. 109.
[48]See *Russell* v. *United States*, 369 U.S. 749 (1962), *Watkins* v. *United States*, 354 U.S. 178 (1957).

goals. For example, in *Watkins* v. *United States*,[49] the Court was confronted with the case of a man who was convicted of contempt of Congress for refusing to answer congressional questions about the political affiliations of his past associates. The Supreme Court reversed his conviction.

## Trespass

Even trespass statutes have been used as a means of addressing affronts against government authority. For example, in *People* v. *Harrison*,[50] a group of Michigan State University students showed up, uninvited and unannounced, at a career fair and protested the Vietnam War in close proximity to a U.S. Marine Corps recruitment table. They apparently blocked students who were interested in conversing with military recruiters. Moreover, the protesting students refused to leave when they were asked to. As such, they were charged with trespassing. The Michigan Supreme Court sided with the university administration:

> For all that defendants may proclaim about their rights of freedom of expression, they had no right to resist the university's exercise of control over its property, to restrict its use for the purpose decided upon by the university, or to speak whenever, however, wherever and to whomever they pleased in violation of directions not to do so by the owner of the public authority in control of the property where the attempt to speak is made. This claim of defendants is without merit.[51]

In these types of cases, the First Amendment rights of freedom of speech and assembly must always be carefully balanced against the potential crime committed.

## Disorderly Conduct

Sometimes state disorderly conduct statutes have been used in an effort to target individuals who threaten the state in some form or fashion. In *Hess* v. *Indiana*,[52] the U.S. Supreme Court was confronted with the question of whether a man's disorderly conduct conviction for loudly stating at a college campus protest that "We'll take the f***ing street later (or again)" should be reversed. The appellant, Hess, claimed that the Indiana disorderly conduct statute under which he was convicted was unconstitutionally vague and prohibits activity protected under the First and Fourteenth Amendments. The Court reversed Hess's conviction, holding, "Appellant's language did not fall within any of the 'narrowly limited classes of speech' that the States may punish without violating the First and Fourteenth Amendments, and since the evidence showed that the words he used were not directed to any person or group and there was no evidence that they were intended and likely to produce *imminent disorder*, application of the statute to appellant violates his rights of free speech."[53] Also see our discussion in chapter two concerning void for vagueness and void for overbreadth.

---

[49]*Watkins v. United States*, 354 U.S. 178 (1957).
[50]*People v. Harrison*, 383 Mich. 585 (1970).
[51]Ibid., p. 593.
[52]*Hess v. Indiana*, 414 U.S. 105 (1973).
[53]Ibid., p. 105

# Threatening the President

Threats against the President of the United States are taken quite seriously. Indeed, federal law prohibits making threats against the President and all successors to the presidency.[54] In one interesting case,[55] however, the U.S. Supreme Court reversed the conviction of an individual for making what at least appeared to be a threat against the President. The Court summarized the facts as follows:

> The incident which led to petitioner's arrest occurred on August 27, 1966, during a public rally on the Washington Monument grounds. The crowd present broke up into small discussion groups and petitioner joined a gathering scheduled to discuss police brutality. Most of those in the group were quite young, either in their teens or early twenties. Petitioner, who himself was 18 years old, entered into the discussion after one member of the group suggested that the young people present should get more education before expressing their views. According to an investigator for the Army Counter Intelligence Corps who was present, petitioner responded: "They always holler at us to get an education. And now I have already received my draft classification as 1-A and I have got to report for my physical this Monday coming. I am not going. If they ever make me carry a rifle the first man I want to get in my sights is L. B. J." "They are not going to make me kill my black brothers." On the basis of this statement, the jury found that petitioner had committed a felony by knowingly and willfully threatening the President.[56]

The Court considered the man's statement "crude political hyperbole which in light of its context and conditional nature did not constitute a knowing and willful threat against the President"[57] under the law.

# Conspiracy and Related Offenses

Traditional criminal conspiracy laws have been used to target would-be terrorists. For example, in *United States* v. *Salameh, et al.*[58] (a pre-9/11 case), the Second Circuit reviewed the case of several men who were indicted and convicted on charges that they conspired to bomb the World Trade Center. Two of them were fugitives at the time of trial but were nevertheless convicted. The evidence against the men was quite overwhelming and their convictions were affirmed.

The federal Racketeer Influenced and Corrupt Organizations (RICO) statute has historically been used against organized crime in all its permutations. It has also been used, more recently, against alleged terrorists. In *United States* v. *Al-Arian*,[59] several members of the "Palestinian Islamic Jihad-Shiqaqi (PIJ) Faction," a purported terrorist organization, were indicted under RICO. The government alleged "that Defendants conspired with the PIJ in the accomplishment of unlawful activities, including, but not limited to, murder, extortion, and money laundering."[60]

---

[54]See 18 U.S.C. Section 871.
[55]*Watts* v. *United States*, 394 U.S. 705 (1969).
[56]Ibid., p. 705.
[57]Ibid.
[58]*United States* v. *Salameh, et al.*, 152 F.3d 88 (2nd Cir. 1998).
[59]*United States* v. *Al-Arian*, 308 F.Supp.2d 1322 (M.D. Fla. 2004).
[60]Ibid., p. 1334.

Still other individuals who have posed threats to the government have been charged with obstruction of justice.[61] Federal law provides, in part, "Whoever corruptly, or by threats or force, or by any threatening letter or communication, endeavors to influence, intimidate, or impede any grand or petit juror, or officer in or of any court of the United States, or officer who may be serving at any examination or other proceeding before any United States magistrate judge . . ., or inures any such officer, magistrate judge, or other committing magistrate . . . shall be punished."[62]

## Extraterritorial Jurisdiction

**extraterritorial jurisdiction** The authority to regulate conduct beyond the territorial boundaries of the United States.

Congress has authority to regulate certain types of conduct that take place beyond the territorial borders of the United States. This is known as **extraterritorial jurisdiction**, or ETJ. For example, the United States has agreements with numerous nations in which its armed forces are stationed. This permits the exercise of jurisdiction over those troops even though they are located in a foreign land. In *United States v. Yousef*,[63] the Second Circuit summarized five specific circumstances in which ETJ is sometimes exercised:

> These five well-recognized bases of criminal jurisdiction are: (1) the "objective territorial principle," which provides for jurisdiction over conduct committed outside a state's borders that has, or is intended to have, a substantial effect within its territory; (2) the "nationality principle," which provides for jurisdiction over extraterritorial acts committed by a State's own citizen; (3) the "protective principle," which provides for jurisdiction over acts committed outside the state that harm the state's interests; (4) the "passive personality principle," which provides for jurisdiction over acts that harm a state's citizens abroad; and (5) the "universality principle," which provides for jurisdiction over extraterritorial acts by a citizen or non-citizen that are so heinous as to be universally condemned by all civilized nations.[64]

As part of the ongoing war on terror, the United States (like many other nations) claims authority to project some of its criminal laws beyond its borders.[65] Likening terrorists to the pirates of days gone by, law professor Anthony Colangelo has explained the logic for ETJ quite eloquently:

> [L]ike the pirate, the terrorist is, in actuality, a national of some state. But by "throw[ing] off his national character" in committing his illegal acts of war, the terrorist has, like the pirate, exposed himself to the enforcement jurisdiction of all states. He too wages a lawless war under the color of no state's authority. While some states doubtlessly may offer support surreptitiously to terrorists, just as some states of old probably secretly supported pirates when it served their political interests, such under-the-table support is not official—indeed far from it: states accused of supporting terrorists often protest vigorously such accusations, and certainly reject being held accountable for terrorist crimes. Thus just as pirates were not privateers acting under the official aegis of sovereign letters of marque and

---

[61] Again see *United States v. Al-Arian*, 308 F.Supp. 2d 1322.
[62] 18 U.S.C. Section 1503(a).
[63] *United States v. Yousef*, 327 F.3d 56 (2nd Cir. 2003).
[64] Ibid., p. 91.
[65] See, e.g., *United States v. Yousef*, 327 F.3d 56 (2nd Cir. 2003); *United States v. Yunis*, 924 F.2d 1086 (D.C. Cir. 1991), p. 1091; *United States v. Bin Laden*, 92 F.Supp.2d 189 (S.D.N.Y. 2000).

reprisal, terrorists are not officially part of any sovereign state's armed forces. Because terrorists operate outside the traditional paradigm of state accountability when they commit their crimes, they are, like pirates, subject to the law of nations, which any state may enforce through criminal prosecution. And just like prosecuting the pirate, prosecuting the terrorist for offenses against the law of nations disrespects no state's sovereignty.[66]

Article I, Section 8, Clause 10 of the Constitution grants Congress the authority "[t]o define and punish . . . offences against the Law of Nations."[67] To the extent terrorist acts fit into this category, then this is the source of the U.S. government's authority to target terrorists in other nations.

Several lower courts have indeed found that Congress has authority to define and punish acts of terrorism committed beyond U.S. borders.[68] Even so, extraterritorial jurisdiction is very limited, and most often to the conduct of U.S. citizens on or in connection with property foreign nations have afforded the U.S. privileges akin to sovereignty (e.g., an embassy). There are some exceptions. For example, Section 804 of the PATRIOT Act extended ETJ to the overseas business premises of federal government entities and the residences of their staffs—but only for crimes committed by or against U.S. citizens. Thus, if a foreign national commits a terrorist act in another country, on a property that falls within the ETJ of the United States, a prosecution may be possible. In some cases, such as the 1989 arrest of Manuel Noriega in Panama, the United States may send troops or law enforcement officials in to another country and make the arrest (it did the former in Noriega's case). However, in most cases, U.S. officials do not have authority to make arrests in foreign countries without the consent of the host country. This area of law is rapidly evolving and an in-depth treatment of the issues is beyond the scope of this text. It is simply important to note that the U.S. criminal law may extend to other nations, particularly when it concerns offenses against the state.

## YOUR DECISION

1. Geraldo is a newsman imbedded with an Army infantry unit in Afghanistan. In an effort to give his network the best coverage of the war on terror, Geraldo draws a map in the sand indicating where his unit is located in relation to the enemy. The U.S. intelligence community is aware that our enemies often watch U.S. television news stations to gain information. Has Geraldo committed a crime? If so, which crime? Does the media reveal too much information regarding our national defense?

2. Julian Assange is the founder of Wikileaks, a nonprofit media organization that releases "leaked" information it receives from a variety of anonymous sources. In November 2010, Wikileaks began releasing 251,287 leaked U.S. embassy cables to a variety of news outlets around the world. The cables were confidential and contained sensitive information regarding national security and relations with other

---

[66]A. J. Colangelo, "Constitutional Limits on Extraterritorial Jurisdiction: Terrorism and the Intersection of National and International Law," *Harvard International Law Journal*, Vol. 48 (2007), pp. 145–146.

[67]The Constitution's foreign commerce clause is also used to justify extraterritorial jurisdiction, as is the United States' treaty power and its foreign affairs power.

[68]See, e.g., *United States* v. *Bin Laden*, 92 F.Supp.2d 189 (S.D.N.Y. 2000); *United States* v. *Yunis*, 681 F.Supp. 896 (D.D.C. 1988).

countries. Although the exact source of the information is unknown, it is presumed Assange received the information from an individual who works for the U.S. government. Assange is not accused of directly accessing or stealing the information from the United States. What crimes, if any, has Assange committed?

## Summary

- Offenses against the state other than terrorism include sedition, sabotage, espionage, criminal syndicalism, and espionage.

- Treason, or "[a] breach of allegiance to one's government, usually committed through levying war against such government or by giving aid or comfort to the enemy,"[69] is the only crime defined in the U.S. Constitution.

- Sedition is akin to inciting rebellion against the government. The government relies primarily on seditious conspiracy statutes to prosecute people for sedition.

- The criminal offense of sabotage is damage to property or obstruction the preparation for war or national defense.

- Syndicalism is an alternative to capitalism, typically a cooperative economic system. Criminal syndicalism is thus the use of unlawful means (sabotage, terrorism, etc.) to accomplish economic or political reform. Interestingly, there is no federal criminal syndicalism statute.

- Espionage, or spying, occurs when one gathers, transmits, and/or "loses" defense information to injure the United States or for the benefit of a foreign power.

- There are several options available for using traditional criminal-law offenses to target threats against the state. Examples include refusal to testify before Congress, trespass, disorderly conduct, threatening the President, conspiracy, RICO, obstruction of justice, and the exercise of extraterritorial jurisdiction.

---

[69] *Black's Law Dictionary*, p. 1501.

# Chapter Review

MODULE **13.1**    **TERRORISM**

### Learning Objectives

- Define terrorism.
- Identify several types of terrorism.
- Explain how the criminal law controls terrorism.

### Review Questions

1. Define terrorism.
2. Compare and contrast five types of terrorism.
3. Explain the U.S. government's "4D" strategy for combating terrorism.
4. What is the role of the PATRIOT Act in combating terrorism?

### Key Terms

domestic terrorism
international terrorism
cyberterrorism
narcoterrorism
ecoterrorism
Antiterrorism and Effective Death Penalty Act (AEDPA)
USA PATRIOT Act

MODULE **13.2**    **OTHER OFFENSES AGAINST THE STATE**

### Learning Objectives

- Distinguish among treason, sedition, and espionage.
- Summarize sabotage and criminal syndicalism.
- Explain how other criminal-law statutes can be used in cases involving threats against the government.

### Review Questions

1. Compare and contrast treason, sedition, and sabotage.
2. Define criminal syndicalism. How is it similar to other offenses against the state?
3. What traditional criminal-law statutes can be used in cases involving threats against the state? How can they be used? What are the limitations?

### Key Terms

treason
sedition
espionage
sabotage

criminal syndicalism
contempt of Congress
extraterritorial jurisdiction

## Chapter Synthesis Questions

1. Which is more important in the war on terror: the criminal law or military intervention? Why?

2. Does the criminal law do enough to control terrorism? Why or why not?

3. Which of the nonterrorism offenses against the state is most serious and why?

4. Which of the following has the most "teeth" in terms of combating terrorism and other offenses against the state: refusal to testify before Congress, trespass, disorderly conduct, threatening the President, conspiracy, RICO, obstruction of justice, or the exercise of extraterritorial jurisdiction? Why?

# GLOSSARY

**accessory after the fact** Under common law, a person who helps the principal after the criminal event takes place.

**accessory before the fact** Under common law, someone solicits, encourages, or commands another to offend.

**accessory** Modern term to describe someone who participates after the crime is already committed.

**accomplice** An individual who aids before or during the commission of a crime.

**actual possession** Property that is either held by the individual or attached to that individual in some fashion.

**actus reus** Latin term meaning "evil act" or criminal act. One of the core requirements of a crime.

**adultery** Sexual intercourse between a male and a female, at least one of who is married to someone else.

**adversarial justice system** A system of justice that pits two parties against each other in pursuit of the truth.

**affirm** In the appeals context, the act of an appellate court agreeing with a lower court's decision.

**affirmative defense** A defense formally raised by the defendant that requires the production of evidence.

**aggravating circumstances** Circumstances that would lend toward a harsher penalty during sentencing.

**Allen charge** Instructions given to jurors after they become deadlocked that instructs them to reexamine their opinions in an effort to reach a verdict.

**American Law Institute** A private organization of lawyers, judges, and legal scholars that wrote and adopted the **Model Penal Code**.

**Antiterrorism and Effective Death Penalty Act (AEDPA)** Federal legislation that defines specific terrorism crimes and penalties.

**apparent safety doctrine** A legal principle that states the defendant is not the legal cause of a resulting harm if the victim reaches a place of "apparent safety," at which point an intervening cause of harm comes into play.

**appellant** The party of appeals.

**appellee** The party appealed against.

**armed robbery** The defendant is in possession of a weapon while committing the crime of robbery.

**arson** Intentionally setting a fire to burn a structure or other physical property.

**asportation** In regard to the crime of kidnapping, the taking and carrying away of another person.

**assault** The threat of bodily harm to another person without physical contact.

**attempt** An inchoate offense in which the defendant has the specific intent to commit the underlying offense and takes some action in furtherance of that intent, but is unsuccessful in completing the crime.

**attempted battery assault** A type of assault in which the criminal attempts to commit the crime of battery but is unsuccessful.

**Bad Samaritan laws** Laws that make it a crime for someone to fail to come to the aid of another who is danger.

**bailee** Person to whom goods or property are entrusted.

**bailor** The individual, usually an employer, who entrust the bailee with his or her property.

**battery** Unlawful offensive touching of another without consent.

**bifurcation** Separating a trial into two parts. In first-degree murder cases, the defendant's guilt or innocence is decided first by the jury. Then, the penalty of life imprisonment or death is decided separately by the jury.

**bigamy** Marriage between two persons when one is married to another.

**bill of attainder** A law that criminalizes conduct without the benefit of a trial.

**Bill of Rights** The first ten amendments to the U.S. Constitution.

**black rage** A criminal defense based on the defendant's past experience with racism that caused him or her to break the law.

**_Blockburger_ rule** An offense is considered the "same offense" for purposes of double jeopardy if two separate statutes that define the offense both contain the same elements.

**bootstrapping** A circular, self-sustaining process.

**breach of peace** An unlawful act that disturbs the peace or harmony of the neighborhood.

**burden of persuasion** In a criminal case, the requirement that the prosecution persuade the jury that the defendant committed the crime.

**burden of production** One party's (the prosecutor's in a criminal case) obligation to present sufficient evidence to have the issue decided by a fact-finder. The burden of production is a question of law.

**burden of proof** The requirement that a particular party convince the jury with regard to a particular issue. In the criminal law context, the burden of proof falls on the prosecutor to establish the defendant's guilt.

**burglary** Breaking and entering into the dwelling or structure of another with the intent to commit a felony inside.

**carjacking** Intentionally taking another person's occupied motor vehicle with the use of a deadly weapon, force, and/or intimidation.

**castle doctrine** A nonaggressor is not required to retreat from his or her home if attacked.

**causation** The requirement that the defendant is responsible for the harm in result crimes.

**chain conspiracy** A type of large-scale conspiracy in which the individuals at one end of the conspiracy are not aware of the individuals at the other end.

**challenge for cause** The opportunity for a prosecutor or defense attorney to excuse a prospective juror for cause (e.g., racial prejudice). Challenges for cause are unlimited.

**child abuse** The physical, sexual, or emotional abuse of a child through voluntary action or failure to act.

**child pornography** Pornography that depicts actual minors in sexually explicit situations.

**circumstantial element** Also known as *attendant circumstances*, the requirement for a specific circumstance to be present.

**circumstantial evidence** Evidence that indirectly proves a fact.

**claim of right** A good-faith belief that the individual has a right to possess the property.

**Code of Hammurabi** The earliest known example of a formal written legal code. It expressed a strong "eye-for-an-eye" philosophy on punishment.

**Combat Methamphetamine Epidemic Act** Federal legislation that primarily restricts access to precursor chemicals used in the manufacture of methamphetamines, particularly ephedrine, pseudoephedrine, and phenylpropanolamine.

**common law** Also known as *case law* or *judge-made law*, the law developed in early England by judges who wrote down their decisions and circulated them to other judges. The law "in common."

**complicity** Involvement in a crime as an accomplice.

**Computer Fraud and Abuse Act (CFAA)** Federal legislation that criminalizes various types of cybercrime.

**concurrence** The *actus rea* and *mens rea* existing simultaneously.

**concurrent jurisdiction** Two courts, namely an adult and juvenile court, both have jurisdiction over a particular case. The prosecutor makes the decision regarding which court to initiate criminal proceedings.

**concurring opinion** An opinion that agrees with the majority decision but for different reasons.

**conduct crimes** Crimes that are complete when the criminal act and criminal intent concur. There is no requirement for resulting harm.

**confederation** A system of government that lacks a strong central authority

**consent** A justification defense in which the victim voluntarily agrees to physical contact with the defendant, such as in the case of rape.

**conspiracy** An inchoate offense in which an agreement is reached to commit a crime.

**constructive possession** The individual has control over the property but is not physically touching it.

**contempt of Congress** A crime for refusing to testify before the U.S. Congress.

**Controlled Substances Act** Federal legislation that classifies illegal narcotics into five different schedules.

**conversion** An unauthorized act that deprives an owner of his property.

**cooperative federalism** A system of federalism in which the lines between federal and state power are blurred.

**corporate vicarious liability** Liability of a corporation for the actions of its agents and employees.

**corrupt motives doctrine** A requirement in some states that defendants have a corrupt motive in order to commit the crime of conspiracy.

**courts of general jurisdiction** Courts that try several types of cases, so-called trial courts.

**courts of limited jurisdiction** Courts that have jurisdiction over relatively minor offenses and infractions. A traffic court fits in this category.

**crime** Anything the criminal law defines as illegal.

**criminal law** Specifies what kinds of behavior are illegal, what punishments are available for dealing with offenders, and what defenses can be invoked by individuals who break it.

**criminal mischief** Intentionally damaging or destroying another's property.

**criminal procedure** A vast system of laws and guidelines that detail how suspected and accused criminals are to be processed and handled by the criminal justice system.

**criminal syndicalism** The use of unlawful means to accomplish economic or political reform.

**cybercrime** A criminal offense committed with the use of a computer or other electronic device.

**cyberstalking** Committing the crime of stalking through electronic communication.

**cyberterrorism** The use of technology, including computers and the Internet, to carry out terroristic attacks.

*de minimus* **infraction defense** A defense that prevents conviction if the defendant's actions were so trivial or minor in relation to the intent of the criminal law.

**defamation** Written or spoken words that damage the reputation of the object of the speech.

**defendant** The individual charged with committing a crime.

**defense of others** A justification defense in which a person is justified using force to protect another from the unlawful use of force by an aggressor.

**demonstrative evidence**  Evidence that seeks to demonstrate a certain point (e.g., drawings, illustrations).

**denunciation**  When society expresses its abhorrence of the crime committed.

**dependent intervening cause**  A cause that is either intended or reasonably foreseen by the defendant.

**derivative liability**  When the defendant derives or obtains his criminal liability from the primary offender.

**diminished capacity**  A failure of proof defense based on the defendant's inability to form the required criminal intent because of a medical disease or defect. It is a unique defense that is not equivalent to the insanity defense.

**direct cause**  The defendant's actions are the direct causal agent that brings about the harm.

**direct evidence**  Evidence that proves a fact without the need for the juror to infer anything from it.

**direct intent**  Intent in which the consequences of a person's actions are desired.

**directed verdict**  A judge's order that one side or the other wins without the need to move on to fact-finding (in which the defense would introduce evidence, call witnesses, and so on).

**discretionary waiver**  The discretion of the juvenile court judge to waive jurisdiction over a criminal case so that the minor can be tried as an adult.

**disorderly conduct**  An individual causes a public disturbance, harm, or annoyance.

**dissent**  A minority opinion that is at odds with the majority opinion

**district court**  Federal trial court. There are 94 in the United States, the District of Columbia, and the U.S. territories.

**domestic terrorism**  Terrorism carried out by an individual or group based and operating within the United States in furtherance of a political or social objective.

**domestic violence**  Assault, battery, or other abusive conduct committed against a family member or intimate partner.

**double jeopardy**  A principle found in the Fifth Amendment to the U.S. Constitution that prevents an individual from being tried twice for the same crime.

**driving under the influence (DUI)**  Operating a motor vehicle with a blood or breath alcohol level over the legal limit of alcohol.

**dual court system**  The American court system, one that separates federal and state courts.

**dual federalism**  A system in which the only powers of the federal government are those explicitly listed, with the rest being left to the states.

**dual federalism**  An interpretation of the U.S. Constitution that suggests a system wherein the only powers vested in the federal government are those explicitly listed in the document, with the remaining powers being left to the states.

**duress**  An excuse defense applicable when the defendant is forced to commit a crime by threat or force.

**ecoterrorism**  Terroristic activities aimed at those perceived to be harming the environment.

**e-mail spoofing**  Altering an e-mail address so that it appears to come from a person other than the sender.

**embezzlement**  Someone in lawful possession of property retains or converts the property for his or her own use with the intent to steal or defraud the rightful owner.

**entrapment**  An excuse defense applicable if the government is found to have manufactured or initiated a crime that would not have otherwise occurred.

**Equal Protection Clause**  A clause in the Fourteenth Amendment of the U.S. Constitution requiring that the government justify any differential treatment on the basis of race, gender, age, sexual orientation, or other characteristic with a state interest.

**espionage**  Spying for the benefit of a foreign government.

**euthanasia**  Purposeful termination of life by someone other than the patient.

***ex post facto* law**  A law enacted in order to retroactively punish behavior. *Ex post facto* is Latin for "after the fact."

**excuse defenses**  A group of defenses in which the defendant admits what he did was wrong but claims he should be excused from criminal liability based on the circumstances.

**extortion**  Also known as *blackmail*; taking property from another with threats of future harm.

**extraterritorial jurisdiction**  The authority to regulate conduct beyond the territorial boundaries of the United States.

**factual causation**  The requirement that the defendant's conduct was the cause in fact of the harm.

**factual impossibility**  Extraneous circumstances prevent the defendant from completing the intended crime.

**failure of proof defense**  A defendant's acquittal is the result of the prosecution failing to prove one or more of the elements of a crime or leaving reasonable doubt in the mind of the jury.

**false imprisonment**  The unlawful detention or restraint of another person.

**false pretenses**  Obtaining the property of another through fraud or deception.

**federalism**  A system of government where power is constitutionally divided between a central governing body and various constituent units.

**felony**  A crime punishable by death or confinement in prison for *more than* 12 months.

**felony murder**  A person is guilty of murder when a death results during that person's commission of a violent felony.

**feticide**  Causing the death of an unborn fetus.

**first-degree murder**  The deliberate, willful, and premeditated killing of another person.

**forgery**  Materially altering a document with the intent to defraud.

**fornication**  Sexual intercourse between unmarried persons.

**gambling**  Making a bet involving monetary risk.

**general deterrence**  The assumption that when would-be offenders see a criminal held accountable, they opt to abide by the law for fear of suffering the same fate.

**general intent**  The intent to commit the *actus reus* or criminal act of the crime only.

**general part of the criminal law**  Broad principles that apply to more than one crime.

**guided-discretion laws**  Laws that provide for the death penalty based on weighing aggravating and mitigating circumstances.

**guilty but mentally ill**  A verdict, short of finding insanity, in which the criminal defendant is mentally ill at the time of the crime.

**hacking**  Breaking into computer systems with the intent to alter or modify settings.

**harassment**  Systematic conduct that intentionally annoys, threatens, and/or intimidates another person.

**Harrison Narcotics Tax Act**  A federal statute passed in 1914 that constituted the federal government's first effort to criminalize opium and cocaine.

**hearsay**  An out-of-court statement admitted in court for the truth of the matter asserted.

**homicide**  The killing of a human being by another human being.

**hung jury**  A deadlocked jury, one that cannot reach a verdict.

**identity theft**  Utilizing personal information of another person to commit fraud or deception.

**imperfect defenses**  Defenses that result in the defendant being convicted of a lesser crime, but do not result in an acquittal.

**incapacitation**  The act of removing an individual from society so that person can no longer offend.

**incest**  Sexual intercourse with certain relatives.

**inchoate crime**  A crime that has not been completed. The three inchoate offenses are **attempt, conspiracy,** and **solicitation.**

**indecent exposure**  Revealing your sexual genitalia to another person.

**independent intervening cause**  A cause that could not be intended or reasonably foreseen by the defendant.

**inherent impossibility**  A defense to a crime of attempt in which the means that the defendant employs to complete the crime are completely implausible and inappropriate.

**inquisitorial system**  The opposite of an adversarial system. The accused does not enjoy the same protections and decision-making authority is placed in the hands of one or very few individuals.

**insanity**  An excuse defense to a criminal charge based on the defendant's mental condition at the time of the crime.

**intellectual property**  Intangible property that can be protected under federal law, such as copyrights, patents, and trademarks.

**intermediate appellate courts**  Courts to which verdicts from courts of general jurisdiction can be appealed.

**intermediate scrutiny**  A test used under the **equal protection clause** of the Fourteenth Amendment for classifications based on gender. The law must be "substantially related" to an "important" government interest.

**international terrorism**  The unlawful use of violence by a group or individual with some connection to a foreign power or group in furtherance of a political or social objective.

**intervening cause**  Another event besides the actions of the defendant that resulted in the harm after the defendant acted.

**intoxication**  An excuse defense applicable only if the intoxication through alcohol, drugs, or other substances is involuntary.

**irresistible impulse test**  An insanity test that focuses on the defendant's ability to conform his or her conduct to the law.

**jury nullification**  Jurors' practice of either ignoring or misapplying the law in a certain situation.

**jury vilification**  The opposite of jury nullification.

**justification defenses**  A group of defenses in which the defendant claims that his actions were right or justified based on the circumstances.

**juvenile waiver**  Trying juveniles as adults in the criminal justice system or waiving them into adult court.

**kidnapping**  The unlawful taking and carrying away of another person with the intent to deprive that person of his or her liberty.

**larceny**  The trespassory taking and carrying away of the person property of another with the intent to permanently deprive the owner of possession.

**last straw rule**  An unlawful killing can be reduced from murder to manslaughter if it was caused by long-standing resentment or humiliation that triggered the crime.

**law enforcement defense**  Defense available to police or other authorized agents for actions committed in the course of law enforcement.

**law**  The formal rules, principles, and guidelines enforced by political authority.

**legal causation**  Also known as *proximate cause*, often the primary act that sets a chain of events in motion. Focuses on whether it is fair to hold the defendant accountable for the resulting harm.

**legal impossibility** A defense to the crime of attempt. The action the defendant intends to perform is not a crime, even if completed.

**legislative exclusion** A statutory requirement that certain juveniles be treated as adults in the criminal justice system.

**libel** Defamation by the written or printed word.

**loitering** The act of lingering aimlessly with no apparent purpose.

**M'Naghten test** An insanity test that focuses on the defendant's ability to appreciate the wrongfulness of his or her conduct based on a mental disease or defect.

**make my day laws** State laws that provide homeowners with considerable latitude to use force to defend their dwelling from unauthorized intruders.

**malice aforethought** Killing another person without justification, excuse, or mitigating circumstances.

**malice** The intent to commit a wrongful act without a legitimate cause or excuse.

**malum in se** An act that is wrong or evil in itself.

**malum prohibitum** An act that is wrong or evil because it is defined as such.

**mandatory waiver** Waiver of a juvenile defendant from juvenile to adult court is mandatory based on the age, offense, or other factors.

**manslaughter** The unlawful killing of another human being without malice aforethought.

**Marijuana Tax Act** A federal statute passed in 1937 that marked the federal government's first effort to regulate marijuana.

**material evidence** Evidence that "is relevant and goes to substantial matters in dispute, or has legitimate influence or bearing on the decision of the case."

**mens rea** Latin term meaning "guilty mind." The mental state or criminal intent of the defendant.

**misdemeanor** A crime punishable by a fine or a period of incarceration *less than* 12 months.

**mistake of fact** A misunderstanding or misinterpretation by the defendant about a relevant fact. Potentially used as a defense or to negate the *mens rea* requirement of a crime.

**mistake of law** The defendant claims to misunderstand or misinterpret the law as it applies to the specific circumstances.

**mistrial** An end to the trial, such as a when the jury becomes hopelessly deadlocked. A new trial is usually held.

**mitigating circumstances** Circumstances that would lend toward a lighter or reduced criminal penalty during sentencing.

**Model Penal Code** A model set of criminal laws adopted by the American Law Institute for states to emulate as they see fit.

**moral rights theory** A theory underlying justification defenses based on the idea that an innocent person has the moral right to act for his or her own benefit in certain situations.

**motivational concurrence** The *mens rea* must be linked to the *actus reus* it is intended to accompany.

**motive** The inducement or reason a defendant chooses to commit a crime.

**murder** The unlawful killing of another person with malice aforethought.

**narcoterrorism** Terroristic activities that result from a collaboration between drug traffickers and traditional terrorist groups.

**natural and probable consequences doctrine** An individual encouraging or assisting a crime can be liable not only for the original crime, but for any other offenses that are the natural and probable consequences of the original crime.

**necessity or choice of evils defense** A justification defense in which the defendant commits a crime out of necessity or to avoid a greater evil.

**negligence** A type of *mens rea* or criminal intent in which the defendant unconsciously creates a risk of harm and does not act like a reasonable person under the circumstances.

**nonexculpatory defense** Defenses unrelated to the elements of the crime or the defendant's alleged fault or guilt.

**nonproxyable offense** A crime that can only be committed by a specific person or class of individuals.

**oblique intent** Intent in which the consequences of a person's actions are not desired, but should have reasonably been foreseen.

**obscenity** Appealing to the prurient interest while lacking in scientific, artistic, or political merit.

**offense modifications** A modification of a criminal offense that shields the defendant from criminal liability.

**omission** The failure to act. In certain circumstances, an omission can satisfy the *actus reus* element of crime.

**opening statements** The statements made by both the prosecutor and defense attorney at the outset of a criminal trial wherein each side lays out for the jury, in overview form, what they will prove throughout the trial.

**opinion** The rationale for an appellate court's decision subscribed to by the majority of judges or justices, usually authored by one judge or justice.

**ostrich instruction** A jury instruction regarding the *mens rea* of accomplice liability that allows the jury to infer knowledge on the part of the defendant from indifference to finding the truth.

**overt act** A voluntary action taken by the defendant in furtherance of the crime of conspiracy.

**panhandling** Public begging for food or money.

**paramour rule** A husband catching his wife in the act of adultery provides adequate provocation to reduce a charge for killing another from murder to manslaughter.

**partial responsibility** A defense that reduces a death sentence to a prison term if the defendant lacked the mental ability to appreciate the wrongfulness of his contact.

**peremptory challenge** The opportunity for a prosecutor or defense attorney to excuse a prospective juror for any reason. Peremptory challenges are limited, and race cannot be used as a basis for exercising peremptory challenges.

**perfect defenses** Defenses that result in the defendant being acquitted of the crime.

**physician-assisted suicide** A patient seeks the assistance of a physician to end his or her own life.

*Pinkerton* **rule** A defendant can be charged both with the crime of conspiracy and the completed offense.

**political authority** Another term for *governmental authority*.

**polygamy** One person being married simultaneously to several others.

**pornography** The depiction of sexual acts or behaviors intending to arouse sexual excitement.

**post-traumatic stress disorder (PTSD)** A potential defense to a crime based on psychological trauma that the defendant suffered after experiencing a traumatic event.

**precedent** In general, some prior action that guides current action. In the context of courts, letting judges' decisions be guided by earlier decisions.

**premenstrual dysphoric disorder (PMDD)** A medical condition creating extreme mental and emotional symptoms prior to menstruation that could potentially be used as a criminal defense to a crime.

**preponderance of evidence** The standard of proof in a civil case, equivalent to "more certain than not."

**presumption** A fact assumed to be true under the law.

**presumption of innocence** A bedrock presumption in the American criminal justice system, the notion that the accused is not guilty until proven as such in a criminal trial.

**presumptive waiver** Waiver of a juvenile defendant from juvenile to adult court is presumed appropriate based on the age, offense, or other factors.

**principal in the first degree** Common law term used to describe the primary offender in a crime.

**principal in the second degree** Under common law, someone who intentionally assists the principal in the first degree with the commission of a crime and who is actually or constructively present at the time of the crime.

**principle of legality** A legal principle stating that a defendant cannot be convicted of a crime unless there is specific legislation making it illegal and defining the potential punishment.

**principle of lenity** A legal principle requiring that any ambiguity in a statute should benefit the defendant, not the government.

**product test** An insanity test that determines whether the criminal activity is the product of a mental disease or defect.

**profanity** Foul language or curse words generally deemed offensive.

**proof beyond a reasonable doubt** The standard of proof necessary in a criminal case, roughly akin to 95% certainty.

**prosecutor** The official who charges the defendant and is tasked with representing the government in court.

**prostitution** Performing or agreeing to perform a sexual act for hire.

**public benefit theory** A theory underlying justification defenses based on the idea that the allegedly criminal action benefits society.

**public intoxication** Appearing in a public place while under the influence of alcohol or substances to a degree where the individual is likely to endanger themselves, others, or property.

**punishment** The infliction of unpleasant consequences on an offender.

**rape** Sexual intercourse without the consent of the victim.

**rape shield laws** Statutes that restrict the admissibility of the victim's past sexual history at trial.

**rational basis** A test used under the **equal protection clause** of the Fourteenth Amendment for classifications. The law must be "reasonably related" to a "legitimate" government interest.

**real evidence** "Any tangible item that can be perceived with the five senses."

**recklessness** A type of *mens rea* or criminal intent in which the defendant consciously creates a risk and chooses to act in disregard of that risk.

**rehabilitation** A planned intervention intended to bring about change in an offender.

**remand** In the appeals context, what happens when an appellate court sends a case back to the lower court for further action consistent with its decision.

*res gestae* Latin term meaning "things done to commit." In regard to felony murder, the sequence of the felony from beginning to end.

*respondeat superior* An employer is liable for the actions of its agents and employees while in the course of employment.

**restoration** The practice of having offenders "face up" to the harm they have caused.

**restorative justice** "A process whereby all the parties with a stake in a particular offence come together to resolve collectively how to deal with the aftermath of the offence and its implications for the future."

**result crimes** Crimes that require actual harm.

**resulting harm** An essential element of a result crime. For example, the resulting harm in homicide is the killing of a human being. Without the killing, it is not homicide.

**retribution** A theory of punishment that believes offenders must be made to suffer, whether by confinement, death, or some other method for their indiscretions.

**reverse** In the appeals context, what happens when an appellate court nullifies or sets aside a lower court's verdict.

**reverse waiver** Waiver of a juvenile defendant from adult court to juvenile court for adjudication.

**riot** A group of three or more people involved in a public disturbance of the peace.

**rout** An unlawfully assembled groups takes a significant step toward rioting.

**sabotage** Damage to property of the United States or obstructing preparation for war or national defense.

**sedition** Advocating the violent overthrow of the U.S. government.

**seditious speech** Speech that advocates rebellion against the government.

**self-defense** A justification defense in which the defendant is permitted to act in order to prevent imminent death or bodily harm.

**sexting** Transmitting sexually explicit images to another person via e-mail or cellular phone.

**sexual assault** A general term that covers a range of nonconsensual sexual offenses against another person.

**social engineering** The practice of obtaining passwords or other sensitive information from individuals through the use of fraud or deception.

**sodomy** Either oral or anal sex between humans, or sexual intercourse between humans and animals.

**solicitation** An inchoate offense that occurs when a person entices, advises, incites, orders, or otherwise encourages someone else to commit a crime.

**special law** In contrast to **common law**, the laws of specific villages and localities that were in effect in medieval England and that were often enforced by canonical (i.e., religious) courts.

**special part of the criminal law** The part of law that defines specific crimes.

**specific deterrence** The idea that when an offender is locked up, that person cannot commit crimes out in society.

**specific intent** The intent to commit an act to achieve a specific criminal result.

**spoke and wheel conspiracy** A type of large-scale conspiracy in which one central actor (the hub) has control of all of the aspects of the conspiracy, while the other members of the conspiracy (the spokes) have control of only one aspect.

**stalking** Intentionally frightening another person by following, harassing, and/or terrorizing.

**stand your ground rule** A legal principle that does not require a person to retreat if that person is the victim of an unprovoked attack.

*stare decisis* A Latin term meaning "to stand by things decided," or to adhere to precedent.

**state supreme court** The highest court in a state.

**statute of limitations** The maximum amount of time allowed by law to seek prosecution for certain crimes or offenses.

**statutory rape** A strict liability crime in which the defendant has sexual intercourse with a minor under the age of consent.

**strict liability** Crimes that do not require *mens rea* or criminal intent.

**strict scrutiny** A test used under the **equal protection clause** of the Fourteenth Amendment for classifications based on race. The law must be "narrowly tailored" to serve a "compelling" government interest. What's more, there must be no "less restrictive" alternative available.

**superior courts** The name commonly used for courts of general jurisdiction. Often found at the county level.

**superior interest theory** A theory underlying justification defenses based on the idea that a superior interest justifies criminal conduct in some situations.

**surreptitious remaining** A person has lawful access the property, but then remains until he or she no longer does, and intends to commit a crime.

**temporal concurrence** The *mens rea* must accompany the *actus reus* in time.

**terrorism** Premeditated, politically motivated violence against noncombatants.

**testimonial evidence** Most often, testimonial evidence consists of verbal statements given by someone who is under oath.

**threatened battery assault** A type of assault in which the criminal intentionally places another person in fear of an imminent battery.

**tort** A private wrong or injury.

**tort-feasor** One who commits a **tort**.

**transferred intent** The defendant's intent to harm one person is transferred to the actual victim of the crime.

**treason** Levying war against the United States or providing aid and comfort to the enemies of the United States.

**trespassing** Physical entry onto another person's property without consent.

**trier of fact** Someone who listens to the evidence and renders a decision, a judge in a bench trial or a jury member in a jury trial. Opposite of trier of law.

**trier of law** One who is tasked with resolving any legal matter that comes before a court, most often a judge. Opposite of a trier of fact.

**Twelve Tables** The first secular written legal code.

**U.S. Court of Appeals** The federal appellate court. There are 13 in the United States: 12 regional courts, and 1 federal circuit.

**U.S. Supreme Court** The highest court in the federal system.

**Uniform Controlled Substances Act** A uniform act drafted to standardize state drug laws. States must affirmatively adopt the act in order for the provisions to becoming binding law.

**unlawful assembly**   A group of people publicly gather unlawfully or for an illegal purpose.

**urban psychosis**   A criminal defense based on the defendant's traumatic upbringing in a violent area.

**urban survival syndrome**   A criminal defense based on the heightened sense of fear that the defendant experiences from being raised in a high-crime urban neighborhood.

**USA PATRIOT Act**   Federal legislation passed in response to the September 11, 2001, terrorist attacks; the act includes expanded tools for law enforcement.

**utilitarian**   In terms of criminal law, the notion that the criminal law should maximize the net happiness of society.

**uttering**   Passing a forged document to another with the intent to defraud.

**vacate**   In the appeals context, basically the same as a reversal.

**vagrancy**   Moving about with no visible means of financial support.

**vandalism**   Sometimes considered a form of *criminal mischief*, willful or malicious acts intended to damage property.

**vicarious liability**   Criminal liability for the acts of another person.

**vice**   Immoral conduct, practices, or habits.

**void for overbreadth**   A constitutional principal requiring that laws do not infringe on constitutionally protected behavior.

**void for vagueness**   A constitutional doctrine based on the Fifth and Fourteenth Amendments to the U.S. Constitution requiring that laws be written with sufficient clarity and specificity.

*voir dire*   The process of examining potential jurors for bias.

**voyeurism**   The act of spying on the intimate activities of other people.

**Wharton's Rule**   A conspiracy cannot occur when two persons are required for the commission of a crime.

**wheel and chain conspiracy**   A type of large-scale conspiracy that has attributes of both the spoke and the wheel and chain types of conspiracies.

**white-collar crime**   Various crimes typically committed by corporate executive or other employees in the course of their employment.

**wobbler**   A criminal offense that can be charged as either a felony or misdemeanor depending on the circumstances.

**XYY chromosome defect**   A criminal defense based on the presence of an extra Y chromosome and hyper-masculinity.

**year-and-a-day rule**   A common law rule stating that a person could not be prosecuted for homicide unless the victim died within a year and a day of the act that was responsible for the fatal injury.

# CASE INDEX

# SUBJECT INDEX